Programming Psion Computers

by

Leigh Edwards

Programming Psion Computers

Copyright ©1997, 1998 Leigh Edwards

ISBN 0 9530663 0 4
Published by:

EMCC
PO Box 109, Sale, Cheshire, M33 4TA, England
Tel +44 (0) 161 969 3205, Fax +44 (0) 161 969 3197
E-mail info@emcc.cix.co.uk

First printed October 1997, first reprint May 1998, second reprint January 1999.

Psion and the Psion logo are registered trademarks, and Psion Series 3, Psion Series 3a, Psion Series 3c, Psion Siena, Psion Series 5, Psion 3Link, SIBO, EPOC16 and EPOC32 are trademarks of Psion PLC. TopSpeed is a registered trademark of TopSpeed Corporation. IBM and IBM PC are registered trademarks of International Business Machines Corp. Microsoft, Microsoft Windows, Microsoft Word and MS-DOS are registered trademarks of Microsoft Corporation. Apple and Macintosh are registered trademarks of Apple Computer Inc.

EMCC acknowledges that some other names referred to are registered trademarks, and are given for information purposes only without commercial interests.

Printed and bound in Great Britain by Deanprint Limited, Stockport, Cheshire

Table of Contents

INDEX

CD-ROM REQUEST FORM

FILES ON OTHER MEDIA

PALMTOP MAGAZINE

THE 3-LIB SHAREWARE LIBRARY

This work is dedicated to Anne, my wife, critic and friend.

1 Introduction

The Psion range of handheld (or palmtop) computers are deceptively powerful and sophisticated systems. A number of key design elements have been responsible for their remarkable popularity and rise to dominance in world markets. One of the most significant features incorporated from the outset is OPL, the in-built BASIC-like programming language. This programmability has been supplemented by the availability of professional quality Software Development Kits (SDKs) from Psion PLC. External SDKs from Psion and programming utilities from third party developers have encouraged users and software houses alike to develop numerous additional applications. An enormous range of freeware, shareware, and commercial applications now exist, thus extending the capabilities of the systems way beyond the range of the excellent built in application programs provided by Psion.

As the Psion range increased and matured the number of options for software development became larger, and the amount of information available to the programmer grew to bewildering proportions. Much of this information has been provided by Psion in various ways. For example, in official documents such as the Psion SDK manuals and programming guides, or in electronic form via a number of on-line support forums (e.g. CIX and CompuServe). In addition a huge amount of knowledge, hard won experience and example code has generously been placed into the public domain by a wide variety of enthusiastic and talented individuals.

During my efforts to become reasonably proficient at writing commercial software for the Psion range I have made use of most of the aforementioned sources of information, including solving a good many problems the hard way. In pouring over the huge mass of information available it was evident that the level of detail, clarity and accessibility varied widely depending on the source and the experience of the contributor. This book represents a serious attempt to provide a comprehensive, up-to-date guide to all of the main options for programming Psion systems. To pass on as much of the key information as possible, adding clarity where required, and give others the benefits of some of my own labours. One of the main motivations for writing this book was that when I started out I would have given my right arm for such a guide.

It is intended to keep this publication current and relevant to future developments from Psion and third party utility developers. If you have any constructive contributions or corrections to this work I would be very grateful to receive them, ideally by e-mail - see the contacts section. All significant contributors will be credited, at least, and may even receive a free copy of a revised edition.

Finally, I am grateful to many people, too many to mention them all here, so in the 'Contacts and Sources' chapter I have acknowledged as many of the key individuals as I can, my apologies to anyone I may have missed.

Purpose and scope

- All of the key methods of writing software for the Psion range of handheld computers are described, i.e. the various languages, development environments and utilities for programmers. The principle focus will be on programming the Series 3, 3a/c and Siena, with references to the Work*about* and HC industrial hand held range where appropriate. Additional chapters have been included to describe the newly released **Series 5** and the options for programming.

- Covers all of the methods for producing and testing of application programs, either exclusively on the Psion or in conjunction with an IBM compatible PC, i.e. each of the programming languages, software development kits (SDKs) or utility programs.

- Covers a wide range of programming topics and techniques that add professional features to your programmes, and can be difficult or time consuming to acquire.

- Describes the main features of each of the key utilities and supplementary SDKs available, to assist the programmer in producing, testing and distributing all types of applications.

- A wide range of miscellaneous programming related topics e.g. getting help from Psion or from the 'on-line' community, up-to-date sources of utilities and example code, file formats for the built in applications etc.

- Includes a PC compatible CD-ROM that contains numerous code examples in OPL, C, OVAL, Macro and some Assembler, including many complete applications. Virtually all of the current freeware and shareware utilities for programmers are supplied for you to use or to evaluate. Numerous additional documents and information files are supplied on disk, and all materials have been meticulously catalogued and indexed.

- This book should be of assistance to all levels of programmer, but it does not aim teach programming for absolute beginners, nor does it attempt to replace all of the detailed information provided in the various language specific manuals. Instead the emphasis is on essential or important concepts and techniques, either because they are unique to the Psion environment or difficult to master. Other topics are included because they are not otherwise well documented, or because they ensure that programs remain consistent with the Psion application 'house style'.

Shareware, freeware and copyrights

Many of the utility programs and larger code examples provided here are expressly covered by embedded Shareware or Copyright notices. See the 'Distributing Your Software' chapter for the principles behind shareware and freeware. Please **do** respect the Copyrights of others. Since shareware is **not** freeware, please register any software that states that it is shareware, if you intend to use it beyond a reasonable evaluation period. If you are unsure, and the developers contact details are included, please check directly with the author. Wherever possible all sources have been acknowledged. Please encourage all contributors, in particular authors of freeware and shareware, with constructive comments or even praise — it will almost certainly be well received.

Using this book

A comprehensive table of contents and index are provided, which should allow the reader to answer specific questions as required. All of the additional information and examples provided on the accompanying CD-ROM is extensively cross-referenced in a specific disk index at the end of the 'Disk Contents' chapter.

It is almost certainly unnecessary to read this book from beginning to end, that is a task reserved for proof-readers and truly dedicated Psion fanatics. However, if you are inexperienced in programming for the Psion range or are considering producing programs for distribution, then close study of the first few chapters is strongly recommended. Particular emphasis should be placed on the 'Fundamental Concepts' and 'Applications, Process and Memory' chapters. Once these chapters have been absorbed you should be well positioned to decide which programming language and development environment is most suited. The appropriate design architecture needed for your particular application should also be somewhat clearer.

Terms used

The majority of handheld systems currently available from Psion use the same hardware architecture, and are collectively known as **SI**xteen **B**it **O**rganisers, or **SIBO** systems. This term will be used throughout the rest of this book, unless it is necessary to refer to specific details of a particular model. In addition, the term Psion Series 3 range, Series 3 or just S3 can be taken to refer to all models in the Series 3 range, exclusions to this will be stated explicitly. Wherever the term EPOC16 is used it refers to operating system of the SIBO range.

The terms Series 5 or S5 refer to the new 32-bit ARM based systems, and EPOC32 refers to the new 32-bit operating system used on the Series 5.

All references to a PC should be taken as referring to an IBM PC compatible. Where PC based software etc. is referred to it will be made clear at the time whether it runs under DOS, Microsoft Windows, both DOS and Windows, or another Operating System.

Since the major software development environments are currently all PC-hosted links to other personal computers, such as Amiga, Atari, Macintosh etc. although acknowledged as possible, are not discussed further.

All references to a PC linked to a SIBO or EPOC32 system should be taken to be via the hardware and associated software methods as supplied by Psion.

Occasionally terms such as E_MAX_PROCESSES will be encountered, they are identifier names which Psion use in their SDKs to refer to constants and standard values e.g. those associated with the operating system. The corresponding numeric values of all such identifiers referred to will either be explicitly stated in the text or will be listed in the Appendix.

To avoid repetitive definitions of specific or technical terms a glossary is provided at the back of the book.

Loading the disk information

Since the disk supplied is in PC compatible format you will need access to a suitable PC to make full use of the information provided. Files on disk are grouped together into specific directories and sub-directories. Groups of related files may also be provided, in the same directory, as compressed archives or .ZIP files. All archive files have been 'unzipped', but the original archive files are provided as well for convenience. 'Zipped' archives can be decompressed using one of the UNZIP programs also located on the disk.

If the CD-ROM was not supplied at the time you purchased this book please request it, free of charge, using the order form supplied inside the back cover.

For an additional charge, to cover the cost of the media and postage, the software and files can be supplied on other PC compatible media, please refer to the order form inside the back cover.

Finding disk-based information

As stated above, the files and information on disk are cross-referenced in a specific index to a high level of detail. Reference to the specific disk index in the chapter 'Disk Contents' should allow you to easily locate the file(s) containing the information or example(s) you require. If you still cannot find the specific item you are searching for, a 'Grep' type search program is also included in the GREPFV10 directory of the disk. Grep programs will do a specific text search through sets of selected files (as specified in the program command line). See the GREPFV10 directory on disk for further details.

Other sources of information

In bringing together much of the information, snippets of code, full program examples, Freeware and Shareware supplied on the disk, I have used many on-line sources such as CIX (Compulink Information eXchange), CompuServe and numerous FTP and Web sites on the Internet. In the Contacts and Sources section I have included details of these sources to enable an interested reader to make contact with other like-minded individuals, to search out additional information and to keep the supplied materials up-to-date.

Disclaimer

While every effort has been made to ensure that the information and materials supplied are accurate and free from defects of any kind, you use the information in this book and in the supplementary materials entirely at your own risk. The author and publisher cannot accept any responsibility for any loss or damage that might be incurred as a result of its use.

2 Development Options

Introduction

If you are new to Psion programming or perhaps starting a large new project, you will have to decide which development platform to use. You may wish to develop your software exclusively on the Psion, on a PC linked to a Psion system, or choose the platform depending on where you are at the time.

For larger projects, PC-based development is recommended, linked to a Psion for evaluation and testing purposes. Using a PC with a Psion ensures that virtually all of the options for software development are available to you. When you're away from base you can still use a Psion system to test the application or specific routines, or even edit sections of source code.

If you don't have access to an IBM compatible PC, or are such a fan of the Psion that you can't bear to use anything else, then your options for choice of language and development environment are considerably more restricted. See the text files in the PSIONFAQ directory on disk for information on options for non PC-based development.

Platforms, overview

The current SIBO development platforms are outlined below. More detailed descriptions of the various platforms, languages and software development environments are provided later in this chapter. Software development options for the new EPOC32 based Series 5 are discussed in the 'Series 5' chapter.

When discussing development issues that involve an attached PC, this book will focus on the use of an IBM PC compatible computer. I risk offending those people who prefer alternative computers as their development system. However, since the PC is the platform preferred by Psion Software PLC, and all of the major development environments are designed for this platform, I feel the limitation is reasonable. A considerable amount of information on the use of alternative computer platforms is provided in the Psionfaq files supplied on disk – see the PSIONFAQ directory.

Notes:
Whatever platform you choose, use of an external power supply for the Psion is highly recommended. There is a particularly high drain on the internal batteries during external communications e.g. to a PC or printer.

For details of how to obtain software development kits and other programming related supplies see the 'Contacts and Sources' chapter.

SIBO system exclusively

It is possible to produce sophisticated OPL programs using just the SIBO machine itself, especially with the OPP pre-processor, covered later. However, apart from the difficulties of working with a small keyboard and screen, this method severely limits your options, and it is not ideal for larger projects. The OPL translation process can be very slow with big source files, although they can be broken up and translated as smaller units. Use of memory can be very efficient since individual translated modules can be loaded and unloaded as required at run time. For security you will need some form of external backup facilities, such as the Cyclone floppy disk unit (from Purple Software Ltd) or Flash RAM, to protect against accidental loss or damage.

It is not possible to develop OVAL (Object-based Visual Application Language) applications on the Series 3c or Work*about* alone.

Writing in 'C' or Assembly Language (8086 machine code) is also possible (although in a somewhat limited manner), using the appropriate third party software (supplied on disk) - see later sections for specific details.

DOS based Psion emulators

Psion have released DOS based SIBO emulators for the Series 3, Series 3a, Siena and the Work*about;* they can be very useful for PC hosted software development, but only for limited testing. Access to an appropriate Psion system is essential for thorough testing of applications.

All of the emulators were released by Psion into the public domain on the understanding that they are used 'as is', and they will **not** be supported by Psion. Copies of the S3a, Siena and Work*about* emulators are included on the disk, on the same unsupported basis.

Note:
If you make use of the SIBO emulators and experience difficulties or have questions, please **do not** contact Psion technical support – see the 'Contacts and Sources' chapter for potential sources of assistance.

PC with a linked SIBO system

If you intend to use the SIBO OPL or C SDKs from Psion, use of a PC linked to a SIBO system is mandatory. Similarly, if you wish to use ODE (the OPL Development Environment) or OVAL (Object-based Visual Application Language), you will need a Windows based PC linked to a SIBO system. ODE and OVAL will also run under other PC-based operating systems - see later. However, when away from home or the office it is obviously possible to write sections of code on the SIBO system itself, for transfer back to the PC when back at base.

Language options

An overview of the language choices is given here, more detail is provided later in the chapter. Beyond your chosen language, further decisions have to be made on the design approach and which development environment to use. A detailed comparison of the various options within each language is given later in this chapter.

The language choice depends upon many factors including previous experience, the development platform you have available, the requirements of the application, the expected processing demands, your objectives in writing the code and even on your target audience.

In order of increasing level, the choices are Assembler (machine code), C, OPL and OVAL. As in many areas of expertise, there is a lot of unnecessary rivalry and snobbery associated with the various programming languages. It is not my intention here to become embroiled with any of that nonsense. The 'levels' given here are purely in terms of the level of abstraction they provide away from the inner workings of the system. In other words, approximately how many lines of source code it takes to achieve some arbitrary result e.g. presenting a bordered window to display information, and receive input from a user.

Here are some probable reasons for making a particular language selection:

Assembly language

- Out of individual enthusiasm or for experience in (8086 family) processor level instructions.
- The need for highest possible processing speed. Typically for small sections of an application, written at a higher level, which have been found (or estimated) to be highly processor intensive and there is a need to optimise them.
- The desired result cannot be achieved in any other way, e.g. writing device drivers.

C programming

- Previous programming experience in C.
- Availability of existing C source code.
- Desire for portability of C source code to other platforms.
- Processing speed.
- Complexity or requirements of the user interface (Psion SIBO OOP C).
- Multiple events have to be handled.

OPL

- No access to a PC.
- Modest project, with no significant processing demands.
- Previous programming experience in BASIC or similar language.
- Speed and flexibility (platform) of development.
- Ease of development and prototyping.

OVAL

- Previous programming experience in Visual BASIC.
- Portability of code from SIBO to Visual BASIC on the PC and vice versa.
- Speed of development.
- Ease of development.
- Project involves Series 3c to PC transfer of data or information.
- Multiple events have to be handled.
- The application is intended for the Series 3c or Work*about* (later models).

Macros

- To automate repetitive tasks on the Psion.
- To automate existing applications.
- Speed of development.
- Ease of development.
- Previous programming experience in OPL.

Use of memory

On the 16-bit SIBO systems, programs are limited to approximately 64K of memory for code, and slightly less than that for data. At first this may seem to be a severe limitation to the production of sophisticated applications, but there are a number of mitigating factors.

Many facilities, provided by the system, enable the production of slick and efficient user interfaces, whilst minimising the code required from the programmer. For example, menu handling and user input via dialogs is very easily achieved, since the system does most of the hard work, based on information supplied by the application.

Languages such as OPL and OVAL provide excellent facilities for modularising programs. Thus an application is not required to have all of its code in memory at once. Some extremely large applications, with a wide range of functionality, have been produced in OPL.

Modularising programs written in C is possible although it is considerably more complex and can be somewhat limiting. Two main options exist: have more than one process running and use inter-process communications between them, make use of dynamic libraries (DYLs) that are akin to DLLs in Window. However, producing DYLs requires the use of object oriented programming (OOP) techniques, and the use of static data (and certain data types) is not allowed in DYLs.

Use of EPOC32 as the basis of the 32-bit Series 5 system removes the 64K limits on code and data.

Portability and re-use of source code

Once you commit to using a particular language and development environment you are likely to generate a large amount of program source code and supporting information. Changing your decision later can involve considerable effort if you wish to make use of the program code and algorithms in another language. Moving program code from one system to another, or converting code into another language is often referred to as 'porting'.

Re-using sections of code and useful algorithms can save considerable time and increase the reliability of your programs. Here are a couple of simple techniques that can make life a lot easier if you intend to re-use or port program code.

- Don't put large amounts of code in monolithic blocks. Instead, split your programs down into small modular units that do specific tasks. For example, making use of small procedures and calling them with parameters will make your code more general purpose. Once a group of procedures have been thoroughly tested they can be used with confidence in other programs.

- Separate a large program into blocks with specific tasks, and avoid mixing code with related but separate purposes. For example, in a game, keep the code that calculates the computer's next move quite separate from the code that displays the move. Similarly, keep the code which handles aspects of the user interface, such as key presses, menus and help etc. separate from the code that redraws the game board.

User interface code and screen display procedures are some of the most difficult to re-use. It is usually relatively easy to port the code that forms the 'engine' of an application, e.g. that calculates the best move in a game of Chess. It is usually much more difficult to port code that forms a major part of the user interface.

In order to get the best out of the Psion environment (particularly in terms of the user interface and asynchronous operation) it may be necessary to adopt an approach that significantly reduces the portability of the code produced. However by careful design and modular programming the effort involved in moving code between languages, to new models or even additional platforms, will be kept to a minimum.

A typical development cycle

With software projects of significant size or complexity, careful design and specification before any code is produced will usually bring significant rewards. Time spent on design will normally drastically reduce the overall time to produce the code. A clear specification can form the basis of an agreement with a customer and will allow a number of programmers to collaborate successfully on a large project. Re-coding because of an unsatisfactory approach is avoided; performance issues and serious bugs can be minimised.

Once the program specification is clear, a typical PC / Psion based development cycle might involve the following stages:

- Production and editing of program code.
- Pre-processing of code (if any - see OPLLINT, AKA, OPP etc.).
- Translation or compilation and linking of source code into executable files.
- Transfer of the application code and other associated files from the PC to the SIBO via a suitable link cable.
- Running and testing of routines or the whole application on the SIBO system.
- Modification or extension of code on the PC, and so on.

The chapter 'Linking to a PC or Printer' discusses the various options for connecting Psion systems to a PC, and the methods available for printing from a Psion computer.

Languages and platforms, in detail

Detailed coverage is provided here on the main programming options for EPOC16 based SIBO systems. Development options relevant to the EPOC32 based Series 5 systems are discussed in the 'Series 5' chapter.

Assembly language options

Apart from enthusiasts who wish to program in assembly language for its own sake, the commonest reasons for resorting to machine level code are:

- The need for highest possible processing speed. Typically for small sections of an application, written at a higher level, which have been found (or estimated) to be highly processor intensive, and there is a need to optimise them.
- The desired result cannot be achieved in other way, e.g. writing device drivers.

If you wish to produce an application (for SIBO) entirely in assembly language it will be necessary to understand the EPOC16 operating system in considerable detail. And, to achieve even a modest level of functionality it will be necessary to make extensive use of operating system calls. Most of the key principles behind EPOC16 are discussed in the 'Fundamental Concepts', 'Processes, Memory and Applications' chapters, and extensive information on operating system calls is provided on disk.

Four main (and one minor) options exist for working in assembly language for SIBO systems:

TopSpeed assembler and linker

Available separately from TopSpeed Corporation or as supplied with the Psion SIBO C SDK professional edition. These tools are PC DOS based. Assembler source code, produced with a selected editor, is assembled and linked to produce an executable that has to be transferred to a SIBO system for testing.

Borland assembler and linker

Programmers who wish to write their own LDD device drivers will need to use assembly language. An interface section in assembly language is essential for device drivers. The assembler code may just provide an appropriate interface to other more extensive code, which could be written in assembly language or in C.

Example device drivers, with assembly language and C source code, are provided with Psion's SIBO C SDK. The recommended development tools for building the device drivers are the PC DOS based assembler and linker from Borland International. The Borland Turbo Assembler (TASM.EXE) and Turbo Linker (TLINK.EXE), required to build the example drivers, have to be purchased separately; they are not supplied as part of the SIBO C SDK from Psion.

S3Asm

S3Asm is a Psion hosted editor and assembler for 8086 class processors, it is suitable for S3a/c systems (and possibly the Siena). S3Asm is shareware and is supplied on disk – see the S3ASM2 directory.

Machine code book

A fourth option for machine level programming is available in the form of a book plus software. A book entitled 'Machine Code Programming on the Psion Series 3a & 3', by John Farrant, explains how to program in 8086 machine code and assembly language. Published by Kuma Books Ltd (ISBN 0-7457-0299-6), the package includes a functional two-pass assembler with text editor and debugger. The Assembler etc. are provided as source listings (in OPL) within the text of the book, although an option to buy the source code on floppy disk is available in the back of the book.

CPOC Assembler

A fifth option for assembly language programmers is to use the Assembler supplied with the CPOC C development system. The CPOC assembler is not designed as a stand-alone program, it has to be used in conjunction with the CPOC 'front end'.

The whole CPOC system, as it currently stands, is provided on disk – see the CPOCALL directory and sub-directories.

C programming

Four options exist for C programmers.

- The CPOC shareware development system, for direct use on a SIBO system.
- The Small C compiler, for direct use on a SIBO system.
- Use a PC based compiler and convert to Psion format with PLINK
- The PC hosted SIBO C SDK from Psion.

Although, for serious/commercial development in C, the only viable option is to use the Psion SIBO C SDK.

CPOC

CPOC is a SIBO hosted C development system that is still being developed. The authors state that they intend to produce a full C development system that can be used to edit and build functioning programs entirely on a Psion system. Some of the components of the CPOC system are not yet functional.

The whole CPOC system, as it currently stands, is provided on disk – see the CPOCALL directory and sub-directories.

S3C111

S3C111 is a SIBO hosted C development system that is complete but very limited; it is based on a public domain SmallC compiler adapted for the Psion Series 3 and 3a/c (and is probably suitable for the Siena). The author states that the S3C111 system can be used to edit and build functioning programs entirely on a Psion system.

The whole S3C111 system is provided on disk – see the S3C111 directory.

PLINK

Code in C compiled with the Microsoft C compiler (or others) can be converted with the PLINK cross-linker to Psion format, which may then be run from inside an OPL program; useful for speeding up time critical sections of an OPL program.

The PLINK cross-linker is provided on disk – see the PLINK directory.

SIBO C SDK options

At the time of going to press the current version of the Psion SIBO C SDK is 2.20, and three variants are available:

- The documentation only version, useful for system related information and details of EPOC system calls. The TopSpeed Corporation C compiler, etc. must be purchased separately before applications can be produced.
- The standard version is a fully usable version including documentation, plus the TopSpeed Corporation C compiler and linker.
- The professional version is as per the standard version, plus the source code for the CLIB library and the TopSpeed Corporation assembler.

SIBO C SDK documentation edition

The documentation variant contains:

- Four A4 sized volumes, divided into nineteen manuals comprising two hundred chapters (see the 'C Programming' chapter for further details).
- The Psion software environment, including libraries, header files and associated software tools.
- A range of example applications and program source code demonstrating the various programming options.

SIBO C SDK standard edition

In addition to the material supplied in the documentation variant, the standard variant has:

- The TopSpeed Corporation C compiler and library.
- The TopSpeed Corporation multi-window editor and project system.

The standard SDK variant contains everything necessary to develop sophisticated SIBO applications in C. The TopSpeed C components may be used independently of the Psion C SDK components to write DOS based programs to run on a PC.

SIBO C SDK professional edition

In addition to the material in the standard variant, the professional variant has:

- The TopSpeed TechKit, including the TopSpeed assembler.
- The TopSpeed C library source, containing the source code (both C and assembler) for the C library that is supplied with the compiler.
- The Psion SIBO CLIB C library source.

OPL

A bewildering array of development options and utilities are now available to OPL developers. Options for the main code development process are described here; see the 'OPL Programming' chapter for more details.

OPL development option	Description	Requirements
SIBO based development.	Editing, OPL pre-processing, translation and testing on a Psion system.	Target SIBO system and an optional OPL pre-processor.
PC DOS SIBO emulator based development.	Editing, pre-processing, translation and provisional testing within a DOS based SIBO emulator.	A DOS based PC, the target SIBO system emulator and an optional OPL pre-processor.
PC DOS based development.	Editing, OPL pre-processing and translation.	A DOS based PC, the target SIBO system, a link cable and file transfer software. An appropriate PC DOS based OPL translator and an optional OPL pre-processor.
PC Windows based development.	Editing, OPL pre-processing and translation.	A Windows based PC, the target SIBO system, a link cable and file transfer software. An appropriate OPL translator and an optional OPL pre-processor.

ODE

The OPL Development Environment (ODE) is an excellent Windows-hosted Integrated Development Environment (IDE) that includes:

- A project manager.
- A powerful multi-file source code editor with coloured syntax highlighting.
- OPLLINT, a code checking utility.
- OPL translators suitable for the S3, S3a/c, Siena, Work*about* and HC.
- Powerful context sensitive help that calls on a full OPL reference library.
- PC to SIBO communications capability via a suitable link cable (not provided).

ODE requires a 386 CPU (or better) based PC compatible and will run under Windows 3.1, 3.11, 95 and NT3.5 or higher, OS/2 or Warp. It requires a VGA display with 4 MB of RAM and 2 MB or more of disk space.

ODE is available as a product in its own right; it is also supplied as part of version 3.0 of the SIBO OPL SDK. ODE is an extremely good development environment for SIBO systems, and is excellent value for money.

SIBO OPL SDK

The current version of the Psion SIBO OPL SDK is version 3.0; it provides all the tools and information necessary to develop sophisticated OPL language applications for Psion SIBO-based systems.

The SIBO OPL SDK contains:

- Two A4 size volumes, comprising thirteen manuals (see the 'OPL Programming' chapter for further details).
- The Psion OPL software environment, including libraries, header files, macro files and utility software.
- A range of example program source code.
- Includes ODE (OPL Development Environment), a Windows PC based Integrated Development Environment.

For serious / commercial development in OPL, purchase of the Psion SIBO OPL SDK is highly recommended.

OPL translators

Psion have produced a range of PC hosted OPL translators for all SIBO systems. The translators are able to pre-process and translate OPL source code into a form suitable for execution on the target SIBO system or DOS based emulator.

All of the available OPL translators are supplied as part of ODE and the SIBO OPL SDK produced by Psion.

The S3tran and S3atran OPL translators are provided on disk – see the OPLTRAN directory.

OPL pre-processors

On a SIBO system, OPL has a number of flaws that can limit its flexibility or allow errors to go undiscovered. A number of OPL pre-processors are available that can significantly improve the usability of the language and eliminate common disastrous errors.

All OPL programmers should seriously consider using a pre-processor. In particular, OPLLINT should be used to check your code before any significant application testing is done.

OPLLINT

An invaluable DOS utility from Psion for checking the syntax and use of variables and procedures, in an OPL program.

OPLLINT is provided on disk – see the OPLLINT directory.

OPP

A SIBO or DOS hosted pre-processor that adds various C-like features to OPL, such as #defines, #includes, 2D arrays and much more. OPP is an excellent OPL programmers' utility for extending the language using operating system calls, and preparing for debugging OPL programs with OPPDBG.

OPP is provided on disk – see the OPP16F directory.

AKA

An excellent DOS hosted utility, AKA is an OPL programmers' tool that will shorten variable and procedure names, reduce the size of OPO or OPA programs, and speed them up slightly.

AKA is provided on disk – see the AKA230 directory.

OPL debugger

Until the arrival of OPPDBG, there was no easy way of debugging OPL code at runtime. OPPDBG provides an excellent OPL programmers' source level debugging utility. However, OPPDBG relies on use of the OPP pre-processor from the same author.

OPPDBG is provided on disk – see the OPPDBG11 directory.

OPLCS editor

OPLCS, short for OPL Code Studio, is a PC Windows based OPL code editor and template-based code generator.

OPLCS is provided on disk – see the OPLCS directory.

Please note:
OPP, OPPDBG, and OPLCS are Shareware programs, so please register any software that you decide to use. Individuals may use AKA free of charge, but commercial users must register it as Shareware.

OVAL

In brief, OVAL is Visual Basic for the Psion; 'Object-based' just refers to the way of working when developing an application. OVAL is code-compatible with Microsoft Visual Basic, it includes over thirty controls that are specially designed for building Psion applications, and takes full advantage of the EPOC operating system. Experienced Visual Basic programmers should be quickly up-to-speed with OVAL.

Developing in OVAL is done in a Windows-based Integrated Development Environment: it features an intelligent source code editor, code translators for Psion computers and over 30 application controls. Developers design applications graphically in the Windows IDE, and test them using a suitable SIBO system computer connected via a serial link cable.

To run OVAL applications, a SIBO system with the OVAL run-time interpreter in ROM (Read Only Memory) is required. Currently, the only systems with OVAL in ROM are the Psion 3c, and recent versions of its industrial relative the Work*about*.

Due to its size, the OVAL runtime engine is not included in the Siena ROM, nor can it be loaded on to earlier machines. OVAL is also absent from the DOS based SIBO emulators and the new Series 5 system.

Developing in OVAL requires a PC-compatible computer with: 80386 or better CPU, a colour VGA display, 4 MB RAM or more (8MB recommended), 2 MB disk space or more and a serial link connection (e.g. 3Link cable, PsiWin etc.). The OVAL IDE will run under the following operating systems: Windows 3.1 or higher, Windows 95, Windows NT 3.5 or higher, OS/2 2.1 or higher. It is not possible to develop OVAL applications directly on the Series 3c, Work*about* or DOS based emulators.

OVAL applications can be distributed, to suitably equipped users, by the usual methods.

Macros

Three options for Macro based automation / programming currently exist for SIBO systems (Non currently exist for the Series 5).

MACSYS

MACSYS is a Freeware Macro system that allows automation of most common Psion tasks. It can record and play back a sequence of keystrokes, but MACSYS macros are actually full OPL programs, and can use all the power available to the system. MACSYS is a little tricky to master, but the effort can be very rewarding.

The complete MACSYS system is supplied on disk with several example Macros – see the MACSYS directory.

KMAC

Is a keystroke Macro record and play back system written in C, and all necessary executable files and full source files are supplied. KMAC can be used as supplied, or used from within programs written in OPL or C. Complete examples are provided that demonstrate the use of KMAC by C or OPL applications; full source is supplied in C and OPL.

The complete KMAC system is supplied on disk with example Macros – see the KMAC directory.

ATS based macros

Starting with the Series 3a, the ATS (Automatic Test System) system was introduced to assist with automated testing of HWIM C applications. Although the process which controls the ATS sequence does not have to be an HWIM application, the process which is being controlled by ATS does have to be a standard HWIM application (or one which mimics the support for ATS).

The ATS system is discussed in more detail in the 'Errors and Debugging' chapter, but is covered in depth in the 'Object Oriented Programming Guide' manual in SIBO C SDK. An example ATS based Macro recording and playback system is provided with the SIBO C SDK. See the OODOC201 directory on disk.

3 Fundamental Concepts

Introduction

With any good idea or exciting new programming project, it's always tempting to dive straight in and produce some actual code; only bothering to read the manuals when you are stuck, or need to look something up. Much of this book can be treated as a resource, to be used only when you need to refer to a particular technique, or solve a programming problem. However, the effort of reading the chapters covering some of the fundamental concepts should repay itself many times over. Not all of the concepts covered will be relevant to all readers. Some more advanced topics may be skipped and returned to as needed, but an understanding of a large proportion of the material presented in this chapter will be of value to all programmers. For example, programming at the client server level will not concern most OPL programmers, but an understanding of the concepts, and how it is used by EPOC16 may be advantageous.

Languages like OPL and OVAL have the distinct advantage of insulating the programmer from the finer details of the operating system. However in order to achieve some of the more advanced results, say in OPL, it may be necessary to use operating system or library function calls. In these circumstances, a more detailed understanding of the concepts behind the calls will make life easier, particularly when problems are experienced.

Wherever possible this chapter will describe key concepts, whilst deliberately staying away from example code. Illustrating a concept to an OPL programmer in terms of code written in C for example, or vice versa, may only serve to confuse. Addressing the specifics of each programming concept or technique will be left to the chapters on each language. However to ensure that each topic is covered in sufficient depth this chapter was written from a general C programming perspective.

When programming in any new environment there is always a learning process to go through, a significant part of that process is to absorb the 'standard' approach to application design in the new environment. One of the most fundamental design issues in the Psion environment is the choice of synchronous versus asynchronous handling of events, such as key presses and general program input/output (I/O). Most programmers like to build on what they have done before and typically will aim to accumulate code that is designed to be reusable, or easily adapted for future uses. A particularly useful section of code to develop and re-use is a basic application framework or template (to handle tasks such as responding to special keys, menus and general I/O). Therefore, I recommend close study of the associated concepts, and of as much example code as possible (in your chosen language) before making a decision about a synchronous/asynchronous design approach.

SIBO architecture

The Series 3 family and Siena handheld computers are all based on the proprietary Psion SIBO (or **SI**xteen **B**it **O**rganiser) architecture, as are the industrial handheld products such as the Work*about* and HC ranges.

The new Series 5 systems have a completely new architecture and operating system, see the 'Series 5' chapter for details.

Key components of SIBO systems

- An 8086 class processor.
- A sophisticated power management system that selectively powers subsystems under control of the operating system.
- A synchronous, high speed, serial protocol for communication between a machine and its peripherals.
- Solid state disks (SSDs) that provide fast mass storage without moving parts.
- Hardware protection of the system from aberrant software processes (Trapping of out of range memory addressing and a watch-dog timer that prevents interrupts being disabled for too long.)
- A real-time clock.
- ROM based system software and applications.
- Graphics LCD display.
- A pointing device (e.g. a mouse pad - on some models only e.g. MC).
- Eight-bit digital sound system (on some models only) e.g. 3a upwards.

The SIBO architecture is physically implemented using a V30H (8086 compatible) processor and custom made integrated circuits called ASICs (Application Specific Integrated Circuits). It is possible, although rarely necessary, to interact with the SIBO hardware system via certain of the ASIC chips, as described the 'Hardware Reference' manual of the Psion SIBO C SDK.

ASICs

The Psion SIBO architecture is unique and very compact because of the use of custom chips called ASICs (Application Specific Integrated Circuits, again all in CMOS). Various ASIC chips handle everything except computation, and provide control over system hardware such as the keyboard, LCD screen, memory, sound, real time clock, peripherals such as SSDs and the serial port etc.

Specialist functions such as auto-switch-off are provided by the ASICs, including one of the most important, hardware memory protection. If a program goes completely ape and attempts to tramp all over areas of memory that it shouldn't have access to, it will be stopped in its tracks by the ASIC hardware. Hardware memory protection is one of the reasons for the above average reliability of Psion handheld computers.

Some ASICs (e.g. ASIC 5) are used in external interfaces and devices such as SSDs. Over time there have been at least ten ASICs. The circuitry became even more closely integrated with the introduction of ASIC 9, this was a composite chip combining a number of the other ASICs including the V30H processor itself!

Processor

The system is sixteen bit, fully 8086 processor instruction set compatible, but the NEC V30H processor used in the Series 3 family has additional instructions available. Approximately 40% higher performance may be expected from the V30H compared to an 8086 chip due to internal design optimisation of the V30H processor. Implemented as an entirely static CMOS (Complimentary Metal Oxide Silicon) design, the processor has no minimum clock speed, therefore the processor clock can be stopped at any time without loss of its internal state. This feature is used extensively as part of the SIBO power saving strategy during periods when the processor is idle (i.e. waiting for an event).

Interrupts

The 8086 class processors have two types of interrupt, software interrupts and hardware interrupts. A vector or jump table at the bottom of memory is used by the processor to look up the address of code designed to handle each type of interrupt. The vector table can contain up to 256 entries each of which is 4 bytes long. The first 33 entries (0 -32) are used for special system and error handling purposes. Interrupts from 33 to 255 are used for the INT xx trap instructions, that are used by EPOC16 to provide the operating system service functions (EPOC16 O/S calls).

A hardware interrupt is a special kind used by peripherals and system hardware (at the electronic level) to signal the processor directly that an event has occurred and must be attended to. For example, the processor is physically signalled, or interrupted, 32 times per second to generate the so called system ticks. Other hardware interrupts may be generated by I/O devices, such as the RS-232 port, to indicate that data has arrived etc.

Memory protection

Special hardware protects the rest of the system from bugged software that tries to write outside of its own allocated data segment. It is possible for a process to modify memory outside of its own data segment, for example by disabling interrupts. However, if a process leaves interrupts disabled for more than 24 system ticks (three quarters of a second) the watch-dog timer hardware will detect this, and the process will be aborted (panicked - see errors later) by the operating system.

Auto-switch-off

The hardware system (e.g. the processor, communications links and peripherals such as storage devices etc.) is interrupt driven to provide a system capable of operating in a multi-tasking mode and should never lose data. To save battery power the SIBO system is designed to shut itself off when certain key activities (e.g. a user key press) have not occurred for a pre-set time.

To make sure that an application does not inadvertently disable the auto switch off mechanism it is necessary to follow a set of programming guidelines for handling events such as key presses - see 'Processes and auto-switch off' in the 'Process, Memory and Applications' chapter.

Storage capabilities

Up to 1Mbyte of memory may be addressed directly on 8086 class processors. In SIBO machines, depending on the model, all or part of this address range may be used. This is why only 512K of memory is available for all running programs, and that any additional memory is allocated to internal disk space.

RAM

The internal memory capacity varies depending on the model. The original Series 3 had 128K or 256K of RAM, the Series 3a offered 256K or 512K and this was later changed to 512K, 1MB or 2MB. The Siena has 512K or 1MB and the 3c has 1MB or 2MB.

On all models the internal RAM memory above 512K is not available as process space i.e. for program code or data, it is reserved for use as internal RAM drive space.

ROM

ROM sizes again vary depending on the model and system options supplied e.g. the Spell checker / thesaurus application and dictionaries were added to the ROM on the larger 3a models (the 1 MB and 2MB RAM variants) available in the UK and US. With the introduction of the Series 3c, with the Oval run-time interpreter included, the ROM was increased to 2MB.

SSDs and files

SIBO machines have 1 to 3 storage drives, depending on the model. All models have a Drive M: , the non removable internal disk, that is actually a section of the internal system memory configured as a RAM drive.

Additional plug in Solid State Disk (SSDs) units are available, and are so-called because they are based on silicon memory with no moving parts. A variety of SSD types and capacities are available. Sizes range from 128K bytes to 8Mb and beyond.

To reduce the entry level cost, the Siena has only the internal RAM drive, it does not have an integral SSD slot. Although, an external SSD drive is an optional extra and connects via the side mounted port.

The different types of removable SSD (in order of decreasing unit cost) are:

- Static RAM with integral Lithium battery
- Flash EPROM
- Solo - one-time-programmable ROM
- PSRAMs Pseudo Static RAM ·
- Masked ROM

An SSD drive can physically and logically mount any type of SSD unit.

SSD interface

The physical interface between an SSD and the drive has only 6 connectors (4 for power, and 2 for data). The 2 data connections are an instance of a high speed serial channel, it is a fundamental part of the SIBO hardware architecture, implemented in custom ASIC chips and can be used to communicate with other peripherals.

The high speed serial channel is driven synchronously by a clock which normally runs at 3.84 MHz, giving a data transfer speed comparable to hard disks on PCs, but without any latency for the drive head to position to the required track. Writing to a Flash SSD is slower because of the time taken to program the EPROM and, in this case, the speed of writing is approaching twice as fast as writing to a typical floppy disk on a PC.

RAM SSDs

RAM SSDs use static RAM backed up by an integral Lithium battery. While the RAM SSD is inserted in an SSD drive, it draws current from the SIBO machine. When the SSD is removed, it relies on its internal battery to maintain its data. Only on later versions of RAM SSD's is it possible to programmatically determine the status of the internal backup battery.

The allocation of the space for directories and files on a RAM SSD is block structured - identical to that used on PC hard disks and floppy disks. Just like floppy disks on a PC, there is a limit to the number of files that may appear in the root directory (where this limit includes directory files). This root directory limit does not limit the number of files that can be stored on a RAM SSD since any number of files may be stored in sub-directories.

The format function automatically allocates the capacity of the root directory as a function of the capacity of the SSD. The number of files that may appear in the root directory depends on SSD size, as follows:

Max files in root	RAM SSD size
16	<128K
32	128K
48	256K
64	512K
128	1M
256	2M
384	4M
512	6M
512	8M

Flash SSDs

Flash SSDs use Flash EPROM chips in which all the data bits are initially set. A particular bit may be cleared by programming but it can not be set again unless all the bits on the chip are set (by erasing the chip). Unlike older generation EPROMs, Flash EPROMs are erased electrically (rather than by exposure to UV light). The speed with which Flash can be programmed is also substantially faster than the old UV erasable EPROMs. A Flash SSDs may be erased in its SSD drive by formatting.

Since Flash memory does not require a battery to maintain it, the data on a Flash SSD is very secure - more so than on RAM SSDs or magnetic media. Flash memory is also cheaper than RAM.

Files stored on Flash RAM cannot be compressed, whereas those on the internal drive or on SRAM devices can be compressed in situ to recover the space used by deleted records or files.

Flash SSDs are particularly attractive for storing program files, read-only data (say for data-referral applications), for securely storing logged data in the field and for archiving data. The storage of files on a Flash SSD is very different from that used on RAM SSDs. The scheme is not at all block structured, but is based on linked variable length records. All this is hidden from the caller and the logical interface to a file on a Flash SSD is the same as for a file on a RAM SSD (or any other medium).

On a Flash SSD, there is no limit on the number of files or directories in the root directory. You will also find that it is possible to fit slightly more data on a freshly formatted Flash SSD than on a RAM SSD of the same nominal capacity. This is due to the fact that files are allocated space in multiples of whole blocks on a RAM SSD, whereas Flash files are stored in exactly sized variable length records.

Solo and ROM SSDs

Solo SSDs (one-time-programmable ROMs) and masked ROMs are used by software publishers to distribute their products and as their names suggest cannot be reformatted once written to (see the chapter on 'Distributing Your Software' for more details).

PSRAM SSDs

PSRAMs are industrial products and are not recommended for use with the S3a S3c or Siena. PSRAMs are available with capacities of 512K, 1MB and 2MBytes. Power consumption is slightly higher than SRAM during read and write operations, but is a lot higher when the machine is switched on because of the refresh oscillator needed to maintain the memory (up to 1/3 rd more power) also a lot more power is needed when the machine is off to maintain the memory. A backup lithium cell has only around 400 hours (17 days) if a PSRAM is taken out of a machine.

SSDs and robust programs

Mass storage devices such as SRAM and Flash RAM can be removed, changed or repositioned at will by the user. Robust programs should be designed to cope with such eventualities without crashing.

Display screens

Depending on the model of SIBO system, the size and resolution of the screen and the availability of a grey plane may vary. The original Series 3 has a screen resolution of 240 pixels wide by 80 pixels deep with no grey plane. With the 3a, the screen was made physically larger, the resolution was doubled to 480 by 160 and a grey plane was added. On the 3c the screen size and resolution are the same as the 3a, but variants with backlighting became available, initially only for US models.

On the Siena the screen size and resolution was reduced to 240 by 160 (also with a grey plane) to accommodate a numeric keypad. Backlighting is not available for the Siena.

The grey plane can be considered to be a layer between a top 'black' layer and a bottom 'white or blank' layer. If a pixel in the top layer is 'on' then a black pixel will be visible. If the same black pixel is 'off', but the grey pixel underneath it is 'on', then a grey pixel will be shown. If both the black and grey pixels are 'off' then a white or blank pixel will result. Black pixels that are 'on' will always obscure the equivalent grey pixel underneath, i.e. in order for a grey pixel to be visible the corresponding black pixel must be off. Programmatic methods for determining the type and resolution of the screen available are described in the relevant language chapters. To help maintain compatibility between newer and older models with lower resolution screens a 'compatibility' mode may be provided.

LCD screens

Model	Resolution in pixels	Pixel pitch in mm	Pixel size in mm	Screen size in mm	Planes	Backlit
HC	160x80	0.34x0.43	0.31x0.40	54.4x34.4	Black only	yes
WA	240x100	0.26x0.30	0.23x0.27	62.4x30.0	Black & Grey	yes
S3	240x80	0.38x0.43	0.35x0.40	92.4x34.4	Black only	no
Siena	240x160	0.25x0.25	0.23x0.23	60.0x40.0	Black & Grey	no
S3a	480x160	0.26x0.26	0.20x0.20	124.8x41.5	Black & Grey	no
S3c	480x160	0.26x0.26	0.20x0.20	124.8x41.5	Black & Grey	yes

Sound hardware

The Series 3, Siena, Series 3a and 3c have varying internal audio hardware and therefore provide distinct sets of sound services, an overview is given here.

Sound on the Siena

The Siena has only a piezoelectric buzzer and so is restricted to emitting warning beeps and other simple sounds, it does not have a speaker or microphone and cannot record or play digital sounds.

Sound on the Series 3

The Series 3 has a piezoelectric buzzer and a loudspeaker, but it can emit only piezo-electric buzzer sounds, DTMF dialling tones, and simple alarm sounds. However, by loading a suitable device driver, such as SNDFRC.LDD which drives the speaker, the machine can also be made to emit sequences of musical notes of variable duration, thus greatly extending its sound capabilities (SNDFRC.LDD is supplied with the SIBO C SDK).

Sound on the Series 3a/c

The Series 3a/c have both a loudspeaker and a microphone, but do not have a piezo-electric buzzer. The Series 3a/c produce buzzer sounds via a piezo buzzer emulation using the speaker which takes more power to drive. Considerably greater sound capabilities are available on the Series 3a/c. In addition to emitting buzzer sounds, DTMF dialling tones and simple alarm sounds, the Series 3a and 3c can play two sequences of musical notes simultaneously, and can play and record compressed digital sound files (WVE files).

Sound on the HC

The HC has a piezoelectric buzzer, amplifier driven loudspeaker and microphone - see Sound on the Series 3a/c above.

Sound on the Work*about*

The Work*about* has only a piezoelectric buzzer and so is restricted to emitting warning beeps and other simple sounds, it does not have a speaker or microphone and cannot record or play digital sounds.

System time and date

The system time is stored (in a 32 bit unsigned ULONG value) as the number of seconds since 00:00:00, January 1, 1970 (compatible with UNIX system time). Obviously the system time will eventually overflow, but not until approximately 136 years after 1970, sometime in the year 2106. A range of system functions are available for accessing the components of the time and date (e.g. year, month, day, hour, minute and second etc.) and for converting between different representations of the date and time.

External communication

All SIBO computers have the ability to connect with external devices such as printers, modems or other computers. Connection methods vary depending on the model and nature of the external device. For example to connect a Series 3c or Siena to another computer, a custom RS232 serial port and cable is used, the Series 3 and 3a are connected through a high speed SIBO serial port via an appropriate conversion device incorporated into the cable. The HC and Workabout industrial handheld units have a variety of connection ports and cables, they can also be connected to external devices through cradles or docking stations.

Opening a channel to the TTY: device provides access to a fully interrupt driven RS-232 serial port. The Siena and Series 3 family recognise only one serial port i.e. the TTY:A port, which supports read / write operations for data, and sensing / setting operations for the serial port parameters and control lines.

A new ASIC, called the CONDOR chip, was introduced with the Series 3c and Siena for serial communications. The new chip, combined with a modifed ROM routines, enabled serial port speeds up to 57.6K baud on the Series 3c (19.2K baud on the Siena).

Opening a channel to the PAR: device provides access to a centronics parallel port, incorporated into a special cable, and is used for printing (see the notes below). The Series 3 family and Siena recognise only one parallel port i.e. the PAR:A port, which is a write only device and does not support read operations.

Bi-directional infrared communications became possible with the introduction of the Series 3c and Siena models. The new CONDOR ASIC described above also handles the serial infrared link. At the time of going to print (September 1997) only Psion to Psion infrared transfers, or infrared printing are possible with suitably IrDA enabled systems. An infrared Psion to PC link has yet to become available as a standard option.

Note:
Problems may be experienced when opening the PAR: device (i.e. the parallel device driver) for printing, for example on the Series 3c or Siena. If you experience an error of the type 'Device not present' it may be necessary to print using the TTY: device instead, even though a parallel cable is being used - see the text file 'FORUM06.TXT' lines 841-1405 in the \ONLINE directory on disk.

The infrared protocols used on the Series 3c and Siena have changed on the Series 5 and data transfers from SIBO to Series 5 are not possible using the standard system software).

The EPOC16 operating system

All applications software on the Siena and Series 3 family of personal organiser run under the control of EPOC16, a 16 bit Operating System which is proprietary to Psion. All other hand held products such as the Workabout and HC ranges from Psion also use EPOC16. The name EPOC is not an acronym, but is a short form of epoch, a name that was intended to reflect the dramatic change from an eight to a sixteen bit operating system that the original grey Psion organiser II used.

Key features

- Pre-emptive multitasking
- MS-DOS compatible file systems
- Installable file systems, including remote file access
- Asynchronous services
- Support for client server services
- A comprehensive I/O (Input / Output) system with many built in I/O devices
- Dynamically loadable device drivers
- Re-entrant function library
- Multiple processes of the same program share a single copy of the executable code.
- Support for a proprietary Object Oriented Programming (OOP) system
- Re-entrant dynamic link libraries.

EPOC versions

EPOC16

There have been several versions of the 16 bit EPOC operating system during the life of the Series 3 range. The version on any particular machine can be obtained by the user from the system screen, or programatically (by an EPOC16 call or using a PLIB library function from within a C program). Similar facilities are available to determine the ROM (Read Only Memory) version, since the Operating System is never released on its own, EPOC16 is always supplied with a number of other files built into the ROM.

Since the machines are sold widely internationally there are also language variants of the ROM (currently around 22 types, see the Appendix for a list). The language of a particular machine can be obtained by specific system calls (examples of these calls are given under the appropriate language section).

An MS-DOS version of EPOC16 is also available to allow the full emulation of the Siena and Series 3/3a on a PC. Copies of the 3a and Siena emulators are supplied on disk.

During the development of EPOC16 and related ROM based facilities, a number of bugs have arisen and in many cases have been fixed, changes in the functionality provided have occurred, some of which are relevant to the programmer. Wherever possible the impact of bugs or changes will be given in the appropriate section.

EPOC32

A new version of EPOC lies at the heart of the newly released Psion Series 5. EPOC32 is a 32-bit operating system developed for high performance products such as high-end palmtops, communicators and smart phones, and is covered in more detail in the 'Series 5' chapter.

The system screen

On a Siena or Series 3 the system screen (also known the Shell Application, SYS$SHLL) is the supervisor process that provides the user interface to the system, and control over the applications running in the system. All of the built-in applications and other suitably constructed third party application programs should communicate with the system screen task for the following reasons:

To display the name, in bold, of any file currently open in the file list under the programs icon, in the system screen.

To ensure that the file name is also displayed in any status window that may be showing.

On receiving a 'Shut down' request from the system screen, an application can close itself down tidily, saving any changes to file as appropriate. Alternatively, applications can be requested to 'Switch files', i.e. to create a new file or change the file the application is currently operating with.

Applications use two mechanisms to communicate their preferences to the system screen concerning any file switching, as well as the name of the file they may currently be using:

During compilation or translation, data is included in the application's .APP or .OPA file; this data may include whether the application is file-based (see Application types later) and if so the default extension of any files to be used, plus the default directory for such files.

Other data is passed in the 'Command line' when the application is started, and this is written to various 'EPOC16 reserved (or magic) static variables', these include the full path name of any file currently in use by the application (see EPOC16 magic statics later).

Processes and priorities

A process is a running program. EPOC16 is a single-user multi-tasking operating system that rapidly switches contexts between a number of independent processes - creating, at times, the illusion of multiple processes running in parallel. When there is more than one process that is ready to run EPOC16 runs the process with the highest priority. If there is more than one ready process with the same highest priority, they take it in turns to run every four system ticks. The initial process priority is normally taken from a value stored in the program file or image, but it may subsequently be changed.

Processes, clients and servers

EPOC16 is a single user, multi-tasking operating system so all active applications with a user interface must share the same screen and keyboard. A 'server' process, called the window server (SYS$WSRV), that runs under EPOC16 provides 'client' processes with shared access to the screen, keyboard and any other user interface devices (e.g. pointing device) that may be present.

Using a server process to share a common resource between a number of clients is a common technique in multi-tasking environments. Another example is the file server, a high priority system process (with process name SYS$FSRV) that performs all file related operations on behalf of 'client' processes i.e. application programs.

The EPOC16 operating system has a number of design features which support client / server relationships.

Processes, foreground and background

At any moment only one client of the window server can be in the foreground, i.e. receiving keyboard input from the user, all other clients are queued in the background. The window of the foreground client is the window that is currently visible, those of the background clients are said to be 'behind' the foreground client window.

When a process starts it normally would come into the foreground (although it is possible to start up a program in the background). Programs can put themselves (or other clients) into the background, or bring themselves (or others) into the foreground. Key press information is not normally received by background programs, but they can opt to capture specific keys by special means.

Events, an introduction

Events significant to EPOC16 are generated by the following occurrences:

- Menu hot key press by the user
- Other key presses of significance to the particular application such as cursor keys etc.
- System screen messages such as 'switch files' or 'close down'
- System messages such as foreground background changes
- System switch on or off etc.

For each client, the Windows Server keeps a queue of events that inform the client of user input and other events. The different types of window server events include:

- Key presses
- Foreground/background changes
- Window redraw events
- Mouse events (if the machine has a pointing device)

Other possible events might include:

- Data arriving from a serial port
- The expiry of a timer or an alarm
- Change of system date
- A process which is ready to run

A program which can react to and process such events, whilst remaining responsive to the user, who may wish to interrupt a process, must be specifically structured to do so and must make use of the asynchronous services provided by EPOC16.

Multi-tasking and multi-threading

Since under EPOC16, its is possible to have several programs apparently running at the same time, each of which may be required to respond to a number of different types of event, it is important to clarify the differences between multi-tasking and multi-threading:

Multi-tasking involves two (or more) different processes; multi-threading involves two (or more) event sources within one process.

EPOC16 takes care of multi-tasking automatically, on behalf of applications; multi-threading requires conscious effort from an application designer.

Multi-tasking is pre-emptive in that a process with a higher priority that is ready to run will always displace a lower priority process that is running.

Multi-threading is non pre-emptive in that an event source with a higher priority may have to wait until a lower priority event source voluntarily releases the processor (gives up the CPU), before it is able to run, since prioritisation of event sources within a multi-threaded application is handled by the application itself. An example might be a game which is currently calculating its next move and a higher priority timer process elapses. Unless the move calculation thread (typically a procedure) voluntarily gives up CPU occasionally, the thread that handles the elapsed timer will not have chance to run.

For complex applications which may involve responding to a number of different event sources, a program designer may decide to use a multi-threaded approach and will therefore be responsible for controlling the priority and activity of each possible thread, usually by using asynchronous requests (see the Applications, Processes and Memory chapter). An alternative approach might be to have a main program that initiates a number of other sub-processes which are responsible for specific tasks. The main program and its sub-processes could use a mechanism such as inter-process messaging to pass signals and information between themselves.

Applications

Executable files exist in several forms: .OPO and .OPA from OPL, .IMG from C or Assembler and .APP from C or Oval. An application (.APP or .OPA) is mainly distinguished from an executable file (.IMG or .OPO) by being installable onto the system screen and having an icon. Applications programs can also be of a variety of types e.g. File based or not file based, and with or without a user interface.

Memory

As processes are created and destroyed, EPOC16 is free to move code and data segments around as necessary, without needing any co-operation from active application programs. Programmers do not need to worry about this, it will have no direct effects on their code or data segments. EPOC16 makes extensive use of the V30H (8086) segment registers (CS,

DS, SS and ES) in its highly efficient manipulation of memory. All programs in the EPOC16 environment must not normally make use of the segment registers.

This limitation restricts C programmers to exclusive use of the small programming model. It is also the reason for the exclusive use of the Topspeed C Compiler that generates pure small model code (which most other compilers do not), that is guaranteed not to use the segment registers.

All programs are limited to code and data segments of 64K (less 32 bytes for data). In the EPOC16 environment this is not as limiting as it may first appear. For programs which require more memory for code or data there are many options and work-arounds that are discussed in the chapters on specific programming languages.

On 8086 class processors up to 1Mb of memory may be addressed directly. On SIBO machines, depending on the model, all or part of this address range may be used. The contents of the internal RAM drive will survive a system reset, most application crashes and even some system crashes. If a hard reset is performed the system will revert to its original state before the batteries were inserted, and all data on the internal RAM drive will be lost. On SIBO systems with more than 512K of RAM, the additional RAM is not available for use by program code or data segments, it is allocated to internal RAM drive space. On a system with more than 512K of memory e.g. a 2M byte machine, the whole of the first 512K of memory will be available for programs and their data. Only when the upper 1.5 M bytes allocated to RAM disk becomes full will the RAM disk space begin to encroach on the 512K of program memory.

Inter-process communications (IPCS)

Any process can send a message to another process, as long as the target process has prepared itself to receive messages by initialising the messaging system provided by EPOC16. The inter-process communication or messaging system was designed to closely follow the I/O System (see later) in terms of its range of synchronous and asynchronous services, i.e. the methods of signalling, use of semaphores and status words. The similarities of operation enable the inter-mingling of asynchronous I/O and asynchronous inter-process messaging.

Files

EPOC16 is said to have a MS-DOS compatible file system, what this means in practise is that it uses the same type of root directory \ sub-directory tree structure, and the same type of file naming convention i.e. the familiar 8.3 or nnnnnnnn.xxx file naming system. Where the file name can be up to eight characters, with an optional period separator, plus an optional file name extension of up to three characters. To accommodate the concepts of 'Installable file systems' and 'Remote file access' EPOC16 also uses node names to specify the location of a filing system.

File specifications

A full EPOC16 file specification has the form <node><device><dir><name><ext> where:

<node> is the file system node e.g. LOC:: in this case referring to local storage on the Psion itself.

<device> is the drive or device name e.g. A: for drive A

<dir> is the directory path e.g. \APP\DOCS\

<name> is the file name e.g. DESIGN

<ext> is the file name extension e.g. .TXT

An example of a complete file specification is:

LOC::A:\APP\DOCS\DESIGN.TXT

Getting suitable filenames is kept simple for the user and for programmers by making use of one of two types of filename specifier, i.e. File Name Selectors and File Name Editors, see the 'Files in EPOC16' chapter.

I/O (input/output) system

A comprehensive input/output (I/O) system is supported by EPOC16, which includes many hardware devices and some software sub-systems. A programmer must (directly or indirectly) use the I/O system to do general file handling, or to interact with various devices and systems within the SIBO environment.

Device drivers

The I/O system is implemented using software interfaces called device drivers, designed to isolate programmers from the details of any underlying hardware, e.g. to print to the parallel port a programmer will open a channel to the PAR: device (see note in the 'External communication' section earlier). EPOC16 hides the complexity of the process from the programmer by means of a suitable device driver. Though the exact implementation of the parallel port hardware may differ across SIBO machines, it will have no effect on the code of an application program. Differences in SIBO hardware are accommodated by using different device drivers for different Psion models.

4 Processes, Memory and Applications

Processes

A process is a running program, normally created by loading a program image file (also called an executable) from the system screen, or via an operating system call such as the PLIB C library call p_execc. After loading the program, the process creator normally calls p_presume to start the process running.

EPOC16 is a single-user multi-tasking operating system that rapidly switches contexts between a number of independent processes - creating, at times, the illusion of multiple processes running in parallel. The maximum number of processes that may exist in a SIBO system is E_MAX_PROCESSES (i.e. 24 on the Series 3 family).

Process priorities

When there is more than one process that is ready to run, the operating system runs the process with the highest priority (an unsigned byte value in the range 1 to 255). Lower priority processes are blocked indefinitely. If there is more than one ready process, with the same highest priority, they take it in turn to run every four system ticks.

Applications should set their priority in the range E_MIN_PRIORITY (i.e. 64) to E_MAX_PRIORITY (i.e. 192) inclusive (the operating system reserves the values outside this range). OPL and OVAL programmers do not normally have to concern themselves directly with process priorities.

The initial process priority is normally taken from a value stored in the program file or image (and is generated by the tool used to build the image) but it may subsequently be changed. (E.g. using the PLIB function p_setpri, p_getpri returns the priority of a process).

Interactive application processes that are clients of the window server are normally created at the priority E_PRIORITY_FORE (i.e. 128) and subsequently leave it to the window server to change their priority depending on whether the process is receiving user input or not.

The supervisor runs at priority 248 and the file server at priority 240. A hardware interrupt runs at the same priority as the process it interrupts. Critical sections of interrupt code are protected by switching off pre-emption.

Semaphores

Semaphores are indicator flags, created and used by EPOC16 to synchronise co-operating processes (where, in this context, a process includes a hardware interrupt). There are three common uses:

- Synchronising access to a shared resource e.g. a storage device.
- Synchronising supplier-consumer relationships e.g. a semaphore associated with a pool of data in a shared data segment.
- Synchronising the completion of asynchronous requests (see later)

The semaphores used by EPOC16 are counting semaphores, having a signed value that can be incremented and decremented via operating system calls or library functions. A semaphore with a negative value implies that a process must wait for the completion of some other event, such as the freeing of a shared resource. The mechanism by which a process waits on a semaphore is part of the overall management of process scheduling.

Asynchronous versus synchronous services

Many system services are implemented in two steps:

- Make the service request.
- Wait for the requested operation to complete - i.e. the waiting process is suspended.

In most cases, as well as providing functions for each step, the system provides a function containing both the above steps. Such combined functions are called 'synchronous' because they automatically cause the requesting process to wait until the operation has completed, i.e. they synchronise it. Functions which queue service requests without waiting for their completion are called 'asynchronous' functions.

Applications use asynchronous requests in situations like the following:

- Make service request A
- Make service request B
- Wait for either of the requested operations to complete - whilst possibly doing some other processing, whilst waiting for one or more of the service requests to complete.

Processes wait for the completion of asynchronous requests by waiting on their I/O semaphore, where each request is associated with a status word - a static variable (or value from the heap) for each request, that is used to indicate the current status of the request that was made. After making one or more asynchronous requests, a process makes an O/S call (e.g. PLIB function `p_iowait`) to wait on the I/O semaphore for one of the requests to complete. A typical application process spends most of its time waiting on its I/O semaphore. For example, an interactive application process that is waiting for user input from the window server is waiting on the I/O semaphore. When the request completes a value will be written into the status word associated with the request that has completed.

The I/O semaphore

When a process is created, the system automatically creates an I/O semaphore on its behalf (a more descriptive name would be the asynchronous request semaphore). Although this semaphore is used for I/O operations, it is used in general for asynchronous requests of other types. The I/O semaphores are stored in the private data space of the operating system, (they can be viewed using the SIBO debugger or the Spy application - discussed elsewhere).

At any particular moment only one process is actually running. When a re-schedule occurs, EPOC16 runs the process with the highest priority that is ready to run. If there is only one ready process at the highest priority it will continue to run indefinitely (and any lower priority processes, that are ready, will wait indefinitely). Pre-emptive multi-tasking means that the running process may be replaced at any time - it does not have to make a system call to yield the processor. A process that becomes ready will immediately run if it has the highest priority.

Therefore it is possible for a process to run for as long as it wants to, and in practice this often happens. However, many events can cause a re-schedule in which the current process is pre-empted, by a higher priority process, without completing its course.

Such events include:

- The fourth consecutive system tick.
- A semaphore being signalled (e.g. as a result of user input) which releases a higher priority waiting process.
- The expiry of a higher priority process in the timer DELTA queue.
- The current process may, by its own action, cause itself to be pre-empted by:
- Signalling the I/O semaphore of a higher priority process (by calling p_iosignalbypid or, for example, by sending it an inter-process message)
- Releasing a higher priority process from the SUSPENDED state (e.g. after loading another process from an image)
- Raising the priority of another process.
- By lowering its' own priority.

If there is more than one ready process with the highest priority, then each process is made current for a fixed time period (4 system ticks), after which the operating system makes the next process of that priority current in what is called a 'round robin' fashion. On a SIBO machine, the system 'ticks' 32 times a second.

Because EPOC16 is a single-user system, the current process is comparatively rarely switched out by the system tick. It is more likely to stop running because an event occurred that made a higher priority process become ready, or because the current process voluntarily gave up its ready status to wait for an event to occur.

In EPOC16, a process consists of at least the following:

- A process control block (described below).
- A data segment, containing the processor stack, static variables and the heap.
- A primary code segment (which is shared if there are one or more other processes of the same program).
- An I/O semaphore (see later).

On SIBO machines, a process that tries to write to a memory segment other than its own data segment is halted with panic number 60. See the end of this chapter for an explanation of panics. (Certain system functions explicitly allow inter-process data transfers - see 'Inter-Process Communication' in the 'Programming Techniques' chapter.)

A code segment may exist in ROM or it may be loaded into a RAM segment from an executable file. A process may acquire other resources during its lifetime - for example, I/O channels or additional code segments. The system automatically releases owned resources such as memory segments, I/O channels and semaphores when a process terminates. Server processes are also designed to clean up client resources when a client process terminates.

System processes

When the operating system initialises itself, it creates a number of system processes, some of which are essential to the operation of EPOC16. After a system reset on a typical machine running EPOC16, the system processes (by process name) are:

SYS$NULL.$01   The zero priority null process runs when no other process is ready to run and switches the machine off (to reduce power consumption) after a period of inactivity.

SYS$MANG.$02   The supervisor has a higher priority than any other process (248) and performs many critical system functions including memory segment moving and resource clean-up when a process terminates.

SYS$FSRV.$03   The file server has the second highest priority (240) and performs all file related operations, including loading a program image to create a process. The file server creates the SYS$WSRV process during start up.

SYS$WSRV.$04   The window server (priority 190) provides shared access to the screen, keyboard and, if present, a pointing device (e.g. a mouse). The window server creates the SYS$SHLL process during start up.

SYS$SHLL.$05   The shell process (priority 112) provides a user interface that allows other processes to be started.

TIME.$06   The time process (priority 144) provides all of the alarm services on the Series 3, Siena and Work*about* systems.

The extension of the process name (e.g. .$01) gives the process number (assigned by the operating system). The structure of process names is described later in this chapter.

Operating System functions are available to change a process name, change a process priority and suspend a process (all of these will fail if they are applied to SYS$NULL, SYS$MANG and SYS$FSRV).

(On systems with a digitiser or mouse, the window server creates a subsidiary process, sharing its data segment, to draw the mouse icon. In EPOC16, a subsidiary process that shares the data segment of its owner is called a 'task', and the window server pointer task has a name such as SYS$WSRV.@05.

The notifier service, p_notify may be provided by the window server itself or it may be provided by a client of the window server. If a separate notifier exists, it has a process name such as SYS$NTFY.$07.)

Process IDs and process control block

Each process is identified by its process ID - a positive 16-bit number containing two bit fields:

The least significant 12 bits is the offset of the process control block in the operating system data segment (also called the process slot).

The most significant 4 bits contains a value in the range 0-7 (note that a valid process ID is positive). This value is incremented modulo 8 each time a process slot is re-used so that an invalid process ID may be rejected if the process being referred to has already terminated.

EPOC16 O/S calls (and C functions such as PLIB p_getpid) are available to return the process ID of the caller, or in fact the ID of any other process. If a system function is passed a process ID that is zero or negative, or in which the least significant 12 bits is outside the range of the process table, the caller is panicked with panic number 7 (invalid process ID).

Process queues

In EPOC16 a process that is not the current process is either suspended or it is held in one of three doubly linked queues i.e. READY, SEMAPHORE or DELTA.

Processes in the READY queue are ordered by the process priority. On a re-schedule, the process at the high priority end of the ready queue runs. If there is more than one ready process at the highest priority, they take it in turns to run every 4 system ticks.

For each semaphore created by processes in the system there is a SEMAPHORE queue. This queue may be empty, or may contain one or more processes in a first-in, first-out order. If the decremented semaphore is negative, the calling process is placed at the end of the appropriate semaphore queue. When that semaphore is subsequently incremented, the process at the head of the semaphore queue is either made current (if it has the highest priority) or it is inserted into the READY queue (after any processes of equal priority).

The time DELTA queue is a special kind of doubly-linked queue. It stores the time interval, in system ticks, between timer entries. The single (possibly empty) time DELTA queue contains both processes and timer device entries. The processes are waiting for a relative or an absolute time i.e. for a specific time period to elapse or for a particular time and date to arrive. The timer device entries are associated with processes that have requested an asynchronous timer. The head of the queue has its DELTA time decremented on every system tick, and is removed when it reaches zero or negative. If it is a process, it is inserted into the READY queue. If it is a timer device entry, the associated process I/O semaphore is signalled.

Process names

A process name has the following form:

```
<name><ext>
```

Where the <name> component contains between one and eight characters and the <ext> component consists of a period, a $ and a two digit number of the form 01, 02, 03 .... This number gives the index (starting from 1) of the process slot.

If the process is a *task* (i.e. a subsidiary process that shares the same data segment), the $ is replaced by a @ where (except for the @) the process name is otherwise the same as the creator of the task.

The maximum length of a process name is E_MAX_NAME (i.e. 12), excluding the zero terminator (buffers normally allow E_MAX_NAME+2 bytes to include the zero terminator, and to keep following variables on an even address).

When a process is created by loading an image, the process is created with a <name> taken from the file name of the image. For example, if a program called LOC::\B:\UTILS\SORT.IMG is loaded twice the process names might be:

SORT.$07
SORT.$11

The <ext> component of a process name guarantees that the process name is unique. Note that the process data segments are given the same unique names, but that data segment names are held independently of the process name.

To convert a process name into a process ID, you use an O/S call (or C library function e.g. PLIB p_pidfind). Since a program cannot anticipate the <ext> component, wild card characters are allowed in a match string. When there is the prospect of more than one process of the same <name> (because a program was loaded more than once), another system service (e.g. PLIB p_pfind) may be used to get the process IDs of all instances.

Processes and auto-switch-off

By default the Siena and Series 3 family auto-switch-off period is set to 300 seconds, system services are available to read (sense), set and disable auto-switch-off e.g. when a mains adapter is connected. It's the zero priority null process (SYS$NULL) which automatically switches the machine off, after the system has been inactive for the auto-switch-off period, to reduce power consumption.

Inactivity counter resets

It may be desirable to have a program running continuously that could contain some regular activity that keeps resetting the inactivity counter of the system. For example, a continuously running clock program might use a repeatedly re-started short interval relative timer. Such programs should not be allowed to stop the system from automatically switching off in the absence of any significant activity. Even if the user was to turn the computer off explicitly, an alarm ringing at some stage would start the program running again, and if the user is not at hand to notice the alarm, the result may be flattened batteries - regardless of the auto-switch-off setting.

Such processes can be marked, via a system service, as not being significant when it comes to determining what constitutes activity. For example the addition of a call to the PLIB function p_unmarka (or the EPOC16 O/S call GenMarkNonActive) will mark the program as apparently inactive and will prevent any activity within the program from resetting the system inactivity counter, resulting in a much more socially responsible program.

SYS$NULL does not get to run

Similarly, situations may arise where the null process does not get an opportunity to run if any other applications are continually running, i.e. the priority of SYS$NULL is lower than that of any other process. Such applications may have to assume responsibility for allowing the machine to switch off, by calling an appropriate EPOC16 system service, e.g. to call the PLIB function p_allowoff from time to time. By doing so, an application assumes responsibility for performing the auto-switch-off that would otherwise be done by SYS$NULL, if it had an opportunity to run.

A real-life example of such an event source would be a re-calculation computation in a spreadsheet, or a reformatting calculation in a word processor. Also a long file operation, such as building the index of a DBF file, should also be broken up into chunks, so allowing the application the chance to respond to other event sources in the meantime. Finally, a game may think indefinitely until such time as it is told to stop.

Programs, which are usually waiting for user input followed by a brief period of processing, will not normally have to worry about these problems.

Idle objects

In applications that handle multiple events, for example, by using asynchronous requests in a fixed order of priority, it is normal practise to put a compute intensive task such as a spreadsheet re-calculation at a low priority position, to avoid the program from becoming unresponsive. The calculation task is considered to be an event source in its own right, i.e. given an opportunity it is always ready to take CPU. Event sources such as this are sometimes referred to as idle objects. This, slightly confusing term, refers to the fact that it will only get a chance to run when the application is otherwise idle, since other event sources are higher in the priority chain. For example, if the application is busy responding to user key presses or other I/O events, it is not idle, and so any idle object e.g. re-calculation has no opportunity to run. Again a process such as a re-calculation should not be allowed to occur as one long uninterrupted task, ideally it should be broken up into sections, with periodic voluntarily returns to the main event processing loop.

Sub-process priorities

Another side-effect of continuous activity is that other processes of lower priority will be locked out. So, consider a program that has launched sub-processes, and is itself about to become compute intensive for an extended period. If it is required that the sub-processes should continue to have an opportunity to run then it is worth considering lowering the priority of the main process (e.g. to `0x70` - using the PLIB call `p_setpri`, where the default is 0x80).

Idle object or sub-process

For larger or more complex applications where a compute-intensive task will occur, the decision to assign it to an idle object within the application, or to a sub-process of the main application has to be made. A number of the following factors may be relevant:

A sub-process will allows a total combined data space greater than 64k.

Fragmentation of the heap is not such a problem for a sub-process since the entire heap will disappear when the sub-process terminates. Whereas for an idle object any heap fragmentation it creates affects the main application.

An idle object is much more tightly bound to the main program than is a sub-process, and communications between the main program and a sub-process have to be more formal. For example, the main process has to check for the existence of the sub-process that may have failed due to an error condition.

An idle object has access to the main application's windows, this is not true for a sub-process.

Memory

As processes are created and destroyed, EPOC16 is free to move code and data segments around as necessary, without needing any co-operation from active application programs. Programmers do not need to worry about this, it will have no direct effect on their code or data segments. EPOC16 makes extensive use of the V30H (8086) segment registers (CS, DS, SS and ES) in its highly efficient manipulation of memory. All programs in the EPOC16 environment must not normally make use of the segment registers.

This limitation restricts C programmers to exclusive use of the small programming model. It is also the reason for the exclusive use of the Topspeed C Compiler that generates pure small model code (which most other compilers do not), that is guaranteed not to use the segment registers.

For Assembler programmers the use of these segment registers is rarely necessary and is obviously very risky. They can only be changed safely by disabling interrupts, otherwise unpredictable and catastrophic effects will result.

OPL and OVAL programmers are largely insulated from detailed considerations of memory usage, unless the program is large or dynamic memory allocation is necessary using functions such as ALLOC.

All programs are limited to code and data segments of 64K (less 32 bytes for data). In the EPOC16 environment this is not as limiting as it may first appear. For programs which require more memory for code or data there are many options and work-arounds that are discussed in the chapters on specific programming languages.

On 8086 class processors up to 1Mb of memory may be addressed directly. On SIBO machines, depending on the model, all or part of this address range may be used, where the available memory (from address zero to 0xfffff) is allocated as follows:

* 1K bytes of interrupt vectors as required by the 8086 architecture.
* The screen bit-map (small display models).
* Operating System data space.
* Allocated memory segments (including application code segments, process data segments and device driver segments).
* Unallocated memory
* The internal RAM drive (LOC::M:).
* Environment variables (up to 4K bytes).
* Any portion of the 1Mb that is not used.
* The screen bit-map (large display models).
* The system ROM.

The contents of the internal RAM drive and the environment variables will survive a system reset (unless a hard reset is performed) and most system crashes. On models with more than 512K of RAM, the additional RAM is not available for use by program code or data segments, it is available as extra internal RAM drive space (accessed by memory bank switching techniques).

Memory that is dynamically allocated is organised into four main sections:

Memory segments
Unallocated memory
RAM drive (M:)
Environment variables

The system maintains all of the unallocated memory in a single chunk - between the allocated memory segments and the memory used by LOC::M:. This means that memory segments have to be moved as a result of other segments being created, deleted or having their size changed. Although application code segments and process data segments can and do move at any time while an application process is running, the operating system automatically adjusts the 8086 segment registers (CS, DS, SS and ES) to follow any movement without explicit support from the application - as discussed above.

When a process is created, a process specific data segment is also created. When that process is running application code, the 8086 DS, SS and ES registers point to the start of the data segment which can not be greater than 0xffe0 bytes long.

The data segment for each process contains (from low to high address):

- The reserved (magic) static variables (0x40 bytes).
- The floating point emulator data space (0x200 bytes from offset 0x100).
- The processor stack.
- Initialised static variables.
- Un-initialised static variables.
- The process heap.

The size of the processor stack is typically in the range 2K to 8K, but it can be varied (e.g. in C by using a different start up modules). Note that the stack size includes the 64 bytes of reserved (magic) static variables and the floating-point emulator data space.

All of the reserved static variables are initialised to zero, except for the word at address zero, which is initialised to 0xDEAD and is otherwise unused. Despite their name, the un-initialised static variables are also initialised to zero.

The bytes in the stack area are initialised to 0xff. The number of 0xff bytes from address 0x40 in the process data segment measures the number of spare bytes on the stack, provided the program is not using the floating point emulator. If the program is using the floating point emulator, the lowest point the stack should legitimately reach is 0x300.

The process heap contains dynamic data structures that are created and destroyed within the lifetime of the process. The heap is placed at the end of the process data segment so that it can be expanded (by expanding the process data segment). Since the data segment is limited to 0xffe0 bytes, the maximum heap size is somewhat smaller than 64K, depending on the size of the stack and the space taken by the static variables.

Magic (or reserved) static variables

The reserved statics (commonly referred to as magic statics) are variables with fixed, known, addresses, existing in the process data space (i.e. a unique set for each process which exist during the lifetime of the process) between addresses 0x00 and 0x40. They are 'magic' in the sense that they are accessible from all parts of the process code, even from dynamic library code (which does not have any data space and therefore may not, normally, access statics).

Some of these variables are used by EPOC16 to manage the process, others are used by system code, such as the window server and the graphics user interface libraries. The specific usage differs depending on the model of SIBO machine.

The remaining reserved statics are freely available for use by the process code. A common use is to provide access from dynamic library code to application-specific data, without the need for it to be passed in function parameters. These locations can also be used by an OPL program as temporary storage e.g. for passing back additional values from function calls. A full list of the reserved statics is given in Appendix.

`0x22` `DatProcessNamePtr`	System user interface library code assumes that this location contains either NULL or a pointer to a zero terminated string that the application wishes to be displayed as its name.
`0x24 DatCommandPtr`	This location contains a pointer, set up by the operating system. It points to an `alloc` cell that contains the full path name, as a zero terminated string, of the .IMG or .APP file from which the process was loaded. Immediately following the zero terminator, the `alloc` cell contains leading byte counted initial command line data.

`0x28 DatApp1`
`0x2a DatApp2`
`0x2c DatApp3`
`0x2e DatApp4`
`0x30 DatApp5`
`0x32 DatApp6`
`0x34 DatApp7`
	These 7 'word' size memory locations exist for each program and are free for application code to use, i.e. 14 bytes in total. They are accessible from anywhere in the applications code (including a DYL library which otherwise cannot have static data).

`0x38 DatGate`	System user interface library code may assume that this location contains an object handle. This is a handle to the Gate Object and can be use by OPL programs to set the Help file name, for access to the printer set up dialogs etc. see the OPL Programming Chapter for more details.
`0x3a DatLocked`	System user interface library code may assume that this location contains a flag indicating whether the application is capable of receiving termination or switch files messages.
`0x3c` `DatStatusNamePtr`	System user interface library code may assume that this location contains a pointer to a zero terminated string that will appear in a status window.
`0x3e` `DatUsedPathNamePtr`	System user interface library code may assume that this location contains a pointer to a fully parsed file name.

The values of the EPOC16 reserved statics `DatProcessNamePtr`, `DatLocked`, `DatStatusNamePtr`, and `DatUsedPathNamePtr` all have special significance for Siena and Series 3 applications. The values of these variables for different applications are read at various times by the system screen and also by the window server.

An application that fails to write suitable data to these statics may find that:

- An incorrect name is displayed in any status window shown in the application
- Instances of the application are shown in the wrong file list in the system screen
- Shut down or switch files messages arrive at inopportune moments from the system screen (see below for more on these messages)
- Assigning an application button to the application in the system screen has no effect.

In general, applications should write to these reserved statics:

- On initialisation (after having analysed the contents of their command line)
- Whenever a new file is opened
- Whenever the application is about to go 'busy' over an extended period of time.

There are routines in the HWIF and HWIM libraries, and functions in OVAL and OPL that assist with keeping these reserved statics up to date.

For more detail see 'Application command lines' later in this chapter.

(While debugging an application written in C using the SIBO Debugger, the values of reserved statics can be determined by using the 'Magic Statics' menu command.)

Re-entrant processes and functions

For efficient memory usage, system code and library function code is re-entrant, i.e. only one copy of the code is loaded, but more than one process may (apparently) be using it concurrently. Each separate program/process has its own unique data segment, but they all may share the same system or function code segment. The multi-tasking nature of EPOC16 gives the illusion of several processes running at the same time, in fact only one process will actually be using the code at any particular moment in time.

Shared code segments

When a second or subsequent 'copy' of the same program is loaded, the existing code segment (which has segment name `<name>.$SC`) is shared and is not loaded again from the program image file (however, a new set of initialised static data values are loaded into a new process data segment for the new 'copy' of the program). The system checks that the existing code segment matches the code in the image file. It compares the checksum of the process control block with the checksum stored in the image header (the checksum in the image header is also used to ensure the integrity of the code when it is first loaded). If the checksums do not match, the load fails. It follows that you cannot run different programs with the same name (or different versions of the same program - i.e. the version number that is stored in the executable file) at the same time.

Environment variables

The system allocates up to 4K bytes for environment variables at the high address end of the system RAM. Environment variables are available to all processes and can be created, deleted, read and set via a number of system services. Environment variables do have a number of valuable attributes but they are a scarce resource and should be used sparingly.

They exist beyond the lifetime of a process and so maybe useful for saving and restoring program settings between separate instances of the program. Hence it is not necessary to use a file if only a small amount of information is to be saved when a program is closed down. They are available to any process and can therefore be used as a simple mechanism for passing a limited amount of information between separate processes.

An environment variable consists of:

a name   of up to E_MAX_ENV_SIZE (i.e. 16) bytes containing any byte except ' * ' or ' ? '

a value   of up to P_ENVMAX-1 (i.e 256) bytes with no restriction on the content

Each environment variable is stored as two successive leading byte count strings (BCS).

Types of environment variable

There are two types of environment variable:

Those with names and values that are both zero terminated strings (ZTSs) i.e. C type strings.

Those whose name or value are other than a ZTS, i.e. contain binary data.

There are also two sets of system service routines for manipulating them - see the appropriate language chapters for examples.

Environment variables can be a powerful programming resource whilst being, at the same time, potentially troublesome. They consume space in a special RAM segment devoted to them - the more environment variables are created (and the larger these are), the greater the chance becomes of other applications failing to work properly, e.g. by not being able to create environment variables as required. Excessive use of environment variables may generate an out of memory condition, either because their own specific area has been exhausted or because the system in general has run out. A file should be used instead if an application wishes to save a large amount of data between invocations.

Naming of environment variables

Name conflicts are possible - data stored in an environment variable by one application may get obliterated by another application, storing different data to an identically named variable.

Psion have reserved the use of the ' $ ' character for use in the names of environment variables that are created and manipulated by Psion system software. All external applications should completely avoid using environment variables with ' $ ' characters in their names - unless they first secure the agreement of Psion. Environment variables can of course have 'simple' names, such as 'table' and 'list', but names such as these are likely to increase the chance of name clashes. It is probably better to use more cryptic names e.g. perhaps based on a derivation of the application name.

System environment variables

A list of all the main Psion system and application environment variables and their functions is given in the Appendix.

Applications

Executable files exist in several forms: .OPO and .OPA from OPL, .IMG from C or Assembler and .APP from C or OVAL. An application (.APP or .OPA) is mainly distinguished from an executable file (.IMG or .OPO) by: being installable onto the system screen and by having an icon.

Applications programs can also be of a variety of types e.g. File based or not file based, and with or without a user interface. All of the various types, the methods by which they communicate with the system screen and the methods of execution are discussed next. This section is rather long and a little complicated but it is an important one to master.

Application types

There are five types of OPAs and APPs:

OPA Type	APP Type	Example Application	Behaviour
0	0	Calc	Does not use files i.e. will have no file list when installed in the system screen - instead there will be only one entry, giving the Public Name of the application. Type 0 applications can have only one copy running at any one time.
1	n/a		Similar to type 0 but uses only one file with the same name as the OPA.
2	2	World	More than one file may exist, but only one may be in use (in bold) at one time. Used to restrict a file based application such that only one copy can run at any one time. Selecting a new file from the list under the icon will send a switch file message to the program which should close the current file and open the new one.

3	3	Agenda, Data, Sheet, Word etc.	More than one file and any number may be open (in bold) at once i.e. If a new file is selected from the list one of the running instances should change to this file. More than one instance of the program may be created (Shift Enter) each with a unique file.
4	4	RunOpl	Many files can be used, and any number may be in use at once. A new instance of the application is run each time a new file is selected. A type of 4 means that the application will have a file list in the system screen, but will never be sent Switch File instructions: however, it should read the command line on its start up.
	5	RunImg	The application is a pure file list application i.e. not a real application at all, but just an icon to group together various applications or utility programs.

Notes:

Initially, the Public Name (see below) appears under the icon. For a file based application, highlighting this name and pressing enter will use a file of this name (if no file exists, the program has the responsibility to create it).

With types 0 - 2 only one instance of the program can be running at any time, whereas types 3 and 4 allow more than one file to be in used at once, but a separate instance of the program will be run for each file.

Types 2, 3 and 4 allow you to create lists of files below the icon, either from within the program itself e.g. by selecting an option from a file menu, or possibly by using the new file option from the system screen.

A user may stop a running application by selecting an emboldened file from the system screen icon list and pressing the delete key. A shut down message (see later) will be sent to the application which should detect the event, save and close any files in use, then exit.

An application's behaviour may be further controlled by adding in additional modifier values to the type number. The type modifiers are described below.

OPL applications

A simple OPL program will generate a corresponding .OPO file when it is translated. On SIBO systems, .OPO files have to be located in an OPO directory to ensure that they appear on the system screen, under the bubble shaped RunOPL icon.

If the .OPO file is not located in an .OPO directory then from the RunOPL icon:

• Press TAB while the highlight is under the RunOPL icon
• Navigate with the file selector until the program file is selected
• Press ENTER to start the selected program.

Sophisticated OPO programs can be created, but they cannot be installed on the system screen, will not receive system messages and do not have icons.

An OPL Application has an `APP...ENDA` header, and when translated will generate a .OPA file containing an embedded icon, plus other essential information to allow it to be installed in the system screen. OPAs are almost exactly equivalent to APP files produced in C or by OVAL (APP files are discussed later).

Non trivial OPL programs, intended for distribution, would normally be of the OPA type. However, OPL applications impose some additional responsibilities on the program designer with respect to the handling of events and system messages - see the 'OPL16 Techniques' chapter for more details.

An OPL16 application source differs from a OPO source file in that it begins with a header of the form:

```
APP Example
    TYPE 3
    PATH "\EXAMPLE"
    EXT "EXA"
    ICON "\OPD\EXAMPLE.PIC"
ENDA
```

Where:

`APP` gives the Public Name of the application, `TYPE` specifies the OPA type (see above), `PATH` gives any default file path, `EXT` specifies the default filename extension, and `ICON` supplies the name and location of a suitable icon file. Once translated, the icon .PIC file is embedded into the .OPA file and so does not have to be supplied separately.

In OPL16, the behaviour of an application can be further modified by adding additional values to the type number, as follows:

OPA Type number, plus	Effect
$1000	Forces the use of a 48x48 pixel, black and grey icon.
$8000	Disables the 'New file' option from the system screen.
$4000	Stops the system screen from terminating the OPA – **do not** use this unless the reason is compelling.
$100	Allows the system screen to terminate the OPA, without sending it a 'shutdown message', i.e. 'X' (see 'Command line processing' later).

Adding in the additional values to the type number must **not** be done in the form of an expression, the values be a constant. For example in the PPCOPL16 application the OPA type is given as $1002, to specify a file based application, with only one file in use at a time and to use the 48x48 black and grey icon.

Note:

OPL32 application headers differ from those in OPL16 and the differences are detailed in the 'OPL32 Techniques' chapter.

C and Assembler programs - IMG and APPs

The system screen usually expects to install .APP files or .OPA files, it will also list all of the .IMG programs under the RunImg icon, provided that the .IMG executable files are located in a top level \IMG directory. You may need to install the RunImg icon, using Psion J, from the system screen.

If the .IMG file is not located in an .IMG directory then from the RunImg icon:

- Press TAB while the highlight is under the RunImg icon
- Navigate with the file selector until the program file is selected
- Press ENTER to start the selected program.

However, a program run via RunImg will receive no special command line from the system screen, nor will it receive any shut down or switch file messages from the system screen (these messages are discussed later). IMG files do not have an icon and so cannot be installed on the system screen. Applications run via RunImg display an empty icon in any Status Window used.

Add files

By convention an .APP file for a C application contains one or more so-called 'add-files' embedded within it, in addition to the core .IMG file itself. Add files include:

A .PIC file providing the icon for the application (.PIC file or a .FON file).

A .RSC or .RZC file providing the resource file for the application.

A .SHD file providing the shell data for the application.

Any add-files would normally be added into the .IMG file automatically during the full 'make' process.

Once built, the icon .PIC file is embedded into the .APP file and does not need to be supplied as a separate file. To be installed on the system screen a .APP file must contain a suitable icon.

Four add file slots are available, and in most cases at least one add-file slot will be free for use for an application specific file. Building additional files into the .APP file diminishes the chance of a user copying the .APP file from one SSD to another and neglecting to copy a vital associated file at the same time. For example, a program that uses special fonts many bind the special font file into the application file.

The .SHD file is a binary file that contains the Public Name of the application, the application's 'type' number and modifiers; for file-based applications it can specify any default file path, default file name extension and the name of a suitable icon file.

The application's behaviour may be further modified, by adding one or more of the following values to the 'type' number:

$8000	Prevents switch-file messages of the Create sort being sent to the application i.e. 'New file' option from the system screen.
$4000	Prevents the application being sent shutdown messages - this will also prevent the application being Killed from the system screen – **do not** use this unless the reason is compelling. (The *Spy* application released as part of the SDK will terminate such an application)
$2000	Indicates that the application's .MS file contains public names for more than one different language version.
$1000	Indicates that the .PIC file contains a 48 by 48 Series 3a/c icon (preceded by a 24 by 24 icon if the application is to run on the Series 3 as well as the Series 3a/c). The Series 3 does not recognise this flag and will simply read the 24 by 24 icon if present.
$100	Allows the system screen to terminate the APP, without sending it a 'shutdown message'. So, for example, pressing DELETE will act as 'Kill application'. The Series 3 does not recognise this flag.
$80	On selecting "Create new list" from the System Screen, the resulting dialog box will contain an extra line, for specifying Text editor or Word processor type. The Series 3 does not recognise this flag.

The .SHD file is a binary file made from a .MS text file using the makeshd.exe utility program provided in the C SDK.

The first line in a .MS file has general form:

```
<Name>[<.EXT>]
```

With the extension .EXT only being present for file-based applications. In that case, .EXT defines the default extension for the application. In all cases, Name is the so-called public name of the application. This must be a valid file name, that is, it must start with a letter and not exceed eight characters.

The second line in a .MS file gives the default directory for an application. This can be left blank for non file-based applications. For example, the .MS file for the built-in Time application could be:

```
Time

8000
```

With the second line left blank.

The third line in a .MS file gives the 'type' number of the application.

An .MS file can have fourth, fifth, sixth ... lines, but only if $2000 has been added to the application type, so that the application has multi-lingual shell data.

Suppose the Data application were to be translated into French, German, and Italian, and that its public names in these languages were to be Fiche, Daten, and Archivi, respectively. In that case, an appropriate .MS file would be as follows:

```
Data.DBF
\DAT\
2003
01Data
02Fiche
03Daten
05Archivi
```

A final step is to rename the .IMG file containing the add-files to have a .APP file name extension.

OVAL applications

OVAL generates fully-fledged applications that have icons and are installed on to the system screen. They can only be run on systems that have the OVAL run-time interpreter and support files available in ROM. All of the properties of an OVAL application, including the application type, the icon and other .PIC files, resource files etc. are specified as options and file names etc. within the OVAL integrated development environment. When the OVAL application is generated all of the options specified are included as part of the .APP file building process.

Public name

The significance of the Public Name of an application is as follows:

This is the name by which the system screen refers to the application, e.g. when allowing an application button to be assigned to the application.

This name will be displayed in the file list for the application, in the system screen, when files have not yet been created and the list would otherwise be empty.

The Public Name of an application must be a valid 8.3 format filename, i.e. FILENAME.EXT with no embedded spaces.

Default extension

The significance of the default extension for a file-based application is as follows:

Files will be shown in the file list for the application in the system screen only if their extension matches the default (with the exception that files are always shown - in bold - if they are currently the open file of an application)

The system screen will pass the specified default extension to the application as part of its command line (see later), when it is started.

Typically, applications will use filename selectors in dialogs which hide extensions matching the default (e.g. showing Example rather than Example.exa), and may even omit other files from the initial list presented.

Default path

Files will be shown in the file list (under the applications icon) in the system screen only if they are located in a directory whose name exactly matches the default path. An exception is that files are always shown (in bold) if they are currently the file that an application has open (e.g the user may have opened a file located in a directory not matching the default path). Default paths for applications are usually top level, as in \EXA. However, they can equally well be sub-directories, as in \EXA\PRIVATE, with the limitation that the total length cannot exceed 20 characters.

Icons

Application icons are bitmap files which have been attached to the executable file, such as Example.pic used in the OPA header above, and may be produced by a variety of means:

- Using one of the many Shareware or Freeware programs available such as Psicon or Draw284 included on the disks.
- Using the Iconed or Iconeda applications that are part of the Psion C SDK.
- Using the window server tool wspcx.exe on the .PCX output of a PC program such as Windows Paintbrush.

Icons are covered in more depth in the 'User Interface' chapter, information on the format of .PIC files is discussed in the 'Utilities and Support Files' chapter.

Help and other program resources

All program text, menu strings, help text and other constant data can be assembled into a program resource script file (.RSS) that is then processed into a 'compiled' (.RSC) or 'compiled and compressed' (.RZC) resource format. Applications can then load text and other information from the resource file as needed, using a unique identifier allocated to each piece of text or data item. A considerable number of advantages arise out of using resource files, including saving memory and simplifying the production of multi lingual applications. Implementing program help, and considerations for multi-lingual applications are covered in more detail in the 'User Interface' chapter. Producing and using resource files is described in the 'Programming Techniques' chapter.

Aliasing applications

Some file-based applications may acquire very large file lists. It may be desirable to separate a long file list into two or more separate lists, for example using the Word application you may wish to have all letters in one file list, all reports in another etc. Separate file lists for the same application could be distinguished on the system screen by having distinct icons, and different application buttons could be used to cycle round running instances of these tasks.

Going further, it may be desirable for the behaviour of an application to alter, depending on which type of file is open. For example, the behaviour of the built-in text editor is different for .WRD files (when the application is seen as Word) from .OPL files (when the application is seen as the OPL programming editor). Jotter, the note taking application on the S3c and Siena is in fact just an alias of the Data application.

The concept of aliasing an application is designed to meet these requirements. For each new file list required, an alias file (.ALS file) should be installed in the system screen. In practice the user can do this on the Series 3a/c or Siena using the 'Create new list' item from the 'Special' menu. Broadly speaking, the contents of a .ALS file match those of a shell data file (or .SHD file): the Public Name, default extension, and default directory are all defined, as well as the application type number. However, the .ALS file goes beyond the .SHD file in that it also specifies:

- The name of the application that is being aliased
- Optionally, some alias information that the system screen should pass to the application when it is run, via the command line, to configure its behaviour in some special way.

Active and passive aliasing

In theory, all applications are capable of being aliased, without them needing to make any specific provision for this possibility. This is known as *passive* aliasing.

Other applications pay explicit attention to any alias information that may be passed to them on their command lines, and adjust their behaviour according to the contents of this information. This is known as *active* aliasing. An example of active aliasing is that of the built-in text editor, as described next. (Jotter on the Series 3c and Siena is an alias of the Data application.)

Any other program that supports active aliasing is free to interpret alias information passed to it in any way that it wishes. There is no obligation to mimic the detailed rules obeyed by the text editor. Parts of the mechanism of aliasing rely on the application paying suitable attention to the details of the command line passed to it. Failure to do this will diminish the effect. Thus even passive aliasing relies on some co-operation from the application being aliased. This is just one reason why all serious applications should analyse the command line passed to them, as part of their initialisation procedures. There are routines in both the HWIF library, the `HWIM.DYL` , OVAL and in OPL to assist with analysing the command line.

Application command lines

Considering the nature of the user interface presented by the system screen the concept of a command line may seem inappropriate at first. However applications launched from the system screen do in fact receive a command line when they are started up, and subsequently may receive messages and new command line information during their lifetime.

The command line communicates the following information to an application that is about to start:

- The public name of the application.
- The default extension for any files used.
- The full path name of any file to open.
- If this file should be opened or created anew.
- Any alias information specified in an alias file.
- Exceptionally, whether the application is to connect to the window server in the background.

When a program starts, its command line is placed in an allocated cell within the heap of the application, the address of this cell is written to the EPOC16 reserved static DatCommandPtr.

The command line for any EPOC16 program always starts with a zero-terminated string containing the full path name of the process being run, the byte immediately after this gives the length of any following data. Ordinarily, when referring to 'the command line', it is this following data that you should have in mind.

For example, suppose the user presses TAB inside the OPL edit file list in the system screen, navigates using the file selector to loc::m:\dat\data.dbf, and then presses ENTER. The full command line passed to the chosen application (actually an alias of *Word*) is as follows:

```
ROM::WORD.APP<0><29>OProgram<0>.OPL OROPO<0>LOC::M:\DAT\DATA.DBF<0>
```

The `<29>` immediately following the zero at the end of the first zero terminated string indicates that the remainder of the command line is `0x29` (41 decimal) bytes long - as is indeed the case when counting all bytes including the terminating zeros, space and point characters but not < or >.

The next byte after this is the command byte:

`'O'` used for a file-based application to indicate that a named file is to be opened

`'C'` used for a file-based application to indicate that a named file is to be created

`'D'` means the application is to connect to the window server in background.

`'Z'` is used for starting an attached application.

(A command byte of `'D'` typically arises for the built-in applications. When it does arise, it is handled automatically by code in HWIM.DYL, which silently translates it into one of the other two cases. A command byte of 'Z' prevents the HWIM application manager from parsing the following command line data. Commands 'Z' and 'D' are not considered again)

After the command byte, there is a zero-terminated string giving the Public Name of the application, followed by another zero-terminated string, containing both the default extension and (if present) the alias information. The alias information, if present, is separated from the default extension by a space. Finally another zero-terminated string gives the full path name of the file to open or create.

In the above example:

- The command byte of the application is 'O'
- The Public Name of the application is 'Program'.
- The default extension is '.OPL'
- The alias information is 'OROPO'
- The name of the file to open is 'LOC::M:\DAT\DATA.DBF'.

In summary, the format of the command line of an application is as follows:

`<cmdbyte><PName><0>[<defextn>[<space><aliasinfo>]<0><fullpath><0>]`

There are routines in the HWIF and HWIM libraries, and functions in OVAL and OPL that assist with analysing the command line.

From command line to magic (reserved) statics

DatProcessNamePtr (0x22)

This static is read by the system screen to determine which file lists a running application (in bold) should be placed into. It is also read by the window server when deciding which action to take when an application button is pressed. Finally, it is read by the system screen in response to any 'Quit application' menu commands, to determine how to implement this request (i.e. how much co-operation the system screen might expect from the application).

System screen file lists

The file lists in the system screen are built as follows:

For each list, the set of all eligible files is compiled; these will all be displayed in normal type. The file list is found for each running application by reading the value of DatProcessNamePtr for each active application. The name of any file that the application currently has open is found by reading the value of DatUsedPathNamePtr and possibly also reading the value of DatProcessNamePtr. If this name matches any entry in the file list, that entry is removed (so that it is no longer displayed) and the name of the open file is added to the list, in bold.

Obviously, the lists will be misleading if the running application is assigned to the wrong list. Assigning a running application to a particular file list is straightforward. The preferred Public Name of the application is read from DatProcessNamePtr, if this matches the Public Name of any existing file list, the application is assigned to that list otherwise, the application is assigned to the *RunImg* list.

To prevent the display of private system processes within the system screen file lists, entries starting with Sys$ are never displayed in a file list, similarly the name Link is never displayed in the RunImg list. Files with the 'hidden' attribute set are never displayed in a system screen file list - unless the file is open within an application (in which case it will be displayed in bold). To check for the existence of hidden files or files starting with Sys$ in a directory, the TAB key should be used to enter 'directory' mode of the system screen. It is also possible to task to an application whose open file starts with Sys$ by repeatedly pressing the SHIFT+SYSTEM key combination, which tasks round *all* running applications (that are clients of the window server).

Assigning application buttons

Suppose that the user has installed the Spy application (see later), and has assigned the application button CONTROL+WORD to it. The system screen updates a data structure that associates each of the possible application buttons to Public Names of applications (e.g. 14 buttons on the Series 3). The address of this data structure, within the system screen data space, is known to the window server (in fact it is kept at DatApp1 in the window servers own data segment).

When the user presses CONTROL+WORD the following happens:

The window server consults this data structure to determine the Public Name that is currently associated with this application button.

It next checks whether the Public Name of the current foreground application matches Spy, reading the Public Name from DatProcessNamePtr. If so, this application is sent a special key-press event, with key code value equal to W_KEY_MODE (as defined in WSKEYS.H) - unless the SHIFT modifier is also held down, in which case the algorithm continues as follows.

The clients of the window server are scanned in current task order, to see whether any can be found with the required Public Name, if one is found it is made the foreground task. Failing this a message is sent to the system screen to position the file list to the application that has the given Public Name. If no such file list exists, the system screen beeps and gives a suitable error message.

The main point is that, the Public Name of the application has to be written to DatProcessNamePtr.

Incidentally, it is now clear why pressing the CONTROL+SYSTEM key (assigned to *RunImg*), or any other application button assigned to a pure file list application, often fails to have the desired effect (of bringing to foreground a running application listed in the relevant file list). The point is that these applications are generally run without any command line being passed to them, so they cannot set up a suitable value at DatProcessNamePtr merely by analysing their command lines.

Also note that the assigned buttons differ in one aspect of their behaviour, depending on the machine used. Consider an application, the built-in database for example, that is currently running in the foreground. On the Series 3, pressing the Data button would change the application from search mode into change mode, and on a second press, back into search mode. On the Series 3a pressing the Data button has no effect when there is currently only one copy of the application running. However when multiple copies are running, then pressing the Data button has the effect of sequentially bringing each copy into foreground - simultaneously holding down the shift key reverses the order of bringing into foreground.

DatUsedPathNamePtr (0x3e)

The EPOC16 reserved static DatUsedPathNamePtr is read solely by the system screen, which assumes that if it is non-null for an application, DatUsedPathNamePtr points to a full path specification of the file currently open in the application. As described above in the section on `DatProcessNamePtr`, these filenames are used when generating the file lists in the system screen:

- Any open file matching an entry in the non-bold section of the file list replaces that entry
- The filename is parsed/rearranged, e.g. from the form `LOC::A:\WRD\SHOPPING.WRD` into Shopping[A].

In case `DatUsedPathNamePtr` is null, the value of the string at `DatProcessNamePtr` (if any) is used instead: failing that, the process name (as returned by the PLIB function call `p_pname`) is used.

Initially, the name of the open file is part of the command line. However, when this has to be changed - either as a result of an Open or Save as command inside the application, or in response to a switch file request from the system screen - a new buffer has to be used for this purpose. (The command line buffer is sized to precisely the right length needed for the initial file.)

Typically, file-based applications will maintain a permanent buffer (or string), of length `P_FNAMESIZE (128 bytes)`, to store any change in the name of the file open. Once the new name has been copied into this buffer, a function call, such as the HWIF function `hSetUpStatusNames` or HWIM or `AM_NEW_FILENAME` method or the OPL SETNAME command, should be used to adjust all EPOC16 statics as appropriate, including `DatUsedPathNamePtr`.

DatStatusNamePtr (0x3c)

The EPOC16 reserved static `DatStatusNamePtr` is used to determine which text string should be displayed as the name of the application in any Status Window shown for that application.

If non-zero, this is assumed to point to a string giving the text to use, with the text being clipped at the first dot encountered, and in any case after eight characters. The text is also converted into standard capitalised form. Thus if `DatStatusNamePtr` points to `"DIARY.AGN"`, the text 'Diary' will be displayed in the Status Window. On the Siena only four characters of the application name can be displayed because of the reduced size of the status window.

The rules for what text to display when `DatStatusNamePtr` is null are the same as those employed when `DatUsedPathNamePtr` is null (see above).

DatLocked (0x3a)

The user may attempt to terminate an application, using the 'Exit application' command in the system screen or by pressing 'Delete' when the cursor is over the name in bold. Or the user may try to change the current application file, by pressing 'Enter' on another entry in the file list for that application.

In either case, the system screen checks the value of the EPOC16 reserved static `DatLocked` for that application. If this is non-zero, a message 'Application is busy' is displayed, and the user's request is refused.

Applications may enter a state in which they are unable to respond to such requests from the system screen. In such case the application should explicitly set `DatLocked` to `TRUE`; OPL programmers should use the LOCK keyword. It is good programming practice to set `DatLocked` back to `FALSE` again as soon as possible afterwards; in OPL by using `UNLOCK`.

As mentioned earlier in this chapter, an application should normally analyse its command line on start-up, and should write various values from this command line into EPOC16 reserved statics as a result.

Applications that disregard their command lines

Simple applications - especially those that are not file based - have no need to pay any attention to the command line passed to them by the system screen. In this case, the various relevant EPOC16 statics are left at their default (zero) values. This fact is picked up by the system screen and by other parts of the operating system, with the following results:

• The name displayed in any status window and in the file list in the system screen is just that of the application .APP or .OPA file
• If the user requests the application to be shut down, from the system screen, the application is shut down by EPOC16, without the application itself being informed of this fact (just as if the user had selected the 'Kill' option in the system screen).

If an application needs to do its own clean up processing in response to a shut down request issued by the user in the system screen, it must analyse its command line during its initialisation, this is true even if the application is not file-based.

One final drawback of an application not processing its command line is that users will be unable to assign application buttons with any effect on that application. Suppose a user assigns `control+world` to a version of the Spy application, for example, that fails to write anything suitable to `DatProcessNamePtr`. If the user subsequently presses the key combination `control+world`, the Spy application will fail to be brought into foreground - thus spoiling the whole purpose of assigning the application button.

Messages from the system screen

Shut down messages

Applications can receive shut down messages from the system screen, as an instruction to quit and close down tidily, saving any changes to file as required. These messages can arise when the user presses DELETE after highlighting a running task in the system screen. However, as mentioned above, if the application has set its DatLocked to TRUE, the system screen instead presents an 'Application is busy' message.

Incidentally, applications are sent shut down messages only if they have a non-zero value of DatProcessNamePtr. The system screen assumes that any application that has left this EPOC16 reserved static at its default (zero) value is unlikely to be prepared to respond to shut down messages. In that case, the system screen instead calls p_pterminate to terminate the application.

Finally, note that any application which has $4000 included in its application type number will never be sent a shut down message from the system screen; instead, the system screen will display the message 'Cannot quit application' - see the appropriate language chapter.

Switch files messages

Applications can receive switch files messages from the system screen, as an instruction to close their existing open file, and to open or create another one. These messages can arise when the user presses ENTER after highlighting a file within that application's file list in the system screen.

Receiving system screen messages

There are two main aspects to applications receiving a shut down or switch files message from the system screen:

- The application must include an event handling mechanism to receive notification that a message from the system screen has been sent to it.
- The application calls a system function (e.g. the window server function wGetCommand, or the OPL c$=CMD$(x%) function, or the OVAL Command$ functions) to determine the contents of the message.

In turn, the initial notification can be received in either of two ways, depending on whether the application is receiving events from the window server directly (by calling wGetEvent or a variant), or as 'extended key presses' via the console device (as occurs for example in HWIF and OPL programs). In either case, the initial event prompts the application to call wGetCommand, to obtain the so-called 'new command line' giving more details about the event.

New command lines from the system screen

The parameter passed to `wGetCommand` (see above) must be the address of a buffer having at least `P_FNAMESIZE` (`128`) bytes. The new command line is written into this buffer.

The first byte of the new command line will be one of `'X'`, `'O'`, or `'C'`:

`'X'`	means the command is a shut down message
`'O'`	means the command is a Switch files message, with a specified file to be opened
`'C'`	means the command is a Switch files message, with a specified file to be created.

In the case of Switch files messages, the remainder of the new command line gives the full path name of the file to open or create.

For OPL programmers one of the aforementioned `c$=CMD$ (x%)` variants may be used to get the appropriate components of new command line. OVAL programmers use the `Command$` functions.

At the time of writing, the command byte is restricted to one of the three values given above. It is possible, however, that some future application might send messages to other applications having different command bytes. In order to be future proof, an application should test explicitly for all expected values of the command byte and should just ignore values other than those expected i.e. should not generate an error on receipt of an unexpected value.

(Note: A new option 'U' is now available on Series 5 – see `GETCMD$` in the 'OPL Reference' chapter).

Client server services

The client - server concept is used quite extensively within EPOC16. For example a 'server' process called the window server (SYS$WSRV) provides its 'client' processes with shared access to the screen, keyboard and any other user interface devices (e.g. pointing device) that may be present. Using a 'server' process to share a common resource between a number of clients is a common technique in multi-tasking environments.

The EPOC16 operating system has a number of design features which support client server relationships e.g. Inter-process messaging in EPOC16 is designed for the efficient implementation of client-server relationships where a particular server may have multiple clients.

EPOC16 starts up with three multi-client servers:

- The supervisor, which performs critical system functions and provides shared access to memory via the memory segment allocator.
- The file server, that provides shared access to file storage devices.
- The window server, that provides shared access to the screen, keyboard and, if present, a pointing device.

A server may also be a client of another server. For example, the window server is a client of the file server (since, for example, it loads bitmap files) and all processes are implicitly clients of the Supervisor.

In order that the relative priorities of client processes have their intended effect, a multi-client server process should run at a higher priority than any of its clients. A client's priority is effectively lowered to that of the server while waiting for completion of a service provided by a low priority server.

Inter-process communications (IPCS)

Any process can send a message to another process, as long as the target process has prepared itself to receive messages by initialising the messaging system provided by EPOC16. The inter-process communication or messaging system was designed to closely follow the I/O System (see later) in terms of its range of synchronous and asynchronous services, i.e. the methods of signalling, use of semaphores and status words. The similarities of operation enable the inter-mingling of asynchronous I/O and asynchronous inter-process messaging.

In the descriptions of object oriented programming in this book and in documentation from Psion, the concept of sending messages to objects is often referred to, this should not be confused with inter-process messaging. In OOP terminology, sending a message to an object just refers to a convention for calling a specific C function that belongs to a particular class of object.

Servers and clients communicate via inter-process messages, and a range of synchronous and asynchronous system services are available to facilitate the receipt and sending of such messages (e.g. via the PLIB function library or as EPOC16 O/S calls). A server process, for example, that wishes to receive messages from client processes would make appropriate system calls to initiate the message system. A server process is usually passive and waits to receive messages from clients, it would not normally initiate a transaction itself by sending a message to a client.

Link paste

An example of another very specific use of inter-process messaging is the 'Link Paste' or 'Bring' capabilities of many of the built-in applications. Data that is highlighted in one application can be brought or pasted into another application, where the user has invoked a 'Bring' command, see the 'Programming Techniques' chapter for further details.

Attached applications

The ability of one application to make use of the functionality of another was introduced with the (OOP) object libraries included in the Series 3a ROM. Only one example of this exists to-date in the built-in applications i.e. where the Agenda application and the Word application co-operate in the production and editing of memos associated with Agenda entries. Agenda starts the Word process as an attached application using a specially modified command byte and line (see Series 3 Command Line above) that contains information such as the process ID of the initiating process, and typically pointers to data items for passing back results. The two applications can then conduct further communications via inter-process messaging if required, see the 'Programming Techniques' chapter for further details.

Automatic test system (ATS)

Starting with the 3a, the ATS system was introduced to assist with automated testing of HWIM (OOP) applications. Although the process which controls the ATS sequence does not have to be an HWIM application, the process which is being controlled by ATS does have to be a standard HWIM application (or one which mimics the support for ATS). Inter-process messaging is used to implement the ATS mechanism and message types include; sending, receiving and recording key presses, running dialogs etc.

ATS can be used for a number of purposes including the following:

- Testing an application by running a pre-determined sequence of operations, such as displaying all the text strings and dialogs belonging to a program, to check the suitability of the resource files contents.
- Producing a rolling demonstration of one or more applications.
- Macro recording and playback.
- Controlling attached applications.

All HWIM applications from the 3a onwards support the receipt of inter-process messaging as standard and are also initialised so that they can be detected as being able to support ATS - see above. See the 'Errors and Debugging' chapter for further details of ATS.

Message slots

An EPOC16 process can open only one message channel for receiving inter-process messages, but messages may arrive from a number of sources. Initialising the message system involves setting up a number of 'message slots' (from the heap) each of which contains a message header (see E_MESSAGE struct as described below) followed by a fixed length buffer. The length and expected structure of the data in the buffer following the message header is defined by the receiver of the message (e.g. the server), and is normally limited to a few words. For example, the file server and the supervisor both use 8 bytes. Note that the sender (i.e. the client) does not control the length of the message sent (a later version of a server could increase the message length to provide additional services while maintaining upward compatibility).

```
typedef struct message
        {
        struct message *next;
        unsigned char *status;
        unsigned int type;
        int pid;
        } E_MESSAGE;
```

When a message from the sender (client) arrives, the message is copied into a previously free message slot, which is also placed in the receiver's message queue. The allocated message slot will contain the message type (as specified by the sender) and the process ID of the sender, followed by the number of bytes of data from the sender (as specified when the process was initiated). Other fields in the E_MESSAGE header are used internally by the message system. It is up to the receiver to act on the message (asynchronously or synchronously), and free up the message slot after processing the message.

The server always removes messages from the front of the queue. Arriving messages are normally inserted at the end of the queue but if the client's priority is 0x80 or more, the arriving message is inserted at the front, overtaking any existing messages, regardless of their sender's priority.

If it is necessary to send more than the small amount of information allowed for by the message length, the message should contain the address of a buffer followed by the length. The server would then copy the data from the client's data segment (e.g. using PLIB function p_pcpyfr which copies data between processes without interruption). A message may also contain the address or addresses of buffers to receive data from the server when the service has been completed. (e.g. the server could use PLIB function p_pcpyto to copy the data to the client's data segment, which copies data between processes without interruption).

When the message has been processed, the server frees the message slot and may also write back a completion status value and signal the sender's I/O semaphore (if a system function call requiring acknowledgement was used). It is usual for servers to request to be informed of the termination of a client (e.g. by calling PLIB function p_logon).

System services are available to allow client process to request a service of the server by sending it typed fixed length messages. If the server does not have any empty message slots, the message sending service waits on a mutual exclusion semaphore until a message slot becomes free. It can therefore be blocked indefinitely, even if the systems service is asynchronous. Multi-client servers avoid this prospect by allocating a slot for each potential client (by allocating say E_MAX_PROCESSES (i.e 24) minus the number of known processes).

Clients need to know the process ID of the server they wish to use. This may be achieved by a number of means: via a system service call specifying the process name (e.g. using PLIB function p_pidfind, for multi-client servers); the client knows the process ID because it created the server process itself; the server created the client and passed its process ID as a parameter during the creation step. For multi-client servers, the client will typically send an opening message to connect to the server.

Synchronous or asynchronous messaging

A client process that sends messages synchronously is effectively suspended from the moment it calls the message sending service, until the server completes processing the message. If completion by the server is dependent on an external event, such as the expiry of a timer or the arrival of serial data, the client may be suspended indefinitely. If the client must remain responsive to other events, such as user input, this will be unacceptable behaviour so the client should use asynchronous messaging. Suppose a client needs to use asynchronous messaging because completion of the processing of the message may be delayed indefinitely by an external event. This implies that the server itself must respond to at least two events (the receipt of a message and the external event) and so must also handle events asynchronously.

A server does not normally have a user interface, so if its only task is to receive and process messages from clients, then synchronous server code may be perfectly acceptable. The server is effectively suspended until a message is received and returns to the suspended state as soon as it has finished processing the message. If the server also has to respond to other events, such as the expiry of a timer, then the receipt of messages must be handled asynchronously.

Errors

EPOC16 is a robust and well protected environment, but errors due to mistakes, design oversights, errors in program code or unexpected user actions are an unfortunate fact of life for software developers. An overview of error reporting is given here, but strategies for avoiding errors and for debugging programs are covered in the chapter on 'Errors and Debugging'.

Fatal errors

Panics

When EPOC16 detects a condition that it determines could have only arisen from a bugged application, it will terminate or panic the process in question. An error code called a panic number in the range 0 - 255 will be reported to the user. See the 'Errors and Debugging' chapter for an overview of panic codes and the Appendix for a complete list of individual panic numbers and their meanings.

OPL

The OPL run-time environment is well protected and panics are rarely generated. Many, but not all, structural and syntax errors are detected by the OPL translator, fatal errors during run-time are usually trapped by the OPL interpreter. See the 'Errors and Debugging' chapter for details of how to avoid and detect OPL errors. See the Appendix for a complete list of the OPL run-time and OPL translator error codes and their meanings.

OVAL

The OVAL run-time environment is well protected and panics should be rare. Many structural and syntax errors are detected by the OVAL translator. Fatal errors during run-time should be trapped by the OVAL interpreter. See the 'Errors and Debugging' chapter for details of how to avoid and detect OVAL errors. See the Appendix for a complete list of the OVAL run-time and OVAL translator error codes and their meanings.

5   User Interface

Application design

Careful design is essential for programs of significant size or complexity, and the time spent planning will normally more than repay itself by dramatically reducing the time needed to produce reliable code. Once the purpose and requirements of the application are clear, it is necessary to decide which language and programming techniques are appropriate. This chapter discusses the key user interface issues in a language independent way, specific examples are provided in appropriate language chapters.

While much of this chapter is also relevant to Series 5, please refer to the 'Series 5' chapter for changes in user interface considerations for EPOC32 systems.

Interface style

Consistency of user interface style between different applications is very important to users, and it should also be important to the application designer who wishes to succeed. Study the built in applications carefully, and do not depart from their normal style unless there is an overwhelming reason to do so. Dramatically varying the way your application appears and reacts to the user will risk alienating them, and may encourage them to use a competitors product instead. See the document 'check.doc' on disk for additional information from Psion on the style and norms expected of Series 3a/c and Siena applications.

Interface elements

Most applications of reasonable complexity that present a user interface are structured in a similar way. They have a main information display window, a main loop that handles user key presses and presents a menu driven interface. Information entered by a user is normally done via dialogs and/or edit windows.

Any application of reasonable complexity, which has a user interface, will normally provide the following interface elements and user features:

- Keystroke handling and data entry.
- A menu handler, with accelerator or 'hot-key' shortcuts.
- Program help information.

- System screen and system message handling.
- At least one window for display of prompts and information.
- Additional dialog windows to receive user input, display messages and modify program options or settings.

This list is not meant to be exhaustive, but represents a likely minimum for an application to be distributed to others.

The first four items in the above list can be considered to be various types of key press e.g. in OPL or HWIF programs. Messages received from the system screen are translated (via the console device) and can be detected by testing for special key codes. (Object oriented programs using the HWIM library receive and process specific messages sent by the window server).

Programs that have other sources of input/output (I/O), but are required to be continually responsive to key presses and other event sources, such as elapsed timers, must adopt an asynchronous design approach for capturing and processing events.

Synchronous or asynchronous design

In the example just outlined, a straightforward synchronous design approach is all that is required. But, if the application has to respond to user input and other event types such as serial data transfers, expiry of timers etc., then an asynchronous approach is required.

Designing a program which handles its I/O asynchronously is more difficult, and may be unnecessary for applications which have only one type of event source such as key presses, or that are never compute bound for long periods. However, if a range of applications is to be developed then designing the basic reusable application framework to operate asynchronously will probably reap rewards later on. Both synchronous and asynchronous I/O techniques are covered in the relevant language chapters.

Example application frameworks of both types can be found on disk, along with a number of text documents which discuss the language statements and techniques in detail. Asynchronous versus synchronous principles is covered in more detail in the chapter 'Processes, Memory and Applications'.

Keyboard input

In all cases it is the window server that handles key presses and routes them to an application, normally the foreground application.

Calling any synchronous input functions such as INPUT, GET or GETEVENT in OPL or the C (PLIB) function p_getch will effectively suspend a program. An application will remain unresponsive to other events or special key presses, such as shut down messages from the system screen, until the input function is satisfied. Programs which use such function calls, but are designed normally to respond to special events such as shut down messages, should surround such synchronous calls with the appropriate lock and unlock functions, to inform the system that they are currently unable to respond.

For example in OPL the LOCK and UNLOCK statements should be used, in C the reserved (or magic) static DatLocked should be set to true. Applications marked as locked will then be reported as 'busy' if sent a shut down message (this does not affect the kill application command for example under Apps from the system menu).

Many programmatic methods exist for reading key presses, even for scanning the keyboard directly, many of these are covered in the chapters on specific programming languages.

Diamond key

Beginning with the Series 3a, the diamond key was introduced to allow applications that have more than one operating mode to switch modes easily e.g. see the built in Data and Agenda applications. Such an application needs to include a check for the diamond key press in its main event-processing loop. Some applications may allow the user to select which modes are to be included in the selection cycle. If a status window (see below) is displayed, the list of operating modes can be used to replace the program icon with a diamond symbol placed next to the current program mode in the list.

Menus

Creating and handling user menus is a relatively painless task for the programmer, since the main part of the menu handling code is incorporated into the EPOC16 system. All the programmer has to do is to provide the menu data, call the appropriate system services or language statement and test for relevant key presses (HWIM based C handles even more of the menu processing automatically).

All menu options (commands) must have an associated accelerator or hot key short cut. On the original Series 3 the twenty six lowercase letter keys and the arithmetic operator keys can be used as menu accelerators i.e. a-z plus +, -, * and / (these may differ on some non English keyboards). Starting with the 3a, the uppercase letters also became available along with the ability to group related menu items together by grey underlining (grey does not need to enabled on the main application window for this to work). Using keys other than those specified above, as accelerators is not recommended and programmers should be particularly careful to avoid duplication of accelerator keys. See the Multi lingual applications section later for comments on choosing accelerator keys.

Windows

A typical application with a user interface will normally have one main window - the parent window- to act as the main information display for the user. In the handheld SIBO systems, only the windows of the foreground process are visible. Windows are rectangular display areas that are created in terms of screen co-ordinates or pixels. Windows can be created in hierarchies or trees, with parent windows having child windows, which themselves may be parents to other windows and so on. Child windows are created relative (in terms of positioning) to their parent window and are clipped to the boundaries of their parent window. For example a child window may be created larger than its parent, but the visible portion of the child will be limited by the boundaries of the parent window. This can be very useful for creating scrolling effects.

For applications that are to run on a range of SIBO machines, with different screen dimensions and resolutions, there are a number of important design factors that must be taken into consideration, see the 'Graphics' section below.

Dialogs

A typical dialog is a modal pop up window that is used to get information or choices from a user. Modal and non modal behaviour is described later. A dialog can have a title and a number of data entry fields (or controls) which can accept specific types of data entry. For example:

- Choice lists
- Action lists of buttons
- Plain text items
- Numeric editors
- Floating point editors
- Date editor
- Time editors
- Text editors - scrolling and non scrolling
- Secret data input fields - e.g. for passwords
- Filename editors or selectors

Dialogs are very flexible objects with a wide range of options and configurable items. For example initial values can be given to items in a dialog and upper and lower limits can be placed on numeric values etc. The list of options is far too great to cover here, but it is worth detailing the differences between dialogs created by OPL or HWIF based C programs and the increased range of options available to the HWIM based C programmer. Dialogs produced by OPL and HWIF programs are essentially the same in terms of what is possible.

HWIM programmers have the following additional facilities:

- Sub-dialogs
- Numeric range editor
- Unsigned integer editor
- Signed integer editor
- Latitude and Longitude editor controls
- Application specific controls can be created.
- A wide range of system supplied dialogs with defined behaviour.
- The contents of dialogs (and menus) can be changed dynamically.
- Locking and dimming of dialog items
- Program activity can continue while a dialog (or menu) is displayed.

Dynamic dialog boxes where the number of controls and their contents change depending on what has been entered already, allow consistency and dependency checks to be carried out before the dialog is allowed to complete, thus creating a more sophisticated interaction with the user. For examples of this type of dynamic dialog box see the built-in Agenda application, in particular the dialogs for creating new Agenda entries and setting repeats.

When a menu, dialog or help screen is active (displayed) in an OPL or HWIF application the program is unable to process other non key press events, such as the expiry of a timer, system shut down messages, link paste requests etc. until the dialog or menu is completed. This is not the case in HWIM or Oval programs. Oval programs are also able to create dynamic dialogs.

Programmers working with HWIF based C can gain access to some of the above HWIM dialog features - see the section 'HWIF with some OOP' in the 'C Programming' chapter for more details.

Alerts

Occasionally an application must get a response from the user before any other processing takes place. For example, when dealing with certain kinds of recoverable error (such as an SSD removed while a file is still open) it may be desirable to lock the application into the foreground, and get an appropriate action or response from the user. One way to achieve this is by using the `wSystemModal(0)` function from the window server library (WLIB). To cancel this state, the program must call `wCancelSystemModal`. However, alerts provide a simple way to achieve this behaviour, they are a special kind of dialog provided by the system.

Dialogs are normally completed by pressing the Enter key to confirm the information typed, or the Esc key to cancel the dialog. Alerts are a simple form of dialog that allows a number of lines of text to be displayed, and to get an appropriate response from the user to a limited set of options. For example: An alert can be used to display a simple message such as 'Are you sure?', and show a choice of two keys such as 'Y' and 'N' that may be selected. An alert can also display a number of lines of text (e.g. up to 4 on a 3a/c) and present three options for the user that are placed above three buttons such as Esc, Space and Enter.

Input focus

If there is more than one window or dialog displayed, and the program is ready to receive user input, then only one window or dialog control can have the 'focus'. The object that currently has the 'focus' is the window or object (e.g. part of a dialog) or menu which is currently responding to user input.

Modal and non modal behaviour

A window or dialog is said to be modal if it requires a suitable input or response from the user before the window or dialog will close or is allowed to lose the input focus. For example modal behaviour is useful when a choice of actions is required from the user to deal with a problem or error condition. While a modal window or dialog is visible the user can only interact with the application via that window or dialog, see 'Alerts' above.

Typical non-modal behaviour is illustrated by a situation where more than one window is displayed but the user is free to move the focus between them at will, by means of the cursor or tab keys. The 'find' mode of the built in Data application is a typical example of such non-modal window behaviour.

System messages

As discussed in the 'Applications, Processes and Memory' chapter, applications should be designed to receive system messages such as switch files and the shut down command, also intercept the command line information and react appropriately.

Switch files messages

Applications can receive switch files messages from the system screen, as an instruction to close the existing open file, and to open or create another one. These messages can arise when the user presses ENTER after highlighting a file within that application's file list in the system screen, see the 'Application file changes' section below for all of the possible options.

Shutdown & foreground/background changes

The very nature of shut down messages implies that the application is currently in the background. For design reasons it may be desirable to ask the user to confirm that the application should be shut down, or to ask whether the current file should be saved. In such cases it will be necessary to force the application into the foreground, this is done using a window server function, examples are provided on disk and are described in the appropriate language chapters.

System messages - failure to respond

When a menu, dialog or help screen is active (displayed) in an OPL or HWIF C application, the program is unable to process other non-key press events until the dialog or menu is completed. For example, the program cannot respond to, the expiry of a timer, a system shutdown message, a link paste (bring) request etc. This is not the case with OVAL or HWIM C applications. (In the case of link paste servers, it is assumed that link paste IPC messages do not remain unacknowledged since the client application may hang.)

Application files

An application is responsible for ensuring that its files, directories and sub-directories exist and, if necessary, for creating them.

Location and naming

Standard directory names are normally used for specific file types e.g. applications are usually placed in a first level \APP directory, digital sound files are usually placed in a \WVE directory etc. An application's own files however, would normally be placed in a specific program directory, usually having the same name as the application and located directly underneath the \APP directory.

For example, an application called Planner.app, which uses files with a default file extension of .PLN could locate its files in a directory such as \APP\PLANNER\ and would specify the directory path as its default.

Although it is possible to use the standard directories for other files of standard types that belong to the example application Planner, e.g. bitmaps (.PIC files), it often more convenient to store them along with the application specific files. In this way they are logically located, and are less likely to be misplaced or deleted and thus cause 'file not found' errors.

See the chapter 'Files in EPOC16' for more details on standard directory names and file name extensions.

Change of files

The current file that an application is using may be determined, or may change, for the following reasons:

From the system screen, when the application is not running
a. The user highlights an exiting file name under the application's icon and presses Enter.
b. The user highlights any file under the application's icon and selects File New from the system menu.

From the system screen when the application is currently running
c. The user highlights a file name under the application's icon, which is not the current file, and presses Enter.
d. The user highlights a file name under the application's icon, which is the currently active file, and presses Delete.
e. The user selects Exit application (or Exit all applications) from the system menu.
f. The user 'kills' the application from the system menu.

From within the application itself
g. The user selects an option from the application's own menu to open a different file, which already exists.
h. The user selects an option from the application's own menu to create a new file.
i. The user selects an option from the application's own menu to exit the application.
j. The user selects an option from the application's own menu to close the current file, but remain in the application.

Option j conflicts with the normal behaviour of SIBO file based applications, and is not usually offered as an option.

A file based application must take steps to intercept messages from the system screen in order to react appropriately to the actions detailed above, however, if the application has set its `DatLocked` to `TRUE` (or used the OPL `LOCK` statement), the system screen presents an 'Application is busy' message instead.

Switch file messages will only ever be sent to applications with basic type number 2 or 3. Applications whose type numbers include $8000 can receive switch file messages of the Open sort, but not of the Create sort.

For most of the options above, it is the responsibility of the programmer to determine what action is taken in response to the event types outlined. The exact behaviour of an application should depend upon the application type number and its purpose. In some cases the program designer may choose not to offer certain file options, and may have no control over certain event types e.g. the kill application options, where the operating system will not inform the application about its impending demise.

It is necessary to keep the system screen informed in the event of changes to the current application file, i.e. by updating the magic statics variable by using the appropriate language function calls. For example in OPL you would use the SETNAME n$ command when the file in use changes. In the system screen the file under the program icon which is currently emboldened would then change to the new file name.

On exiting, or on receipt of a shut down message (see options d, e and i above), an application would normally save its current file before closing down.

Note:
One important note, on program files, worthy of mention is that many applications have a 'Save as' option on their file menu. In SIBO systems the 'standard' response to selecting this option is to ask the user for a new name, and to save a copy of the current file under the new name, while the application continues to work with the original file. In many other systems, including the Series 5, the 'standard' behaviour differs in that on using 'Save as' the application will switch to using the new file, having saved and closed the original file.

Icons

Icons are initially produced as bitmap files that are bound to the executable file when it is translated or compiled. Icons may be produced by a variety of means:

- Using one of the many Shareware or Freeware programs available such as Psicon or Draw284, included on the disks.
- Using the Iconed or Iconeda applications that are part of the Psion C SDK.
- Using the Window Server tool wspcx.exe on the .PCX output of a PC program such as Windows Paintbrush.

An icon (.PIC) file can contain:

- A 24x24 bitmap for a Series 3 icon.
- two 48x48 bitmaps for icons from the Siena and Series 3a onwards - the first and second bitmaps in the icon .PIC file specify the black and grey planes respectively.
- A 24x24 bitmap for a Series 3 icon followed by two 48x48 bitmaps for a Series 3a icon.
- If an OPA or APP (series 3a onwards) has a 48 x 48 black / grey icon then $1000 should be added into the application TYPE number, see the 'Applications, Processes and Memory' chapter for a discussion of application types.

For example, for an OPA header:

```
APP Example
    TYPE 3
    PATH "\EXAMPLE"
    EXT "EXA"
    ICON "\OPD\EXAMPLE.PIC"
ENDA
```

The TYPE statement would become:

```
APP Example
    TYPE $1003
    PATH "\EXAMPLE"
    EXT "EXA"
    ICON "\OPD\EXAMPLE.PIC"
ENDA
```

If $1000 is not added and the application is installed on a 3a or above then a scaled up 24 x 24 icon will be used (as per the original series 3 icon).

If no extension is given in the icon file name then .PIC is assumed. If an icon is not provided for an OPA it will be shown on the system screen with a standard OPA icon. The system screen will refuse to install an APP file that does not contain an icon.

It's also possible to attach many other bitmap files to the icon .PIC file and read in the appropriate bitmaps in as needed during program execution, see the 'Programming Techniques' chapter for details of WSPCX.EXE and for information on the format of .PIC files.

After compilation/translation a copy of the icon is bound into the application. The icon .PIC file need not be loaded on to the Psion for it to be visible when the program is installed. See the section below on 'Status windows' for details of the display of program icons in status windows.

Graphics

Windows can be created to be of a specific size and at a particular position in terms of horizontal and vertical pixels. They can be created with or without a grey plane and to be initially visible or invisible.

The visibility of a window may be changed as required. It can be useful to make a window invisible while modifying its contents, only making it visible again when the update is complete. Numerous facilities exist (e.g. in OPL, C and OVAL) for drawing lines, borders, setting and clearing pixels and copying areas of one window to another or between bitmaps and windows or vice versa, and the various options are described in the 'OPL16 Techniques' chapter.

Collectively windows and bitmaps (see later) are referred to as drawables, each of which has a unique identifier. In OPL the default window is always identified as number 1, the other drawables have unique identifying numbers, which are allocated when they are created or loaded. A total of eight simultaneous drawables are supported by OPL16, i.e. the total number of bitmaps and windows (in OPL32 the limit is 64).

A discussion of different techniques used for graphics manipulation can be found in the 'OPL16 Techniques' chapter.

Screen sizes and compatibility

All original Series 3 applications are fully compatible with the Series 3a/c and Work*about*. These machines automatically recognise such applications and run them in compatibility mode (via the window server) - both the icon, as displayed on the system screen, and the main display are expanded linearly by a factor of two in each dimension. On the Siena, Work*about* and the Series 3a/c, compatibility mode consists of borders left across the top and bottom of the screen to restrict the area to 240x80 pixels.

Applications written in C that wish to use the full screen capabilities of the Series 3a or 3c must explicitly turn off the compatibility mode by calling the window server `wCompatibilityMode` function. In OPL applications this is taken care of automatically by using the appropriate OPL translator.

An application can identify which model it is running on using an EPOC16 O/S call `GenLcdType` or PLIB function `p_getlcd` and using the value returned to determine the screen resolution. In OPL, getting dimensions of the default window with the `gHEIGHT` and `gWIDTH` functions can be used as a clue to the machine type, see the 'OPL16 Techniques' chapter for more details.

It is quite feasible, although possibly more difficult, to write applications that run on the whole SIBO range using the screen of each machine to the full. However, care should be taken to ensure that such an application does not use any machine specific features e.g. the grey plane when running on a Series 3 or enhanced sound capabilities on a Siena.

In addition to scaling the size of windows to be appropriate for each SIBO machine, consideration should also be given to the width of all textual information, for example:

- The combined length of menu titles and menu item strings.
- The width of dialog titles and prompt strings.
- The width of program related help text.
- The effects of language translation on the length of text.

It is wise not to make screen text layouts too cramped in the primary language, and it's better to dynamically calculate various screen positions and dimensions at run time rather than hard code them in. Particularly if the application is to be multi lingual, - see the 'Resource files' section later.

The various screen sizes, resolutions and availability of a grey plane are discussed in the 'Fundamental Concepts' chapter.

Bitmaps

In addition to windows, EPOC16 supports structures called bitmaps. The concepts behind bitmaps can seem a little confusing at first, but for graphics programming it is essential to master them. The following is not meant an exhaustive description of bitmaps, but should illustrate most of the key concepts (see also Sprites below).

Bitmaps are just two-dimensional arrays of pixels (held in memory), any of which may be either on or off. They can be treated as off screen windows but with only one plane. Like windows, they are rectangular objects created in terms of 'x' and 'y' co-ordinates, and are also referred to as drawables because, like windows, they can also be drawn to.

Bitmaps are not visible until they are copied into a current window. When held in memory bitmaps have only one plane, i.e. they **cannot** have a grey plane. This is source of considerable confusion, probably due to references to bitmap files, such as icon files, which apparently contain both black and grey bitmaps. In fact, all this means is that there are two bitmaps in the file, and when the system loads the icon, one bitmap will be copied into the black plane of the window and the other will be copied into the grey plane.

In OPL the plane to be used e.g. for the bitmap copy command is selected using gGREY. Also, the nature of the copy process can be changed so that each pixel copied from the bitmap to the display has a particular effect i.e. it sets, clears, inverts or replaces the corresponding pixel in the plane of the window.

Once a bitmap is created, and drawn to by setting or re-setting its pixels, it can be saved to a bitmap file, retrieved from a file or copied into an area of a window. Bitmap files, or a collection of bitmaps in one file, can be appended to an OPA or APP file (e.g. including the program icon) to reduce the number of files included in the set that makes up a complete application. The relevant bitmaps can then be loaded as required from a combined bitmap file or from the OPA or APP file, see the relevant programming language chapter. For details of how to create, convert and combine bitmaps see the 'Programming Techniques' chapter.

Even though the boundary defined for a bitmap is rectangular, any shape or pattern of bits can be created within that area to produce more complex shapes. By default all pixels are off when a bitmap is first created, but bits may be set or re-set using a number of graphics drawing commands as required. For more complex shapes it is normal to use a graphics drawing program, e.g. Draw284 (see the 'Disk Contents' chapter) to create the desired shapes and then save them to bitmap files. At run-time the bitmaps can be loaded into memory and used as required.

A bitmap (or a rectangular section of it) can be copied into a window to create the pattern required on screen. Normally, a bitmap is copied into the required plane i.e. black, grey if available or sometimes both. So, even though bitmaps themselves only have one plane, they can be used to affect either the black plane or the grey plane in a window. Therefore, if grey is used in an application it may be necessary to use more than one bitmap to create the desired effect in a section of the display.

Finally, each pixel in the bitmap can be made to affect a corresponding pixel in the destination area (and plane) to which it is copied, in one of several ways, i.e. replace, set, clear or invert. For example with replace mode, every pixel in the section of the bitmap copied, would replace each of the corresponding pixels in the display. Whereas set mode, would take each pixel in the bitmap that was 'on' and set the corresponding pixel in the display to 'on'. Any bitmap pixels that were not 'on' would have no effect on the corresponding display pixels.

Screen drawing, re-drawing and memory

There is only one physical display screen, but windows may overlap, menus appear and disappear, dialog boxes come and go, so the screen has to be re-drawn after such changes. For programmers working in OPL and C programmers working in HWIF re-drawing is taken care of automatically. In OPL and HWIF, and optionally in OVAL, this is done with windows that have backup bitmaps that are managed automatically.

Whilst having the clear advantage of being simpler for the programmer, using backup bitmaps does slow down screen displays slightly and consumes much more memory, since all drawing processes and display information is duplicated. For example: on a Series 3a/c using a full size window (480 x 160 pixels) with grey enabled, two backup bitmaps are needed (one for each plane) consuming an extra 19200 bytes of memory. In many cases by careful selection of window dimensions and selective use of grey these disadvantageous effects can be minimised. However, since it is possible to create windows that are much bigger than the actual display area the problems may become very significant. For example, an application that used a scrolling view of a large map could easily run out of available memory.

Using C it is possible to create windows without backup bitmaps, but the process of redrawing areas which have been overwritten may have to be handled by the programmer explicitly. Adopting an HWIM C design approach for the map example described above would avoid the memory problem.

When a program starts its default window usually occupies the whole screen. It's always a good idea to reduce the memory used by windows, by making them only as big as required.

You can consider the default window as having two components, a graphics window with a slightly smaller text window inside it. To write to the text window you use statements such as FONT and PRINT, but you can only use one font on screen at once. A much more flexible approach is to ignore the text window and use the graphics window instead, for example in OPL by using statements such as gFONT, gPRINT and gPRINTB etc.

Cursors

Non destructive text or graphics cursors can be created. System supplied cursors can be off, on and flashing or on but not flashing. For special cursors and cursor shapes see the sections on bitmaps and sprites.

Sprites

To fully comprehend sprites you should have a clear understanding of bitmaps and screen display planes, see Bitmaps above. Sprites were introduced with the Series 3a (version 4 of the window server). A sprite is a graphic object of variable size and shape that can be attached to a window, but does not disturb the underlying display and instead appears to 'float' above it. Sprites can be animated and managed automatically by the window server, which is responsible for maintaining the contents of the display underneath it. They can be of any shape, of variable size and animated without affecting the rest of the display.

A sprite consists of one to thirteen bitmap sets. If animation is not required then only one bitmap set is needed. Each set consists of up to six bitmaps, each of which must be the same size. In each set of six bitmaps the first three control the appearance of the black plane and next three bitmaps control the grey plane. e.g. considering the black plane, the first of the three bitmaps specifies which pixels should be set, the second bitmap specifies which pixels should be cleared and the third bitmap determines which pixels are to be inverted. The next group of three (out of the six in the set) control the pixels to set, clear and invert in the grey plane. Within any set you only have to supply a bitmap where you wish to affect the characteristic of the particular display plane i.e. some of the bitmaps in a set can be empty.

If a sequence of bitmaps sets is used (i.e. up to thirteen), then each set may vary in size from each other, but all bitmaps within any particular set must be of the same size. In use, each bitmap in a set of six will be drawn to the screen at the same time, at a specified position, and will remain displayed for a specified duration. If a sequence of bitmaps is used, then each set will be displayed in a cycle for the specified duration, and optionally at a specified pixel offset from the notional position thus creating the apparent movement.

Only one sprite can exist for each client of the window server at any particular time (i.e. one sprite per process), but different individual sprites can be created and destroyed as required.

(Using Psion C it is also possible to create animation on any SIBO system by attaching a sequence of up to twelve bitmaps to a window, the reader is referred to the window server manual of C SDK documentation.)

Fonts

ROM based fonts

The various SIBO systems provide a variety of ROM based text fonts i.e. built in fonts. On the original Series 3 there are three ROM based fonts, with the 3a this was increased to thirteen. Each font has an identifying number that specifies the typeface and size (in pixels) of the characters in the font set. All characters in a font set are of the same height but may have either a constant width (mono spaced font) or variable width (proportional font) which will depend upon the specific character displayed.

The default font or 'system font' for the Series 3 is stored in the environment variable $WS_SF (i.e. font 1), from the 3a onwards various fonts are used by the system for different purposes - the list is held in $WS_FNTS.

See the 'Programming Techniques' chapter for specific details of the available fonts.

Font files

An application that requires custom fonts can load them from font files that may contain one or more font sets. Font files typically have a .FON file name extension.

Custom fonts

A text font is in fact a set of up to 256 pixel patterns, each of which defines a symbol, an alphanumeric character or graphic. New fonts may be defined in a text font sources file (typically with a .FSC extension) which are used with the PC based font compiler wsfcomp.exe , to produce a .FON file containing one or more font sets. A SIBO font compiler and example font source filer are supplied on disk - see the \WSFCOMP directory.

Status windows

On the Siena, Series 3 range and Work*about* the window server supports two kinds of status window, temporary or permanent. A typical permanent Status Window can be seen on the Series 3 range by pressing Ctrl+Menu from the system screen. From the 3a onwards a status window can be re-sized. Repeatedly pressing Ctrl+Menu will cycle through: full size, small and no status window. A temporary status window (if temporary status windows are enabled) can be viewed as a transient pop up window by pressing Psion+Menu at any point, it will remain in front of the clients existing windows for approximately 2.5 seconds. On the Siena only one size of status window is available.

While enabled, the window server maintains a permanent status window to the right of the screen and behind existing windows. If the main window of an application occupies the whole of the screen it will obscure any permanent Status Window which may be enabled. In other words the Status Window will be hidden behind the applications window. If an application is to support a permanent status window, it should be 'tiled' with the main top-level window, i.e. the width of the main window should be reduced from the right hand side by an appropriate amount to allow the current status window to be seen. See the 'OPL16 Techniques' chapter for an example.

Any other windows you create may also obscure a status window that is open. If you think of open windows as a series of layers, one above the other, then any permanent status window is always positioned as the lowest layer, and so it will always be obscured if any other windows occupy the same 'x,y' co-ordinates.

If a large status window is displayed, for example on a Series 3a/c, the program icon is usually displayed at the top, although this can be disabled or changed to show the current operating mode of the program (diamond list). Many of the 'built-in' Applications have different 'modes' of operation, the precise definition being dependent on the application. As well as using menu options and 'hot' keys to switch between the different modes, an application can set the diamond key to cycle around some or all of them - see the Data or Agenda applications for examples of diamond lists. Changing the status window display in this way (from the 3a onwards) can be done in C programs using window server functions, in OPL by specific language keywords and in OVAL programs by language statements and by changing items of property.

Note that the Workabout status window does not display either the application's icon or a list of modes, the Siena only has a narrow status window and the HC does not have a status window.

Compatibility mode status window

In version 4 of the window server (3a onwards), applications on the S3a/c and Workabout can run in S3 compatibility mode. This allows an application to have the 'look' and 'feel' of the same application running on a S3. On the S3a/c, this is achieved by doubling up the pixels. For example, a line that is 10 x 1 pixels on the S3 will be drawn 20 x 2 pixels on the S3a/c and should 'look' the same. On the Workabout, applications running in compatibility mode will normally exactly match the S3 appearance.

If an application is running in compatibility mode on the S3a/c or Workabout, then a call to the window server wsEnable function creates a compatibility mode status window that looks and behaves like an S3 status window. Alternatively, the version 4 function wStatusWindow can be used to create a compatibility status window.

Printing

To allow user flexibility in choice of printer model, printer settings (such as page size, margins headers etc.) and print device configuration (e.g. via serial, parallel, infrared or to a file) an application should provide access to the standard Print Set Up dialog. After invoking the print set up dialog, an application is not normally required to keep a record of the selections or changes made by the user, ROM-based system code will take care of this (the choices are actually held in environment variables - see the Appendix for details).

However it is the responsibility of an application to obtain, and to record, information about the users detailed printing requirement (usually via a dialog), for example to confirm that printing is definitely required, to select what should be printed and possibly the way in which it should be done.

Sound

On SIBO systems the sound production and recording capabilities vary quite widely depending on the model, these differences are discussed in the 'Fundamental Concepts' chapter.

Depending upon the purpose of an application and decisions made during the design process sound may play no part in the user interface, or may be a fundamental part of the functionality of the application.

Where sound is not fundamental to the purpose of the program, e.g. it is just used to provide warning beeps etc. it is advisable to provide a user option to disable the program sound, even though disabling all sound may be possible as a system wide option.

All Series 3 and HC models have an internal amplifier driven loudspeaker that can be driven by the SND: device driver. On the original Series 3 the sound driver is limited to providing DTMF dialling tones or simple alarm sounds.

Enhanced hardware and software included in the Series 3a and 3c enable the built-in SND: device driver to simultaneously play two tunes on the built-in speaker. Although the sound quality is not as high as with digital sound files, the memory requirements are much less. For example to play a tune lasting six seconds would require a digital sound file of size 49,184 bytes. A comparable figure using the SND: device driver would be less than 1 Kb.

The 3a and 3c models also include a microphone and can record sounds into compressed digital sound (.WVE) files which can be replayed. Note that digital sounds cannot be recorded to Flash SSDs although once copied to a Flash SSD they can be played back.

If digital sound files are played, say as part of a game, the absence of the appropriate sound files should not cause a run time failure. Digital sound files can require a considerable amount of storage space and consume much more battery current when played; the user should retain the option to disable their use or even to delete them. In particular, the Siena and Work*about* are restricted to emitting warning beeps and other simple sounds, they do not have speakers or microphones and cannot record or play digital sounds.

See the 'Programming Techniques' and 'I/O System' chapters for specific details of using the various sound production and recording services.

Resource files

Applications with a user interface have to present prompt strings, menu tiles/items, dialog title/descriptions, user help and other text based information to the user. Embedding this type of information directly in the code as literal strings is generally considered not ideal practice, even when the application is intended to be mono-lingual. Several distinct advantages can be derived form using resource files, they are described in the chapter on 'Programming Techniques'.

User help information

Providing 'on line' application help to users, possibly even context sensitive help, has become the norm for applications of any reasonable sophistication. Users have come to expect specific guidance in response to pressing the Help key on a Siena or Series 3 (Shift

Esc on the Work*about*). As a program designer you obviously have to detect the help key press itself, but providing appropriate help text etc could be done in any number of ways. As usual there is a 'standard' way of doing this, i.e. by including the help information in the program resource file, see the 'Programming Techniques' chapter for more details on implementing program help.

Multi-lingual applications

For multi lingual applications the help information and all other program text will have to be provided in all supported languages. Using resource files allows all of the language specific information to be separated out from the program code, thus making the translation process easier and modular. Examples of loading language specific information are covered in the appropriate programming language chapters.

Care has to be taken to consider the effects of translation on text string lengths and hence on program buffer sizes, on screen layouts, menu text, button text, dialogs and help window widths, see also the Graphics section above.

Keyboards and menu accelerators

The set of possible menu accelerators may vary from language to language due to the keyboard changing.

All languages must support the 30 accelerators 'a' through 'z', together with '+', '-', '*', and '/'. Exceptions to this are French, Spanish and Belgian which uses the French keyboard:

- French   replaces '/' with '?'
- Spanish   replaces '*' with '>' and '/' with 'ñ'.

Applications that fail to take account of these differences when they are translated into another language will find they end up carrying a 'lame' accelerator. The accelerator will be visible on the menu, but there may be no way for the user to press the required key combination.

Note: It is very important to avoid duplicating an accelerator key for more than one menu item, the system has no way of detecting this and it can lead to unexpected and confusing behaviour.

On the Series 3a/c, Siena and Work*about* the uppercase alpha characters may also be used i.e. A through Z, giving a total of 56 possible accelerator keys.

In choosing accelerator keys it is advisable to study those used by the built in applications, and where possible use the same hot key for an identical (or very similar) menu option in your own application. Unshifted accelerator keys should be used, preferably corresponding to the first letter of the menu item, although this is not always possible. If the first lowercase letter cannot be used it may be appropriate to use the shifted uppercase letter. If the first letter is not available in either form then the second letter of the menu item may be a suitable alternative.

If the application has a 'diamond' menu, then shifted accelerator keys should be used by convention, and where possible the keys used should match the first letter of the items shown in the status window diamond list.

In translating an application into another language it will be necessary to change many of the accelerator keys. Using specific program resource files to hold all of the accelerator keys and all other menu text makes life much easier for the programmer and the translator alike.

Co-operating programs

As previously discussed in the 'Process, Memory and Application' chapter, EPOC16 provides many facilities in support of inter-process communications (IPCS) or messaging between programs. IPCS is used by the built in applications to implement 'Bring' i.e. highlighting and pasting information from one application into another and to allow one application to make use of the functions provided by another e.g. Agenda uses Word for memo editing. Application programmers may also make use of the IPCS services to provide similar functionality or for other purposes.

Bring or link paste

An example of a very specific use of inter-process messaging is the 'Link Paste or Bring' capabilities of many of the built-in applications, where data that is highlighted in one application can be brought or pasted into another application, where the user has invoked a 'Bring' command. See the 'Programming Techniques' chapter for further details.

Attached applications

The ability of one application to make use of the functionality of another was introduced with the (OOP) object libraries included in the Series 3a ROM. Only one example of this exists to-date in the built-in applications i.e. where the Agenda application and the Word application co-operate in the production and editing of memos associated with Agenda entries. Agenda starts the Word program as an attached application, using a specially modified command byte and command line. Additional information is supplied in the command line, such as the process ID of the initiating process and pointers to data items for passing back results. The two applications can then conduct further communications via inter-process messaging if required.

Running other programs

Occasionally it may be desirable to have your application run another program in response to the needs of the user, or to avoid duplicating functionality provided elsewhere, and then return to your program when the user has completed their task. This can be achieved without any real difficulty and is covered in the 'Programming Techniques' chapter.

Aliasing applications

Some file-based applications may end up with large file lists. It may be desirable to separate a file list into two or more separate lists, for example: with the Word application, all correspondence could go in one file list, all the chapters of your novel in another, and so on. These file lists could be distinguished, on the System Screen, by having distinct icons, and different application buttons could be used to cycle round running instances of these tasks.

Going further, it may be desirable for the behaviour of the application to alter, depending on which type of file is open. For example, the behaviour of the built-in text editor is different for .WRD files (when the application is seen as Word) from .OPL files (when the application is seen as Prog).

The concept of aliasing an application is designed to meet these requirements. For each new file list required, an alias file (.ALS file) should be installed in the system screen. In practice the user can do this on the Series 3a/c or Siena using the 'Create new list' item from the 'Special' menu. Aliasing is covered in more detail in the 'Programming Techniques' chapter.

6 Files in EPOC16

Introduction

EPOC16 is said to have an MS-DOS compatible file system. What this means in practice is that it uses the same type of root directory \ sub-directory tree structure and the same type of file naming convention. File names can be up to eight characters, with an optional period separator, plus a file name extension of up to three characters i.e. the familiar 8.3 or nnnnnnnn.xxx file naming system.

To accommodate the concepts of 'Installable file systems' and 'Remote file access' EPOC16 also uses node names to specify the location of a filing system.

File specifications

A full EPOC16 file specification has the form `<node><device><dir><name><ext>` where:

`<node>`	is the file system node e.g. `LOC::` in this case referring to local storage on the Psion itself.
`<device>`	is the drive or device name e.g. A: for drive A
`<dir>`	is the directory path e.g. `\APP\DOCS\`
`<name>`	is the file name e.g. `DESIGN`
`<ext>`	is the file name extension e.g. `.TXT`

An example of a complete file specification is:

`LOC::A:\APP\DOCS\DESIGN.TXT`

Note:
File specifications can be in upper or lower case, or a mixture.

Getting suitable filenames is kept simple for the user and for programmers by making use of one of two types of filename specifier, i.e. File Name Selectors and File Name Editors.

File name selectors and editors

Access to file name selectors and file name editors is provided as part of the EPOC16 operating system and OPL, C and OVAL provide methods to invoke them.

In a dialog box a file name selector can constrain the user by only allowing the selection of a file name from those that already exist, as appropriate for commands such as Open or Merge.

File name editors allow the user to type in the name of a file that may or may not already exist, as appropriate for commands such as 'Save as' and 'New'.

With either method a user can bring up a full file list by pressing the Tab key, or Control+Tab for more detailed file system navigation. In both cases, a disk selector is presented to allow the user to select the appropriate drive and directory. Using a file name selector or editor allows ROM based code to handle the selection of a filename and path.

File name parsing

File name parsing functions are available in C and OPL and will supply any file specification information that is missing or not explicitly supplied by the user. Parsing is also useful where you want to avoid making any assumptions about the syntax of the file specification e.g. when full files names may involve remote filing system nodes etc. The current node, drive and default directory are used to fill in the blanks if the file name information supplied to the parse function is incomplete. Applications usually specify their default directory path and file name extension as part of the program source code or build information. When the program is compiled or translated, the file specification details become available to the operating system and hence to the parsing functions.

Parse functions can also provide easy access to the component parts of a file specification see the PARSE$ function in the OPL programming section for an example.

OVAL does not have a parse function, the `FileSelector` and `FileNamEditor` control property settings determine the final composition of the file specification.

Note:
At least 128 bytes of storage space should be allocated for each file specification in your program.

File name extensions, standard

A number of standard filename extensions may be used by the internal applications provided by Psion, and are recognised by the system:

.AGN	Agenda files
.APP	Applications which are installable e.g. have icons
.DBF	Database files
.DBS	.DBS database sever files
.IMG	Programs – will be listed under the Runimg icon
.JOT	Jotter data files
.O	Word template files
.ODB	Application specific data files
.OPL	OPL program source files
.OPO	Translated OPL programs – will be listed under the Runopl icon
.PIC	Bitmap files
.SPR	Spreadsheet files
.WDR	Printer drivers
.WLD	World database files
.WRD	Word document files
.WVE	Digital sound files

Other file name extensions may of course be used, it is up to the program designer. See the 'User Interface' chapter for general principles of locating and naming of application specific files and directories.

Wildcards

When searching for a file or files, parts of the file name or extension can be replaced with wildcards i.e.

Use   *   to replace zero or more characters.

Use   ?   to replace individual characters.

Thus, a file search for .DBF will find all files with the .DBF file name extension, whatever the name. BG*.DBF will find all files beginning with BG and ending with DBF. Using *LES.DBF will match all DBF file name ending in LES e.g. SALES.DBF and TRIBBLES.DBF. The last example differs from wildcard searches on MS-DOS based systems where the characters in the name following the * are lost, and so the search would effectively find all files matching *.DBF.

A search for .D?? will find all files where 'D' is the first character of the file name extension.

Wild cards can only be used as components of file names, not directory names.

Directories

In contrast to file selectors on other systems, those on SIBO systems such as the Siena and Series 3 family allow users to specify paths that do not yet exist. This can happen fairly commonly, for example as follows:

1. The user inserts a brand new SSD into drive A
2. A 'Save as' or 'New file' menu option is selected
3. The user adjusts the disk selector to drive A: and hence the new disk
4. The user types e.g. 'Design' into the filename editor

Assuming the default directory for the application is `\DOC\` and the default file name extension is .TXT, the filename returned to the application (after internal parsing) would be: `LOC::A:\DOC\DESIGN.TXT` even though the directory `\DOC\` does not currently exist on the disk in the A: drive. It is the responsibility of application programs to test for such conditions and to create the required directories.

Directory names, standard

A number of standard first level directories may be used by the internal applications provided by Psion, and are recognised by the system and by the applications i.e.

`\AGN`	Agenda files
`\APP`	Applications which are installable e.g. have icons
`\DAT`	.DBF database files
`\DBS`	.DBS database server files
`\GPK`	Games pack settings files
`\IMG`	Programs – will be listed under the Runimg icon
`\JOT`	Jotter data files
`\OPD`	Application specific data files and bitmaps
`\OPL`	OPL program source files
`\OPO`	Translated OPL programs – will be listed under the Runopl icon
`\SPR`	Spreadsheet files
`\WDR`	Printer drivers, Word templates and spell checker dictionaries.
`\WLD`	World database files
`\WRD`	Word document files
`\WVE`	Digital sound files

Other directory names may of course be used, it is up to the program designer. See the 'User Interface' chapter for general principles of locating and naming of application specific files and directories.

General file management

EPOC16 provides a wide range of functions and services for the general management of files and directories. Access to file management facilities is fairly straight forward, but varies considerably depending upon the programming language you are using.

In C, OPL and OVAL keywords are available to:
- Get lists of file and directory names
- Test for the existence of a specific file or directory
- Copy, delete or rename files
- Create or remove directories
- Change the current path i.e. node, drive and directory
- Compress database files to remove all records marked as deleted

In C and OVAL, functions are available to:
- Get and set file attributes
- Get file information such as size, date and time
- Find the amount of internal memory available

In C and OPL, functions are available to:
- Find the free disk space. Although strangely, the OPL SPACE function can only be used in association with an open database file.

The file server

The file server is a high priority system process (with process name SYS$FSRV) that performs all file related operations on behalf of 'client' processes. An application process must connect to the file server before using its services, this is normally taken care of by the program start up code. (For example in C, the start up module is the code that precedes the main() function, and is supplied as standard for use with the PLIB library). Most applications need the services of the file server, and the overhead of automatically connecting to the file server by default is modest.

Installable file systems and remote file access

The file server supports multiple installable file systems or nodes. To-date three file systems have been implemented on the Siena and Series 3:

LOC::   The local filing system with devices M: (the internal RAM drive) and SSD drives A:, B:

REM::   The remote filing system, available while the file server is connected to a remote file server. The structure of the filing system depends upon what the remote system is. If the remote system is a PC or another SIBO machine, the structure is the same as for LOC::. Remote file servers have been implemented for PCs running DOS or MS Windows and the Apple Macintosh.

ROM::   The ROM filing system, used to access ROM-based files. This filing system is not normally visible to the user and does not support devices or directories.

SSDs are driven by the LOC:: file system using a number of subsidiary physical device drivers (PDDs) handling the different SSD types and the internal M: device i.e.

LOC.TY0   the RAM SSD PDD

LOC.TY1   the Flash SSD PDD

LOC.TYM   the internal RAM (M:) PDD

As previously stated, the devices and directory structures within the LOC:: file system are compatible with the MSDOS filing system.

SSD drive doors have switches that keep the file server informed of possible SSD removals and insertions. After an SSD drive door has been opened and closed, the file server checks each drive to see if it contains a new SSD. When the file server detects a new SSD, it automatically mounts it.

File operations - asynchronous

The file server is essentially asynchronous in its operations, and most system service functions for the filing system are provided in both asynchronous and synchronous forms. Because the file server has a higher priority than any of its clients, any operation that does not wait for a slow external device will have completed by the time an asynchronous request has returned. This includes any operation on the ROM:: file system or where the LOC:: file system accesses SSDs or the internal RAM drive (M:). However, when accessing the REM:: file system where the connection is via an RS232 cable, any asynchronous request is almost certain to return before the operation is complete.

Although, in practice, most file operations complete in a fraction of a second, a particular file request may take an extended time. For example, a read of 60K bytes from a REM:: file, connected over a 9600 baud serial link, would take around a minute. However, a request will never take an indefinite time to complete (as, for example, a write to the parallel port can do when the printer is off line). For these reasons, the file server does not actively support a cancel I/O request service, because the file may be left in an indeterminate state if a partially completed write operation is cancelled.

File types and formats in EPOC16

Psion application file formats

Apart from ASCII text files and .RTF files, the file formats used by the built-in applications such as Word and Sheet are proprietary to Psion. Some of the Psion applications do provide options to import data in other formats, or to save their data in formats other than their normal standard. For example, the Data application can export a database file (in .dbf format) to records in a text file, with delimiters (such as commas) between the record fields. Similarly Data can import (or merge in) database records from text files that have field delimiters.

Conversion of file formats

An increasing number of applications with in built file conversion facilities are appearing, both from Psion and from third party software companies. A prime example of file format conversions is demonstrated by the Psiwin application suite from Psion which has file conversion to and from Psion's proprietary file types to and from the formats for major PC based applications, such as Microsoft Word, Excel, Schedule+, WordPerfect, Lotus 123, Organiser etc. See the 'Linking to a PC or Printer' chapter for more details of PsiWin.

More file converters are appearing with time, but Psion have provided a set of guidelines for programmers who wish to produce additional file format converters for use with PsiWin (version 1.x), see the 'Programming Techniques' chapter.

For information on file formats and conversion between file formats see the 'Programming Techniques' chapter.

Binary files

A binary file is one where the bytes in the file are not treated with any special significance or interpretation by the EPOC16 filing system. Applications manipulating binary files are free to treat the bytes of data read or written in any way they choose. If the content of the file has any internal structure, then it is a format designated by the application designer. In OPL or C programs, data from binary files may be read or written in blocks of up to 16K bytes. In OVAL programs, it is possible to read up to 65534 bytes at a time. Text files may be treated as binary files, but it is more usual to open the file for I/O in text mode – see below.

Text files

Text files under EPOC16 follow broadly the same format conventions as in many other systems. For example, PC DOS text files are record based files, with each record terminated by a CR/LF sequence - a carriage return code (CR, decimal 13) followed by a line feed code (LF, decimal 10). The end of file (EOF) may optionally be marked by a SUB code (SUB, decimal 26), although this is becoming less common on systems that record the logical file length.

Text files can be treated as flat binary files, where the programmer takes care of all bytes in the data stream, including the record terminator sequences (e.g. CR/LF). However, it more usual to make use of the support provided by EPOC16 for handling individual text records. In the latter case, the terminating sequences are hidden from the programmer, who just reads and writes text records of up to 256 bytes in length (255 bytes if holding records in OPL strings).

Since text files are record based, and the length of any given record can vary, it is not possible to delete individual text records or replace amended records in their original positions. New text records are always appended to the end of a file. The simplest solution to modifying a section of text embedded within a file is by reading, amending and re-writing the whole file. Thus, applications that involve writing data to text files are potentially non flash-friendly (see later).

Binary or text file I/O

The specific details of reading or writing to a binary file or a text file depend upon the language used, and is covered in more detail elsewhere. However, many of the general principles of file I/O are independent of the language and so are discussed here.

Note:
Access to Psion database files (.DBF format) is quite different to general file I/O, and is handled through specific database functions, an overview of which is given later.

All general file handling is done via the I/O system using the `FIL:` device driver, although references to the `FIL:` device are not usually made explicitly, and it is largely hidden from the programmer. Opening a channel to the `FIL:` device provides access to file operations. Application processes must connect to the file server before they can use its services. However this is normally taken care of by the program start up code, and is normally included automatically i.e. in OPL, OVAL, or C programs that use PLIB (see the file server section earlier in this chapter).

Before the file I/O functions can be used, it is necessary to open a channel to the file. For example, with a call to a system service function e.g. the OPL keyword IOOPEN, the PLIB C function `p_open` or the OVAL Open statement.

Open modes

Files can be opened for access in one of three modes:

- Binary   data is accessed as a sequence of bytes with no apparent structure.
- Random   data is treated as a series of fixed length records.
- Sequential   variable length records, typically for text files.

Files can be opened for read only or shared access, read and write access or append mode. In C or OPL, opening a file as unique will create a new file with a unique name, which can be very useful for creating temporary working files.

Attempting to open a file that does not exist will create it, unless the file is being opened in shared or read only mode, in which case an error will be generated.

Note:
Once a file is open, references to the open file channel are made using the file identifier or handle. See the 'I/O System' chapter for more a detailed discussion of I/O function numbers, handles and error values.

Reading and writing

Data can be read from and written to the file using functions such as the OPL functions IOREAD() and IOWRITE() or the C functions p_read() and p_write(). In OVAL, reading and writing to the file is achieved via specific keywords such as GET, PUT, INPUT and PRINT, depending on the type of data and the file mode.

Flushing file buffers

To optimise file I/O speed, data to be written to text files is buffered in memory until a defined block size is reached. An I/O request such as:

```
r% = IOW(handle%, FFLUSH, #0, #0)   REM FFLUSH = 9
```

may be used to force the text to be written to the file, say just before a file is closed. This has the advantage of detecting, and being able to recover from, any file errors that would not be possible after using IOCLOSE.

Flushing of file buffers is only relevant to text files opened for update, and should be used sparingly to avoid reductions in performance and undue fragmentation of Flash SSDs.

Data for binary files is not buffered, so the FFLUSH operation is not normally used, with the exception that it also causes the file modification details (date and time) to be written, for both text and binary files.

Positioning within a file

When a file is opened for random access, the current position in the file for the next read or write operation can be set, e.g. in OPL with the IOSEEK() function. In OVAL, the current position can be set and sensed using the Seek() function; the Loc() function returns the most recent seek position of the file.

Setting a new end of file

For binary stream files it is possible to truncate, extend or reserve space in a file using the FSETEOF function e.g.

```
r% = IOW(handle%, FSETEOF, nEOF&, #0)   REM FSETEOF = 11
```

Where the variable nEOF& specifies the new end of file (i.e. the offset in bytes). If the value of nEOF& is beyond the current end of file it will be extended, and shortened if it is within the current end of file.

Closing

Once the interaction is finished, the I/O channel to the file is closed using an appropriate function call, e.g. using the OPL function IOCLOSE(), PLIB function p_close() or Close in OVAL. It is good practice to close a file as soon as it is no longer being accessed. Unless there are specific reasons to the contrary, it is advisable not to keep files permanently open. It is better to close a file as soon as possible, re-opening it again each time it is needed. Closing a file releases memory and other resources back to the system.

Avoiding file I/O errors

General file I/O may seem complex at first, but in practice it is not; more details are provided elsewhere in the book and example code is provided on disk; see the main index and the disk specific index in the 'Disk Contents' chapter. A couple of important points should be noted however. The file handle or identifier is the vital link to any particular open file and it should not be 'lost' by over writing it, or by holding it in a local variable and then referring to it outside of the scope of the procedure that declared the variable. Always design your programs to handle errors that may arise during file handling. For example with OPL, the I/O functions such as IOREAD(), IOWRITE() do not generate errors that can be caught using the TRAP or ONERROR statements. Virtually all of the OPL I/O keywords return a value, if the return value from the I/O call is negative, an error has occurred. Additional code should be included to examine the return value for error conditions, and act accordingly. A full list of possible error codes is given in the Appendix.

Database files

Psion .DBF files

Database files created by the built in applications (such as 'Data') consist of individual records, which may be split into sub-records called fields. Such files are manipulated by adding, deleting and updating individual records, unlike applications such as Word which read and write whole files at once. This behaviour ensures that DBF files are Flash-friendly (see below), but it also has a number of other consequences to the programmer:

- New records are always appended to the end of the file.
- Deleted records are only marked as deleted, and the space they used will not be recovered until the whole file is compressed.
- Updating the contents of a record actually results (automatically) in the modified record being written to the end of the file as a new record, and the old record is marked as deleted.
- Keeping records in a particular order (e.g. sorted) is not a trivial problem.

Thus, even though it is possible to 'position the current record pointer' so that it is pointing at a specific record number in the file, you cannot rely on using record numbers to keep track of a specific data record after changes have been made to the file. This is not normally a significant problem since the EPOC16 DBF database services do provide excellent searching facilities. Programmers who wish to use an equivalent to record numbers should include a field to act as a record number field, or another unique identifier, in each data record and maintain it within the application code. The identifier field may then be used with the DBF search facilities to read records in the required way.

Database files may be created and manipulated by the built in 'Data' application, or via your own application code, in C, OPL or OVAL, by making use of the .DBF service functions provided. OVAL programmers have automatic access to the database server (DBS) functions that are discussed later in this chapter.

Records produced by the Psion 'Data' application are limited, in that only string fields are used. However, database files produced by other applications may use field types of integer, long integer, floating point and string.

For a more detailed discussion of the .DBF file format see the 'Programming Techniques' chapter.

Maximum records

The maximum number of records that can be handled by the standard .DBF functions is 65,534.

Database compression

In OPL programs, if a DBF file is located on the internal RAM drive or on a RAM SSD it is compressed by default when the file is closed, or if a user invokes a 'Compress' option provided by the application. In other words, all of the space used by the deleted records will be recovered. Applications written in C have to explicitly specify the file compress action.

It is not possible to compress a .DBF file stored on Flash RAM automatically in this way. Database files on Flash RAM can be compressed by using a 'File - Save as' option or by using a .DBF services compress function, to 'copy' the .DBF file under another name (or with the same name, but in a new location). All of the 'deleted' records will be removed during the 'Save as' or compress process, whereas a simple copy operation will copy all data including the records marked as deleted.

ISAM database files

The ISAM (Indexed Sequential Access Method) library is a set of functions for efficient access and indexing of .DBF database files. Such files consist of multiple records containing one or more structured fields; they can be created, maintained and accessed from OPL and C programs on the S3, S3a/c, Siena, HC and Workabout. The ISAM library is supplied in the form of a dynamic library i.e. ISAM.DYL.

OVAL applications cannot use the ISAM library; it uses the more recent DBS database format instead.

The ISAM library uses B-tree index files to provide rapid indexed and sequential access to DBF files. It is the most widely used form of index file simply because it is the most efficient general method of accessing database files. B-tree index files minimise the number of disk accesses per retrieval. In general B-tree index files should not be constructed or maintained on a Flash SSD (but index files can be read from a Flash SSD).

The ISAM library functions provide the following:

- Fast record retrieval on a key. For example, a DBF file can be searched for all records containing the key 'Smith'.
- Very little degradation of the speed of retrieval occurs as the number of records increases.
- Sequential access to records that are ordered by the key (i.e. next, back, first and last).
- The ability to see a selection of the records in the file (by constructing a selective or sparse index).
- Access to record fields with automatic conversion from numbers to text (and vice-versa) if required.
- Powerful key definitions based on combinations of up to eight fields, giving highly ordered access.
- The opening multiple (up to 31) index files for a DBF file at any one time. For example, a DBF file containing customer details can have two indexes, one for searching on customer occupation and related details and the other for searching on customer location and related details.

- The adding, erasing, and updating of records with the appropriate updating of all associated index files carried out automatically.

Field types

The following field types are available:

> BYTE, UBYTE, WORD, UWORD, LONG, ULONG, DOUBLE, STRING.

However, if compatibility with existing OPL or PLIB DBF functions is required, the field types must be restricted to:

> WORD, LONG, DOUBLE, STRING

Maximum records

The maximum number of records that can be handled by the standard .DBF functions is 65,534. However, in ISAM the maximum number of database records is 2,147,483,647. The ISAM library and example code in C and OPL is supplied on disk.

DBS database files

DBS is a Database server from Psion that allows access to dBase III and IV format files in addition to the usual Psion DBF files. DBS is the replacement for the ISAM library, and runs on the Series 3, Series 3a/c, Siena, HC and Work*about*.

DBS is a database server (a separate process on the Psion), with full multi-client support, including simultaneous access to the same data and index files, which ISAM does not provide. DBS has extended the ISAM functionality by adding:

- Database level support.
- Index tracking.
- Multiple record buffers on the same table, with record locking during editing.
- DynaViews, which give a filtered and/or sorted view of records in a table.
- Extra field flags.
- Three new field types: Date, Logical and LongBinary (LongBinary not currently supported by Psion DBF).
- Text based expressions can be used with DBS to specify filters and sorting.

Because DBS is a separate process, each function call has the overhead of an inter-process message, but DBS is mostly faster (particularly at indexing) than ISAM. However, field data access is slower using DBS than ISAM.

The DBS server is 'built in' to OVAL, but the DBS tools are provided by Psion free of charge to allow the same functionality from both C and OPL programs. The Psion Database Server tools (DBS_105) are provided on disk, but are subject to certain license conditions – see the license.txt file included. Other documentation describing how to use DBS is included with the server software, along with example code in C and OPL.

All DBS files should be located in a \DBS directory i.e. off the root directory of a drive.

DBS cannot read index files written by ISAM.

dBase files

Although the dBase file format is not ideal for handheld machines, DBS supports it so that data can be used directly from PC based applications without having to be first translated into Psion DBF format.

Data files in dBase format tend to be 2-3 times bigger than an equivalent Psion DBF data file and dBase indexes can also be up to 2 times larger than Psion ones (depends very much on the sorting key). Text based fixed-width format field types are used by dBase for all field types, this makes the data access slower than .DBF field access. Because of other overheads, this is most noticeable when indexing a table, when using dBase format files can be 2-3 times slower than using the Psion .DBF format files.

SSDs and robust applications

Mass storage devices such as SRAM and Flash RAM can be removed, changed or repositioned at will by the user. SSD drive doors have switches that keep the file server informed of possible SSD changes. Robust programs are designed to cope with such eventualities without crashing.

In general, the filing system is robust and reasonably secure, as illustrated by the following:

The RAM SSD physical device driver (PDD) on the LOC:: file system (see File specifications above) does not buffer written data. This protects the integrity of the SSD contents from being corrupted by crashes (application or system) that may occur while files are open, or by the removal of the SSD while files are open on it. Similarly, the data in each write to a file on a Flash SSD is written straight to the SSD, i.e. it is not buffered (This may not be the case for text files, which are handled by a layer over the FIL: device. The buffering of such files is thus outside the file server's control). However, in the interests of efficient storage, the record just written is kept open for as long as possible - until the file channel is closed, flushed or until a write to another file on the same SSD occurs. File date and time stamps are not written until the file channel is flushed or closed. If the SSD is removed or the machine resets while there is an open file channel with an write outstanding, the record is closed when the file is next accessed (the file is then also stamped with the current date and time).

Flash friendly applications

The Flash filing system is designed such that the logical interface to files on a Flash SSD (whether reading or writing) is entirely equivalent to that on other devices (RAM SSD, hard disk etc.). However, when overwriting or when deleting a file, space is consumed and is not recovered until the Flash SSD is next formatted.

Note also that renaming a file, setting the date and time or setting the file attributes all use up additional space and can therefore fail through lack of remaining capacity. However, deleting a file does not consume any further space.

Storage space on Flash RAM devices can only be recovered by reformatting the whole device, so applications such as Word Processors and Spreadsheets which usually re-write the whole file on update should avoid using Flash devices. File based applications such as Databases etc. which operate on a record by record basis can use Flash RAM without a significant problem. However, space used by records that have been deleted or updated (which typically involves the addition of a new record and deletion of the old) will not be recoverable until a reformat is performed. Files stored on Flash RAM cannot be compressed, whereas those on the internal drive or on SRAM devices can be compressed in situ to recover the space used by deleted records.

Flash SSDs are particularly attractive for storing program files, read-only data (say for data-referral applications), for securely storing logged data in the field and for archiving data. The storage of files on a Flash SSD is very different from that used on RAM SSDs. The scheme is not at all block structured, but is based on linked variable length records. All this is hidden from the caller and the logical interface to a file on a Flash SSD is the same as for a file on a RAM SSD (or any other medium).

On a Flash SSD, there is no limit on the number of files or directories in the root directory. You will also find that it is possible to fit slightly more data on a freshly formatted Flash SSD than on a RAM SSD of the same nominal capacity. This is due to the fact that files are allocated space in multiples of whole blocks on a RAM SSD whereas Flash files are stored in exactly sized variable length records.

7 I/O System

Introduction

A programmer must use the input/output (I/O) system (directly or indirectly) to do general file handling, or to interact with various devices and systems within the SIBO environment. A comprehensive I/O system is supported by EPOC16, which includes many hardware devices and some software sub-systems. For example, to print to the parallel port a programmer would open a channel to the PAR: device.

Note, this chapter covers the principles of device I/O. To simplify the description of I/O processing and signalling, the OPL function names and terms will be used; although C and OVAL programmers will have no problems in recognising the equivalent terms and function names.

The principles of general file I/O are covered in the chapter – 'Files in EPOC16'.

I/O devices

CON:	for access to basic screen and keyboard services
FIL:	for operating on files
PAR:	for accessing the parallel port
TTY:	for access to an RS232 serial port
XMD:	for access to the Xmodem or Ymodem serial data transfer protocols
NCP:	for establishing a link to a remote system
SND:	for access to sound via a loudspeaker - for non-digital sounds
TIM:	for using an asynchronous timer
ALM:	for setting Alarms
FRC:	the free running counter – e.g. for use as a high-resolution timer
WLD:	to access the built-in World application database
SIR:	for low level to access the serial infrared port.
AIR:	for protocol controlled access to the serial infrared port
IRP:	for infrared printing port services e.g. point and shoot printing.

Listed above is a comprehensive, although not exhaustive, list of the I/O devices in a SIBO system. Other I/O devices may be used for interaction with additional peripherals, such as bar code readers, docking stations (e.g. for the Work*about* and HC systems) or even software services such as the DBS database server (described in the 'Files in EPOC16' chapter).

Some of the devices in the list above are included for completeness, e.g. the `FIL:` device, since file operations are not normally done explicitly by direct reference to this device.

More detailed descriptions of the I/O devices listed above are provided later in this chapter, and example code is supplied on disk to demonstrate a wide range of interactions with most of the devices. See the index for references to the relevant example file names.

Device drivers

The I/O system is implemented in EPOC16 using software interfaces called device drivers, that are designed to isolate the programmer from the details of any underlying hardware. Thus, although the exact implementation of the parallel port hardware may differ across SIBO machines, it will have no effect on the code of an application program. Differences in SIBO hardware are accommodated by using different device drivers for different Psion models.

To use I/O devices it is not necessary to understand the details of the associated device drivers, you just need to know the name of the device and the functions that it provides.

For those who wish to know more about device drivers, or even how to produce their own, more detail is provided at the end of this chapter.

Using the I/O system

Device I/O may seem complex at first but in practise it is not; more specific details are provided elsewhere, and example code for a number of common I/O tasks is provided on disk.

Before the functions of an I/O device can be used it is necessary to get a handle or identifier for the device. Unless a 'standard' handle exists for the device, a channel must be opened to the device with a call to a system service function (e.g. the OPL keyword `IOOPEN()` or the PLIB `p_open()` function).

If the I/O device is not recognised as valid, the system will pass the open call on to the file server to see if the device specified was a file name. Setting the mode parameter to −1 in the function call to open the device will prevent this behaviour. For example in OPL:

```
IOOPEN(handle%, name$, -1) REM open a device not a file
```

In OVAL, many of the I/O devices in the system, such as the serial port, are used via specific OVAL controls. Opening a channel to a device is done through the Open method of the DeviceIO control and a number of I/O related methods are available to interact with the device.

Handles

Opening a channel to a device or file will return a handle or identifier; all further references to the channel are then made using the handle.

In OPL, the console device may be referred to using a handle of –2, and a handle of –1 can be used to refer to the last device channel that was opened with LOPEN. (Note: Do not use handles of –2 or –1 if you are using the I/O macros in the OPL SDK.)

I/O functions

Specific functions or actions of the I/O device are accessed via synchronous functions such as IOW() or asynchronous I/O service functions such as IOC() or IOA(). These functions make various types of request on the I/O channel. For example, to read from or write to the device.

The particular I/O function requested is specified by a function number parameter. Some I/O functions are specific to a particular device, for example FSEEK, which sets the file position on an open file channel. Some I/O functions apply to more than one device, including:

Function ID	Value	Action
FREAD	1	Read data from a channel
FWRITE	2	Write data to a channel
FCLOSE	3	Close a channel
FCANCEL	4	Cancel outstanding asynchronous request on a channel
FSET	7	Set channel characteristics
FSENSE	8	Sense channel characteristics
FFLUSH	9	Flush out the data buffers

In OPL the most commonly used I/O functions are supported by their own synchronous convenience functions as follows:

IOCLOSE	i.e. IOW(FCLOSE)
IOREAD	i.e. IOW(FREAD)
IOWRITE	i.e. IOW(FWRITE)
IOSEEK	i.e. IOW(FSEEK)

The functions IOCLOSE, IOREAD and IOWRITE are used with many devices.

The function IOCLOSE (or p_close() in C) is applicable to all devices; IOSEEK only applies to open files, and is described in the 'Files in EPOC16' chapter.

Closing the channel

Once the interaction is finished, the I/O channel to the device is closed using an appropriate function call e.g. the OPL function IOCLOSE(), PLIB function p_close() or Close in OVAL. It is good practice to close the I/O channel as soon as it is no longer being accessed. Closing a channel will release memory and other resources back to the system.

Avoiding I/O errors

The device handle is the vital link to any particular I/O channel. A handle may be 'lost' by overwriting it, or by holding it in a local variable and then trying to refer to it outside of the scope of the procedure that declared the variable.

Always design your programs to handle errors that may arise during I/O device handling. For example with OPL the I/O functions such as IOW(), IOC() do not generate errors that can be caught using the TRAP or ONERROR statements. Virtually all of the OPL I/O keywords return a value. If the return value is negative, an error has occurred. Additional code should be included to examine the return value for error conditions and act accordingly. A full list of possible error codes is given in the Appendix.

Synchronous I/O

Synchronous I/O, using a function such as IOW() (or p_iow() in C), is relatively simple. However, if you are planning to use asynchronous device I/O, and particularly if multiple I/O requests are to be made, it is essential to understand I/O semaphores, status words and the differences between synchronous and asynchronous operations.

Some I/O system services are implemented in two steps:

1. Make the service request.
2. Wait for the requested operation to complete - i.e. the waiting process is suspended.

In most cases, as well as providing functions for each step, the system provides a function containing both the above steps. Such combined functions are called *synchronous*, because they automatically cause the requesting process to wait until the operation has completed, i.e. they synchronise it.

Note:
If you only intend to make synchronous I/O calls (i.e. using functions such as IOW() or p_iow()), then matters are usually much simpler, and you don't have to worry about I/O semaphores and status words.

Asynchronous I/O

For asynchronous I/O, always use functions calls of the type IOC() or its equivalent p_ioc(), unless it is absolutely necessary to test for the successful start of the I/O request. Functions such as IOC() assume that the I/O request will start correctly, but will still return an error condition if it did not start or fails to complete.

Functions that queue multiple service requests, without waiting for their completion, are called asynchronous functions.

Applications use asynchronous requests in situations like the following:

1. Make service request A
2. Make service request B
3. Wait for either of the requested operations to complete - whilst possibly doing some other processing, while waiting for one or more of the service requests to complete.

Processes wait for the completion of asynchronous requests by waiting on their I/O semaphore. Each request has an associated with a status word - a static variable (or value from the heap) that is used to indicate the current status of the request that was made.

Semaphores and status words

Semaphores are indicator flags created and used by EPOC16 to synchronise co-operating processes; they have three common uses:

• Synchronising access to a shared resource e.g. a storage device.
• Synchronising supplier-consumer relationships e.g. a semaphore associated with a pool of data in a shared data segment.
• Synchronising the completion of asynchronous requests.

The semaphores used by EPOC16 are counting semaphores, having a signed value that can be incremented and decremented via operating system calls or functions. A semaphore with a negative value implies that a process must wait for the completion of some other event, such as the freeing of a shared resource. The mechanism by which a process waits on a semaphore is part of the overall management of process scheduling.

I/O Semaphores

When a process is created, the system creates a single I/O semaphore on its behalf, initially with a value of zero. Although this semaphore is used for I/O operations, it is used in general for asynchronous requests of other types. The I/O semaphores for all processes are stored in the private data space of the operating system, (they can be viewed using the SIBO debugger or the Spy application - discussed elsewhere).

After making one or more asynchronous requests, for example using IOC() or IOA() in OPL, a program could call IOWAIT (in C the PLIB function p_iowait() would be used) to wait for one or more of the I/O requests to complete.

In fact, a typical application process spends most of its time waiting on its I/O semaphore. For example, an interactive application process that is waiting for user input is waiting on its I/O semaphore.

Each call to the `IOWAIT` function (or PLIB `p_iowait()`) decrements the I/O semaphore and suspends the process. The call to `IOWAIT` will return when **any** outstanding asynchronous request completes, and so it may return immediately. A negative value for an I/O semaphore means that the process is waiting on one or more I/O requests. A call to `IOWAIT` will only return when the I/O semaphore is non-negative i.e. when something has happened.

When asynchronous I/O requests complete, the system signals the event by incrementing the I/O semaphore for the process. Therefore, if you are making more than one I/O request, it is essential to check the status word associated with each I/O request to ensure that it was one of your requests that completed.

I/O status words

Each asynchronous request will have its own status word that **must** remain available to the to the I/O function (usually by declaring it as a global variable). When any particular I/O request completes, a value will be written into the status word associated with that request. Status words are used to indicate the current state of the request, or the result of a completed I/O request.

While the I/O request is still pending i.e. before the call to `IOWAIT` has returned, a negative value for a status word indicates that request is still outstanding.

When a call to `IOWAIT` has returned, the status word for each outstanding I/O request should be examined (this is sometimes called polling). If the status word for a particular I/O request has the value `E_FILE_PENDING` (i.e. -46), then that request has not completed, and it may be another of the outstanding requests that has completed. Any other negative value indicates that an error has occurred, whereas a zero or positive value indicates it completed successfully.

Note:
If you are only making one asynchronous I/O request at a time, use `IOWAITSTAT` instead of `IOWAIT`, since a call to `IOWAITSTAT` will only return when the I/O request associated with the specific status word completes.

Once an asynchronous I/O request has completed, and a status word with an appropriate value has been detected, the 'on completion code' is then executed. The order in which the various status words are examined, and therefore acted upon, will determine the order of priority associated with the various I/O requests.

When the processing of a completed I/O request is done, it is usual to re-queue the I/O request and call `IOWAIT` again, to wait for the next completion. For example, to wait for the receipt of more data from a serial port, or for the next key press etc.

Always be sure **not** to re-queue the same I/O request again unless the status word indicates it has definitely completed. Making a new I/O request while a previous one on the same status word is still pending will almost certainly cause the program to be panicked.

However, some drivers will allow both a read and a write request to be pending at the same time, the serial port (TTY:) for example.

If none of the status words correspond to one of the outstanding I/O requests, then the return from IOWAIT was a 'false alarm' for your purposes. Such a program would usually loop round and call IOWAIT again. This of course, will decrement the I/O semaphore again, potentially raising a 'stray signal'. If so, you must keep a count of each time IOWAIT returned on a 'false alarm' (i.e. due to other functions completing and signalling, outside of your code).

When one of the status words finally shows that IOWAIT returned due to an I/O request made by your program, IOSIGNAL (p_iosignal() in C) must then be called once for each of the other 'false alarm' returns. This will correctly increment the I/O semaphore to replace each of the decrement signals caused by any repeated 'false alarm' calls to IOWAIT.

Cancelling an asynchronous request

Most asynchronous request operations have a corresponding cancel function, and the following principles are applicable:

- The cancel function will only precipitate the completion of the I/O request.
- It may be too late to cancel the I/O operation, it may have already completed before the cancel function was processed.
- In either case, the completion of the I/O request must still be 'processed', since the I/O semaphore will have been signalled.

The I/O request can be cancelled with a call such as:

IOW(handle%, FCANCEL, #0, #0), where FCANCEL = 4. With the Series 3, 3a/c, Siena or Work*about* the IOCANCEL(handle%) function could be used.

If the I/O request has already completed the cancel function will do nothing; otherwise it will only precipitate the completion of the I/O request, but with the status word set to E_FILE_CANCEL (i.e. -48).

Important note:
To ensure any stray I/O signal is 'used up', a call should be made to:

IOWAITSTAT handle% (or p_waitstat(&handle)) immediately following the call to cancel.

I/O and compute intensive processes

An alternative strategy, to making asynchronous I/O requests and then waiting for a return from IOWAIT, could be to make the I/O requests and then go round in a loop testing (polling) the value of the corresponding status words. However, in a multi-tasking environment this is usually considered anti-social, because it can hog a lot of processor bandwidth.

In some situations it may be desirable to remain responsive to user key presses, whilst continuing to do some other compute intensive task, for example calculating the next move in a game. In the situation just described, a looping and polling design may be more appropriate.

If this approach is used, you need to be aware that in some cases asynchronous requests are completed by functions known as wait handlers. Therefore, it is necessary to call IOYIELD before each poll of the status word, to give any wait handlers a chance to run.

Wait handlers are functions that process the completion of asynchronous requests from within IOWAIT (or IOWAITSTAT). Any active wait handlers are called just before IOWAIT would have otherwise returned.

While an application performs a computationally intensive task that takes an extended time, it should call IOYIELD, because wait handlers are only called when the process calls IOWAIT or IOWAITSTAT. The IOYIELD function is effectively a combination call to IOSIGNAL, followed by a call to IOWAIT. Thus, IOYIELD allows any wait handlers to run.

For example:

```
...
IOA(handle%,func%,stat%,#pBuf%,len%)
DO
    nextmove:    /* calculate part of next game move */
                 /* this task must not be continuous, */
                 /* i.e. it should be broken up into sections */
                 /* so IOYIELD gets to run quite often */
    IOYIELD      /* allow any I/O wait handlers to run */
UNTIL stat%<>E_FILE_PENDING
...
```

In example above, completion of the I/O function is indicated by the status word becoming zero or positive. Remember that the I/O semaphore will have been incremented, so it is obligatory to 'use up' that signal by calling IOWAIT, to avoid a 'stray signal' later.

Console services

The CON: device provides a basic set of screen and keyboard handling services, e.g. for simple character based C or assembler applications. Programs written in OPL, HWIF C, HWIM C and Oval spare the programmer from any need to make direct use of the console CON: device. In I/O calls made to the console device from an OPL program, a handle of –2 can be used as the default.

(A C program that makes use of the CLIB start up module will automatically open a channel to the CON: device. This is not the case if the PLIB start up module is used, but the first PLIB console I/O function call that is made will automatically open a channel, if one is not already open. A process that attempts to explicitly open a console channel when it already has a channel open will be panicked - see the 'Errors and Debugging' chapter).

File services

All general file handling is done via the I/O system using the FIL: device driver, although references to the FIL: device are not usually made explicitly, and are largely hidden from the programmer. Opening a channel to the FIL: device provides access to file operations. Application processes must connect to the file server before they can use its services. However, this is normally taken care of by the program start up code and is included automatically, i.e. in OPL, OVAL, or C programs that use PLIB. See the chapter entitled 'Files in EPOC\16' for more details on general file I/O.

Parallel port

Opening a channel to the PAR: device provides access to a centronics parallel port, normally just used for printing. The Siena and Series 3 family recognise only one parallel port i.e. the PAR:A port, which is a write only device and does not support read operations. Other SIBO machines may support more than one parallel port e.g. PAR:B or PAR:C in addition to PAR:A.

In OPL, it is more usual to interact with the parallel port using the synchronous keywords such as LOPEN, LCLOSE and LPRINT. If the PAR: device port has been 'opened' with LOPEN, a handle of −1 may then be used in any subsequent I/O requests made with functions such as IOW(). However, if the port is opened with IOOPEN, then the handle returned by that call should be used for all subsequent I/O service calls.

See Infrared communications later for details of printing via the infrared port.

Serial port

Opening a channel to the TTY: device provides access to a fully interrupt-driven RS-232 serial port. The Siena and Series 3 family recognise only one serial port i.e. the TTY:A port, which supports read / write operations for data, and sensing / setting operations for the serial port parameters and control lines. Other SIBO systems, such as the HC and Work*about,* may support more than one serial port e.g. TTY:B or TTY:C in addition to TTY:A.

In OPL, it is more usual to interact with the serial port using the synchronous keywords such as LOPEN, LCLOSE and LPRINT. If the TTY: device port has been 'opened' with LOPEN, a handle of −1 may then be used in any subsequent I/O requests made with functions such as IOW(). However, if the port is opened with IOOPEN, then the handle returned by that call should be used for all subsequent I/O service calls.

See Infrared communications later for details of sending data via the serial infrared device.

Xmodem and Ymodem transfers

The XMD: device driver supports the industry standard Xmodem and Ymodem serial data transfer protocols, for transfer of data (files) between similar or dissimilar computers. Applications that intend to use the file transfer I/O services must first open a channel to the XMD: device driver. (The XMD: driver is an example of an attached device driver that automatically makes use of the serial port device driver to which it attaches.)

Link and NCP

The Link application is the process that controls the connection of a SIBO system to a remote system such as a PC. The Link application has no visible user interface. On the Series 3 family, Siena and Work*about* the user is able to turn the link on or off, as well as setting up link parameters such as the baud rate, from a remote link option on the system screen 'Special' menu. The Link and SYS$NCP processes are started and stopped by the system process (SYS$MANG) in accordance with the user settings. Link monitors changes in the SYS$NCP process, and sets up the remote filing system once a connection is established.

It is the SYS$NCP process that actually handles the details of the communication at the Psion end, and provides the NCP: device driver functions to the applications programmer. The SYS$NCP process establishes the remote connection and manages the data transfer. It is Link processes (one at each end) that (via SYS$RFSV processes) create a client server type connection between the local file system (i.e. the Psion) and the remote file system (e.g. a PC). Applications which require to make use of the NCP: I/O services must first open a channel to the NCP: device driver. A document (called NCP.DOC) is provided on disk which give more details on Link and NCP.

Sound

Different SIBO systems have varying internal sound hardware and therefore provide distinct sets of sound services. Producing sound via a buzzer or via the SND: driver is described here. Recording and playback of digital sounds is described in the 'Programming Techniques' chapter.

Sound mechanisms

In all cases, sounds produced by the buzzer (or buzzer emulation) are generated via the PLIB p_sound function, the GenSound OS call, the OPL BEEP function or the Oval Beep function.

Sounds made via a speaker (if fitted), such as DTMF dialling tones and some alarm sounds, are controlled via I/O functions using the SND: device driver.

Playing and recording of digital sound files (.WVE files) is achieved using appropriate O/S calls or PLIB C function calls.

Sound example code, in OPL and C, is provided on disk, see the disk index in the 'Disk Contents' chapter.

Alarm sounds

When setting an alarm on the Series 3a/c, there are five standard alarm sounds available (apart from silent), i.e. rings, chimes, fanfare, soft bell and church bell. Rings and chimes are two standard sounds produced using I/O calls to the SND: device, the other three sounds are produced by playing digital sound files. The 'standard' alarm sound .WVE files are in ROM and have the names SYS$AL01.WVE, SYS$AL02.WVE and SYS$AL03.WVE. An example OPL program (ALARMSND.OPL) is supplied on disk to demonstrate playing both types of sound. See the Alarms section below for details of how to set alarms from your own programs.

Dialling (DTMF) sounds

Dialling tones are produced using I/O calls to the SND: device. An example OPL program (DTMF.OPL) is supplied on disk that demonstrates generating DTMF dialling sounds on Series 3, 3a or 3c machines.

Timers and processes

A process can be suspended because it is waiting for a timer to elapse, or it may still be active and operating asynchronously but is ready for its I/O semaphore to be signalled when a timer device entry elapses. The timer entries are held in the time DELTA queue - see the 'Processes, Memory and Applications' chapter.

Two types of timer are supported by EPOC16, using the TIM: device driver:

Absolute timers

- Expiry times are specified as a specific number of seconds after time 00:00:00 on January 1, 1970.
- When an absolute timer elapses, a SIBO machine that is currently off, will switch on again.
- Putting the system time forward may cause an absolute timer to expire.
- They are used for alarms in the Agenda and Time applications - see Alarms below.

Relative timers

- Expiry times are specified as a time interval (in number of system ticks), relative to the system time, at the moment it is queued. Since they are stored as a signed 32 long integer they have a range of approximately 2.1 years (at the SIBO rate of 32 ticks per second).

- If the SIBO machine is turned off, any relative timers effectively stop running so they cannot switch the machine on.

- Altering the system time has no effect on the expiry time.

- Relative timers with intervals less than the auto-switch-off time can stop the system switching off - see 'Processes and auto-switch-off' in the 'Processes, Memory and Applications' chapter.

Asynchronous and synchronous timers

Synchronous timers will wait until the specified time period elapses before returning to the calling program. The synchronous function IOW() can be used on an open channel to the TIM: device to set a timer. However, it is simpler and more reliable to use the OPL PAUSE command, or the PLIB C functions such as p_sleep, p_sleepa and p_sleept; all are examples of synchronous timer functions.

Asynchronous I/O calls to set timers (e.g. with IOC() or IOA()) will return immediately. Other processing may then be done, such as queuing other asynchronous requests, before using IOWAIT to wait for the completion of one of the requests.

Timer functions

To use a timer (e.g. in OPL) you first open a channel to the TIM: device e.g.

r% = IOOPEN(handle%, "TIM:", -1)

Then make an I/O request (e.g. IOW(), IOC() or IOA()) to call one of the following functions:

Function ID	Value	Action
FRELATIVE	1	Set a relative timer
FABSOLUTE	2	Set an absolute timer
FCANCEL	4	Cancel a timer e.g. IOW(handle%, FCANCEL)

By opening a new device channel for each timer required, it is possible to have many timers running.

In OVAL, a timer control can be used to signal your program each time a set time interval elapses. The timer control has a resolution of $1/10^{th}$ of a second, so the shortest time interval that is allowed is 100 milliseconds. Specifying a time interval of less than $1/10^{th}$ of second will generate an error 380.

To close the timer channel you would use, IOCLOSE(handle%).

Free running counter (FRC)

For programmers who need access to a high-resolution timer, a device driver for a built-in free running counter (FRC) became available with Series 3a and Workabout systems (i.e. it is not available on the HC or Series 3).

The FRC: device has a resolution of 1/1024 seconds, and is accurate to 2.6 seconds per month. Applications should only make use of the FRC if they need a resolution of 1/32 seconds or greater. The FRC should only be used for as long is it absolutely necessary, since the it can only support one process at any one time. A relative or absolute timer should be used instead of the FRC: device unless a very high resolution is mandatory e.g. for an application such a stopwatch. Example programs that demonstrate the FRC: device are provided on disk.

Alarms

Timers are an integral part of EPOC16. However, all alarm services, a specific use of timers, are provided by the built-in 'Time' application on the Siena and Series 3 systems, rather than having alarms as an fundamental part of EPOC16. Alarm services are accessed by opening an I/O channel to the ALM: device driver and using an I/O request (such as IOW(), IOC() or IOA()) to set the properties.

Alarms may have the following properties:

- An absolute time for the alarm.
- An optional message to be displayed.
- For timed alarms, an actual appointment time to be shown
- For alarms on the 3a/c and Siena, an alarm sound (which may be silent)

A process setting an alarm may request a timed or an un-timed alarm – this may seem a little confusing at first. The only difference between an un-timed and a timed alarm is that a timed alarm can display the 'time due', in addition to the day and month information. So a timed alarm can give advanced warning of the actual time at which something is due.

All alarms have an absolute time in the future at which they should expire. If a program sets an alarm but terminates before it expires, the alarm remains in effect, and is referred to as orphaned.

A zero terminated (ZTS) text message of up to 64 characters can be attached to an alarm on a Series 3 system. With alarms from the Series 3a onwards, the message can be up to 160 characters long, and can have a sound associated with them. Sounds can be rings, chimes, silent or a digital sound file, including one of the ROM based alarm sounds; for more details see the section on Alarm sounds earlier.

Alarm functions

Function ID	Value	Action
A_FTIMED	1	Series 3 timed alarm
A_FUNTIMED	2	Series 3 un-timed alarm
A_FTIMED_X	10	Series 3a/c or Siena timed alarm
A_FUNTIMED_X	11	Series 3a/c or Siena un-timed alarm
FCANCEL	4	Cancel an alarm e.g. IOW(handle%, FCANCEL,#0,#0)

With a Series 3a system or later, all of the alarm functions above may be used. With an original Series 3 system, only the first two types of alarm function can be used.

The structure of the data passed to the alarm device driver will depend upon whether it is a for an alarm on a Series 3 or on a Series 3a or later. A number of OPL programs (e.g. AALARMA.OPL and EX_ALARM.OPL) are supplied on disk to demonstrate setting alarms with messages and sounds, and give details of the data structures needed.

World database

Applications can have access to the information held on a large number of countries and many of their major cities, that is contained in the database of the built-in World application.

The data is in a ROM based file with the name ROM::WORLD.WLD, unless the ROM is a multi-lingual ROM - see later. By default, a WORLD.WLD extension file will be created to hold updated information such as new cities and changes to countries. The additional files should contain a maximum of 32 entries each to maintain optimum access efficiency. New World extension files, with different names, may have been created by the user to hold new of updated information. The World database server will read these files, and the data the extension file contains will override that in the main World file. The data in the main World database file is held in compressed form. Opening a channel to the WLD: device driver allows an application to access and update the information held. Applications are able to set the current home city and the current default country.

Information in the World database includes:

For each country
- National telephone dialling codes.
- International prefix dialling code.
- National prefixes for long distance calls.

For each city
- Time deviation from GMT.
- The zone for day light saving time (DST).
- Sunset and sunrise times calculated and returned as local time.
- Latitude, longitude and the co-ordinates of the city on the world map.

A number of OPL examples are provided on disk, they illustrate access to the data in the World database. Of particular interest are FDIAL.OPL and FDIAL.TXT which demonstrate getting country specific dialling information. The file WLD.TXT contains the I/O function numbers and details of the data structures used when making requests on the WLD: device.

In a multi-lingual ROM, there will be multiple world data files. The English data will be in ROM::WORLD.WLD, and the other languages in files with names of the form ROM::WORLD._xx, where xx is replaced by the language number. For example, a French world data file would have the name ROM::WORLD._02, a Dutch data file would be called ROM::WORLD._18. A full list of the country codes is provided in the Appendix.

Infrared communications

A bi-directional infrared communications port was introduced with the Series 3c and Siena, access to the infrared services is provided through the following I/O devices:

SIR: Gives low level access to the serial infrared port.
AIR: Provides protocol controlled access to the serial infrared port.
IRP: For infrared printing port services e.g. point and shoot printing.

Infrared printing support is provided to applications via the IRP: I/O device (using the IRLPT.LDD device driver), in a similar way to printing via the PAR: parallel port device.

IRP uses the AccessIR API services, which is a protocol controlled link mechanism provided by Psion, over the top of the IrDA (Infrared Data Association) standards. AccessIR provides a higher level link designed to simplify the connection of IrDA enabled devices e.g. printers, PCs or other Psion computers. The AccessIR API is used via the AIR: I/O device, and itself makes use of the low-level SIR: I/O device to talk to the infrared hardware.

Device drivers are provided in the Series 3c and Siena for SIR:, but the drivers for the IRP: and the AIR: I/O device (ACCESSIR.LDD) are only provided in the Series 3c, they are not present in the Siena ROM. On the Siena the drivers for IRP: and AIR: have to be installed and loaded into memory as required. The IR device drivers required for the Siena are supplied on disk, see the SIEIRPR directory and the notes below.

The SIR: I/O device also handles the 'beaming' function for transmission and receipt of data and files between Psion IrDA capable machines. An example program is provided on disk that demonstrates Serial infrared (via SIR:) chat between two people typing on two systems see IRCHAT.OPL.

Another demonstration program IRCOPY.OPL will receive a file transmitted via infrared from another system.

An alternative method is available for infrared communications that uses the IrMUX API, where communication between the application and the IrMUX API is via IPCS (Inter Process Communications). IrMUX is more flexible than AccessIR but more complex to use and is designed to be used by programmers using HWIM C.

Note:

The infrared protocols used on the Series 3c and Siena are different to those used on the Series 5. Data transfer between SIBO and Series 5 systems is not possible with the standard system software.

The Siena infrared printer drivers are provided on the supplied disk. They are installed as follows:

Copy accessx.ldd, irlpt.ldd and loadlpt.img into the img directory of your machine. You must be create this directory if it does not already exist. 'Loadlpt' should appear under the IMG icon in the System screen. Run the Loadlpt program by highlighting it and pressing 'Enter'. Follow the program instructions to install the infrared drivers. It is not necessary to keep the loader program (loadlpt.img) on the Siena once it has been run, although you will need to run it again if the machine is ever reset.

After installation infrared printing will be possible from any printing enabled Siena application. To print using infrared: select the 'Print setup' menu option within an application, and tab through the range of devices until "Infrared" appears. Still within the print set-up dialog, select the correct printer model and align the Siena with the printer's IR port, then select 'Print' to start IrDA printing.

Device drivers, in more detail

The I/O system is implemented using software interfaces called device drivers, which are designed to isolate the programmer from the details of any underlying hardware.

In EPOC16, device drivers are usually implemented as two layers; the logical device driver (LDD) layer with which the programmer interfaces and is hardware independent; and the physical device drivers (PDDs) which are hardware dependent.

An LDD may make use of several PDDs that are hardware specific. For example, to open a file the programmer will interface with the FIL: LDD, which will use an appropriate PDD for access to Flash SSDs, RAM SSDs or Internal RAM disk files etc. Exactly which PDD is used is transparent to the programmer.

By layering the device driver system, it is possible to present the same interface (via a common LDD) to the programmer; even though the exact implementation of a hardware device may differ across SIBO machines. (The differences are accommodated by using different PDDs for different models.)

EPOC16 supports the concept of attached device drivers, where a device driver attaches itself to another device driver and makes use of its functionality. For example, the XMD driver makes use of the serial port driver TTY: in order to provide Xmodem and Ymodem data transfers.

Some device drivers do not access hardware at all, but the driver mechanisms are used to add additional functionality to the system. For example, the standard C floating point library is implemented as a device driver, and the interface to the DBS database library is via an LDD.

External device drivers

Many device drivers are 'internal', i.e. they are built into the ROM. For example, the RS232 LDD and its PDD are in ROM, but other 'external' device drivers may have to be loaded from a file e.g. a bar code reader device driver. Such dynamically loadable and removable device drivers are a key feature of EPOC16, and system service functions are provided to load and delete (unload from memory) external LDDs and PDDs.

When a channel is opened to a device driver, a loaded (external) device driver will be used in preference to any existing (internal) device driver of the same name. Hence, it is possible to write replacement device drivers for those provided as standard - see Writing device drivers below.

Writing device drivers

Programmers who wish to write their own LDD device drivers will need to use assembly language. A small section of assembler code may just provide an appropriate interface to other more extensive code, which may be written in assembly language or in C.

Example device drivers, with assembly language and C source, are provided with Psion's EPOC16 C SDK; although it is necessary to have the Borland Turbo Assembler (TASM.EXE), and the Turbo Linker (TLINK.EXE) to re-build the drivers from the source code.

8 OPL Programming

Introduction

Programmers working in OPL have the widest range of platform choices for developing applications. An outline of the options is given in the 'Platforms' chapter; here each of the options are described in more detail, including some 'how to' information.

Comments are given on the advantages and disadvantages of each way of working, plus more details of the software and documentation supplied. For example, the Psion SIBO OPL SDK is described in considerable a detail.

OPL has evolved considerably with each generation of systems from Psion, to become powerful and flexible programming tool that still remains easy to use. Evidence of the growth in power can be seen from the ROM space the language requires. On the Organiser II it took a mere 8K, 19K on the HC, 23K on the Series 3, 29K on the Work*about*, S3a/c and Siena. A major change occurred in OPL as implemented on Psion Series 5 systems and it has now grown to occupy 140K of ROM memory.

OPL on 16-bit SIBO machines will be referred to as OPL16 (or SIBO OPL), on the 32-bit Series 5 systems it will be called OPL32. A detailed description of the entire OPL language is given in the 'OPL Reference' chapter.

Examples of more advanced OPL16 techniques are covered in the 'OPL16 Techniques' chapter using a full application as an example.

Differences between OPL16 and OPL32, and programming for Series 5 are discussed in the 'OPL32 Techniques' chapter. In addition the chapter contains a detailed description of a full Series 5 example application in OPL32.

You will find a wide range of OPL programming examples on disk. The examples vary: There are countless small snippets of OPL code to demonstrate a specific technique. Some are complete OPL applications. Some are very sophisticated combination examples that call the operating system or even sections of code written in C. All of the examples are described and indexed in the 'Disk Contents' chapter.

OPL manuals

In the past Psion supplied a printed copy of the OPL programming manual with each 'consumer' machine. When it became apparent that most users made no use of their OPL manual, Psion stopped supplying it by default in the UK. Printed copies of the Series 3a

OPL programming manual can be purchased from Psion for around £10. Psion also put the text of the Series 3a OPL manual into the public domain (whilst retaining the copyright); it is supplied in its complete form on disk – see the OPLMAN directory.

For Siena, Series 3c and Series 5 programmers the latest OPL programming manual is available for download from the Psion PLC Website. An edition of the manual in Microsoft Word format, obtained in June 97, is available on disk - see the OPLMAN32 directory.

Note:
You are referred to the Psion Website for the latest version of all documentation and examples originating from Psion – see the 'Contacts and Sources' chapter for access details.

Purchasers of the Series 5 system are supplied with the OPL32 manual on the PsiWin 2.0 (Explorer) CD-ROM.

SIBO based development

As stated elsewhere you can develop software using a SIBO system exclusively, and many successful Freeware and Shareware authors do just that. Some very sophisticated applications have been produced entirely on Psion computers.

Using the built in OPL editor/translation system is so straight forward that I will not waste words describing the process (see the text files in the OPLMAN directory for details), other than to stress the need for making regular backup copies of your source code and related files. Be sure to backup any files from the internal RAM drive to Flash or RAM SSDs, or a PC if you have one, especially if you make calls to the operating system or to sections of assembler code. A severe crash and reset, although rare, could wipe out weeks of hard work.

SIBO with OPP/OPPDBG

OPP and OPPDBG are shareware products from Andy Clarkson. OPP is a sophisticated OPL development system that provides alternative programming editors, adds new capability to the OPL editing / translation process, extends the OPL syntax and hides the complexity of operating system calls. Use of OPP also enables (optional) debugging of OPL programs at the source code level via OPPDBG - see later.

After OPP is installed a programmer works with the OPP editor (actually an alias of Word) to produce program source code files, with a filename extension of OPP. Similarly, an OPH editor is used to produce header files with an OPH extension. A new #include instruction allows references in OPP program files to the OPH files. During the OPP translation process the OPH files are opened, and the contents treated as though they were part of the source file in which they are 'included'. Header files are extremely useful for defining constants and macros (via #define) and for 'including' standard sections of macro/library code.

Working with OPP on a SIBO system is almost exactly like using the built in OPL editor and translator, but with greatly increased functionality. For example, the system allows definition of C-like data structures and language extensions such as 2D arrays. A huge number of pre-defined OPH include files are supplied which provide simple access to virtually all of the EPOC16 system calls.

OPP also has an option to make translated programs less prone to reverse translation by the REVTRAN program (see the REVTRAN directory on disk).

OPP is an excellent and very impressive system, I am only aware of two slight disadvantages associated with its use. The first and most important is that it makes programs OPP specific and dependent. Porting OPP code to new Psion machines may be more difficult, and will rely on the author of OPP being willing and able (dependent on Psion) to port it to any new systems. A second minor disadvantage is the lack of an outline view in the OPP and OPH editors.

The OPP pre-processor is also available in DOS form – see later under 'PC based development'.

OPPDBG

A run-time source level OPL debugger that can display the lines of OPL code currently being executed and enables 'break points' to be set at specific points of interest in the code. OPP allows examination / changing of local variables in the running program; it depends upon the use of OPP.

Both OPP and OPPDBG are provided on disk for your evaluation – see OPP16f and OPPDBG11.

Please note:
OPP and OPPDBG are shareware programs, if you decide to use them please register them.

PC based development

The basis for PC based OPL development is:

- A PC running either DOS or Windows
- The target SIBO computer, or DOS based emulator
- A SIBO to PC link and PC based software (see the chapter 'Linking to a PC or Printer')
- An external power supply for the Psion computer
- Your chosen PC based development tools – discussed below

DOS based development

Editing

Since SIBO OPL source code is just plain ASCII text, you may use the text or programmers editor of your choice. One point is worth noting here: be careful about the size of your source files if you wish to be able move source code back and forth between the PC and a SIBO system. The SIBO based OPL (or OPP) program editors (which are aliases of Word) are limited to files of around 40K bytes or less.

After producing the OPL code it is translated using one of the PC hosted translators. Testing may be done using a DOS based emulator or using a SIBO system, after transfer of the OPO or OPA executable to the target system.

Translation

PC based translation of OPL to SIBO executable code is via one of the machine specific translators produced by Psion. PC hosted OPL translators exist for:

Series 3	S3TRAN.EXE
Series 3a/c + Siena	S3ATRAN.EXE
Work*about*	WATRAN.EXE
HC	HCTRAN.EXE
(MC	MCTRAN.EXE)

Production of an executable from OPL source files is done using an appropriate translator from the DOS prompt, with file names and control parameters on the command line. More usually, translation is done from a batch file containing instructions to translate a number of related source files. The translators are capable of pre-processing OPL source files to an intermediate source code form, which are given a .PRP file extension. Pre-processing resolves and incorporates all of the 'include' file information and any 'defined' information. It can be useful to pre-process the files as a pre-check before final translation. Pre-processed files are used as input to AKA, the variable and procedure name compactor, described later.

'C' style comments may be used as an alternative to using the REM statement. Text between the pre-processor comment delimiters /* and */ is treated as comment text. Comments of this type can extend over several lines, for example:

```
/*
Multi-line Comment
Stripped out by pre-processor
*/
```

Note that 'C' style comments cannot be nested, so that the pre-processors will not allow the following:

```
/*
PRINT "Press any key" :g%=get /* more comments */
*/
```

The translators described above accommodate the development and changes that have occurred in OPL with time, and are supplied as part of the SIBO OPL SDK and ODE available from Psion. In fact, ODE uses the translators listed above; they are run from within Windows in DOS session hidden from the user – sometimes this is responsible for misleading or missing error messages in ODE.

Two of the translators (S3TRAN and S3ATRAN) were placed into the public domain some years ago and are provided on disk – see the OPLTRAN directory.

Note:
Although translators such as S3ATRAN can handle much bigger source files than on a SIBO system (over 120K), there are limits on the amount of code, and in particular symbol information, they can handle.

OPLLINT

OPLLINT is a tool to check OPL source code for common problems such as variables that are not initialised or referenced, procedures that are never called, code that is never executed, and global variable clashes. One of the most insidious sources of errors in OPL programs comes from undefined variables, usually they are only detected at run-time (and therefore may be a long time in showing themselves). Undefined variable errors arise from the failure of the OPL translator to check that each variable, as used in a section of code, has a corresponding Local or Global declaration statement. However, this type of error, plus others, can be eliminated by the use of the DOS based OPLLINT program from Psion. OPLLINT is supplied with the SIBO OPL SDK and ODE.

OPLLINIT has been put into the public domain and is provided on disk – see the OPLLINT directory.

DOS based OPP

The OPP pre-processor is also available in DOS form, it can be used in combination with a SIBO computer, a DOS based emulator or even in combination with ODE - the Windows hosted development environment. Use of the DOS version of OPP requires the availability of DOS based OPL translators such as S3ATRAN – see translation above. A more detailed description of OPP is given earlier.

OPP is provided on disk for your evaluation –see OPP16f.

Please note:
OPP is Shareware, if you decide to use it please register it.

AKA

AKA (Also Known As) is an excellent DOS hosted utility by David Palmer. It is an OPL programmers' tool that will shorten variable and procedure names, reduce the final size of OPO or OPA program, and speed them up slightly. Use of AKA requires the availability of DOS based OPL translators such as S3ATRAN – see translation above. AKA has the added advantage of also making OPL programs less understandable if reverse translated with the REVTRAN program (see the REVTRAN directory).

AKA is provided on disk – see the AKA230 directory.

Please note:
For personal use AKA is Freeware, used for commercial purposes or for personal gain it is Shareware, if you decide to use it for business use please register it.

DOS based SIBO emulator

The SIBO emulators from Psion, such the Series 3a emulator, provide a facsimile of the SIBO machine running under a DOS implementation of the EPOC16 operating system. An IBM compatible PC is needed, with at least 4 Mbytes of memory and a 386 processor or better. They were designed as in house development tools to enable software authors to develop and test programs more quickly and conveniently than on a real machine. Psion released them on an unsupported royalty free basis, and as such you should **not** contact Psion with questions regarding the emulators.

SIBO emulators will not run under Windows 3.x, Windows 95, OS/2, NT, or under most DOS emulation's running on non-PC machines. The emulators use DPMI to access the required amount of memory, and DOS boxes in windows do not support DPMI to the extent required. Applications installed during an emulation session will not remain installed on the system screen. Each time emulator is started it is equivalent to a hard reset of a real SIBO system. However the Macsys macro system can be used to re-install other applications required.

The Series 3a emulator will not record sound and, because of hardware differences, they do not support some low level operating system calls such as the GetScanCodes call (as documented in the OPL manual). Caution is also required because certain tests conducted while running under emulator, e.g. for machine type or screen size, do not conform to the values that would be returned on a SIBO machine.

Notes:
For more convenient OPL editing a large screen format can be used with the emulators by modifying the settings in the HHSERVER.PAR file supplied with the system. Change the line beginning with SERVER_PARAMS to:

SERVER_PARAMS −X640 −Y480 −D

The OPL pre-processor and debugging utilities OPP / OPPDBG described earlier can be used under the DOS SIBO emulators.

OPLCS Windows editor

OPLCS, short for OPL Code Studio, is a PC Windows based OPL code editor and template based code generator by Jonathan Fisher. Production of executable code OPLCS requires the availability of DOS based OPL translators such as S3ATRAN – see translation above. For PC to SIBO system communication and file transfers OPLCS relies upon other software such as Psiman which is part of the PsiWin package from Psion.

OPLCS is provided on disk – see the OPLCS directory.

Please note:
OPLCS is a Shareware program, please register it if you decide to use it.

ODE

The OPL Development Environment (ODE) is an excellent MS Windows hosted Integrated Development Environment (IDE) from Psion that includes:

- A project manager.
- A powerful multi-file source code editor with coloured syntax highlighting.
- Source code for a range of illustrative OPL examples, including an excellent asynchronous application framework.
- OPLLINT, an OPL source-code checking utility.
- OPL translators suitable for the S3, S3a/c, Siena, Work*about* and HC.
- A set of utility programs for sound and graphics file conversions, plus a font compiler for producing custom font sets.
- Powerful context sensitive help that calls on a full OPL reference library.
- PC to SIBO communications capability – (a link cable is not included).

You start writing a new program in ODE by creating a new project file, adding source files and other application related files as they are created. Editing is done through a remarkably good multi-window editor that has many powerful features – such as an outline view of program procedures, colour syntax highlighting and an excellent multi-file text search facility. A useful text search and replace option is available, but I found that using the 'replace all' option would crash the ODE system.

Data files associated with the application can also form part of the project information, and files may be flagged for transfer to the SIBO system. The project file tracking system will update all files on the SIBO machine, replacing them with their more up-to-date PC versions as required. Additional information and code macros can be '#included' from other source files. Constants with long identifier names may be '#defined' and conditional translation is supported.

When you wish to test the code, the build options can be configured to translate all the source files, run the OPLLINT checker, transfer the executables and related files to the SIBO system and start up the application on the machine.

A number of example projects are supplied to demonstrate the use of the ODE project system as well as a range of programming techniques.

The OPL source code checker OPLLINT supplied with ODE can optionally be integrated into the project build process. Other DOS based utilities provided for sound file conversions, font-file compilation and bitmap conversion are run from the DOS command line.

Printed documentation supplied with ODE is minimal, but extensive 'online' help is provided as Windows help files. A particularly useful feature is the language-related help. If you need to check the syntax / parameter details for an OPL statement, position the cursor over the keyword in question and press 'F1'. A help file will open at the point that gives details of the keyword or function under the cursor.

ODE is available as a product in its own right; it is also supplied as part of version 3.0 of the SIBO OPL SDK – see below for details. ODE is an extremely good development environment for SIBO systems, and is excellent value for money.

ODE with OPP

The OPP pre-processor system (DOS version) described above may be easily integrated into the Psion ODE development system. Although, inclusion of OPP within the ODE build process requires the OPLLINT utility to be disabled.

The Psion SIBO OPL16 SDK

The OPL16 SDK provides the richest source of information and software available for the development of OPL applications for Psion SIBO-based systems. Purchase of the SIBO OPL SDK is highly recommended for all serious / commercial OPL developers.

Version 3.0 of the SIBO OPL16 SDK contains:

- ODE (OPL Development Environment) a Windows PC based Integrated Development Environment – see details of ODE above.
- Two A4 size volumes, comprising thirteen manuals (see below for further details).
- The Psion OPL software environment, including OPL libraries, header files, macro files, device drivers and a range of utility software.
- A wide range of example source code.
- OPL translators suitable for the S3, S3a/c, Siena, Workabout, HC and MC systems.
- OPLLINT, an OPL source-code checking utility.
- A SIBO database file of the OPL language keywords and syntax.
- A comprehensive set of utility programs including: Sound and graphics file converters; database/text file converters; a printer driver compiler; a TLV file editor and a font compiler for producing custom font sets.
- RCom and RPrint, PC DOS to SIBO communications and printing utilities – (a link cable is not included).
- Flash and RAM SSD utilities.

Note:
There is one strange omission from the SIBO OPL SDK, the resource compiler (Rcomp.exe) and its associated documentation is not included, however, it has been put into the public domain by Psion - see the HELPKIT directory on disk.

OPL16 SDK manuals

The OPL16 SDK documentation (version 3.0) consists of thirteen manuals, in two volumes that cover a wide range of features of the SIBO architecture and development system.

Getting Started

- SDK registration and support
- SDK contents and hardware requirements
- Installation and PC directory structure
- ODE and non ODE based development
- Linking a PC to a SIBO system
- A hello world example

SIBO Programmers Reference

- Describes the SIBO family of computers
- Solid state disks
- The basic software and terms explained
- Support for remote file access
- Connecting to other computers
- Technical specifications

HC Programmers Reference

This manual contains information that is specific to the development of applications for the rugged and highly configurable HC range of hand-held computers. The topics discussed include:

- Introduction to the HC concept
- The HC command shell
- The HC in a Cradle or Docking Station
- Customising the HC ROM
- Technical specifications for the HC and its peripherals

Series 3 Programmers Reference

This manual contains information that is specific to the Series 3 and Series 3a palmtop computers. The topics discussed include:

- Introduction to the Series 3 range

- Connecting to other computers
- The Series 3 user interface
- Series 3 programming overview – OPAs Vs OPOs
- Communicating with the System Screen - including the differences between file-based and non-file based applications
- The receipt by applications of Shut-down and Switch-files messages, and the modification of an application's behaviour by means of the technique of aliasing,
- Technical specifications for the Series 3 and its peripherals.

Work*about* Programmers Reference

This manual contains information that is specific to the Work*about* handheld computer and its peripherals. It describes the principal features of the Work*about* and the various user interfaces that are available to the developer.

- Introduction to the Work*about* software and hardware
- Connecting to other computers
- Customising the Work*about*
- The Work*about* command processor
- The Work*about* docking station
- Work*about* software development
- Technical specifications for the Work*about* and its peripherals
- The Work*about* command processor Vs HC command processor Vs MS-DOS

OPL Programming Guide

The OPL Programming Guide describes program development in OPL for all SIBO machines, including advice on writing machine-independent programs.

- Introduction to OPL
- OPL program development
- Variables, constants and expressions
- Loops and branches
- Calling procedures
- Errors and error handling
- Data file handling
- Operators and logical expressions
- Graphics, fonts and sprites
- Menus, dialog boxes, shadowed boxes and status windows
- Asynchronous requests and semaphores
- Devices and the I/O system
- General file handling
- Time, timers and dates
- OPL applications - OPAs
- Miscellaneous advanced topics
- Debugging OPL programs

OPL Library

This manual documents the supplied library procedures and macros; provided to facilitate development and cover most areas of programming. Source code for all of the library code and macros is included on disk.

- Introduction and overview
- File and directory handling
- Serial communication
- Processes and inter-process messaging
- Window server
- Link handling
- General utilities
- Recording and playback of sounds
- Development tools
- Menu handling
- Device handling
- Bar-code device driver
- Environment variables

OPL Language Reference

A comprehensive alphabetic listing of all OPL keywords, a keyword summary, listed by task, and an OPL quick reference guide. Appendices cover printing from OPL, and character codes and fonts.

- Overview of functions and commands
- OPL summary, listed by task
- OPL alphabetic listing
- OPL quick reference
- OPL different implementations
- Character codes and fonts
- Printing from OPL

OPL Technical Reference

The OPL Technical Reference manual describes the technical aspects of the implementation of OPL for the SIBO range of computers. Topics include:

- Introduction and OPL translator
- Operation of the OPL translator
- The OPL runtime interpreter mechanism
- Optimising for speed
- Variables and constant storage
- Database files
- Graphics implementation

Tools Reference

A full description of the software tools supplied with the OPL SDK. The tools include:

- OPL pre-processing translators SIBO machines
- The OPLLINT source-code checking tool
- PC linking and printing with RCom and RPrint
- PC linking and printing with MCLink, SLink and MCPrint
- PsiWin file transfer and conversion
- Window server and PCX converter
- Printer driver compiler
- Font compiler
- Database file to text and text to database conversion utilities
- File editor / dumping
- OPL SIBO reference database and Windows help files
- Sound file conversion

EPOC16 O/S System Services

Provides a complete description of the software interrupt interface to ROM-based system services, classified into 21 areas of functionality.

An appendix lists the services both alphabetically, by service name, and numerically, by interrupt and function number. This will be of particular interest to programmers who wish to use EPOC16 calls and to assembly language programmers.

- Introduction to O/S calls
- Segmented memory management
- Heap memory management
- Semaphore management
- Message management
- Dynamic Library, category and object management
- Device management
- Input / output management
- File management
- Process management
- Date and time management
- Conversion management
- Long integer management
- Floating point number handling
- Floating point function interface
- Character management
- Buffer management
- String management
- General management
- Database file management

- Hardware management
- EPOC interrupt function numbers, alpha and numeric listings

I/O Devices Reference

Describes the I/O device drivers that have been written by Psion. The description of each driver includes a full explanation of the services that it supports, together with example code.

- Introduction to devices and drivers
- Console
- Parallel port
- Serial port
- Sound
- Xmodem and Ymodem
- Cradle and docking station
- Magnetic card reader
- Bar-code reader
- HC Intelligent bar code reader / RS232 port
- HC Printer

Hardware Reference

The Hardware Reference manual contains a description of the SIBO computer hardware, including the principal chip-set, expansion ports and the SIBO serial protocol.

- The principal chip set
- The SIBO serial protocol
- The SIBO expansion ports

Source code protection

Revtran is a reverse translator for OPL16 programs. Written by Mike Rudin, it turns OPO or OPA modules back into OPL source code, although original local variable names will be lost and substituted with generated names. This application allows programmers to see how others have implemented their programs, and may give valuable insight into useful programming techniques.

Revtran is supplied on disk, but please note that you should **not** use it to circumvent protection mechanisms; to avoid paying shareware fees; to steal complete programs; or to do anything illegal or anti-social.

Some OPL programs are protected against reverse translation. The author of REVTRAN gives some hints protecting programs from reverse translation in the manual; these suggestions are detailed below along with some additional options.

Anti-Revtran strategies

To make a reverse translated program less readable, modify all procedure and global variable names to make them meaningless. This can be done before translation, or using a program such as AKA. After translation it is possible to replace alphabetic characters in names with non-printing control characters for greater obscurity.

Replace some non-executed parts of the translated program with garbage by using a binary file editor on the OPA or OPO file, so that a reverse-translator such as Revtran will stop or crash. A dedicated hacker will be able to overcome this, although possibly only after considerable effort.

For example,

```
GOTO SKIP
  PRINT "NO REVTRAN" REM code never executed
SKIP::
```

or

```
IF 1 > 2
  a$="NO REVTRAN"   REM should never get here!
ENDIF
```

Filling the "NO REVTRAN" string and the byte immediately before it with garbage values will stop Revtran in its tracks.

Find some limit or bug in Revtran, and include code that crashes Revtran by exploiting it. This is unreliable, as a future version of Revtran may have bugs fixed, and there are other reverse-translation tools.

Build your program using OPP and set the option to include anti-Revtran information in the translated program.

Use a program such as OPLprot or Norev14 to protect the translated program. OPLprot is available from Marco Aicardi – see the 'Contacts and Sources' chapter. Norev14 is supplied on disk for information, but it is Shareware and is effectively disabled until you have registered it with Raymond Stone the author.

9 OPL Reference

Introduction

All of the OPL functions and commands are described in detail; they are grouped by the nature of their task or function. Occasional items may be repeated if they are associated with more than one function.

The OPL language has gone through a number of developments and enhancements during its lifetime. Also, implementation of OPL on different Psion computers can also vary.

All of the OPL functions and commands in this chapter are labelled to indicate which Psion machines they apply to. If a keyword or command is **not** labelled with the identifier of the machine you are working with then it **does not** apply.

A major change occurred in OPL as implemented on Psion Series 5 systems. OPL on 16-bit SIBO machines will be referred to as OPL16 (or SIBO OPL) and OPL on the 32-bit Series 5 systems will be called OPL32.

On Series 5 systems some aspects of OPL16 have gone, some new features have been added, and the syntax of some language statements has changed due to extra options, or the effects of 32-bit addressing. For example, the CALL function is not available in OPL32 since direct calls to the operating system have gone. (Most operating system calls have been replaced by language extensions called OPXs – see the 'OPL32 Techniques' chapter for more details of OPXs).

Syntax differences may exist between OPL16 and OPL32 implementations of the same command or function; wherever this occurs it will be clearly indicated, occasionally a separate description will be provided.

Where necessary brief OPL examples are given, however, error-handling code is not usually included to keep the examples short and simple. For reliable programs it is always advisable to include code that tests for errors, attempts to recover or closes down gracefully – for more details see the 'Errors and Debugging' chapter.

Use the main index to locate specific OPL keywords and commands alphabetically. All of the OPL keywords in the index and are also listed alphabetically under the heading 'OPL statement'. The general category or task to which groups of OPL keywords belong can be found under the heading 'OPL'.

Note: **OPL SDKs**
A number of OPL keywords described in this chapter are not available on the HC, e.g. MENU, mCARD etc. However most, if not all, of the missing functionality is provided via

OPL library procedures supplied with the Psion SIBO OPL SDK. A wide range of additional functionality is provided via the SIBO OPL SDK library procedures and macros, as outlined in the 'OPL Programming' chapter.

It is recommended that all commercial OPL programmers should invest in a copy of the relevant OPL SDK (SIBO or EPOC32) from Psion.

Functions, commands and procedures

OPL functions are so called because they return a value, e.g.

```
s = SIN(angle)
```

Returns the sine of `angle` (in radians) to the variable `s`.

OPL commands carry out a specific task e.g.

```
CLS
```

Clears the text screen, `CLS` takes no arguments.

Or

```
AT x%,y%
```

Positions the cursor in the text window. The `AT` command takes two arguments to position the cursor at `x%` characters across and `y%` lines down the screen.

Arguments are any values required as part of a command or function call. Parameters are values passed to a procedure. In programming related text the terms 'arguments' and 'parameters' are often used interchangeably.

OPL procedures are sections of OPL code that you define; they can take a number of parameters and may return a single numeric or string value.

Notation used

For each command or function, all of the alternative options are given, where necessary the alternatives are marked which are only applicable to a particular machine or version of OPL.

Commands and functions can be entered in any combination of lower and upper case, except where clearly stated to the contrary.

Commands must be separated from their parameters by inserting a space character. Each parameter must be separated from the next by a comma (,).

Function keywords are followed immediately by an opening bracket '('. Parameters must be separated from each other by a comma and the list of function parameters must be terminated with a closing bracket ')'.

Default values may be assumed if some parameters are not supplied. Default values for particular commands and functions are given in the individual command/function descriptions that follow.

Note: **'var' variables and # prefixes**
If a parameter is preceded by 'var' you don't need to type in 'var', it just indicates that a local or global variable must be used and not a constant. When you see 'var' the address of the variable is passed (see BYREF below), not the value held (it happens automatically, you don't have to use ADDR).

However, if you already hold the address of the variable, you can add a '#' prefix to a 'var' argument, this tells OPL that the expression following is the address to be used, not a variable whose address is to be taken.

Single elements of arrays may also be used for parameters labelled as 'var', but not database field variables or procedure parameters.

Note: **BYREF**
BYREF, is used to indicate that variables are passed by reference (typically to an OPX procedure) i.e. to pass the address of the variable to allow the called procedure to modify the variable's contents.

Note: **OPL32 constants**
OPL32 allows the inclusion of header files, and many useful OPL32 related constants are provided with the Series 5 in a ROM based header file named CONST.OPH. Many of the 'standard' constants are used in the OPL32 examples given here - see the 'OPL32 Techniques' chapter for details of using and reading this file.

Program control

Procedures

PROC...ENDP	Define the start and end of a procedure.
#INCLUDE	Include other files into an OPL16 source file.
	DOS based OPL translators only.
#DEFINE....	Define a symbolic name for a constant value OPL16. Also undefine a
#UNDEF	symbol.
	DOS based OPL translators only.
#IFNDEF...	Test for previous definition of a symbol
#ELSE...	Take alternative action
#ENDIF	End test clause
	DOS based OPL translators only.
CONST	Declare a constant with global scope – OPL32
INCLUDE	Include other files into an OPL32 source file.
DECLARE OPX	Used in OPX header files to define its name etc. OPL32

Notes:
OPL32 see DECLARE EXTERNAL and EXTERNAL for detecting procedures called before they have been defined.

PROC .. ENDP   S3, S3a/c, Siena, S5, WA, HC

```
PROC pname:
...
ENDP
```

The PROC keyword declares the beginning of a new procedure, ENDP defines its end, and the pname: parameter defines its name. In OPL16, procedure names can be up to 8 characters long, including any variable type specifier. In OPL32, names of procedures can be up to 32 characters long, including any variable type specifier.

#INCLUDE   S3, S3a/c, Siena, WA, HC

```
#INCLUDE <extras.oph>
#INCLUDE "\opl\mystuff\extras.oph"
```

Used with the DOS based OPL translators only.

Causes the specified text file to be read in, as if it were part of the file 'including' it. The included file may contain definitions for symbolic names and their values, using the #DEFINE statement, or even additional OPL code.

Including a file is logically identical to replacing the #INCLUDE statement with the file's contents.

If the filename is specified inside angle brackets (e.g. `<extras.oph>`) the header file will be read from the include directory specified with the –i flag on the translator command line.

If the filename is specified in quotes (e.g. `"extras.oph"`) the header file will be read from the current directory, unless a path is specified (e.g. `"\opl\mystuff\extras.oph"`), where the file will be read from the exact location given.

See `#DEFINE,` `#IFNDEF` and the 'OPL16 Techniques' chapter for more details.

#DEFINE   S3, S3a/c, Siena, WA, HC

```
#DEFINE symbolicname value
```

Used with the DOS based OPL translators only.

A pre-processor directive, that will substitute the defined symbol with its assigned value wherever the symbol occurs. A number of values are usually `#DEFINE`d in a separate file, and the file is `#include`d in an OPL source file (this must be before the point at which the symbols are used). For example:

```
#DEFINE Days_in_Week 7
```

Previously defined symbols may be 'undefined' with `#UNDEF` statements. For example:

```
#UNDEF Days_in_Week
```

See `#INCLUDE,` `#IFNDEF` and the 'OPL16 Techniques' chapter for more details.

#IFNDEF   S3, S3a/c, Siena, WA, HC

```
#IFNDEF symbolicname
    . . . .
#ELSE
    . . . .
#ENDIF
```

Used with the DOS based OPL translators only.

A pre-processor directive, that will test for the existence of the defined symbol and take some action if not true, and optionally `#ELSE` some alternative action. For example:

```
#IFNDEF English_Ver
   #INCLUDE <English.oph>
#ELSE
   #INCLUDE "\opl\French\French.oph"
#ENDIF
```

See `#INCLUDE,` `#DEFINE.`

CONST

```
CONST KConstantName=value
```

Declares constants that are treated as literal values, and are not stored as data. CONST declarations must be made outside any procedure, usually at the beginning of the module. KConstantName uses the normal type-specifiers (%, &, $ or non for floating-point values) as for variables. CONST values have global scope, and are not overridden by local or global variables with the same name: in fact the translator will not allow the declaration of a local or global variable with the same name. By convention, all constants are usually named with a leading K to distinguish them from variables.

Note that it is not possible to define constants with values -32768 (for integers) and -214748648 (for long integers) in decimal notation, but hexadecimal notation may be used instead (i.e. values of $8000 and &80000000 respectively).

See INCLUDE, EXTERNAL and the 'OPL32 Techniques' chapter for more details.

INCLUDE

```
INCLUDE file$
```

Includes a file, file$, which may contain CONST definitions, prototypes for OPX procedures and prototypes for module procedures. The included file may **not** include module procedures themselves. Procedure and OPX procedure prototypes allow the translator to check parameters and coerce numeric parameters (that are not passed by reference) to the required type.

Including a file is logically identical to replacing the INCLUDE statement with the file's contents.

The filename of the header may or may not include a path. If it does include a path, then OPL will only scan the specified folder for the file. However, the default path for INLCUDE is \System\Opl\, so when INCLUDE is called without specifying a path, OPL looks for the file firstly in the current folder and then in \System\Opl\ in all drives from Y: to A: and then in Z:, excluding any remote drives.

Note:
Individual INCLUDE statements are needed in all program modules (loaded with LOADM) where the CONST and prototype information is used, not just in the main program module.

See CONST, EXTERNAL and the 'OPL32 Techniques' chapter for more details.

DECLARE OPX

```
DECLARE OPX opxname,opxUid&,opxVersion&

    . . .

END DECLARE
```

Declares an OPX. `opxname` is the name of the OPX, `opxUid&` its UID and `opxVersion&` its version number. Declarations of the OPX's procedures should be made inside this structure.

See the 'OPL32 Techniques' chapter for more details.

Program settings

SETFLAGS	Change the behaviour of a running program
CLEARFLAGS	Clear flags set to affect the behaviour of a running program

SETFLAGS   S5

`SETFLAGS flags&`

Sets flags to produce various effects when running programs. Use CLEARFLAGS to clear any flags which have been set. The effects that can be achieved are as follows:

flags&	effect
1	Restricts the memory available to your application to 64K, emulating SIBO systems. Should only be used, if required, at the beginning of a program. Changing this setting repeatedly will have unpredictable effects.
2	Enables auto-compaction on closing databases. This can be slow, but it is advisable to use this setting when lots of changes have been made to a database.
4	Enables raising of overflow errors when floating-point values are greater than or equal to 1.0E+100 in magnitude, instead of allowing 3-digit exponents (for backwards compatibility).
65536 or &10000	Enables GETEVENT, GETEVENT32 and GETEVENT32A to return the event code $403 to ev&(1) when the machine switches on.

By default these flags are cleared.

See also GETEVENT32, CLEARFLAGS.

CLEARFLAGS   S5

`CLEARFLAGS flags&`

Clears the flags given in `flags&` if they have previously been set by SETFLAGS, returning to the default.

See SETFLAGS.

Loops, branches and jumps

	Repeat a set of instructions:
DO...UNTIL	until a condition is true
WHILE...ENDW	while a condition is true
BREAK	Break to the end of a repeating set of instructions
CONTINUE	Continue at the start of a repeating set of instructions
IF...ELSEIF...ELSE...ENDIF	Perform instructions according conditional tests
GOTO	Go to a specified label
VECTOR...ENDV	Jump to one of a list of labels
@ operator	Call a procedure according to the name in a string expression.
RETURN	To the calling procedure
STOP	Stop the program

DO...UNTIL   S3, S3a/c, Siena, S5, WA, HC

```
DO
   statement
   statement
   .
   .
UNTIL condition
```

DO causes the set of statements which follow it to execute repeatedly until the condition specified by UNTIL is met, in which case execution continues from the statement following UNTIL. Each DO must have a matching UNTIL to end the loop. This type of loop construct will always execute the statements in between the DO and UNTIL at least once.

If the tested condition is never met, the program will loop forever.

If the limit of eight DO... UNTIL levels of nesting is exceeded a 'too complex' error will be generated.

See BREAK and CONTINUE.

WHILE...ENDWH   S3, S3a/c, Siena, S5, WA, HC

```
WHILE condition
   ..
   ..
   ..
ENDWH
```

Loop, and repeatedly perform the set of instructions between the WHILE and the ENDWH statements, as long as the expression condition returns logical TRUE - non-zero.

If `expression` is not true (zero or FALSE), the program jumps to the statement after the ENDWH statement. Each WHILE must be closed with a matching ENDWH.

If the tested condition is never met, the program will loop forever.

If the limit of eight WHILE... ENDWH levels of nesting is exceeded a 'too complex' error will be generated.

See BREAK and CONTINUE.

BREAK   S3, S3a/c, Siena, S5, WA, HC

BREAK

Exit from a program DO...UNTIL loop or a WHILE...ENDWH loop to exit the loop and immediately execute the line following the UNTIL or ENDWH statement.

For example:

```
DO
 ...
 IF a=b
  BREAK   REM break out of loop to x%=3 statement
 ENDIF
 ...
UNTIL KEY
x%=3
 ...
```

CONTINUE   S3, S3a/c, Siena, S5, WA, HC

CONTINUE

Jump to the test condition of a program loop, i.e. go immediately to the UNTIL... statement of a DO...UNTIL loop, or to the WHILE... statement of a WHILE...ENDWH loop.

For example:

```
DO
  ...
  ...
  IF a<3.5
    CONTINUE REM continue loop at UNTIL
  ENDIF
  ...
  ...
UNTIL a>b
```

IF...ENDIF S3, S3a/c, Siena, S5, WA, HC

```
IF condition1
  ...
ELSEIF condition2
  ...
ELSE
  ...
ENDIF
```

Control the execution of program statements depending on one or more specified conditions. The program executes one of the following, depending on which condition (if any) is true:

- • The statements following the IF condition.

or

- • The statements following one of the ELSEIF conditions. There may be any number of ELSEIF statements, including none at all.

or

- • The statements following ELSE (or, if there is no ELSE, nothing at all). There may be either one ELSE statement or none.

After the ENDIF statement, execution of following statements continues as normal.

IF, ELSEIF, ELSE and ENDIF must be in that order.

Every IF statement **must** be matched with an ENDIF.

IF...ENDIF constructs may be nested inside others, for example:

```
IF condition1
  ...
ELSE
  IF condition2
    ...
  ENDIF
  ...
ENDIF
```

If the limit of eight IF... ENDIF levels of nesting is exceeded a 'too complex' error will be generated.

GOTO S3, S3a/c, Siena, S5, WA, HC

```
GOTO label or GOTO label::
..
..
label::
```

Goes to the line following the label:: and continues from there.

The label:

- must be in the current procedure
- must start with a letter and end with a double colon, although the double colon is not necessary in the GOTO statement
- may be up to 8 characters long excluding the colons in OPL16 or 32 characters in OPL32

VECTOR   S3, S3a/c, Siena, S5, WA, HC

```
VECTOR index%
  label1,label2,...
  labelN
ENDV
```

Jump to a label in a list, depending on the value of index%.

The VECTOR and ENDV statements enclose a list of names of labels, where the labels themselves appear elsewhere in the same procedure. The list may spread over several lines, with a comma separating consecutive names in any one line. The last name in a line should not have a following comma.

VECTOR index% jumps to the label corresponding to number index% in the list that follows - if index% is 1 this will be the label matching the first name in the list, and so on.

If index% is not in the range 1 to N, where N is the number of labels, the program continues with the statement after the ENDV statement.

Using VECTOR...ENDV can avoid the need to write a very long IF...ENDIF constructs, with ELSEIF used many times.

For example:

```
...
VECTOR p%
  FUNCA,FUNCX
  FUNCR
ENDV
PRINT "p% was not 1/2/3" :GET :GOTO end
FUNCA::
PRINT "p% was 1" :GET :GOTO end
FUNCX::
PRINT "p% was 2" :GET :GOTO end
FUNCR::
PRINT "p% was 3" :GET :GOTO end
...
end::
...
```

Here, if p% is 1, VECTOR jumps to the label FUNCA::. If it is 2, it jumps to FUNCX::, and if 3, to FUNCR::. If p% is any other value, the program continues with the statement after the ENDV statement.

Problems with VECTOR (HC and Series 3 only)

The VECTOR command leaves two spurious bytes on the runtime stack if the index is out of range, causing unpredictable problems in certain circumstances. This problem applies to the HC and Series 3 only. A workaround is provided in the Psion SIBO OPL SDK.

@ operator   S3, S3a/c, Siena, S5, WA, HC

```
r% = @%(procn$):(parameters)
```

Call a procedure by name, where a string expression holds the procedure name. This allows a program to 'derive' the name of a procedure to call under particular circumstances.

Use an @ symbol, optionally followed by a character to show what type of value is returned. For example, use a % character to return an integer value. The following examples show the four types of value that can be returned:

```
r% = @%(procn$):(parameters)      for integer
r& = @&(procn$):(parameters)      for long integer
r$ = @$(procn$):(parameters)      for string
r  = @(procn$):(parameters)       for floating-point
```

For example, if procn$ = "myproc" then:

```
r$ = @$(procn$):(a$,b$)  REM is equivalent to
r$ = myproc:(a$,b$)
```

Upper or lower case characters can be used (the case is ignored), and the string expression must not include the symbol for the return type (i.e. %, & or $).

RETURN   S3, S3a/c, Siena, S5, WA, HC

```
RETURN
RETURN variable
```

Terminate the execution of a procedure and return control to the point where that procedure was called (ENDP does this automatically).

RETURN variable, in addition to returning control to the calling procedure, passes the value of variable back to the calling procedure. The variable may be of any type and may be an array element, for example RETURN x%(3). **Only one value may be returned.**

RETURN on its own, and the default return through ENDP, causes the procedure to return the value 0 or a null string (" ").

For example:

```
PROC price:
  LOCAL x
  PRINT "Enter price:",
  INPUT x
  x=vat:(x)
  PRINT x
  GET
ENDP

PROC vat:(exclude)
  RETURN exclude+17.5%
ENDP
```

STOP   S3, S3a/c, Siena, S5, WA, HC

```
STOP
```

Terminates the running program as soon as the command is encountered.

Note:
In OPL32 STOP may not be used during an OPX callback; if it is used it will raise a 'STOP used in callback' error.

Error handling

ERR	After an error, get the error number
ERR$	error message
ERRX$	extended error message – OPL32
ONERR	Declare or remove an error-handler
RAISE	Raise an error
TRAP	Let the program continue after an error
REM	Put an explanatory comment in your program
or /* */	with DOS based translators

ERR   S3, S3a/c, Siena, S5, WA, HC

```
error% = ERR
```

Return the number of the last error that occurred or 0 if no error had occurred.

For example:
```
...
PRINT "Enter age in years>",
DO
  TRAP INPUT age%
  IF ERR=-1
    PRINT "Number please>",
  ENDIF
UNTIL ERR=0
...
```

To clear the value of ERR on the SIBO, you can do the following,

```
    ONERR e0
    RAISE 0
e0::
    ONERR OFF
```

In OPL32 you can set the value returned by ERR to 0 (or any other value) by using:

```
TRAP RAISE 0.
```

See also: ERR$, ERRX$.

ERR$ S3, S3a/c, Siena, S5, WA, HC

```
error$ = ERR$(error%)
```

Return the error message for the specified error code, error%.

ERR$ (ERR) gives the message for the last error which occurred.

For example:

```
    ...
    TRAP OPEN "B:\FILE",A,field1$
    IF ERR
      PRINT ERR$(ERR)
      RETURN
    ENDIF
    ...
```

ERRX$ S5

```
x$ = ERRX$
```

Returns the current extended error message (when an error has been trapped), e.g.

'Error in MODULE\PROCEDURE,EXTERN1,EXTERN2,...'

would be presented in an Alert dialog if such an error had not been trapped. Allows the list of missing externals, missing procedure names, etc. to be found when an error is trapped by a handler.

Return the number of the last error that occurred or 0 if no error had occurred.

See also: ERR, ERR$.

ONERR   S3, S3a/c, Siena, S5, WA, HC

```
ONERR label or ONERR label::
..
..
ONERR OFF
...
```

The ONERR label instruction establishes an error handler in a procedure.

Normally when an error occurs the program is halted with an error message. If an error handler is declared with ONERR then an error will cause the program to jump to label:: instead. The code following label:: can then find out the error code and handle matters appropriately.

The label may be up to 8 characters long in OPL16 (32 in OPL32), starting with a letter. It ends in a double colon (::), although the colons are not needed in the ONERR statement.

ONERR OFF disables the ONERR command, so that any errors occurring after the ONERR OFF statement no longer jump to the label.

It is advisable to use the command ONERR OFF immediately after the label. This is to prevent an error in the error handling code causing an infinite loop.

For example:

```
ONERR argerr
PRINT SQR(-1) REM error handled
argerr::
ONERR OFF
```

The ONERR command has a lower priority than TRAP. In other words, a TRAPped command will not trigger the error handler, but any others will.

The following example uses RAISE to forcibly invoke the error handler installed with ONERR.

```
PROC test:
ONERR errh::
    PRINT "Error occurs here"
    RAISE -1        REM General failure
    REM this line will never be reached

errh::
    PRINT "Error handling code"
ENDP
```

RAISE   S3, S3a/c, Siena, S5, WA, HC

RAISE error%

Raise an error.

The error raised is error number error%. This may be one of the errors listed in the error handling chapter, or a new error number defined by the programmer.

The error is handled by the error processing mechanism currently in use - either OPL's own, which stops the program and displays an error message, or the ONERR handler if ONERR is on.

TRAP   S3, S3a/c, Siena, S5, WA, HC

TRAP command

Trap errors from a command. The TRAP command may precede any of these commands:

Data file commands
APPEND, UPDATE, COMPRESS, DELETE, BACK, NEXT, LAST, FIRST, POSITION, USE, CREATE, OPEN, OPENR, CLOSE. Also with OPL32 MODIFY, INSERT, PUT, CANCEL.

File and device commands
COPY, ERASE, RENAME, LOPEN, LCLOSE, LOADM, UNLOADM, CACHE

Directory commands
MKDIR, RMDIR

Data entry commands
EDIT, INPUT

Graphics commands
gSAVEBIT, gCLOSE, gUSE, gUNLOADFONT, gFONT, gPATT, gCOPY

For example, TRAP DELETE "fred.txt".

Any error resulting from the execution of the associated command will be trapped. Program execution will continue at the statement after the TRAP statement, but ERR will be set to the error code.

TRAP has a **higher priority** than any ONERR that has been set.

In OPL32 you can set the value returned by ERR to 0 (or any other value) by using:

TRAP RAISE x% REM Sets the value of ERR to x% and clears the trap flag.

REM   S3, S3a/c, Siena, S5, WA, HC

REM comment

Designate text as a program comment.

The REM keyword precedes a remark included to explain how a program works. All text after the REM up to the end of the line is ignored.

If REM follows a statement on the same line it need only be preceded by a space, not a space and a colon.

For example:
```
INPUT a
b=a*.175   REM b = VAT
```

The REM keyword may also be used to temporarily disable a program statement during debugging.

Note:
If you are using the DOS based translators (e.g. in ODE) you may also use 'C' style comments of the form: /* useful remarks go here */

For example:
```
INPUT a
b=a*.175  /* b=VAT */
```
Comments of this type may span multiple lines, but cannot be nested.

Screen and keyboard control

SCREEN	Set the size and position of the text window
CLS	Clear the text window
SCREENINFO	Get text window information
FONT	Set text window font
STYLE	Set text window character style
gUPDATE	Control when the window server updates the screen
AT	Position the cursor
CURSOR ON/OFF	Display or hide the cursor
EDIT	Display a string to be edited and get a value from the keyboard
INPUT	Get a value from the keyboard
PRINT	Display text, numbers etc.
PAUSE	For a number of 1/20ths of seconds
	Wait until a key is pressed and return the key pressed
GET	- as a character code
GET$	- as a character string
GETEVENT	For key press events see the section on Event handling later.
	Find out which key was pressed, if any
KEY	- as a character code (no pause)
KEY$	- as a character string (no pause)
GET	- as a character code (pause for keypress)
GET$	- as a character string (pause for keypress)
KMOD	Find out what combination of key modifiers was pressed
ESCAPE OFF	Disable or enable PSION-ESC from quitting a running program
ESCAPE ON	
OFF	Turn the Psion off

SCREEN   S3, S3a/c, Siena, S5, WA, HC

```
SCREEN width%,height%
SCREEN width%,height%,xchar%,ychar%
```

Changes the size of the window in which text is displayed using PRINT, AT etc.

The arguments xchar% and ychar% specify the character position of the top left corner. If these arguments are not supplied, the text window is centred in the screen.

An OPL program can initially display text to the whole screen.

CLS S3, S3a/c, Siena, S5, WA, HC

```
CLS
```

Clears the contents of the text window.

The cursor is moved to the beginning of the top line. If you have used CURSOR OFF the cursor is still positioned there, but is not displayed.

SCREENINFO S3a/c, Siena, S5, WA

```
SCREENINFO var info%()
```

Get information about the text window.

This information is useful when doing PRINT commands, etc.

This keyword allows you to mix text and graphics. It is required because while the default window (ID 1) is the same size as the physical screen, the text window is slightly smaller and is centred in the default window. The gaps of a few pixels around the text screen, referred to as the left margin and top margin, depend upon the font in use.

On return, the array info%(), which must have at least 10 elements, contains the following information for OPL16 and OPL32:

Info%(1)	Left margin in pixels
Info%(2)	Top margin in pixels
Info%(3)	Text window width in character units
Info%(4)	Text window height in character units
Info%(5)	Reserved (window server id for default window)

In OPL16

Info%(6)	Font id (as set by FONT)
Info%(7)	Pixel width of text window character cell
Info%(8)	Pixel height of text window line
Info%(9)	Reserved
Info%(10)	Reserved

In OPL32 font ID is a 32-bit integer and therefore will not fit into a single element of info%(). Hence, the least significant 16 bits of the font ID are returned to info%(9) and the most significant 16 bits to info%(10).

Info%(6)	unused
Info%(7)	Pixel width of text window character cell
Info%(8)	Pixel height of text window line
Info%(9)	Least significant 16 bits of the font ID
Info%(10)	Most significant 16 bits of the font ID

Initially SCREENINFO returns the values for the initial text screen. Subsequently any keyword that changes the size of the text screen font, such as FONT, will change some of these values and SCREENINFO should therefore be called again.

FONT   S3a/c, Siena, S5, WA

FONT font%,style%

FONT **font&**,style% - **in OPL32**

Set the font and style for the default text window.

FONT clears the screen and automatically resizes the text window and the default graphics windows to the maximum size, excluding any status window. On SIBO systems it should be called after enabling a status window, because the new size of the text and graphics windows depends on the size of the status window.

Note:
FONT -$3fff,0 leaves the current font and style, it just adjusts the window sizes and clears them.

The font number, font% or font&, is the same as for gFONT, and the style, style%, is the same as for gSTYLE.

The table below lists the fonts provided in the system ROMs, (and in Series 3 ROM, though FONT is not available on that machine – see below).

Note:
Fonts on the Series 5 are identified by a 32-bit UID, rather than by a 16-bit value representing the font position in the ROM as on SIBO systems. However, OPL32 does provide some mapping where possible between OPL16 font IDs and Series 5 OPL32 font UIDs. A **full list of the Series 5 fonts** is provided in a ROM based header file CONST.OPH, see the 'OPL32 Techniques' chapter for details of using and reading this file.

In the table below, Swiss and Arial refer to fonts without serifs while Roman and Times fonts either have serifs (e.g. font 6) or are in a style designed for serifs, but are too small to show them (e.g. font 5 on the Series 3c). Courier is a mono-spaced font, i.e. has characters that are all the same width (and have their pixel size as **width x height**). With proportional fonts, each character can have a different width.

Fonts 1 to 3 are the Series 3 fonts, and are used when running in compatibility mode on the Series 3a/c, Siena and Work*about*. Initially font 4 is used on the text screen of the Series 3a/c and Siena, Courier 11 is used on the Series 5.

Font	Name	Pixels WxH or H only	System	Name Series 5 only	Pixels WxH or H only
1	Series 3 normal	8	S3, S3a/c, Siena, WA	N/A	
2	Series 3 bold	8	S3, S3a/c, Siena, WA	N/A	
3	Series 3 digits	6x6	S3, S3a/c, Siena, WA	N/A	
4	Mono	8x8	S3a/c, Siena, WA	Courier	8
5	Roman	8	S3a/c, Siena, WA	Times	8
6	Roman	11	S3a/c, Siena, WA	Times	11
7	Roman	13	S3a/c, Siena, WA	Times	13
8	Roman	16	S3a/c, Siena, WA	Times	15
9	Swiss	8	S3a/c, Siena, WA	Arial	8
10	Swiss	11	S3a/c, Siena, WA	Arial	11
11	Swiss	13	S3a/c, Siena, WA	Arial	13
12	Swiss	16	S3a/c, Siena, WA	Arial	15
13	Mono	6x6	S3a/c, Siena, WA	Tiny (mono)	3x4

The font style can be modified according to the following table.

style%	effect	OPL32 constant
0	normal style	KgStyleNormal%
1	Bold	KgStyleBold%
2	Underlined	KgStyleUnder%
4	Inverse	KgStyleInverse%
8	double height	KgStyleDoubleHeight%
16	Mono	KgStyleMonoFont%
32	Italic	KgStyleItalic%

These styles can be combined by ORing their values together for example, to set underlined and double height and Times Roman 8 point, use:

```
FONT 5, 2 OR 8
```

Alternatively add the style% values together. For example, to set bold underlined and double height use:

```
FONT 5,11          (as 1+2+8=11)
```

To change fonts on a Series 3 the IOW function can be used.

See also STYLE, gFONT and gSTYLE.

STYLE   S3a/c, Siena, S5, WA

```
STYLE style%
```

Set the text window character style.

The style% argument can be 2 for underlined, or 4 for inverse.

gUPDATE S3, S3a/c, Siena, S5, WA, HC

```
gUPDATE ON
gUPDATE OFF
gUPDATE
```

Update the screen, or switch screen-updating on/off.

The screen of the Psion in OPL is, by default, updated whenever anything is drawn to it.

The gUPDATE OFF command switches off this feature. Drawing commands are buffered and the screen is automatically updated only when the command buffer is full, or when a screen or keyboard **function** that has to return a value immediately is called. The screen will be updated as few times as possible (though some keywords will always cause an update).

Switching updating off can result in a considerable speed improvement in some cases, for example, where a program contains sequences of graphics commands. In such a case, each sequence should be followed by gUPDATE. It is certainly advantageous to use gUPDATE OFF when about to write exclusively to bitmaps. An update can be forced at any time by using the gUPDATE command on its own, and gUPDATE ON returns to normal screen updating.

The gUPDATE command affects anything that displays to the screen. If a program uses a lot of PRINT commands, gUPDATE OFF may make a significant difference in speed.

Note:
With gUPDATE OFF, the buffering of graphics commands may delay the detection of runtime errors, thus causing the location of such errors to be incorrectly reported. For this reason, gUPDATE OFF is best used in the final stages of program development, and even then you may have to remove it to locate some errors.

AT S3, S3a/c, Siena, S5, WA, HC

```
AT indent%,rowsdown%
```

Position the cursor at indent% characters across the text window and rowsdown% rows down.

The command AT(1,1) always moves to the top left corner of the text window. Initially the text window is the full size of the screen. The size and position of the text window is changed using the SCREEN command.

A common use of AT is to display strings at particular positions in the text window, for example:

```
AT 5,10
PRINT "Fixed message"
```

- PRINT statements **without** an AT display at the left edge of the window on the line below the last PRINT statement (unless you use ',' or ';') and strings displayed at the top of the window eventually scroll off as more strings are displayed at the bottom of the window.

- Strings always overwrite anything that is on the screen - they do not cause things below them on the screen to scroll down.

For example:

```
PROC records:
LOCAL k%
OPEN "M:\ODB\CLIENTS.ODB",A,nm$,tl$
DO
  CLS
  AT 1,7
  PRINT "Press a key to"
  PRINT "step to next record"
  PRINT or Q to quit"
  AT 2,3 :PRINT A.nm$
  AT 2,4 :PRINT A.tl$
  NEXT
  IF EOF
    AT 1,6 : PRINT "End of file"
    FIRST
  ENDIF
  k% = GET
UNTIL k% = %Q OR k% = %q
CLOSE
ENDP
```

CURSOR   S3, S3a/c, Siena, S5, WA, HC

CURSOR OFF	
CURSOR ON	
CURSOR winId%	HC,S3
CURSOR winId%,ascent%,width%,height%	HC,S3
CURSOR winId%,ascent%,width%,height%,type%	S3a/c, Siena, S5, WA

CURSOR ON switches the text cursor on at the current cursor position. Initially no cursor is displayed.

You can switch on a graphics cursor in a window by following CURSOR with the ID of the window, winId%. This replaces any text cursor. At the same time, you can also specify the cursor's shape, and its position relative to the baseline of text.

The ascent% argument is the ascent - the number of pixels (-128 to 127) by which the top of the cursor should be above the baseline of the current font.

The height% and width% arguments (both from 0 to 255) are the cursor's height and width.

An error is raised if winId% specifies a bitmap rather than a window.

If you do not specify these three parameters, the following default values are used:

```
ascent%     = font ascent
height%     = font height
width%      = 2
```

If `type%` is given (S3a/c, Siena, S5, WA) it can have the following effects:

type%	cursor type
1	obloid (**not S5**)
2	not flashing
4	grey

The values can be added together to combine effects, e.g. if `type%` is 6 a grey non-flashing cursor is drawn.

The instruction CURSOR OFF switches off any cursor.

For a text cursor see also AT. For a graphics cursor see also gAT, gX, gY.

EDIT   S3, S3a/c, Siena, S5, WA, HC

```
EDIT string_variable$
EDIT log.field$
```

Display a string variable that the user can edit directly on the screen. All the usual editing keys are available - the arrow keys move along the line, Esc clears the line, and so on.

When the user has finished editing, Enter is pressed to confirm the changes. If Enter is pressed before any changes have been made, then the string will be unaltered.

If EDIT is used in conjunction with a PRINT statement, a comma should be used at the end of the PRINT statement, so that the string to be edited appears on the same line as the displayed string), e.g.:

```
PRINT "Edit address:",
EDIT A.address$
```

TRAP EDIT
If the Esc key is pressed while no text is on the input line, the 'Escape key pressed' error (number -114) will be returned by ERR - provided that the EDIT has been trapped, using TRAP EDIT. This feature can used to allow the user to press the Esc key to abandon editing a string.

INPUT   S3, S3a/c, Siena, S5, WA, HC

```
INPUT variable
INPUT log.field
```

Wait for a value to be entered at the keyboard, and then assign the value entered to a variable or data file field. The value can be edited as it is typed in. All the usual editing keys are available - the arrow keys move along the line, ESC key clears the line and so on.

If inappropriate input is entered (for example, a string when the input was to be assigned to an integer variable) a '?' is displayed and a new value can be entered. (See also the following description of `TRAP INPUT`).

The `INPUT` command is usually used in conjunction with a `PRINT` statement:

```
PROC temp:
LOCAL cent
DO
  PRINT "Temperature? "
  PRINT " (centigrade)";
  INPUT cent
  PRINT "That's ";32+cent*9/5,"fahrenheit."
  GET
UNTIL 0
ENDP
```

Note:
The ';' at the end of the `PRINT` statement, so that the cursor waiting for input appears on the same line as the message.

TRAP INPUT
If a bad value is entered (for example "abc" for `a%`) in response to a `TRAP INPUT`, the '?' is not displayed. Instead, the value of the variable is unchanged, the appropriate error condition is set and control passes on to the next line of the procedure.

The error number of any error that has occurred can be found by calling the `ERR` function. For example, if the ESC key is pressed while no text is on the input line, the 'Escape key pressed' error (number -114) will be returned by `ERR` (provided that the `INPUT` has been trapped). This feature could be used to allow someone to press the ESC key to avoid inputting a value.

See also `EDIT`. This works in a similar way to `INPUT`, except that it displays a string to be edited and then assigns it to a variable or field. It can only be used with strings. Use `dEDIT`, for editable string input in a dialog.

PRINT   S3, S3a/c, Siena, S5, WA, HC

`PRINT list`

Display the results of a list of expressions in the OPL text window.

The list can be punctuated in one of these ways:

- Items separated by commas are printed with a space between them.
- Items separated by semicolons are printed with no space between them.
- Each `PRINT` statement prints on a new line, unless the preceding `PRINT` ended with a semicolon or comma.

There can be as many items as needed in the list. A single `PRINT` on its own just moves to the next line.

For example, on 1st January 1990:

```
PRINT "TODAY is",
PRINT DAY;".";"MONTH;".";YEAR
```

would display:

```
TODAY is 1.1.1990.
```

Furthermore:

PRINT 1	displays 1
PRINT "Hello"	displays Hello
PRINT "Number",1	displays Number 1

Use LPRINT to print to an attached device, such as a printer, or to a file.

The output from the PRINT command is governed by the text attributes set by FONT and STYLE.

PAUSE   S3, S3a/c, Siena, S5, WA, HC

```
PAUSE timcode%
```

Pause the program for a certain time, (or until a key is pressed), depending on the value of timcode%:

timcode%	action
0	wait for a key to be pressed
+ve	pause for timcode% twentieths of a second
-ve	pause for timcode% twentieths of a second, or until a key is pressed.

So PAUSE 100 would make the program pause for 5 seconds (i.e. $^{100}/_{20}$) , and PAUSE - 100 would make the program pause for 5 seconds, or until a key is pressed.

If timcode% is 0 or negative, a following GET, GET$, KEY, KEY$, etc. will return the key press which terminated the pause. To discard this key press, if it is not required, clear the buffer after the PAUSE with a single KEY function:

```
PAUSE 0 :KEY
```

GET   S3, S3a/c, Siena, S5, WA, HC

```
keycode% = GET
```

Wait for a key to be pressed and return the character code for that key.

For example, if the 'A' key is pressed with Caps Lock off, the integer returned is 97 (a), or 65 (A) is returned if 'A' was pressed with the Shift key down.

See also KMOD for modifier key testing e.g., Shift, Ctrl etc.

GET$ S3, S3a/c, Siena, S5, WA, HC

```
keypress$ = GET$
```

Wait until a key is pressed and then return which key was pressed, as a string. For example, if the 'A' key is pressed in lower case mode, the string returned is "a".

See also KMOD for modifier key testing e.g., Shift, Ctrl etc.

KEY   S3, S3a/c, Siena, S5, WA, HC

`keycode% = KEY`

Returns the character code of the last key pressed, if there has been one since last calling one of the keyboard functions INPUT, EDIT, GET, GET$, KEY, KEY$ or GETEVENT, (and the menu and dialog input handling keywords).

If no key has been pressed, zero is returned.

See KMOD to check whether modifier keys (Shift, Ctrl, Psion or Caps Lock) were used.

This command does not wait for a key to be pressed, unlike GET.

KEY$ S3, S3a/c, Siena, S5, WA, HC

`k$ = KEY$`

Returns the last key pressed as a string, if there has been a keypress since last calling one of the keyboard functions INPUT, EDIT, GET, GET$, KEY, KEY$ or GETEVENT, (and the menu and dialog input handling keywords).

If no key has been pressed, a null string ("") is returned.

See KMOD to check whether modifier keys (Shift, Ctrl, Psion or Caps Lock) were used.

This command does not wait for a key to be pressed, unlike GET$.

KMOD   S3, S3a/c, Siena, S5, WA, HC

`modcode% = KMOD`

Return a code representing the state of the modifier keys (whether they were pressed or not) at the time of the last keyboard access, (such as a GET or a KEY function).

The modifiers have these codes:

Key state	decimal	hex	OPL32 constant
Shift key down	2	$2	KkmodShift%
Control key down (not HC)	4	$4	KkmodControl%
Psion key down – SIBO only	8	$8	KkmodPsion%
Caps Lock on	16	$10	KkmodCaps%
Fn down – Series 5 only	128	$80	KkmodFn%

If there was no modifier, the function returns 0. If a combination of modifiers was pressed, the sum of their codes is returned - for example 26 is returned if Psion (8) and Shift (2) were pressed, and Caps Lock was on (16).

The KMOD function should only be used **immediately** after a KEY, KEY$, GET or GET$ statement.

The value returned by KMOD has one binary bit set for each modifier key used. To see which modifier keys were held down the bits that are set can be tested using the logical operator AND on the value returned by KMOD.

For example:

```
PROC modifier:
  LOCAL k%,mod%
  PRINT "Press a key"
  k% = GET
  CLS
  mod% = KMOD
  PRINT "You pressed",k%,"with"
  IF mod% = 0
    PRINT "no modifier"
  ENDIF
  IF mod% AND 2
    PRINT "Shift down"
  ENDIF
  IF mod% AND 4
    PRINT "Control down"
  ENDIF
  IF mod% AND 8
    PRINT "Psion down"
  ENDIF
  IF mod% AND 16
    PRINT "Caps Lock on"
  ENDIF
ENDP
```

If KMOD returns 24 (i.e. 16+8) to mod%, the expression mod% AND 8 returns 8, that is logical TRUE, so "Psion down" is displayed; mod% AND 2 returns 0, so "Shift down" is **not** displayed.

ESCAPE OFF/ON   S3, S3a/c, Siena, S5, WA, HC

```
ESCAPE OFF
ESCAPE ON
```

Stop Psion-Esc being used to break out of the program when it is running, (ESCAPE OFF). The ESCAPE ON command re-enables this feature.

ESCAPE OFF takes effect only in the program in which it occurs. The Psion-Esc hotkey is automatically enabled again when you run another program.

Note:

If your program enters a loop that has no logical exit, and ESCAPE OFF has been used, you cannot exit the program. You can terminate the OPL process from the Command Processor (HC/WA), if it is running. Alternatively you can terminate the OPL process from the System Screen (S3, S3a/c, Siena, WA), or by going to the filename under the RunOPL icon and pressing Delete, (however, if LOCK ON has been used, this will not work). The Ctrl-Psion-Shift-K key combination may also be used. On the Series 5 the process can be ended from the task list.

OFF S3, S3a/c, Siena, S5, WA, HC

```
OFF
OFF seconds%
```

Switch the Psion off.

When the machine is switched on again, the statement following the OFF command is executed, for example:

```
OFF :PRINT "Back on again"
```

By specifying an integer, seconds%, between 3 and 16383, the machine can be switched off for that number of seconds and then automatically turns back on and continues with the next line of the program (16383 seconds is about 4½ hours). The machine can be turned on before the expiry of this period with a normal switch-on keypress.

On the Series 5 the minimum time to switch off is 5 seconds. EPOC32 also prevents switch off if there's an absolute timer outstanding and due to go off in less than 5 seconds.

Warning:
Take care with the use of the OFF command. If, due to a programming mistake, a program uses OFF in a loop, the user may find it impossible to switch the Psion back on, and may have to reset the computer.

The OFF command is fairly brutal. Don't use it if there could be other processes running which aren't expecting the computer to suddenly or repeatedly switch off. This is almost always the case, so use OFF with care.

Files

File management

COPY	Copy files
DELETE	Delete files
RENAME	Rename files
EXIST	Check if certain files exist
DIR$	Find out what files exist
PARSE$	Generate a full filename specification and get information on the components
SPACE	Find out how much free space there is on a device

COPY   S3, S3a/c, Siena, S5, WA, HC

```
COPY source$,dest$
```

Copy the file `source$`, which may be of any type, to the file `dest$`. Any existing file with the name `dest$` is deleted. You can copy from one device to another.

Use the appropriate file extensions to indicate the type of file, and wild cards if you wish to copy more than one file at a time:

- If `source$` contains wild cards, `dest$` must not specify a filename, just the device and directory to which the files are to be copied under their original names.

- You must specify either an explicit extension or the wild card extension `.*` on the first (source) filename.

To copy all the OPL files from the root directory of *a:* to *b:\backup*, for example:

```
COPY "A:\*.OPL","B:\BACKUP\"
```

On Series 5 if `source$` contains wildcards, `dest$` may specify either a filename similarly containing wildcards or just the device and directory to which the files are to be copied under their original names.

Example: To copy all the files from internal memory (in `\OPL`) to `D:\ME\`:

```
COPY "C:\OPL\*","D:\ME\"
```

See `COMPRESS` for more control over copying Data files. If you use `COPY` to copy a data file, erased records are always copied and you cannot append to another data file.

Note:
Remember the final backslash on the directory name.

DELETE   S3, S3a/c, Siena, S5, WA, HC

```
DELETE file$
```

Deletes any type of file.

You can use wild cards - for example, to delete all the OPL files in A:\

```
DELETE "A:\*.OPL"   REM SIBO
DELETE "C:\OPL\*"   REM EPOC32
```
See `DELETE` under Data files for deleting a table from an OPL32 database.

RENAME   S3, S3a/c, Siena, S5, WA, HC

```
RENAME file1$,file2$
```
Renames `file1$` to `file2$`.

Any type of file can be renamed, but the names may not include wild cards.

Renaming across directories, for example:
```
RENAME "\dat\x.odb","\n\x.odb"
```

is valid. If you're renaming across directories, you can leave out the destination filename. The source filename will be used by default.

For example:
```
PRINT "Old name:" :INPUT a$
PRINT "New name:" :INPUT b$
RENAME a$,b$
```

EXIST   S3, S3a/c, Siena, S5, WA, HC

```
e% = EXIST(filename$)
```

Check to see that a file or directory exists – **see note below**.

Returns -1 (true) if the file exists and 0 (false) if it doesn't.

Use this function when creating a file to check that a file of the same name does not already exist, or when opening a file to check that it has already been created:

```
...
IF NOT EXIST("CLIENTS")
   CREATE "CLIENTS",A,nm$
ELSE
   OPEN "CLIENTS",A,nm$
ENDIF
...
```

Note:
Always include the file extension in the file name – a default extension of .ODB is assumed by OPL16.

If testing for the existence of a directory you **may** need to append a period to the end of the name, e.g. dirnam$ + " . " to prevent the above behaviour interfering with the directory test. The need for the trailing " . " in directory names appears to have been eliminated in later versions of OPL16 and in OPL32.

DIR$ S3, S3a/c, Siena, S5, WA, HC

```
file$ = DIR$(spec$) then
file$ = DIR$("")
```

Lists filenames, including subdirectory names, matching a file specification. You can include wild cards in the file specification. If spec$ is just a directory name, include the final path delimiter on the end - for example, `"M:\TEMP\"` with trailing backslash on a DOS-type filing system, such as the Series 3a. Use the function like this:

- `DIR$(spec$)` returns the name of the first file matching the file specification.
- `DIR$("")` then returns the name of the second file in the directory.
- `DIR$("")` again returns the third, and so on.
- When there are no more matching files in the directory, `DIR$("")` returns a null string.

In OPL16, to list all the .DBF files in M:\DAT\, for example:

```
PROC dir:
    LOCAL d$(128)
    d$=DIR$("M:\DAT\*.DBF")
    WHILE d$<>""
        PRINT d$
        d$=DIR$("")
    ENDWH
    GET
ENDP
```

In OPL32, to list all the files whose names begin with A in C:\ME\

```
PROC dir:
    LOCAL d$(255)
    d$=DIR$("C:\ME\A*")
    WHILE d$<>""
        PRINT d$
        d$=DIR$("")
    ENDWH
    GET.
ENDP
```

PARSE$ S3, S3a/c, Siena, S5, WA, HC

`p$ = PARSE$(file$,rel$,var off%())`

Return a full file specification from the filename `file$`.

Any missing information is filled in from `rel$`.

The offsets to the various file specification components in the returned string are returned in `off%()` which must be declared with at least 6 integers:

`off%(1)`	Filing system offset (1 always)
`off%(2)`	device offset
`off%(3)`	path offset
`off%(4)`	filename offset
`off%(5)`	file extension offset
`off%(6)`	flags for wild cards in the returned string

For example on SIBO, after this call:

```
p$=PARSE$("datafile", "B:\", off%())
```

the string p$ might be set to `LOC::B:\datafile.dat`. The contents of `off%(4)` in this case would be 9, because the filename starts at character position 9 in p$.

The flag values in `off%(6)` are given below.

Off%(6)	Meaning
0	no wild cards
1	wildcard in filename
2	wildcard in file extension
3	wildcard in both

If rel$ is not itself a complete file specification, the current filing system, device and or path are used as necessary to fill in the missing parts. It is essential that file$ and rel$ should be separate string variables.

As a further SIBO example:

```
p$=PARSE$("NEW","LOC::M:\ODB\*.ODB",offsets%())sets p$ to
"LOC::M:\ODB\NEW.ODB" and offsets%() to (1,6,8,13,16,0).
```

Note that the filename extension is considered to start at, and include, the full stop.

In OPL32 for example:

```
p$=PARSE$("NEW","C:\Documents\*.MBM",x%())sets p$ to
C:\Documents\NEW.MBM and x%() to (1,1,3,14,17,0).
```

SPACE   S3, S3a/c, Siena, S5, WA, HC

```
bytes& = SPACE
```

Return the number of free bytes on the device on which the current (open) data file is held.

For example:

```
PROC stock:
OPEN "C:\stock",A,a$,b%
WHILE 1
  PRINT "Item name:";
  INPUT A.a$
  PRINT "Number:";
  INPUT A.b%
  IF RECSIZE>SPACE
    PRINT "Disk full"
    CLOSE
    BREAK
  ELSE
    APPEND
  ENDIF
ENDWH
ENDP
```

Problems with SPACE (S3, HC)

There are two problems with the SPACE function.

The SPACE function returns the space on the device last used for OPEN or CREATE, rather than the space on the device associated with the current file. In other words, the USE command does not change the device interrogated by the SPACE function.

The SPACE function cannot be used to sense the space on a remote computer that uses a filing system requiring more than 8 characters to specify the filing system and device. For example, SPACE would fail on a Macintosh device called REM::HD40.

Directory management

MKDIR	Create directory
RMDIR	Remove directory
SETPATH	Set current directory
EXIST	See General file management above

MKDIR   S3, S3a/c, Siena, S5, WA, HC

MKDIR dir$

Create a new directory.

For example, MKDIR "M:\MINE\TEMP" creates the directory m:\mine\temp, also creating m:\mine if it does not already exist. Use "C:\MINE\TEMP" on Series 5.

RMDIR   S3, S3a/c, Siena, S5, WA, HC

RMDIR dir$

Remove the directory specified by dir$.

If the directory is not empty, it is not removed and an error is raised.

SETPATH   S3, S3a/c, Siena, S5, WA, HC

SETPATH path$

Set the current directory for file access.

For example:
in OPL16, SETPATH "A:\docs\"
in OPL32, SETPATH "C:\docs\"

The LOADM command continues to use the directory of the initial module, but all other file access will be to the new directory.

Note:
Remember the final backslash on the directory name.

Database files

CREATE	Create a new data file
	Open a data file
OPEN, OPL16	to read or write data
OPEN, OPL32	to read or write data
OPENR	read only
USE	Use a different data file that has already been opened
COMPRESS	Copy a data file, optionally appending to another data file and removing erased records
APPEND	Make a new record
UPDATE	Change a record
	Search for records containing a certain string
FIND	- simple search
FINDFIELD	- controlled search
ERASE	Erase a record
	Move to a different record in a file
FIRST	- first record
LAST	- last record
NEXT	- next record
BACK	- previous record
POSITION	- a specific record
COUNT	Count the records
CLOSE	Close a data file
EOF	Detects the end of file has been reached
ODBINFO	Get database information
POS	Get current record number
RECSIZE	Get the current record size in bytes
	New OPL32 database keywords – see notes below
DELETE	Delete a table from a data file
INSERT	Insert a new blank record into a database.
MODIFY	Modify the current record without moving it.
PUT	Makes the database changes permanent.
CANCEL	Discards database changes made
BOOKMARK	Puts a bookmark at the current record
GOTOMARK	Make bookmarked record current
KILLMARK	Remove a bookmark from a record
BEGINTRANS	Begins a transaction on the current database
COMMITTRANS	Commits the database transactions
INTRANS	Finds out if the current view is in a transaction
ROLLBACK	Cancels transaction(s) on the current view
COMPACT	Compacts the database file

Notes:

For general file operations (I/O) on text or binary type files, see the later section on 'I/O operations on files and devices'.

A number of new of new database keywords have been added to OPL32. On the Series 5, INSERT, PUT and CANCEL should be used in preference to APPEND and UPDATE, although APPEND and UPDATE are still supported.

Additionally, OPL32 has a **database OPX** that provides considerably more database functionality – see the 'OPL32 Techniques' chapter for more details.

CREATE, OPL16   S3, S3a/c, Siena, S5, WA, HC

```
CREATE file$,ID,field1,field2,...
```

- Creates a data file called `file$`.
- If you don't give a file extension, the default extension .ODB will be used. The file name may be a full file specification up to 128 characters long.
- The file may have up to 32 fields, as specified by field1,field2,... and field names may be up to 8 letters/numbers. If viewed in the Data application (Series 3, 3a/c, Siena and Work*about*), field1 starts on the top line of the window, field2 is below it, etc.
- Variable-naming rules apply also to the field names field1,field2... in that the type of the field is indicated by a suffix character. For example:
- `CREATE "myfile", A, name$, age%, nhsno&, addr$`
- Note that string fields are automatically 255 characters long, so no size need be specified in brackets after a string field.
- The ID argument specifies the logical file identifier - `A`, `B`, `C` or `D`. This is used as an abbreviation for the file name when you use other data file commands such as USE.

Immediately after the `CREATE` statement, the file is open at the first record and can be accessed.

For example:

```
CREATE "M:\CLIENTS",B,NAME$,PHONE$
```

would create a data file in the internal RAM drive, with the name clients.odb and the logical file ID of `B`.

CREATE, OPL32   S5

```
CREATE tableSpec$,ID,f1,f2,...
```

Creates a table in a database. The database is also created if necessary. Immediately after calling `CREATE`, the file and view (or table) is open and ready for access.

`tableSpec$` contains the database filename and optionally a table name and the field names to be created within that table. For example:

```
CREATE "clients FIELDS name(40), tel TO phone", D, n$, t$
```

The filename is `clients`. The table to be created within the file is `phone`. The comma-separated list, between the keywords `FIELDS` and `TO`, specifies the field names whose types are specified by the field handles (i.e. `n$`, `t$`). The `name` field has a length of 40 bytes, as specified within the brackets that follow it. The `tel` field has the default length of 255 bytes. This mechanism is necessary for creating some indexes.

- The filename may be a full file specification of up to 255 characters. A field name may be up to a maximum of 64 characters long. Text fields have a default length of 255 bytes.
- `ID` specifies the logical file identifier `A` to `Z`. This is used as an abbreviation for the file name when using other data file commands such as `USE`.

SIBO compatibility

As in OPL16, the table specification may contain just the filename. In this case the table name will default to `Table1` and the field names will be derived from the handles: "$" replaced by "s", "%" by "i", and "&" by "a". E.g. `n$` becomes `ns`. Knowing this allow views to be opened on tables (called `Table1`) that were created with the OPL16 method. However, it would be better to create the fields with proper names in the first place.

For example:

```
CREATE "clients",A,n$,t%,d&
```

is a short version of

```
CREATE "clients FIELDS ns,ti,da TO Table1",A,n$,t%,d&
```

both creating `Table1`. The database `clients` is also created if it does not exist already.

OPEN, OPL16   S3, S3a/c, Siena, S5, WA, HC

```
OPEN file$,ID,field1,field2...
```

Opens an existing data file called `file$`.

The file is given the logical file name `ID`. The opened file is then referred to within the program by its logical name (`A`, `B`, `C` or `D`).

The fields are given the names `field1`, `field2`..., etc. Variable-naming rules apply to these field names, in that the type of the field is indicated by a suffix character. For example:

```
OPEN "myfile", A, name$, age%, nhsno&, addr$
```

Note that string fields are automatically 255 characters long, so no size need be specified in brackets after a string field.

Field names need not be supplied for trailing fields that are not accessed by the program. It is allowable to specify field names for all the leading fields only - up to and including the last one that needs to be updated or appended. Up to 4 files can be open at once on SIBO systems.

For example:

```
OPEN "M:\CLIENTS",A,name$,addr$,credit&
```

OPEN, OPL32   S5

```
OPEN query$,ID,field1,field2...
```

Opens an existing table (or a 'view' of a table) from an existing database, giving it the logical view name ID and handles for the fields `field1`, `field2`..., etc. ID can be any letter in the range A to Z (i.e. up to 26 files open concurrently). `query$` specifies the database file, the required table and fields to be selected.

For example:

```
OPEN "clients SELECT name, tel FROM phone",D,n$,t$
```

The database name here is `clients` and the table name is `phone`. The field names are enclosed by the keywords SELECT and FROM and their types should correspond with the list of handles (i.e. n$ indicates that the name field is a string).

Replacing the list of field names with ★ selects all the fields from the table.

`query$` is also used to specify an ordered view and if a suitable index has been created, then it will be used. For example:

```
OPEN "people SELECT name,number FROM phoneBook ORDER BY name
ASC, number DESC",G,n$,num%
```

would open a view with name fields in ascending alphabetical order and if any names were the same then the number field would be used to order these records in descending numerical order.

SIBO compatibility

As in OPL16, `query$` may contain just the filename. In this case a table with the default name Table1 would be opened if it exists. The field names would then be unimportant, as access will be given to as many fields as there are supplied handles. The type indicators on the field handles must match the types of the fields.

OPENR   S3, S3a/c, Siena, S5, WA, HC

```
OPENR file$,ID,field1,field2..   OPL16
OPENR query$,ID,field1,field2..   OPL32
```

This command works exactly like OPEN except that the opened file is read-only; OPL may not APPEND, UPDATE or PUT the records it contains.

Using OPENR, however, means that two or more separate programs, running at the same time, can share the same file.

USE   S3, S3a/c, Siena, S5, WA, HC

USE ID

In OPL16, selects the data file with the ID A, B, C or D.

In OPL32, selects the data file with the ID A - Z.

The file must previously have been opened with OPEN, OPENR or CREATE and not yet be closed. All of the record handling commands (such as POSITION, UPDATE, and GOTOMARK, INSERT, MODIFY, CANCEL, and PUT in OPL32) then operate on this file.

COMPRESS   S3, S3a/c, Siena, WA, HC

COMPRESS source$,dest$

Copy data file source$ to another data file dest$. If dest$ already exists, the records in source$ are appended to the end of dest$.

Erased records are not copied. This makes COMPRESS particularly useful when copying from a Flash SSD. Note: the space used by erased records on a RAM SSD or in internal memory is automatically freed when you close the file.

If you want source$ to replace dest$ rather than appending to it, use:

    TRAP DELETE dest$

before the COMPRESS statement.

You can use wild cards if you wish to copy more than one file at a time. But if the first name contains any wild cards, the second name must not include a filename, just the device and directory to which the files are to be copied under their original names.

To copy all the OPL data files from the root directory of a: to b:\backup\, for example:

    COMPRESS "A:*.ODB","B:\BACKUP\"

Notes:
Remember the final backslash on the directory name.

In OPL32, COMPRESS has been replaced with COMPACT. Where possible the new database keywords in OPL32 should be used in preference to some of those in OPL16. See also SETFLAGS for details of how to set auto-compaction on closing files.

In OPL16, to disable the compress feature and optimise the speed of closing files use:

P%=PEEKW($1C)+$1E

POKEW p%,PEEKW(p%) OR 1

To re-enable compression on closing files use:

P%=PEEKW($1C)+$1E

POKEW p%,PEEKW(p%) AND $FFFE

APPEND   S3, S3a/c, Siena, S5, WA, HC

APPEND

Add a new record to the end of the current data file (without affecting the current record). The record added is made from the current values of the field variables A.field1$, A.field2$, and so on, of the current data file. If a field has not been assigned a value:

- zero will be assigned to it if it is a numeric field
- a null string will be assigned if it is a string field.

For example:

```
PROC add:
  OPEN "M:\add",A,f1$,f2$,f3$
  PRINT "ADD NEW RECORD"
  PRINT "Enter name:",
  INPUT A.f1$
  PRINT "Enter street:",
  INPUT A.f2$
  PRINT "Enter town:",
  INPUT A.f3$
  APPEND
  CLOSE
ENDP
```

To overwrite the current record with new field values, use UPDATE.

Note:
In OPL32 the new database keywords should be used in preference to APPEND.

UPDATE   S3, S3a/c, Siena, S5, WA, HC

UPDATE

Erases the current record in the current data file and saves the current field values as a new record at the end of the file. This record, now the last in the file, remains the current record.

For example:

```
A.count=129
A.name$="Brown"
UPDATE
```

Use APPEND to save the current field values as a new record.

Note:
In OPL32 the new database keywords should be used in preference to UPDATE. Using UPDATE may produce a lot of erased records. COMPACT should be used to remove them, or alternatively use SETFLAGS to set auto-compaction on.

Problems with UPDATE (S3, HC)

UPDATE can cause a subsequent POSITION call to go to the wrong record in some circumstances. A workaround is to use POSITION 1 after every call to UPDATE. You may need to use POS to save the current position before using UPDATE so that you can restore that position after the POSITION 1 call.

FIND   S3, S3a/c, Siena, S5, WA, HC

```
record% = FIND(string$)
```

Search the current data file for a record in which any string field matches string$. The search starts from the current record, so use NEXT to progress to subsequent records. FIND makes the next record containing string$ the current record and returns the number of the record found, (or zero if not found). The search is case-independent.

The following wild cards may be included:

 ?   matches any single character

 *   matches any group of characters.

So to find a record with a field containing both Dr and either BROWN or BRAUN, use:

```
F% = FIND("*DR*BR??N*")
```

FIND("BROWN") will find only those records with a field consisting solely of the string BROWN.

FIND may only be used to search string fields.

Problems with FIND (S5)

On early versions of the Series 5 FIND may cause a 'User error 23' if used on a database with more than 16 fields.

Workaround

Use FINDFIELD instead which does not seem to suffer from this problem.

FINDFIELD   S3a/c, Siena, S5, WA

```
record% = FINDFIELD(string$,start%,no%,flags%)
```

Find a string in specified fields of a data file, make the record with this string the current record, and return the number of this record or zero if not found.

The string to look for is string$, as for FIND.

The number of the string field to start looking in is start% (1 for the first string field).

The number of string fields to search in is no%, (starting from the string field specified by the start%). If you want to search in all fields, use start%=1 and for no% use the number of fields you used in the OPEN/CREATE command.

The type of search is defined by the code in `flags%`, which adds together two values:

0	for a case independent match, where capitals and lower-case letters match
16	for a case dependent match.
0	to search backwards from the current record.
1	to search forwards from the current record.
2	to search backwards from the end of the file.
3	to search forwards from the start of the file.

For example, if a file is opened with:

```
OPEN "fred",a,i1%,s1$,i2%,i3%,s2$,s3$
```

Then the command:

```
FINDFIELD("x",1,2,1)
```

tries to find the string "x" in the two fields `s1$` and `s2$`.

Problems with FINDFIELD (S3a)

You may experience a number of problems using `FINDFIELD` when the command fails to find a match on searching backwards. You are advised therefore not to use `FINDFIELD` when this condition could occur.

On failing to find when searching backwards, `FINDFIELD` discards the first record in its internal buffer, so that a call to `FIRST` always causes all fields to be empty (in the case of strings) or zero (in the case of numeric fields).

On failing to find when searching backwards, `FINDFIELD` does not, as expected, return 0. Instead it positions to the first record and returns 1.

`FINDFIELD` does a `FIND` in some cases.

Workaround

Before each call to `FINDFIELD` you should have the following line:

```
POKEB PEEKW($1c)+7,0
```

ERASE   S3, S3a/c, Siena, S5, WA, HC

ERASE

Erase the current record in the current file.

The next record is then current. If the erased record was the last record in a file, then following this command all fields in the current record will be 0 or null strings, and `EOF` will return true.

Problems with ERASE (S3, HC)

`ERASE` causes a subsequent `POSITION` call to go to the wrong record in some circumstances. A workaround is to use `POSITION 1` after every call to `ERASE`. You may need to use `POS` to save the current position before using `ERASE` so that you can restore that position after the `POSITION 1` call.

FIRST   S3, S3a/c, Siena, S5, WA, HC

FIRST

Position to the first record in the current data file.

LAST   S3, S3a/c, Siena, S5, WA, HC

LAST

Positions to the last record in a data file.

NEXT   S3, S3a/c, Siena, S5, WA, HC

NEXT

Position to the next record in the current data file, and make it current. If NEXT is used after the end of a file has been reached, no error is reported but the current record is null and the EOF function returns true.

BACK   S3, S3a/c, Siena, S5, WA, HC

BACK

Make the previous record in the current data file the current record. If the current record is the first record in the file, then the current record does not change.

POSITION   S3, S3a/c, Siena, S5, WA, HC

POSITION record%

Makes record number record% the current record in the current data file. If record% is greater than the number of records in the file then the EOF function will return true.

Makes record number record% the current record in the current view.

On the Series 5, by using bookmarks and editing the same table via different views, positional accuracy can be lost and POSITION x% could access the wrong record. Accuracy can be restored by using FIRST or LAST on the current view. POS and POSITION still exist mainly for reasons of SIBO compatibility and **it is better to use bookmarks instead on the Series 5.**

IN OPL32, see BOOKMARK, GOTOMARK, KILLMARK.

Problems with POSITION (S3, HC)

ERASE and UPDATE can cause a subsequent POSITION call to go to the wrong record in some circumstances. A workaround is to use POSITION 1 after every call to ERASE or UPDATE. You may need to use POS to save the current position before using ERASE so that you can restore that position after the POSITION 1 call.

COUNT   S3, S3a/c, Siena, S5, WA, HC

`reccnt% = COUNT`

Return the number of records in the current data file. This number will be 0 if the file is empty.

In OPL32 trying to count the number of records in a view while updating the view will raise an 'Incompatible update mode' error (This will occur between assignment and APPEND / UPDATE or between MODIFY / INSERT and PUT).

CLOSE   S3, S3a/c, Siena, S5, WA, HC

`CLOSE`

In OPL16 close the current data file (that is, the one that has been CREATEd or OPENed and most recently USEd).

In OPL32 close the current view on a database. If there are no other views open on the database then the database itself will be closed.

If some records have been deleted using ERASE, CLOSE recovers the memory taken up by the erased records, (provided that the file is held either in the internal memory drive m: or on a SIBO RAM SSD or a S5 Compact Flash disk).

Note:
To disable this feature on SIBO and optimise the speed of closing files use:

```
P%=PEEKW($1C)+$1E
POKEW p%,PEEKW(p%) OR 1
```

To re-enable compression on closing files use:

```
P%=PEEKW($1C)+$1E

POKEW p%,PEEKW(p%) AND $FFFE
```

In OPL32 see SETFLAGS for details of how to set auto-compaction on closing files.

EOF   S3, S3a/c, Siena, S5, WA, HC

`end% = EOF`

Find out whether the end of a file has been reached. Returns -1 (true) if the end of the file has been reached, or 0 (false) if it hasn't.

When reading records from a file, you should test whether there are still records left to read, otherwise you may get an error.

For example:

```
PROC eoftest:
OPEN "myfile",A,a$,b%
DO
     PRINT A.a$
     PRINT A.b%
     NEXT
     PAUSE -40
UNTIL EOF
PRINT "The last record"
GET
RETURN
ENDP
```

ODBINFO   S3a/c, Siena, WA

```
ODBINFO var info%()
```

Get DBF database information; returns pointers to logical file data blocks. This keyword is provided for advanced use only. It facilitates the use of OS and CALL to access data file interrupt functions not accessible with OPL keywords.

The info%() array must have four elements. Pointers to data blocks for each of the four data files with logical names A, B, C and D are returned in this array.

Take extreme care not to corrupt these blocks of memory, as they are the actual data structures used by the OPL runtime interpreter.

A data block which has no open file using it has zero in the first two bytes.

Otherwise, the block of data for each file has the following structure, giving the offset to each component from the start of the block and with offset 0 for the 1st byte of the block:

Offset	Bytes	Description
0	2	DBF system's file control block (handle) or zero if file not open.
2	2	Offset in the record buffer to the current record.
4	2	Pointer to the field name buffer.
6	2	Number of fields.
8	2	Pointer to start of record buffer.
10	2	Length of a NULL record.
12	1	Non-zero if all fields are text.
13	1	Non-zero for read-only file.
14	1	Non-zero if record has been copied down.
15	1	Number of text fields.
16	2	Pointer to device name.

POS   S3, S3a/c, Siena, S5, WA, HC

```
record% = POS
```

In OPL16, returns the number of the current record in the current data file. The first record in a data file is 1, the second 2 and so on.

In OPL32, POS returns the number of the current record in the current view. It is better to use bookmarks instead of POS on the Series 5.

On SIBO systems, a file can have up to 65534 records. However POS returns an integer and integers can only be in the range -32768 to +32767. Record numbers above 32767 are therefore returned as follows:

record	value returned by POS
32767	32767
32768	-32768
32769	-32767
32770	-32766
.	.
.	.
65534	-2

To print record numbers, the following could be used:

```
...
IF POS<0
  PRINT 65536+POS
ELSE
  PRINT POS
ENDIF
...
```

In OPL32 the number of the current record may be greater than or equal to 65535 and hence values may need to be truncated to fit into p%, giving inaccurate results. **It is better to use bookmarks when dealing with a large number of records.** Note, however, that the value returned by POS can become inaccurate if used in conjunction with bookmarks and multiple views on a table. The accuracy can be restored by using FIRST or LAST on the current view.

In OPL2 see BOOKMARK, GOTOMARK, KILLMARK.

RECSIZE   S3, S3a/c, Siena, WA, HC

```
bytes% = RECSIZE
```

Return the number of bytes occupied by the current record. This function may be used, for example, to check that a record may have data added to it without overstepping the 1022-character limit:

```
PROC rectest:
LOCAL name$(20)
OPEN "M:\odb\name",A,name$,a$,b$,c$,d$
PRINT "Enter name:",
INPUT name$
IF RECSIZE<=(1022-LEN(name$))
  A.name$=name$
  APPEND
ELSE
  PRINT "Won't fit in record"
  ENDIF
ENDP
```

Note:
RECSIZE is not supported in OPL32. Where possible the new database keywords in OPL32 should be used in preference to some of those in OPL16.

Problems with RECSIZE (S3, HC)

RECSIZE sometimes does not return the correct value.

Workaround

When the record contains a string field, assign it to itself. For example:

    a.a$=a.a$

This forces RECSIZE to produce the correct result.

DELETE   S5

    DELETE dbase$,table$

This deletes the table, table$, from the database, dbase$. All views of the database, and hence the database itself, must be closed.

INSERT   S5

    INSERT

Inserts a new, blank record into the current view of a database. The fields can then be assigned to before using PUT or CANCEL.

MODIFY   S5

    MODIFY

Allows the current record of a view to be modified without moving the record. The fields can then be assigned to before using PUT or CANCEL.

PUT   S5

    PUT

Marks the end of a database's INSERT or MODIFY phase and makes the changes permanent.

See INSERT, MODIFY, CANCEL.

CANCEL   S5

    CANCEL

Marks the end of a database's INSERT or MODIFY phase and discards the changes made during that phase.

BOOKMARK   S5

b%=BOOKMARK

Puts a bookmark at the current record of the current database view. The value returned can be used in GOTOMARK to make the record current again. Use KILLMARK to delete the bookmark.

GOTOMARK   S5

GOTOMARK b%

Makes the record with bookmark b%, as returned by BOOKMARK, the current record. b% must be a bookmark in the current view.

KILLMARK   S5

KILLMARK b%

Removes the bookmark b%, which has previously been returned by BOOKMARK, from the current view of a database.

See BOOKMARK, GOTOMARK.

BEGINTRANS   S5

BEGINTRANS

Begins a transaction on the current OPL32 database; allow changes to a database to be committed in stages. Once a transaction has been started on a view (or table) then all database keywords will function as usual, but the changes to that view will not be made until COMMITTRANS is used.

See also COMMITTRANS, ROLLBACK, INTRANS.

COMMITTRANS   S5

COMMITTRANS

Commits the OPL32 database transactions on the current view.

See also BEGINTRANS, ROLLBACK, INTRANS.

INTRANS   S5

i&=INTRANS

Finds out whether the current view is in a transaction. Returns -1 if it is in a transaction or 0 if it is not.

See also BEGINTRANS.

ROLLBACK   S5

ROLLBACK

Cancels the current transaction on the current view. Changes made to the database with respect to this particular view since BEGINTRANS was called will be discarded.

See also BEGINTRANS, COMMITTRANS.

COMPACT   S5

COMPACT file$

Compacts the database file$, rewriting the file in place. All views on the database and the hence the file itself should be closed before calling this command. This should not be done too often since it uses considerable processor power.

Compaction can also be done automatically on closing a file by setting the appropriate flag using SETFLAGS.

OPL program modules

LOADM   Load an OPL module so you can use the procedures in it
UNLOADM   Remove a module from memory

LOADM   S3, S3a/c, Siena, S5, WA, HC

LOADM module$

Load a translated OPL module file so that procedures in that module can be called. The module$ argument is a string containing the name of the OPO file.

Until a module has been loaded with LOADM, calling a procedure in that module will give an error.

In OPL16, the default directory for LOADM is that of the top-level module which is automatically loaded (the directory of the initial running program, or the one specified by an OPA application.). It is not affected by the SETPATH command. The default file name extension is .OPO. Specify the full file name only where necessary.

In OPL32, LOADM uses the folder of the top-level module. It is not affected by the SETPATH command. Once LOADM has been called, procedures loaded stay in memory until the module is unloaded, so significantly more memory can be used than on SIBO, where procedures are unloaded when the cache is full (or on return if caching is not used).

Notes:
Up to eight modules can be in memory at any one time; that includes the main program module. An error will occur on trying to LOADM a ninth module. Hence, in addition to the

main program module, you may use LOADM seven times before having to use UNLOADM to remove a module from memory in order to load another one.

LOADM loads an index table containing the names and file addresses of the procedures; it does **not** load the whole module. The file is then left open. Each procedure is loaded only when it is called.

When a procedure is called, OPL searches the module indexes for the procedure name in the order that modules were LOADMed.

With OPLLINT, you are strongly advised to specify the module name for LOADM as a literal string rather than as a string expression or variable. This allows OPLLINT to check the procedures in the named module.

For example:

```
LOADM "A:\RP\NEWMODUL"
LOADM "FILEH" REM in same directory as top-level module
```

UNLOADM   S3, S3a/c, Siena, S5, WA, HC

```
UNLOADM module$
```

Remove from memory the OPL module module$, previously loaded with LOADM. The UNLOADM command also removes all procedures in the module from the cache. The module$ argument is a string containing the name of the translated module.

In OPL16 the extension .OPO is assumed, and need not be included.

In OPL32, once LOADM has been called, procedures loaded stay in memory until the module is unloaded, so significantly more memory can be used than on SIBO, where procedures are unloaded when the cache is full (or on return if caching is not used).

The procedures in an unloaded module cannot then be called by another procedure.

Note:
It is considered bad practice to unload a module containing procedures that are still running - e.g. for a procedure to unload its own module.

Problems with UNLOADM (S3, S3a, HC)

The statement:

```
UNLOADM ""
```

Will unload the top-level module rather than raising an error.

OPL procedure cacheing

CACHE   Set up a procedure cache, or enable/disable procedure cacheing
CACHETIDY   Remove returned procedures from a cache
CACHEHDR   Read cache index header
CACHEREC   Read cache index record

Note:
Cache commands are not available on the **Series 5** since procedure cacheing is automatic in OPL32.

CACHE   S3a/c, Siena, WA

```
CACHE ON
CACHE init%,max%
CACHE OFF
```

Create a procedure cache of a specified initial number of bytes init% which may grow up to the maximum size max%. You should usually TRAP this.

The minimum cache size is 2000 bytes, which is used if any lower value is specified. If the maximum size specified is less than the initial size, the maximum is set to the initial size. The maximum cache size cannot be changed once the cache has been created and an error is returned if you attempt to do so. Once a cache has been created, CACHE OFF prevents further cacheing, although the cache is still searched when calling subsequent procedures. CACHE ON may then be used to re-enable cacheing.

You can specify init% and max% up to 32,767 bytes, although this limit can be exceeded if you use hexadecimal, as in this example:

```
CACHE $9000,$9000
```

Note:
You cannot exceed the total memory limit of each process.

CACHEHDR   S3a/c, Siena, WA

```
CACHEHDR ADDR(hdr%())
```

Read the procedure cache header record.

The cache index begins with a header, then has one index record for each procedure cached. The CACHEHDR command reads the header into array hdr%(), which must have at least 11 integer elements:

Element	Contents
hdr%(1)	Current address of the cache itself.
hdr%(2)	Number of procedures currently cached.
hdr%(3)	Maximum size of the cache in bytes.
hdr%(4)	Current size of the cache in bytes.

hdr%(5)	Number of free bytes in the cache.
hdr%(6)	Total number of bytes in cached procedures that can be freed (i.e. not running).
hdr%(7)	Offset from the start of the cache index to the first free index record.
hdr%(8)	Offset from start of cache index to most recently used procedure's record; zero if none.
hdr%(9)	Offset from start of cache index to least recently used procedure's record; zero if none.
hdr%(10)	Address of the cache index, or zero if no cache created yet.
hdr%(11)	Non-zero if cacheing is on, and zero if it is off.

All offsets mentioned give the number of bytes from the start of the index to the procedure record specified.

If no cache has yet been created, hdr%(10)=0 and the other data read is meaningless.

Note:
Any information returned is liable to change whenever a procedure is called, so you cannot save these values over a procedure call.

CACHEREC   S3a/c, Siena, WA

CACHEREC ADDR(rec%()),offset%

Read the cache index record at offset offset% into array rec%().

The array must have at least 18 integer elements.

This is an advanced command, intended for use during program development only.

Element	Contents
rec%(1)	Offset to less recently used procedure's record or zero if on LRU.
rec%(2)	Offset to more recently used procedure's record or zero if on MRU.
rec%(3)	Usage count - zero if not running.
rec%(4)	Offset in cache itself to descriptor for building the procedure frame.
rec%(5)	Offset in cache itself to translated code for the procedure.
rec%(6)	Offset in cache itself to the end of the translated code for the procedure.
rec%(7)	Number of bytes used by the procedure in the cache itself.
rec%(8-15)	Leading byte counted procedure name, followed by some private data.
rec%(16)	Address of the procedure's leading byte counted module name.
rec%(17)	Address of the cache index, or zero if no cache created yet.
rec%(18)	Non-zero if cacheing is on, and zero if it is off.

Alternatively offset%=0 specifies the most recently used (MRU) procedure's record, if any, and offset%<0 the least recently used procedure (LRU) procedure's record, if any.

For a free index record only rec%(1) is significant, giving the offset of the next free index record.

The data returned by CACHEREC is meaningless if no cache exists (in which case rec%(17)=0) or if there are no procedures cached yet, (when hdr%(8)=0 as returned by CACHEHDR).

Note:
Any information returned is liable to change whenever a procedure is called, so you cannot save these values over a procedure call.

The index records for cached procedures form a doubly-linked list, starting from first the most recently used procedure (MRU), then from the least recently used procedure (LRU). A further singly linked list gives the offsets to free index records.

CACHETIDY   S3a/c, Siena, WA

CACHETIDY

Remove from the cache any procedures that have returned to their callers.

This might be called after performing a large, self-contained action in the program that required many procedures.

Note:
A procedure that has returned is automatically removed from the cache if you unload the module it is in.

Dynamic library (DYL) handling

LOADLIB	Load (and optionally link) a DYL
LINKLIB	Link a DYL
UNLOADLIB	Unload a DYL
FINDLIB	Get a DYL category handle for a DYL category name

Note:
Dynamic libraries are not available on the **Series 5** - see the section on OPL extensions, i.e. OPXs in the 'OPL32 Techniques' chapter.

LOADLIB   S3a/c, Siena, WA

ret% = LOADLIB(var cathand%,name$,link%)

Load and optionally link a DYL, name$, that is not in the ROM.

If successful, this writes the category handle to cathand% and returns zero. The DYL is shared in memory if already loaded by another process. The link% argument specifies if the loaded library is to be linked immediately after loading:

0	do not link
1	Link

LINKLIB

```
LINKLIB cathand%
```

Link any libraries that have been loaded using LOADLIB.

UNLOADLIB

```
ret% = UNLOADLIB(var cathand%)
```

Unload a DYL from memory. If successful, returns zero. The category handle (cathand%), is that returned by LOADLIB.

FINDLIB

```
ret% = FINDLIB(var cathand%,catname$)
```

Find the DYL category catname$ (including .DYL extension) in the ROM. On success return zero and write the category handle to cathand%.

To get the handle of a RAM-based DYL, use LOADLIB, to guarantee that the DYL remains loaded in RAM. FINDLIB will get the handle of a RAM-based DYL but does not keep it in RAM.

Memory management

	Declare variables
GLOBAL	- global
LOCAL	- local
CONST	Declare a constant with global scope – OPL32
DECLARE EXTERNAL	Allow detection of undefined variables or procedures – OPL32
EXTERNAL	Declares variables or procedures as external – OPL32
ALLOC	Allocate a heap cell
FREEALLOC	Free an allocated heap cell
REALLOC	Change the size of an allocated a heap cell
ADJUSTALLOC	Insert or delete a section of an allocated heap cell
LENALLOC	Get the length of an allocated heap cell
ADDR	Address of a variable in memory
BYREF	Pass a variable to an OPX by reference – OPL32
UADD	Addition to a pointer - add an integer value
USUB	Subtraction from a pointer - subtract an integer value
POKE commands	Store a value in a specific place in memory
PEEK commands	Find out the value stored at a certain place in memory
USR and USR$	Machine code calls
OS and CALL	Operating system calls

Variable declaration

GLOBAL   S3, S3a/c, Siena, S5, WA, HC

GLOBAL variables

Declare variables to be used in the current procedure, in any procedures called by the current procedure, or procedures called by those procedures. In contrast, LOCAL declaration sets up variables that can only be used in the current procedure.

The variables may be of 4 types, depending on the symbol their name ends with:

- Variable names **not** ending with $ % & or () are floating-point variables, for example price, x.
- Those ending with a % are integer variables, for example x%, sales92%.
- Those ending with an & are long integer variables, for example x&, sales92&.
- Those ending with a $ are string variables. String variable names must be followed by the maximum length of the string in brackets, - for example names$(12), a$(3).

Array variables have a number immediately following them in brackets which specifies the number of elements in the array. Array variables may of any type described above, for example: GLOBAL x(6),y%(5),f$(5,12),z&(3)

When declaring string arrays, two numbers must be supplied, enclosed in brackets. The first declares the number of elements, the second declares the maximum length of each element. For example `surname$(5,8)` declares five elements, each up to 8 characters long.

OPL16 variable names may be any combination of up to 8 numbers and alphabetic letters. They **must** start with a letter. The length includes the `%` `&` or `$` sign, but not the `()` in string and array variables.

OPL32 variable names may be any combination of up to 32 numbers, alphabetic letters and the underscore character. They **must** start with a letter or an underscore. The length includes the `%`, `&` or `$` sign, but not the `()` in string and array variables.

The case (upper or lower) of characters in variable names is ignored.

More than one GLOBAL or LOCAL statement may be used, but they **must** be on separate lines, after the procedure name and before any executable code.

LOCAL   S3, S3a/c, Siena, S5, WA, HC

`LOCAL variables`

Declare variables that can be referenced only in the current procedure.

Any procedure may create a variable with the same name as one declared elsewhere by means of LOCAL. Use GLOBAL to declare variables that may be referenced in all called procedures.

The naming and types of LOCAL variables are as for GLOBAL variables above.

CONST   S5

`CONST KConstantName=value`

Declares constants that are treated as literal values, and are not stored as data. CONST declarations must be made outside any procedure, usually at the beginning of the module. `KConstantName` uses the normal type-specifiers (`%`, `&`, `$` or non for floating-point values) as for variables. CONST values have global scope, and are not overridden by local or global variables with the same name: in fact the translator will not allow the declaration of a local or global variable with the same name. By convention, all constants are usually named with a leading `K` to distinguish them from variables.

Note: that it is not possible to define constants with values `-32768` (for integers) and `-214748648` (for long integers) in decimal notation, but hexadecimal notation may be used instead (i.e. values of `$8000` and `&80000000` respectively).

See INCLUDE, EXTERNAL and the 'OPL32 Techniques' chapter for more details.

DECLARE EXTERNAL   S5

DECLARE EXTERNAL

Causes the OPL32 translator to report an error if any variables or procedures are used before they are declared. It should be used at the beginning of the module to which it applies, before the first procedure. It is useful for detecting 'Undefined externals' errors at translate-time rather than at runtime.

For example, without 'DECLARE EXTERNAL', the following example code would raise an error, "Undefined externals, i " at run-time. Including the declaration as shown ensures the error is detected at translate-time.

```
DECLARE EXTERNAL
PROC main:
    LOCAL i%
    i%=10
    PRINT i   REM  i used by mistake instead of i%
    GET
ENDP
```

If DECLARE EXTERNAL is used, all subsequent variables and procedures used in the module will have to be declared using EXTERNAL. See EXTERNAL.

EXTERNAL   S5

```
EXTERNAL variable    REM must be used inside each procedure body
EXTERNAL prototype   REM must be used outside of any procedure body
```

Required if DECLARE EXTERNAL is specified in the module.

The first version above declares a variable as external. For variables you must use EXTERNAL inside the body of each procedure that uses that variable, in similar way to the use of LOCAL and GLOBAL statements. For example:

```
DECLARE EXTERNAL
EXTERNAL myProc:

PROC main:
  GLOBAL var%
  ...
  myProc:
  PRINT var%
ENDP

PROC myProc:
  EXTERNAL var%
  var%=1
ENDP
```

The second version above declares the prototype of a procedure (prototype includes the final : and the argument list). The procedure may then be referred to before it is defined. This allows the procedures parameters to be type-checked at translate-time rather than at runtime, and also provides the necessary information for the translator to coerce (automatically convert) numeric argument types.

A header file should be 'included' that declares prototypes of all the procedures. The header file is 'included' at the beginning of the module that defines the declared procedures, it is also be 'included' in any other modules that call the procedures. DECLARE EXTERNAL is used at the beginning of modules that 'include' the header file so that the translator can ensure that the procedures are called with correct parameter types or types which can be coerced.

For example:

```
DECLARE EXTERNAL
EXTERNAL myProc%:(i%,l&)
REM or INCLUDE "myproc.oph" that defines all your procedures

PROC test:
   LOCAL i%,j%,s$(10)

   REM j% is coerced to a long integer as specified by the
   prototype.
   myProc%:(i%,j%)

   REM translator 'Type mismatch' error:
   REM string can't be coerced to numeric type
   myProc%:(i%,s$)

   REM wrong argument count gives translator error
   myProc%:(i%)
ENDP

PROC myProc%:(i%,l&)
   REM Translator checks consistency with prototype above
   ...
ENDP
```

See also DECLARE EXTERNAL.

Memory, dynamic allocation

ALLOC   S3a/c, Siena, S5, WA

```
pcell% = ALLOC(size%)
pcell& = ALLOC(size&) in OPL32
```

Allocates a cell on the heap of the specified size in bytes, (size% or size&). A pointer to the cell is returned or zero if there is not enough memory. Note that the new cell is not initialised.

The number of bytes allocated is restricted to 64K in OPL16.

In OPL32 this restriction is removed and therefore the return type must be a long integer. Also cells are allocated lengths that are the smallest multiple of four greater than the size requested. An error will be raised if the cell address argument is not in the range known by the heap.

In OPL32 cells are allocated lengths that are the smallest multiple of four greater than the size requested. An error will be raised if the cell address argument is not in the range known by the heap.

FREEALLOC   S3a/c, Siena, S5, WA

```
FREEALLOC pcell%
FREEALLOC pcell&
```
in OPL32

Free a previously allocated heap cell at `pcell%` or `pcell&`.

The number of bytes allocated is restricted to 64K in OPL16. In OPL32 this restriction is removed and therefore the input type must be a long integer.

See also SETFLAGS if you require the 64K limit to be enforced on the Series 5. If the flag is set to restrict the limit, `pcell&` is guaranteed to fit into a short integer.

REALLOC   S3a/c, Siena, S5, WA

```
pcelln% = REALLOC(pcell%,size%)
pcelln& = REALLOC(pcell&,size&)
```
in OPL32

Change the size of a previously allocated cell at `pcell%` (`pcell&`) to `size%` (`size&`), returning the new cell address or zero if there is not enough memory. If out of memory, the old cell at `pcell%` (`pcell&`) is left as it was. If the size of `pcell%` (`pcell&`) is being decreased, `pcell%` (`pcell&`) and `pcelln%` (`pcelln&`) will be the same.

In OPL32 cells are allocated lengths that are the smallest multiple of four greater than the size requested. An error will be raised if the cell address argument is not in the range known by the heap.

ADJUSTALLOC   S3a/c, Siena, S5, WA

```
pcelln% = ADJUSTALLOC(pcell%,offset%,amount%)
pcelln& = ADJUSTALLOC(pcell&,offset&,amount&)
```
in OPL32

Open or close a gap in a memory cell.

The gap is at offset `offset%` (`offset&`) within the allocated cell `pcell%` (`pcell&`). The offset is zero for the first byte in the cell. The gap is opened if the amount (`amount%` or `amount&`) is positive, and closed if it is negative. The function returns the new cell address in `pcelln%` (`pcelln&`), or zero if out of memory.

The number of bytes allocated is restricted to 64K in OPL16.

In OPL32 this restriction is removed and therefore the return type must be a long integer. Also cells are allocated lengths that are the smallest multiple of four greater than the size requested. An error will be raised if the cell address argument is not in the range known by the heap.

LENALLOC   S3a/c, Siena, S5, WA

```
lencell% = LENALLOC(pcell%)
lencell& = LENALLOC(pcell&) in OPL32
```

Return the length of the previously allocated heap cell at `pcell%` (`pcell&`).

In OPL32 cells are allocated lengths that are the smallest multiple of four greater than the size requested. An error will be raised if the cell address argument is not in the range known by the heap.

Memory, addresses & pointer arithmetic

Note:
UADD and USUB should **not** be used for pointer arithmetic in OPL32 unless SETFLAGS has been used to enforce the 64K memory limit. Long integer arithmetic should be used for pointer arithmetic on the Series 5.

ADDR   S3, S3a/c, Siena, S5, WA, HC

```
pvar% = ADDR(variable)
pvar& = ADDR(variable) in OPL32
```

Return the address at which the variable is stored in memory.

The values of different types of variables are stored in bytes starting at `ADDR(variable)`. See the PEEK functions for details.

The ADDR function may be used to find the address of the first element in an array, as in `ADDR(x%())`. It is also possible to find the address of a specific element of the array, for example `ADDR(x%(2))`.

This command is principally useful for passing variables to procedures that need to modify them. To pass a variable by reference rather than by value, you need to pass a pointer - ADDR returns a pointer to its argument.

In the case of strings, the address pointed to by `pvar%` holds the length-byte prefix.

See SETFLAGS for enforcing the 64K limit on the Series 5.

See also UADD and USUB, and the PEEK functions.

BYREF   S5

```
BYREF variable
```

BYREF, is used to indicate that `variable` will be passed by reference (typically to an OPX procedure) i.e. to pass the address of the variable to allow the called procedure to modify the variables contents.

UADD   S3a/c, Siena, WA

`i% = UADD(val1%,val2%)`

Add `val1%` and `val2%`, as if both were unsigned integers with values from 0 to 65535. Using this function prevents integer overflow for pointer arithmetic, e.g.:

    UADD(ADDR(text$),1)

should be used instead of

    ADDR(text$)+1

One argument would normally be a pointer and the other an offset expression.

See also `USUB` and `ADDR`.

USUB   S3a/c, Siena, WA

`i% = USUB(val1%, val2%)`

Subtract `val2%` from `val1%`, as if both were unsigned integers with values from 0 to 65535.

Using this function prevents integer overflow for pointer arithmetic, e.g.:

    USUB(ADDR(text$),1)

should be used instead of

    ADDR(text$)-1

One argument would normally be a pointer and the other an offset expression.

See also `UADD` and `ADDR`.

Memory, reading and writing

The various POKE commands are able to store different data types into memory locations, usually into a memory location of a previously declared variable.

Note:
Casual use of the POKE commands can result in the loss of data in the Psion.

The various PEEK commands are able to read different data types from memory locations, usually from the location of a previously declared variable. See the corresponding PEEK functions for more details of how the different variable types are stored in memory.

The ADDR function is used to find out the address of a particular variable in memory, it may also be used to find the address of the first element in an array, as in `ADDR(x%())`. It is additionally possible to find the address of a specific element of the array, for example `ADDR(x%(2))`.

POKEB   S3, S3a/c, Siena, S5, WA, HC

```
POKEB address%,intv%
POKEB address&,intv% - in OPL32
```

Store the integer value `intv%` (less than 256) in the single byte at `address%` or `address&`.

POKEF   S3, S3a/c, Siena, S5, WA, HC

```
POKEF address%,floatv
POKEF address&,floatv - in OPL32
```

Store the floating-point value `floatv` in bytes starting at `address%` or `address&`.

POKEL   S3, S3a/c, Siena, S5, WA, HC

```
POKEL address%,long&
POKEL address&,long& - in OPL32
```

Store the long-integer `long&` in bytes starting at `address%` or `address&`.

POKEW   S3, S3a/c, Siena, S5, WA, HC

```
POKEW address%,int%
POKEW address&,int% - in OPL32
```

Store the integer `int%` across two consecutive bytes, with the least significant byte in the lower address, that is `address%` or `address&`.

POKE$ S3, S3a/c, Siena, S5, WA, HC

```
POKE$ address%,string$
POKE$ address&,string$ - in OPL32
```

Store the string `string$` in bytes starting at `address%` or `address&`.

PEEKB   S3, S3a/c, Siena, S5, WA, HC

```
intval% = PEEKB(address%)
intval% = PEEKB(address&) - in OPL32
```

Return the integer value of the byte at `address%` or `address&`.

PEEKF   S3, S3a/c, Siena, S5, WA, HC

```
float = PEEKF(address%)
float = PEEKF(address&) - in OPL32
```

Return the floating-point value at `address%` or `address&`.

Floating-point numbers are stored in `IEEE` format for doubles, across eight bytes. `PEEKF` automatically reads all eight bytes and returns the number as a floating-point value. For example, if `var=1.3` then `PEEKF(ADDR(var))` returns 1.3.

PEEKL   S3, S3a/c, Siena, S5, WA, HC

```
long& = PEEKL(address%)
long& = PEEKL(address&) - in OPL32
```

Return the long integer value at `address%` or `address&`.

Long integers are stored in four bytes, the least significant first and the most significant last, for example:

$01 $00 $00 $00 = 1
$00 $00 $01 $00 = 65536

PEEKW   S3, S3a/c, Siena, S5, WA, HC

```
int% = PEEKW(address%)
int% = PEEKW(address&) - in OPL32
```

Return the integer at `address%` or `address&`.

Integers are stored in two bytes, the first of which is the least significant, so that:
$01 $00 = 1
$00 $01 = 256

The `ADDR` function returns the address of the first (least significant) byte.

PEEK$ S3, S3a/c, Siena, S5, WA, HC

```
string$ = PEEK$(address%)
string$ = PEEK$(address&) - in OPL32
```

Return the string at `address%` or `address&`.

For example, if `var$="ABC"`, then `PEEK$(ADDR(var$))` would return the string `"ABC"`.

Strings are stored as one character per byte, with a leading byte containing the string length e.g. the length byte is 3 in the example below. Each letter is stored as its character code (that is, `A` is stored as 65, `B` as 66, and so on). Thus:

12	3	65	66	67

represents the string `"ABC"`.

The byte value prior to the length byte, i.e. 12 is the maximum declared size of the string. For example in:

```
LOCAL var$(12)
```

Note:
ADDR(var$) returns the address of the length byte and USUB(ADDR(vars$),1) gives the address of the maximum string length.

Machine code calls

USR   Call a machine code routine returning an integer
USR$ Call a machine code routine returning a string

Notes:
The OPL16 machine code keywords are no longer supported in OPL32, they have been replaced by OPL extensions called OPXs.

Casual use of these functions can result in the loss of data in the Psion.

USR   S3, S3a/c, Siena, WA, HC

```
u% = USR(addr%,ax%,bx%,cx%,dx%)
```

Execute machine code written by the developer, returning an integer.

The USR code (i.e. the assembler code written by the developer) must return with a **far RET**, otherwise the program will crash.

The values of ax%,bx%... are passed to the AX,BX,... 8086 registers. The microprocessor then executes the machine code starting at addr%. At the end of the routine, the value in the AX register is passed back to u%.

This example shows a simple operation with a far RET:

```
PROC trivial:
  LOCAL triv%(2),u%,ax%
  triv%(1)=$c032    REM xor al,al
  triv%(2)=$cb      REM retf
  ax%=$1ab
  u%=USR(ADDR(triv%()),ax%,0,0,0)
  REM returns(ax% AND $FF00)
  PRINT u% REM displays 256 ($100)
  GET
ENDP
```

See also USR$, ADDR, PEEK commands, POKE commands, OS, CALL.

USR$ ·   S3, S3a/c, Siena, WA, HC

```
u$ = USR$(addr%,ax%,bx%,cx%,dx%)
```

Execute machine code written by the developer, returning a string.

The USR$ code written by the developer must return with a **far RET**, otherwise the program will crash.

The values of ax%, bx%, cx% and dx% are passed to the AX, BX, CX and DX 8086 registers. The microprocessor then executes the machine code starting at addr%. At the end of the routine, the value in the AX register must point to a length-byte preceded string. This string is then copied to u$.

See USR for an example. See also ADDR, PEEK commands, POKE commands, OS, CALL.

Operating system calls

OS   Call a system interrupt number returning all registers and flags
CALL   Call a system interrupt number returning AX only

OS   S3, S3a/c, Siena, WA, HC

```
flags% = OS(inter%,pRegIn%)
flags% = OS(inter%,pRegIn%,pRegOut%)
```

Calls the Operating System interrupt number inter%, reading the values of all returned 8086 registers and flags.

The CALL function, although simpler to use, does not allow the AL register to be passed and returns only the AX register. This makes it suitable only for certain interrupts. For instance, CALL is not suitable for calling any interrupt that can return the CARRY flag set on error.

The input registers are passed at the address pRegIn%. The output registers are passed at the address pRegOut% if supplied, otherwise they are returned at address pRegIn%. Both addresses can be of an array, or of six consecutive integers.

Register values are stored sequentially as 6 integers and represent the registers **in this order**: AX, BX, CX, DX, SI, and DI. The interrupt's function number, if required, is passed in register AH.

The output array must be large enough to store the 6 integers in all cases irrespective of the interrupt being called. The pRegIn% and pRegOut% arguments can point to the same memory location. The value returned by OS is the 8086 flags register.

The Carry flag which is relevant in most cases, is in bit 0 of the returned value, so the expression:

```
flags% AND 1
```

will be non-zero if Carry is set. Similarly the Zero flag is in bit 6 (flags% AND 64), the Sign flag in bit 7 (flags% AND 128), and the Overflow flag in bit 10 (flags% AND 1024). Error codes are returned where appropriate in the 8-bit AL register - the high-byte AH register is not defined on error. To extend the negative error code from AL into AH, use the expression:

```
AX OR $FF00
```

For example, to find the number of days in the month in a given year, call EPOC16 O/S System Service TimDaysInMonth, which is function number 8 of interrupt $89 (which is the TimManager interrupt):

```
PROC dim%:
  LOCAL ax%,bx%,cx%,dx%,si%,di%   REM this order is essential
  LOCAL flags%                    REM returned 8086 flags
  LOCAL m%,y%
  PRINT "Month (1-12)>", :INPUT m%
  PRINT "Year  (1900+)>", :INPUT y%
  cx%=y%-1900                     REM CL register,year
  POKEB ADDR(cx%)+1,m%-1          REM CH register,month
  ax%=$0800                       REM AH=8 for TimDaysInMonth
  flags%=OS($89,ADDR(ax%))        REM $89 for TimManager
  IF flags% AND 1                 REM carry set?
    PRINT ERR$(ax% OR $ff00)      REM AL=error;extend to integer
  ELSE
    PRINT ax%,"days in",MONTH$(m%),y%
  ENDIF
  GET
ENDP
```

See also CALL.

Using OS with OPLLINT

The OS keyword requires that CPU registers (AX, BX, CX, DX, SI or DI) are passed as variables. Although these registers must be declared - for example:

```
LOCAL ax%,bx%,cx%,dx%,si%,di%
```

not all of them may be in use in any one particular line of code. OPLLINT will warn you about, for example:

```
flags%=OS(140,addr(ax%))
```

because the variables bx%, cx%, dx%, si% and di% are not referenced. The way around this is to fool OPLLINT into thinking the variables have been used, with a piece of code such as:

```
#ifdef _OPLLINT
    bx%=cx%=dx%=si%=di%=ax%
#endif
```

CALL S3, S3a/c, Siena, WA, HC

```
err% = CALL(service%,bx%,cx%,dx%,si%,di%)
```

Make an Operating System call from an OPL program.

The CALL command returns the 8086 AX register only, and is therefore suitable only for O/S services that do not return errors (or any flags or registers that you are interested in). Furthermore, the AL register cannot be set for CALL. The alternative OPL function OS overcomes these difficulties, but is more complicated to use.

The interrupt number itself is the least significant byte of service%. The AH value (the sub-function number) is the most significant byte of service%. The values of the other arguments are passed to the corresponding 8086 registers.

The Call function should not be used if:

- You need the return values of other registers than AX.
- Errors are flagged with Carry.
- You need the return values of other flags
- You need to pass the AL register.

Problems with CALL (S3, HC)

The CALL function does not support setting the AL register. Certain system services require that AL be set to 0, so CALL cannot be used for them.

Workaround

The AL register happens to be copied from the low byte of the SI register. This is now guaranteed for future versions of OPL on the 8086. This workaround can only be used when the system service does not require the SI register itself to be passed.

Printing

LOPEN	Prepare a device or file to print to
LCLOSE	Close the print device or file opened with LOPEN
LPRINT	Print to an attached device or file

LOPEN S3, S3a/c, Siena, S5, WA, HC

```
LOPEN port$
LOPEN file$
```

Open the port or file to which LPRINTs are to be sent.

No LPRINTs can be sent until a port or file has been LOPENed.

You can open any of these devices:

- The parallel port, with either LOPEN `"PAR:A"` (or LOPEN `"PAR:B"` if the Psion has this port).
- The serial port, with either LOPEN `"TTY:A"` (or LOPEN `"TTY:B"` if the Psion has this port).
- A file on the Psion or an attached computer. LOPEN the file name, e.g. on a PC:
  ```
  LOPEN "REM::C:\BAK\MEMO.TXT"
  ```
  or on an Apple Macintosh:
  ```
  LOPEN "REM::HD40:MY BAK:MEMO5"
  ```

Any existing file of the same name will be overwritten when you print to it.

Only one device may be open at any one time. Use LCLOSE to close the device (if left open it is closed automatically when a program finishes running).

Note:
All the I/O calls, e.g. IOW() can be passed a handle of -1 to use the LOPENed device, for example:
```
IOW(-1,FREAD,...)
```

LCLOSE   S3, S3a/c, Siena, S5, WA, HC

```
LCLOSE
```

Close the device or file opened with LOPEN. The device or file is also closed automatically when a program ends.

LPRINT   S3, S3a/c, Siena, S5, WA, HC

```
LPRINT list
```

Prints a list of items, in the same way as PRINT, except that the data is sent to the file or device most recently opened with LOPEN.

The list of items may be quoted strings, variables, or the evaluated results of expressions. The punctuation of the LPRINT statement (commas, semi-colons and new lines) determines the layout of the printed text, in the same way as PRINT statements.

An error is raised if no device has been opened with LOPEN.

Numeric functions

Trigonometric functions

```
COS, SIN, TAN,
ACOS, ASIN, ATAN

RAD
DEG
```

Cosine, Sine, Tangent,
Arccosine, Arcsine, Arctangent
Note: All trig function arguments are in radians
Convert angles   - from degrees to radians
                  - from radians to degrees

COS   S3, S3a/c, Siena, S5, WA, HC

```
cosine = COS(radians)
```

Return the cosine of `radians`, an angle in radians.

SIN   S3, S3a/c, Siena, S5, WA, HC

```
sine = SIN(radians)
```

Return the sine of `radians`, an angle expressed in radians.

TAN   S3, S3a/c, Siena, S5, WA, HC

```
tangent = TAN(radians)
```

Return the tangent of `radians`, an angle expressed in radians.

ACOS function   S3, S3a/c, Siena, S5, WA, HC

```
radians = ACOS(x)
```

Return the arc cosine, or inverse cosine $(\cos^{-1})$ of x.

The value of x must be in the range -1 to $+1$. The number returned is an angle in radians.

ASIN   S3, S3a/c, Siena, S5, WA, HC

```
radians = ASIN(x)
```

Return the arc sine, or inverse sine $(\sin^{-1})$ of x.

The value of x must be in the range -1 to $+1$. The number returned is an angle in radians.

ATAN

```
radians = ATAN(x)
```

Return the arc tangent, or inverse tangent (TAN^{-1}) of x.

The number returned is an angle in radians.

RAD

```
radians = RAD(degrees)
```

Convert from degrees to radians.

All the trigonometric functions assume angles are specified in radians, but it may be more convenient to enter angles in degrees and then convert with RAD. For example:

```
PROC xcosine:
  LOCAL angle
  PRINT "Enter angle in degrees:";
  INPUT angle
  PRINT "COS of",angle,"degrees is",
  angle=RAD(angle)
  PRINT COS(angle)
  GET
ENDP
```

The formula used is (PI*x)/180.

To convert from radians to degrees use DEG.

DEG

```
degrees = DEG(radians)
```

Converts from radians to degrees.

Returns radians, an angle in radians, as a number of degrees, degrees. The formula used is:

```
radians*180/PI
```

All the trigonometric functions (SIN, COS, etc.) work in radians, not degrees. You can use DEG to convert an angle returned by a trigonometric function back to degrees. For example:

```
PROC xarctan:
    LOCAL arg,angle
    PRINT "Enter argument:";
    INPUT arg
    PRINT "ARCTAN of",arg,"is"
    angle=ATAN(arg)
    PRINT angle,"radians"
    PRINT DEG(angle),"degrees"
    GET
ENDP
```

To convert from degrees to radians, use RAD.

General numeric functions

EXP	Raise the number *e* to a power
LN	Logarithms — natural (base *e*)
LOG	— decimal (base 10)
PI	*Pi* as a constant (π)
SQR	Square root
	Use random numbers
RND	— generate a random floating point number ($0 \leq x < 1$)
RANDOMIZE	— set a seed for random number generation

EXP   S3, S3a/c, Siena, S5, WA, HC

`e = EXP(x)`

Returns e^x - that is, the value of the arithmetic constant e (2.71828...) raised to the power of x.

LN   S3, S3a/c, Siena, S5, WA, HC

`a = LN(x)`

Return the natural (base e) logarithm of x. Use LOG to return the base 10 logarithm of a number.

LOG   S3, S3a/c, Siena, S5, WA, HC

`a = LOG(x)`

Return the base 10 logarithm of x. Use LN to find the base e (natural) logarithm.

PI   S3, S3a/c, Siena, S5, WA, HC

`p = PI`

Return the value of π (3.14159265358979...).

SQR   S3, S3a/c, Siena, S5, WA, HC

`s = SQR(x)`

Returns the square root of x, which must be greater than or equal to zero.

RND   S3, S3a/c, Siena, S5, WA, HC

```
random = RND
```

Return a random floating-point number in the range 0 (inclusive) to 1 (exclusive).

To produce random numbers between 1 and n - e.g. between 1 and 6 for a dice - use the following statement: `f%=1+INT(RND*n)`

The `RND` function produces a different random number every time it is called within a program. A fixed sequence can be generated by using `RANDOMIZE`. Alternatively, `RANDOMIZE` could be supplied with an argument generated from, for example, `MINUTE` and `SECOND` to seed the sequence differently each time.

For example:

```
PROC rndvals:
LOCAL i%
PRINT "Random test values are:"
DO
  PRINT RND
  i%=i%+1
  GET
UNTIL i%=10
ENDP
```

Note:

In OPL32 (very early versions on the Series 5) the **first** call to RND produced an unreliable value. **Workaround** – call the RANDOMISE function to set the random seed (usually during program initialisation) and immediately follow it with a call to RND to dump the first value. For example:

```
RANDOMISE second+1+minute+1+hour+1
RND
```

RANDOMIZE   S3, S3a/c, Siena, S5, WA, HC

```
RANDOMIZE seed&
```

Set the 'seed' (start-value) for `RND` to `seed&`.

Successive calls of the `RND` function produce a sequence of pseudo-random numbers. If `RANDOMIZE` is used to set the seed back to what it was at the beginning of the sequence, the same sequence will be repeated.

To seed the sequence differently each time, you could begin by using `RANDOMIZE` with an argument generated from `MINUTE` and `SECOND`. In a game program you would typically use `RANDOMIZE` in this way, but only once, e.g. when the game first initialises.

The same set of 'random' values <u>might</u> be needed to test new versions of a procedure. To do this, precede the set of `RND` statements with the statement `RANDOMIZE value&`. Then to repeat the sequence, use `RANDOMIZE value&` again, using the same value.

For example:

```
PROC seq:
LOCAL g$(1)

WHILE 1
  PRINT "S: set seed to 1"
  PRINT "Q: quit"   ·
  PRINT "other key: continue"
  g$=UPPER$(GET$)
  IF g$="Q"
    BREAK
  IF g$="S"
    PRINT "Setting seed to 1"
    RANDOMIZE 1
    PRINT "First random no:"
  ELSE
    PRINT "Next random no:"
  ENDIF
  PRINT RND
ENDWH
ENDP
```

See also RND.

Statistical numeric functions

MAX	Find the greatest value in the list
MIN	Find the smallest value in the list
MEAN	Average the list
SUM	Add up the list
STD	Find the standard deviation
VAR	Find the variance

MAX   S3, S3a/c, Siena, S5, WA, HC

```
m = MAX(list_of_numbers)
m = MAX(array(),count%)
```

Return the greatest of a list of numeric items.

The list can be either:

- A list of variables, values and expressions, separated by commas

or

- The elements of a floating point array

When operating on an array, the first argument must be the array name followed by (). The second argument count%, separated from the first by a comma, is the number of array elements you wish to operate on - for example m=MAX(arr(),3) would return the value of the largest of elements arr(1), arr(2) and arr(3).

MIN S3, S3a/c, Siena, S5, WA, HC

```
m = MIN(list_of_numbers)
m = MIN(array(),count%)
```

Return the smallest of a list of numeric items.

The list can be either:

- List of variables, values and expressions, separated by commas

or

- The elements of a floating point array.

When operating on an array, the first argument must be the array name followed by (). The second argument `count%`, separated from the first by a comma, is the number of array elements you wish to operate on - for example `m=MIN(arr(),3)` would return the minimum of elements `arr(1)`, `arr(2)` and `arr(3)`.

MEAN S3, S3a/c, Siena, S5, WA, HC

```
m = MEAN(list_of_numbers)
m = MEAN(array(),count%)
```

Return the arithmetic mean (average) of a list of numeric items.

The list can be either:

- A list of variables, values and expressions, separated by commas

or

- The elements of a floating point array.

When operating on an array, the first argument must be the array name followed by (). The second argument `count%`, separated from the first by a comma, is the number of array elements you wish to operate on - for example `m=MEAN(arr(),3)` would return the average of elements `arr(1)`, `arr(2)` and `arr(3)`.

This example displays 15.0:

```
arr(1) = 10
arr(2) = 15
arr(3) = 20
PRINT MEAN(arr(),3)
```

SUM S3, S3a/c, Siena, S5, WA, HC

```
s = SUM(list_of_numbers)
s = SUM(array(),count%)
```

Return the sum of a list of numeric items.

The list can be either:

- A list of variables, values and expressions, separated by commas

or

- The elements of a floating point array.

When operating on an array, the first argument must be the array name followed by (). The second argument `count%`, separated from the first by a comma, is the number of array elements you wish to operate on - for example `m=SUM(arr(),3)` would return the sum of elements `arr(1)`, `arr(2)` and `arr(3)`.

STD S3, S3a/c, Siena, S5, WA, HC

```
s = STD(list_of_numbers)
s = STD(array(),count%)
```

Return the sample standard deviation of a list of numeric items. The list can be either:

- A list of variables, values and expressions, separated by commas

or

- The elements of a floating point array.

When operating on an array, the first argument must be the array name followed by (). The second argument `count%`, separated from the first by a comma, is the number of array elements you wish to operate on - for example `m=STD(arr(),3)` would return the standard deviation of elements `arr(1)`, `arr(2)` and `arr(3)`.

This function gives the sample standard deviation using the formula:

$$\mathrm{SQR}\left(\sum((x_i-(\sum x_i/\mathtt{count\%}))^2/(\mathtt{count\%}-1)\right)$$

where `count%` is the number of elements in the list. To convert to population standard deviation, multiply the result by `SQR((count%-1)/count%)`.

VAR S3, S3a/c, Siena, S5, WA, HC

```
v = VAR(list)
v = VAR(array(),count%)
```

Return the *sample* variance of a list of numeric items. The list can be either:

- A list of variables, values and expressions, separated by commas

or

- The elements of a floating point array.

When operating on an array, the first argument must be the array name followed by (). The second argument count%, separated from the first by a comma, is the number of array elements you wish to operate on - for example m=VAR(arr(),3) would return the variance of elements arr(1), arr(2) and arr(3).

This function gives the sample variance, using the formula:

$$\sum (x_i-(\sum x_i/\text{count\%}))^2/(\text{count\%}-1)$$

where n is the number of elements in the list.

To convert to population variance, multiply the result by (count%-1)/count%.

Numeric conversion

	Convert negative number to positive
ABS	- floating point or integer, returning a floating point
IABS	- integer or long integer, returning a long integer
	Take floating point number, removing any fractional part
INT	- returning a long integer
INTF	- returning a floating point number
FLT	Convert an integer into floating-point
HEX$	Convert an integer into hexadecimal string
	Convert a number into a string (with controlled justification)
FIX$	- fixed decimal places/maximum length
GEN$	- fixed maximum length
NUM$	- as a rounded integer, fixed maximum length
SCI$	- scientific format, fixed decimal place /maximum length

ABS function   S3, S3a/c, Siena, S5, WA, HC

```
absval = ABS(float)
```

Return the absolute value of a floating-point expression. That is, negative numbers are converted to positive.

For example, ABS(-10.099) returns 10.099.

If x is an integer, no error is returned, but the result will is converted to floating point. For example ABS(-6) returns 6.0.

Use IABS to return the absolute value as a long integer.

IABS   S3, S3a/c, Siena, S5, WA, HC

```
i& = IABS(x&)
```

Return the absolute value of an integer or long integer expression x&. That is, negative numbers are converted to positive.

For example IABS(-10) returns 10.

See also ABS, which returns the absolute value as a floating-point value.

INT   S3, S3a/c, Siena, S5, WA, HC

```
integer& = INT(x)
```

Returns the integer (in other words the whole number part) of the floating-point expression x. The number is returned as a long integer.

Positive numbers are rounded down, and negative numbers are rounded up. This may be undesirable - for example INT(-5.9) returns -5 and INT(2.9) returns 2. If you want to round a number to the nearest integer, add 0.5 to it (or subtract 0.5 if it is negative) before you use INT.

See also INTF.

INTF   S3, S3a/c, Siena, S5, WA, HC

```
float = INTF(x)
```

Used in the same way as the INT function, but the value returned is a floating-point number. This may be needed in cases where a calculation is required to have an integer result, but the value could exceed the Psion's normal range for integers.

For example, INTF(1234567890123.4) returns 1234567890123.0

See also INT.

FLT   S3, S3a/c, Siena, S5, WA, HC

```
float = FLT(x&)
```

Convert an integer expression (either integer or long integer) into a floating-point number. For example:

```
PROC gamma:(v)
  LOCAL c
  c = 3E8
  RETURN 1/SQR(1-(v*v)/(c*c))
ENDP
```

This procedure could be called as:

```
gamma:(FLT(a%))
```

to pass it the value of an integer variable without having first to assign the integer value to a floating point variable.

See also INT and INTF.

HEX$ S3, S3a/c, Siena, S5, WA, HC

```
h$ = HEX$(x&)
```

Return a string containing the hexadecimal (base 16) representation of integer or long integer x&.

For example HEX$(255) returns the string "FF".

Notes:
To enter integer hexadecimal constants (16 bit) put a $ in front of them. For example $FF is 255 in decimal. (Don't confuse this use of $ with string variable names).

To enter long integer hexadecimal constants (32 bit) put an & in front of them. For example &FFFFF is 1048575 in decimal, and &10000 is 65536. Counting in hexadecimal is as follows:

```
0 1 2 3 4 5 6 7 8 9 A B C D E F 10 ...
```

The hexadecimal digit A stands for decimal 10, B for decimal 11, C for decimal 12 ... up to F for decimal 15. After F comes 10, which is equivalent to decimal 16. To understand numbers greater than hexadecimal 10, again compare hexadecimals with decimals. Conventional algebraic notation is used for the following examples - 10^2 means 10x10, 10^3 means 10x10x10 and so on.

253 in decimal is: $(2x10^2)+(5x10^1)+(3x10^0)$ - that is:

$(2x100)+(5x10)+(3x1)$ in other words: 200+50+3.

By analogy, &253 in hexadecimal is:
$(\&2x16^2)+(\&5x16^1)+(\&3x16^0)$
= (2x256)+(5x16)+(3x1)
= 512+80+3
= 595 in decimal.

Similarly, &A6B in hexadecimal is:
$(\&Ax16^2)+(\&6x16^1)+(\&Bx16^0)$
= (10x256)+(6x16)+(11x1)
= 2560+96+11
= 2667 in decimal.

You may also find this table useful for converting between hex and decimal:

hex.	decimal	
&1	1	$= 16^0$
&10	16	$= 16^1$
&100	256	$= 16^2$
&1000	4096	$= 16^3$

For example,

&20F9 is (2x&1000)+(0x&100)+(15x&10)+9 which in decimal is
(2x4096)+(0x256)+(15x16)+9 = 8441.

All hexadecimal constants are either of type integer (if preceded by $) or of type long (if preceded by &). So, arithmetic operations involving hexadecimal numbers behave in the usual way. For example, &3/&2 returns 1, &3/2.0 returns 1.5, 3/$2 returns 1.

FIX$ S3, S3a/c, Siena, S5, WA, HC

float$ = FIX$(number,places%,width%)

Return a string representation of a number, number, to places% decimal places. The string will be up to width% characters long.

For example

    f$=FIX$(123.456,2,7)

returns the string "123.46" in f$.

If width% is negative the string is right-justified, for example:

    FIX$(1,2,-6) returns " 1.00" where there are two spaces to the left of the 1.

If width% is positive the string is left-justified, for example FIX$(1,2,6) returns "1.00".

If the number x will not fit in the width specified by width%, then the string will contain asterisks, for example:

    FIX$(256.99,2,4) returns "****".

See also GEN$, NUM$ and SCI$.

GEN$ S3, S3a/c, Siena, S5, WA, HC

`number$ = GEN$(number,width%)`

Return a string representation of a number, (`number`). The string will be up to `length%` characters long.

For example GEN$(`123.456,7`) returns `"123.456"` and GEN$(`243,5`) returns `"243"`. Also:

- If `length%` is negative then the string is right-justified, for example GEN$(`1,-6`) returns `"     1"` where there are five spaces to the left of the 1.
- If `length%` is positive then the string is left-justified, (no spaces are added), for example GEN$(`1,6`) returns `"1"`.
- If the number (`number`) will not fit in the width specified by `length%`, then the returned string will just be `length%` asterisks, for example GEN$(`256.99,4`) returns `"****"`.

See also FIX$, NUM$ and SCI$.

NUM$ S3, S3a/c, Siena, S5, WA, HC

`n$ = NUM$(x,length%)`

Return a string representation of the integer part of the floating-point number x, rounded to the nearest whole number.

The string will be `length%` characters wide:

- If `length%` is negative then the string is right-justified, for example NUM$(`1.9,-3`) returns `"  2"` where there are two spaces to the left of the 2.
- If `length%` is positive then the string is left-justified, for example NUM$(`-3.7,3`) returns `"-4"`.
- If the string returned to n$ will not fit in the width specified by `length%`, then the string will just contain asterisks, for example NUM$(`256.99,2`) returns `"**"`.

See also FIX$, GEN$ and SCI$.

SCI$ S3, S3a/c, Siena, S5, WA, HC

`s$ = SCI$(number,places%,length%)`

Return a string representation of the floating point expression `number` in scientific format, to `places%` decimal places in a string `length%` characters long. If `length%` is negative then the string is right-justified.

For example:

```
SCI$(123456,2,8) returns "1.23E+05"
SCI$(1,2,8) returns "1.00E+00"
SCI$(1234567,2,-9) returns " 1.23E+06"
```

If the number does not fit in the width specified then the returned string contains asterisks.

```
SCI$(1234567,1,6) returns "******"
```

See also FIX$, GEN$, and NUM$.

String handling

	Get characters from a string
LEFT$	- from the left
MID$	- from the middle
RIGHT$	- from the right
REPT$	Repeat a string
LOWER$	Convert a string to all lower case
UPPER$	Convert a string to all upper case
LEN	Return the length of a string
ASC	Return the character code of the first character of a string
LOC	Locate a string is within another string
	Convert a string into a number
VAL	- string contains no functions/operators
EVAL	- string contains functions/operators
CHR$	Get the character with a certain character code

LEFT$ S3, S3a/c, Siena, S5, WA, HC

```
leftchr$ = LEFT$(string$,length%)
```

Return the leftmost length% characters from the string string$.

For example if filen$ has the value "mydoc.txt", then b$=LEFT$(filen$,5) assigns "mydoc" to b$.

See also MID$ and RIGHT$.

MID$ S3, S3a/c, Siena, S5, WA, HC

```
m$ = MID$(string$,start_position%,length%)
```

Return a string comprising length% characters of string$, starting with the character at position start_position%.

E.g. MID$("mydoc.txt",6,4) would return the string ".txt".

See also LEFT$ and RIGHT$.

RIGHT$ S3, S3a/c, Siena, S5, WA, HC

```
r$ = RIGHT$(string$,length%)
```

Return the rightmost `length%` characters of `string$`.

For example:

```
PRINT "Enter name/reference",
INPUT c$
ref$=RIGHT$(c$,4)
name$=LEFT$(c$,LEN(c$)-4)
```

See also `LEFT$` and `MID$`.

REPT$ S3, S3a/c, Siena, S5, WA, HC

```
r$ = REPT$(string$,repeats%)
```

Return a string comprising of `repeats%` repetitions of `string$`.

E.g. if `string$="ex"` then `r$=REPT$(string$,5)` returns "exexexexex".

LOWER$ S3, S3a/c, Siena, S5, WA, HC

```
l$ = LOWER$(string$)
```

Convert any upper case characters in the string `string$` to lower-case and returns the completely lower-case string.

E.g. `LOWER$("PRICE")` returns the string "price".

Use `UPPER$` to convert a string to upper case.

UPPER$ S3, S3a/c, Siena, S5, WA, HC

```
u$ = UPPER$(string$)
```

Converts any lower case characters in `string$` to upper-case, and returns the completely upper-case string. For example `UPPER$("price")` returns PRICE.

For example:

```
...
PRINT "Y to continue"
PRINT "or N to stop."
g$=UPPER$(GET$)
IF g$="Y"
  nextproc:
ELSEIF g$="N"
  RETURN
ENDIF
...
```

Use `LOWER$` to convert to lower case.

LEN   S3, S3a/c, Siena, S5, WA, HC

`length% = LEN(string$)`

Return the number of characters in `string$`.

E.g. if `addr$` has the value "10 Downing Street" then `LEN(address$)` returns 17.

This function could be used, for example, to check that a data file string field is not empty before displaying it:

```
IF LEN(A.client$)
  PRINT A.client$
ENDIF
```

ASC   S3, S3a/c, Siena, S5, WA, HC

`chcode% = ASC(a$)`

Return the character code of the first character of `a$`. If `a$` is a null string ("") `ASC` returns the value 0. For example, `ASC("hello")` returns 104, the code for 'h'.

Alternatively, use a statement such as: `A%=%char` to find the code for `char` - e.g. `%X` for 'X'.

LOC   S3, S3a/c, Siena, S5, WA, HC

`pos% = LOC(string$,search$)`

Return an integer showing the position in `string$` where `search$` occurs.

Zero is returned if `search$` doesn't occur in `string$`. The search is case insensitive.

For example:

```
LOC("STANDING","AND")
```

would return the value 3, because the sub-string `"AND"` starts at the third character of the string `"STANDING"`.

VAL   S3, S3a/c, Siena, S5, WA, HC

`v = VAL(nstring$)`

Return the floating-point number corresponding to a numeric string.

The string must be a valid number - that is, not `"5.6.7"` or `"196f"`, nor expressions like `"45.6*3.1"`. But scientific notation, such as `"1.3E10"`, is valid.

For example: `VAL("470.0")` returns 470.0.

See `EVAL` for evaluating expressions.

EVAL   S3, S3a/c, Siena, S5, WA, HC

```
float = EVAL(expr$)
```

Evaluate the mathematical string expression expr$ and return the floating-point result.
The expr$ argument may include any mathematical function or operator
(e.g. sin(x)/(2**3)). Note that floating-point arithmetic is always performed.

For example:

```
DO
  AT 10,5 : print "Calc:"
  TRAP INPUT n$
  IF ERR
    BREAK
  ENDIF
  AT 10,7
  ONERR badExp
  PRINT "Res=";EVAL(n$)
  ONERR OFF
  CONTINUE
badExp::
  ONERR OFF
  PRINT "Bad expression"
UNTIL 0  REM Loop forever
```

Note:
In OPL32, EVAL runs in the "context" of the current procedure, so globals and externals
can be used in expr$, procedures in loaded modules can be called and the current values
of gX and gY, can be used etc. LOCAL variables **cannot** be used in expr$.

See also VAL.

CHR$ S3, S3a/c, Siena, S5, WA, HC

```
char$ = CHR$(chrcode%)
```

Return the character with character code chrcode%. This function may be used to display
characters not easily available from the keyboard. For example, the instruction:

```
PRINT CHR$(150) REM displays: û
```

Similarly the instruction:

```
PRINT CHR$(174) REM displays: ®
```

Date and time

DATIM$	Get the current date and time as a string
SECOND, MINUTE, HOUR	Get the current time components
DAY, MONTH, YEAR	Get the current date components
DAYS	Get the number of days between two dates
DOW	Return what day of the week,
WEEK	or what week number, a certain date falls in
MONTH$	Return the month name for a month number
DAYNAME$	Return the day name for a day of the week number
DATETOSECS	Convert between time formats
SECSTODATE	
DAYSTODATE	Convert number of days since 1/1/1900 to date string – OPL32

Note:
In OPL32 a Date OPX provides a large set of procedures for manipulating dates and for accurate timing. See the 'OPL32 techniques' chapter for more details.

DATIM$ S3, S3a/c, Siena, S5, WA, HC

datetim$ = DATIM$

Return the current date and time from the system clock as a string.

For example:

    "Tue 26 May 1992 13:01:44"

The string returned always has this format - 3 mixed case characters for the day, then a space, then 2 digits for the day of the month, and so on.

See also DAY, MONTH, YEAR, SECOND, MINUTE, HOUR, DOW, gCLOCK.

SECOND   S3, S3a/c, Siena, S5, WA, HC

secs% = SECOND

Return the current 'seconds' component of the time from the system clock (0 to 59).

E.g. at 6:00:33, SECOND returns 33.

See also DAY, MONTH, YEAR, MINUTE, HOUR, DOW, gCLOCK.

MINUTE   S3, S3a/c, Siena, S5, WA, HC

minutes% = MINUTE

Return the current minute number from the system clock (0 to 59).

E.g. at 8.54 am, MINUTE returns 54.

See also DAY, MONTH, YEAR, SECOND, HOUR, DOW and gCLOCK for drawing an on-screen clock.

HOUR   S3, S3a/c, Siena, S5, WA, HC

`h% = HOUR`

Return the number of the current hour from the system clock as an integer between 0 and 23.

For example, at 8.54 am HOUR returns 8.

See also, DAY, DATETOSECS, SECSTODATE, MONTH, YEAR, SECOND, MINUTE, DOW, gCLOCK.

DAY   S3, S3a/c, Siena, S5, WA, HC

`daymth% = DAY`

Return the current day of the month (1 to 31) from the system clock. For example, on the 23rd April 1996 DAY returns 23.

See also MONTH, YEAR, SECOND, MINUTE, HOUR, DOW, gCLOCK.

MONTH   S3, S3a/c, Siena, S5, WA, HC

`mthnum% = MONTH`

Returns the current month from the system clock as an integer between 1 and 12. E.g. on 12th March 1990, MONTH returns 3.

OPL32 constant	value
Kjanuary%	1
Kfebruary%	2
Kmarch%	3
Kapril%	4
Kmay%	5
Kjune%	6
Kjuly%	7
Kaugust%	8
Kseptember%	9
Koctober%	10
Knovember%	11
Kdecember%	12

See also DAY, YEAR, SECOND, MINUTE, HOUR, DOW.

YEAR   S3, S3a/c, Siena, S5, WA, HC

```
yearnum% = YEAR
```

Return the current year as an integer between 1900 and 2155 from the system clock. For example, on 9th April 1996, `y%=YEAR` assigns 1996 to `y%`.

See also DAY, MONTH, SECOND, MINUTE, HOUR, DOW, gCLOCK.

DAYS   S3, S3a/c, Siena, S5, WA, HC

```
days& = DAYS(day%,month%,year%)
```

Return the number of days since 01/01/1900. For example, to find out the number of days between two dates:

```
PROC deadline:
    LOCAL a%,b%,c%,deadlin&
    LOCAL today&,togo%
    PRINT "Day? (1-31)"
    INPUT a%
    PRINT "Month?"
    PRINT "(1-12)"
    INPUT b%
    PRINT "Year?(19??)"
    INPUT c%
    deadlin&=DAYS(a%,b%,1900+c%)
    today&=DAYS(DAY,MONTH,YEAR)
    togo%=deadlin&-today&
    PRINT togo%,"days to go"
    GET
ENDP
```
See also dDATE, SECSTODATE.

DOW   S3, S3a/c, Siena, S5, WA, HC

```
daynum% = DOW(day%,month%,year%)
```

Returns the day of the week number, 1 for Monday to 7 for Sunday, - given the date.

The `day%` argument must be between 1 and 31, `month%` from 1 to 12 and `year%` from 1900 to 2155.

For example:

```
D% = DOW(26,5,1996)
```

returns 7, meaning Sunday.

OPL32 constant	value
KMonday%	1
KTuesday%	2
KWednesday%	3
KThursday%	4
KFriday%	5
KSaturday%	6
KSunday%	7

See also DAY, MONTH, YEAR, SECOND, MINUTE, HOUR, gCLOCK.

WEEK   S3, S3a/c, Siena, S5, WA, HC

`weeknum% = WEEK(day%,month%,year%)`

Return the week number in which the specified day falls, as an integer between 1 and 53.

The `day%` argument must be between 1 and 31, `month%` between 1 and 12, and `year%` between 1900 and 2155.

For example on the 9th February 1995, `w%=WEEK(9,2,1995)` returns 6 in `w%`.

Each week is taken to begin on the 'Start of week' day, as specified in the Time application. On machines without a Time application, Monday is taken to be the start of the week by default. When a year begins on a different day, it counts as week 1 if there are four or more days before the next week starts, (i.e. the first Thursday of each year is in week 1).

See also DAY, MONTH, YEAR, DAYS, DATIM$.

MONTH$ S3, S3a/c, Siena, S5, WA, HC

`mthname$ = MONTH$(mthnum%)`

Convert `mthnum%`, a number from 1 to 12, to the month name, expressed as a three-letter mixed case string. For example

    `MONTH$(1)` returns the string `"Jan"`.

See also MONTH, DATIM$.

DAYNAME$ S3, S3a/c, Siena, S5, WA, HC

day$ = DAYNAME$(daynum%)

Convert daynum%, a number from 1 to 7, to the day of the week, expressed as a three letter string. E.g. d$ = DAYNAME$(1) returns "Mon".

For example:

```
PROC Birthday:
    LOCAL d&,m&,y&,dWk%
    DO
        dINIT
        dTEXT "","Date of birth",2
        dTEXT "","eg 23 12 1963",$202
        dLONG d&,"Day",1,31
        dLONG m&,"Month",1,12
        dLONG y&,"Year",1900,2155
        IF DIALOG=0 :BREAK :ENDIF
        dWk%=DOW(d&,m&,y&)
        CLS :PRINT DAYNAME$(dWk%),
        PRINT d&,m&,y&
        dINIT
        dTEXT "","Again?",$202
        dBUTTONS "No",%N,"Yes",%Y
    UNTIL DIALOG<>%y
ENDP
```

See also DOW, DAY, DATIM$.

DATETOSECS   S3, S3a/c, Siena, S5, WA, HC

Secs& = DATETOSECS(year%,month%,day%,hour%,minute%,second%)

Return the number of seconds since 00:00 on 1 January 1970 at the date/time specified. Raises an error for dates before 1 January 1970.

The value returned is an unsigned integer. (Values up to +2,147,483,647, which is 03:14:07 on 19/1/2038, are returned as expected. Those from +2,147,483,648 upwards are returned as negative numbers starting from -2,147,483,648 and increasing towards 0.)

See also SECSTODATE, HOUR, MINUTE, SECOND, DAYS, dDATE.

SECSTODATE   S3, S3a/c, Siena, S5, WA, HC

SECSTODATE s&,var year%,var month%,var day%,var hour%,var minute%,var second%,var yearday%

Set the variables, (year%, month%, day%, hour%, minute%, second%), to the date and time corresponding to s&. The s& argument is expressed as the number of seconds since 00:00 on 1 January 1970.

The yearday% variable is set to the day in the year (1-366).

The $s\&$ argument is an **unsigned** long integer. To use values greater than +2,147,483,647, subtract 4,294,967,296 from the value.

See also DATETOSECS, HOUR, MINUTE, SECOND, dDATE, DAYS.

DAYSTODATE   S5

DAYSTODATE days&,year%,month%,day%

This converts days&, the number of days since 1/1/1900, to the corresponding date, returning the day of the month to day%, the month to month% and the year to year%. This is useful for converting the value set by dDATE, which also gives days since 1/1/1900.

Sound

BEEP   Sound the buzzer

BEEP   S3, S3a/c, Siena, S5, WA, HC

BEEP duration%,pitch%

Sound the buzzer. The beep lasts for duration%/32 seconds.

For a one second long beep make duration% = 32. The maximum is 3840 (2 minutes). The pitch (frequency) of the beep is 512/(pitch%+1) KHz. The command:

BEEP 5,300

gives a short, comfortably pitched, beep.

If time% is made negative, BEEP first checks whether the sound system is in use (perhaps by another OPL program) and returns if it is. Otherwise, BEEP waits until the sound system is free. The following example gives a scale from middle C:

```
PROC scale:
LOCAL freq
LOCAL n%
REM n% is key relative to middle A
n%=3   REM start at middle C
WHILE n%<16
  freq=440*2**(n%/12.0)
  REM middle A = frequency 440Hz
  BEEP 8,512000/freq-1.0
  n%=n%+1
  IF n%=4 OR n%=6 OR n%=9 OR n%=11 OR n%=13
    n%=n%+1   REM 1 extra for semi-tone
  ENDIF
ENDWH
ENDP
```

If the batteries are low on a Series 5, BEEP may not produce the desired effect, the buzzer will be used instead and it produces a higher pitched sound. Buzzer sounds are generated using extra circuitry, via the same speaker, but with less drain on the batteries.

Alternatively, sound the buzzer with this statement: PRINT CHR$(7). On SIBO this beeps at a fixed pitch for a fixed length of time, whereas on Series 5 it produces a click.

Graphics

Window and bitmap manipulation

gCREATE	Create a window
gSETWIN	Change size and position of window
gORDER	Set order to show windows
gRANK	Get order in which a window is shown
gVISIBLE ON	Make window visible
gVISIBLE OFF	Make window invisible
	Get screen position of a window
gORIGINX	- gap between left of screen and left of window
gORIGINY	- gap between top of screen and top of window
gCREATEBIT	Create a bitmap
gLOADBIT	Load a bitmap from file
gSAVEBIT	Save window/bitmap to bitmap file
gCLOSE	Close window/bitmap
gUSE	Set which window/bitmap to use
	Control the use of grey / colour mode
DEFAULTWIN	- in the default window
gGREY	- in the current window

gCREATE   S3, S3a/c, Siena, S5, WA, HC

id% = gCREATE(xpos%,ypos%,width%,height%,vis%) **– OPL16 or OPL32**
id% = gCREATE(xpos%,ypos%,width%,height%,vis%,grey%) **OPL16**
id% = gCREATE(xpos%,ypos%,width%,height%,vis%,flags%) **- OPL32**

Create a window with specified screen position (xpos%,ypos%), and dimensions (width%, height%) and make it both current and foreground. Set the current graphics cursor position to 0,0, its top left corner. If vis% is 1, the window will be visible immediately; if 0, it will be invisible (see gVISIBLE).

Returns id% (2 to 8 in OPL16, 2-64 in OPL32), the drawable ID, which identifies this window for other keywords (the default window is 1). Note that in OPL32 63 windows may be open at any time and it is recommended that you use many small windows rather than a few large ones.

In **OPL16**, if `grey%` is not given or is 0, the window will not have a grey plane. If `grey%` is 1, it will have one.

In **OPL32**, `flags%` specifies the graphics mode to use and shadowing on the window. By default the graphics mode is 2-colour and there is no shadow. The least significant 4 bits of `flags%` gives the colour-mode as before 0 (2 colour-mode), 1 (4 colour-mode), 2 (16 colour-mode). The next 4 bits may be set to specify the shadowing on the window. If 0, the window has no shadow. The next 4 bits give the shadow height relative to the window behind it (a height of *N* units gives a shadow of *N*×2 pixels).

The components of the `flags%` argument are most easily specified as a combination of hexadecimal digits. For example:

flags%	description
$412	16 colour-mode ($2), shadowed window ($1), with height 4 units ($4) above the previous window with a shadow of 8 pixels.
$010	2 colour-mode (black and white) shadowed window at the same height as the previous window.
$101	4 colour mode window with no shadow (height ignored if shadow disabled).
$111	4 colour mode window with shadow of 1 unit above window behind, i.e. 2 pixel shadow.

See also `gCLOSE`, `gGREY`, `DEFAULTWIN`, `gUSE`, `gORDER`

Problems with gCREATE (S3a)

When a window is created, its grey flag is sometimes erroneously set. If the window was created with a black plane only, this causes problems when you call `gFONT`, `gSTYLE`, `gTMODE` or `gGMODE`. **Workaround** - as soon as you create the window, use `gGREY 0` to clear the grey setting.

gSETWIN   S3, S3a/c, Siena, S5, WA, HC

```
gSETWIN xpos%,ypos%,width%,height%
gSETWIN xpos%,ypos%
```

Change the position and, optionally, the size of the current window. Raises an error if the current drawable is a bitmap. The current cursor position is unaffected.

If this command is used on the default window, the SCREEN command must be used to ensure that the area in which PRINT commands display text is wholly contained within the default window.

gORDER   S3, S3a/c, Siena, S5, WA, HC

```
gORDER winId%,rank%
```

Set the window specified by the window ID `winId%` to the selected foreground/background position (`rank%`), and redraw the screen. Position 1 is the foreground window, position 2 is next, and so on. Any position greater than the number of windows is interpreted as specifying the end of the list. Raises an error if `winId%` is a bitmap.

On creation, a window is at position 1 in the list.

Note: This only affects overlapping windows in the running OPL program and cannot be used to move the program to foreground.

See also `gRANK`, `gUSE`.

gRANK   S3, S3a/c, Siena, S5, WA, HC

`rank% = gRANK`

Return the current windows foreground/background position (that is the rank), from 1 to 8. The rank is 1 for the foreground window. Raises an error if the current drawable is a bitmap.

See also `gORDER`.

gVISIBLE ON/OFF   S3, S3a/c, Siena, S5, WA, HC

`gVISIBLE ON`
`gVISIBLE OFF`

Make current window visible or invisible. Raises an error if the current drawable is a bitmap.

gORIGINX   S3, S3a/c, Siena, S5, WA, HC

`leftgap% = gORIGINX`

Return the gap in pixels between the left side of the screen and the left side of the current window. A negative value is returned if the left side of the window is to the left of the screen. Raises an error if the current drawable is a bitmap.

See also `gORIGINY`.

gORIGINY   S3, S3a/c, Siena, S5, WA, HC

`topgap% = gORIGINY`

Return the gap in pixels between the top of the screen and the top of the current window. A negative value is returned if the top of the window is above the top of the screen. Raises an error if the current drawable is a bitmap.

See also `gORIGINX`.

gCREATEBIT   S3, S3a/c, Siena, S5, WA, HC

```
id% = gCREATEBIT(width%,height%) - OPL16 and OPL32
id% = gCREATEBIT(width%,height%,mode%) - OPL32
```

Create a bitmap with specified dimensions `width%` and `height%`, and makes it the current drawable. Sets the current graphics cursor position to `0,0`, its top left corner. Returns `id%`, the drawable ID, that identifies this bitmap for other keywords.

In OPL32 `gCREATEBIT` may be used with an optional third parameter which specifies the graphics mode of the bitmap to be created. The values of these are as given in `gCREATE`. By default the graphics mode of a bitmap is 2-colour.

See also `gCLOSE`, `gLOADBIT`, `gSAVEBIT`, `gUSE`.

gLOADBIT   S3, S3a/c, Siena, S5, WA, HC

```
id% = gLOADBIT(name$,write%,index%)
id% = gLOADBIT(name$,write%)
id% = gLOADBIT(name$)
```

Load a bitmap from the named bitmap file and makes it the current drawable. Sets the current graphics cursor position to `0,0`, the top left corner. Returns `id%` that identifies the drawable for other keywords.

In OPL16, if `name$` has no file extension, .PIC is used.

In OPL32 `gLOADBIT` does **not** add a default filename extension to the input argument name.

Note than on the Series 5, `gLOADBIT` loads EPOC32 picture files, in the same file format that is saved by `gSAVEBIT`. EPOC32 picture files can also be generated by exporting files created by the Sketch application. These are called multi-bitmap files (MBMs), though often containing just one bitmap as in the case of `gSAVEBIT` or Sketch files, and usually have an .MBM extension.

The bitmap is kept as a local copy in memory.

The optional `write%` argument specifies read/write access to the bitmap:

> `write%=0`   For read-only access. Attempts to write to the bitmap in memory will be ignored, but the bitmap can be used by other programs without using more memory.
>
> `write%=1`   Allows writing to and re-saving the bitmap; the default case.

For bitmap files that contain more than one bitmap, `index%` specifies which one to load. For the first bitmap, use `index%=0`; the default value.

In OPL16, bitmap files saved from an in memory bitmap with `gSAVEBIT` have only one bitmap. Saving a bitmap from a window with a grey plane will save two bitmaps, black with `index%=0` and grey with `index%=1`.

See also `gCLOSE`.

gSAVEBIT
S3, S3a/c, Siena, S5, WA, HC

```
gSAVEBIT name$,width%,height%
gSAVEBIT name$
```

Save the current drawable as the named bitmap file. If `width%` and `height%` are given, then only the rectangle of that size (in pixels) from the current cursor is copied.

In OPL16, if `name$` has no filename extension, .PIC is used. Saving a window to file that includes grey will save both planes to the file, black bitmap first followed by grey.

OPL32 does not supply a default file name extension, but the convension is to use a .MBM filename extension.

See also `gLOADBIT`, `gCREATEBIT`.

gCLOSE
S3, S3a/c, Siena, S5, WA, HC

```
gCLOSE drawid%
```

Close the specified drawable (identified by its ID number, `drawid%`) that was previously opened by `gCREATE`, `gCREATEBIT` or `gOPENBIT`. If you close the current drawable, the default window (`ID=1`) becomes current. An error is raised if you try to close the default window.

On the HC, Series 3 and Series 3a, prior to using `gCLOSE`, you should:

- Close any clock that is open in the window.
- Set `gGREY 0` if the window has a grey plane.

See also `gCREATE`, `gCREATEBIT` or `gOPENBIT`.

gUSE
S3, S3a/c, Siena, S5, WA, HC

```
gUSE drawid%
```

Make the drawable `drawid%` current. Graphics drawing commands will now use this drawable. The `gUSE` command does not bring the drawable to foreground (use `gORDER 0` for this).

DEFAULTWIN
S3a/c, Siena, S5, WA

```
DEFAULTWIN grmode%
```

Change the default window (`ID=1`) to enable or disable the use of grey on SIBO or change the colour mode on Series 5.

In OPL16 grey cannot be used initially in the default window.

> `grmode%=1` enables the use of grey.
> `grmode%=0` disables the use of grey.

A side-effect of DEFAULTWIN is to clear the default window.

Using grey does use more memory than using only black.

If you need to use grey you are advised to call DEFAULTWIN once only at the start of the program. If it fails with an 'Out of memory' error, the program can then exit cleanly without losing vital information.

In OPL32 the default window uses 4-colour mode initially.

grmode%=0 changes to 2-colour mode (results in a mapping of greys to white or black)
grmode%=1 just clears the screen, leaving the window in 4-colour mode.
grmode%=2 changes to 16-colour mode.

Using DEFAULTWIN with either of these values also clears the screen to ensure compatibility with SIBO.

Using 4-colour mode uses more power than using 2-colour mode and 16-colour mode uses even more.

See also gGREY, gCREATE and , gCOLOR.

gGREY   S3a/c, Siena, S5, WA

gGREY mode%

In OPL16, controls whether all subsequent graphics drawing and graphics text in the current window draw to the black plane, the grey plane, or both. The gGREY command cannot be used with bitmaps (i.e. in memory as opposed to bitmap files), because they have only one plane. It is helpful to think of the black plane being in front of the grey plane, so a pixel set in both planes will appear black. To enable the use of grey in the default window (ID=1) use DEFAULTWIN 1 at the start of your program. If grey is required in other windows you must create the windows with a grey plane using gCREATE.

In OPL32, gGREY changes the pen colour between black and light grey (i.e. equivalent to the effect of using gCOLOR $aa,$aa,$aa).

All subsequent graphics drawing is determined by the value of mode%:

mode%	OPL16 - plane(s) drawn to	OPL32 – pen colour
0	Black plane only (the default)	Black pen
1	Grey plane only	Light grey pen
2	Both planes	Black – and all other values of mode%

See also DEFAULTWIN and gCREATE.

Window and bitmap characteristics

gLOADFONT, OPL16	Load and unload user-defined fonts
gLOADFONT, OPL32	
gUNLOADFONT	
gFONT	Set font to use
gSTYLE	Set style of text
gGMODE	Set graphics mode
gTMODE	Set text mode

gLOADFONT, OPL16   S3, S3a/c, Siena, WA, HC

`fontId%=gLOADFONT(name$)`

Load the user-defined font `name$`. Returns a font ID number, which can be used with gFONT to make the current drawable use that font. If `name$` does not contain a file extension, .FON is used.

gFONT itself is very efficient, so all required fonts should normally be loaded at the start of the program.

Note that built-in Psion fonts in ROM are automatically available, and do not need to be loaded.

Also see gUNLOADFONT, gFONT.

gLOADFONT, OPL32   S5

`fileId%=gLOADFONT(filename$)`

Loads the user-defined fonts in the file `filename$` and returns the `fileId%`, which is only used with gUNLOADFONT. The built-in Psion fonts in ROM are automatically available, and do not need to be loaded.

A maximum of 16 font files may be loaded simultaneously. A set of published font UIDs are supplied with font files to enable the use of the loaded fonts with gFONT. Typically the UIDs are included from a header file e.g. CONST.OPH. For example:

```
fileId%=gLOADFONT("Music1")
gFONT KMusic1Font1&
...
gUNLOADFONT fileId%
```

gFONT itself is very efficient, so all required fonts should normally be loaded at the start of the program.

Also see gUNLOADFONT, gFONT.

gUNLOADFONT   S3, S3a/c, Siena, S5, WA, HC

gUNLOADFONT fontId% - **OPL16**
gUNLOADFONT fileId% - **OPL32**

Unload a user-defined font that was previously loaded using gLOADFONT. Raises an error
if the font has not been loaded. The built-in Psion fonts are not held in memory and cannot
be unloaded.

See also gLOADFONT.

gFONT   S3, S3a/c, Siena, S5, WA, HC

gFONT fontId%
gFONT fontId& - **in OPL32**

Set the font for the current drawable to fontId% or fontId&. The font may be one of the
predefined fonts in the ROM or a user-defined font. User-defined fonts must first be
loaded by gLOADFONT, which returns the font ID needed for gFONT.

Font numbering is **different on the HC** from that on the Series 3 family, Siena and
Work*about*. The HC fonts are listed below.

Font	Name	Pixel WxH or H only	System
1	HC standard font	15	HC
2	HC small font	11	HC
3	HC Mono	6x8	HC
4	HC Mono 2 font	7x10	HC
5	Series 3 normal	8	HC
6	Series 3 bold	8	HC

In the table below, Swiss and Arial refer to fonts without serifs while Roman and Times
fonts either have serifs (e.g. font 6) or are in a style designed for serifs, but are too small to
show them (e.g. font 5 on the Series 3c). Courier is a mono-spaced font, i.e. has characters
that are all the same width (and have their pixel size as **width x height**). With proportional
fonts, each character can have a different width.

Fonts 1 to 3 are the Series 3 fonts, and are used when running in compatibility mode on
the Series 3a/c, Siena and Work*about*.

Initially font 4 is used on the text screen of the Series 3a/c and Siena, Courier 11 is used
on the Series 5.

Font	Name	Pixels WxH or H only	System	Name Series 5 only	Pixels WxH or H only
1	Series 3 normal	8	S3, S3a/c, Siena, WA	N/A	
2	Series 3 bold	8	S3, S3a/c, Siena, WA	N/A	
3	Series 3 digits	6x6	S3, S3a/c, Siena, WA	N/A	
4	Mono	8x8	S3a/c, Siena, WA	Courier	8
5	Roman	8	S3a/c, Siena, WA	Times	8
6	Roman	11	S3a/c, Siena, WA	Times	11
7	Roman	13	S3a/c, Siena, WA	Times	13
8	Roman	16	S3a/c, Siena, WA	Times	15
9	Swiss	8	S3a/c, Siena, WA	Arial	8
10	Swiss	11	S3a/c, Siena, WA	Arial	11
11	Swiss	13	S3a/c, Siena, WA	Arial	13
12	Swiss	16	S3a/c, Siena, WA	Arial	15
13	Mono	6x6	S3a/c, Siena, WA	Tiny (mono)	3x4

The special font number $9a is set aside to give a machine's default graphics font; this is the font used initially for graphics text. The actual font may vary from machine to machine - e.g. it is font 1 on the Series 3 and font 11 on the Series 3a. The default font is 11 (Swiss 13) for the Series 3c, and 12 (Arial 15) for the Series 5. So gFONT 12 or gFONT &9a both set the Series 5 standard font, which gPRINT normally uses. (gFONT 11 or $9a on the Series 3a/c or Siena)

Note:
Fonts on the Series 5 are identified by a 32-bit UID, rather than by a 16-bit value representing the font position in the ROM as on SIBO systems. However OPL32 does provide some mapping where possible between OPL16 font IDs and Series 5 OPL32 font UIDs. A full list of the Series 5 font IDs is provided in a ROM based header file CONST.OPH, – see the 'OPL32 Techniques' chapter for details of using and reading this file.

See also gLOADFONT, gSTYLE and FONT.

gSTYLE   S3, S3a/c, Siena, S5, WA, HC

gSTYLE style%

Set the style of text displayed in subsequent gPRINT, gPRINTB, gXPRINT and gPRINTCLIP commands on the current drawable.

style%	effect	OPL32 constant
0	Normal style	KgStyleNormal%
1	Bold	KgStyleBold%
2	Underlined	KgStyleUnder%
4	Inverse	KgStyleInverse%
8	Double height	KgStyleDoubleHeight%
16	Monospaced	KgStyleMonoFont%
32	Italic	KgStyleItalic%

These styles can be combined by ORing their symbolically defined constants - for example, to set underlined and double height, use:

```
gSTYLE 2 or 8
```

Alternatively add the `style%` values together. For example, to set bold underlined and double height use:

```
gSTYLE 11            (as 1+2+8=11)
```

Note that the Series 3 fonts 1 and 2 (see gFONT) are the normal and bold font versions of each other and bold i.e., style%=1 should not be used with them. Also mono i.e., style%=1 was designed for use with these two proportional fonts to change them to monospaced fonts algorithmically.

This command does not affect non-graphic commands, like PRINT.

See also gFONT, gTMODE.

gGMODE   S3, S3a/c, Siena, S5, WA, HC

```
gGMODE mode%
```

Set the graphics mode for the current drawable. This sets the effect of **all** subsequent drawing commands - gLINEBY, gBOX, etc. - on the current drawable.

mode%	pixels will be :
0	Set
1	Cleared
2	Inverted

By default, the drawing commands **set** the pixels in the drawable. Use gGMODE to change this. For example, if you have drawn a black background, you can draw a white box outline inside it with either:

```
. . .
gGMODE 1
gBOX
. . .
```

or:

```
. . .
gGMODE 2
gBOX
. . .
```

See also gBOX, gTMODE, gFILL

gTMODE S3, S3a/c, Siena, S5, WA, HC

gTMODE mode%

Set the mode in which text is displayed for the current drawable. Subsequent gPRINT and gPRINTCLIP commands will draw in this mode.

mode%	pixels will be:
0	Set
1	Cleared
2	Inverted
3	Replaced

Before the first use of gTMODE in a program, mode% = 0, i.e. set. Graphics text commands cause a pixel to be set in the drawable for each dot in a character.

When mode% is 1 or 2, graphics text commands cause a pixel to be cleared (or inverted) for each dot in a character. When mode% is 3, entire character 'boxes' are displayed in the drawable; character pixels are set, and the background 'box' is cleared.

This command does not affect GIPRINT, gPRINTB, gXPRINT and the non-graphics commands, like PRINT.

See also gMODE, gSTYLE, gFONT.

Window and bitmap information

gIDENTITY	Get identity of current window/bitmap
	Get graphics cursor position
gX	- x position
gY	- y position
gWIDTH	Get width or height of window/bitmap
gHEIGHT	
gINFO	Get general information about current drawable – OPL16
gINFO32	Get general information about current drawable – OPL32

Note:

If used on the default window at program start up, gWIDTH and gHEIGHT can give useful information about the particular machine that a program is running on. E.g. a Siena would return values of 240 and 160 pixels repectively.

gIDENTITY S3, S3a/c, Siena, S5, WA, HC

drawid% = gIDENTITY

Return the ID of the current drawable. The default window has ID=1.

gWIDTH S3, S3a/c, Siena, S5, WA, HC

```
width% = gWIDTH
```

Returns the width of the current drawable.

gHEIGHT S3, S3a/c, Siena, S5, WA, HC

```
height% = gHEIGHT
```

Return the height of the current drawable.

gINFO S3, S3a/c, Siena, WA, HC

```
gINFO var i%()
```

Gets general information about the current drawable and about the graphics cursor (whichever window it is in). See gINFO32 for OPL32.

The information is returned in the array i%() which must be at least 32 integers long. The information is about the drawable in its current state, so e.g. the font information is for the current font in the current style.

The following information is returned:

i%(1)	lowest character in font (changed when gFONT is used)
i%(2)	highest character in font (changed when gFONT is used)
i%(3)	height of font (changed when gFONT is used)
i%(4)	descent of font (changed when gFONT is used)
i%(5)	ascent of font (changed when gFONT is used)
i%(6)	width of zero character (changed when gFONT is used)
i%(7)	maximum character width (changed when gFONT is used)
i%(8)	flags for font (see below, changed when gFONT is used)
i%(9-17)	name of font (see below, set by gFONT)
i%(18)	current graphics mode (set by gGMODE)
i%(19)	current text mode (set by gTMODE)
i%(20)	current style (set by gSTYLE)
i%(21)	cursor state (ON=1,OFF=0, set by CURSOR ON/OFF)
i%(22)	ID of the window containing the cursor (-1 for text cursor)
i%(23)	cursor width (set by CURSOR)
i%(24)	cursor height (set by CURSOR)
i%(25)	cursor ascent (set by CURSOR)
i%(26)	cursor x position in window
i%(27)	cursor y position in window
i%(28)	1 if drawable is a bitmap
i%(29)	cursor effects (S3a/c, Siena, WA only, set by CURSOR)
i%(30)	gGREY settings (S3a/c, Siena, WA only)
i%(31)	reserved (window server ID of drawable)
i%(32)	Reserved

If the cursor state if OFF, (i%(21)=0), or is a text cursor (i%(22)=-1), then i%(23) to i%(27) and i%(29) should be ignored. If the cursor state is ON, (i%(21)=1), it is visible in the window identified by i%(22).

Array element i%(29) has bit 0 set (i%(29) AND 1) if the cursor is obloid, bit 1 set (i%(29) AND 2) if not flashing, and bit 2 set (i%(29) AND 4) if grey.

i%(8) contains certain flags that can **optionally** be stored in the font by its designer. There is therefore no guarantee that these flags are meaningful. If the font designer has followed the conventions for the flags, then i%(8) specifies a combination of the following font characteristics:

1	Standard ASCII character set (32-126)
2	Contains Code Page 850 character set (128-255)
4	Font is bold
8	Font is italic
16	Font is serifed
32	Font is monospaced (S3/S3a/WA)
$8000	Font is stored expanded for quick drawing (S3a/c, Siena, WA)

Use PEEK$(ADDR(i%(9))) to read the name of the font as a string.

See also gGMODE, gTMODE, gSTYLE, gGREY.

gINFO32   S5

```
gINFO32 var i&()
```

Gets general information about the current drawable and about the graphics cursor (whichever window it is in). This replaces gINFO because the information returned has changed. i&() must have 48 elements. The same information is returned to the array elements as for gINFO except for the following,

I&(1)	reserved
I&(2)	reserved
I&(9)	the font UID as used in gFONT
I&(10-17)	unused
I&(30)	graphics colour-mode of current window
i&(31)	gCOLOR red% of foreground
i&(32)	gCOLOR green% of foreground
i&(33)	gCOLOR blue% of foreground
i&(34)	gCOLOR red% of background
i&(35)	gCOLOR green% of background
i&(36)	gCOLOR blue% of background
I&(37-48)	elements 37 to 48 are currently unused

Additionally note that on the Series 5, i&(8)=2 means that Code Page 1252 is used (rather than Code Page 850) and also that there is no obloid cursor, so bit 0 will never be set in i&(29).

See also gINFO, gFONT, gCOLOR, gCREATE.

Graphics 'cursor' positioning

gAT   Set absolute graphics cursor position
gMOVE   Move graphics cursor
gX   Get current graphics cursor position
gY

gAT   S3, S3a/c, Siena, S5, WA, HC

gAT xpos%,ypos%

Set the graphics cursor position for the current window, using absolute co-ordinates.

gAT 0,0 sets the cursor position to the top left of the current drawable.

See also gMOVE.

gMOVE   S3, S3a/c, Siena, S5, WA, HC

gMOVE dx%,dy%

Moves the current graphics cursor position dx% to the right and dy% down, in the current drawable. Negative dx% and dy% move left and up respectively.

See also gAT.

gX   S3, S3a/c, Siena, S5, WA, HC

xpos% = gX

Returns the current x position, the offset from the left side of the current drawable.

gY   S3, S3a/c, Siena, S5, WA, HC

ypos% = gY

Returns the current y position, the offset from the top of the current drawable.

Graphics text

gPRINT	Display a list of expressions
gPRINTCLIP	Display text neatly clipped in rectangle
gPRINTB	Clear a box and display text within it
gTWIDTH	Get width of text
gXPRINT	Display text neatly underlined/highlighted

gPRINT   S3, S3a/c, Siena, S5, WA, HC

`gPRINT list`

Display a list of expressions at the current graphics cursor position in the current drawable. All variable types are formatted as for PRINT. Unlike PRINT, gPRINT does not end by moving to a new line. A comma between expressions is still displayed as a space, but a semi-colon has no effect. Without a list of expressions, gPRINT does nothing.

Text displayed with gPRINT will be shown in the current text mode (as set by gTMODE) and font (as set by gFONT).

See also gPRINTB, gPRINTCLIP, gTWIDTH, gXPRINT, GIPRINT.

gPRINTCLIP   S3, S3a/c, Siena, S5, WA, HC

`dischrs% = gPRINTCLIP(text$,width%)`

Display text$ at the current graphics cursor position, displaying only as many characters as will fit inside width% pixels. Returns the number of characters displayed.

See also gPRINT, gPRINTB, gTWIDTH, gXPRINT, GIPRINT, gTMODE.

gPRINTB   S3, S3a/c, Siena, S5, WA, HC

```
gPRINTB text$,width%
gPRINTB text$,width%,align%
gPRINTB text$,width%,align%,top%
gPRINTB text$,width%,align%,top%,bottom%
gPRINTB text$,width%,align%,top%,bottom%,margin%
```

Display text text$ in a cleared box of width width% pixels. The current graphics cursor position is used for the left side of the box and for the baseline of the text.

The align% argument controls the alignment of the text in the box:

align%	effect
1	right aligned
2	left aligned
3	centred.

The `top%` and `bottom%` arguments are the clearances (in pixels) from the text to the top and bottom of the box. Together with the current font size, they control the height of the box. An error is raised if `top%` plus the font ascent is greater than 255.

The `margin%` argument controls the margins:

alignment	margin%
Left	The offset (in pixels) from the left of the box to the start of the text
Right	The offset (in pixels) from the right of the box to the end of the text
Centred	The offset (in pixels) from the left or right of the box to the region in which to centre, with positive `margin%` meaning left and negative meaning right.

If values are not supplied for some arguments, the following defaults are used:

`align%`	left
`top%`	0
`bottom%`	0
`margin%`	0

`gPRINTB` is not affected by the text mode set using `gTMODE`.

See also `gPRINT`, `gPRINTCLIP`, `gTWIDTH`, `gXPRINT`.

gTWIDTH   S3, S3a/c, Siena, S5, WA, HC

`width% = gTWIDTH(text$)`

Return the width in pixels of `text$` for the current font and style.

See also `gPRINT`, `gPRINTB`, `gPRINTCLIP`, `gXPRINT`.

gXPRINT   S3, S3a/c, Siena, S5, WA, HC

`gXPRINT string$,flags%`

Display `string$` at the current graphics cursor position in the current drawable, with precise highlighting or underlining. The current font and style are still used, even if the style itself is inverse or underlined. Text mode 3 (replace) is used - both set and cleared pixels in the text are drawn.

The `flags%` argument has the following effect:

flags%	effect
0	Normal, as with `gPRINT`
1	Inverse
2	Inverse, rounded (corner pixels not inverse)
3	Inverse, thin
4	Inverse, thin, rounded (corner pixels not inverse)
5	Underlined
6	Thin, underlined

Where lines of text are separated by a single pixel, the **thin** options maintain the separation between lines.

The gXPRINT command does not support the display of a list of expressions of various types - use NUM$, GEN$, FIX$ and SCI$ to convert numbers to strings first. The gXPRINT command is not affected by the current text mode set using gTMODE.

See also gPRINT.

Graphics drawing commands

gCLS	Clear current window/bitmap
GLINEBY	Draw a line - relative to the current cursor position
gLINETO	- to a specific point
gBOX	Draw a box
gBORDER	Draw borders
gXBORDER	
gPOLY	Draw a set of lines
gFILL	Fill a rectangle
gINVERT	Invert the pixels in a rectangle
gPATT	Fill a rectangle with a pattern
gCOLOR	Set pen drawing colour – white, black or grey level - OPL32
gSETPENWIDTH	Set pen drawing width in pixels
gCOPY	Copy a rectangle
gPEEKLINE	Read a horizontal line from a window/bitmap/screen
gSCROLL	Scroll a window/bitmap (also see gSETWIN)
gBUTTON	Draw a 3-D button/key
gDRAWOBJECT	Draw a lozenge
gCIRCLE	Draw a circle – OPL32
gELLIPSE	Draw an ellipse – OPL32
gCLOCK	Display or remove a running clock – see variants

gCLS   S3, S3a/c, Siena, S5, WA, HC

gCLS

Clear the whole of the current drawable and set the current graphics cursor position to 0,0 i.e., the top left corner.

gLINEBY   S3, S3a/c, Siena, S5, WA, HC

gLINEBY dx%,dy%

Draw a line from the current graphics cursor position to the point dx% to the right and dy% down in the current mode. Negative dx% and dy% mean left and up respectively. The current cursor position moves to the end of the line drawn.

The Series 5 never draws the end point, so for `gLINEBY` `dx%,dy%`, point `gX+dx%,gY+dy%` is not drawn. However, OPL32 specially plots the point when the start and end-point coincide.

`gLINEBY 0,0` plots (sets) the pixel at the current cursor position.

See also `gLINETO, gPOLY`.

gLINETO   S3, S3a/c, Siena, S5, WA, HC

`gLINETO xpos%,ypos%`

Draw a line from the current graphics cursor position to the point `xpos%,ypos%`. The current cursor position moves to `xpos%,ypos%`.

For horizontal lines in OPL16, the line includes the pixel with the lower x co-ordinate and excludes the pixel with the higher x co-ordinate. Similarly for vertical lines, the line includes the pixel with the lower y co-ordinate and excludes the pixel with the higher y co-ordinate. For oblique lines (where the x and y co-ordinates change), the line is drawn minus one or both end points.

The Series 5 never draws the end point, so for `gLINETO dx%,dy%`, point `x%,y%` is not drawn. However, OPL32 specially plots the point when the start and end-point coincide.

To plot a single point, use `gLINETO gX,gY` (or `gLINEBY 0,0`).

See also `gLINEBY, gPOLY`.

gBOX   S3, S3a/c, Siena, S5, WA, HC

`gBOX width%,height%`

Draw a box from the current graphics cursor position to the pixel `width%` to the right and `height%` down. The current cursor position is unaffected.

See also `gBORDER`, and `gXBORDER`.

gBORDER   S3, S3a/c, Siena, S5, WA, HC

`gBORDER flags%`
`gBORDER flags%,width%,height%`

Draw a one-pixel wide border around the edge of the current drawable. If `width%` and `height%` are supplied, a border shape of this size is drawn, with the top left corner at the current cursor position for graphics. If they are not supplied, the border is drawn around the whole of the current drawable.

The flags% parameter controls three attributes of the border - a shadow to the right and beneath, a one-pixel gap all around, and the type of corners used:

flags%	effect	OPL32 constant
1	single pixel shadow	KbordSglShadow%
2	gap for single pixel shadow	KbordSglGap%
3	double pixel shadow	KbordDblShadow%
4	gap for double pixel shadow	KbordDblGap%
$100	one-pixel gap all around	KbordGapAllRound%
$200	more rounded corners	KbordRoundCorners%

Flag values may be combined to control the three different effects. For example, for rounded corners and a gap for a double pixel shadow, use: flags%=$204.

Set flags%=0 for no shadow, no gap and sharper corners.

To de-emphasise a previously emphasised border, for example, use gBORDER with the shadow turned off:

```
gBORDER 3 REM show border
GET
gBORDER 4 REM border off
```

Shadows on Series 5 windows will not show in the same way as shadows on other objects such as dialogs and menu panes. To display such shadows on a window, you must specify them when using gCREATE. Hence you should use gCREATE (and gXBORDER) in preference to gBORDER on the Series 5.

See also gBOX and gXBORDER.

gXBORDER   S3a/c, Siena, S5, WA

```
gXBORDER type%,flags%,width%,height%
gXBORDER type%,flags%
```

Draws a border in the current drawable of a specified type. The border fits inside a rectangle of the specified dimensions (width%, height%), or has the size of the current drawable if no dimensions are specified. Two types of border are available:

type%	description
0	For drawing the Series 3 type border. flags% are as for gBORDER.
1	For drawing the Series 3a/c, Siena and Work*about* 3-D grey and black border. A shadow or a gap for a shadow is always assumed. flags%=1,2,3,4 are as for gBORDER. When the shadow is enabled (1 or 3) only the grey and black parts of the border are drawn; you should pre-clear the background for the white parts. When the shadow is disabled (2 or 4) the outer and inner border lines are drawn, but the areas covered by grey/black when the shadow is enabled are now cleared. This allows a shadow to be turned off simply by calling gXBORDER again.
2	For Series 5 type borders.

The following values of flags% apply to **Series 5** border types:

flags%	effect
0	none
$01	single black
$42	shallow sunken
$44	deep sunken
$54	deep sunken with outline
$82	shallow raised
$84	deep raised
$94	deep raised with outline
$22	vertical bar
$2a	horizontal bar

The following values of flags% apply to all border types:

flags%	effect	OPL32 constant
0	normal corners	
Add $100	leave 1 pixel gap around the border.	KbordGapAllRound%
Add $200	more rounded corners	KbordRoundCorners%
Add $400	lose a single pixel at each corner of the rectangle, making it look slightly rounded.	KbordLosePixel%

If both $400 and $200 are mistakenly supplied, $200 has priority. On SIBO systems an error is raised if the current window has no grey plane.

See also gBORDER.

gPOLY   S3, S3a/c, Siena, S5, WA, HC

```
gPOLY a%()
```

Draw a sequence of lines as defined by the array a%(). The command is equivalent to gAT
followed by multiple gLINEBY and gMOVE commands, but it is quicker and more efficient.

The array is set up as follows:

```
a%(1)        starting x position
a%(2)        starting y position
a%(3)        number of pairs of offsets
a%(4)        dx1%
a%(5)        dy1%
a%(6)        dx2%
a%(7)        dy2% etc.
```

Elements a%(4) onwards specify pairs of offsets and the operation to be performed. Each
pair specifies the amount by which to move. Positive dx% and dy% values indicate to the
right and down respectively: negative values indicate to the left and up.

The dx% value also indicates the operation:

- to **draw** a line, multiply the corresponding dx% by 2
- to **move** by an amount, multiply the corresponding dx% by 2 and add 1

The current graphics cursor position is left at the start x, y position.

For example, to draw two horizontal lines 50 pixels long and 30 pixels apart starting at
position 20,10:

```
a%(1)=20    : a%(2)=10   REM start x,y
a%(3)=3                  REM 3 operations
a%(4)=50*2  : a%(5)= 0   REM draw right 50
a%(6)=0*2+1 : a%(7)=30   REM move down 30
a%(8)=-50*2 : a%(9)= 0   REM draw left 50
gPOLY a%()
```

gFILL   S3, S3a/c, Siena, S5, WA, HC

```
gFILL width%,height%,mode%
```

Fill the rectangle of the specified dimensions (width%, height%) from the current
graphics cursor position, according to the graphics mode (mode%) specified. The current
cursor position is unaffected.

mode%	pixels are:
0	set
1	cleared
2	inverted

See also gBOX, gPATT.

gINVERT   S3, S3a/c, Siena, S5, WA, HC

`gINVERT width%,height%`

Invert the rectangle `width%` to the right and `height%` down from the current graphics
cursor position, except for the four corner pixels.

gPATT   S3, S3a/c, Siena, S5, WA, HC

`gPATT pattid%,width%,height%,mode%`

Fill the rectangle of the specified size from the current graphics cursor position, with
repetitions of the drawable `pattid%`. Set `pattid%=-1` to use a pre-defined grey pattern.
As with `gCOPY`, this command can copy both set and clear pixels, so the same modes are
available as when displaying text:

mode%	pixels are:
0	set
1	cleared
2	inverted
3	replaced

If `mode%` is 3, the entire source drawable is copied, with set and clear pixels. For `mode%`
values of 0, 1 and 2 only the pixels which are set in the pattern are acted on.

The cursor position is unaffected.

In OPL16, `gPATT` is affected by the setting of `gGREY` (in the current window) in the same
way as `gCOPY`:

gGREY	effect
0	copies black to black
1	copies grey to grey, or black to grey if source is black only
2	copies grey to grey and black to black, or black to both if source is black only.

See also `gFILL`.

gCOLOR   S5

`gCOLOR red%,green%,blue%`

Sets the pen colour of the current window. The `red%,green%,blue%` values specify a
colour which will be mapped to white, black or one of the greys on non-colour screens.
Note that if the values of `red%`, `green%` and `blue%` are equal, then a pure grey results,
ranging from black (0) to white (255). The exact effect will depend upon the grey levels
set when the window is created. For example:

`gCOLOR 0,0,0 REM now draw in solid black`

gSETPENWIDTH   S5

gSETPENWIDTH width%

Sets the pen drawing width in the current drawable to width% pixels. The valid range is
from 0 to 32767. A value of 2 gives a distinct line. Touching a single point on the screen
with a value of 10 will give an approximately round spot.

gCOPY   S3, S3a/c, Siena, S5, WA, HC

gCOPY drawid%,xpos%,ypos%,width%,height%,mode%

Copy a rectangle of the specified dimensions (width%,height%) from the point
xpos%,ypos% in drawable drawid%, to the current cursor position for graphics in the
current drawable. As this command can copy both set and clear pixels, the same modes are
available as when displaying text.

mode%	pixels are:
0	set
1	cleared
2	inverted
3	replaced

Replace copies the entire rectangle, with set and clear pixels. The other modes act only on
set pixels in the source pattern.

The current cursor position is not affected in either drawable.

For the Series 3a/c, Siena, Series 5 and Work*about*, gCOPY is affected by the setting of
gGREY (in the current window) as follows:

gGREY	effect
0	copies black to black
1	copies grey to grey, or black to grey if source is black only
2	copies grey to grey and black to black, or black to both if source is black only.

Note:
On the Series 5, it is inadvisable to use gCOPY to copy **from** windows as it is very slow. It
should only be used for copying from bitmaps to windows or other bitmaps.

See also gSCROLL.

gPEEKLINE   S3, S3a/c, Siena, S5, WA, HC

gPEEKLINE drawid%,xpos%,ypos%,var data%(),width%
gPEEKLINE drawid%,xpos%,ypos%,var data%(),width%,mode% - **OPL32**

Read a horizontal line from the drawable drawid%, starting at xpos%,ypos%, with
width% specifying the number of pixels to be read. The leftmost 16 pixels are read into
data%(1), with the first pixel read into the least significant bit. The array data%() must

be long enough to hold the data. The number of integers required is given by the (integer division) formula `(length%+15)/16`.

On SIBO systems if `drawid%` is set to 0, the whole screen itself is read, not any particular window, and if `$8000` is added to `drawid%`, the grey plane (not the black plane) will be peeked. The `$8000` option will raise an 'invalid arguments error' in OPL32.

If `width%` is not a multiple of 16, `data%()` will contain some random values. For example, if `width%` is 1, as in this case:

```
gPEEKLINE drawid%,xpos%,ypos%,data%(),1
```

bit 0 of `data%(1)` will be meaningful, and the other 15 bits will not.

In OPL32, `gPEEKLINE` has an extra optional parameter `mode%` to specify the colour mode:

mode%	colour mode	colour of pixel which sets bits
-1	black and white	black
0	black and white	white
1	4-colour mode	white
2	16-colour mode	white

The default `mode%` is -1. For 4 and 16-colour modes, 2 and 4 bits per pixel respectively are used. This is to enable the colour of the pixel to be ascertained from the bits that are set. White results in all 2 or 4 bits being set, while black sets none of them. For example, in a 4-colour window, with the colour set by

```
gCOLOR 16,16,16
```

a pixel of a line would peek as `0001` in binary. Similarly, a pixel of a line with the colour set to

```
gCOLOR 80,80,80
```

would result in the value `0101` in binary when peeked.

Note:
If the optional parameter `mode%` is used on the Series 5, the array size allowed must be adjusted accordingly: it must be at least twice as long as the array needed for black and white if the line you wish to peek in 4-colour mode and four times as long in 16-colour mode.

gSCROLL   S3, S3a/c, Siena, S5, WA, HC

```
gSCROLL dx%,dy%
gSCROLL dx%,dy%,xpos%,ypos%,width%,height%
```

Scroll the pixels within the current drawable by offset `dx%,dy%`. Positive `dx%,dy%` indicate right and down respectively. The drawable itself does not change position and the current cursor position is unaffected.

If a rectangle within the current drawable is specified, at `xpos%,ypos%` with dimensions `width%,height%`, (in pixels), only this rectangle is scrolled.

The gSCROLL command may be viewed as providing the capability to move a rectangle to a new position within the same drawable. The region "left behind" by the scroll is cleared, so if you are using gSCROLL to perform vertical text scrolling for example, you must display the appropriate line in the cleared region yourself.

If there is only a small amount of text in a window it may be more appropriate to use gSETWIN to move the whole window, containing **all** the text, up and down relative to the screen.

Pixels that scroll off the screen are lost. If you want to be able to scroll back, use gSETWIN.

See also gSETWIN.

gBUTTON   S3a/c, Siena, S5, WA

```
gBUTTON text$,ty%,width%,height%,st%
```

in OPL32

```
gBUTTON text$,ty%,width%,height%,st%,bitmapId&
gBUTTON text$,ty%,width%,height%,st%,bitmapId&,maskId&
gBUTTON text$,ty%,width%,height%,st%,bitmapId&,maskId&,layout%
```

Draw a 3-D black and grey button.

This is a key, not an application button. It is drawn at the current position in a rectangle of size width%, and height%, which fully encloses the button in all its states. The label text$ specifies up to 64 characters to be drawn in the button in the current font and style. You must ensure that the text will fit in the button.

To draw a Series 3 style button use ty%=0, to draw a Series 3a/c type button use ty%=1, use ty%=2 for a Series 5 type button.

The meaning of st% varies according to ty%:

button type	ty%	OPL32 constant	button state	st %	OPL32 constant
S3 style	0	KButtS3%	raised button	0	KbuttS3Raised%
S3 style	0	KButtS3%	depressed (flat) button.	1	KbuttS3Pressed%
S3a/c style	1	KButtS3a%	raised button	0	KbuttS3aRaised%
S3a/c style	1	KButtS3a%	semi-depressed (flat) button	1	KbuttS3aSemiPressed%
S3a/c style	1	KButtS3a%	fully-depressed (sunken) button.	2	KbuttS3aSunken%
S5 style	2	KButtS5%	raised button	0	KbuttS5Raised%
S5 style	2	KButtS5%	semi-depressed (flat) button	1	KbuttS5SemiPressed%
S5 style	2	KButtS5%	fully-depressed (sunken) button	2	KbuttS5Sunken%

On SIBO systems an error is raised if the current window has no grey plane.

On the Series 5, there is added support so that bitmaps may be used on buttons. Three extra optional arguments can be passed which give the bitmap ID, the mask ID and the layout for the button respectively. `maskId%` can be 0 to specify no mask.

The following constants should be used for `layout%` to specify relative positions of the text and icon on a button,

position of text	layout%
right	0
bottom	1
top	2
left	3

The following constants can be added to the values above to specify how a button's excess space is to be allocated,

share	0
to text	$10
to picture	$20

When the layout is such that the text is at the top or the bottom, then text and picture are centred vertically and horizontally in the space allotted to them. If the layout has text to the left or right, then the text is left aligned in the space allotted to it and the picture is right or left aligned respectively. Both text and picture are centred vertically in this case.

Examples:

layout%	description
$13	a button with text on the left and left aligned in any excess space.
$20	a button with text on the right and the picture left aligned in any excess space.
$10	a standard toolbar button, putting the text on the right.

For a picture only with no text use `text$=""`.

An 'Invalid arguments' error is raised if you use the ID of a window with gBUTTON. Read-only bitmaps may also be loaded using the Bitmap OPX. See the 'OPL32 Techniques' chapter for more details using OPX's.

gDRAWOBJECT   S3a/c, Siena, WA

`gDRAWOBJECT type%,flags%,width%,height%`

Draw the scalable graphics object specified by `type%`, scaled to fit in the rectangle with top left at the current graphics cursor position and with the specified dimensions `width%` and `height%`.

There is only one object type (set `type%=0`) a 'lozenge'. This is a 3-D rounded box lit from the top left, with a shadow at bottom right and a grey body.

The flags% argument specifies the corner roundness:

flags%	effect
0	For normal roundness
1	For more rounded
2	For a single pixel removed from each corner.

An error is raised if the current window has no grey plane.

gCIRCLE   S5

gCIRCLE radius%
gCIRCLE radius%,fill%

Draws a circle with the centre at the current position in the current drawable. If the value of radius% is negative then no circle is drawn.

If fill% is supplied and if fill%<>0 then the circle is filled with the current pen colour.

See gELLIPSE, gCOLOR.

gELLIPSE   S5

gELLIPSE hRadius%,vRadius%
gELLIPSE hRadius%,vRadius%,fill%

Draws an ellipse with the centre at the current position in the current drawable. hRadius% is the horizontal distance in pixels from the centre of the ellipse to the left (and right) of the ellipse. vRadius% is the vertical distance from the centre of the ellipse to the top (and bottom). If the length of either radius is less than zero, then no ellipse is drawn.

If fill% is supplied and if fill%<>0 then the ellipse is filled with the current pen colour.

See gCIRCLE, gCOLOR.

gCLOCK   See machine variants below

See machine specific sections for the exact syntax.

Display or remove a running clock showing the system time. The clock is drawn at the current graphics cursor position in the current window. Only one clock may be displayed in each window. In order to replace a clock with a new type, you first need to call gCLOCK OFF.

The mode% argument controls the type of clock.

The offset% argument specifies an offset in minutes from the system time to the displayed time. This allows you to display a clock showing a time other than the system time (e.g. the time in another country).

The defaults are: mode% = 1, and offset% = 0.

Notes:
Do not use gSCROLL to scroll the region containing a clock. When the time is updated, the old position would be used. The whole window may, however, be moved using gSETWIN.

On systems with a grey plane it is possible to draw clocks that include grey in windows created without a grey plane.

gCLOCK   S3 and HC

```
gCLOCK ON,mode%
gCLOCK ON,mode%,offset%
gCLOCK OFF
```

mode%	clock type
1	Small digital
2	Medium, system setting
3	Medium, analog
4	Medium, digital
5	Large, analog

The clock type (analog or digital) may be set for the system. This system setting can then be used by all programs run on the Psion by using mode%=2

The above values may be ORed with a combination of:

$10   To include a display of the date on small and medium clocks only. The date is displayed to the left of the current graphics cursor position on a digital clock.

$20   To include a display of seconds on small and large clocks only.

$40   To show am/pm on medium clocks only.

For example:

```
gCLOCK ON,$10 or $20 or 1
```

specifies a small digital clock, showing both date and seconds, and:

```
gCLOCK ON,$20 or 5
```

is a large analog clock with a moving second hand.

gCLOCK   S3a/c, Siena and WA

```
gCLOCK ON
gCLOCK ON,mode%
gCLOCK ON,mode%,offset%
gCLOCK ON,mode%,offset%,format$
gCLOCK ON,mode%,offset%,format$,font%
gCLOCK ON,mode%,offset%,format$,font%,style%
gCLOCK OFF
```

The gCLOCK command for the Series 3a/c, Siena and Workabout has extended mode% values and further arguments. The format$, font% and style% arguments are used for formatted digital clocks **only,** as described below.

Modes 1 to 5 (as for S3 and HC above) are provided for HC and Series 3 compatibility, and produce HC/Series 3 clocks. Other values are:

mode%	clock type
6	Black and grey medium, system setting
7	Black and grey medium, analog
8	Second type medium, digital
9	Black and grey extra large
10	Formatted digital (described below)

You can OR the value with any of these:

$10	Shows the date in all except the extra large and formatted clocks
$20	Shows seconds in small digital, large analog, black and grey medium analog and extra large clocks
$40	Shows am/pm in small digital and black medium clocks only.
$80	Specifies that a clock is to be drawn in the grey plane (only for clocks that do not contain both black and grey, i.e. all except the black and grey, medium, analog clock and the extra large clock).

Digital clocks display in 24-hour or 12-hour mode according to the system-wide setting, e.g. in Time. The 'am/pm' flag ($40) can be used with digital clocks in 12-hour mode, and with medium analog clocks.

The default font for gCLOCK is the system font (value $9a). The default style is normal (0).

For the formatted digital clock (mode%=10), you may optionally specify font% and style% with values as for gFONT and gSTYLE. A format string (up to 255 characters long) specifies how the clock is to be displayed. The format string contains a number of format specifiers in the form of a % followed by a letter. (Upper or lower case may be used.) For example, %H means "hours" and %T means "minutes";

Thus, at 11:05 pm:

```
gCLOCK ON,10,0,"h:%H, m:%T"
```

displays a running clock as:

```
h:23, m:05
```

To make each item as abbreviated as possible, you can use a * after the %. For example, "%*T" at 11:05 pm abbreviates '05' to '5'.

In the following list of specifiers, those which produce numbers will do so without any leading zero if you use %* instead of %. Other abbreviations are given in brackets as appropriate:

specifier	displays	abbreviated display
%%	Inserts a % character.	none
%*	Abbreviate next item, e.g. %*1. Omits leading zeros, or truncates names to three characters.	none
%: and %/	Time and date separators, as set in the system	none
%A	'am' or 'pm' text	1st letter only
%D	Day number as two digits, 01-31	no leading zero
%W	Week number as two digits, 01-53	no leading zero
%M	Month number as two digits, 01-12	no leading zero
%E	Day name	1st 3 characters
%N	Month name	1st 3 characters
%H	Hour in 24-hour, 00-23	no leading zero
%I	Hour in 12-hour format, 01-12	no leading zero
%S	Seconds, 00-59	no leading zero
%T	Minutes, 00-59	no leading zero
%X	Suffix string for day number, e.g. '1st', '2nd'	none
%Y	Year as a four digits	two digits - no century

specifier	displays
%1	First item of the date format as per the system format settings, as a number
%2	Second item of the date format as per the system format settings, as a number
%3	Third item of the date format as per the system format settings, as a number
%4	Day or month number, i.e. the first item as per the system format settings.
%5	Day or month number, i.e. the second item as per the system format settings.

specifier	effect
%G	Toggles the day whether its %1, %2, %3, %4 or %5 between long form and abbreviation.
%P	Toggles the month whether its %1, %2, %3, %4 or %5 between long form and abbreviation.
%U	Toggles the year whether its %1, %2, or %3 between long form and abbreviation.
%F	Toggles days between numeric and name formats.
%O	Toggles months between numeric and name formats.
%L	Toggles the suffix on a day number whether its %1, %2, %3, %4 or %5.

If the system settings are for 12 hour format %6 sets the hour and %7 set am or pm. If the settings are for 24 hour format %6 sets the hour and %7 has no effect.

So the format string `"%1%/%2%/%3"` automatically generates a clock with day, month and year in the order as set in the system settings. `"%4%/%5"` gives a clock with just day and month in selected order. Similarly, `"%6%:%T%:%S%7"` gives a clock with hour, minute and second automatically conforming to the system configuration.

Note that for those specifiers that toggle between two different options (e.g. %F), the state of toggle is remembered only within one format string and not from one string to the next. In other words the toggle state is restored to the default setting when displaying a new clock.

As a final example, assuming that the system setting is for 'Day/month/year' date format, 'am-pm' time format and ':' time separator and that the time is 11:30:05 pm on 9th March 1996:

```
"%G%L%P%O%*E, %1 %2 %3 %6%:%T:%S%"
```

generates:

```
Sat, 9th Mar 1996 11:30:05pm
```

With the same set-up, except for 'Month/day/year' date format in '24-hour' mode, the same string generates:

```
Sat, Mar 9th 1996 23:30:05
```

Problems with gCLOCK (S3, S3a, HC)

OPL can raise a runtime error in gCLOCK because it mistakenly thinks that a window already has a clock. The problem derives from the fact that, when a window with a clock in it is closed, the "slot" which that window occupied retains the clock data. When another window is opened using that slot, OPL believes a clock is still present and will therefore raise an error when gCLOCK is called. To avoid the problem **always use gCLOCK OFF** to remove the clock before closing a window that has a clock.

See also DAY, MONTH, YEAR, SECOND, MINUTE, HOUR, DATIM$, DAYS, DOW.

gCLOCK

```
gCLOCK ON
gCLOCK ON,mode%
gCLOCK ON,mode%,offset&
gCLOCK ON,mode%,offset&,format$
gCLOCK ON,mode%,offset&,format$,font&
gCLOCK ON,mode%,offset&,format$,font&,style%
gCLOCK OFF
```

Modes 1 to 5 (as for S3 and HC above) are no longer available and mode 10 has been replaced with a richer mode 11. An `offset&` of up to a whole day can be specified.

mode%	clock type
6	Black and grey medium, system setting
7	Black and grey medium, analog
8	Second type medium, digital, automatically displays of day of week and day of month below the time
9	Black and grey extra large, automatically displays a second hand
11	Formatted digital (described below) replaces `mode%=10` in OPL16.

You can OR the value of `mode%` with:

$100	To allow `offset&` to be specified in seconds

The values $10, $20, $40 and $80 used with `mode%` in OPL16 (see above) are no longer supported.

format	effect
%%	Insert a single % character in the string
%*	Abbreviate following item, e.g. %*1. Omits leading zeros, or truncates names to three characters.
%:n	Insert a system time separator character. n is an integer between zero and three that indicates which time separator character is to be used. For European time settings, only n=1 and n=2 are used, giving the hours/minutes separator and minutes/seconds separator respectively.
%/n	Insert a system date separator character. n is an integer between zero and three that indicates which date separator character is to be used. For European time settings, only n=1 and n=2 are used, giving the day/month separator and month/year separator respectively.
%1	Insert the first component of a three component date (i.e. day, month and year) where the order of the components is determined by the system settings. The possibilities are: dd/mm/yyyy, (European), mm/dd/yyyy (American), yyyy/mm/dd (Japanese).
%2	Insert the second component of a three component date where the order has been determined by the system settings. See %1.
%3	Insert the third component of a three component date where the order has been determined by the system settings. See %1.

format	effect
%4	Insert the first component of a two component date (i.e. day and month only) where the order has been determined by system settings. The possibilities are: dd/mm, (European), mm/dd (American), mm/dd (Japanese).
%5	Insert the second component of a two component date where the order has been determined by the system settings. See %4.
%A	Insert am or pm according to the current language and time of day. Text is printed even if 24 hour clock is in use. May be placed before or after the time, and a trailing or leading space as appropriate will be added. The abbreviated version (%*A) removes this space. Optionally, a minus or plus sign may be inserted between the % and the A. This operates as follows: %-A causes am/pm text to be inserted only if the system setting of the am/pm symbol position is set to display **before** the time. Similarly, %+A causes am/pm text to be inserted only if the system setting of the am/pm symbol is set to display **after** the time. No am/pm text will be inserted before the time if a + is inserted in the string. For example you could use, "%-A%H%:1%T%+A" to insert the am/pm symbol **either** before or after the time, according to the system setting. %+A and %-A cannot be abbreviated.
%B	As %A, except that the am/pm text is only inserted if the system clock setting is 12 hour. (This should be used in conjunction with %J.)
%D	Insert the two-digit day number in month (in conjunction with %1 etc.).
%E	Insert the day name. Abbreviation is language specific (3 letters in English).
%F	Use this at the beginning of a format string to make the date/time formatting independent of the system setting. This fixes the order of the following day/month/year component(s) in their given order, removing the need to use %1 to %5, allowing individual components of the date to be printed.
%H	Insert the two-digit hour component of the time in 24 hour clock format.
%I	Insert the two-digit hour component of the time in 12 hour clock format. Any leading zero is automatically suppressed, regardless of whether an asterisk is inserted or not.
%J	Insert the two-digit hour component of time in either 12 or 24 hour clock format depending on the corresponding system setting. When the clock has been set to 12 hour format, the hour's leading zero is automatically suppressed regardless of whether an asterisk has been inserted between the % and J.
%M	Insert the two-digit month number (in conjunction with %1 etc.).
%N	Insert the month name (in conjunction with %1 etc.). When using system settings (i.e. not using %F) this causes all months following %N in the string to be written in words. When using fixed format (i.e. when using %F) %N may be used alone to insert a month name. Abbreviation is language specific (3 letters in English).
%S	Insert the two-digit second component of the time.

format	effect
%T	Insert the two-digit minute component of the time.
%W	Insert the two-digit week number in year, counting the first (part) week as week 1.
%X	Insert the date suffix. When using system settings (i.e. not using %F), this causes a suffix to be put on any date following %X in the string. When using fixed format (i.e. using %F), %X following any date appends a suffix for that particular date. Cannot be abbreviated.
%Y	Insert the four digit year number (in conjunction with %1 etc.). The abbreviation is the last two digits of the year.
%Z	Insert the three digit day number in year.

Example format strings are as follows:

The example used is 1:30:05 pm on Wednesday, 1st January 1997, with the system setting of European dates and with am/pm after the time:

"%-A%I:%T:%S%+A" will print the time in 12 hour clock, including seconds, with the am/pm either inserted before or after the time, depending on the system setting. So the example time would appear as, 1:30:05 pm.

"%F%E %*D%X %N %Y" will print the day of the week followed by the date with suffix, the month as a word and the year. For example, Wednesday 1st January 1997.

"%E %D%X%N%Y %1 %2 %3 " will use the locale setting for ordering the elements of the date, but will use a suffix on the day and the month in words. For example, Wednesday 01st January 1997.

"%*E %*D%X%*N%*Y %1 %2 '%3 " will be similar to 3., but will abbreviate the day of the week, the day, the month and the year, so the example becomes "Wed 1st Jan 97".

"%M%Y%D%1%/0%2%/0%3" will appear as 01/01/1997. This demonstrates that the ordering of the %D, %M and %Y is irrelevant when using locale-dependent formatting. Instead the ordering of the date components is determined by the order of the %1, %2, and %3 formatting commands.

style% may take any of the values used to specify gSTYLE, other than 2 (underlined).

Note:
A 'General Failure' error will result if you attempt to use an invalid format. Invalid formats include using %: and %/ followed by 0 or 3 when in European locale setting (when these separators are without meaning) and using %+ and %- followed by characters other than A or B.

Graphics sprites

CREATESPRITE	Create a sprite
APPENDSPRITE	Append bitmap to sprite
CHANGESPRITE	Change bitmap set of sprite
DRAWSPRITE	Draw a sprite
POSSPRITE	Position a sprite
CLOSESPRITE	Close a sprite

Note:
The OPL16 sprite keywords are no longer supported in OPL32, they have been replaced by superior sprite handling functions via an OPX.

CREATESPRITE   S3a/c, Siena, WA

sprId% = CREATESPRITE

Create a sprite, returning the sprite ID, sprId%.

Note:
Only one sprite is currently available in OPL16.

See also APPENDSPRITE, CHANGESPRITE, CLOSESPRITE, DRAWSPRITE, POSSPRITE.

APPENDSPRITE   S3a/c, Siena, WA

APPENDSPRITE time%,var bit$()
APPENDSPRITE time%,var bit$(),dx%,dy%

Append a single bitmap-set to the sprite.

The duration time%, (in tenths of a second), is the time that the bitmap set is to be displayed before going on to the next bitmap-set in the sequence. The names of the bitmap files in the set (or "" to specify no bitmap) are held in bit$(). The array must have at least 6 elements:

bit$(1)	for setting black pixels
bit$(2)	for clearing black pixels
bit$(3)	for inverting black pixels
bit$(4)	for setting grey pixels
bit$(5)	for clearing grey pixels
bit$(6)	for inverting grey pixels

All the bitmaps in a single bitmap-set must be the same size else 'Argument' error (-2) is raised on attempting to draw the sprite. Bitmaps in different bitmap-sets may differ in size.

If supplied, dx% and dy% are the (x,y) offsets from the sprite position to the top-left of the bitmap-set. Positive values are for offsets to the right and downwards. The default value of both offsets is zero.

See also CHANGESPRITE, CLOSESPRITE, CREATESPRITE, DRAWSPRITE, POSSPRITE.

Problems with APPENDSPRITE (3a, WA)

A sprite larger than the screen can "crash" the machine. (Series 3a screen size: 480 x 160; Workabout screen size: 240 x 100)

CHANGESPRITE S3a/c, Siena, WA

```
CHANGESPRITE ix%,time%,var bit$()
CHANGESPRITE ix%,time%,var bit$(),dx%,dy%
```

Change a bitmap-set in the sprite.

The bitmap-set is specified by ix%, (1 for the first bitmap-set). The names of the bitmap files in the set (or "" to specify o bitmap) are held in bit$(). The array must have at least 6 elements:

bit$(1)	for setting black pixels
bit$(2)	for clearing black pixels
bit$(3)	for inverting black pixels
bit$(4)	for setting grey pixels
bit$(5)	for clearing grey pixels
bit$(6)	for inverting grey pixels

All the bitmaps in a single bitmap-set must be the same size else 'Argument' error (-2) is raised on attempting to draw the sprite. Bitmaps in different bitmap-sets may differ in size.

If supplied, dx% and dy% are the (x,y) offsets from the sprite position to the top-left of the bitmap-set. Positive values are for offsets to the right and downwards. The default value of both offsets is zero.

The CHANGESPRITE command can be called only after DRAWSPRITE.

Note:
The time% argument is ignored.

See also APPENDSPRITE, CLOSESPRITE, CREATESPRITE, DRAWSPRITE, POSSPRITE.

DRAWSPRITE S3a/c, Siena, WA

```
DRAWSPRITE xpos%,ypos%
```

Draw the sprite in the current window with top-left at pixel position xpos%,ypos%. If any bitmap-set contains bitmaps with different sizes, DRAWSPRITE raises an 'Invalid arguments' error (-2). Once the sprite has been drawn, no further file access is performed, even when it is animated.

See also APPENDSPRITE, CHANGESPRITE, CLOSESPRITE, CREATESPRITE, POSSPRITE.

POSSPRITE S3a/c, Siena, WA

POSSPRITE xpos%,ypos%

Set the position of the sprite to pixel xpos%,ypos%.

See also APPENDSPRITE, CHANGESPRITE, CLOSESPRITE, CREATESPRITE, DRAWSPRITE.

CLOSESPRITE S3a/c, Siena, WA

CLOSESPRITE sprId%

Close the sprite with ID sprId%. Only one sprite is currently available in OPL. See also APPENDSPRITE, CHANGESPRITE, CREATESPRITE, DRAWSPRITE, POSSPRITE.

Menus

mINIT	Start a new set of menus
mCARD	Define a menu
mCASC	Define a cascade menu – OPL32
MENU	Display menus
mPOPUP	Define and display a popup menu – OPL32

Note:
The Menu statements are not available on the HC, menus can be created and used via the OPL16 SDK library procedures.

mINIT S3, S3a/c, Siena, S5, WA

mINIT

Cancel any existing menus, in preparation for the definition of new menus. Use mCARD and mCASC (Series 5 only) to define each menu, then MENU to display them.

On the Series 5, it is incorrect to ignore mCARD and mCASC errors by having an ONERR label around an mCARD or mCASC call. If you do, the menu is discarded and a 'Structure fault' will be raised on using mCARD, mCASC or MENU without first using mINIT again - see MENU.

mCARD S3, S3a/c, Siena, S5, WA

mCARD title$,item1$,hotkey1%
mCARD title$,item1$,hotkey1%,item2$,hotkey2%...

Define a menu which has been initialised using mINIT. When all of the menus have been defined, MENU is used to display them.

The titles$ argument is the name of the menu. A maximum number of items on the menu may be defined, depending on which Psion is the target machine:

Psion	Maximum
S3	6
S3a/c, S5	8
WA	6

Each menu item is specified by two arguments. The first is the item name, and the second the key code for a hot-key. This specifies a key which, when pressed together with the Psion key on SIBO or Ctrl on Series 5, will select the option. If the key code is for an upper case key, the hot-key will use both the Shift and Psion (Ctrl) keys together (except S3).

Options can be divided into logical groups by displaying a grey line under the final option in a group. To do this, pass the negative value corresponding to the hot-key code for the final option in the group. For example, -%A specifies hot-key Shift-Psion-A (Ctrl-Shift-A) and displays a grey line under the associated option in the menu.

Series 5 supports the following menu features:

- Menu items without shortcuts, by specifying shortcut values between 1 and 32. For these items the value specified is still returned if the item is selected.

- Menu items which are dimmed, or which have checkboxes or option buttons (sometimes known as radio buttons).

The extra properties are controlled by adding the following bits to the shortcut key key-code.

Effect	value	OPL32 constant
menu item dimmed	$1000	KmenuDimmed%
item has check-box	$0800	KmenuCheckBox%
start of an option button list	$0900	KmenuOptionStart%
middle of an option button list	$0A00	KmenuOptionMiddle%
end of an option button list	$0B00	KmenuOptionEnd%
checkbox/option button symbol on	$2000	KmenuSymbolOn%
checkbox/option button symbol indeterminate	$4000	KmenuSymbolIndeterminate%

The start, middle and end option buttons are for specifying a group of related items that can be selected exclusively (i.e. if one item is selected then the others are deselected). The number of middle option buttons is variable. A single menu card can have more than one set of option buttons and checkboxes, but option buttons in a set should be kept together. For speed, OPL does not check the consistency of these items' specification.

If a separating line is required when any of these effects had been added, you must be sure to negate the whole value, not just the shortcut key key-code.

In the example,

```
mCARD   "Options","View1",%A   OR   $2900,"View2",-(%B   OR   $B00),
        "Another option",%C
```

the second shortcut key key-code and its flag value is correctly negated to display a separating line.

A 'Too wide' error is raised if the menu title length is greater than or equal to 40. Shortcut values must be alphabetic character codes or numbers between the values of 1 and 32. Any other values will raise an 'Invalid arguments' error.

If any menu item fails to be added successfully, a menu is discarded. It is therefore incorrect to ignore mCARD errors by having an ONERR label around an mCARD call on the Series 5. If you do, the menu is discarded and a 'Structure fault' will be raised on using mCARD without first using mINIT again. See MENU for an example of this.

See also mINIT, MENU and mCASC for cascaded menu items.

mCASC   S5

mCASC title$,item1$,hotkey1%,item2$,hotkey2%

Creates a cascade for a menu, on which less important menu items can be displayed. The cascade must be defined before use in a menu card. For example, a 'Bitmap' cascade under the File menu of a possible OPL drawing application could be defined like this:

mCASC "Bitmap","Load",%L,"Merge",%M

mCARD "File","New",%n,"Open",%o,"Save",%s,"Bitmap>",16,"Exit",%e

The trailing > character specifies that a previously defined cascade item is to be used in the menu at this point: it is not displayed in the menu item. A cascade has a filled arrow head displayed along side it in the menu. The cascade title in mCASC is also used only for identification purposes and is not displayed in the cascade itself. This title needs to be identical to the menu item text apart from the >. For efficiency, OPL doesn't check that a defined cascade has been used in a menu and an unused cascade will simply be ignored. To display a > in a cascaded menu item, you can use >>.

Shortcut keys used in cascades may be added to the appropriate constant values as for mCARD to enable checkboxes, option buttons and dimming of cascade items.

As is typical for cascade titles, a shortcut value of 16 is used in the example above. This prevents the display or specification of any shortcut key. However, it is possible to define a shortcut key for a cascade title if required, for example to cycle through the options available in a cascade.

See mCARD, MENU, mINIT.

MENU

```
val% = MENU
val% = MENU(var init%)
```

Displays the menus defined by mINIT, mCARD and mCASC, and waits for you to select an item. Returns the hot-key key code of the item selected, as defined in mCARD, in lower case. If the menu is cancelled by pressing Esc, MENU returns 0.

If init% is passed it sets the initial menu pane and item to be highlighted. The init% argument should be 256*(menu%)+item%; for both menu% and item%, 0 specifies the first, 1 the second and so on. If init% is 517 (=256*2+5), for example, this specifies the 6th item on the third menu.

If init% was passed, MENU writes back to init% the value for the item that was last highlighted on the menu. You can then use this value when calling the menu again.

In OPL16, you only need to use this technique if you have more than one menu in your program, maintaining one variable for each menu.

In OPL32, It is necessary to use MENU(init%), passing back the same variable each time the menu is opened if you wish the menu to reopen with the highlight set on the last selected item.

On the Series 5, it is incorrect to ignore mCARD and mCASC errors by having an ONERR label around an mCARD or mCASC call. If you do, the menu is discarded and a 'Structure fault' will be raised on using mCARD, mCASC or MENU without first using mINIT again.

The following bad code will not display the menu:

```
        mINIT
        ONERR errIgnore1
        mCARD "Xxx","ItemA",0 REM bad shortcut
errIgnore1::
        ONERR errIgnore2
        mCARD "Yyy",""           REM 'Structure fault' error (mINIT
        discarded)
errIgnore2::
        ONERR OFF
        MENU                     REM 'Structure fault' again
```

See also mCARD and mINIT. On the HC the menu%: SIBO OPL16 SDK library procedure is used.

Problems with MENU (S3, HC)

There are some circumstances in which OPL programs with menus can gradually lose small amounts of system memory. All memory lost in this way is fully recovered when the OPL application exits, but if the application runs for a long time without exiting, it is possible that the cumulative amount of memory lost will in time adversely affect the performance of the application.

Solution

By adding a few extra lines of OPL code to a program, it can be ensured that no memory loss of this sort will occur. The changes required are as follows:

a) Declare three global arrays pt1&(7), pt2&(7), pt3&(8).

b) Before MENU is called for the first time, you should call the procedure ptinit: (source code given below).

c) Instead of calling MENU directly, define a procedure menu%: (example source code given below) and call that instead.

Note:

To simplify the patch code, the contents of ptinit: could be moved inside menu%:, with virtually no detectable speed degradation, but with the advantage that the three global arrays can become local variables inside menu%:.

Example of Menu patch code

```
PROC test:
  GLOBAL pt1&(7),pt2&(7),pt3&(8)
  LOCAL m%
  ptinit:
  DO
    mINIT
    mCARD "Menu 1","Option 1",%a
    mCARD "Menu 2","Exit",%x

    m%=menu%:
    IF m%=%a
      GIPRINT "Option 1 selected"
    ENDIF
  UNTIL m%=%x
ENDP

PROC ptinit:
  pt1&(1)=&8BF88BFC
  pt1&(2)=&8B00121E
  pt1&(3)=&778B205F
  pt1&(4)=&E42AAC0C
  pt1&(5)=&A5ABC88B
  pt1&(6)=&75C084AC
  pt1&(7)=&CBF8E2FB
  pt2&(1)=&00B4F08B
  pt2&(2)=&FC808BCD
  pt2&(3)=&AD0D7330
  pt2&(4)=&C932D08B
  pt2&(5)=&CDD88BAD
  pt2&(6)=&F8754ACF
  pt2&(7)=&CB
ENDP
PROC menu%:
  LOCAL r%
  USR(ADDR(pt1&(1)),ADDR(pt3&(1)),0,0,0)
  r%=menu
  USR(ADDR(pt2&(1)),ADDR(pt3&(1)),0,0,0)
  RETURN(r%)
ENDP
```

mPOPUP

```
mPOPUP(x%,y%,posType%,item1$,hotkey1%,item2$,hotkey2%,...)
```

Presents a popup menu. mPOPUP returns the value of the keypress used to exit the popup menu, this being 0 if Esc is pressed.

mPOPUP defines and presents the menu itself, and **should not** and **need not** be called from inside the mINIT...MENU structure. posType% is the position type controlling which corner of the popup menu x%,y% specifies and can take the values,

posType%	corner	OPL32 constant
0	top left	KMPopupPosTopLeft%
1	top right	KMPopupPosTopRight%
2	bottom left	KMPopupPosBottomLeft%
3	bottom right	KMPopupPosBottomRight%

item$ and key% can take the same values as for mCARD, with key% taking the same constant values to specify checkboxes, option buttons and dimmed items. However, cascades in popup menus are not supported.

For example:

```
mPOPUP (0,0,0,"Continue",%c,"Exit",%e)
```

specifies a popup menu with 0,0 as its top left-hand corner with the items 'Continue' and 'Exit', with the shortcut keys Ctrl+C and Ctrl+E respectively.

See also mCARD.

Dialogs

dINIT	Start a new dialog
dINITS	Start a new dialog using small font – WA only
dPOSITION	Position a dialog
dTEXT	Define text for dialog
dEDIT	Define a text edit box for dialog
dEDITMULTI	Define a multi-line text edit box for dialog – OPL32
dXINPUT	Define a secret edit box for a dialog
dFILE,OPL16	Define a filename edit box for a dialog
dFILE,OPL32	Define a filename edit box for a dialog
dCHOICE	Define a choice list for a dialog
dFLOAT	Define a floating point numeric edit box for a dialog
dLONG	Define a long numeric edit box for a dialog
dDATE	Define a date edit box for a dialog
dTIME	Define a time edit box for a dialog
dBUTTONS	Define exit keys for a dialog
dCHECKBOX	Define a check box for a dialog – OPL32
DIALOG	Display a dialog
ALERT	Display a simple alert dialog

Notes:

- Only one dialog may be in use at a time.
- A dialog must be initialised with dINIT, items defined e.g. dLONG and displayed with DIALOG within in the same procedure.
- In OPL16 i the width of any line would make the dialog too wide, a 'Too wide' **error is** raised when DIALOG is called. In OPL32 **no error** is raised if the dialog is too wide or too long to fit on the screen; it is up to the programmer to ensure the dialog is displayed in a suitable way.
- In OPL16 a dialog may consist of up to nine lines, including any title. Filename editors count as two lines, and exit keys count as three. A 'Too many items' **error is** raised if this limit is exceeded.

dINIT   S3, S3a/c, Siena, S5, WA

```
dINIT
dINIT title$
dINIT title$,flags% – in OPL32
```

Prepare for the definition of a dialog, cancelling any existing one.

Use dTEXT, dCHOICE, etc. to define each item in the dialog, then DIALOG to display the dialog. If title$ is supplied, it will be displayed at the top of the dialog, centred and with a line across the dialog below it.

The maximum number of lines of text that the dialog can have depends on which Psion computer the program will be run on:

System	maximum lines
S3	7
S3a/c, Siena and S5	9
WA	6
	(8 with dINITS)

In OPL32 `flags%` can be any ORed combination of the following:

flags%	effect	OPL32 constant
1	Buttons on right rather than at bottom	KDlgButRight%
2	No title, any title in dINIT is ignored	KDlgNoTitle%
4	Use the full screen	KDlgFillScreen%
8	Don't allow dialog box to be dragged	KDlgNoDrag%
16	Pack dialog densely (not buttons) for more lines	KDlgDensePack%

Series 5 dialogs without titles cannot be dragged regardless of value of `flags%`.

Note:
Errors that occurred when adding items to a dialog in OPL16 did not cause dINIT to fail. In OPL32 if such errors occur, the dialog will be deleted a 'Structure fault' error is raised, and dINIT will have to be called again.

dINITS   WA

```
dINITS
dINITS title$
```

Prepare for the definition of a dialog using the small font, cancelling any existing one.

Use dTEXT, dCHOICE, etc. to define each item in the dialog, then DIALOG to display the dialog.

If `title$` is supplied, it will be displayed at the top of the dialog, centred and with a line across the dialog below it.

This command is specifically for the Work*about*, so that a dialog can have eight lines instead of six on the restricted screen, (see dINIT above). The top and bottom border will be significantly clipped with nine items, so dINITS dialogs should only use a maximum of eight items.

dPOSITION   S3, S3a/c, Siena, S5, WA

```
dPOSITION posx%,posy%
```

Position a dialog.

Use dPOSITION at any time between dINIT and DIALOG. The dPOSITION command uses two integer values. The first, `posx%`, specifies the horizontal position, and the second, `posy%`, the vertical position.

For example:

command	dialog screen position	OPL32 constants
dPOSITION -1,-1	top left	KDPositionLeft%,KDPositionLeft%
dPOSITION 1,1	bottom right	KDPositionRight%,KDPositionRight%
dPOSITION 0,0	central, the default position for dialogs.	KDPositionCentre%,KDPositionCentre%
dPOSITION 1,0	right-hand edge, and centred half way up the screen.	KDPositionRight%,KDPositionCentre%

dTEXT   S3, S3a/c, Siena, S5, WA

```
dTEXT prompt$,body$
dTEXT prompt$,body$,format%
```

Define a line of text to be displayed in a dialog.

The prompt, `prompt$`, will be displayed on the left side of the line, and `body$` on the right side. If you only want to display a single string, use a null string (`""`) for `prompt$`, and pass the desired string in `body$`. It will then have the whole width of the dialog to itself. An error is raised if `body$` is a null string. The text in `body$` is normally displayed left aligned (although usually in the right column). You can override this by specifying `format%`:

format%	effect	OPL32 constant
0	left align body$	KDTextLeft%
1	right align body$	KDTextRight%
2	centre body$	KDTextCentre%

Note that on the Series 5, alignment of `body$` is only supported when `prompt$` is null, with the body being left aligned otherwise. In addition, you can add any or all of the following three values to `format%`, for these effects:

format%	effect	OPL32 constant
$100	use bold text for body$, **not OPL32**	KDTextBold%
$200	draw a line below this item	KDTextLineBelow%
$400	allow prompt$ item to be selected	KDTextAllowSelection%
$800	specify this item as a text separator, **OPL32 only**	KDTextSeparator%

On the SIBO family, only one line can be drawn across a dialog using the flag $200. It will be below the last item that requests it, whether the title from `dINIT` or a `dTEXT` item. Setting `format%` = $400 allows only the prompt, and not the body, to be selected.

On the Series 5, bold dialog text is not supported. You can display a line separator between any dialog items by setting the flag $800 on an item where `p$` and `body$` are null. (If `p$` and/or `body$` are not null, then the flag is ignored and no separator is drawn.) The separator counts as an item in the value returned by DIALOG. OPL32 still supports

OPL16's underlining of dTEXT items by setting format% = $200. Setting format% = $400 allows the only the prompt, but not the body, to be selected.

See also dEDIT.

dEDIT S3, S3a/c, Siena, S5, WA

```
dEDIT var string$,prompt$
dEDIT var string$,prompt$,width%
```

Define a string edit box, to go in a dialog.

The prompt, prompt$, will be displayed on the left side of the line. The string variable to edit is string$. Its initial contents will appear in the dialog. The length used when string$ was defined is the maximum length you can type in. On exiting the dialog, the string$ variable will hold the value entered by the user.

The value width%, if supplied, gives the width (in pixels) of the edit box (allowing for widest possible character in the font). The string will scroll inside the edit box, if necessary. If width% is not supplied, the edit box is made wide enough for the maximum width string$ could possibly be.

See also dTEXT, dXINPUT.

dEDITMULTI S5

```
dEDITMULTI ptrdata&,prompt$,width%,lines%,maxlen%
```

Defines a multi-line edit box to go into a dialog. Normally the resulting text would be used in a subsequent dialog, saved to file or printed using the Printer OPX.

Ptrdata&	Holds the address of the buffer for the text.
prompt$	Displayed on the left side of the edit box.
width%	Specifies the width of the edit box within which the text is wrapped, using a notional average character width. The actual number of characters that will fit will depend on the character widths.
lines%	Specifies the number of full lines displayed. Any more lines will be scrolled.
maxlen%	The length in bytes of the buffer excluding the bytes used to store the length.

Note that the edit box uses any Enter key pressed when it has the focus, so Enter can't be used to exit the dialog. Another item is needed that can take the focus without using the Enter key. For example, a button that does not use the Enter key to exit a dialog whenever it contains a multi-line edit box. The Enter key is used by a multi-line edit box that has the focus before being offered to any buttons. However, the Esc key will always cancel a dialog, even when it contains a multi-line edit box.

ptrdata& is the address of a buffer to take the edited data. It could be the address of an array as returned by ADDR, or of a heap cell, as returned by ALLOC (see ADDR and ALLOC). The buffer may not be specified directly as a string, and may not be read as such; it should be peeked, byte by byte. It is convenient to use a long integer array as the buffer, with at least 1+(maxlen%+3)/4 elements. The leading 4 bytes at `ptrdata&` contains the initial number of bytes of data following. The first four bytes are set by `dEDITMULTI` to the actual number of bytes edited. Hence the first element of the array should specify the initial length.

If an allocated cell is used (probably because more than 64K is required), the first 4 bytes of the cell **must** be set to the initial length of the data. If this length is not set then an error will be raised. For example if a 100000 byte cell is allocated, you would need to poke a zero long integer in the start to specify that there is initially no text in the cell. For example:

```
ptrdata&=ALLOC(100000)
POKEL ptrdata&,0          REM Text starts at ptrdata& + 4
```

A number of special characters (defined in `CONST.OPH`) may appear in the buffer:

A paragraph delimiter marks the end of a paragraph. A line break is a new line that does not signify a new paragraph. Non-breaking characters guarantee that no line break will occur at the point they are inserted. A potential hyphen marks the place where a hyphen may be inserted if the word occurs on the break of a line. A visible space character is the character that is displayed when spaces are set to be visible. The following example presents a three-line edit box that is about 10 characters wide and allows up to 399 characters:

```
CONST KLenBuffer%=399
PROC dEditM:
  LOCAL buffer&(101)      REM 101=1+(399+3)/4 in integer
  arithmetic
  LOCAL pLen&,pText&
  LOCAL i%
  LOCAL c%
  pLen&=ADDR(buffer&(1))
  pText&=ADDR(buffer&(2))
  WHILE 1
    dINIT "Try dEditMulti"
    dEDITMULTI pLen&,"Prompt",10,3,KLenBuffer%
    dBUTTONS "Done",%d REM button needed to exit dialog
    IF DIALOG=0 :BREAK :ENDIF
    PRINT "Length:";buffer&(1)
    PRINT "Text:"
    i%=0
    WHILE i%<buffer&(1)
      c%=PEEKB(pText&+i%)
      IF c%>=32
        PRINT CHR$(c%);
      ELSE
        PRINT "."; REM just print a dot for special characters
      ENDIF
      i%=i%+1
    ENDWH
  ENDWH
ENDP
```

dXINPUT

`dXINPUT var string$,prompt$`

Define a secret string edit box, such as for a password, to go in a dialog. The prompt, `prompt$`, will be displayed on the left side of the line. The `string$` parameter is the string variable to take the string that the user types in.

Initially the dialog does not show any characters for the string; the initial contents of `string$` are ignored. A special symbol will be displayed for each character you type, to preserve the secrecy of the string.

Note:
`string$` must be at least eight characters long on SIBO systems and must be less than 16 characters long on the Series 5 (OPL32 identifier `KDXInputMaxLen%`).

dFILE, OPL16

`dFILE var file$,prompt$,flags%`

Define a filename edit box, to go in a dialog. A 'Disk' selector is automatically added on the line below. The `file$` variable must be declared to be at least 128 bytes long, or an error will be raised. The prompt, `prompt$`, will be displayed on the left side of the line.

The type of file editor is controlled by `flags%`, and the kind of input allowed. You can add together any of the following values:

flags%	meaning
1	use an edit box
2	allow directory names
4	directory names only
8	disallow existing files
16	query existing files
32	allow null string input
64	don't display extension
128	obey/allow wildcards

The first of the list is the most crucial. If you add 1 into `flags%`, you will see a file edit box, as when creating a new file. If you do not add 1, you will see the 'matching file' selector, used when choosing an existing file.

If performing a 'copy to' operation, you might use 1+2+16, to specify a file edit box for the target file, (in which you can type the name of a directory to copy to), and which will produce a query if you type the name of an existing file.

If asking for the name of a directory to remove, you might use 4, to allow an existing directory name only.

'Query existing' is ignored if 'disallow existing' is set. These two, as well as 'allow null string input', only work with file edit boxes, not 'matching file' selectors.

The string variable to edit is file$. Its initial contents always control the initial drive and directory used. For a file edit box, any filename part of file$ is shown. For a 'matching file' selector, you can use wildcards in the filename part (such as *.tmp) to control which filenames are matched. To do this, you must add 128 to flags%. Adding 128 also allows wildcard specifications to be entered (returned in file$), for both 'matching' and 'new file' selectors.

If file$ does not contain any drive or directory information, the path as set by SETPATH is used. If SETPATH has not been used, the \OPD directory on the default drive (usually *m:*, 'Internal') is used.

With a 'matching file' selector (as opposed to an edit box) the value 8 restricts the selection to files which match the filename/extension in file$. 'Matching file' selectors can also use 64, in which case files with the same extension as that in file$ are shown without this extension. (Many Series 3, Series 3a/c, Siena and Work*about* file selectors are like this.)

You can always press Tab to produce the full file selector with a dFILE item.

See also dEDIT.

dFILE, OPL32   S5

```
dFILE file$,prompt$,flags%
dFILE file$,prompt$,flags%,Uid1=0,Uid2=0,Uid3=0
```

Defines a filename edit box or selector, to go in a dialog. A 'Folder' and 'Disk' selector are automatically added on the following lines.

file$ must be declared to be 255 bytes long, since file names may be up to this length, and if it is shorter an error will be raised. The prompt, prompt$, will be displayed on the left side of the line. By default no prompts are displayed for the file, folder and disk selectors on the Series 5. A comma-separated prompt list should be supplied.

For example, for a filename editor with the standard prompts use:

```
dFILE file$,"File,Folder,Disk",1
```

The type of file editor is controlled by flags%, and the kind of input allowed. You can add (OR) together any of the following values:

flags%	meaning	OPL32 constant
1	use an edit box	KDFileEditBox%
2	allow folder names	KDFileAllowFolders%
4	folder names only	KDFileFoldersOnly%
8	disallow existing files	KDFileEditorDisallowExisting%
16	query existing files	KDFileEditorQueryExisting%
32	allow null string input	KDFileAllowNullStrings%
~~64~~	~~not S5 (don't display extension) file name extensions are not significant~~	
128	obey/allow wildcards	KDFileAllowWildCards%

| 256 | to allow ROM files to be selected | `KDFileSelectorWithRom%` |
| 512 | to allow files in the System folder to be selected | `KDFileSelectorWithSystem%` |

The first of the list is the most important. Adding 1 into `flags%` will present a file edit box, as when creating a new file. If you do not add 1, a 'matching file' selector is presented, i.e. for choosing an existing file.

If performing a 'copy to' operation, you might use 1+2+16, to specify a file edit box for the target file, (in which you can type the name of a folder to copy to), and which will produce a query if you type the name of an existing file. If asking for the name of a folder to remove, you might use 4, to allow an existing folder name only. 'Query existing' is ignored if 'disallow existing' is set. These two, as well as 'allow null string input', only work with file edit boxes, not 'matching file' selectors.

The string variable to edit is `file$`. Its initial contents always control the initial drive and folder used. For a file edit box, any filename part of `file$` is shown. For a 'matching file' selector, you can use wildcards in the filename part (such as `*.tmp`) to control which filenames are matched. To do this, you must add 128 to `flags%`. Adding 128 also allows wildcard specifications to be entered (returned in `file$`), for both 'matching' and 'new file' selectors. You can always press Tab to produce the full file selector with a `dFILE` item.

UIDs are used to identify files in the system for many purposes. The System screen uses Uid2 to distinguish between applications of various types and documents:

- Eikon applications
- Eikon applications' documents
- OPL applications
- OPL applications' documents

Uid3 is used by the System screen to identify particular applications.

For file selectors, dFILE supports file restriction by **UID**, or by **type** from the user's point of view. Documents are identified by three UIDs which identify which application created the document and what kind of file it is. Specifying all three UIDs will restrict the files as much as is possible, and specifying fewer will provide less restriction. You can supply 0 for `uid1&` and `uid2&` if you only want to restrict the list to `uid3&`. This may be useful when dealing with documents from one of your own applications: you can easily find out the third UID as it will be the UID you specified in the APP statement. **Note that UIDs are ignored for file name editors.**

Here are some OPL32-related UID constants:

OPL32 constant	**value**
`KuidOPLInterpreter&`	268435816
`KuidOPLApp&`	268435572
`KuidOPLDoc&`	268435573
`KuidOPO&`	268435571
`KuidOPLFile&`	268435594
`KuidOpxDll&`	268435549

For example, if the application is UID `KUidMyApp&`, then the following will list only application-specific documents:

```
dFILE file$,prompt$,flags%,0,KUidOplDoc&,KUidMyApp&
```

See also `dEDIT`.

dCHOICE   S3, S3a/c, Siena, S5, WA

```
dCHOICE var choice%,prompt$,list$
dCHOICE var choice%,prompt$,list$+",..." - in OPL32
```

Define a choice list to go in a dialog.

The prompt, `prompt$`, will be displayed on the left side of the line. The string `list$` should contain the possible choices, separated by commas, for example:

```
"Yes,No"
```

One of these will be displayed on the right side of the line, and the LEFT and RIGHT arrow keys can be used to move between the choices. The `choice%` parameter must be a LOCAL or a GLOBAL variable. It specifies which choice should initially be shown: 1 for the first choice, 2 for the second choice, and so on. When you finish using the dialog, `choice%` is given a value indicating which choice was selected - again, 1 for the first choice, and so on.

On the Series 5, `dCHOICE` supports an unrestricted number of items (up to memory limits). To extend a `dCHOICE` list, add a comma after the last item on the line followed by " . . . " (three full-stops), as shown in the usage above. `choice%` must be the same on all the lines, otherwise an error is raised.

For example, the following specifies items i1, i2, i3, i4, i5, i6:

```
dCHOICE ch%,prompt$,"i1,i2,..."
dCHOICE ch%,"","i3,i4,..."
dCHOICE ch%,"","i5,i6"
```

dFLOAT   S3, S3a/c, Siena, S5, WA

```
dFLOAT var float,prompt$,min,max
```

Define an edit box for a floating-point number, to go in a dialog.

The prompt, `prompt$`, will be displayed on the left side of the line. The `min` and `max` parameters give the minimum and maximum values that are to be allowed. An error is raised if `min` is higher than `max`. The floating-point variable `float` must be a LOCAL or a GLOBAL variable. It specifies the value to be shown initially. When you finish using the dialog, the value you entered is returned in `float`.

dLONG S3, S3a/c, Siena, S5, WA

```
dLONG var long&,prompt$,min&,max&
```

Defines an edit box for a long integer, to go in a dialog.

The prompt `prompt$` will be displayed on the left side of the line.

The `min&` and `max&` parameters give the minimum and maximum values which are to be allowed. An error is raised if `min&` is higher than `max&`.

The variable `long&` must be a LOCAL or a GLOBAL variable. It specifies the value to be shown initially. When the user finishes using the dialog, the value they entered is returned in `long&`.

dDATE S3, S3a/c, Siena, S5, WA

```
dDATE var disdays&,prompt$,mindays&,maxdays&
```

Define an edit box for a date, to go in a dialog.

The prompt, `prompt$`, will be displayed on the left side of the line. The LOCAL or a GLOBAL variable, `disdays&`, specifies the date to be shown initially. Although it will appear on the screen like a normal date, for example "15/03/92", `disdays&` must be specified as "days since 1/1/1900". The `mindays&` and `maxdays&` parameters specify the minimum and maximum values which are to be allowed. Again, these are in days since 1/1/1900. An error is raised if `mindays&` is higher than `maxdays&`. When the user has finished using the dialog, the date entered is returned in `disdays&`, in days since 1/1/1900. The system setting determines whether years, months or days are displayed first.

Note:
The day number of 1 January 1970 is 25567. This is required when converting from a dialog date to a system date/time, e.g.:

```
system_time = (dialog_date-
25567)*86400+(seconds_from_start_of_day)
```

If you're collecting a date/time from a dialog, it's a good idea to set the minimum input date to this (25567) figure. In OPL32 use DAYSTODATE which converts a number of days since 1/1/1900, to the corresponding date.

See also DAYS, SECSTODATE, DATETOSECS, DAYSTODATE.

dTIME S3, S3a/c, Siena, S5, WA

```
dTIME var disecs&,prompt$,type%,minsecs&,maxsecs&
```

Define an edit box for a time, to go in a dialog.

The prompt, (`prompt$`), will be displayed on the left side of the line.

The `disecs&` parameter, which must be a LOCAL or a GLOBAL variable, specifies the time to be shown initially. Although it will appear on the screen like a normal time, for example 18:27, the value of `disecs&` must be specified as seconds after 00:00. A value of 60 means one minute past midnight; 3600 means one o'clock, and so on.

The `minsecs&` and `maxsecs&` parameters give the minimum and maximum values which are to be allowed. Again, these are in seconds after 00:00. An error is raised if `minsecs&` is higher than `maxsecs&`.

When the user has finished using the dialog, the time that they entered is returned in `disecs&`, in seconds after 00:00.

The `type%` parameter specifies the type of display required, as follows:

type%	time display	OPL32 constant
0	absolute time, no seconds	KDTimeAbsNoSecs%
1	absolute time with seconds	KDTimeWithSeconds%
2	duration, no seconds	KDTimeDuration%
3	duration with seconds	KDTimeDurationWithSecs%
4	**S5 only** - time displayed without hours	KDTimeNoHours%
8	**S5 only** - time displayed in 24 hour format	KDTime24Hour%

For example, 03:45 represents an absolute time while 3 hours 45 minutes represents a duration. Absolute times always display am or pm as appropriate, unless 24 hour clock is specified. Duration's never display am or pm. Note, however, that if you use the `type%` KDTimeNoHours% then the am/pm symbol will be displayed and the `type%` KDTimeDuration% must be ORed in if you wish to hide it.

See also dDATE.

dBUTTONS   S3, S3a/c, Siena, S5, WA

```
dBUTTONS prompt1$,keycode1%
dBUTTONS prompt1$,keycode1%,prompt2$,keycode2%
dBUTTONS prompt1$,keycode1%,prompt2$,keycode2%,prompt3$,keycode3%
```

Define exit keys to go at the bottom of a dialog.

One, two or three exit keys may be defined. Each pair of `prompt$` and `keycode%` specifies an exit key; `prompt$` being the text to be displayed above it, while `keycode%` is the key code of the key.

OPL32 allows more than 3 buttons; they are added in the same way, using more prompt / key code pairs.

The DIALOG function returns the key code of the key pressed (in lower case for letters).

For alphabetic keys, use the % sign: %A means the code of "A"', and so on. The shortcut key is then Ctrl+alphabetic key on the Series 5. If you use the code for keys such as Tab or Enter, its name (e.g. 'Tab', or 'Enter') will be shown in the picture of the key.

In OPL32, the following effects may be obtained by adding the appropriate constants to the shortcut key key-code:

constant	effect	OPL32 identifier
256	display a button with no shortcut key label underneath it	KDButtonNoLabel%
512	use the key alone (without the Ctrl modification) as the shortcut key	KDButtonPlainKey%

If you use a negative value for a keycode% argument, that key is a 'Cancel' key. The corresponding positive value is used for the key to display and the value for DIALOG to return, but if you do press this key to exit, the var variables used in commands like dEDIT, dTIME, etc. will not be set. For OPL32, when using a negative shortcut to specify the cancel button, you must negate the shortcut together with any added flags.

The Esc key will always cancel a dialog box, with DIALOG returning 0. If you want to show the Esc key as one of the exit keys, use -27 as the keycode% argument (its key code is 27) so that the var variables will not be set if Esc is pressed.

In OPL16 there can be only one dBUTTONS item per dialog, and it takes up three lines on the screen. The dBUTTONS item must be the last dialog command you use before DIALOG itself.

In OPL32 the buttons take up two lines on the screen. The dBUTTONS item may be used anywhere between dINIT and DIALOG; where it is used will not affect the position of the buttons in the dialog.

Some key presses, such as those using the Control key on SIBO, cannot be specified.

This example presents a simple query, returning TRUE for Yes, or FALSE for No.

```
PROC query:
    dINIT
    dTEXT "","FORGET CHANGES",2
    dTEXT "","Sure?",$202
    dBUTTONS "No",%N,"Yes",%Y
    RETURN DIALOG=%y
ENDP
```

See also ALERT.

dCHECKBOX   S5

dCHECKBOX chk%,prompt$

Creates a dialog checkbox entry with two states i.e. the tick is either on or off. The state of the checkbox is maintained across calls to the dialog. Initially you should set the live variable chk% to 0 to set the tick symbol off and to any other value to set it on. chk% is then automatically set to 0 if the box is unchecked or -1 if it is checked when the dialog is closed.

See also dINIT.

DIALOG S3, S3a/c, Siena, S5, WA

`n% = DIALOG`

Present the dialog prepared by `dINIT` and commands such as `dTEXT` and `dCHOICE`.

If the user completes the dialog by pressing Enter, the settings are stored in the variables specified in `dTEXT`, `dCHOICE`, etc., although the developer can prevent this with `dBUTTONS`.

If `dBUTTONS` was used when preparing the dialog, the key code that ended the dialog is returned. Otherwise, `DIALOG` returns the line number of the item that was current when Enter was pressed. The top item (or the title line, if present), has line number 1.

If the user cancels the dialog by pressing Esc, the variables are not changed, and 0 is returned (OPL32 constant `KDlgCancel%`).

ALERT S3, S3a/c, Siena, S5, WA

```
ret% = ALERT(msg1$)
ret% = ALERT(msg1$,msg2$)
ret% = ALERT(msg1$,msg2$,caption1$)
ret% = ALERT(msg1$,msg2$,caption1$,caption2$)
ret% = ALERT(msg1$,msg2$,caption1$,caption2$,caption3$)
```

Present an alert, (a simple dialog), with the messages and key captions specified, and wait for a response. The message to be displayed on the first line is `msg1%`. The message to be displayed on the second line is `msg2%`. If this is not supplied or is a null string then the second message line is left blank. Up to three keys may be used out of Esc, Enter and Space:

- Esc only
- Esc and Enter
- Esc, Enter and Space

The strings to be displayed on screen over the key legends are:

`caption1$`	Esc
`caption2$`	Enter
`caption3$`	Space

If no key captions are supplied then the word CONTINUE is used above an Esc key legend. The key return values are:

key press	return value	OPL32 identifier
Esc	1	KAlertEsc%
Enter	2	KAlertEnter%
Space	3	KAlertSpace%

See also BUSY, dBUTTONS and GIPRINT.

Screen messages

BUSY   Display busy message in a screen corner

GIPRINT   Display general information text for ~2 seconds in a screen corner

BUSY   S3, S3a/c, Siena, S5, WA

```
BUSY message$
BUSY message$,c%
BUSY message$,c%,delay%
BUSY OFF
```

Display or cancel a 'Busy' message in a corner of the screen.

This is used to indicate to the user periods when an OPL program is going to be temporarily unresponsive to key presses. To display a message in the bottom left of the screen use BUSY message$. To cancel the message use BUSY OFF.

The string to display, message$, may be up to 19 characters long, 80 in OPL32 (KBusyMaxText% = 80). Only one message can be displayed at a time.

If c% is given, it controls the corner in which the message appears:

c%	corner	OPL32 constant
0	top left	KBusyTopLeft%
1	bottom left	KbusyBottomLeft%
2	top right	KBusyTopRight%
3	bottom right (default)	KBusyBottomRight%

A delay time (in half seconds) before the message is displayed, can be specified using delay%. This may be used to prevent 'Busy' messages from continually appearing very briefly on the screen.

See also GIPRINT.

GIPRINT   S3, S3a/c, Siena, S5, WA, HC

```
GIPRINT string$
GIPRINT string$,c%
```

Display an general information message (string$) for about two seconds, in the bottom right (or other specified) corner of the screen. For example:

```
GIPRINT "Not found"
```
displays:
```
Not found
```

The string specified (string$) can be up to 64 characters. If a string is too long for the screen, it will be clipped. Only one message can be shown at a time. The message can be cleared - for example, when a key is pressed - with GIPRINT "". GIPRINT is not affected by the text mode set using gTMODE.

If c% is given, it controls the corner in which the message appears:

c%	corner	OPL32 constant
0	top left	KbusyTopLeft%
1	bottom left	KbusyBottomLeft%
2	top right	KbusyTopRight%
3	bottom right (default)	KbusyBottomRight%

See also BUSY, ALERT.

OPL applications (OPAs)

APP, OPL16	Start an OPA definition; code that follows defines an OPA
APP, OPL32	Start an OPA definition; code that follows defines an OPA
CAPTION	Define the name of an application for specific languages OPL32
TYPE	Define OPA type OPL16 only
FLAGS	Define a file or non file based application, OPL32 only
PATH	Define directory for files created/used by an OPA OPL16 only
EXT	Define filename extension for files created/used by an OPA OPL16 only
ICON	Define name of bitmap file containing the icon for an OPA
ENDA	End an OPA definition; code that precedes defines an OPA
CMD$	Get command-line information, usually on start up
GETCMD$	Return new command line arguments to a running OPA
SETNAME	Set a program's name and update system screen file list, OPL16 only
SETDOC	Set a file as a document and update system screen task list, OPL32 only
GETDOC$	Returns the name of the current application document, OPL32 only
LOCK	Lock/unlock an OPA

APP, OPL16   S3, S3a/c, Siena, WA

APP name

Begins the definition of an OPL16 application or OPA.

The public name of the OPA, as used by the system screen, is given by name. This is **not** the file name. Note also that it does not have surrounding quote marks.

The APP command must be used in conjunction with ENDA:

```
APP name
...
ENDA
```

The APP line may be followed by any or all of the keywords PATH, EXT, ICON and TYPE

See also the entry for the CMD$ function, for the use of CMD$(5) to return an OPA's public name.

APP, OPL32 S5

```
APP pname,uid&
```

Begins the definition of an OPL32 application (OPA).

The public name of the OPA, as used by the system screen, is given by pname. Note that the pname string does **not** have surrounding quote marks and may be up to 250 characters. The name supplied in pname is the applications' name in its default language – see the OPL32 keyword CAPTION for other languages.

The APP command must be used in conjunction with ENDA for example:

```
APP pname,uid&
...
ENDA
```

uid& is the application's unique identifier or UID. For distributed applications, official reserved UIDs must be used. These can be obtained by contacting Psion Software PLC – see the 'Series 5' chapter for details.

The APP line may be followed by the keywords ICON and FLAGS. The arguments to any of the keywords between APP and ENDA must be constants and not expressions. All information included in the APP…ENDA structure will be used to generate an AIF file that specifies the applications caption (possibly in various languages), its icons for use on the System screen and its setting of FLAGS.

See CAPTION, ICON, FLAGS.

CAPTION S5

```
CAPTION pname$,language%
```

Specifies an OPA's public name (or caption) for a particular language, which will appear below its icon on the Extras bar and in the list of 'Programs' in the 'New File' dialog (assuming the setting of FLAGS allows these) when the language is that used by the machine. CAPTION statements may only be used inside an APP...ENDA construct.

The language code specifies the language variant of each pname$, so that the application name need not be changed when used on a different language machine. If used, CAPTION causes the default name given in the APP declaration to be discarded. Therefore CAPTION statements must be supplied for **every** language variant, including the language of the machine on which the application is originally developed. The maximum length of pname$ is 255 characters. However, a name longer than about 8 characters will not fit neatly below the application's icon on the Extras bar.

See APP.

TYPE

TYPE opatype%

Set the type of an OPA – **OPL16 only**.

The type can be from 0 to 4, and this is defined by the value of opatype%. The opatype% parameter must be a constant, as the translator cannot evaluate variables or expressions.

On the Series 3a/c, Siena or Work*about* opatype% should be set to a value from $1000 to $1004, to set the type to 0 to 4 respectively. The $1000 allows a 48x48 black and grey icon to be used. OPA types are discussed in the 'Processes, Memory and Applications' chapter.

This can only be used between APP and ENDA.

OPL32 / Series 5 users – see Flags.

FLAGS

FLAGS flags%

Replaces TYPE used on SIBO systems. Constants for these flags are supplied in CONST.OPH; possible values for flags% are:

flags% = 1 for applications that can create files. Your application will then be included in the list of applications offered when the user creates a new file from the System screen.

flags% = 2 to prevent the application from appearing in the Extras bar. It is not usual to set flags% to this value.

This can only be used between APP and ENDA on Series 5.

PATH

PATH dir$

Give the directory for the System Screen to use when listing files used by an OPA – OPL16 only.

If you do not use this, the normal \OPD directory will be used. The maximum length, including a final \, is 19 characters. Don't include a node name or drive name in this path. This command can only be used between APP and ENDA.

EXT

EXT name$

Define the file extension of files to be used by an OPA – OPL16 only.

This can only be used between APP and ENDA when defining an OPA. If you do not specify this, .ODB is used. Note that the files used by an OPA do not have to be data files, as the I/O commands give access to files of all kinds.

ICON   S3, S3a/c, Siena, S5, WA, HC

ICON name$

Give the name of the bitmap file to use as the icon for an OPA.

This can only be used between APP and ENDA. For SIBO systems see the 'OPL16 Techniques' chapter for more details.

On the Series 5, name$ is a multi-bitmap file (.MBM) that contains up to three bitmap/mask pairs – see the 'OPL32 Techniques' chapter for more details.

ENDA   S3, S3a/c, Siena, S5, WA, HC

ENDA

End of an OPA clause – see APP above.

CMD$ S3, S3a/c, Siena, S5, WA, HC

command$ = CMD$(x%)

Return the command-line arguments passed when starting a program.

Null strings may be returned. The x% parameter should be from 1 to 3, plus 4 and 5 on SIBO systems. The arguments CMD$(2) and CMD$(5) are only for OPAs (OPL applications).

The argument returned by CMD$(1), is the full path name used to start the running program. This will usually be the full path name of the image file used to run the OPL process - rom::exop1.img. The second argument, returned by CMD$(2), is the full path name of the file to be used by an OPA.

The third argument, returned by CMD$(3), may be 'C' for "Create file" or 'O' for "Open file". If the OPA is being run with a new filename, this will be 'C'. This happens when the OPA is run for the first time and whenever a new filename is used to run it. Otherwise the OPA is being run with the name of an existing file, and CMD$(3) will return 'O'.

On Series 5 'R' is returned if the application has been run from the Program editor or has been selected via the 'Extras bar', and not by the selection or creation of one the applications' documents from the system screen. If the CMD$(3)='R', a default filename, including path, is passed in CMD$(2).

On SIBO the fourth argument, returned by CMD$(4), is the alias information, if any. In practice this has no relevance to OPAs. The fifth argument (SIBO only), returned by CMD$(5), is the application name, as declared with the APP keyword.

See also the GETCMD$ function.

GETCMD$ S3, S3a/c, Siena, S5, WA

`arg$ = GETCMD$`

Returns new command-line arguments to a running OPA, after a "change files" or "shut down" event have occurred.

The first character has the following meaning:

`"C"`	close down the current file, and create the specified new file.
`"O"`	close down the current file, and open the specified existing file.
`"X"`	close down the current file (if any) and quit the OPA.
`"U"`	Letter unknown – Series 5 only.

If it is `"C"` or `"O"`, the rest of the string is a filename. You can only call GETCMD$ once for each system message.

See also CMD$, GETEVENT, TESTEVENT.

SETNAME   S3, S3a/c, Siena, WA

`SETNAME opaname$`

Set the name of the running OPA to `opaname$` and redraw any status window, using that name below the icon. Used to update the system screen file lists with the current file in use by the application.

For OPL32 see SETDOC.

See also CMD$, GETCMD$, GETEVENT.

SETDOC   S5

`SETDOC file$`

Sets the file `file$` to be a document. This command should be called immediately before the creation of `file$` if it is to be recognised as a document. SETDOC may be used with the commands CREATE, gSAVEBIT and IOOPEN.

The string passed to SETDOC must be identical to the name passed to the following CREATE or gSAVEBIT otherwise a non-document file will be created - see note below.

Example of document creation:

```
SETDOC "myfile"
CREATE "myfile",a,a$,b$
```

SETDOC should also be called after successfully opening a document to allow the System screen to display the correct document name in its task list.

In case of failure in creating or opening the required file, you should take the following action:

- Creating - try to re-open the last file and if this fails display an appropriate error dialog and exit. On reopening, call SETDOC back to the original file so the Task list is correct.
- Opening - as for creating, but calling SETDOC again is not strictly required.

Database documents, created using CREATE, and multi-bitmap documents, created using gSAVEBIT, will automatically contain your application UID in the file header. For binary and text file documents created using IOOPEN and LOPEN, it is the programmer's responsibility to save the appropriate header in the file. See the 'OPL32 Techniques' chapter for details.

Note:
To ensure the application's UID is incorporated into the document header, you are **strongly** advised to use the PARSE$ function on the file name before using it with the SETDOC and subsequent CREATE commands.

GETDOC$ S5

doc$=GETDOC$

Returns the name of the current application document.

See also SETDOC.

LOCK   S3, S3a/c, Siena, S5, WA

LOCK ON
LOCK OFF

Mark an OPA or OPO program as locked or unlocked.

When an OPA is locked with LOCK ON, the System screen will not send it events to change files or shut down. For example on a S3, if you move to the file list in the System screen and press Delete to try to stop that running OPA, a message appears, indicating that the OPA cannot close down. On a S5, if you move to the task list or the document name in the system screen try to stop the OPA by using the 'Close file' button or Ctrl+E respectively, a message appears indicating that the program is busy.

You should use LOCK ON if your OPA uses a command that waits for a user response - e.g. EDIT, DIALOG, GET, or ALERT. When one of these commands is waiting, the OPA can't respond to System Screen messages, so use LOCK ON to make sure you don't get any. You might also use it when the OPA is about to go busy for a considerable length of time, or at any other point where a clean exit is not possible. Use LOCK OFF as soon as possible afterwards.

Don't use LOCK ON before a call to GETEVENT.

'Foreground', 'Background' and 'Machine on' events may still occur while the OPA is accessing the keyboard, and will be discarded.

An OPA or OPO program is initially unlocked.

Event handling

TESTEVENT	Test whether an event has occurred
GETEVENT	Wait until an event occurs and return event information
GETEVENT32	Wait until an event occurs and return event information – OPL32 only
GETEVENTA32	Asynchronous version of GETEVENT32 – OPL32 only
GETEVENTC	Cancel previous call to GETEVENTA32 – OPL32 only
POINTERFILTER	Selectively filters pointer type events

Important note:
When programming in OPL32 you should always use GETEVENT32 rather than using GETEVENT. All events are sensed by GETEVENT, but it cannot supply the pointer event information and is supported on Series 5 only for backward compatibility.

Date change events are not detected by the Series 5.

TESTEVENT   S3, S3a/c, Siena, S5, WA, HC

```
t% = TESTEVENT
```

Test whether an event has occurred. Returns -1 (true) if an event has occurred, otherwise returns 0 (false).

Note:
Use TESTEVENT with caution; for example, placing it inside loops can prevent a machine from switching off, and may lead to very high power consumption. Events are detected but **not** read by TESTEVENT - use functions such as GETEVENT or GETEVENT32 to read them.

GETEVENT   S3, S3a/c, Siena, S5, WA, HC

```
GETEVENT var ev%()
```

Waits for an event to occur. Returns with ev%() specifying the event.

The array ev%() (or string of integers) must be at least 6 integers long. Although only two elements of ev%() are currently used, the other four are reserved for future expansion.

The GETEVENT command passes control to the operating system, which waits for an event to occur. When it gets one, it puts the details into ev%() and returns control to the application. The data returned in ev%() depends on the type of event that occurred.

There are two classes of events: keypress events and system events. On a keypress event, ev%(1) contains the key code. Modifier keys and auto-repeat count are returned in ev%(2). On a system event (foreground, background, switch-on, change files, exit, or date change), ev%(1) contains a code specifying the event.

If the event is a keypress, the expression:

```
(ev%(1) AND $400)
```

is guaranteed to be zero. For any other events this expression is guaranteed to be non-zero.

If a key has been pressed, the values in `ev%()` are:

`ev%(1)`	key code (as for GET)
`ev%(2) AND $00ff`	modifier (as for KMOD)
`ev%(2)/256`	auto-repeat count (ignored by GET)

You can't use KMOD after GETEVENT to find out what the keypress modifiers were, because GETEVENT returns the modifier in the array passed to it and doesn't store the value for later retrieval using KMOD.

The table below gives the actual value of array item `ev%(1)` after a system event.

event description	value in ev%(1)
Application has moved to foreground	$401
Application has moved to background	$402
The Psion has switched on	$403
If a Series 3, 3a/c, Siena or Work*about* wants an OPA to change files or exit (use GETCMD$ to determine which)	$404
Date has changed, Series 3a/c, Siena or Work*about*, **not** Series 5	$405

Future versions of OPL may add other event numbers, so you should **not** raise an error if the event number is not one of the currently known ones, but should ignore that unknown type of event.

Note:

If a non-key event such as 'foreground' occurs while a keyboard keyword such as GET, GET$, EDIT, INPUT, MENU or DIALOG is being used, the event is discarded. So GETEVENT must be used exclusively if both key and non-key events need to be monitored. If you need to use the above keywords in OPAs, use LOCK ON / LOCK OFF around them. See the LOCK command for more details.

See also TESTEVENT, GETEVENT32, GETCMD$.

GETEVENT32   S5

`GETEVENT32 var ev&()`

Waits for and returns all event types, including pointer (pen) events.

Returns with `ev&()` specifying the event, `ev&()` must have at least 16 elements. All events return a 32-bit time-stamp. GETEVENT32 returns more information than GETEVENT, as listed below:

If a key has been pressed: `(ev&(1) AND &400)=0`

`ev&(1)`	key code
`ev&(2)`	time stamp
`ev&(3)`	scan code
`ev&(4)`	modifier e.g. Shift, see below
`ev&(5)`	repeat

Unlike the key repeat for GETEVENT, the repeat for GETEVENT32 is strictly that, i.e. if there is only one keypress, then the repeat value in ev&(5) = 0.

For all the other event types, ev&(1) is greater than &400:

event description	ev&(1)	ev&(2)
Application to foreground	$401	time stamp
Application to background	$402	time stamp
Psion has switched on	$403	time stamp
Application to change files or exit	$404	time stamp
~~Date changed — not available in Series 5~~	~~$405~~	

By default the machine switch on event is **not** enabled, the appropriate flag should be set to enable it - see SETFLAGS. If the change files / exit event is received, GETCMD$ should be called to find out what action should be taken.

If a key is pressed down: ev&(1)=&406
    ev&(2)   time stamp
    ev&(3)   scan code
    ev&(4)   modifiers e.g. Shift, see below

If a key is released: ev&(1)=&407
    ev&(2)   time stamp
    ev&(3)   scan code
    ev&(4)   modifiers e.g. Shift, see below

If a pen event occurs: ev&(1)=&408
    ev&(2)   time-stamp
    ev&(3)   window ID, as returned by the gCREATE keyword.
    ev&(4)   pointer type, 0 = pen down, 1 = pen up, 6 = pen drag
    ev&(5)   modifiers e.g. Shift, see below
    ev&(6)   x-co-ordinate
    ev&(7)   y-co-ordinate
    ev&(8)   x-co-ordinate relative to parent window
    ev&(9)   y-co-ordinate relative to parent window

If a pen enters contact with the screen: ev&(1)=&409
    ev&(2)   time stamp
    ev&(3)   window ID

If a pen exits contact with the screen: ev&(1)=&40A
    ev&(2)   time stamp
    ev&(3)   window ID

Modifiers, in ev&(4) for key presses and in ev&(5) for pointer (pen) events, have values as follows:

modifier	value	OPL32 constant
Shift	2	KkmodShift%
Control	4	KKmodControl%
Caps	16	KKmodCaps%
Fn	32	KKmodFn%

Each even type has an OPL32 constant that may be used to make your code more readable, their names are as follows.

```
OPL32 event type constant          value
KEvNotKeyMask&                     &400
KEvFocusGained&                    &401
KEvFocusLost&                      &402
KEvSwitchOn&                       &403
KEvCommand&                        &404
KEvDateChanged&                    &405
KEvKeyDown&                        &406
KEvKeyUp&                          &407
KEvPtr&                            &408
KEvPtrEnter&                       &409
KEvPtrExit&                        &40A
```

Notes:

Some events; such as pointer events, pointer enters and pointer exits, can be filtered out to avoid being swamped by unwanted event types. See POINTERFILTER.

For other unknown events, ev&(1) contains &1400 added to the code returned by the window server. ev&(2) is the timestamp and ev&(3) is the window ID, and the rest of the data returned by the window server is put into ev&(4), ev&(5), etc.

If a non-key event such as 'foreground' occurs while an entry keyword such as GET, GET$, EDIT, INPUT, MENU or DIALOG is being used, the event is discarded. So GETEVENT32 must be used exclusively if both key and non-key events need to be monitored. If you need to use the above keywords in OPAs, use LOCK ON/OFF around them so that the System screen won't send messages to switch files or shutdown while the application cannot respond. See the LOCK command for more details.

See also GETEVENT, GETEVENTA32, GETCMD$.

GETEVENTA32   S5

GETEVENTA32 var status%,var ev&()

Asynchronous version of GETEVENT32, returns the same information to the array ev&() as GETEVENT32. See GETEVENTC, GETEVENT32, GETEVENT. See also the 'I/O System' chapter for details of asynchronous I/O functions.

GETEVENTC   S5

GETEVENTC(var stat%)

Cancels a previous call to the GETEVENTA32 function, with status stat%. Note that GETEVENTC consumes the signal (unlike IOCANCEL), so IOWAITSTAT should not be used after GETEVENTC.

POINTERFILTER

`POINTERFILTER filter%,mask%`

Allow filtering of pointer events in the current window.

Some events; such as pointer events, pointer screen enter and pointer screen exit, can be filtered in or out to avoid being swamped by unwanted event types. By default pointer events are not filtered out. Add the following values together to achieve the desired `filter%` and `mask%`:

pointer event	value
none	0
enter/exit	1
drag	4

The bits set in `filter%` specify the settings to be used, 1 to filter out the event and 0 to remove the filter. Only those bits set in `mask%` will be used for filtering. This allows the current setting of a particular bit to be left unchanged if that bit is zero in the mask. (i.e. `mask%` dictates what to change and `filter%` specifies the setting to which it should be changed). For example,

```
mask%=5 REM =1+4 - allows enter/exit and drag settings to be changed
POINTERFILTER 1,mask% REM filters out enter/exit, but not dragging
...
POINTERFILTER 4,mask% REM filters out drag and reinstates enter/exit
```

See also GETEVENT32, GETEVENTA32.

Status windows

STATUSWIN	Display / hide status window
STATWININFO	Get status window information
SETNAME	Set a program's name and update system screen file list, OPL16
DIAMINIT	Initialise a 'diamond' list and redraw the status window
DIAMPOS	Position 'diamond' symbol on a 'diamond' list

Note:
The OPL16 status window keywords are no longer supported in OPL32, status windows have been replaced by toolbars via a toolbar .OPO support module in ROM – see the 'OPL32 Techniques' chapter for details. Diamond lists are not supported under OPL32.

STATUSWIN   S3, S3a/c, Siena, WA

```
STATUSWIN ON
STATUSWIN ON,swtype%
STATUSWIN OFF
```

Display or remove a 'permanent' Status window.

If `swtype%=1` the small Status window is shown. If `swtype%=2` the large Status window is shown. The `STATUSWIN ON` instruction on its own displays an appropriate Status window; on the Series 3a/c models and Work*about* this will always be the large Status window. The `type%` argument cannot be used on machines below the Series 3a. Only one type of Status window is available on the Siena. The `STATUSWIN OFF` command removes the Status window.

The permanent status window is behind all other OPL windows. In order to see it, you must use FONT, or both SCREEN and gSETWIN, to reduce the size of the text and graphics windows. When creating windows in your program, make sure you don't accidentally obscure any Status window present.

Note:
The standard key combination for invoking a permanent Status window is Ctrl-Menu. This cycles through the available types (e.g. large, small, none on the Series 3a/c). A temporary Status window is displayed for a few seconds by pressing Psion-Menu.

See also STATWININFO.

STATWININFO   S3a/c, Siena, WA

`t% = STATWININFO(type%, var xy%())`

Gets information about the Status window.

Sets `xy%(1)`, `xy%(2)`, `xy%(3)` and `xy%(4)` to the top left x, top left y, width and height respectively of the specified type of status window. There are the following four possible values of `type%` for the status window:

type%	description
1	the Series 3a style small status window
2	the Series 3a style large status window
3	the Series 3 compatibility mode status window
-1	whichever type of status window is current

The STATWININFO function returns `t%`, the type of the current status window (with values as for `type%`, or zero if there is no current status window). If `type%=-1` is used to get information about the current status window and there is none enabled, STATWININFO returns consistent information in `xy%()` corresponding to a status window of width zero and full screen height positioned one pixel to the right of the physical screen.

See also STATUSWIN.

SETNAME   S3, S3a/c, Siena, WA

`SETNAME opaname$`

Set the name of the running OPA to `opaname$` and redraw any status window, using that name below the icon. Used to update the system screen file lists with the current file in use by the application. See SETDOC for OPL32.

See also CMD$, GETCMD$, GETEVENT.

DIAMINIT   S3a/c, Siena

DIAMINIT pos%,string1$,string2$...

Initialises the Diamond list (discarding any existing list).

The strings string1$, string2$, etc. contain the text to be displayed in the status window for each item in the list. The pos% parameter specifies the initial item against which the *Diamond indicator* (♦) should be positioned, with pos%=1 specifying the first item. (Any value greater than the number of strings specifies the final item.) If pos%>=1 you must supply at least this many strings. If pos% is not supplied or if pos%=0, or if DIAMINIT is used on its own with no arguments, no bar is defined.

If pos%=-1 the list is replaced by the icon instead in the large status window.

See also DIAMPOS.

DIAMPOS   S3a/c, Siena

DIAMPOS pos%

Positions the *Diamond indicator* (♦) on the *Diamond list*.

Positioning outside the range of the items wraps around in the appropriate way. The parameter value pos%=0 causes the Diamond symbol to disappear.

See also DIAMINIT.

I/O operations on files and devices

IOOPEN	Open any type of file or device
IOREAD	Read from a file or device opened with IOOPEN
IOWRITE	Write to a file or device opened with IOOPEN
IOCLOSE	Close a file opened with IOOPEN
IOSEEK	Position within a file opened with IOOPEN
IOA	Perform an asynchronous I/O operation
IOC	Perform an asynchronous I/O operation with guaranteed completion
IOCANCEL	Cancel an asynchronous I/O function
IOYIELD	Allow I/O wait handlers to complete requests and update status words
IOWAIT	Wait for completion of any asynchronous operation by IOA or IOC
IOWAITSTAT	Wait for completion of a specific asynchronous operation by IOA or IOC
IOWAITSTAT32	Wait for completion of a specific asynchronous operation by IOA or IOC OPL32 only
IOSIGNAL	Signal completion of an I/O operation
IOW	Perform a synchronous I/O operation
KEYA	Perform an asynchronous keyboard read
KEYC	Cancel a KEYA

Notes:
The concepts behind the use of the I/O functions and commands are covered in the 'I/O System' chapter and the 'Files in EPOC16' chapter.

In OPL32, the I/O keywords provide the same access to files as in OPL16, but only the SIBO device drivers "TIM:", "TTY:A", "CON:" and "FIL:" are emulated. A handle of -1 for the LOPENed device or -2 for "CON:" can be used as in OPL16.

In OPL32 IOYIELD must always be called before polling status words, i.e. before reading a 16-bit status word, if IOWAIT or IOWAITSTAT have not been used first. This is because OPL32 needs to set the 16-bit status word based on the value of the actual EPOC32 32-bit status word.

IOOPEN   S3, S3a/c, Siena, S5, WA, HC

```
r% = IOOPEN(var h%,name$,mode%)
```

Create or open a file, or open an I/O device driver called name$.

Returns the handle of the file or device in h%, for use by subsequent I/O function calls. mode% specifies how to open the file.

For creation of a file with a unique name, use IOOPEN(var h%,address%,mode%) where address% is the **address** of a string, specifying **only** the path of the file to be created. The string must be at least 130 characters long, to take the unique full file name specification. Typically used to create a temporary file that will later be renamed or deleted.

The mode in which the file is to be opened is specified by mode%, formed by ORing together values which fall into the three following categories: Open mode, file format and access flags.

Open mode – select one value only

$0000   Open an existing file (or device). The initial current position is set to the start of the file.

$0001   Create a file (which must not already exist).

$0002   Replace a file (truncate it to zero length) or create it if it does not exist.

$0003   Open an existing file for appending. The initial current position is set to the end of the file. For text format files (see $0020 below) this is the only way to position to end of file.

$0004   Creates a file with a unique name. For this case, you must use addr%, the address of a string at least 130 characters long, (the maximum file specification), instead of name$. This string specifies only the path of the file to be created (any filename in the string is ignored). IOOPEN then sets the string to the unique filename generated (including the full path).

File format – select one value only

$0000   Binary. Up to 16K can be read from or written to the file in a single operation.

$0020   Text. Lines are terminated by any combination of the CR and LF ($0D, $0A) characters. The maximum record length is 256 bytes and Ctrl-Z ($1A) marks the end of the file.

Access flags – select any combination of one values

$0100   Update flag - Allows the file to be written to as well as read. If not set, the file is opened for reading only. You **must** use this flag when creating or replacing a file.

$0200   Random access flag – the file is opened for random access (not sequential access), using the IOSEEK function.

$0400   Share flag - the file can still be opened by any process. If not specified, the file is locked and cannot be opened again by any process until either the owning process exits, or the file is closed with IOCLOSE. If the file is opened for writing ($0100 above), this flag is ignored, since sharing is then not feasible.

See also IOCLOSE.

Problems with IOOPEN (S3, HC)

On error, IOOPEN writes the error code into the handle variable as well as returning the error code. This is not a problem when opening files, it only causes problems with attached device drivers. A workaround is provided in the Psion SIBO OPL SDK.

IOREAD   S3, S3a/c, Siena, S5, WA, HC

```
r% = IOREAD(h%,addr%,maxLen%)
r% = IOREAD(h%,addr&,length%)
```
- in OPL32

Read from the file with the handle `h%`.

The `addr%` argument is the address of a buffer large enough to hold a maximum of `maxLen%` bytes. The buffer could be an array or even a single integer as required. No more than 16K bytes can be read at a time. If the value returned to `r%` is negative it is an error value, otherwise it is the actual number of bytes read.

For text files

If `maxLen%` exceeds the current record length, data only up to the end of the record is read into the buffer; no error is returned and the file position is set to the next record.

If a record is longer than `maxLen%`, the error value 'Record too large' (-43) is returned. In this case the data read is valid but is truncated to length `maxLen%`, and the file position is set to the next record.

A string array `buffer$(255)` can be used for the buffer. Pass the address `UADD(ADDR(buffer$),1)` to `IOREAD`. You can then `POKEB` the first byte of the string with the length (returned to `r%`) so that the string conforms to normal OPL string format. In this case, `maxLen%` should be 255 because the record length can be 256. If a 'Record too large' error is returned, you must read the extra byte separately. (Often you will know that the record length in your file will be not be greater than 255, in which case you don't need to check for this error).

For binary files

If you request more bytes than are left in the file, the number of bytes actually read (even zero) will be less than the number requested.

So if `r%<maxLen%`, end of file has been reached. No error is returned by `IOREAD` in this case, but the next `IOREAD` would return the error value 'End of file' (-36).

IOWRITE   S3, S3a/c, Siena, S5, WA, HC

```
r% = IOWRITE(h%,addr%,length%)
r% = IOWRITE(h%,addr&,length%)
```
in OPL32

Write `length%` bytes from a buffer at `addr%` to the file or device driver with the handle `h%`.

When a file is opened as a binary file, the data written by `IOWRITE` overwrites data at the current position. When a file is opened as a text file, `IOWRITE` writes a single record. The closing CR/LF is automatically added.

IOCLOSE   S3, S3a/c, Siena, S5, WA, HC

```
r% = IOCLOSE(h%)
```

Close the file or device driver with the handle `h%`. Returns zero if successful, otherwise an error code is returned.

See also `IOOPEN`.

IOSEEK   S3, S3a/c, Siena, S5, WA, HC

```
r% = IOSEEK(h%,mode%,var offset&)
```

Seek to a position in the file with handle `h%` that has been opened for random access. The `mode%` argument specifies how `offset&` is to be used. The `offset&` parameter may be positive to move forwards or negative to move backwards. The values you can use for `mode%` are:

mode%	effect
1	Set position in a binary file to the absolute value specified in `offset&`, with 0 for the first byte in the file.
2	Set position in a binary file to `offset&` bytes from the end of the file.
3	Set position in a binary file to `offset&` bytes relative to the current position.
6	Rewind a text file to the first record. `offset&` is ignored, but you must still pass it as a argument, for compatibility with the other cases.

`IOSEEK` sets the variable `offset&` to the absolute position set.

Note:
If you are using # to pass the value of the offset rather than have OPL use its address:

In OPL16 you would call IOSEEK using,

```
r% = IOSEEK(h%,mode%,#offset%)
```

In OPL32 you should use,

```
r% = IOSEEK(h%,mode%,#offset&)
```

i.e. pass the long integer `#offset&`.

See also `IOOPEN`

IOA   S3, S3a/c, Siena, S5, WA, HC

```
r% = IOA(h%,func%,var status%,var arg1,var arg2)
```

Get the device driver opened with handle `h%` to perform the asynchronous I/O function `func%` with the two further arguments, `arg1` and `arg2` as specified in the driver documentation.

The argument `status%` is set by the device driver when the function completes or fails.

The usual setting of status% will be -46, which means that the function is still pending. When, at some later time, the function completes, status% is automatically changed. For this reason, status% should usually be global - if the program is still running, status% must be available when the request completes, or the program will probably crash.

If status%>=0, the function completed without error. If status%<0, the function completed with error. The error number is specific to the device driver. At the same time, a signal is sent to the running OPL program.

In most cases, you cannot perform another I/O read/write function to this device until you first read the signal of this function's completion.

An IOWAIT or IOWAITSTAT must be performed for each IOA. If this is the only I/O device with a function pending, wait for the signal with IOWAITSTAT status%. If you have other functions pending on other devices, you must use IOWAIT and IOSIGNAL.

Alternatively, you can cancel the pending function with IOW(h%,4). The program will still receive a signal, which should be read with IOWAITSTAT or IOWAIT.

If an OPL program is ready to exit, it does not have to wait for any signals from pending IOA calls.

Note:
For S3a/c, Siena, S5 and WA, using IOC is more convenient than IOA.

IOC   S3a/c, Siena, S5, WA

```
r% = IOC(h%,func%,var status%,var arg1,var arg2)
```

Make an I/O request with guaranteed completion. Gets the device driver opened with handle h% to perform the asynchronous I/O function func% with the two further arguments, arg1 and arg2 as specified in the driver documentation.

The IOC function allows you to assume that the request started successfully. Since the return value is always zero it can be ignored. Any error is always given in the status word status%. The argument status% is set by the device driver, when the function completes or fails.

An IOWAIT or IOWAITSTAT must be performed for each IOC. If there was an error, status% contains the error code and the next IOWAIT will return immediately as if the error occurred after completion.

There is seldom a requirement to know whether an error occurred on starting a function, and IOC should therefore be used in preference to IOA.

Problems with IOC (S3a, WA)

Calling this function with the wrong number of arguments, or arguments of the wrong type, can cause serious problems in your OPL program.

IOCANCEL   S3a/c, Siena, S5, WA

`r% = IOCANCEL(h%)`

Cancel any outstanding asynchronous I/O requests (made with `IOA` or `IOC`) on the channel specified by `h%`, causing them to complete. Zero is always returned, and can therefore be ignored.

The completion status word contains `-48` (meaning "I/O cancelled") after `IOCANCEL` has been called.

Device drivers that support truly asynchronous services provide a cancel service. The detailed effect of the cancel depends on the device driver. However, the following general principles apply:

- The cancel precipitates the completion of the request (it does not stop the request from completing).
- The cancel may or may not be effective (i.e. the request may complete naturally before the cancel is processed; the status word will be set as for `IOA`/`IOC`).
- After a cancel, you must still process the completion of the asynchronous request (typically by immediately calling `IOWAITSTAT` to "use up" the signal).

The `IOCANCEL` function is harmless if no request is outstanding (e.g. if the function completed just before cancellation requested).

See also `IOA, IOC`.

IOYIELD   S3, S3a/c, Siena, S5, WA, HC

`IOYIELD`

Ensure that any asynchronous I/O functions, queued using `IOA` or `IOC`, are given a chance to run and their status words are updated.

The `IOYIELD` command is logically equivalent to:

`IOSIGNAL :IOWAIT.`

which returns immediately, but causes any asynchronous handlers to run.

Some devices are unable to perform an asynchronous request if an OPL program becomes computationally intensive, using no I/O (screen, keyboard etc.) at all. In such cases, the OPL program should use `IOYIELD` before checking the `status%` variables passed to `IOC` or `IOA`.

IOWAIT   S3, S3a/c, Siena, S5, WA, HC

`IOWAIT`

Wait for any asynchronous I/O function to signal completion.

If you've got an `IOA` or `IOC` request pending, use `IOWAIT` to await its completion.

Signals are generated (and thus `IOWAIT` returns) when **any** pending I/O request finishes, so you'll need to check whether this signal was meant for you or not.

To do this, look at the value of the `status%` variable you passed to `IOA` or `IOC`. If the signal wasn't for you, you'll need to call `IOWAIT` again.

The best way to handle 'wrong numbers' or 'stray signals' is to have a loop, like this:

```
loop
    call IOWAIT
    check status%
    is the signal for me?
until the signal is for me
```

You must keep count of the 'wrong numbers' you receive, because `IOWAIT` intercepted those signals before they ever got to their waiting processes. When you have got your signal, you will need to generate a fresh signal with `IOSIGNAL` for each 'wrong number' you received. If you don't do this, you will interfere with other processes' I/O.

If you have no other functions pending on different I/O handles, use `IOWAITSTAT` or (`IOWAITSTAT32`) instead.

IOWAITSTAT   S3, S3a/c, Siena, S5, WA, HC

`IOWAITSTAT var status%`

Wait for the specific asynchronous I/O function (called with `IOA` or `IOC`) with status word `status%`, to signal completion.

IOWAITSTAT32   S5

`IOWAITSTAT32 var status&`

Similar to IOWAITSTAT but takes a 32-bit status word. IOWAITSTAT32 should be called only when you need to wait for completion of a request made using a 32-bit status word when calling an asynchronous OPX procedure. `status&` will be `&80000001` (`KStatusPending32&`) while the function is still pending, and on completion will be set to the appropriate EPOC32 error code. For a 16-bit status word the 'pending value' is -46 (`KErrFilePending%`).

IOSIGNAL   S3, S3a/c, Siena, S5, WA, HC

`IOSIGNAL`

Signal an I/O function's completion.

See also `IOWAIT`.

IOW   S3, S3a/c, Siena, S5, WA, HC

r% = IOW(h%,func%,var arg1,var arg2)

Perform the synchronous I/O function func% using the device driver opened with handle h%, the two further arguments, arg1 and arg2, are as specified for the particular device driver.

KEYA   S3, S3a/c, Siena, S5, WA, HC

error% = KEYA(var status%,var key%())

This is an asynchronous keyboard read function.

The array key%() must be declared with at least two elements.

When the function completes, key%(1) contains the character code of the key pressed. The least significant byte of key%(2) takes the key modifier. The most significant byte of key%(2) takes the count of keys pressed (0 or 1). Thus key%(2) AND $FF is the modifier, using the same codes as KMOD (2 for Shift-, 4 for Control- and so on). If a key was pressed key%(2)*256 is 1, or else 0.

The KMOD function cannot be used with KEYA.

The KEYA function needs an IOWAIT in the same way as IOA.

The KEYA function is included in OPL because the handle of the keyboard driver is unknown to the casual programmer.

Note that

        KEYA(status%,key%(1))

is almost equivalent to

        IOA(-2,status%,key%(1),#0)

where -2 specifies the Console device driver (which handles the OPL keyboard). The only difference is that any key pressed to exit from PAUSE (when called with a negative argument) is used up by KEYA but not by the above IOA call.

Cancel with KEYC.

KEYC   S3, S3a/c, Siena, S5, WA, HC

error% = KEYC(var status%)

Cancel the previously called KEYA function with status word status%.

After cancelling the request, IOWAITSTAT status% must still be called to consume the signal.

Note that

```
KEYC
```

is equivalent to

```
IOW(-2,FCANCEL,#0,#0)
```

where -2 specifies the Console device driver (which handles the OPL keyboard) and
FCANCEL = 4.

Object handling

NEWOBJ	Create a new object by category number
NEWOBJH	Create a new object by category handle
SEND	Send a message to an object
ENTERSEND	Send a message to an object, returning an error if method leaves
ENTERSEND0	Send a message to an object, returning 0 if method doesn't leave

Note:
These OPL16 functions are not supported in OPL32, access to the operating system
functions, and system related objects, is via OPL extensions called OPXs.

NEWOBJ   S3a/c, Siena, WA

```
objhand% = NEWOBJ(objcatno%,objclass%)
```

Create a new object by category number objcatno% belonging to the class objclass%.

Returns the object handle on success, or zero if out of memory.

See also LOADLIB, FINDLIB, SEND, ENTERSEND, ENTERSEND0, NEWOBJH.

NEWOBJH   S3a/c, Siena, WA

```
objhand% = NEWOBJH(objcath%,objclass%)
```

Create a new object by category handle objcath% belonging to the class objclass%.

Returns the object handle on success or zero if out of memory.

See also LOADLIB, FINDLIB, SEND, ENTERSEND, ENTERSEND0, NEWOBJ.

SEND   S3a/c, Siena, WA

```
ret% = SEND(pobj%,method%,var p1,...)
```

Send a message to the object pobj% to call the method number method%, passing between
zero and three arguments (p1...) depending on the requirements of the method, and
returning the value returned by the selected method.

If the method requires a pointer to a variable, just pass the variable (not the address of it).

If the method requires a value (not a pointer) then use the # prefix. For example, to pass the value 3 as p1 use:

```
ret% = SEND(pobj%,method%,#3)
```

See also NEWOBJ, NEWOBJH, ENTERSEND, ENTERSEND0, LOADLIB, LINKLIB, FINDLIB, UNLOADLIB.

Problems with SEND (S3a, WA)

Calling this function with the wrong number of arguments, or arguments of the wrong type, can cause serious problems in your OPL program. The OPL translator cannot check the number of arguments or the types required.

ENTERSEND   S3a/c, Siena, WA

```
ret% = ENTERSEND(pobj%,method%,var p1,...)
```

Send a message to the object pobj% to call the method number method%, passing between zero and three arguments (p1, p2, p3) depending on the requirements of the method.

This is the same as SEND except that, if the method leaves, the error code is returned to the caller. Otherwise the value returned is as returned by the method.

If the method requires a pointer to a variable, just pass the variable (not the address of it).

If the method requires a value (not a pointer) then use the # prefix. For example, to pass the value 3 as p1 use:

```
ret% = ENTERSEND(pobj%,method%,#3)
```

See also ENTERSEND0, SEND , NEWOBJ, NEWOBJH, LOADLIB, LINKLIB, FINDLIB, UNLOADLIB.

Problems with ENTERSEND (S3a, WA)

Calling this function with the wrong number of arguments, or arguments of the wrong type, can cause serious problems in your OPL program. The OPL translator cannot check the number of arguments or the types required.

ENTERSEND0   S3a/c, Siena, WA

```
ret% = ENTERSEND0(pobj%,method%,var p1,...)
```

Send a message to the object pobj% to call the method number method%, passing between zero and three arguments (p1, p2, p3) depending on the requirements of the method.

This is the same as ENTERSEND except that, if the method does not leave, zero is returned.

If the method requires a pointer to a variable, just pass the variable (not the address of it). If the method requires a value (not a pointer) then use the # prefix.

For example, to pass the value 3 as p1 use:

```
ret% = ENTERSEND0(pobj%,method%,#3)
```

See also ENTERSEND, SEND ,NEWOBJ, NEWOBJH, LOADLIB, LINKLIB, FINDLIB, UNLOADLIB.

Problems with ENTERSEND0 (S3a, WA)

Calling this function with the wrong number of arguments, or arguments of the wrong type, can cause serious problems in your OPL program. The OPL translator cannot check the number of arguments or the types required.

10   OPL16 Techniques

Introduction to PPCOPL16

The primary objective of this chapter is to describe the structure of a demonstration OPL application (PPCOPL16.OPA) to illustrate a wide range of OPL16 programming techniques. To gain maximum benefit from this chapter, it is best read whilst referring to the source code of the PPCOPL16 application. I recommend loading the source files into the program editor on a SIBO system and using the find function to assist in following the program flow.

The full application and all necessary files are supplied on disk, including extensively commented source code in OPL and C - see the directory named PPCOPL16.

Techniques covered

As will be evident when you install and run PPCOPL16, that the icon, much of the code and some of the graphics objects used in PPCOPL16 originated during the development of a Backgammon game for the Series 3a/c, Siena and Work*about*. In the Backgammon application, OPL was used to provide all elements of the user interface and file handling, but C was used (via a DYL) for the game 'engine' to ensure the move calculations are done very quickly. Because of the range of techniques used, the framework of the game was chosen as an illustrative OPL application framework.

Taken as a whole this a comprehensive and somewhat complex example. However, taken in stages, with frequent references to the commented source code, the reader should easily be able to absorb most, if not all, of the techniques demonstrated. You may then incorporate just the relevant routines into your own application. For example, the application is not dependent on any code written in C. Use of the DYL can be easily removed if it is not required. However, readers who are conversant with C, and have the SIBO C SDK, may choose to extend or replace the DYL methods with their own.

OPL application (OPA)

- Type 2 i.e. file based - only one instance running and one file in use at a time
- Default file path located under the APP directory
- Default file extension of .EXT
- A 48x48 pixel icon with grey (3a onwards)

Event handling

- Key press events, including a wide range of special keys such as menu, diamond and status windows.
- System messages, start command line and new command line information e.g. Create a new file, switch files, shut down program.

Background to foreground program changes

Machine detection

- S3, S3a, S3c, Siena or Workabout
- Screen and graphics size adjustment based on screen resolution

Status window toggling and screen resizing

Menu handling

- Including dynamically changing menu items

Multi-lingual techniques

- Machine language detection
- Use of language specific resource files

Graphics techniques

- Use of grey and black planes
- Use of drawing modes to set, clear or invert pixels
- Drawing graphics objects directly
- Drawing graphics with bitmaps
- Creating, saving and loading bitmap files
- Animation

Sound

- Error beeps - toggling on or off
- Asynchronous digital sound playback

File handling

- Detection of the existence of files and directories
- Locating program file and drive origin
- Determination of the users default drive
- Getting and selecting file names
- Creation of files and directories as needed
- Data file handling for saving a restoring user program preferences and settings
- Use of simple dialogs for data entry

Miscellaneous techniques
- Use of EPOC16 operating system calls
- Calls to C functions via a DYL
- Help facilities - including multi-lingual help text
- Error trapping and handling
- Use of random numbers

Source files

If you wish to view or even modify the PPCOPL16 example application, it is best done using ODE, and a suitable project file is supplied (it has a .MAK file name extension). Alternatively the program can be translated using S3ATRAN.EXE. If you wish to use PPCOPL16 on a SIBO system it will be necessary to substitute all of the information from the 'include' files into the main source code files.

All of the OPL source code is contained in two files, PPCOPL16.OPL and PPCMOD01.OPL, other identifier and constant information is 'included' from three header files with .OPH extensions.

Virtually all language specific text for the user interface, including messages, menu titles, menu items and accelerator keys, is located in the English language resource file i.e. PPCOPL01.RSS - see the section on 'PPCOPL16 language text' below.

The C source code and related files for the DYL are in a PPCOPL16\\DYL subdirectory. Note that the PPCOPL16.C file is an automatically generated source file, the main C source files for the DYL are PPCOPL01.C, PPCOPL16.CAT and PPCOPL16.H. Two other files are worthy of particular note: The TS.RED file tells the SIBO C SDK where other files are located; it will have to be modified to reflect your system set up. A MAKE.BAT file is provided (along with others) to handle building of the DYL from the source files.

Important note:
It is most important that any C source code files associated with a DYL (or an OOP C application) **do not** have the same name as the category file (i.e. the .CAT file). When the project is built, a source code file is automatically generated with the same name as the .CAT file but with a .C extension. For example, PPCOPL16.CAT will produce a file called PPCOPL16.C. **Any .C source code file you have laboured to create, that happens to have the same name as the .CAT file, will be overwritten!**

Executable files

The \APP directory and its \PPCOPL16 subdirectory contain all of the files required to run the demonstration application on a SIBO system. Any other files required by the application will be created at run-time.

Language text

Virtually all language specific text for the user interface, including messages, menu titles, menu items and accelerator keys, is located in the English language resource file i.e. PPCOPL01.RSS. This file is converted into a .RSC file by the resource compiler RCOMP.EXE. The .RSC file is then converted into a compressed form using RCHUF.EXE. If you do not have this program (it is supplied with the SIBO C SDK), then the file can be used in its .RSC form, but all references to the .RZC file extension in the OPL program code will have to be modified to .RSC.

The RZC.BAT file handles the process of resource file compilation and compression (it also renames the .RSG file, automatically produced by the resource compiler, to .OPH so its contents can be <u>viewed</u> using the ODE editor).

If other languages are to be supported, the text in the .RSS file will have to be translated into each of the supported languages, being very careful to stay within the text sizes indicated in the file itself. Each specific version of the file should be given a name that incorporates the corresponding country code e.g. the English file is named PPCOPL01.RSS, the corresponding French resource file should be named PPCOPL02.RSS, and will generate corresponding .RSC and .RZC file during compilation. A full list of language codes is given in the Appendix.

Structure overview

Execution begins in the START: procedure where all of the program global variables are declared, program exit via Psion Esc is disabled with the ESCAPE OFF statement, and the other OPL program module is loaded. The extra module (PPCMOD01) initialises all program global variables, file/directory names and much more besides. When PPCMOD01 has done its work it is unloaded and is never called again, thus saving precious memory.

Processing returns from INITOBJ: to START: which sets up the default ONERR error handling (outside of any deliberate trapping/handling), then an endless loop is entered using KEYPRES%: to handle all events and key presses. All other program functionality is provided via routines called from within the KEYPRES%: procedure.

As stated elsewhere in the book, it's the window server that handles passing keyboard information to the foreground process. Applications can be structured to receive such event information synchronously; i.e. they can just sit and wait for a key press, in which case the program is effectively suspended. Alternatively they may need to receive event information, such as key presses, asynchronously, i.e. register more than one I/O request and then go round in a loop doing other tasks until signalled that an event such as a key press has occurred.

In OPL, statements such as GET, GET$ or even GETEVENT are synchronous, whereas KEYA is an asynchronous keyboard read (a more complex alternative would be to use the asynchronous I/O function IOA()).

Many other asynchronous services are provided by EPOC16. Most OPL programmers don't need to use asynchronous techniques, but if the program has to do other tasks such as handling serial port transfers, while remaining responsive to key presses, then asynchronous methods are essential.

Complete source code for an asynchronous application framework is provided amongst the examples supplied with the ODE OPL development environment from Psion.

The PPCOPL16 application is structured to respond to a number of event types synchronously.

Initialisation in detail

The INITOBJ: procedure starts by setting aside some memory for procedure cacheing, not really needed in this application, useful if program speed is affected when loading and unloading program modules with LOADM and UNLOADM.

Error handling

Notice the use of the TRAP command before the CACHE statement to override any ONERR processing that may have been set up. The ERR value will still be set if CACHE fails but the pferr: procedure will get to process any error that occurs. Calling a procedure such as pferr: allows for controlled handling and reporting of errors, and leaves open the potential for error recovery to take place. Relying solely on the system to 'crash out' when an error occurs is very unfriendly. If no error has actually occurred, pferr: will just return without taking any action.

Another point to note here is the use of the ERR in the pferr: procedure call after the CACHE statement. If an error occurs at this point it will probably be error −10 which corresponds to "No system memory". Using ERR is handy at this point, because as yet we have not loaded any language specific text, so any program supplied error message might not be meaningful to the user. Instead, the system error message will be used, and it will be in the correct language for the machine.

File locations

Next, the getlocs: procedure is called to find out where various files and directories are located, and to get the users default disk so it can be used to store the program settings file. Information on disks, directories and file names are stored in a series of global string variables that will be used extensively elsewhere for a wide range file handling tasks. Two points are of particular interest here: The use of an operating system call (i.e. CALL($0387)) to find the users default path, including the default disk drive letter. Also, including a period '.' at the end of a directory name string, when testing for the existence of a directory - to prevent OPL automatically appending a .ODB file extension on to the directory name. For the same reason, when testing for the presence of a particular file, it is always wise to explicitly include the file name extension in the file name (see the PARSE$ function in the 'OPL Reference' chapter).

Languages

All language specific text is located and loaded from an appropriate language resource file by the `loadlang`: procedure. An operating system call is used to get the language code for the machine, the code is converted into a two character string (with a leading '0' if needed), and the string is used as the last two characters of the resource file name, to ensure it is language specific. See the 'Language text' section above for examples, and the 'Appendix' for a list of language codes. If a language specific resource file is not found the program will default to using the English file.

OPL16 does not directly support the use of program resource files, but the EPOC16 system does. To load strings and other data from the resource file it is necessary to call procedures located in the ROM based '`OLIB.DYL`' library. Hence, the use of the OPL16 `FINDLIB` and `NEWOBJH` keywords to locate and utilise the Object Oriented Methods in the OLIB dynamic link library. Methods in the library (e.g. to open/close the resource file and load data) are called using the `ENTERSEND` keyword. Identifiers such as `RS_OPEN` and `RS_CLOSE` are just the numbers of the library methods. Other identifiers such as `PROG_TITLE` are used to load specific items of information. All of the identifiers for method numbers and text strings etc. are '`#defined`' in files with .OPH extensions. If you wish, the corresponding numeric values can be substituted directly into the OPL source code.

A range of individual `ENTERSEND` calls are used to load up specific strings, then all of the user messages, menu strings and menu accelerators are loaded into string arrays inside three loop structures. An alternative approach, to the use of message arrays, would be to have a procedure to load specific message strings at the time they are needed. Calls to the OLIB library are completed very quickly and the user would see no noticeable delay in the program's response. However, the use of an array is virtually essential for menu information for reasons of overall speed, and to avoid the `mCARD` source lines becoming too long for the OPL translator. Finally, identifiers such as `A_OPEN_A` and `M_OPEN_T` are used to access the specific elements of the string arrays, they are calculated from related identifiers (such as `A_OPEN`) in the 'included' file named PPCMENU.OPH.

(See the HELPKIT directory on disk for more details on the use of resource and help files in OPL16.)

Screen resolution and window sizes

When any OPL program starts its default window (i.e. window ID = 1) occupies the whole screen. Since OPL uses a system of backup bitmaps, to simplify window re-drawing when the display is updated, windows can use quite a lot of memory. Twice as much memory is needed if grey is enabled (via the `DEFAULTWIN` command). It's always a good idea to reduce the memory used by windows, by making them only as big as required.

You can consider the default window as having two components, a graphics window with a slightly smaller text window inside it. To write to the text window you use statements such as `FONT` and `PRINT`, but you can only use one font on screen at once. Ignoring the text window and using the graphics window instead with statements such as `gFONT`, `gPRINT` and `gPRINTB` is much more flexible.

To accommodate the different screen sizes and resolutions of SIBO machines, the program now establishes what machine it is running on. Having established the system is suitable; the machine identity is used to set a number of global variables to values appropriate for the fonts and graphics objects to be used. Since some of the objects will be loaded from bitmap files, an appropriate file name prefix is also selected.

Next, the presence of a several essential files is established, and if some of the simpler bitmap files are not found the program calls `crBits:` to create and save them (i.e. `circle.pic`, `cross.pic` and `spot.pic`).

Machine detection

A useful side effect of the start up default window is that the `w%=gWIDTH` and `h%=gHEIGHT` commands will indicate which machine a program is running on. For example, values of `w%,h%:` 240,80 = Series 3; 480,160 = Series 3a/c; 240,160 = Siena; 240,100 = Work*about*.

However, a further test is needed to distinguish between a program running on a S3a or on a S3c. Testing for the presence or otherwise of the ROM based file `ROM::SYS$IRDA.IMG`, associated with S3c infrared capability, is a reasonably good method.

Status windows

The default window will initially obscure any status window, this can be remedied by reducing the size of the default window using the OPL FONT (or `gSETWIN` and `SCREEN`) statements (see also the `SCREENINFO`, `STATUSWIN` and `STATWININFO` statements). Any other windows you create may also obscure a status window that is open. If you think of open windows as a series of layers, one above the other, then any permanent status window is always positioned as the lowest layer, and so it will always be obscured if any other windows occupy the same x y co-ordinates. FONT automatically resizes the default window to the maximum size excluding any status window. It should be called after creating the status window because the new size of the text and graphics windows depends on the size of the status window. Note that FONT `-$3fff,0` does not change the current font and style, it just changes the window sizes and clears them. If you use SCREEN and `gSETWIN` instead of FONT, you should use the `STATWININFO` keyword to find out the size of the status window – see the `setdisp:` procedure for details.

Loading the DYL

After ensuring that the .DYL file exists, the `LOADLIB` function is called to load the dynamic link library into memory and return a category handle for the library into the variable `PgCat%`. A category handle is just an identifying number for the group (category) of methods in the library. A non-zero value returned into `su%`, from the call to `LOADLIB`, indicates that an error occurred. A call to `NEWOBJH` is used to create the library 'object' and return a handle (identifier) for it; the handle is then used to refer to the library object when making calls to its methods (procedures) via the SEND function. To keep things simple there is only one method in the example DYL, i.e. `O_GETRAM` that returns a number of statistics about the current allocation of system memory.

Command line processing

When the program is started (i.e. not already running) from the System Screen, a command line is passed to the program containing a command byte and a file name. The command line information will depend on how the program was started up.

The command byte will be 'C' if the user used the 'New file' option from the system screen menu while the highlight was under the program's icon. The user will have been asked to provide a file name after selecting 'New file' and that name will be passed to the program in the command line. A command byte of 'O' results from the user selecting a file with the highlight from the list under the icon and pressing enter. Again the name of the selected file is passed to the program.

Two functions are used to get this information from the command line: CMD$(3) returns the command byte and CMD(2) returns the file name and path. Note the use of the PARSE$ function to add in any missing file name information and build a full file specification.

Program settings file

Program settings are restored by calling the getpdefs: procedure; if the file name (passed as in the cpfn$ parameter) does not exist the procedure will create one using default settings. Settings stored are the state of the error beep (on or off) and whether a status window should be shown or not. After loading or creating the settings file initp: is called to initialise some parameters including the variable menu item strings such as 'Beep on' or 'Beep off', it also uses the SETNAME command to tell the system screen name of the file now in use. The width of the display is set according to the presence of a status window or not by the setdisp: procedure, and the string for the status window menu item is adjusted accordingly.

Random seed

A new random seed is initialised at program start up because the program uses some random numbers (via the RND function) for dice, and to get random screen co-ordinates for graphics. To avoid the same sequence of random numbers being generated every time the program is run, the initrnd: procedure uses a combination of hour, minute and second as a seed value in RANDOMIZE.

Program credits

After displaying some credits and application information, by calling the about: procedure, the program returns to the original start: procedure and enters an endless loop that repeatedly calls keypress%: to handle system events and user key presses.

Events and user input

All program functionality, including exit from the program, is provided via procedures called from within the `keypres%:` procedure.

The first action taken by `keypres%:` is to call the `GETEVENT:` command, a synchronous call that only returns when an event of some kind has happened. Effectively (as far as EPOC16 is concerned) the program is suspended and is waiting for the system to pass on the details of system events or key presses. A program only normally receives key presses (from the window server) when it is the foreground process, so if the program goes into the background (e.g. by the user pressing the system key) it is only able to process system events, not key presses.

On receipt of an event of some kind, `keypres%:` tests the value in `a%(1)` to see if it was a system message event, and if so it tests the command byte in the new command line for one of three types of command. Valid commands received from the system screen (while the program was running in the background) are:

- 'X' to shutdown the program
- 'C' to create a new file, i.e. using the name entered by the user in the dialog presented by the system screen
- 'O' to open the file picked from the list under the program's icon.

Shutdown messages may arrive due a user selecting the emboldened file from the icon list and pressing the delete key, or may be sent from the system, for example in response to an 'Exit application' command (the 'Kill application' does not send any message before terminating the application).

The new command line is returned by the `GETCMD$` function. The command byte is the first character of the new command line string (in `w$`), and is retrieved into `t$` with the `LEFT$` string function. The remainder of the new command line is the file name, and it is put back into `w$` by getting the next 128 characters with the `MID$` string function.

Next, the procedure tests for key presses. Of particular interest are special keys such as: Ctrl+Menu, Menu, Help, the Diamond key (or Psion+* for Work*about*) or the Psion key plus a menu accelerator key. Key press modifiers are returned by `GETEVENT`, hence the tests for Ctrl+Menu involves testing the values returned in `a%(2)`.

The special key presses have the following effects:

Ctrl+menu, Diamond, Psion+* or the menu hot key Shift+Psion+S, toggle the state of the status window on or off and resize the screen (note how the Status Win menu item changes when this happens).

Help brings up the help menu using the program related help items and text located in the language specific resource file. Calling the internal help system is discussed in detail later in the section on 'Application functions'.

Menu brings up the program menu. Selecting a menu item from under one of the menu titles will return a corresponding accelerator key. All menu related text and accelerator keys are defined in the resource file. Thus, all menu text and accelerator keys can be language specific without affecting the program code in any way.

Note the use of LOCK ON and LOCK OFF surrounding the use of the MENU keyword to tell the system that the application cannot currently process system messages. Attempting to send shutdown messages etc. while a menu is open (and marked with LOCK ON) will result in an 'xxxxxx is busy' message; this is a limitation imposed by OPL16.

Menu hot key presses

Once the other key tests have been done (and responded to if found) the Psion key modifier is tested for. If the Psion key press is detected, the Psion key code is removed and the Shift modifier is tested for; if found the value of the key pressed is converted to lower case. The key value remaining in k% is then equivalent to the key value that would be returned by the MENU function itself.

A series of IF-ELSEIF tests are done to check for menu accelerators, or special keys such as Enter and Space. Many alternatives to an IF-ELSEIF test sequence can be used, and some may be considered more elegant or be more efficient e.g. using the VECTOR command or the @ operator.

When the key value in k% matches a menu key or menu hot key combination, the appropriate procedure is called. On return from the procedure the keypres% loop is entered again ready for the next system event or key press.

Application functions

As stated earlier, the PPCOPL16 application is provided as an illustrative example application, and the functionality included is simply designed to demonstrate a number of significant programming techniques. Many approaches can be used for the overall design of an application. If you find the approach illustrated by PPCOPL16 to your liking please feel free to use the code as a framework for your own applications.

File menu

Options are: **Open, Save as and Save**

These options simply allow the user to manage the program's settings file. That is, to open another settings file, to save the current file under a new name, but stay with the current file (Note: this typical of SIBO behaviour, but a S5 application should swap to the new file). Save, just saves the current program settings and stays with the same file.

Edit menu

Options are: **Owner and Telephone**

Provides simple string editing using dialogs. Note the use of LOCK ON and LOCK OFF surrounding the use of the DIALOG keyword to tell the system that the application cannot currently process system messages. Attempting to send shutdown messages etc. while a dialog is open (and marked with LOCK ON) will result in an 'xxxxxx is busy' message; this is a limitation imposed by OPL16.

The Owner and Telephone information is automatically saved in the program's settings file whenever the user quits the program, or changes the file in use via the File menu options, changes the state of any settings such as error beep or the status window state.

Wherever possible program data and information should be saved automatically without the user having to do it explicitly. Unless of course you wish to provide options for the user to quit the application without saving or revert to a previously unchanged version.

Game menu

Options are: **Clear screen, Throw dice, Graphics and Sound**

Clear screen does precisely that, but it clears whatever is the current window, and can be used to clear only the black plane, the grey plane or both. Try altering the value of the plns% parameter in clear: in the call at the start of the blobs: procedure. Also note that clear: does not clear or otherwise affect the state of any status window.

Throw dice function (dice:) generates two random dice values (i.e. in the range 1-6) using calls to the RND function. Dice value one will always be the larger value, and a flag will be set if a double is thrown.

Two different methods are used to draw the dice. Method one (called from dicedrwb:) uses bitmap-copying techniques. First the two dice are drawn, one black and one white, and then the source of the bitmap objects are drawn to show the origin of the component parts of the dice. Method two (called from dicedrww:) uses direct drawing of graphics into a hidden window, and then window to window copies. The pros and cons of the two techniques are described next in the Graphics discussion.

Graphics shows a number of techniques, illustrated in four main procedures (triang: blobs: bmpfile: and animicon:) that are all called from the graphics: procedure.

The first procedure triang: draws solid grey, solid black, and 'hollow' triangles in the black and grey planes using bitmap copying. Next, the same types of triangle are drawn, using direct graphics drawing commands instead. One important factor here is the relative speed of drawing, particularly with the filled shapes.

Procedure blobs: draws twenty filled and twenty hollow 'circles' of various relative heights, then it draws twenty solid pieces and twenty 'white' pieces all of the same size. All objects are drawn at random screen co-ordinates. The first set of 'blobs' were drawn by direct graphics commands, and the second set of uniform pieces were placed on the screen by copying from bitmaps held in memory. Points to note are; again the obvious speed differences, but the possibility for dynamic sizing of the objects when using direct drawing and the more sophisticated shapes possible with hand-crafted bitmaps.

Procedure bmpffile: shows that when drawing with bitmaps they do not have to be held in memory, they can be loaded from bitmap files as needed. Copying from bitmaps already held in memory is quickest, but using gLOADBIT to bring them in as needed is not so far behind.

Incidentally, the three bitmap files used (i.e. `circle.pic`, `cross.pic` and `spot.pic`) will all be drawn directly and saved to disk if the files don't exist when the program starts up – see the `crBits:` procedure.

Procedure `animicon:` uses the two bitmaps from the program's icon file to do some simple animation. Movement is simulated by alternately copying each bitmap into the screen in set mode followed by a delay and then again in invert mode. By moving the 'cursor' co-ordinates slightly and repeating the process the two halves of the icon appear to move towards each other and finally coalesce. The smoothness, speed of movement and degree of screen flicker can be modified by varying the pause duration and the number of pixels between successive screen positions. Of course any other objects or information displayed in the path of the bitmaps being 'moved' will have to be redrawn. Screen areas disturbed by animation can be restored in various ways. Principally you have two main options, either to call the procedures that draw specific areas of the screen as needed, or to copy the area of the screen about to be disturbed and then replace it when the moving object has passed moved on. Animation, which does not disturb the underlying display, can be done using sprites. Using sprites is a little complex at first, made more so if you have several objects to move, since only one sprite may exist at once in OPL16 (in OPL32 this restriction has gone).

In summary, the particular graphics techniques employed will depend upon the end result required, but some other factors may play a part in the final decision.

Drawing graphics directly allows dynamic scaling of objects, but will limit the complexity of the objects used, without resorting to a huge amount of very specific drawing code.

With bitmaps, much more complex shapes can be manipulated, but you can only scale objects by having multiple bitmap sets, and you are fixed to the range of sizes available in the pre-defined bitmaps. Hand crafted bitmaps are almost always superior in appearance. A pixel changed here and there in a bitmap can have dramatic and subtle effects on its final appearance on the screen. An alternative method of using bitmaps is via a set of custom made fonts (which are just bitmap sets anyway), then using commands such as gPRINT to present the objects on screen. See the 'User Interface' chapter for details of custom fonts.

Note:
Bitmap files **do not** contain black and grey bitmaps, they may contain one or more bitmaps, but what happens to them when they are loaded is up to the programmer. For example, purely by convention icon files contain two bitmaps (Series 3a onwards), the first of which is loaded into the black plane and the second is loaded into the grey plane of the screen. Bitmaps in memory or in files do not have planes, only display screens (on suitable systems) support the concept of grey and black planes.

Sound calls the `psound:` procedure to demonstrate the asynchronous playback of a digital sound file (i.e. GROMIT.WVE). While the sound is playing other activities can still take place, illustrated by running the icon animation procedure at the same time as playing the sound. Before attempting to play the sound, the procedure ensures that the file exists and that the machine is of a suitable type.

Control menu

Options are: **Beep off/on and Status Win off/on**

Beep demonstrates toggling the state of the program error or warning beep to on or off, and modifying the 'Beep' menu item to reflect the change. Note also that the state of the beep may be modified from the menu item or via its corresponding hot key. Either of these options will cause the menu item to be changed to 'Beep on / off, i.e. to reflect the action it will next perform if selected. All calls within the program to issue a beep sound (i.e. via the `sound:` procedure) will only take effect if beep is set to on.

Status Win demonstrates toggling the state of the status window on and off, resizing the screen and modifying the 'Status Win' menu item to reflect the change. Note also that a number of ways are provided to toggle the state of the status window i.e. from the menu item, via its corresponding hot-key, with the Diamond key and with the Ctrl+Menu key combination. Any of these options will cause the menu item to be changed to 'Status Win on / off', i.e. to reflect the action it will next perform if selected.

Any changes to the state of the status window or beep sound are saved into the current program settings file and are restored whenever the program is run again with the same file.

Special menu

Options are: **Memory, About and Exit**

Memory uses the getmem: procedure to call a method (procedure) in the DYL. When the method is called (i.e. `O_GETRAM`), the address of the `mem%(4)` array is passed (in the variable `memaddr%`) so that the DYL can put multiple return values directly into the OPL array. Written in OOP C, the DYL uses some PLIB functions to get some statistics about the use of system memory, i.e. the first 512 Kbytes of memory normally available for programs. Some of the first 512 Kbytes of memory will be used for RAM disk on systems with total memory of 512 K or less. On systems with more than 512 Kbytes of memory, non-of the first 512 Kbytes will be used as RAM disk until all of the memory above 512K is filled.

The `about:` procedure is used in a special mode to display the memory statistics obtained:

- 'Total usable' - is all of the system memory, not including any available memory above 512K.
- 'For programs' - is the amount currently in use by programs and their data.
- 'For RAM disk' - is the proportion of the first 512K currently occupied as RAM disk, on larger memory systems this will almost always be zero.
- 'Free' - is the amount of memory available for use by new programs and their data.

About uses the `about:` procedure to display application credits / information, and the current settings for 'Owner' and 'Telephone'. The same procedure is used for a few seconds at program start up, but when called from the menu it waits for a key to be pressed (i.e. by calling the `waitkey:` procedure) before returning. Note the use of `GETEVENT` in `waitkey:` to allow the program to respond to system screen shut down messages whilst waiting for the user to press a key.

Exit quits from the program via the `endit:` procedure. Note the use of a call to `choose%:` to get a confirmation to quit from the user, and in particular the operating system call (i.e. `CALL($998d,0,0)`) to force the program to the foreground. Since the program wants to confirm the exit option, if the application is in the background and a system shut down message is received the user would not see the dialog asking for confirmation. Hence the application must force itself to the foreground to show the message and get a response. In fact, this is not good practise and was just done to demonstrate the foreground switch. It is much better to design the application so it saves any information and shuts down without requiring any user involvement.

Help key

Pressing the help key calls `help%:` procedure to bring up the application's help menu. In fact the code in `help%:` may look a little odd, but it is similar to using the procedures (method) in the PPCOPL16.DYL library. Instead, methods provided by the operating system's 'gate object' are used to: register the name of the application help file (i.e. the program's resource file), display a list of help topics and in turn display the text for the items selected by the user.

11 C Programming

An outline of the options for programming in C for SIBO systems is given in the 'Platforms' chapter. Although SIBO based development environments do exist they are not yet fully developed, and are certainly not suitable for the development of complete applications. The other C development systems are included on disk with their own documentation and are therefore not considered further in this chapter.

For application development in C the only realistic option is to use the SIBO C SDK from Psion. This chapter begins by describing the contents of the C SDK in some detail and goes on to describe and contrast the development options it presents to you as a prospective user.

Some of the key steps and issues involved in the development process are then outlined. Finally a guide is given to the wide array of examples included in the C SDK. The SIBO C SDK covers a lot of ground and includes a lot of useful example code, but the information about what you actually 'have in your hands' is widely scattered throughout the extensive manuals and the disk based information files.

In addition to the example code provided in the SIBO C SDK, you will find a wide range of C programming examples on disk. The examples vary: There are small snippets of C code to demonstrate a specific technique. Some are complete C applications (in HWIF and HWIM). All of the additional examples provided are described and indexed in the 'Disk Contents' chapter.

ROM-resident libraries

Looking at the size of the sophisticated built-in applications on a SIBO system leads to a surprise, they are very small. There are two main reasons for this: the very efficient TopSpeed compiler produces compact code, virtually all applications make extensive use of the ROM-resident libraries, thus there is no need to append large run-time/library modules to the executable file. Two basic types of library are available in ROM, C-type type and object-oriented (OOP) type libraries. The exact libraries available (and versions thereof) will depend on the machine in use. Use of the SIBO C SDK revolves around the use of the ROM-resident libraries and they are all fully documented in version 2.20 of the SDK.

C libraries

CLIB	Standard 'C' library. In all machines.	Easiest for porting existing C programs. Restricted I/O. Most applications will avoid CLIB.
PLIB	Psion 'C' library. In all machines.	Library functions designed to utilise the features of the SIBO system. Generates much smaller code than CLIB because it is a thin layer over ROM code.
WLIB	Windows server library. In all machines.	Provides graphical access to the screen and keyboard.
HWIF	Handheld WIMP interface library. Not built into any machine, but is supplied with the SIBO C SDK.	Gives 'C' access to dialogs, menus and edit boxes. A 'C' layer over the object-oriented HWIM, providing much - but by no means all - of HWIM's functionality.

Object-oriented libraries

OLIB	Psion Object Library OLIB services may be used from otherwise non-object-oriented C programs. In all machines.	Provides services that are independent of the user interface including, data storage, file management, basic text editing, event scheduling, inter-process communication, time management and timers.
HWIM	Handheld Windows Icons and Menus. In all machines.	User interface and application framework library. Called by HWIF.
FORM	Formatted text and printing. Not in HC machines.	For more sophisticated treatment of editable text.
XADD	The XADD library extends the functionality of the HWIM and FORM libraries. Not in S3 or HC systems.	Provides print preview facilities, a calendar window that can display one or more months, grid classes, active objects and ATS.

Psion SIBO C SDK

The SDK is available in three variants as discussed in the 'Development Options' chapter. The standard and professional versions of the C SDK provide all of the information and software tools necessary to develop C language applications for Psion SIBO-based products.

SIBO C SDK software

The software and related files supplied in the package are actually from two sources, TopSpeed Corporation and Psion Software. TopSpeed Corporation supply a specially packaged version of their compiler, linker and project system to Psion who supply it as part of the C SDK, after adding in their libraries specialist utilities and example source code. The exact contents of the package depend upon the variant purchased, as described in the 'Development Options' chapter. Further details of the example source code and utilities are given later in this chapter.

SIBO C SDK documentation

Version 2.20 (February 1997) of the SIBO C SDK documentation consists of nineteen manuals, in four volumes, covering a wide range of features of the SIBO architecture and development system. These are described below.

A full electronic index to the documentation in the SIBO C SDK is provided on disk. This index is extensively cross-referenced and contains over 14,000 entries - see the CSDK directory. The C SDK index was produced by EMCC as a commercial product, purchasers of this book are free to use the index for their own individual purposes. However do not distribute the C SDK index to others, doing so by whatever means, will be in breach of international copyright laws.

General Programming Manual

This manual explains how to install the SDK and how, by means of simple examples, to build an application that will run on a Psion SIBO machine.

It describes in detail the differences between the CLIB and PLIB C libraries and also gives guidance on copy protection. The important 'Fundamental Programming Guidelines' chapter explains the basic principles that should be understood by all developers of SIBO applications. The General Programming Manual has sections on the following topics:

- Installation and overview of the SIBO C SDK
- Building an application
- Notes on CLIB

- Fundamental programming guidelines, includes advice on how to ensure that an application remains responsive to user input, is robust against run-time errors, such as shortage of memory.
- Copy protecting software
- Application / machine compatibility

HC Programming Guide

This manual contains information that is specific to the development of applications for the rugged and highly configurable HC range of hand-held computers. The topics discussed include:

- Introduction to the HC, basic hardware and software concepts
- Writing software for the HC
- The HC command Shell, overview, files, directories and alphabetical listing
- The HC in the Cradle
- Customising the HC ROM
- Technical specifications

Series 3/3a Programming Guide

This manual contains information that is specific to the Series 3, 3a/c and Siena handheld computers. The topics discussed include:

- Series 3 Programming Overview - including advice on writing multi-lingual applications
- Communicating with the System Screen - including the differences between file-based and non-file based applications,
- The receipt by applications of shutdown and switch-files messages, and the modification of an application's behaviour by means of the technique of aliasing
- Enhanced sound output
- Use of the Spy application
- Technical specifications and the differences between the Series 3 models

Work*about* Programming Guide

This manual contains information that is specific to the Work*about* handheld computer. It describes the principal features of the Work*about* and the various user interfaces that are available to the developer. In addition to guidelines for customising the machine for a particular application. The topics discussed include:

- Introduction to the Work*about,* basic hardware and software
- Writing software for the Work*about,* basic programming and customising options
- Full description of the built-in Command Processor software
- Technical specifications, VIC (Vehicle Interface Cradle) and Docking Station

EPOC O/S System Services

This manual contains a complete description of the software interrupt interface to ROM-based system services. An appendix lists the EPOC16 services both alphabetically, by service name, and numerically, by interrupt and function number. This will be of particular interest to assembly language programmers.

Topics in the EPOC O/S System Services manual include:

- Introduction and documentation conventions
- Segmented memory management
- Heap memory, semaphore and message management
- Dynamic library, category and object management
- Device Management
- Input / output management
- File and process management
- Date and time management
- Conversion management
- Long integer management
- Floating point number handling and function interface
- Character, Buffer and string management
- General management
- Database file management
- Hardware management
- Interrupt and function numbers
- Environment variables

Additional System Information

The Additional System Information manual explains a variety of topics, including communications software, resource files, printer drivers, the file formats used by applications and the writing of device drivers, in particular

- MCLink, MCPrint and Slink
- Resource files
- WDR printing
- DBF files
- Series 3a Agenda and word processor file format
- Series 3/3a MC spreadsheet file format
- Writing and example device drivers
- Word file format conversion DYL's
- Agenda file format updates

Tools Reference

This manual contains chapters describing a number of communications and file conversion tools useful for developers including:

- RCom introduction, selection and advanced use
- PsiWin, a suite of three software packages
- File editor
- Sound and data file conversion utilities

PLIB Reference

This manual contains a comprehensive description of the PLIB C function library. The library routines are classified into fourteen areas of functionality and each group is accompanied by background information, usage recommendations and example code.

- Introduction to PLIB, SIBO and EPOC
- Characters, strings and buffers
- Arrays and queues
- Integer conversion and rectangle functions
- Floating point C, long integer and scientific functions
- Error handling
- Memory allocation
- Asynchronous requests and semaphores
- Input / output system
- Time, timers and dates
- EPOC files
- Processes and inter process messaging
- General system services
- Database files
- Object oriented programming
- PLIB reference update

Window Server Reference

The Window Server is a separate built-in process that is always running on each SIBO machine. It provides access to the screen and keyboard for all running applications. The Window Server Reference manual describes the WLIB library that provides the interface between an application and the window server. Topics discussed include:

- Comprehensive introduction and description
- General window server functions
- Windows
- Graphics output, bitmaps, text fonts
- Events and keyboard input
- Window server reference update

I/O Devices Reference

This manual describes the I/O device drivers that have been written by Psion. The description of each driver includes a full explanation of the services that it supports, together with example code.

- Introduction
- Console services
- Parallel port
- Serial port
- Sound
- Alarm device driver
- Free running counter
- Series 3 world database
- Xmodem and Ymodem
- NCP and link
- Cradle and docking station
- HC Magnetic card reader
- HC Bar code reader
- HC intelligent bar code reader / RS232 port
- Introductions to Psion Infrared communications
- The AccessIR API
- The IrMUX API
- Fast charger

The SIBO Debugger

The SIBO C source-level debugger supplied with the SDK runs on a PC. It is normally used for remote debugging of an application running on a SIBO machine but may, in some circumstances, also be used to debug SIBO applications running on the PC.

The debugger is specifically designed to facilitate the debugging of applications running in the EPOC environment, in which the application's code segment may be relocated at any time. This manual describes the facilities provided by the debugger and explains its use.

- Introduction and starting up the Debugger
- The graphics interface
- Top level views
- The process window
- The file manager
- Troubleshooting

Hardware Reference

The Hardware Reference manual contains a description of the SIBO computer hardware, including the principal chip-set, expansion ports and the SIBO serial protocol.

- The principal chip set
- The SIBO serial protocol
- The SIBO expansion ports

Programming in HWIF

HWIF (the Handheld WIMP Interface) is a library of user interface routines suitable for use by C developers producing applications for the Work*about*, Series 3 and Siena range of computers. The HWIF library provides easy and efficient access to many aspects of the functionality of these machines, including sophisticated printing and the presentation of menu bars, dialog boxes and edit boxes. The manual contains a range of worked examples as well as a comprehensive description of all HWIF routines.

- Introduction to and overview of HWIF
- Worked examples in HWIF, getting started and getting serious
- Advanced use of HWIF
- The HWIF reference documentation

Object Oriented Programming Guide

The Object Oriented Programming Guide describes the development of applications for SIBO machines using Psion's proprietary Object Oriented programming techniques. It contains a general introduction to the concepts of object-oriented programming and full practical details of how to build an object-oriented application. Later chapters describe the use of many of the classes supplied in the built-in object libraries, including menus, dialogs, edit boxes, resource files and the print services. One chapter provides some advice on application design using the Series 3a/c 'Record' application as a model.

- Introduction and basic concepts
- Building an object-oriented application
- Building a Dynamic Library (DYL)
- An HWIM example - Hello World
- Commands and command menus
- Windows
- Dialogs and Dialog controls
- Active objects
- Error handling and recovery
- File based applications
- Edit windows
- Printing
- Link paste
- HWIM resource files

- Application design
- Series 3a attached applications
- Series 3a automatic test system
- Category and method function source files
- Mechanisms

An earlier version (v2.01) of the chapters in this manual can be found in the OOPDOC201 directory on disk.

ISAM Reference

The ISAM (Indexed Sequential Access Method) object library provides a powerful set of functions to access record and field structured files of the type that are manipulated by OPL programs and the Data application on SIBO machines.

The ISAM Reference manual explains, with the aid of example code, how to load and use the ISAM library, and contains a complete description of the ISAM functions.

- Introduction and overview
- ISAM functions, general, data file and index file functions

OLIB Reference

The OLIB library contains a collection of object classes that provide services that are independent of the user interface, and are therefore suitable for use in the 'engine' code of any application. These services include data storage in a segmented buffer, arrays with a variable number of elements, basic text editing, event management and scheduling, file management, timers and time management and inter-process communication.

This manual contains complete descriptions of the object classes in the OLIB library. The classes described include:

- Introduction using OLIB classes
- The ROOT class
- The TIME class
- The SGBUF segmented buffer class
- Variable array classes (similar to container classes in C++)
- Editable documents
- Resource files (.RSC and .RZC)
- Binary file management
- The CLEANUP class - aids to error recovery
- The APPMAN - applications manager class
- The ACTIVE class and active objects
- Idle objects and the AIDLE class
- TIMER active object classes
- File active objects
- File lists
- File management classes

- The LOCS local file scan class
- System services
- IPCS - Inter-process communication
- Link paste

This library is built into all SIBO machines.

FORM Reference

The FORM library contains classes used in the storage, layout, display and printing (including print preview) of formatted editable text. This manual contains descriptions of the object classes in the FORM library. These classes provide the ability to store, display and print formatted document text. Supports printing to any printers that are supported by a printer device driver. Essentially FORM implements much of the engine of the word processor on the Series 3 family.

FORM depends on the window server but is independent of the higher level HWIM. It is used widely by HWIM to implement edit boxes, for example, and is thus used indirectly by all applications. It is used directly by the word processor and by other applications for text processing and for printing.

The topics include:

- Introduction, using form classes
- The Formatted document content classes
- The Document layout classes
- The Document printing classes
- The Print preview class
- The Calendar image class
- The Polytext classes

The library is built into the Work*about*, and into all members of the Series 3 family and Siena.

HWIM Reference

The HWIM Reference manual contains descriptions of more than seventy classes that provide the basic management of an event-driven application and the whole of an application's user interface. The HWIM Reference manual contains descriptions of the rich set of object classes that provide the application management environment and a sophisticated user interface for all machines in the Series 3 range. It contains classes that implement the Series 3 interface style, including menus and dialog boxes. Many of the commonly required dialogs are provided - for example, for print set-up, page layout and for presenting help. There is extensive support for file selection.

The range of topics includes:

- Introduction, using HWIM classes
- The HWIMMAN Application Manager

- The WSERV class
- The Command Manager
- Windows
- List Boxes and Menus
- Dialog Boxes
- Labels, buttons and choice lists
- Numeric editors
- Text Editors
- Gauge classes
- File selectors
- File list generator classes
- The FILELIST window class
- General system dialogs
- Print classes
- Dialling dialogs
- Help Classes
- OPL and comms script support
- Incremental matchers
- Link paste support
- Representations of time and date
- The GATE class
- HWIM utility functions
- HWIM reference update for Siena and Series 3c

The library is built into the Work*about*, and into all members of the Series 3 family and Siena.

XADD Reference

The XADD library consists of extensions to the HWIM and FORM libraries that are available on the Work*about,* Series 3a/c and Siena. The XADD library was introduced in the Series 3a machine and is not present in Series 3 machines. The contents include:

- Introduction, using XADD classes
- Print preview classes
- Calendar classes
- Automatic test system classes
- Additional active object classes
- Tabular grid display

The development process

An application written in C with the SIBO SDK must be developed on a PC. The TopSpeed Corporation's TopSpeed C compiler provides specific support for the generation of executables that are to run under the EPOC16 operating system.

Programs are written on the PC, using either the TopSpeed Environment or another program editor. When successfully compiled and linked the program is transferred to, and run on the machine. See the chapter 'Linking to a PC or Printer' for details of suitable cables and software. Transfer and testing may also be done under the control of the SIBO source level debugger that is provided with the SIBO C SDK.

Applications running on the machine may be remotely debugged from the PC, using the SIBO debugger. Those parts of the software that do not depend on the user interface code specific to the SIBO machine may be debugged locally on the PC.

If an appropriate SIBO emulator is available, it may be used for initial testing, but final testing should always take place on the machine itself.

Usually the various development steps: of editing, compilation, linking etc. are done in the DOS environment. It is possible operate in DOS sessions, for example launched from Windows 3.x, but this is not the most secure way of working. Most of the example programs and applications are built using a combination of project files (with .PR extensions) using DOS batch files to automate the 'make' process.

Programming options

In general terms, there are five different levels at which C programs can be written (using the C SDK) for SIBO systems:

- Using CLIB, with user interface restricted to console I/O of the `getchar` and `puts` variety
- Using PLIB, again with user interface restricted to console I/O.
- Using PLIB with WLIB, to access the graphics and windowing capabilities of the Window Server.
- Using HWIF, with its support for menus and dialogs similar to those available in OPL.
- Using object-oriented programming (OOP) i.e. the HWIM, FORM, OLIB and XADD DYLs built into the ROM.

CLIB

The CLIB library contains standard functions, familiar to most C developers, and is described in the TopSpeed C Library Reference manual supplied with the SIBO C SDK. A developer who wishes to port an existing application to a SIBO machine with a minimum amount of effort would use CLIB. However, a pure CLIB program is restricted to using a simple user interface with row and column text-based display.

PLIB

The PLIB library provides functions with equivalent behaviour to those supplied in CLIB. It is, however, more closely matched to the EPOC O/S and will, in general, result in a significantly smaller program than the equivalent version using CLIB. In addition, PLIB provides access to many of the EPOC system services that are not available in CLIB and can thus be used, for example, to develop applications with more sophisticated user interfaces. There is, however, more to learn for a programmer already familiar with standard C libraries. A compromise route is possible, since a CLIB program may also use a mix of PLIB functions.

Because of the advantages of code size and greater power, use of the PLIB library is the recommended route for most types of application development. Choosing this route opens up a range of further options.

The first of these is to use only the PLIB and WLIB libraries. In addition to PLIB's provision of full access to the EPOC system services, this approach allows complete flexibility in the design of an application's user interface. Development of a user interface comparable with that used by the built-in applications will, however, require a considerable programming effort. A second option is to use the services provided by the HWIF library in addition to PLIB.

HWIF

HWIF provides a C function interface to many user interface services of the built-in object libraries. It allows applications to make use of, for example, windows, command menus and dialogs, without the need to use object-oriented techniques or for an intimate knowledge of the object libraries themselves. Programs written in this way will generally use more memory than programs making direct use of the object libraries and will, in certain circumstances, lack some responsiveness to multiple event sources. HWIF is the C equivalent to OPL programs.

Dialog and menu interactions

An HWIF application enters a special mode when it makes the calls uPresentMenus, uRunDialog, hPrint or hPrintSetupDialog or calls the system help routines:

- System screen messages are blocked, the user is told that the application is 'busy'
- The application will not be made aware of background/foreground or switch on/off events.
- If a timer expires, or another non-key press event occurs, the application is only aware of this when the user concludes the menu or dialog interaction.

Processing of events passes to a central get-event loop in ROM code. This ROM get-event loop can only process events from event sources it explicitly knows about - and this excludes any timers, alarms, or other non-key press event sources installed by the application.

Programmers working with HWIF based C can gain access to some of the HWIM dialog features (as described in the 'User Interface' chapter) see the section 'HWIF with some OOP' in the 'C SDK examples' section later in this chapter.

Note that the HWIF library is not built into any machine, but is supplied with the SIBO C SDK.

Object-oriented programming (OOP)

A third option is to make use of Psion's object-oriented programming system. This allows developers to take advantage of the OLIB, HWIM, FORM and XADD object libraries that are built into most machines. Applications developed in this way derive the maximum benefit from the built-in system software, but at the cost of an appreciable learning curve.

Applications written using OOP and the object libraries have a number of advantages over those written in OPL and those written in HWIF C. Some of the more significant advantages are:

- By default an HWIM application maintains its screen's appearance by using a dynamic redrawing technique. OPL and HWIF use backed-up bitmaps, using more memory and slowing down drawing to the screen.
- A number of classes such as dialog boxes and dialog box controls already exist, with default behaviour. As such, they can be used directly, or sub-classed as required for more specialised behaviour. Such classes permit quite sophisticated applications to be built fairly quickly.
- The contents of dialog boxes and menus can be changed dynamically, allowing a more sophisticated dialog with the user. Also, consistency and dependency checks can be performed before allowing the user to exit from a dialog. Both of these are difficult, if not impossible, with HWIF.
- Program activity may continue while a menu or a dialog is being displayed.
- All resources are placed in resource files. This encourages the creation of language independent applications.
- OOP permits software to be re-used. Standard classes can be developed for one application and can be re-used in another.
- The object paradigm is well suited to the design process, particularly for interactive event-driven programs with graphical interfaces.

OOP options

An application can make use of OOP techniques in one of a number of different ways. This section explains the main options that are available.

Using existing object libraries

An otherwise non-object oriented C application can simply create and use one or more objects from existing object libraries. A typical example of this kind of usage is the using the ISAM DYL library for database access. Example code is provided on disk to illustrate how to create an instance of a class from an external category and send messages to it. Note that, since the ISAM DYL is not in the ROM, it has to be explicitly loaded before being linked.

In principle, this technique can be used with any class from an existing object library. However, in practice it is restricted to classes that do not depend on the user interface. The ISAM example is typical in this respect, in that it uses the console services to supply its user interface.

The technique is particularly suitable for creating and using instances of classes such as the variable array (container) classes in OLIB. In such a case, where the class library being used is in the ROM, there is no need to load it before linking. Examples of using array classes are provided on disk.

One of the main advantages of this technique is that it requires very little additional knowledge, other than the details of the particular class or classes that are being used.

Application-specific classes

Rather than simply using an existing class, an application may define one or more application-specific classes. These classes may, by sub-classing, add value to other existing library classes or may be totally new classes (although a 'new' class is, in fact, a subclass of the OLIB ROOT class). Such an application may also make use of existing object libraries, as described above.

Although it is possible to write a fully object oriented application of this type, a typical application will still be largely written in non-object oriented code. As for applications that simply use existing classes, the technique is better suited to classes that do not depend on the user interface.

A simple example of an application of this type appears in the 'Building an Object Oriented Application' chapter of the 'OOP Guide' manual in the C SDK. The example code is provided in the \sibosdk\oopdemo directory of the C SDK.

Using a DYL

Instead of using the classes of an existing object library, an application can use objects in a custom object library (or DYL). The way to create and use a custom DYL is described in the 'Building a Dynamic Library' chapter of the 'OOP Guide' manual in the C SDK. The example code is provided in the \sibosdk\oopdemo directory of the C SDK.

The classes in the DYL may be any combination of 'new' classes or subclasses of existing library classes. This technique may be combined with the use both of custom libraries and of custom classes in the application itself, as described above.

In addition to the advantages of the previous techniques, writing one or more parts of an application as separate DYLs allows for easier code sharing and re-use and allows large applications to be written (a single code segment may not exceed 64 Kbytes).

See the 'Example' sections later in this chapter.

Using HWIM

A developer who wishes to create an application with an object oriented user interface should make use of the HWIM class library.

This case is qualitatively different from those described above, in that many of the classes in the HWIM library are designed to be used together, and are not particularly suited to being used in isolation. Some of the classes rely on the existence of instances of other classes and on certain specific initialisation having been performed. This is the reason why the techniques described above are not recommended for the HWIM user interface classes.

An HWIM application always contains a basic framework of objects to provide those features that are common to all HWIM applications. These features include the provision of command menus and dialogs, the handling of multiple event sources and the direction of keyboard events to the appropriate object(s) within the application. Such an application requires a specific form of start-up code in its `main()` function to create the basic framework and perform the necessary initialisation.

Many of the HWIM application framework classes can be used directly, but an application will always define and use application-specific classes, including sub-classes of the classes supplied by HWIM. The application may also, of course, use or subclass the classes from other object libraries - either the standard libraries that are in the ROM, or application-specific DYLs.

See the 'Example' sections later in this chapter.

Code and data size limits

The TopSpeed C compiler was chosen by Psion because it supports a pure small model, for which the code generator totally abstains from manipulating the 8086 segment registers. Other C compilers occasionally save and restore the segment registers to memory when generating small model code.

As it happens there are other benefits to using the TopSpeed C compiler:

- In the EPOC environment, the code generated by the TopSpeed C compiler is typically 20% more compact than that produced by Turbo C or Microsoft C.
- It supports register-based (rather than just stack-based) calling conventions which contribute to its compact code generation and also reduce execution times.
- Psion used its capability to define custom calling conventions (via `#pragma` statements) to interface efficiently with the software interrupts of the system services (in some cases removing entirely the need for interfacing code)

Because the functions in the PLIB library for TopSpeed C use custom calling conventions, **the use of C prototypes is mandatory**.

When programming in C for EPOC, you **must** program using the small model, in which the code and the data segment are each limited to 64K bytes. The restriction to the small model allows EPOC to move memory segments, including the process code and data segments, without any co-operation from applications. Being able to move memory segments around in a multitasking system (for example, as processes are created and destroyed) is vital for efficient RAM usage.

For reasons described earlier, program executables tend to be significantly smaller when built in EPOC compared to other environments (such as a PC) and the 64K code segment limit is less likely to be a problem than you might have first thought. It is also true that small model code is in any case more compact because function and variable addresses are 16-bit words.

Notwithstanding the above, if an application does require more than 64K of code, there are the following options:

- Break up the application into a main process with multiple transient sub-processes.
- Implement part of the functionality in a server process where the services are accessed using inter-process messaging.
- Implement part of the functionality as a device driver, accessed via I/O system calls.
- When using object-oriented programming (OOP) or otherwise, break up the program into multiple dynamic libraries containing external classes that are accessed by OOP message sending.

The 64K data segment limit is normally large enough for the stack and miscellaneous data structures. Dynamic data structures are typically allocated from the 'heap'. This resides at the high address end of the data segment and can grow as the need arises.

When a program does require more than 64K of data, it is often because of a single data structure that can grow to a large size (such as, for example, a word processor document). Such potentially large data structures may be implemented in external memory segments where a particular segment can grow up to a limit of 512K bytes. However, the access to data in an external segment is not as convenient as it is for data in the process data segment. Library functions are available for the management of memory segment.

Directories in the C SDK

The full set of sub-directories under the \SIBOSDK directory are listed in the table below. The contents of each sub-directory are summarised in the table. Some directories may be optional or are specific to the SDK version. Where appropriate, the contents of the sub-directories listed in the following table are described in more detail. For example, the contents of each sub-directory that contains significant example programs/applications is discussed in the text following the table.

Sub-directory	Contents
\ATS	Automatic Test System demo macro recorder/player
\DEMO	Various standard demo programs – from very simple to more complex
\EWDEMO	Simple edit windows example – use of some OOP techniques
\FCONV	OOP source code for the creation of file format conversion DYLs for Word
\FONT	Font file source code examples
\HCMAST	Software allowing alternative versions of the HC ROM to be built
\HWDEMO	HWIF source code demonstrating extensive use of the HWIF library
\HWIFOOD	HWIF examples making use of OOP techniques
\HWIFSRC	The entire, build-able, source of the HWIF library, for interest and/or to allow the writing of extensions to HWIF
\HWIMDEMO	Source code demonstrating use of Date and Gauge classes in HWIM
\INCLUDE	Header and include files - .h, .g, .rg, .rh, .rsg, .inc, .hpp, ing etc.
\LDD	Assembler source code for some example LDD logical device drivers
\LIB	Standard libraries, startup objects, and some loadable device drivers (dynamic extensions to the SIBO operating system)
\NOTES	A full HWIM version of Notes program (HWIF version is in \HWDEMO)
\OOPDEMO	Programs demonstrating the basic use of the Object Oriented Programming system (other directories contain more advanced examples)
\PR	Some standard/example project files
\RECORD	Source of the Object Oriented Series 3a Record application. This is build-able, provided that the \sibosdk\oop directory has also been installed
\RESOURCE	System resource script files (.RSS) for English machine ROMS
\S3ATOOL	Series 3a versions of an Icon editor and the Spy applications
\SRC	Source code for the CLIB (standard C) library (not present in all versions)
\SYS	The SIBO Debugger and many other programming tools and file converters
\TPRINT	OOP source code demonstrating use of LPRINTER classes
\WD	Printer script source for some WDR printer driver files
\WDRPRINT	OOP source code demonstrating use of XPRINTER classes plus the saving of print settings
\WKDEMO	HWIF (Tables) and HWIM (Lcdtest) examples for the Work*about*

Example programs in the C SDK

The examples supplied with the Psion C SDK are listed below by directory and typically with the title of manual\chapter where they are discussed.

\sibosdk\demo	
General Programming Manual – Fundamental Programming Guidelines	
HELLO.C	A first example application using CLIB
P_HELLO.C	A PLIB version of Hello World
EVENTS.C	First version of Events
EVENTS2.C	Second version of Events
EVENTS3.C	Third version of Events
EVENTS4.C	Fourth version of Events
Writing for the HC	
W_HELLO.C	A graphics version of Hello World
GAUGE.C	Graphics and timers illustrated
LINED.C	Line editor code and test code
Series3/3a Programming Guide	
SOUND.C	Using the SND: device driver on the Series 3a
Additional System Info	
READRSC.C	Reading the contents of a resource file
PLIB Reference	
P_DLIST.C	Using p_dinfo to list devices
P_PRNDIR.C	Using p_open(P_FDIR) to list a directory
P_COMP.C	Binary file access (comparing two files)
P_SEARCH.C	Text file access (p_read to search a text file)
Window Server Reference	
PCXSAVE.C	Capturing the screen directly to a PCX file
SCAPT.C	Screen capture program using MCLINK RUN
FONTS.C	The program used to generate the font pictures in the manuals
HC Programming Guide - Replacing the shell on the HC	
HCSHELL.C	Sample shell/application
LKSHELL.C	Minimal shell for remote debugging on the HC
General window server funcs	
ALERT.C	Alert3 example of calling wsAlertW
Windows Server – Clocks	
CLOCK.C	Clocks demonstration for the HC
Window Server – Graphics output	
BUTTON.C	Intended use of wDrawButton

\sibosdk\ats

Demonstrates the use of the ATS mechanisms (outside of an OOP application) by operating as a Macro recorder/player. See 'The Series 3a Automatic Test System in the OOP guide.

\sibosdk\ewdemo

The source code for a simple edit window example ehello.img. This program draws a one-line edit window in the middle of the screen, and diverts most incoming key presses to that window. Demonstrates use of some OOP techniques - see the 'OOP Guide' manual in the C SDK. See the \Notes directory for a more complex example OOP program.

\sibosdk\hwdemo

Each paragraph in the following section is headed by the name (in bold type) of an HWIF application. The associated text describes the principle characteristics of each application and the particular programming techniques that it illustrates. Although these are HWIF applications the methods employed are likely to be useful for non-HWIF applications, for instance, in HWIM programs.

Query focuses almost exclusively on the basic **menu** and **dialog functionality** of HWIF (use of the HWIF **time-text utility functions** is also illustrated). Examples are given of **each of the possible items that can be included in dialogs**. There are only **a few graphics calls**, and these are completely straightforward. There is no file-handling (likewise in fact for all of the first four example applications). The application itself provides answers to questions that a user may wish to pose, such as the **conversion of centigrade values into Fahrenheit** or **miles into kilometres**; the next **occurrence of a certain date** combination (e.g. Friday the 13th); the **size of a specified file**, and the **encryption** and **decryption** (using a supplied key) **of given text** messages. Query also demonstrates **PLIB functions that avoid the floating-point emulator**. Note that **QU1.C** to **QU4.C** are development stages leading up to the **Query** application.

Tables, introduces **reading a key asynchronously**. It involves the user typing in the answer to a multiplication problem (such as '4 times 9') before **a timer** that is ticking away on screen runs out completely. Also introduces use of a simple HWIF **edit box** (with double height characters), and includes examples of **several useful graphics techniques** - with an **animated action button** and a **growing gauge display** outside of the context of a dialog. On exit, the **state of the application is recorded in an environment variable**, which is used to re-initialise the application the next time it is run. Note that **TA1.C** to **TA3.C** are development stages leading up to the **Tables** application.

Remind, functions as a half-way-house between the built-in **Agenda** application and the built-in **Time** application. Allows users to **set alarms** with text strings, that **can be 'snoozed'** by specified time intervals. Illustrates access to the **alarm server device**. It demonstrates more of the **important concepts concerning asynchronous I/O**. Also introduces another large subject: **printing and access to the Print Setup dialog**. The main screen display is a **scrolling list** of all reminders scheduled by the user, automatically **sorted into chronological order**. The graphics calls employed demonstrate how to achieve **smooth scrolling** (without undue screen flicker). Finally, on receipt of the key-press control+menu, Remind hides or shows a **permanent status window**, and adjusts the rest of its display accordingly.

In Remind, all text has been removed from the source module remind.c and placed in suitable structures in the **remind.rss resource file**. Code in remind.c ensures that the resources are loaded as needed. Several aspects should be noted: The custom project file remind.pr contains the instruction 'runrs remind' which has the result of **creating the binary file remind.rsc** from the plain text file remind.rss using the batch file rs.bat which in turn invokes the **resource compiler rcomp.exe**. The binary file remind.rsc is listed in the **add-file-list** file remind.afl to ensure that it is automatically linked together with the object code as part of the application file remind.app. The routine LoadMenus in remind.c **loads the menu text out of the resource file** into static data structures and then 'walks' the data structures, converting them into the form required by the HWIF menu sub-system. In contrast, **string data is only loaded** into memory **when required** using the function LoadStr. The code in remind.c is copiously commented.

Notes is another application that functions as a half-way house between the functionality of two of the built-in applications: it straddles **some of the characteristics of the built-in Database and Word applications**. The screen is divided up into **three edit windows**, Title, Notes, and Find, with the data for a series of notes being directly **edited in place** (as opposed to being manipulated only through dialogs). As well as providing a wide-ranging survey of the editing facilities available via HWIF, the Notes application also gives **a further example of printing**. An **HWIM version of Notes** is located in the \sibosdk\notes directory.

Dump produces a **Hex dump of a nominated file;** displayed on the screen in the first instance, but a selected portion of the dump can be **written out to a nominated file**. The dump can be **scrolled in any direction**, it is possible to **search it, either for strings of text, or for byte streams**. The application **introduces file-handling**, both of the file to be dumped (initially chosen from the system screen), and of the file to receive a written record of the dump. Finally, the use of a **special mode** is illustrated, in which repeated cursor key-presses may cause the display to be drawn in its new position only when there is a suitable delay in receiving keys.

Tele and **Days** are two applications illustrating different uses of the **.DBF database sub-system**. These applications differ from both Notes and Remind in that **they make permanent copies of their data on file** (whereas Notes and Remind just operate with in-memory data). Both of these applications **deal with Shutdown and Switchfile messages** from the system screen.

Tele is a simple example of a **fixed field database**, with fields for a name, a department code, and a telephone extension number. **Records can be added, deleted, updated, searched for, and even sorted (using quicksort)**. A couple of other .DBF file options are also illustrated: **Merge and Copy**. Telephone numbers, once found, can have corresponding **DTMF tones emitted**. The main screen display is straightforward, involving **double height characters**.

Days illustrates a .DBF database that stores peoples' birthdays (or other days of interest), along with a notes field. The application **maintains an in-memory index** that **sorts the entries** by date to facilitate a more meaningful presentation of the contents of the database. The **main screen view is somewhat elaborate**: it can be **toggled between a series of edit**

boxes (as in Notes) and **a scrolling list** (as in Remind). Alteration of the data takes place by direct manipulation in the **edit boxes**.

Spy reveals many secrets of the inner workings of the Series 3, which present a **list of all the processes running** at any one time, together with specified information, such as the **number of cells in the allocator heap of that process**, and the **watermark on its stack**. This list can be **refreshed on a timer**, the application also provides an additional example of **asynchronous keyboard reads**.

Joker is a maverick application, whose main role is to instantiate all the **special cases tested for by Spy**. For example, Joker can **corrupt its allocator heap on demand**, in a variety of different ways.

Iconed is a full-blown **icon editor**, which can be used to **design icons for new applications** and to improve the icons shipped with the example applications. This illustrates a whole variety of **more advanced graphics calls**, as well as **another set of possibilities in file-based applications**.

\sibosdk\hwifood - HWIF with some OOP

It is possible to arrange for an HWIF program to use parts of the built-in object-oriented libraries OLIB, FORM, HWIM and (from 3a onwards) XADD. For example, to use the object-oriented dialogs, via the `hOODialog` function. The techniques involved are described in the 'Advanced Use of HWIF' chapter in the 'Programming in HWIF' manual of the C SDK. The 'oquery' is derived from the HWIF 'query' example, but 'oquery' uses an OOP style dialog by using a DYL. The 'gbar' example uses a growing scroll bar gauge and uses OOP techniques by modifying the HWIF category itself.

\sibosdk\notes

The example application Notes.app. Full source code and supporting resource and project files for an HWIM OOP application to demonstrate three edit windows. This application is an HWIM version of the HWIF notes example program in the \sibosdk\hwdemo directory.

\sibosdk\oopdemo

Simpler demonstrations of OOP techniques than found in the Notes and Record examples.

The 'prndir' example application is written largely in non-object oriented code and is described in the 'Building an Object Oriented Application' chapter of the 'OOP Guide' manual.

Two 'hello world' example HWIM programs are provided.

The 'timer' demonstration application uses a timer to illustrate the use of **active object techniques**.

The 'sort and rsort' examples demonstrate two ways to create and use **a custom DYL** and are described in the 'Building a Dynamic Library' chapter of the 'OOP Guide' manual.

\sibosdk\record

Full build-able source code for a 'Record' application built-in to the Series 3a. Full Object Oriented Series 3a Record application. The design of this application is described in detail in the 'Application Design' chapter of the OOP Guide manual.

\sibosdk\wkdemo

HWIF version of the 'Tables' application and an HWIM program 'Lcdtest' tailored for the Work*about*.

'Charger.c' is a Work*about* program to monitor and control the fast charger circuitry in the docking station. Allows the main battery, or spare battery to be charged, or the main battery to be discharged, and the status of both batteries to be monitored.

Examples from the text of the I/O Devices Reference manual

The examples described below only exist as listings in the text of the C SDK manuals; they are not provided in source file format.

Console chapter, P16-18 simple Console example. A short program consisting of two parts, the first part simply receives keys typed by the user and reports them by type on the screen. The second part enables the user to scroll a part of the display and to set the console attributes (scroll lock, line wrap etc) to see how they affect the way typed characters are displayed.

Parallel Port chapter P21-22. Simple use of the Parallel port.

Serial Port chapter, P32-36. Simple use of the Serial port

Sound chapter, P40. 'Ice cream van' dual tone sound.

Sound chapter, P41-42. DTMF Dialling tones.

Xmodem and Ymodem chapter, P69-71. Simple file transfers.

NCP and Link chapter, P82-83. Client server link example.

HC Intelligent bar code chapter, P110-111. Bar code reading.

AccessIR API chapter, P125-128. Infrared inter-machine transfers.

Examples on disk

A wide range of general C examples are supplied on disk, including full applications in HWIF and HWIM C. There are also numerous C snippets and examples of using C with OPL, in particular by calling DYLs. See the descriptive lists and the index in the 'Disk Contents' chapter.

12 OVAL Programming

Introduction

OVAL is short for 'Object-based Visual Application Language'; it is a relatively new visual programming system from Psion. In brief, it's Visual Basic for the Psion; 'Object-based' just refers to the way of working when developing an application. OVAL is code-compatible with Microsoft Visual Basic and includes over thirty controls that are specially designed for building Psion applications, and take full advantage of the EPOC16 operating system. In general, if you know VB, you will be well on your way with OVAL.

OVAL introduces visual programming, rapid application development and application prototyping to the Psion environment. It appears to be a very powerful and flexible programming system, that is designed to dramatically speed up application development.

OVAL applications are only currently applicable to the Series 3c and later Work*about* machines. A 32-bit implementation OVAL for EPOC32 based system is planned, but it is not expected until the first half of 1998.

To run OVAL applications the run-time system has to be present in the machine, since OVAL (like OPL) is an interpreted language. OVAL code is translated into tokenised code rather than compiled into machine code as with C or C++. On the Series 3c and Work*about* machines the ROMs are considerably bigger than in earlier SIBO systems, because the OVAL run-time interpreter is very large. Putting so much 'library code' in ROM has the benefit of minimising the size of OVAL applications themselves.

Developing in OVAL

It is not possible to produce OVAL applications on the SIBO system directly. To develop in OVAL, you'll need the Windows-based development environment; it features an intelligent source code editor, code translators for Psion computers and over 30 application controls. Developers design applications graphically in a PC based integrated development environment (IDE) and test them using a suitable Psion computer connected via a serial link cable.

OVAL platform

Developing in OVAL requires a PC-compatible computer with: 80386 or better CPU, a colour VGA display, 4 MB RAM or more (8MB recommended), 2 MB disk space or more and a serial link connection (e.g. Link cable – see the 'Linking to a PC or Printer' chapter).

The OVAL IDE will run under the following operating systems: Windows 3.1 or higher, Windows 95, Windows NT 3.5 or higher, OS/2 2.1 or higher.

OVAL and events

Graphical user-driven interfaces, of the type found on SIBO systems demand a particular approach to programming. The conventional linear program structure of: user data input, processing of the data and the display of the results is not suitable for use with OVAL. In addition to user actions and input, 'events' of other types may occur and they all have to be handled by the application. For example, the expiry of a timer or the receipt of a system message are also events to be detected and processed. To be able to process a range of events of the type described, the application will typically have an 'event loop' in which it will wait for an event to occur, process it and then return to waiting for the next event. OVAL is designed to operate in this way, and will not take kindly to being 'bent out of shape' and forced to operate according to the old linear approach.

By their very nature OVAL applications are event driven, that is they are capable of handling a range of user actions plus other events arriving from multiple sources. Event driven applications will remain responsive to user input and events from other sources e.g. timers and input/output from devices such as the serial port. This, so-called asynchronous operation, is difficult to achieve in OPL (or HWIF C) and usually requires the use of Object Oriented Programming in C (e.g. HWIM C); it is fundamental to OVAL.

OVAL makes the task of handling multiple events easier. I recommend that you carefully study the design and operation of the example applications provided, and then construct your own according to the same fundamental structure.

OVAL IDE

The OVAL development system consists of an excellent MS Windows hosted Integrated Development Environment (IDE) from Psion that includes:

- A project manager.
- A powerful multi-file source code editor with coloured syntax highlighting.
- Powerful context sensitive help that calls on an OVAL reference library.
- PC to SIBO communications capability – (a link cable is not included).
- Source code for a range of illustrative OVAL examples.
- A set of utility programs for sound and graphics file conversions, plus a font compiler for producing custom font sets.

Note:

The **Ovaldemo** directory on disk contains a fully functional OVAL integrated development environment (IDE) from Psion Software; the only restriction is that you can use a maximum of two forms and two modules in each project. For the most up-to-date copy of the OVAL evaluation IDE you should visit the Psion Website - see the 'Contacts and Sources' chapter for details.

The development process

Applications are produced graphically using the PC based IDE and are tested after translation using a suitable Psion computer connected via a serial link cable.

You start writing a new program in OVAL by creating a new project file, adding source files and other application related files as they are created.

OVAL applications are held in project files that .OVP file extensions. The components of a project include: Forms, Dialogs, Modules, Resources, Pictures and Files.

To help you get started a number of example applications are provided with the IDE. A screen shot below shows a database example OVDATA.OVP loaded into the OVAL IDE.

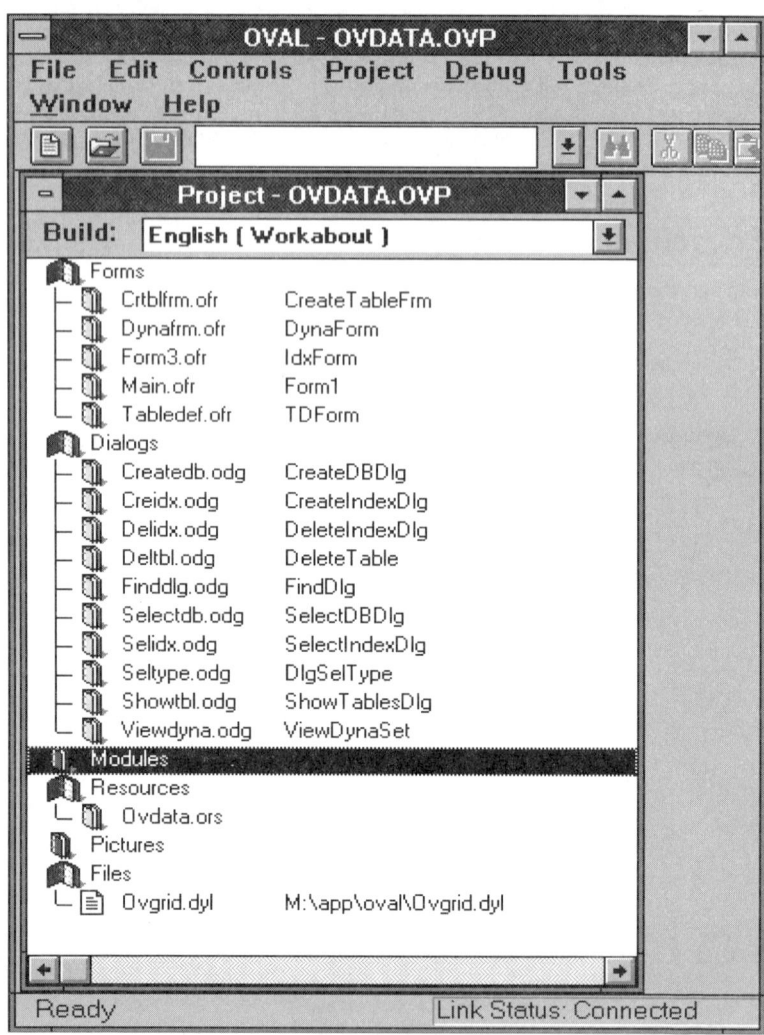

OVAL provides facilities to the programmer via a very extensive range of keywords and functions within the language itself, but also via the numerous controls available plus their associated property. The fundamental elements of an OVAL application are 'forms' and 'controls'. Every program usually has at least one form, to act as the graphical backdrop on which the interface elements (or controls) are placed, for example: menus, user input, text, graphics etc. A form appears as a window when the application is run, and a separate form is required for each window in the application. A form is a 'container' for controls; dialogs and frames are other types of container.

In the screen shot below, the main form is open for editing; also shown is the control selection palette.

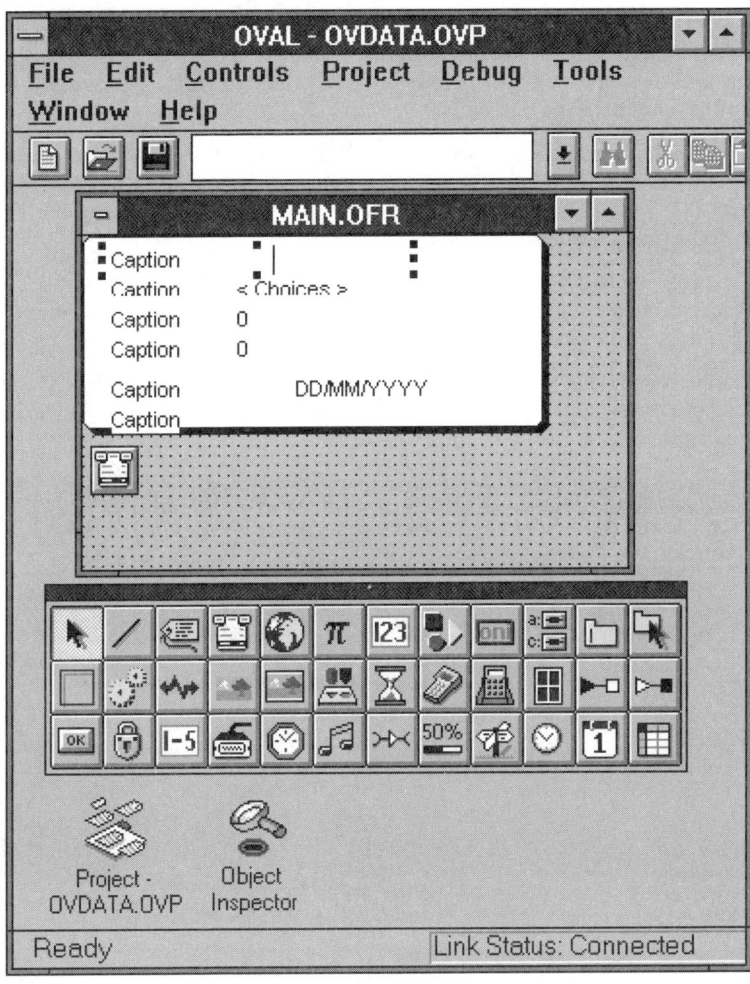

Examples controls are: text, menus, buttons, input fields, each control has information associated with it: its physical appearance, its current state, the things the user can do to it and with it (its events), and the code that determines what the application does in response to a given event.

All the information relating to a control is stored in its properties (i.e. associated data). For example, the pressed or un-pressed state of a button is a property element, so is its size, position on the form, its colour etc.

Imagine a control such as a button; it has an appearance and a state - on or off. It responds to one event: when it gets pressed. When the button is pressed, OVAL changes its appearance and state, then generates a suitable event.

Usually a procedure will have been written, in OVAL BASIC, to specifically handle such an event, OVAL then executes that procedure. The procedure might, for example, display a dialog box, or quit the program etc.

You can get information from a control by looking at its properties, and you can also set the properties in order to change the appearance, behaviour or state of the control. If your code sets the 'state property' of the button to 'on', OVAL will change the buttons' appearance just as if it had been pressed.

Some controls are hidden and do not actually appear on the screen, but are useful nonetheless. A good example is the Timer control, which simply generates an event after a specified period of time.

In the form example shown above a date edit field can be seen, indicated by dd/mm/yyyy, the specific characteristics of that field can be seen, and modified by using the object inspector shown below.

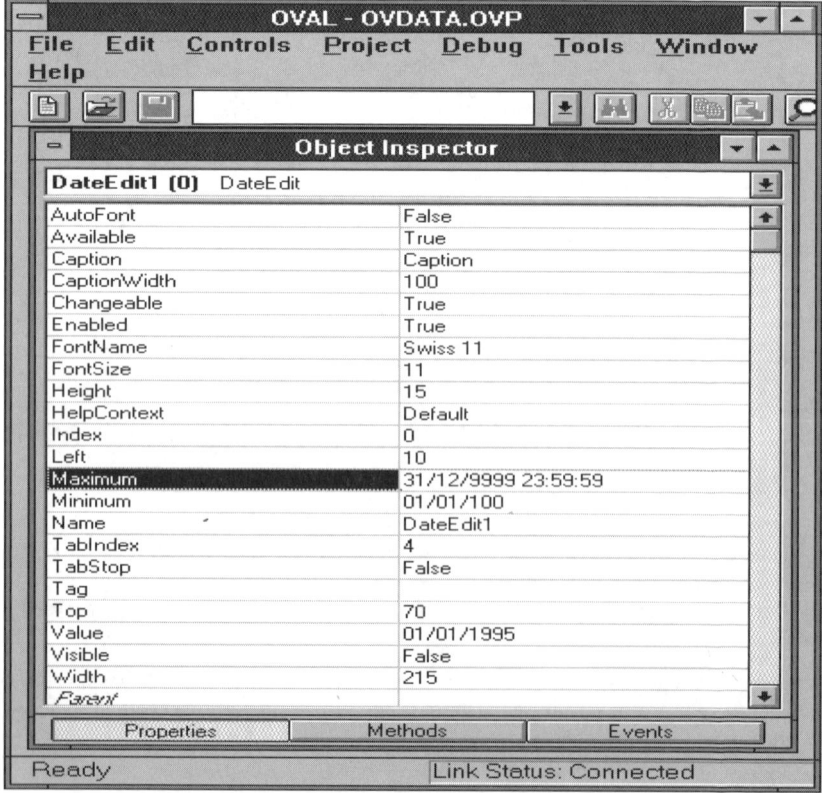

As can be seen, a wide range of object attributes can be varied, including the initial date value, the minimum and maximum values for the field etc.

Creating sophisticated menus is easily achieved using the menu editor, as shown in the example screen below.

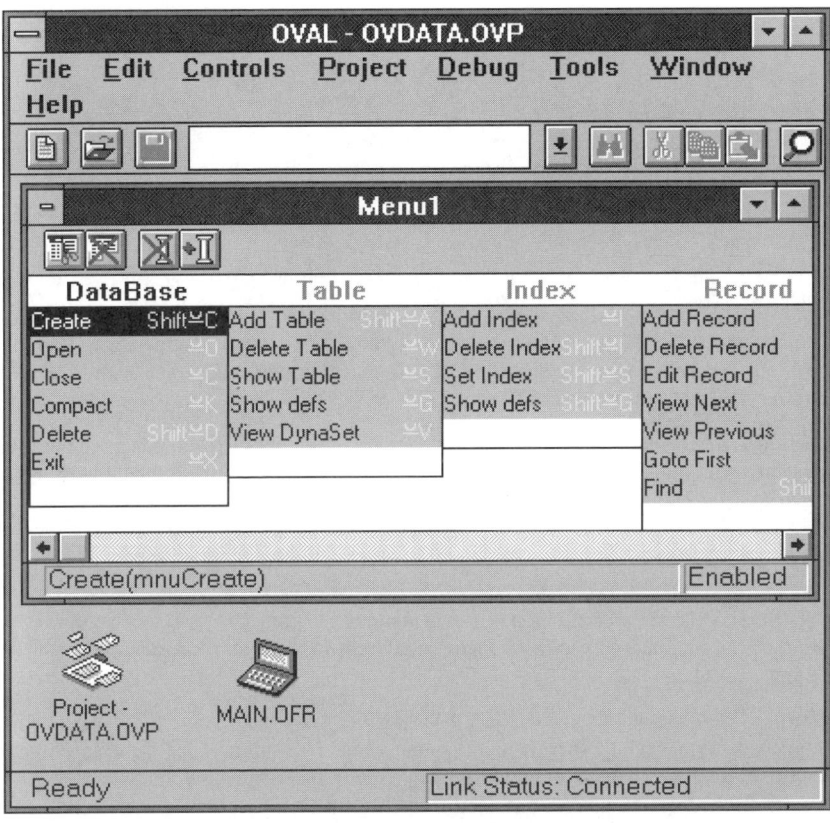

Accelerator keys and corresponding sub-routines are associated with each of the menu options created within the application. In the menu item dialog box above, the accelerator key for the menu option is set to 'Psion C' and the sub-routine mnuCreate (show below) is called when the menu option is selected.

```
Sub mnuCreate_Click ()
    Dbload = DATA_CREATE
    CreateDBDlg.Show
End Sub
```

The sub-routine mnuCreate opens a user dialog to get details of the database to be created. The dialog box opened, CreateDBDlg, is the first one listed in the main project view (the very first screen shot) shown under the heading 'Dialogs'.

Editing of OVAL BASIC program code is done through a very good multi-window editor that has many powerful features, such as an outline view of program procedures, colour syntax highlighting and an excellent multi-file text search facility.

Data files associated with the application can also form part of the project information, and files may be flagged for transfer to the SIBO system. The project file tracking system will update all earlier versions of files on the SIBO machine, replacing them with their more up-to-date PC versions as required.

Additional information and code macros can be '#included' from other source files. Constants with long identifier names may be '#defined' and conditional translation is supported.

IDE extras

In addition to allowing the creation of forms, dialogs, program code and menus, the OVAL IDE contains a number of very useful additional 'project sections' i.e. Modules, Resources, Pictures and Files.

Modules: are containers for code and data. An OVAL project consists of one or more modules. A form module, for example, contains the description of the form, information about it, and all the controls and code associated with that form. Each module resides in a separate file associated with the project. Code attached to a particular form is private to that form - that is, code in other forms cannot access it. Sections of program code placed in a code module is accessible to all parts of an OVAL program i.e. they are used for code which you want to be able to access from several forms.

Resources: are used to store program specific string information, constant data and user help text. Resources and help text can be edited from within the IDE. When the application is built the resource information can be included in the resulting .APP file. Separating this type of information away from the program code eases the production of multi-lingual applications.

Pictures: holds the file names for bitmap files, such as the program icon and any other bitmaps that may be used by the application. An icon editor is included within the IDE. PC type bitmap (.BMP) files may also be included and they will be converted to the Psion (.PIC) format before being transferred to the Psion.

Files: may hold the names of any other files required by the application, they will be copied over to the Psion as required.

Builds: You can specify different 'builds' for a given OVAL project, with whatever associated files you want. For example, incorporating language specific resource files to produce a multi-lingual application.

Running applications

OVAL generates fully-fledged applications that have icons and can be installed on to the system screen. All of the properties of an OVAL application including the application type, the icon and other .PIC files, resource files etc. are specified as options and file names etc. within the Oval integrated development environment. When the Oval application is generated they are included as part of the .APP file.

To run OVAL applications the Psion **must** contain the OVAL run-time interpreter, this is currently limited to the Psion 3c and its industrial relative the Work*about*.

When you wish to test the code, the build options can be configured to translate all the source files, transfer the executables and related files to the SIBO system, and start up the application on the machine.

Oval applications can be distributed without attached royalties, to suitably equipped users, either on SSD or on floppy disk for installation from a PC. There are no restrictions attached to any OVAL applications that you may develop but Psion retain the copyright over the development environment and documentation. Since the OVAL run-time system is ROM based, it will occasionally be necessary to distribute other OVAL components, such as updated libraries (.DYLs), along with your application. Psion do not normally place any restrictions on the developer in doing this.

Debugging

OVAL provides extensive facilities for PC hosted source code debugging of applications including: breakpoints, debug messages, step execution, watches and immediate code.

- A breakpoint is a point in the code where OVAL will stop and allow you to inspect variables, see the call stack and execute immediate code (see below).
- Debug messages allow you to print information to the Debug window from within your application.
- Step execution allows 'Step over' and 'Step into' options to execute one line of code at a time - rather as if every line in your application was set as a breakpoint. 'Step into' traces every single line, while 'Step over' treats a procedure call as a single line and does not trace through the procedure itself.
- Watches show the value of a variable or expression, or allow you to pause the application under certain conditions (as though OVAL had encountered a breakpoint).

- Immediate code - while the application is paused in debugging mode, you can enter any legal OVAL statements into the Debug window and see the result. For example, you could use it to inspect a variable local to the current procedure.

Performance

On a Series 3c OVAL for example, applications can take a surprisingly long time to start up, this can be disconcerting at first. However, when the application has initialised and is running, the overall speed can seem to be quite good. Simple OVAL applications are probably a little slower than an OPL equivalent. However, the demonstration Formula 1 database application was very slow to respond to certain user actions.

Reliability

Version 1.0 of the OVAL translator and run-time system had a number of fairly significant reliability problems. In particular, there were problems with the integral database management system and an interim fix was released by Psion to address these specific problems (see the OVAL section in the 'Disk Contents' chapter for details of the fixed files).

At the time of going to print (September 1997) version 1.1 of OVAL is undergoing final testing, and is due for release before the end of the year. Version 1.1 is not intended to be comprehensive revision of OVAL, instead Psion have concentrated on addressing the reliability issues.

Manuals and documentation

OVAL is supplied with a single manual (180 pages) in a format that is slightly wider than A5. The manual is designed to take a user, who is new to visual programming, through each of the stages required to build a simple application. Later chapters describe key concepts such as variables and objects, controls, files, graphics, databases etc. However, all of the detailed information required for in-depth programming is located in three very large Windows help files. These files cover:

- OVAL help – a guide to using and developing with OVAL that supplements the printed manual.
- OVAL Control Reference – a detailed guide to the available controls, their properties and methods.
- OVAL Language Reference – a detailed guide to the OVAL BASIC language keywords and syntax.

In general the help files are very useful, and at first they seem to be quite comprehensive. However, when put into practical use, the Language Reference file supplied with version 1.00 of OVAL was incomplete in a number of important areas, and contained quite a few syntax errors. Since the Windows help files are the programmers' only reference it is very important that they should be fully comprehensive, and most of all correct. Hopefully, version 1.1 of OVAL will address this situation.

Support

The main source of information and support from Psion for programmers and developers is supposed to be via the Psion Websites, in particular the EPOC World Website. However, no specific provisions currently seem to be in place on the EPOC World Website for OVAL developers.

In the past, support for OVAL from Psion has been somewhat limited. The best source of help and advice for OVAL developers is probably available from the 'on-line' discussion forums. For example, active Psion programming related discussions take place on CIX, CompuServe and Usenet. If you are considering a commercial project based on OVAL, going 'on-line' to seek the experiences of other developers could be very valuable. See the 'Contacts and Sources' chapter for details of how to access the on-line services and the Psion Websites.

OVAL IDE examples

A number of example projects are supplied with the OVAL development environment and demonstrate a range of programming techniques. Although it is puzzling that the applications provided with OVAL do not seem to be documented in any way.

Examples supplied with version 1.0 of OVAL include:

DEMO1.OVP – A small graphics demonstration, using an animated butterfly bitmap and a timer to control the animation interval.

WALK.OVP – A small graphics demonstration, using an animated figure with a timer to control the animation interval. The application starts up with an opening 'splash' screen.

BALL.OVP – A small animated graphics demonstration, using a variable shaped ball with a timer to control the animation interval.

PICVIEW.OVP – Uses a file selection dialog to allow the selection of a bitmap file (.PIC) and then displays the selected bitmap on screen.

IPCCLNT and **IPCSRVR.OVP** – used together illustrate inter-process messaging in the form of a client process and a server process that may send and receive messages.

OVSERIAL.OVP – Used with the Visual BASIC application **VBSERIAL.EXE**, demonstrate serial communications between a Psion machine and a PC.

OVDATA.OVP – Demonstrates a simple database creation application that allows the definition of tables with named fields.

DATABASE.OVP – A comprehensive demonstration of the OVAL database functionality using a database of Formula 1 motor-racing information. This is a complex and impressive application, but it was very slow to respond to certain information requests when run on a Psion 3c.

Examples on disk

Some additional OVAL example projects, programmers hint files and database patches are supplied on disk. Many of the examples and information files have come from the Psion Inc (USA) Website. See the descriptive lists and the index in the 'Disk Contents' chapter, and the 'Contacts and Sources' chapter for details of the Psion Website addresses.

The **Ovaldemo** directory on disk contains a fully functional OVAL integrated development environment (IDE) from Psion Software; the only restriction is that you can use a maximum of two forms and two modules in each project. For the most up-to-date copy of the OVAL evaluation IDE you should visit the Psion Website - see the 'Contacts and Sources' chapter for details.

Developing new OVAL controls

OVAL may be extended by adding new controls, this can only be done using the Psion SIBO C SDK in combination with a specific 'OVAL Controls SDK'. The new OVAL controls SDK is due out before the end of 1997. An extensive knowledge of HWIM C will be a pre-requisite for building new OVAL controls.

13   Series 5

Hardware

The Series 5 is fractionally larger (at 6.7" x 3.5" x 0.9") and a little heavier than a Series 3c, but it is still easily stowed in a pocket or handbag. Despite having the same form factor as the earlier machines the real innovations are revealed when the unit is opened out. The huge screen fills the upper half of the unit, and the keyboard seems too large to fit inside the shell when closed again.

The general outward appearance may be similar, but the internals of the Series 5 are radically different from previous SIBO machines. The central large scale device in the Series 5 is a CL-PS7110 manufactured by Cirrus Logic Inc, based around an ARM 7100 (Advanced RISC Machines Ltd) which is a 32-bit high-integration, application specific micro-controller, with very low power consumption. The CL-PS7110 device was developed by a close collaboration between Psion Computers and ARM.

Series 5 machines run under EPOC32, a completely new 32-bit operating system designed and written by Psion Software. EPOC32 on the Series 5 uses a new Graphical User Interface called EIKON.

The higher CPU performance allows the Series 5 to cope with the increased software demands imposed by friendlier user interfaces, WYSIWYG applications, increased functionality and advanced communication protocols. A high performance CPU removes the need for expensive and power hungry floating point or DSP (Digital Signal Processing) units.

Power
Series 5 machines are powered by 2 x AA batteries (giving up to 35 hours life) with a 2032 3V lithium backup cell and an optional external AC adapter (6V DC).

Machine IDs
Programmers interested in copy protection or Shareware registration will be intrigued by the possibilities presented by 16-digit unique machine identifiers included in Series 5 machines.

ARM processor and sub-systems

The 32-bit RISC (Reduced Instruction Set Computer) processor runs at 18.432 MHz giving 15-MIPS (Million Instructions Per Second), equivalent to a 33MHz Intel 486 based PC.

The ARM 7100 device is based around the ARM 710a processor core, which includes a MMU (Memory Management Unit) and 8-Kbytes of on chip unified instruction and data cache. Despite containing 570,000 transistors, the ARM710a chip is very small. Outside the ARM710a core, the ARM7100 uses the AMBA bus to access the integrated peripherals. The ARM7100 is only a little larger than the ARM710a processor itself.

Besides improving performance from inexpensive memory systems, the on-chip cache also saves power by reducing the need to drive the power-hungry external busses. In addition to efficient memory management the MMU provides hardware memory protection to the operating system and other processes from bugged applications.

The ARM 7100 chip supports a large memory address space (3072MBytes total) it can directly interface to four banks of DRAM (Dynamic Random Access Memory). Each bank is 32-bits wide and up to 256Mbytes in size. Self-refresh DRAM is also supported as well as SRAM/ROM flash memory.

Using the ROM/expansion interface, eight separate linear memory segments are decoded, each segment being 256Mbytes. Memory segments can be programmed to be 8, 16 or 32-bits wide. Wait states can be included, either programmed or using a ready pin. This interface could be called a static memory interface, it can connect SRAM but not DRAM. Like the DRAM interface, no additional glue logic is required.

The ARM7100 typically delivers 10 times the CPU performance of the 16-bit architectures on which many of today's electronic organisers are based. These processors are not cached, have no memory management and have relatively slow clock speeds.

The ARM7100 has exceptionally low power demands (only 66mW full speed), it delivers 270 MIPS of performance per Watt of power consumed, much greater than the best of its competitors at 150 MIPS/Watt. It has two low power modes (down to 33uW) to further maximise battery life. During the development of the EPOC32 operating system, Psion collaborated very closely with the chip designers to ensure that EPOC32 took full advantage of all of the features of the CL-PS7110, including its unique ultra low-power consumption modes to maximise battery life. Advanced power management technology ensures lowest power consumption in standby, idle and normal operating modes. The CL-PS7110 allows the Series 5 system to consume one-half to one-tenth the energy compared to the requirements of similar systems.

The ARM7100 typically consumes only 20mA in normal operation at 18.432MHz, equating to only 66mW at 3.3v. It is specified to 2.2v in standby, where the main oscillator and display are shut off.

An internal PLL (Phase Locked Loop) is used to generate the main system clock. Mechanical devices like the quartz crystal are very power hungry and the faster they are driven the hungrier they are. Using a PLL to multiply the clock frequency by five, system power consumption is reduced since the external crystal runs at a lower speed.

The ARM7100 is designed to have a second very low speed external clock crystal (32kHz) to save more power when in standby mode than if the main clock frequency was just divided down. This second clock is designed to use a very cheap and low power quartz watch crystal. The 32kHz oscillator maintains the real-time clock and the ability to wake up for interrupts. Typical current consumption is 10uA.

Idle mode is where the display is still being driven, but the clock to the CPU core is stopped. The system can respond to any interrupt, e.g. a tap on the screen. Typical current consumption is 1.5mA. Two pins on the chip can be used to force the device into standby mode - synchronised with the DRAM cycles. Transition from standby back to normal operation is only allowed if the appropriate pins indicate no power problem, thus avoiding a restart when the battery is flat.

Improved user interface features are accommodated by the integral high resolution (640 by 240 pixels), 16 grey scale LCD controller. The keyboard connects via a parallel interface, the analog-to-digital converter for pen input is connected via a synchronous serial port.

There are five FIFO (First in First Out) buffers on the ARM7100, two for UART (Universal Asynchronous Receiver Transmitter), two for CODEC interface and one for the LCD controller. (CODEC is short for Coding and Decoding of analog data streams to and from digital data.)

Connection to other devices, such as a desktop PC or modem, is achieved through an RS232 port driven by the on-chip UART. The internal UART has similar functionality to the 16C550, supporting bit rates up to 115.2kbits/sec. The UART includes an IrDA (Infrared Data Association) SIR (Serial Infrared) protocol encoder. Transmit and receive pins are used to directly drive an infrared interface for links to printers and other IrDA enabled equipment.

PC-card (PCMCIA) slots are essential in many handheld devices. For example, to enable the user to plug in adapters such as a modem, Ethernet card, memory device and so on. The ARM7100 contains all the necessary logic to support a PC-card interface, only requiring an external buffer on the main system bus.

The interrupt controller supports high and low priority interrupt requests. There are a total of sixteen interrupt sources, including 4 external interrupt pins.

A CODEC interface allows direct connection to a telephony type CODEC chip. This is full duplex with two separate 16-byte FIFO buffers. Speech recording/playback (and possibly voice control) is via the CODEC interface which is connected to the internal speaker and microphone.

A DMA (Direct Memory Access) controller is used to service the LCD without software and CPU overhead, freeing the processor for other tasks. When the FIFO buffer local to the LCD controller is half-empty, a DMA request is generated to transfer the next part of the video buffer located in the external RAM. Main system RAM is used for display storage to keep the system flexible and cost low.

A power management/state control block controls the start-up and shutdown of the main oscillator and all power management features. These include hardware shutdown (to avoid starting-up with low batteries) and battery-low interrupt generation.

Other ARM 7100 peripherals are: Two 16-bit timer/counters with two modes of operation, a real-time clock and match register, DC-DC converter interface (2 channels) and a watchdog timer. For parallel I/O, there are 36 bits of programmable I/O (four 8-bit ports, one 4-bit port).

Hardware block diagram

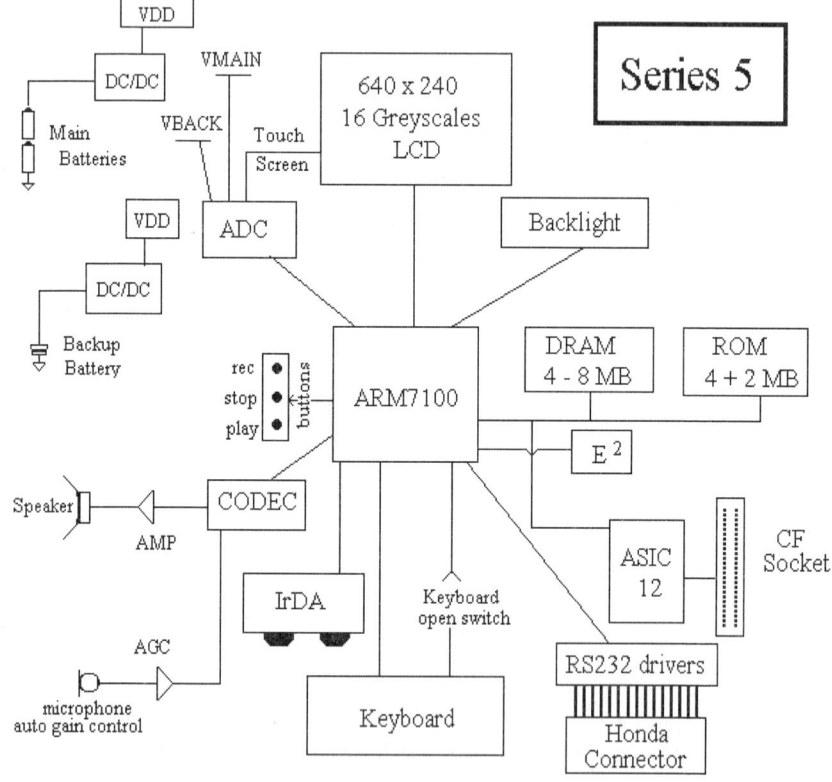

Notes:

The device labelled E2 contains information such as the unique machine ID and configuration information such as whether the operating system is in ROM or Flash RAM (the speed of access is different).

Memory and storage

Current Series 5 machines are available with 4Mb or 8Mb internal RAM memory which approximates to 2000 pages of text; 40,000 appointments; 20,000 database entries; or 30 minutes of digital audio.

The 32-bit architecture removes the 64K memory constraints on programs and data found on SIBO system. The Series 5 ROM is now a relatively massive 6 Mbytes.

A section of the internal RAM drive is designated as drive C:, the single compact flash slot is seen as drive D:, any other drives may be assigned letters E: to Y: (The ROM drive is referred to as drive Z:).

Storage space is sub-divided into folders instead of directories and filenames can be very long; up to 255 characters including embedded spaces. Application documents now have names without the usual filename extension.

Compact flash

Psion have abandoned the use of their proprietary SSD storage units for Series 5, in favour of industry standard compact flash storage (CF) devices. Compact flash refers to a form factor for plug in cards that measure approximately 36mm deep by 43mm wide by 3.3mm thick. The CF format has been adopted as a standard by companies such as Kodak, Canon, NEC etc, for digital still cameras. CF is also being taken up by manufacturers of other handheld devices such as organisers, pocket computers and mobile phones.

Concerns about storing certain types of data, such as text and document files, on Flash RAM are a thing of the past. Media reformatting is not required with CF storage; deleted file space is recovered automatically. Data on CF disks is very secure, the devices feature dynamic defect management and error correction. Transfer rates with CF storage are very high, reading at up to 3.0 Mbytes/sec and writing at up to 1.0 Mbyte/sec.

A single CF card slot (50-pin connector) is provided under the right-hand-side of the Series 5. CF cards are available from Psion (Sandisk manufactured) and others such as Simple Technology. Typical capacities are 2, 4, 8, 10, 12 and 16 Mbytes. Higher capacity CF devices will soon be available from a number of sources, capacities in excess of 32 Mbytes are planned.

Note:
Not all CF units are made equal. Read/write performance and power demands can vary widely between manufacturers, it is wise to compare the specifications before purchasing from untried sources.

Screen

Series 5 has a backlit LCD screen, 134-mm wide by 50-mm high, with a resolution of 640x240 pixels (100 x 26 characters) and 16 grey levels. A touch sensitive digitiser (ADC) overlays the screen, the sidebar and the application icons. The sensitive area is therefore larger than the display area, it is approximately 142-mm wide by 58-mm high, to allow for the icon bar and the sidebar at the left edge side of the screen.

The screen resolution of 640x240 pixels is referred to as half VGA and contains twice as many pixels as Series 3a/c (153600 versus 76800). The sensitive area has a higher resolution of 695x280, so the icon-bar and sidebar do not take up valuable display area.

Three graphics drawing modes are possible:
- Two 'colour', black and white, no grey (1 bit per pixel).
- Four 'colour', black, white, light grey and dark grey (2 bits per pixel).
- Sixteen 'colour', black, white, and 14 grey levels (4 bits per pixel).

For graphics, four-colour mode (grey-levels) is preferable. Although sixteen-colour mode may apparently lead to more impressive graphics, there are a number of reasons not to use this mode:
- The battery load is very much higher
- Bitmaps occupy far more memory and disk space.
- Because of contrast limitations on LCD displays the difference between four-colour mode and sixteen-colour mode is hardly noticeable.

A new bitmap file format is used; the new .MBM files can hold multiple bitmaps in compressed format (by a factor of two over the EPOC16 format). Utilities are supplied on the PsiWin 2 CD-ROM for converting bitmaps between PC .BMP formats to S5 .MBM and vice-versa. Icons and bitmaps may be imported and exported from the built in Sketch application. Icons and bitmaps are discussed in more detail in the 'Programming Techniques' chapter.

User input

A 53 key full-travel laptop-style keyboard extends out of the case when the 'clam shell' style case is opened. A pointing device or stylus is stored in the right-hand-side of the unit.

The user interface of the Series 5 is designed to make maximum use of the integral touch sensitive areas including the screen, the sidebar and the icons buttons just above the top row of keys. However, the system can be driven equally well through the keyboard, either via selecting menu options or better still by use of menu short-cuts, also known as hot-keys.

Touch sensitivity has a slight down side; to use it your programs must be event driven. Series 5 applications should respond to key presses, pointer events (called pen taps), and system events, e.g. messages to switch documents, shut down etc. Event driven programming is discussed in detail in the 'OPL32 Techniques' chapter.

Hot-keys

The Psion key, familiar to SIBO users as the 'hot-key' modifier, is replaced on the Series 5 by the Ctrl key. For alphabetic keys the Ctrl modified value is the ordinal position in the alphabet ignoring upper and lower case. For example:

Ctrl+A or Shift+Ctrl+A will return 1

Ctrl+B or Shift+Ctrl+B will return 2 etc.

This value can be found by ANDing the ASCII value of the alphabetic character with (NOT $60). So the key code of upper and lower case letters is the same when pressed together with Ctrl, with only the value of the modifier differing. For example, pressing Ctrl+J returns 10 which is (6A AND (NOT $60)).

The following table lists the default hot-key standards for the Series 5. Not all applications support every one of these, so typically a number of these may frequently do application specific things instead.

Key	Ctrl+key	Ctrl+Shift+key
A	Select all	About Program <name>
B	Bold	
C	Copy	Insert special character
D	Delete	
E	Close	
F	Find	Font
G	Go to	
H	Replace	Help on Program <name>
I	Italic	Merge in
J	Find next	Format object
K	Preferences	
L	Spell	Thesaurus
M	Zoom in	Zoom out
N	Create new	
O	Open	Insert object
P	Print	Print set-up
Q	Switch view	Password
R	Revert to saved	
S	Save	Save as
T	Show toolbar	Show top toolbar
U	Underline	Page set-up
V	Paste	Print preview
W	Wrap	
X	Cut	
Y	Redo	
Z	Undo	Edit object

Special keys

The codes returned for various special keys are as follows:

key	Hex code	decimal code
Home	1002	4098
End	1003	4099
PgUp	1004	4100
PgDn	1005	4101
←	1007	4103
→	1008	4104
↑	1009	4105
↓	100A	4106
Menu	1036	4150

Notes:
Repeatedly pressing the Menu key does not cycle through the menu 'cards' as it does on SIBO systems. Pressing the menu key a second time will cancel the menu in a similar manner to pressing the Esc key.

Pressing the Help-key on Series 5 will always call system related help, hence the Help-key cannot be used for application specific help. Application related help should now be provided as an application menu option, via a hot-key press (Ctrl+Shift+H is recommended) and preferably also via a help button on the application's Toolbar. Providing application specific help is described and demonstrated in the 'OPL32 Techniques' chapter.

Audio

An internal speaker and microphone are present in the Series 5 and are linked through a CODEC chip to provide a digital audio system. Sound may be recorded and replayed from digital sound files that are compressed/decompressed in real-time. External record, play/stop, rewind buttons provide 'Dictaphone' type capabilities without needing to open the unit up.

Audio record/play application software is provided as standard and the digital sound capabilities are available for use by application programmers.

If the batteries are low on a Series 5 making a beep sound via a system function call may not produce the desired effect, the buzzer will be used instead, it produces a higher pitched sound. Buzzer sounds are generated via the same speaker using additional circuitry, designed to place a lower drain on the batteries.

Series 5 digital-sound files are more compact than the SIBO equivalents. Utilities are provided on the PsiWin 2 CD for converting Series 3a/c (.WVE) to Series 5 formats and vice versa. Sound files from the PC (.WAV) can also be transferred in either direction.

Sound files and conversion utilities are discussed in more detail in the 'Programming Techniques' chapter.

Communications

A single combined serial/parallel port is supplied at the back of the Series 5. It uses the same 15-pin 'Honda-format' connector as the Series 3c.

Since connectivity is a fundamental objective for Series 5 systems, all machines are supplied with a serial cable plus Psion's Explorer software on CD-ROM.

Psion Software's EPOC Connect software runs on a Microsoft Windows-based PC (Win 95 or NT only) to provide integration facilities (EPOC Connect is 'badged' variously by licensees: Psion Computers' PsiWin 2.0 product is an example).

Using EPOC Connect, the PC and EPOC32 machine can see each other's disks, and access and transfer data. Backup and restore for the EPOC32 machine is supported, with a range of partial restore options. File format conversion, and agenda synchronisation at record and even field level, are supported. The EPOC32 machine may use the Windows printing system to print: this avoids the inconvenience of changing printer cables, and allows EPOC32 to drive any Windows-supported printer in addition to those it supports natively.

EPOC Connect supports a range of file formats from Microsoft, Lotus and Corel and a range of applications; word processors, spreadsheets, databases and PIMs. Round-trip format conversions preserve many features. The architecture of EPOC Connect is extensible, so that converters for new releases, or different vendors' products, may be written.

IrDA infrared links
At the time of going to print only Psion to Psion infrared data transfers or infrared printing is possible with suitably IrDA enabled systems. An infrared Psion to PC link adapter for use with the Series 5, and software such as PsiWin 2 is due become available (Autumn 97) as an option from Psion. The infrared protocols used on the Series 3c and Siena have changed on the Series 5 and data transfers from SIBO to Series 5 are not possible using the standard system software.

The RS232 serial port and the infrared link are capable of transfer speed up to 115.2Kbps.

Series 5 has a built-in VT100 terminal emulator.

Software

The Series 5 is based on EPOC32, Psion's new 32-bit multi-tasking operating system. EPOC32 is based on a small highly optimised real time micro-kernel.

The micro-kernel schedules threads pre-emptively, and uses a memory management unit (MMU) to provide separate address spaces for each process, therefore isolating all processes from each other.

EPOC32 is based on a client server model. A few vital system-wide services, such as thread creation, semaphores and timers, are provided by the kernel. Most other system services are provided by a variety of servers, such as the file server, window server, serial communications server and others. The kernel and all servers keep track of the resources used by their clients, and when a client thread terminates all associated resources are cleaned up.

The 'native' language of EPOC32 is C++. The 'standard' Series 5 applications and the vast majority of EPOC32 is written in C++, even the device drivers, only the kernel is written in assembly language.

The structure and operations of EPOC32 are discussed in more detail later in this chapter.

System interface

EIKON is the default GUI (Graphical User Interface) for EPOC32. It builds on a number of central operating system components described later in the chapter.

Displays on handheld machines impose a number of unique constraints; including smaller screen sizes, grey scale or more restricted colour capabilities, and sometimes lower contrast. Handheld systems are also used in a wide variety of lighting conditions ranging from outdoors, through brightly lit offices, to subtly lit rooms at home.

EIKON makes good use of screen space by displaying menus only when needed, and allowing the toolbar to be optionally turned off. Since the task bar is off-screen, there is no need to permanently waste screen space displaying the applications currently running. Cascaded menus allow the length of menu panes to be shortened to fit within a shallow screen depth. Multi-page dialogs, besides being a valuable GUI paradigm in their own right, also help to conserve space.

To compensate for displays with lower contrast, EIKON makes use of strong contrasts for its user interface elements. Available options are displayed in black on white, in a reasonable-sized font.

Almost all application views support zooming to three, four or five magnification states. This allows the zoom-state to be tailored to the best compromise between amount of information displayed, and visibility, depending on lighting conditions, the application's data, and the user's eyesight. Since easy adjustment is a critical comfort factor, zooming is a sidebar function, always instantly available.

Psion Software designed EIKON specifically for the requirements of handheld machines. It provides the look and feel for users, a framework for programmers, and an environment for applications.

EIKON defines the look and feel of the Series 5 machine. It is designed to make this as attractive as possible. Although in some circumstances, an EPOC32 machine may use a different GUI.

A wide range of interface elements are available to an OPL32 developer, and they are determined by those implemented in EIKON. However, more flexibility and options are available to a C++ developer.

EIKON uses real-world metaphors for some things, however, as PCs are now part of the real world, PC metaphors such as menus, dialogs and toolbars are also used, these can be quickly learned. Experience of other platforms has demonstrated that complete departure from PC to other 'real-world' metaphors, while they may be fun initially, severely compromise the overall usability of the machine.

Psion have paid considerable attention to the wording and layout of text in menus, dialogs and error messages. Dialogs are navigated using arrow keys rather than TAB. Cues are given when keyboard shortcuts are available, except for standard keys such as ESCAPE and ENTER.

The I/O devices of a handheld machine are different from those of a PC: EIKON has been designed to make EPOC32 machines easy to use with both the keyboard and pen, and to make optimal use of display 'real estate'.

Series 5 applications

The 'standard' Series 5 applications include: enhanced database, time management, calculator, time/world clock, word processor, spreadsheet, sketch/draw tool, VT100 communications, audio software, spell checker and the OPL32 programming language. Due to the additional processing power available the applications 'built in' to the Series 5 are now WYSIWYG wherever appropriate.

Under EPOC16 there is a confusing array of application 'types' and associated 'type' modifiers. (See the 'Processes, Memory and Applications' chapter). The situation is simplified under EPOC32, only two application types are now recognised; applications that use documents and those that don't. Also the 'type' modifiers have gone.

Applications, as well as folders and files, can have long names up to a maximum of 250 characters. In practise using names that are above the usual maximum of eight characters will create a number of difficulties. For example, when the name is presented in certain elements of the user interface, such as the Toolbar title and the Extras bar, it will be truncated.

Under the new system, all applications for distribution should have a unique identifier numbers (UID) and hold program information and settings in a Windows-style .INI file.

Application UIDs

All applications must specify a unique identifier, and they are used in a number of ways with the Series 5 system. Applications developed for personal use may safely use any UID in the range &0100000 to &0fffffff. Psion will issue a UIDs for applications that are to be distributed; they are guaranteed to be unique and start at &10000000. To obtain a reserved UID you should contact Psion Software – see the 'Contacts and Sources' chapter.

OPX UIDs

All OPL extensions (OPXs) have UIDs to avoid confusion between OPXs that might have the same name.

AIF files

Application information files (AIFs) are associated with all applications and contain supporting data such as the icons/masks, the application name(s) and type. The OPL32 translator creates this file automatically based on the details supplied in the APP...ENDA header.

User interface

The basic user interface metaphor used for Series 5 has changed from that used on most SIBO systems, i.e.: Icons in the system screen with file lists underneath them, application files that depend on specific file name extensions that are typically located in specific application directories. EPOC32 uses a desktop metaphor that is very reminiscent of Windows 95.

Before designing a new application time spent carefully studying the operation and user interface of the system, and of the 'standard' applications will be time well spent. It is important, wherever possible, to closely model the 'look and feel' of your applications on the 'house style' demonstrated by Psion.

When porting a SIBO application to EPOC32 it is tempting to do the minimum to get the application 'up and running', and to avoid the additional complexity involved in adopting the new user interface model. If you take the easier approach, for example to leave out options for a pen driven interface, the application will immediately stand out as an anachronism to the user. It may be acceptable to those who are familiar with SIBO applications, but it will be particularly irksome to users who are not familiar with applications on earlier Psion systems.

Files

Some changes on the Series 5 are in name only. For example, directories are now known as folders. Series 5 folders and files can have long names up to a maximum of 250 characters.

However, other changes are a little more complex than they may seem at first. Files created and used by applications are now known as documents and appear on the system screen next to the corresponding application icon. They contain unique header information to allow the system to launch the correct application when the user selects a document.

Non document files, i.e. those that do not launch applications when selected, are marked with the default 'question mark' icon (except for certain application related files in the system folder).

Application documents can be put anywhere the user wishes, conventionally they do not have nor do they depend on specific extensions to the document name. It is the programmers' responsibility to ensure that any necessary folder\file paths are created as required. New documents created from within a running application should inherit the current program settings. If an application has a 'Save as' option it should save the current file, create a copy of the current file with the new name and switch to using the new file. This 'Save as' behaviour differs from SIBO applications which stay with the original document.

Despite the fact that the files an application creates/uses are referred to as documents, the term file should still be used in any text or prompts in the user interface. For example in menus, dialogs and other user prompts.

Some aspects of SIBO-style behaviour have been retained. For example, applications and the files that support them often have specific extensions and are located together in a specific folder. All applications have a .APP extension (including OPL applications); resource files end in .RSC; bitmap files end in .MBM and program settings are held in files with a .INI extension.

Applications and their support files are typically held in a specific folder located directly under the \system\apps folder. Programmers may still find file name extensions useful. For example, to distinguish the nature and contents of non-document files that hold other 'internal' data required by an application.

Using file name extensions for application support files may simplify the installation of an application when using PsiWin 2. Early versions of PsiWin 2 may confuse the user by failing to transfer some files, or even attempting to convert non-document files, during the installation of an application from a PC to a Series 5. File transfers may be made more reliable, for the user, if file name extensions are used for non-document files.

Assuming they are located correctly, applications are automatically 'installed' on the Extras bar. For simple OPL programs the RunOPL icon has gone. When a folder is open, any OPO programs will appear on the system screen next to a default OPL icon.

Keyboard conventions

Although it is one of EPOC32's key features that it supports pen-based devices, keyboard operation is still critically important. A good quality keyboard is still the fastest and most accurate way to enter large amounts of text. In some conditions, the environment may not allow pens to be used with great accuracy.

EIKON provides powerful dialog facilities. However, dialogs are navigated using the arrow keys rather than the tab key (as in Windows). Left and right arrow keys are often used to navigate within a control, but up and down arrow keys navigate between individual controls within a dialog. This provides more obvious behaviour to the users, and is a more natural use of the keyboard within a dialog. As a consequence, dialogs provide only a one-dimensional vertical array of controls. In practice, this is not an onerous constraint. Multi-page dialogs provide a natural interface, especially for rich features such as print set-up or agenda entry settings. Custom controls may be written, containing existing controls if necessary, that provide horizontal navigation for some dialog lines. The one-dimensional control list may be extended by using a scrolling dialog.

The most common application commands are available from both the menu and via keyboard shortcuts. Some keyboard shortcuts are defined earlier in this chapter. For instance, Copy from the Edit menu is CTRL+C, which will be familiar to users of Microsoft Windows applications. Other keyboard shortcuts may be application-specific.

Menu items and buttons in dialogs, that have keyboard shortcuts associated with them, are indicated by an appropriate label. EIKON provides this support automatically, without programmer intervention.

Pen conventions

EIKON has been optimised for pen usage. Because a pen is not a mouse, different gestures are appropriate. Pens are good for freehand drawing, but bad for accurate double-clicks and for drag-and-drop. Clearly, a pen cannot do a right-click. EIKON keeps the pen interface simple by supporting only the simplest operations with the pen.

The double-click operation familiar to mouse users is replaced in EPOC32 by select and open. A pen tap on an unselected object will select it. A pen tap on a selected object will open it. The time interval between selecting and opening is irrelevant.

EIKON makes further use of the pen by presenting an application-specific toolbar to the right of an application's window: the toolbar provides a clock, and commonly used functions at the press of a button.

EPOC32 allows the digitizer to be extended beyond the visible area of the screen. EIKON uses this to provide a pen-activated side bar on the left with menu, clipboard, infrared and zooming functions. The digitizer is also extended below the visible area of the screen, to provide a task bar with application-switching icons.

Standard controls and views provide many active elements. For instance, clocks in the toolbar may be changed from analog to digital by tapping them. The time may be set from the Time application by tapping on the clock. 'Dog-ears' are available on the Agenda views to turn pages.

The majority of pen-enabled interface elements are sufficiently large to select comfortably with a pen, even under unfavourable conditions. Buttons on screen, side bar and task bar may even be selected with a finger.

INI files

Series 5 applications should store program information and current settings in .INI files. For example, if the application uses documents it should save the name and path of the last file used by the application. When an application starts up or closes down information in the program .INI file should be read or updated respectively. Application .INI files should have the same name as the application and be located using the same path. All active .INI files (other than a .INI file used as an initial template) should be stored on the internal drive, i.e. drive C:. So for example, PPCOPL32.APP has a PPCOPL32.INI file located in the C:\System\Apps\PPCOPL32\ folder.

In maintaining information in .INI files it is important to remember that multiple invocations of an application may be running, but there should only be one .INI file. Therefore, information should only be saved to the .INI file when the application (or any copy of it) closes. This way, the information stored will always correctly reflect the latest user preferences and record the document that was last in use. For this reason, .INI files should be opened, read and closed immediately, they should never be kept open during the lifetime of an application.

If a .INI file does not exist, or is corrupt, a new file should be created containing suitable defaults. Creating a .INI file may be done by writing default data into a new file, or by making a copy from a prepared 'template' file (as per the 'standard' applications). In the case of missing or corrupt .INI files, simply recreate a new one but do not confuse the user with an error message.

Command line information

Command line information is passed to Series 5 applications when they start up, in a similar manner to SIBO applications. In addition to the Create and Open command bytes (i.e., 'C' and 'O'), a new Run command byte ('R') may be encountered by Series 5 applications. Run signifies that the application has been run from the Program editor, or has been selected via the Application's icon on the Series 5 'Extras' bar. It also signifies that the application was not launched by the selection or creation of a document from the System screen. A default filename, including path, is passed in to the application by the system (and is retrieved in OPL32 using CMD$(2)).

On receipt of the 'R' command, an application should always try to open the document that was in use when the program last exited, as recorded in its .INI file. If the .INI file does not exist (see above), or if the 'last file used' no longer exists, you should create a new document using default file name supplied by the system. (i.e. in OPL32 in CMD$(2)). The default file name provided by the system screen is based on your application's name or caption.

Whenever an application changes to another document it should inform the operating system to allow the system screen to embolden the current document name, and to correctly show it in the task list (in OPL32 this is done using the SETDOC command).

New command line information

In EPOC32 a running application may receive messages from the system screen as on SIBO systems. Valid commands received (typically while the program is running in the background) are:

- 'X' to shutdown the program
- 'C' to create a new file, i.e. using the name entered by the user in the dialog presented by the system screen
- 'O' to open the file picked from those displayed on the system screen.
- 'U' unknown command.

On arrival of the shutdown message ('X') the application should save and close its current document, save the information and current setting in the .INI file and then close down. For example, if the user selects the file from the task list and chooses the close option, or because the message had been sent by the system itself.

For create ('C') the application should save and close its current document, create the specified new document and restore all program settings to the defaults.

For open ('O') the application should save and close its current document, open the specified existing document and restore all program settings to the defaults.

Document UIDs

Files that belong to an application are referred to as documents, and are identified by having the programs' UID embedded in the document (file) header, rather than by their location and/or file name extension. Documents display their application's icon and will launch the application if selected. A document header may contain up to four UIDs; you should always assume the first 32 bytes of a document file, at least, are allocated to UIDs.

The various UIDs are used to identify files in the system for many purposes.

UID1 is the most general identifier, and indicates the type of file structure used (see Store later). For example:

Database files have UID1=10000050h (KPermanentFileStoreLayoutUid).
Bitmaps are stored with UID1=10000037h (KDirectFileStoreLayout).

UID2 is used by the system screen uses to distinguish between applications of various types and documents:

Document identifier	UID2
EIKON applications	1000006Ch
EIKON applications' documents	1000006Dh
OPL applications	268435572h
OPL applications' documents	268435573h

For non-documents files, the value in UID2 indicates that the file is an 'external file'. In OPL32, if SETDOC is used, the OPL document UID (KUidOplDoc&=268435573h) is used instead. External or non-document files do not have an application UIDs, and are displayed on the system screen beside a question mark icon to indicate that they are unrecognised.

UID3 is used by the system screen to identify a specific application.

UID4 is a checksum and is system generated (by Store, see later).

A small Series 5 utility program (Uidread), for reading the four UIDs from Series 5 files, is provided on disk with source code in OPL32 format in \Ppcopl32\ppcopl32, and in text format in Ppcopl32\dosutils\ppctxt.

Icons

Series 5 icons typically contain three sizes, i.e., 24x24, 32x32 and 48x48 pixels, to accommodate the different zoom levels in the system screen. The sizes are read from the .AIF file, if the exact size required is not provided, or if some sizes are missing the most suitable size is used. Production of Series 5 icons is discussed in the 'Programming Techniques' chapter and more information for OPL32 programmers is provided in the 'OPL32 Techniques' chapter.

Toolbars

Status windows used on SIBO systems have been replaced by Toolbars on Series 5. Toolbars, like status windows, are also located on the right hand side of the screen. The system screen usually displays a Toolbar (try pressing Ctrl+T). A typical application Toolbar window will have a title, four application related buttons and a clock. Options on the Toolbar may be context or mode sensitive i.e.; the options/buttons presented may change to reflect the current operating 'mode' of an application. EPOC32 provides support for the use of Toolbars to application developers. Use of Toolbars in OPL32 is described and demonstrated in the 'OPL32 Techniques' chapter.

EPOC32

Series 5 machines run under the control of EPOC32, Psion's new 32-bit multi-tasking operating system, that is based on a small highly optimised real time micro-kernel. The following section is an overview of EPOC32 and its principal components. If you are new to programming the Series 5 you should spend some time reading this (possibly difficult) section to familiarise yourself with the new terms and concepts involved.

OPL32 programmers are largely isolated from the intricacies of the operating system, but C++ programmers will have to become closely acquainted with EPOC32 concepts and terminology.

A hierarchical diagram of EPOC32 is given below, and it can be seen that the 'Base' is the central core of EPOC32. The base provides the programming framework for all other components in EPOC32.

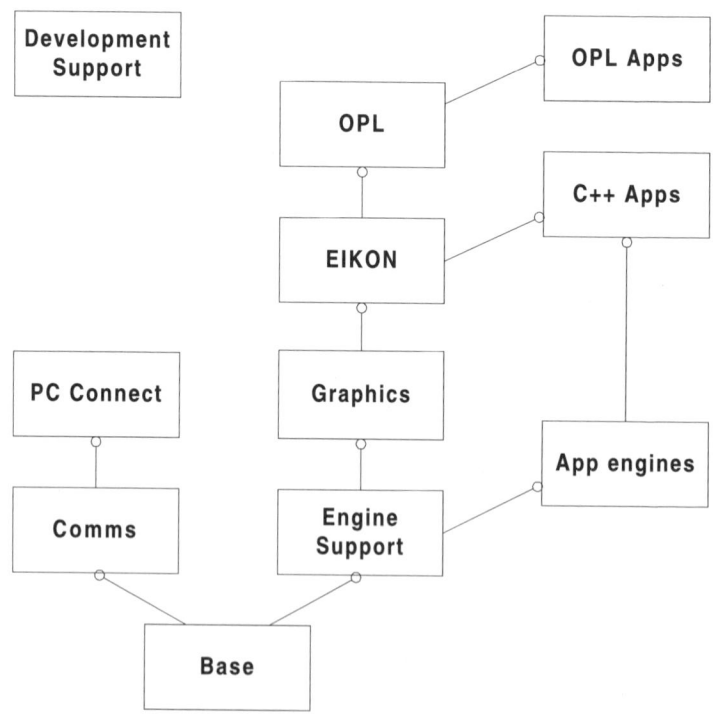

Base	The core of EPOC32 that acts as the overall system supervisor and executive. It provides the hardware abstraction layer, user libraries and the file services.
Comms	Serial comms (RS232 and IrCOMM) and sockets (IrDA, TCP/IP, PLP Psion Link Protocol).
Engine support for data	Streams, Store and DBMS services.
Engine support for graphics	Device independent e.g. same for screen and printing.
Engine support	Utilities for resource files, clipboard, alarm and world servers, sound compression etc.
App engines	e.g. ShEng.dll the spreadsheet engine – access to application data is through App engines (OPL would use an OPX for engine access).
EIKON	EPOC32's graphical user interface and policy/graphics layer, providing elements such as dialogs, menus, toolbars etc. CONE – CONtrol Environment supports EIKON with very abstract user-interface elements.

Threads and processes

The EPOC32 micro-kernel schedules threads pre-emptively, and uses a memory management unit (MMU) to provide separate address spaces for each process, therefore isolating all processes from each other.

A 'process' is a unit of memory protection (an application for example), that may have a number of associated 'threads' that are units of execution, and 'own' resources. A process may just consist of a single thread, and in that case the two terms are effectively interchangeable.

Each different application started from the system screen, the icon bar or from the extra's bar goes into its own process. The individual processes are protected from each other. So if the user opens two Word documents and one Sheet document three separate processes will be running. If one instance of the Word application failed, there would be little if any risk to the other processes or their data.

However, the user may embed some Sheet data inside a Word document (effectively inside the Word application). In this case the instance of the Sheet application, that edits the embedded sheet data, will be running in the same process as the Word application, i.e. as a separate thread. If the embedded Sheet thread was to fail then there is a definite risk to the data of the 'containing' Word application, and possibly to the Word process as well.

Finally, the above discussion only applies to ARM based processes and threads. In the WINS emulation the 'S' in WINS stands for 'Single process', hence all applications run in the same process.

The base

The main components of the base are:

- The kernel
- User library
- Device drivers
- File server

EPOC32 is designed to run on more than one platform, for example the ARM 710 processor and PC platforms. Regardless of the platform on which the base is implemented the user library and file server present a consistent interface to user programs.

The kernel

The kernel and all servers keep track of the resources used by their clients, and when a client thread terminates all associated resources are cleaned up. Memory is a precious commodity in all hand held systems. Resources must be freed when they are finished with; leakage could cause a system failure eventually. It is especially important that partially allocated resources should be freed when an operation fails because of insufficient resources. Within each thread, errors are reported by a `leave()` function, and may be trapped by either system or application code. As part of `leave()` processing, automatic cleanup deals with partially allocated resources, and prevents memory and other resource leakage.

EPOC32 achieves its excellent real-time performance in two ways. Firstly, its server-based architecture allows it to run with processor interrupts always enabled, except for a few short instruction sequences. Thus interrupt latency, the time between an interrupt occurring and an interrupt service routine being scheduled, is typically a few tens of microseconds (for an ARM 7100 at 18MHz). Typical thread latency is only a little longer than this. If no higher priority thread is running, the thread latency is limited by the time it takes the interrupt service routine to decide what to do, to post the thread's request semaphore, and have the executive schedule the thread.

EPOC32 provides 'superthreads', which run as kernel extensions at a higher priority than the kernel server. 'Superthreads' maximum latency is 100 microseconds on an 18MHz ARM 7100. By contrast, user threads running at a lower priority than the kernel-server, have a maximum latency limited by the longest running kernel service, which at 35 milliseconds is still very respectable.

The kernel and executive run in privileged state, and can directly access all parts of the system. User threads run for the most part in unprivileged state. User threads access the kernel via the kernel executive, whose services are presented through the user library API (Application Programmers Interface). A user thread can only directly access its own data, plus data belonging to other threads in the same process.

The kernel server thread is always present. It is the highest-priority thread in the system, and performs services on behalf of other threads. The kernel server owns all kernel resources, which reside on the kernel heap. Kernel resources may be used by the executive, operating in the context of any thread, or by other kernel-side threads. However, kernel resources may only be allocated by the kernel server to minimise context switching and locking in the system. It allows the system to run essentially without disabling interrupts, so that interrupt latency is in the order of a few microseconds.

Power management is a key activity of EPOC32. A 'null thread' is always present; it is the lowest-priority thread in the system and therefore only runs when there is nothing else to do. It stops the CPU clock to save power, and sets an inactivity timer that will turn the machine off if no user activity occurs within a given time interval.

User library

A user thread may use services provided by the kernel, by I/O devices, or from other threads that function as servers. User-threads request kernel services by using the user library application programmer's interface (API). The services are carried out by the kernel server thread. Such services include: extending the heap, timers, semaphores, creating processes and threads; anything fundamental to the operation of the machine.

The user library makes facilities available to user threads and, in some cases, provides services to the kernel as well. The user library provides the `leave()` function, and cleanup facilities which make it easy for programs to detect errors such as out-of-memory, and to clean up partially allocated resources. Strings and fixed-length data buffers are supported by a unified class hierarchy: the descriptor classes. In addition to active objects, EPOC32's cleanup support and descriptors are among its most distinctive aspects.

Support functions for DLLs, threads and processes are provided. Data structures include lists, dynamic memory buffers, and extensible arrays that build on the memory buffers. C++ templates are used to provide type-safe collection classes. Math functions manipulate IEEE754 double-precision floating-point numbers. Text support functions similar to `sprintf()` in standard C, and a parser like `sscanf()` are provided.

Device drivers

Machine resources are managed by the kernel, and device drivers interface with hardware. Device drivers are mainly used by the kernel, but the drivers have associated libraries to allow user threads to access the driver's facilities. User threads request services from I/O devices by using an API provided by a user-side device driver library. The device request is handled by a device driver under kernel control.

Current device drivers include:

Keyboard	Pointer digitizer	Screen	Sound	Timer
RS232	Parallel	Infrared	ATA	TCP/IP

The kernel and device drivers implement the required EPOC32 functions in different ways depending on the hardware platform. The base is responsible for providing the same interface to user programs, regardless of the particular EPOC32 platform. On each platform, the base interfaces with underlying hardware or software in a different way. EPOC32 provides all of the drivers for the CL-PS7110 peripherals.

File server

The file server manages files on behalf of all client threads in the system, and on behalf of the kernel. The file server presents an object oriented API to its clients, through which clients may manipulate drives, volumes, directories and files. Volumes are formatted using VFAT: filenames, including their drive and path, may be up to 256 characters long.

On a machine platform, the ROM is mapped to drive Z:, and contains an unlimited VFAT directory tree. The RAM is dynamically allocated between user threads and between the C: drive. Removable media are supported in the form of CF cards (compact flash). Remote drives, on another computer, connected by a communications link, are supported through installable file systems.

The file server implements the program loader which supports both .EXEs and .DLLs. Both are executed in-place from ROM, and loaded as needed from RAM or from removable or remote drives. On machine platforms, DLLs are restricted to linking by ordinal, rather than by name to prevent potentially long names wasting memory. Production of link-by-ordinal DLLs, and maintenance of binary compatible enhancements to them, is fully supported by the EPOC32 tool chain. On machine platforms, DLLs may not have write-able static data: instead, object handles must be passed directly, or thread-local storage (TLS) must be used: there is one machine word of TLS per DLL per thread.

Support services

A few vital system-wide services, such as thread creation, semaphores and timers, are provided by the kernel. Most other system services are provided by a variety of servers. Whatever method is used to provide a service, communication between the service provider and the service requestor is essential.

Message passing

Services provided by servers are referred to as objects, and they are identified using handles that consist of one or two machine words. Client threads use handle objects to identify the service requested from the provider. Service request functions, made via a library, are translated by the library into a message, which may consist of a request code and up to four machine-word parameters. The executive sends the message to the service provider. The service provider may respond with a single machine word, which is used as a return value to the client. For services requiring more parameters or bulk data transfer, inter-thread read/write functions are available.

The service provider may represent the object with a potentially complex and large class. Depending on the type of service, objects may be shared so that different client threads may access them, each client using its own handle for the object. The service provider must monitor all its client threads so that, if any of them terminates, whether normally or abnormally, all the server-side resources it currently owns may be released.

Client/server model

EPOC32 is based on a client server model, for example:

File server	Window server	Font/bitmap server	Process server	Sound Server
Comms server	Alarm server	World server	Database server	Socket server

User threads request services from server threads by using an API provided by the server's client interface library. The service is carried out within the server thread. Servers are used for all high-level services: in EPOC32, this means anything that does not interface directly with the kernel or with a device. Servers are often used to manage a single resource on behalf of multiple clients, controlling sharing or exclusive access where necessary. In turn, these servers often own and drive I/O devices on behalf of their clients.

For example, the file server is responsible for sharing and manipulating all files, file systems, devices and media. The window server shares the screen, keyboard and pointer between processes. The client-server framework is so easy to use that, if you need to write a multi-threaded application it's often easier to structure the dependent threads as servers rather than to use basic thread services.

Asynchronous operation

Asynchronous operations are fundamental to EPOC32, as they were in EPOC16. Many kernel, I/O and server-provided services complete asynchronously. Monitoring the state of a number of objects that may have outstanding requests by polling in a tight loop uses a lot of battery current. To save power, EPOC32 makes extensive use of its own asynchronous services. Clients wait for completion of asynchronous services, rather than polling. All threads spend most of their time waiting for one of a number of outstanding requests, and then briefly handle requests as they are completed.

The mechanism EPOC32 provides to handle asynchronous requests (active objects) is the 'active object' system; a design pioneered by Psion in EPOC16. Most threads use an active scheduler to manage one or more active objects. Each active object is responsible for requesting a particular service, and then handling its completion. Handling completion may take from a few tens of instructions, to a couple of seconds: often, handling completion will result in issuing more requests for asynchronous service. Using an active scheduler to manage one or more active objects it is possible to produce applications that always remain responsive to the user.

Stream store

The stream store is fundamental for engine support. Data from applications is stored in a network of streams, and streams are held in a store. A store may be a file, or it may be a clipboard, undo buffer, or other implementation.

File stores include two types:

- Direct file store in which streams are written just once and is suitable for most applications
- Permanent file store in which streams can be manipulated at will and is suitable as a foundation for a database.

All EPOC32 applications use file stores for their main documents. Embedded documents are supported by embedded stores, whose interface is similar to that for a direct file store.

The stream store is used for all data storage requirements in the system, and it is a requirement of any component, or application engine, that it be able to store its data in a stream, or in a store using a network of streams. Therefore, all other engine support components use the stream store.

In a conventional system, data is stored in files. For instance, a word processor document containing an embedded bitmap and an embedded chart may be stored in a file containing three segments as follows:

For conventional direct access to the file, the word processor would save all the data sequentially, starting with the embedded objects, and ending with the text stream itself. References within the file would use seek positions, and would all be backward: useful, because by the time they are needed, they are already known. The seek position for the top-level text stream would be stored in a reserved location at the beginning of the file: this is also possible, if you reserve a fixed amount of space (say, four bytes) at the head of the file before writing the other data. A file format like this is relatively easy to produce. It is efficient, and has an important advantage: the embedded objects do not have to be loaded along with the main text stream, until they are needed. A stream store may be thought of as an abstraction of such a file, and Psion represent it as follows:

Each stream in the store is identified by a stream ID and the whole store has a single root stream. One stream may refer to another using its stream ID.

The store interface is abstract, but has a number of concrete implementations. The 'Direct file store', provides exactly the function required by the word processor above: the streams are written in sequence, the stream ID is represented by a seek position, and the root stream is stored in the file store's header. The 'Direct File store' is used by most applications with load/save behaviour; such as a word processor. When the application saves its data, the old file store is replaced entirely (usually, for safety, it is renamed until the new file store has been written successfully).

Another concrete store implementation is the 'Permanent file store'; this uses a much more complex implementation, allowing streams to be manipulated, added, deleted, extended and re-written etc., at will. Great care has been taken in the implementation to ensure that updates are atomic, even under failure conditions. As a result of these complexities, stream

IDs bear no relation to seek position, in fact, you should make no such assumptions about stream IDs. Such stores are suitable for database type applications, in which entries are loaded, manipulated and saved a few at a time. It is called a 'Permanent file store' because, although entries may be replaced when they are saved, the file store itself is not replaced.

Other store types are used to implement the system clipboard, in-memory buffers used sometimes for undo processing, buffers used for communications (e.g., infrared beaming of application data), and system .INI files.

Most classes in EPOC32 are either 'stream-aware' (they can externalise to and internalise from streams), or are 'store-aware' (they can store to and restore from stores, creating and manipulating streams as necessary). As a result, and because there are so many types of store, the system is very flexible and promotes re-use in many ways. Provider interfaces allow new types of stream and store to be written, which further extends the possibilities for re-use.

Embedding objects

Application data files are referred to as 'documents', and are stored in stream stores. The environment constructs the stream store, and the application uses it without knowing what type of store it is. For a main document, the environment may construct either a direct file store or a permanent file store, depending on the requirements of the application.

For an embedded document, the environment constructs another type of store, an 'embedded store'. The embedded store uses, as its underlying medium, a stream in the containing store. An embedded store supports the same kind of operations as a direct file store. Therefore, any application whose main document uses a direct file store may also be embedded.

The advantage of using an embedded store is that, if the embedding document uses a permanent file store and wants to delete an embedded document, it needs only to delete a stream. Or, if it wants to copy an embedded document, it needs only to copy the stream data. Compared to opening the embedded document during these operations, this saves RAM, saves having to specify passwords on encrypted embedded documents, and allows deletion and copying of embedded documents even if their associated application is not available.

Doors, glass or iconic

Documents with an embedded object must indicate the presence of the object to the user. This representation is referred to as a 'door'. If you open a door, you move into the embedded document. Some embedded documents may only be represented by an 'iconic door', which show an icon associated with the embedded application. Iconic doors are suitable, for instance, for voice memos, or for long word processor documents. Some embedded documents are represented by a 'glass door'; you can see what is behind a glass door without opening it. A glass door presents a picture of the embedded data.

Application architecture

The application architecture specifies the methods by which embeddable applications can be found when you wish to embed something in document. In addition it specifies the methods by which the embedding application can be found again when a glass door is drawn, or when a door is opened. It also provides the means to manage an application thread that may have loaded several applications, representing the main document, any glass doors that are being displayed, and any embedded documents that are open. For this reason, embeddable applications are all DLLs that run in an existing thread, rather than programs that would each require a separate process.

Implementing embedding

Object embedding works by re-using several existing components of EPOC32. In turn applications re-use parts of EPOC32, and parts of their existing code, to support embedding.

The embedding system is extensible, with no fixed set of embeddable applications. To make your own application embeddable, you need to create a door for it. An iconic door is very simple to add. A glass door is slightly more work; most glass-door code benefits from re-use of application view code that must be written to support on-screen display and printing.

You also support embedding from your own application: re-use rich text as a component of your application, and EIKON's rich text editors will handle the embedding of any application's data. The power that this system delivers to users can be seen by detailed study of the applications built-in to a Series 5 machine.

DBMS

The stream store is also the basis for the database management system (DBMS), which uses a permanent file store to provide a relational database containing an arbitrary number of tables. Commit and rollback are supported, together with incremental compaction and space reclamation. An SQL subset is provided to allow views to be constructed on data from a table in the database. The database makes very efficient use of RAM and file space, and can recover from operations that were interrupted, for example by an emergency power-off.

Graphics

EPOC32's graphics components fulfil the requirements of a GDI (Graphics Device Interface), for two main devices, the screen device and printers. Together, the graphics components form the basis for the EIKON GUI.

The font and bitmap server and BITGDI provide the low-level data management and rendering needed to produce graphics on screen, or off-screen bitmap. The ARM processor's RISC instruction set enables the BITGDI to perform as an extremely effective blitter and graphics renderer.

The window server builds on these components, using the BITGDI to draw graphics on the screen, clipping each operation to the boundaries of its window, whether that window is fully visible, or partially hidden by others higher up in the window order. CONE, the CONtrol Environment, provides the abstract base class used by all GUI controls: a control is a rectangular region that may be either a whole window, or just a part of it. Additionally, any control may contain zero or more component controls.

As well as graphics, the window server drives the keyboard and pen. Keystrokes are sent to the application with focus, and pointer events are sent to the application owning the window in which they occurred. CONE packages these facilities, offering each key event to a stack of controls in turn, and routing each pointer event to the control in which it occurred. Together, CONE provides sufficient framework for both individual controls, and controls in the context of a thread that may be running multiple embedded applications.

These facilities provide a powerful programming framework. However, the central graphics components do not impose the user interface policy: menus, dialogs, toolbars, buttons, window borders etc are all the responsibility of the EIKON GUI, which uses the facilities of the graphics components.

Views

Built on the graphics system are several high-level views, all available for applications' use.

Text views provide an interface for displaying, editing and rapidly reformatting text content. This is a complex process, but because it is provided as a system component of EPOC32, it is available for use in any application.

Chart provides business graphics, and is used, for example, by the Sheet application, to provide charts data based on a spreadsheet range.

Grid provides a grid of rich text data. It is the basic component of a spreadsheet, but can also be used for other applications.

Clock provides self-updating digital or analog clocks.

Fonts

The font store supports a variety of ROM fonts and also allows applications to define their own and add them to the font and bitmap server until they are no longer required. EPOC32 provides Times New Roman, Arial and Courier New, plus some symbol fonts and special UI fonts, such as LED-type digits for the calculator and similar applications.

Rich text

All operating systems and class libraries provide some support for strings. Real text, however, is much more than strings. EPOC32's text content and views provide a rich text model that is used by most EPOC32 applications.

A rich text object consists of characters, paragraphs and pictures. A wide range of character and paragraph formatting options are available. Any picture derived from the GDI-provided abstract base class may be included in rich text.

Text content may be stored in a stream store, and may therefore form part of any application's data model. An EPOC32 application such as the word processor has a data model which is simply a rich text object, plus some UI settings such as the cursor location and zoom state. An application such as the spreadsheet may use several hundred rich text objects to represent its cell data.

Rich text provides a full range of functions to support inserting, deleting and formatting text content. An application that manipulates text interactively should co-ordinate its text content updates with calls to the text views formatting engine, which maintains a display on the screen. The text views API has been designed for convenience in use, and enables editors to be written which manipulate large documents with no noticeable performance degradation when compared with small ones.

EIKON provides standard editors for rich text, available either stand-alone or as components of dialogs, for re-use by any application which manipulates rich text.

Re-usable rich text is a technology that Psion Software pioneered in EPOC16. It is a difficult technology. In conventional systems, application authors who wish to present a non-trivial interface to their users often end up with one of two undesirable situations. Either they do not attempt the task at all, or they achieve only a minimal and quirky implementation, and pay a relatively high price even for that. EPOC32's facilities are ready for re-use, and allow developers to present a consistent, efficient and usable interface to applications.

From a technology point of view, rich text also presents another convenient aspect of re-use: the text views do not use the text content model directly, but through a carefully defined interface. This interface may be provided by another content model, such as a web browser or large-scale text browsing application. This allows the application to provide the text content in an application-optimised way (perhaps implementing dynamic decompression from a read-only database), but to re-use the layout and formatting capabilities of text views for display and printing.

Printing

The GDI defines a conventional banded printing model. All graphics devices support zooming and scaling, and a print device is not fundamentally different from any other type of device. An application's view code can therefore be re-used to draw to a banded printer.

EIKON provides a set of re-usable printing components, available to any application. Print preview uses a print device that maps to a window on the screen. A print settings dialog specifies which pages to print, and print set-up specifies paper size and margins, headings and footings. Print settings are 'stream-aware', and so may be stored along with an application's other data in the application's stream store.

EPOC32 provides many printer drivers to drive printers directly, over a serial link or, for maximum convenience, using infrared. If you already have a printer connected to a PC, EPOC Connect provides the facilities to re-use any printer driver written for Windows, and any TrueType font, for printing from your PC.

A generic print component provides printer support and several printer drivers for popular printer families.

Each printer driver provides its own font metrics, and turns the GDI commands issued by an application when printing, into the relevant instructions for the target printer. It is possible to use the printer font metrics when formatting for the screen: the text views component does this, to provide genuine WYSIWYG for the word processor and other applications. A print job may have a header and a footer, each optionally hidden on the first page: the header and footer each use rich text, and so support rich content, including fields for the page number and total number of pages. All print settings can be stored in a stream, and therefore contained as part of any application's document content.

A special type of printer driver provides an on-screen preview of any print job. It is therefore easy for all applications to support print preview.

Another printer driver drives a Windows-hosted printer through EPOC Connect. EPOC Connect also allows font metrics of any TrueType font to be downloaded to the EPOC32 machine, so that WYSIWYG formatting on the EPOC32 machine is still possible.

A final special case is fax; any application that can print documents may also output to fax.

Component re-use

The components described above provide particularly powerful re-use which may be appreciated by all developers and users of an EPOC32 system, and which help to make EPOC32 significantly more powerful than any of its competitors.

More conventional components are also available for re-use, ranging from collection classes for arrays and lists, in the user library, to hierarchical list boxes and other GUI elements in EIKON.

For developers, this presents enormous benefit. An EPOC32 developer should assume that a component is available to do a certain task, and spend some time looking for it. At first, this may take a while. However, within a short time, this leads to enormously productive programming, and applications that deliver power to users, in a compact package.

GDI

The GDI does not implement graphics, but it is fundamental because it provides the abstract base classes used by all graphics on the system. These include a graphics device, a graphics context (used for all drawing), colour, measurement and zooming support, printer support and fonts.

Text content

The GDI's definitions are used in turn by the text content model. This is a powerful component of EPOC32, which allows rich text to be manipulated with ease. This supports a variety of applications ranging from the word processor (which simply manipulates a single rich text object) to entries in databases, agendas and spreadsheet cells. Text content may also be stored in any stream store.

Application architecture

The application architecture specifies all the architectural issues to do with finding applications, tracking running applications, file locations, icons and captions, and object embedding. It provides an extensible system of language environment support: each language environment provides its own plug-in facilities to recognise and run applications. Currently, EIKON, OPL and .exe programs are supported. A future language environment such as Java could provide its own recogniser and run under the present application architecture without changing it.

Engine utilities

Finally, the engine utilities provide more useful tools, including resource file support (used for specifying GUI components and translatable text strings), clipboard support, sound utilities, specialised array classes, an alarm server, and a world data server.

Comms

EPOC32's communications support is based on two servers: the serial communications server (comms server) and the sockets-server.

Serial communications

The comms server provides a client API and several serial protocol implementations, each of which is written to a provider interface.

The serial client API provides a virtualisation of the RS232 device. On the one hand, this allows the full function of the device to be accessed by any client thread. On the other hand, it allows any number of threads to have the device open concurrently, provided only that no two clients attempt to read or write simultaneously. This port sharing gives increased flexibility: for instance, a dial-up application may use a scripting engine running in one thread to log onto a service, and then hand the port over to the sockets server to handle communications during a session.

The provider interface allows any serial protocol to be written, running as part of the comms server. The serial protocol may be implemented as an active object system running in the same thread as the comms server or, when pre-emptive response is necessary, it may launch threads of its own.

Two serial protocols are provided by EPOC32. The RS232 protocol drives the built-in RS232 device at speeds up to 115kbps on an 18MHz ARM 7100. A full implementation of IrCOMM is also provided.

On the client side, XMODEM and YMODEM are supported.

Sockets and networking

The socket server's client API provides an object-oriented sockets interface, with its cultural heritage in the BSD sockets API. A provider interface provides, in layered form, support for any sockets protocol. Implementations include TCP/IP, IrDA, and Psion Link Protocol (PLP).

The TCP/IP implementation supports a rich variety of protocols, including SLIP and PPP.

PLP is a proprietary protocol, used for compatibility with EPOC16, and for communication to the PC using EPOC Connect.

Dial-up and scripting

Dial-up connections are supported by a telephone dialler using a dial-engine to perform transformations on telephone numbers to dial the correct tone sequence. The same engine can be used for DTMF dialling for voice connections. A scripting engine supports the potentially complex process of signing on to a dial-up service.

EIKON

EIKON is the default GUI (Graphical User Interface) for EPOC32. It builds on the central components represented by the base, engine utilities and graphics components. It also uses other machine facilities, notably comms (i.e. for printing).

GUI elements

EIKON provides a rich set of GUI elements. Users can send commands to applications using menus, shortcut keys, or toolbar buttons. Menus support cascades. Dialog support includes single and multi-page dialogs and even scrolling dialogs for special applications.

Many standard controls are available, including number and text editors, list boxes and combo boxes, font and sound selectors, and controls optimised for personal information management, such as convenient time/date navigation, and latitude and longitude editors.

Scroll bars have dynamically-sized grab handles, and scroll application data automatically.

Many types of list are supported, including hierarchical lists, multi-column lists in which each entry has several aligned fields, and snaking lists, that wrap vertically into a container. A variety of standard lists are provided, and owner-draw lists may be written.

A console is available for displaying comms terminals and text-based shells, like an MS-DOS prompt under Windows 95.

Standard higher-level components include file browsers, 'Open' and 'Save As' dialogs, print settings and print preview.

These standard components, plus the flexibility for programmers to define their own controls, make EIKON the most powerful GUI available for handheld use.

Programmers framework

EIKON provides a powerful framework for programmers. To a first approximation, any application program may be thought of as an engine plus a GUI. GUI programming in turn divides into issuing and handling commands, drawing application views, and handling commands with dialogs.

In EPOC32, separate engine development is encouraged. A well-structured application's engine will be completely independent of EIKON.

Commands may be issued using menus, the toolbar or via shortcut keys. It is easy to specify any of these methods, using a resource file. An EIKON application provides a single function to handle all commands: typically, this identifies the command and invokes another function to process it.

Application views consist of one or more controls, which allow the application to draw its data, and to handle interaction through keyboard and pointer. Usually, the application re-uses the same drawing code for the control used in the view, for printing, and for drawing as a glass door.

Many commands are handled using a dialog to specify some further parameters, before doing some action. Dialogs are specified in a resource file and implemented by deriving from EIKON's abstract dialog base class. Facilities are provided to get data into and out of dialogs, validate controls individually, and ensure consistency across controls. In addition to the wide range of controls provided by EIKON, you may include custom controls in a dialog. Dialogs are automatically laid out when they are constructed, so that it is not necessary to specify pixel positions and sizes in the application. An additional benefit of automatic layout is that dialogs adjust automatically, when the application is localised into new languages.

EPOC32 variants

EPOC32 has been optimised for handheld mobile devices. Today, such devices require considerable software power and robustness. Psion have stated that EPOC32's robust design was inspired by industrial-strength workstation environments such as Unix, or Windows NT. Its multi-processing architecture allows EPOC32 to be scaled upwards to meet very high demands for personal computing power.

EPOC32 also supports lower-end scalability. Its resources are all owned by threads rather than processes; this allows EPOC32 to be configured as a single-process system with relative ease. As it happens, such a single-process system is also much easier to implement under Win32 than a full multi-process system. The WINS development environment is therefore a single-process variant of EPOC32.

EPOC32 is an international operating system. It supports localisation in a variety of Western languages using the Windows Latin 1 and Windows Latin 2 character sets. These are the 'narrow' builds of EPOC32, which allow text data to be represented compactly in Western markets.

EPOC32 is also designed for 'wide' builds, using the UNICODE character set for all internal purposes, and additionally a variety of other character sets (such as shift-JIS) for data interchange. Psion Software, together with Psion's Far Eastern subsidiaries are working on the input method editors and enhancements to text formatting and GUIs, required to support Far Eastern locales.

On a machine platform (referred to as MARM, MX86 etc.), the 'Base' functions as a real and complete operating system. The kernel and device drivers use the machine's hardware. The file server presents the ROM as drive Z:, and uses the RAM for drive C:, shared dynamically with other applications' use of RAM. The file server may also use removable media for other drives. A hardware abstraction layer (HAL) is used to allow much of the base to be re-used without change, even for radically different underlying platforms. On machine platforms that share a common instruction set, such as ARM variants, different implementations require only slight alterations to some device drivers and configuration files.

WINS

WINS is an emulation of a machine platform. For example on a Windows 95/NT PC it is used as the basis of the OPL and C++ SDKs (software development kits). The user library API and the client interface to the file server are essentially identical. User programs built on the WINS base use exactly the same source code and binaries as for MX86, and the same source code as for MARM.

The WINS kernel and device drivers use the Win32 API to provide services. For example, the EPOC32 screen is mapped to a window on the PC screen: the size and background bitmap for the window may be configured to represent a variety of EPOC32 target machines. In all other respects, the emulator window functions just like any other Win32 window. The HAL presents various intended hardware emulations to higher-level parts of the base.

The WINS file server maps drive C: onto \epoc32\wins\c\ on whatever drive the SDK is installed. Z: is mapped onto a directory whose name depends on the variant of the WINS platform: for narrow debug builds, Z:\ is mapped to \epoc32\release\wins\deb\z\. This means that an EPOC32 program under development, even if it has serious bugs, will not be able to damage the users' PC-based files, or even the installed EPOC32 SDK.

WINC

WINC is designed to run the WINS application engine libraries(DLLs), driving them with format conversion programs that form part of desktop connectivity software. For example, WINC is the basis of PsiWin 2. The user library and file server provide substantially the same API for WINC as on a machine platform. The kernel and device drivers use the Win32 API to provide services to WINC. Unlike WINS or the machine platform, there is no support for graphics and no need for a screen window. Also, since the driving program is not an EPOC32 user program, but a Windows application, the WINC file server does not attempt to map file references into safe areas. Instead, the whole PC file system is available to WINC and the driving software is responsible for using it correctly.

The WINC platform relies on another EPOC32 concept: that of application 'engines'. In C++, it's sometimes appropriate to think of the member functions of a class as the only way to access its member variables. On a much larger scale, the API of the application engine is the only way to access an application's data, including its file format. Therefore, instead of publishing file formats for such purposes as format conversion on the PC, EPOC32 applications simply make their application engines available for use.

An app engine may also be used to promote rapid application development on a machine. In EPOC16, many programs were written to access files produced by the built-in applications and so provide an interface between PIM data and some other application. Under EPOC32, this can be achieved in the OPL language by writing an OPX to provide some of the app engine's API to an OPL program. Users of this technique must be aware that EPOC32 applications do not support concurrent access to a single data file.

For converting file formats, the engine is run under the WINC platform. For converting formats, only the data is needed; graphics components and the GUI itself are unnecessary. The application engine is driven by a converter, that on a PC will usually be a Windows program. The same basic set up is used for conversion both to and from EPOC32 formats, and also for synchronisation at field and record level.

Software development

Initially there are two main options for Series 5, OPL32 the 32-bit successor to OPL16, or C++ that succeeds the SIBO C SDK.

OPL32 options

Programmers can develop full applications on the Series 5 itself, but a PC based OPL32 SDK is available for commercial developers or anyone who wants a PC hosted development environment. The OPL SDK supports more comfortable development of OPL programs on a PC.

The Psion OPL32 SDK includes:

- The PC based WINS emulation of the Psion Series 5 in several configurations
- Tools (for resource file compilation, bitmap and font manipulation, etc.)
- Examples not found on EPOC32 machines
- Documentation, in HTML and RTF formats.

A PC running under Windows 95, Windows NT 3.51 or Windows NT 4.0 is needed with 25MB of free disk space.

An equivalent to the OPL16 SDK libraries is not supplied with the EPOC32 OPL SDK. Also, calls to the operating system are not available directly in OPL32. An OPX must be used to replace any essential EPOC16 OPL library functions or OS calls. Any facility available to a C++ program may be made available to an OPL program through an appropriate OPL extension, or OPX. The C++ SDK is needed to develop OPXs. An OPL programmer does not need the C++ SDK in order to use OPXs.

OPP and OPPDBG for Series 5

Andy Clarkson, the author of OPP and OPPDBG for SIBO systems, will be investigating the possibility of producing versions for Series 5 in the near future. See the 'Contacts and Sources' chapter.

C++

C++ is EPOC32's native language. Software development relies on ideas as well as tools. The most powerful idea in EPOC32 is object orientation and its theoretical corollary, re-use. Object orientation is an extremely powerful design tool: viewed at all levels, EPOC32 is a system of objects. C++ is a natural, mainstream, object-oriented language, which allows object-oriented designs to be implemented easily. Although C++ has a reputation in some quarters for being slow and bloated, this is by no means necessarily the case. EPOC32 demonstrates that, by achieving re-use of source code and object code, C++ may be used to write highly efficient, compact systems.

The Psion C++ SDK includes:

- All user-side class libraries
- The WINS emulation of the Psion Series 5 in several configurations
- Tools (for project control, resource compilation, bitmap and font manipulation, etc.)
- Example code
- Documentation, supplied in HTML. Object orientation results in tightly interwoven class relationships; in turn, the documentation needs to be tightly interwoven also. The documentation is delivered in HTML, and includes many navigational aids including links to class definitions from all their references. However, unfortunately there are no document search facilities.

The C++ SDK includes the GNU tool chain required to compile for MARM. You will also need Microsoft Visual C++ to compile programs for WINS, the Windows version of EPOC32. The standard or learning editions of Microsoft Visual C++ may be used (because WINS does not use MFC libraries). You will need a fairly high specification PC running Windows NT or Windows 95.

Applications are developed first under Microsoft Visual C++ for the WINS platform, on a PC running Microsoft Windows 95/NT, and are debugged with the aid of Microsoft's powerful debugger. Then, the same source code is cross-compiled using the highly effective GNU C++ compiler for the target MARM processor, and uploaded to a target machine for execution.

Other languages

OVAL

The OVAL run-time system is not available in the first Series 5 systems, although this is likely to be remedied in the not too distant future in the form of OVAL32.

Java

Psion Software PLC recently announced they had licensed Java technologies from Sun Microsystems Inc, and intend to port it to the EPOC32 platform. Java is a cross-platform industry standard development language allowing the development of fully featured programs. Java's strong Internet support will make it easier to develop Internet centric applications for EPOC32 platforms.

Developer support

EPOC World, Psion Software's developer support organisation, was officially launched on 1st July 1997. Two types of EPOC World subscription are available, at the time of going to print (September 97) was priced as follows:

'C++ Developer' subscription   GBP 200.00
'OPL Developer' subscription   GBP 75.00

An EPOC World subscription is for a year, and includes access to the EPOC World Website, a copy of the latest SDK on CD-ROM and one update to that SDK (when the next version is released).

The EPOC World web-site includes:

- The latest EPOC32 C++ and OPL SDK documentation and tools
- Extra utilities, example code, documents and how-to guides
- Knowledge-bases
- Contact details for defect reporting
- Administrative services
- Training course timetables
- Conference details

See the 'Contacts and Sources' chapter for details of how to subscribe to EPOC World.

14   OPL32 Techniques

Introduction

New OPL programmers will benefit considerably from reading the 'OPL16 Techniques' chapter before this one, since the emphasis here is on changes from OPL16. All OPL32 programmers should gain more from this chapter if they have read the 'Series 5' chapter first.

There are two main sections in this chapter, the first concentrates on the changes, deletions and additions to OPL. The second section describes an example application, in considerable detail, with the aim of illustrating the primary changes and new features of OPL32.

All source code and supporting files for the example application are provided on disk - see the PPCOPL32 directory.

The syntax of the OPL32 keywords and functions is described in the 'OPL Reference' chapter. More detailed information, including the functions provided in the 'standard' OPXs, is provided in the OPL32 manuals from Psion (they are provided on the PsiWin 2 CD-ROM and are available from Psion's Website) - also see the OPL32MAN directory on disk.

OPL, the changes

Some OPL16 programs will need only minor modification to run under EPOC32; it will depend upon the complexity of the code, the dependence on operating system calls and possible use of OPL16 SDK library functions.

Extensions to OPL have been made to allow programmers to take advantage of the touch sensitive high resolution display on the Series 5. Also, some OPL keywords have been modified and new ones added for controlling the new grey level graphics modes.

In addition to the graphics changes, menus, dialogs and database handling have been improved to take advantage of the abilities of EPOC32.

Some aspects of OPL16 have gone, some new features have been added, and the syntax of some language statements has changed to provide extra options due to the effects of 32-bit addressing. For example, direct calls to the operating system have gone, but most have been replaced by language extensions called OPXs.

One of the major difference between OPL32 and earlier other versions of OPL is the influence of 32-bit addressing. This means that the arguments and return values of quite a number of OPL keywords have changed from being integers to long integers.

An indirect effect of the 32-bit architecture is that folder names, file names and program names can very long. In OPL source code, identifier names, i.e. names of variables, parameters, constants and procedures, can be up to 32 characters long, including any variable type specifier.

Header files may be 'included', e.g. for the definition of constants, variables and even procedure prototypes. In fact, many system-related constants relevant to OPL32 programmers are supplied in a ROM-based file CONST.OPH that can be included in OPL32 programs.

The new 32-bit memory model has enabled the 64K limits on program and data space to be removed, which is great news, but this should not have a major influence over the structure of an OPL application. It should still be part of a responsible designers remit to avoid producing applications that hog a large proportion of available memory.

To make the best of the new pointer driven interface a slightly modified approach to application design is also recommended. For existing applications to incorporate features such as pen input and to behave in a similar manner to the built-in applications, a fair amount of modification will be required.

Crunching code

A burning question for many existing OPL16 programmers will be: 'How fast is OPL32 compared to OPL16'. My simplistic benchmarks (S3c vs Series 5) confirm statements from Psion, that over-all OPL32 is about three times faster. However, the really good news is reserved for lovers of structured programming, because the time overhead on procedure calls has come right down. In OPL32 calls to procedures are implemented up to fourteen times faster. Also, calling OPX functions is said to be as fast as calling OPL's built in functions. Incidentally, auto-switch-off now functions even inside tight loops, you have to deliberately disable it in OPL32.

Keywords removed

- RECSIZE and COMPRESS (replaced by COMPACT).
- gDRAWOBJECT.
- gINFO is replaced by gINFO32.
- STATUSWIN, STATWININFO, DIAMINIT and DIAMPOS. The Series 5 does not have status windows, Toolbars are used instead - see later in this chapter for details.
- TYPE, PATH and EXT. On many SIBO machines the information provided via these statements was only used by the System screen. The Series 5 does not require this information. A new command FLAGS has a similar function to TYPE. On the Series 5, applications do not have types, application-specific paths or filename extensions. An application and its associated documents are identified by a UID (unique identifier) instead.

- CMD$ (4) returned alias information, which is no longer supported on Series 5. The application name returned by CMD$(5) on SIBO is not supported - see APP and CAPTION.
- SETNAME. The new SETDOC, serves a similar purpose, and should be called before saving your main document.
- Named Calculator memories and M0,...,M9. The Series 5 Calculator does not use OPL to evaluate expressions.
- CACHE, CACHETIDY, CACHEHDR and CACHEREC have gone since procedures are automatically cached on Series 5.
- CREATESPRITE, APPENDSPRITE, CHANGESPRITE, DRAWSPRITE, POSSPRITE and CLOSESPRITE. Superior sprite-handling OPX functions are provided.
- OS and CALL. The Series 5 provides extensibility using special OPL DLLs. Five OPXs are supplied with Series 5 systems as standard, and more are set to emerge from a range of sources. OPXs are discussed in more detail later in this chapter.
- USR and USR$.
- ODBINFO. Available on S3a/c, Siena and Work*about*.
- LOADLIB, LINKLIB, UNLOADLIB, FINDLIB, GETLIBH, NEWOBJ, NEWOBJH, SEND, ENTERSEND and ENTERSEND0. OPXs are now used for calling language extensions and creating object instances.
- Printing via the PAR: device is possible, but the device is no longer directly available to OPL32. All printing from OPL32 programs is best done using the standard printer OPX. A sophisticated set of functions are available including access to the four standard print dialogs and facilities for sending text, bitmaps and formatting information to a printer.

Keywords added

- DECLARE EXTERNAL, EXTERNAL, INCLUDE and CONST allow the use of header files which include the definition of constants and procedure prototypes.
- mCASC and mPOPUP provide new menu features.
- dCHECKBOX and dEDITMULTI provide new dialogs entry items.
- DAYSTODATE allows easy conversion of "days since 1/1/1990" to a date.
- gCOLOR, gCIRCLE, gELLIPSE and gSETPENWIDTH provide new graphics functionality.
- gINFO32 replaces gINFO.
- SETFLAGS and CLEARFLAGS allow for increased SIBO compatibility
- IOWAITSTAT32.

Database commands:

- DELETE allows deletion of a table.
- INSERT, MODIFY, PUT and CANCEL allow the construction and management of more flexible databases.
- BOOKMARK, KILLMARK, GOTOMARK support the identification/marking of specific records in databases.

- BEGINTRANS, COMMITTRANS, INTRANS and ROLLBACK support transactions and recovery in databases.
- COMPACT replaces COMPRESS.

OPL applications:

- CAPTION and FLAGS allow definition of OPL applications; FLAGS is similar to TYPE.
- SETDOC and GETDOC$ allow files to be created as application documents.
- GETEVENT32, GETEVENTA32 and POINTERFILTER provide increased support for handling of events, including pointer (pen) events.

Two other significant additions are:

- Support for Toolbars (to replace status windows). See the example application section later in this chapter.
- Support for language extensions in separate EPOC32 DLLs called OPXs.

Keywords amended

The following keywords have undergone some changes, although many of these are related to modified argument types and remain functionally compatible with earlier versions of OPL.

- ADDR, ALLOC, ADJUSTALLOC, REALLOC, LENALLOC and FREEALLOC
- APP and ICON
- CMD$ (3)
- To manage pointer events (pen taps) a new function GETEVENT32 has been added. All of the old information and more is supplied by GETEVENT32, so the OPL16 function GETEVENT is essentially redundant in OPL32. Also GETEVENT32 has an asynchronous equivalent GETEVENTA32.
- BUSY
- OFF
- SCREENINFO
- dBUTTONS, dCHOICE, dFILE, dINIT, dTEXT, dTIME and dXINPUT
- mCARD
- CLOSE, COUNT, CREATE, OPEN, POS and POSITION
- CURSOR, DEFAULTWIN, gBORDER, gBUTTON, gCLOCK, gCREATE, gCREATEBIT, gFONT, gGREY, gLINETO, gLINEBY, gLOADBIT, gSAVEBIT, gLOADFONT, gUNLOADFONT, gPEEKLINE and gXBORDER.
- LOADM now 'officially' supports up to seven program modules to be loaded concurrently, in addition to the main program module. Although, this was possible 'unofficially' on earlier systems. If speed is an issue though it's wise to keep this to minimum.

OPA header changes

As discussed in the 'Processes, Memory and Applications' chapter, OPL applications are distinguished from OPL programs by the presence of an APP...ENDA header. In OPL32 these headers have changed in a number of ways.

```
APP pname,UID&
    CAPTION appname1$,language1
    CAPTION appname2$,language2
    FLAGS flags%
    ICON filename$
ENDA
```

CAPTION

In the example header above, the pname string (without surrounding quotes) specifies the default public name for the application. Any subsequent occurrences of the CAPTION keyword will override the default pname with language specific names. If you wish to have the name of the application dependent on the language in which it is operating then you must use CAPTION. However, you must supply a CAPTION statement for all language variants including the original language in which the application was developed.

UID&

This the unique identifier for the application, as discussed in the 'Series 5' chapter.

Applications developed for personal use may safely use any UID in the range &0100000 to &0fffffff. Psion will issue a UIDs for applications that are to be distributed; they are guaranteed to be unique and start at &10000000. To obtain a reserved UID you should contact Psion Software - see the 'Series 5' chapter.

FLAGS

FLAGS replaces TYPE used on SIBO systems; possible values for flags% are:

flags% = 1 for applications that can create files. Your application will then be included in the list of applications offered when the user creates a new file from the System screen.

flags% = 2 to prevent the application from appearing in the Extras bar. It is not usual to set FLAGS to this value.

ICON

On the Series 5, filename$ following the ICON statement is typically the filename of a multi-bitmap file (.MBM) that contains up to three bitmap/mask pairs. Three sizes are included, 24x24, 32x32 and 48x48 pixels, to accommodate the different zoom levels in the system screen. The sizes are read from the .MBM file, if the exact size required is not provided, or if some sizes are missing the most suitable size is used.

In fact, you can use ICON more than once within the `APP...ENDA` construct on the Series 5. The OPL32 translator only insists that each icon bitmap is paired with a mask of the same size in the final ICON list. This allows you to use pairs of MBMs containing just one bitmap as produced and exported from the Sketch application.

For example, you could specify them individually:

```
APP ...
    ICON "icon24.mbm"
    ICON "mask24.mbm"
    ICON "icon32.mbm"
    ICON "mask32.mbm"
    ICON "icon48.mbm"
    ICON "mask48.mbm"
ENDA
```

or with an icon/mask pair in each MBM:

```
APP ...
    ICON "iconMask24.mbm"
    ICON "iconMask32.mbm"
    ICON "iconMask48.mbm"
ENDA
```

Or with all the bitmaps and masks as just one MBM, as would normally be the case if the icon and masks were prepared on the PC, and then processed using the BMCONV tool. For example.

```
APP ...
    ICON "filename.mbm"
ENDA
```

Once translated, the icon .MBM file is embedded into the .AIF file and so does not have to be supplied separately.

Production of icons is discussed in more detail in the 'Programming Techniques' chapter.

Toolbars

Status windows have been replaced by Toolbars located on the right hand side of the screen. A typical OPL application Toolbar will have a title, four application specific buttons and a clock. Support for Toolbars in OPL applications is provided via the ROM-based `Toolbar.opo` program module and the toolbar.oph header file. Use of a Toolbar is illustrated in the example application described later in this chapter.

Graphics

Up to sixty-four drawables (windows and bitmaps) can be used at once, the previous maximum in OPL16 was eight. Animating graphics is easier, multiple 'Sprites' can be used simultaneously - I can't find a stated limit, but for speed reasons it is not recommended to use more than 20 at once!

Three graphics drawing modes are possible:

- Two 'colour', black and white, no grey.
- Four 'colour', black, white, light grey and dark grey.
- Sixteen 'colour', black, white, and 14 grey levels.

For graphics, four grey-level mode is preferable. Although sixteen 'colour' mode may apparently lead to more impressive graphics, there are a number of reason not to use this mode:

- The battery load is very much higher
- Bitmaps occupy far more memory and disk space.
- Because of contrast limitations on LCD displays the difference between four colour mode and sixteen colour mode is hardly noticeable.

Databases

Operations on twenty-six simultaneous data files are now supported by OPL32 - using the logical identifiers A to Z. Native Psion .DBF databases can be used, but they have to be converted to an EPOC32 file format. PsiWin 2.0 does not convert SIBO .ODB files yet, but I believe a converter may be in production. I recommend the use of JBdata (an excellent Series 3 freeware program by John Boyce) to save the data in delimited text format on a Series 3a/c. Then copy the text file to a Series 5 and import it into a database on the Series 5.

A much improved database server is available to OPL32, with many new keywords - see the 'OPL Reference' chapter. A number of more advanced database features (such as indexes) are provided via a database OPX - see the documentation in the OPLMAN32 directory on disk.

Application help

Unfortunately, pressing the main help-key on the Series 5 when in an application will take you to generic system help, not to application specific help. Application related help should now be provided as an application menu option, via a hot-key press (Ctrl+Shift+H is recommended) and preferably also via a help button on the application's Toolbar. Providing application specific help is demonstrated later in this chapter.

OPXs

OPL is now extendible through libraries called OPXs. Five OPXs are supplied as standard with the first Series 5 machines, they provide support function for:

- Date & time handling .
- System related - i.e. many of the functions that were only available in OPL16 through operating system calls, e.g. foreground/background switching, backlight control, sound control, file and application control, etc.
- Bitmaps for use with buttons and Sprites
- Database extras - including a sub-set of SQL
- Printing - text, bitmaps, formatting information and print preview

Using the functions provided by OPXs is very easy and is demonstrated later in this chapter. The OPX supplier provides an OXH header file and the INCLUDE keyword is used to include these header files into your program source. OXH header files provide the declaration information required by your program when calling the OPX routines. The declaration information for the OPX specifies its name, UID and version number, followed by the procedure prototypes.

Alternatively, the OPX declaration details can be inserted directly into your OPL source code file(s) - see OPH headers below.

The five 'standard' OPXs and their OXH header files have default paths in the ROM (Z:), but the full path for any OPX may be supplied. These are \System\Opl\ for the header files and \System\Opx\ for the OPXs themselves. The OPX header files are stored in the ROM, but may be copied into RAM - see 'OPL32 example files' below.

With the standard OPXs, the OPL programmer is sometimes given direct access to objects via pointers (i.e. memory addresses used for direct access and efficiency). Otherwise Sprites, for example, could not be set up using an array of IDs. These objects can be explicitly deleted (through procedures provided by the OPX) to free memory or else they will be deleted when the program exits.

All of the functions provided in the 'standard' OPXs are detailed in the OPL32 manuals from Psion (they are provided on the PsiWin 2 CD-ROM and are available from Psion's Website) - also see the OPLMAN32 directory on disk.

OPX headers

As an alternative to INCLUDEing the OPX header information, the OPX declarations can be inserted directly into an OPL source file for example:

```
DECLARE OPX <opxName>,<uid>,<version>
    <protoType1> : <ordinal1>
    <protoType2> : <ordinal2>
    . . .
END DECLARE
```

where,

`<opxName>` is the name of the OPX without the .OPX extension. The OPX is stored in a \System\Opx\ folder on any drive, with the drives scanned from Y: to A: and then Z: if no path is specified. This allows ROM OPXs (in Z:) to be overridden if required.

`<uid>` is the UID of the OPX. The specification of a UID as well as a name guards against OPXs with the same name being confused, which could otherwise cause serious problems. The UID is checked on loading the OPX, a 'Not supported' error will result if the UIDs in the header file and in the OPX itself do not match.

`<version>` is the version number of the OPX. The version number of an OPX will be increased when any new procedures are added. OPL will refuse to load an OPX which reports that it can't support the version number given in the declaration. The version number expressed in hex is e.g. $0100 to represent version 1.00, $0102 for version 1.02 etc. In general, an OPX supplier will increment the 2 low digits (the so-called minor version number) for backward compatible changes, and will increment the 2 high digits for major incompatible changes.

`<prototype>` specifies the name, return type and parameters of an OPX procedure in the same way as for an OPL procedure when using the EXTERNAL keyword. Numeric parameters to OPX procedure can be passed by reference using BYREF. This means that the OPX is able to change the value of the variable. The OPX procedure prototype is followed additionally by a colon.

`<ordinal>` specifies the number of the procedure in the OPX itself and is used to call the correct procedure.

OPX name clashes

If an OPX procedure name clashes with one of your OPL procedures, or with that of another OPX procedure, you can make a copy of the OXH file and change the name of the offending procedures, but **not** the return type, parameter list or ordinal. You should then include this new OXH file in your module and the new name can then be used to refer to the procedure in your code.

For example, consider the OPX declaration,

```
DECLARE OPX XXOpx,XXOpxUid&,XXOpxVersion&
    XXClose%:(id&) : 1
    ProcWithLongParam:(aLong&) : 2
    AddOneToParams:(BYREF par1%,BYREF par2&, BYREF par3) : 3
END DECLARE
```

If a short integer is passed to `ProcWithLongParam:`, the translator will automatically convert it to a long integer.

The `AddOneToParams:` procedure adds one to each of the parameters. This is possible because the parameters are passed by reference. Parameters passed by reference must be variables rather than constant values because the OPX will write back to the variable. The variable type must always be the same as given in the declaration.

Callbacks from OPX procedures

An OPX procedure can call-back to a OPL procedure. This may be useful if an OPX needs some information that is not known when the procedure is initially called, or if it requires a large amount of data that needs to be sent piecemeal.

The OPX provider will specify the exact form for the OPL procedure that you must provide for the call-back to be completed successfully.

Developing OPXs

OPXs are (Dynamic Link Libraries) DLLs that are written in C++, they must conform to a series of standard interface conventions. Information and OPX source code examples are provided with the Series 5 C++ SDK available from Psion - see the 'Series 5' chapter for more details.

Series 5 OPL source files

Unlike OPL source code files on SIBO systems, OPL files on the Series 5 are not plain ASCII text. Instead they conform to the EPOC32 document conventions by having a binary header containing UIDs. The UID header identifies the files as belonging to the OPL editor program. Hence, reading Series OPL source files directly on other systems is not possible. However, the OPL editor on the Series 5 has options to import text files into a editor file and export OPL source code as plain text.

Notes:
A 'Shifted' space character is not treated as equivalent to an unshifted space character, and it is very easy to accidentally include them when entering OPL code. Shifted space characters in a Series 5 source file will give an 'Illegal character' error on translation. Fortunately, even though they are not visible any illegal characters are flagged and are therefore easily removed.

A REM comment on the same line as an INCLUDE statement will give a 'Not found' error on translation. Comments can be put on separate lines, before or after an INCLUDE statement, but not on the same line.

OPL32 example files

A number of OPL32 example programs and associated header files are supplied in the ROM of each Series 5 machine. If you wish to learn from them, or to use some of the example code in your own applications, there a two methods of getting access to the files. You can load them individually into the program editor, using the method described below for reading ROM-based files, or they can be easily transferred into a folder of your choice as follows:

- Create a new folder to hold the files
- Switch to the OPL program editor

- Select 'Create standard files' from the Tools menu and choose the folder name you created in the dialog that is presented.

Reading ROM-based files

Go to the system screen and press Ctrl+K (to select Tools, preferences), ensure that the 'Show system folder' option is checked (i.e. set) and tap 'OK', which will take you back to the system screen. Press Ctrl+Tab, this will take you to the folder browser. Select Disk Z in the disk select box at the top of the screen. The contents of the ROM folders will now be shown. Select the top level OPL folder, the Const.oph file will be listed along with many other header files (i.e. OPH and OPX files). Quit from the browser view by tapping 'OK', and all of the files in the OPL ROM folder will now be displayed on the system screen.

Double tap on the Const.oph file and it will be loaded into the OPL programming editor as a read only file. Use the 'Save as' option from the file menu to save the selected file in a folder of your choice.

Introduction to PPCOPL32

The rest of this chapter provides a detailed description of the structure of a demonstration OPL32 application. PPCOPL32 is based upon the 'Demo' application supplied by Psion with each Series 5 machine - see the 'OPL32 example files' section above. PPCOPL32 is designed to illustrate the structure of an OPL32 application and to demonstrate many of the new features of OPL32, including handling pointer and other events.

I have extensively commented the original source code, fixed a bug or two and extended the range of techniques used. For example, the application now uses an .INI file to store and retrieve its settings between invocations. It also incorporates the use of help Data files, which themselves contain information that describes how to implement program help. Additional error handling has been added, the editing of very long text data through a dialog box, plus the basis for multi-lingual support is included.

The full application and all necessary supporting files are supplied on disk. Included are extensively commented source code in Series 5 OPL format as well as in text format. In addition, the DOS and Series 5 bitmap files needed to build the 'zoomable' program icon are provided, plus the other graphical items used by the application such the 'EPOC' logo and the bitmaps for the Toolbar buttons. DOS batch files are available to build the .MBM files on a PC. All files are located in the directory structure named PPCOPL32.

To gain maximum benefit from the discussion that follows, the rest of this chapter is best read whilst referring to the comments and OPL source code of the PPCOPL32 application. I recommend loading the source files into the program editor on a Series 5 and using the find function to assist in following the program flow.

Note:

If you wish to view the PPCOPL32 source code in the Series 5 editor I recommend the following editor settings: From the Tools preferences menu set 'Mono fonts only' with all other options unchecked. From the Format menu set the Font to 'Courier 8pt bold' and the text colour to 'black'.

Techniques covered

Taken as a whole this a comprehensive and somewhat complex example. However, taken in stages, with frequent references to the commented source code, the reader should easily be able to absorb most, if not all, of the techniques demonstrated. You may then incorporate just the relevant routines into your own application.

OPL application (OPA)

- Application UIDs
- FLAGS 1 i.e. file based - although the application does not use 'Documents', and more than one instance of the application may be running.
- Zoom-able icon i.e. 48x48, 32x32 and 24x24 pixel icons
- Include files - OPX headers, system constants and application specific constants

Event handling

- Key press events, including a wide range of special keys such as menu and menu hot-keys.
- Pointer events
- Machine switch on event
- Foreground / background (gained focus / lost focus) events
- System messages, new command line information i.e. shut down program.

Toolbar use

- Toggling on/off
- Retaining the Toolbar state
- Button bitmaps

Menu handling

- Cascaded menus
- Dynamically changing menu items
- Popup menus

Multi-lingual techniques

- Language specific application names
- Resource file selection

Graphics techniques

- Use of four and sixteen grey levels
- Drawing with a pen
- Loading and displaying bitmap files
- Ordering of multiple windows

Sound
- Error beeps - toggling on or off
- Retaining sound state

File handling
- Detection of the existence of files and directories
- File name PARSE$ing for file and drive origin
- Program .INI file
- Use of dialog flags for file name editors / selectors

OPX calls
- For microsecond resolution timer
- Running, monitoring and ending other programs
- Resource file handling (limited)

Miscellaneous techniques
- Editing of very long text through a dialog box
- New dialog time editors
- Application help facilities
- Error trapping and handling

Source files

If you wish to modify or experiment with the PPCOPL32 example application the files will have to be loaded from the CD-ROM on to a Series 5 system or into the WINS directory structure on a PC.

All of the OPL source code is contained in two Series 5 format files, PPCOPL32 and PPCOPL32.OPH - see the \PPCOPL32\PPCOPL32 sub-directory on disk.

Text versions of the files are also provided for convenient viewing on a PC - see the \PPCOPL32\DOSUTILS\PPCTXT sub-directory.

The translated application is located in \PPCOPL32\SYSTEM\APPS\PPCOPL32. Other support files for building the icon and the other .MBM files are located in sub directories such as \PPCOPL32\DOSUTILS\ICONMBM etc.

Structure overview

At the top of the PPCOPL32 source file there are a number of INCLUDE statements to link in constants and header information for the OPXs used by the application. Of particular note is the inclusion of CONST.OPH, a ROM-based file that defines the values of a wide range of system constants. For details of the contents of the CONST.OPH file see the section 'OPL32 example files' earlier in this chapter. The PPCOPL32.OPH header file contains a number of application specific numeric and string constants, in particular the UID for the application with the identifier name KUidEmcc00& and the 32-bit hexadecimal value &100002A5.

The APP..ENDA header uses a default 'public name' of PPCOPL32 for the application, followed by its UID. Three CAPTION statements are language specific names/country codes for the application and will override the default name. The exact name used will depend on the language code returned by the machine and is taken care of by the system. Application names can be very long (250 characters) but it is advisable to keep them quite short to prevent them from being truncated on the 'Extras' bar and possibly in the Toolbar title.

ICONs for the application are declared to be in the multi-bitmap file PPCOPL32.MBM. This file contains three bitmap/mask pairs for three icon sizes, to allow for 'zooming' of the system screen display. Production of icons is discussed in more detail in the 'Programming Techniques' chapter.

The APP...ENDA construct is used by the OPL translator to generate an Application Information File (.AIF) containing 3 icon and mask pairs, the application name and the setting of FLAGS. The .AIF file is created in the application directory together with the .APP file itself. For example, the .AIF for PPCOPL32.APP is:

\System\Apps\PPCOPL32\PPCOPL32.AIF

The translator will generate an .AIF based on all the information available in the APP...ENDA header. However, if any is missing, then the following defaults are be used:

- for ICON: the 'question mark' icon
- for CAPTION: the caption specified in the APP declaration
- for FLAGS: the default value of 0.

Application headers are discussed in more detail under 'OPA header changes' earlier in the chapter.

Execution begins in the main: procedure where many of the program global variables are declared. The ROM-based Toolbar.opo module is loaded with LOADM, then TBarLink: one of its procedures is called to link in some GLOBAL variables needed for the toolbar routines. Note that processing never returns to this point. Instead, a procedure name is passed as an argument in the call to TBarLink: and it is in the KAppCont1: procedure where processing will resume. After TBarLink: has completed its tasks it will call KAppCont1: using the OPL procedure calling operator @. More GLOBAL variables are set up by KAppCont1:, and myInit%: an initialisation procedure is called. Finally KAppCont1: enters an endless loop to repeatedly call the nextEv%: procedure, that in turn uses the new GETEVENT32 function to wait for the next event. All other program functionality is provided via command procedures called by the Toolbar.opo procedure TBarOffer%: or from within the offrCmd%: procedure. The clockwise and anti-clockwise graphics options are available from the Menu and the Toolbar buttons, but the Pop-up menu demonstration is only available from the Toolbar button.

Processing in detail

The first three actions in `main:` are to get the width and height of the full screen (the default window), to use the `SETFLAGS` statement to enable `GETEVENT32` to see machine switch on events (not seen by default), and to disable program exit via Psion Esc with the `ESCAPE OFF` statement.

Language text

Next `Getlang:` is called to get the machines language code and hence derive the name of a language specific resource file. Currently no OPX function is available to return the language code for a Series 5 (as I write this one is in production by Psion), therefore the `Getlang:` procedure is incomplete. Currently it just determines the name of the resource file and briefly displays it during program initialisation.

Assuming the language code for the machine has been obtained, the code is converted into a two character string (with a leading '0' if needed), and the string is used as the last two characters of the resource file name, to ensure it is language specific. See the 'Language text' section in the 'OPL16 Techniques' chapter for examples, and the 'Appendix' chapter for a list of language codes. If a language specific resource file is not found the program will default to using the English file, if that is not found the program would normally quit out with an error message via the `pferr:` procedure.

Support for the use of program resource files is included in the SYSTEM.OPX library, and example calls to the procedures involved are included in `Getlang:` for information but are REMed out so they are not executed.

Toolbar support

All Series 5 applications should support a toolbar. `Toolbar.opo` is supplied in the ROM and provides the set of procedures required for this support. The key procedures in `Toolbar.opo` are described as they are encountered.

The `Toolbar.opo` support module is now loaded and `TBarLink:("AppCont1")` is called as described earlier. Processing resumes in the `AppCont1:` procedure which calls the procedure `myInit:` that in turn calls `Read_ini:` to restore program settings (or set up and use the defaults) from the programs' .INI file.

Application files

Program settings are restored by calling the `Read_ini:` procedure. Settings stored are the state of the error beep (on or off) and whether a Toolbar window should be shown or not. The width of the display is set according to the presence of a Toolbar or not.

All applications should ensure that they handle corrupt or missing .INI files correctly. When starting up, the program tries to open the .INI file. If this fails for **any** reason the procedure will use the default settings. It is not useful to report an error to the user, they will probably not understand the error or know how to fix it.

Series 5 applications should save non-document files (external files) to their so-called application directory. So, in the case of PPCOPL32, the application directory is \System\Apps\ppcopl32\, this is also the directory where the application itself should be located. Note, you can determine the full file specification of a file by using the PARSE$ function.

Documents and UIDs

Although PPCOPL32 does not create or use 'document' files it is worth an aside here to describe how they may be created. A document is a file that is specific to a particular application and may be used to launch the application. Documents do not normally have a filename extension and are identified as belonging to a particular application via a file header that may contain up to four UIDs. If a file header contains the UID of an application the appropriate icon will appear beside the file name when it is visible on the system screen.

Database documents, produced using CREATE, and multi-bitmap documents, created using gSAVEBIT, will automatically contain your application UID in the file header, providing the SETDOC command is used immediately before the command to produce the file. For example:

```
file$ ="myfile"
SETDOC file$
CREATE file$,a,a$,b$
```

Sets the file myfile to be a document. SETDOC may be used with the commands CREATE, gSAVEBIT to ensure the document header is created correctly. However, documents created with IOOPEN represent a special case and are described later.

Note:
The string passed to SETDOC must be identical in **every** respect to the name passed to the following CREATE or gSAVEBIT otherwise a non-document file will be created. So you are **strongly** advised to use the PARSE$ function on the file name before using it with the SETDOC and subsequent CREATE commands. For example:

```
file$ ="myfile" REM ensure file$ string is at maximum size
file$=PARSE$(file$,LEFT$(CMD$(1),LEN(CMD$(1))-4),off%())
SETDOC file$
CREATE file$,a,a$,b$
```

SETDOC should also be called after successfully opening a document to allow the System screen to display the correct document name in its task list.

In case of failure in creating or opening the required file, you should take the following action:

- Creating - try to re-open the last file and if this fails display an appropriate error dialog and exit. On re-opening, call SETDOC naming the original file so the Task-list is correct.
- Opening - as for creating, but calling SETDOC again is not strictly required.

For binary and text file documents created using IOOPEN and LOPEN, it is the programmer's responsibility to save the appropriate header in the file. This is a fairly straight-forward process and the following suggests one way of finding out what the header should be:

- Create a database or bitmap document in a test run of your application using SETDOC as described above.
- Run the program described below to read the four long integer UIDs from the test document.
- Write these four long integers to the start of the file you create using IOOPEN.

A small Series 5 utility program (Uidread) for reading the four UIDs from Series 5 files is provided on disk with source code in OPL32 format in \Ppcopl32\ppcopl32, and in text format in Ppcopl32\dosutils\ppctxt.

Creating text file documents using IOOPEN or LOPEN has two special requirements:

- You will need to save the required header as the first text record. This will insert the standard text file line delimiters CR LF (hex 0D 0A) at the end of the record.

- The specific 16 bytes required for your application may itself however contain CR LF. Since you should know when this is the case, you will need to read records until you have reached byte 16 in the document. This is clearly not a desirable state of affairs, but is inescapable given that text files were not designed to have headers. It is recommended by Psion that you request a replacement UID for your application if it contains bytes equivalent to CR LF.

Once a document has been open/created using IOOPEN, and the header written as described above, you should still use the SETDOC command to inform the system screen/task list about the document that is now being used by the application.

Toolbar initialisation

After loading the .INI file information, processing continues in myInit: by setting the values of a number of global variables and sets the pen line drawing width to two pixels. Then myInit: calls one of the application's own procedures initTBar:, to initialise the Toolbar.

After loading two button bitmaps from the 'buttons.mbm' multi-bitmap file, the TBarInit: procedure (from the Toolbar.opo module) is called, passing the application name and the full screen dimensions as parameters. This call sets the Toolbar title to the application name and creates an invisible toolbar window with a clock. By default OPL32 programs have compute mode on (i.e. they run at background priority even when in foreground). Note that TBarInit: sets compute mode off (see SETCOMPUTEMODE: in SYSTEM.OXH) allowing the program to run at foreground priority when in foreground.

Four Toolbar buttons are then set up by calling TBarButt:, two of the buttons use the bitmaps loaded at the start of the TBarInit: procedure. The first argument in the list passed to TBarButt: is the hot-key (or menu shortcut key) that corresponds to the action to be taken, i.e., the procedure to be called inside your application.

Finally the Toolbar is either made visible or left hidden depending on the setting of the `TbVis%` flag established by the `Read_ini:` procedure.

Windows

When any OPL program starts its default window (i.e. window ID = 1) occupies the whole screen. To simplify window re-drawing when the display is updated OPL uses a system of backup bitmaps. Each window created will use twice as much memory as you might expect. Therefore, it is always a good idea to make windows only as big as required to minimise your programs use of memory.

You can consider the default window as having two components, a graphics window with a slightly smaller text window inside it. FONT clears the window and sets the text window font and style. To write to the text window you use statements such as FONT and PRINT, but you can only use one font on screen at once. Ignoring the text window and using the graphics window instead with statements such as `gFONT`, `gPRINT` and `gPRINTB` is much more flexible.

Next, the `myInit:` procedure calls the `makeWins:` procedure to load the 'EPOC' bitmap from a file into memory. The `makeWin%:` procedure is then called twelve times to create an arrangement of small windows arranged in a circular pattern, each displaying the 'EPOC logo' copied from the bitmap held in memory. Control returns to the `AppCont1:` procedure after the main window is positioned last in the order.

Events and user input

The `AppCont1:` procedure now enters an endless loop calling `nextEv%:` to wait for the next event to occur. When events of particular type occur the control will BREAK from the loop in the `nextEv%:` procedure and return control to `AppCont1:`. Together these two procedures act as filters, testing for and reacting to different types of event.

`AppCont1:` displays any text characters that are typed in, draws lines on the screen in response to pen actions on the main window, and displays numeric information about other events not handled by the `nextEv%:` procedure.

`nextEv%:` calls GETEVENT32 to detect all events including: key presses, shutdown messages from the system, pen events, machine switch on and other events such as foreground and background changes. It is the `nextEv%:` procedure that is responsible for offering all pointer events (pen taps) to the Toolbar procedure `TBarOffer%:`. All pen taps on the side-bar menu tab, possible menu key presses, or hot-key short cuts are passed to the `offrCmd%:` procedure. All program functionality, including exit from the program, is provided via procedures called by `offrCmd%:`.

The GETEVENT32 command is a synchronous call that only returns when an event of some kind has happened. Effectively (as far as EPOC32 is concerned) the program is suspended and is waiting for the system to pass on the details of system events or key presses. A program only normally receives key presses (from the window server) when it is the foreground process, so if the program goes into the background (e.g. by the user pressing the system key) it is only able to process system events, not key presses.

In OPL, statements such as GET, GET$ or even GETEVENT32 are synchronous, whereas GETEVENTA32 and KEYA are asynchronous. Most OPL programmers don't need to use asynchronous techniques, but if the program has to do other tasks such as handling serial port transfers, while remaining responsive to key presses, then asynchronous methods are essential (see GETEVENTA32). The PPCOPL32 application is structured to respond to a number of event types synchronously.

System messages

On receipt of an event of some kind, nextEv%: tests the value in event&(1) to see if it was a system message event, if so it tests the command byte in the new command line. Valid commands received from the system screen (typically while the program is running in the background) are:

- 'X' to shutdown the program
- 'C' to create a new file, i.e. using the name entered by the user in the dialog presented by the system screen
- 'O' to open the file picked from those displayed on the system screen.
- 'U' unknown command.

Since this application does not open or create documents it only tests for the arrival of the shutdown message ('X') from the system. For example, if the user selects the file from the task list and chooses the close option, or because message has been sent by the system.

New command line information is returned by the GETCMD$ function. The command byte is the first character of the new command line string (in command$), and is retrieved with the LEFT$ string function. The remainder of the new command line is ignored.

Test are done for special key press events such as Menu or the Ctrl key plus a menu accelerator key. Key press modifiers are returned by GETEVENT32, hence the tests for Ctrl+Menu involves testing the values returned in event&(2).

Menu commands

In the PPCOPL32 application, pressing the Menu key or tapping the Menu tab on the side-bar will bring up the program menu. Selecting a menu item from under one of the menu titles will return a corresponding accelerator key or hot-key character code. All menu related text and accelerator keys are defined as literal strings and character codes in the offrCmd%: procedure. For a multi-lingual application such data should be read from a specific resource file. Thus allowing all menu text and accelerator keys to be language specific without affecting the program code in any way. Use of program resource files is demonstrated in the 'OPL16 Techniques' chapter and is not implemented in PPCOPL32 for two reasons: The language code for the machine cannot be obtained in OPL32 (an additional OPX is due from Psion to address this oversight), and the resource file compiler is only available with the OPL and C++ SDKs from Psion.

All pen taps are sent to the Toolbar procedure `TBarOffer%:`, if it corresponds to one of the Toolbar buttons the appropriate command procedure is called. The same procedure also detects taps on the clock or Toolbar title and takes the appropriate action to change the clock type or bring up the task list.

If the menu key or a hot-key is pressed the `offrCmd%:` procedure is called to decode it. For valid entries a corresponding command procedure will be called. Matching procedures are called via the @ operator which is designed to call a procedure named in a string variable. Selecting a menu option or using a valid accelerator key results in a single ASCII character; the selection is decoded in `offrCmd%:`. The character returned is added to the command procedure root string (in `cmdRoot$`) to arrive at a unique string that will be the name of the procedure provided to handle the menu option selected. For example, pressing Ctrl+E (i.e., to exit the program) will generate the character 'E' which when added to the command root string gives `'cmdE'`, the name of the program exit procedure. Two types of command procedure root names exist, `'cmd'` for lower case hot-key presses and `'cmds'` for shifted key presses.

The Toolbar procedures also use this mechanism to call the procedure assigned to each button during Toolbar initialisation by calls to the `TBarButt:` procedure. Each button has a short cut or hot-key letter associated with a corresponding command procedure in your application, that will be called by `Toolbar.opo` when a toolbar button is selected.

A number of points about the `offrCmd%:` procedure are worthy of note: The key stroke and key stroke modifier are passed as parameters and are used to detect if the menu key, menu pen tab or a hot-key was pressed. If the menu key is detected or the menu side bar tab was tapped the procedure will present a menu. Note the LOCK ON and LOCK OFF statements around the MENU function call to inform the system that the application is busy and cannot process system messages. Attempting to send shutdown messages etc. while a menu is open (and marked with LOCK ON) will result in an 'xxxxxx is busy' message; this is a limitation imposed by OPL32.

Two of the menu items have check boxes so the state of the `snd%` and `TbVis%` flags are tested to see if the check boxes should ticked or not when the menu is displayed. If a tick should be shown a value of $2000 is put into the appropriate flag variables i.e., `TbOn%` and/or `SOn%` and the flags are used in the mCARD line.

If the key press was a hot-key (i.e., the Ctrl key modifier was used) the key value has to be converted. Pressing Ctrl+A will return the number 1, corresponding to the first letter of the alphabet, Ctrl+B returns 2 and so on (try the 'Events' option on the PPCOPL32 menu and look at the numeric values returned for key presses with the Ctrl key). By subtracting 1 from the hot-key value and adding in the ASCII value for the character 'a' the result of a hot-key press will be equivalent to the value returned by the call to MENU where the same option was selected.

Error handling

In a number of critical places sections of error handling code are included to deal with abnormal situations. For example, at the end of the `offrCmd%:` procedure, to deal with illegal options or variables being encountered that have not been defined. Error handling is enabled with the ONERR eNotCmd statement and control will jump to the labelled section of code in the event of an error.

Notice also the use of the TRAP command before certain keywords. The TRAP command will override any ONERR processing that may have been set up. The ERR value will still be set if the function or command fails but the pferr: procedure will get to process any error that occurs. Calling a procedure such as pferr: allows for controlled handling and reporting of errors, and leaves open the potential for error recovery to take place. Relying solely on the system to 'crash out' when an error occurs is very unfriendly. If no error has actually occurred, pferr: will just return without taking any action.

Another point to note is the use of the ERR code with calls to the pferr: procedure. Using ERR as the error code is handy at certain points, e.g. before any language specific text has been loaded because any program supplied error text will not be available. Instead, the system error code (ERR) and message can be used, by default it will be in the correct language for the machine.

Menu options

As stated earlier, the PPCOPL32 application is provided as an illustrative example application, and the functionality included is simply designed to demonstrate the features of OPL32 plus a number of significant programming techniques. Many approaches can be used for the overall design of an application. If you find the approach illustrated by PPCOPL32 to your liking you may wish to use some of the ideas or code in the framework of your own applications.

File menu

Options are: **Close**

Program exit is handled by the cmdE%: procedure. All routes out of the PPCOPL32 application are via this procedure. First, the .INI file is saved, then tests are done to see if the application help was used and whether the help 'thread' is still running. When help is started a thread ID is returned in HelpThrdID&, this value will be non-zero. A call to IOYIELD is used to allow the status word Hstatus& to be updated for the help thread. If help is still active the status word will be equal to KStatusPending32&, so the thread is ended using an OPX routine called ENDTASK&: using the identifier (ID) for the help thread obtained when help was called.

The above code is included to deal with the situation where the user has ended the help thread (via the help menu or through the task list) before quitting from the application. In these circumstances the status word will be reset to zero after the call to IOYIELD, therefore trying to end the help thread would result in an error.

Edit menu

Options are: **Clear screen**

Clear screen is handled by the `cmdSC%:` procedure which makes the Toolbar window the first in rank order and the main window second in rank order, thus hiding the 'EPOC' windows behind the main window. The main window is then made current and is cleared.

Dialogs

Options are: **New flags, Edit boxes - cascades to Text editor, Date/Time and Filename**

The first thing to note is the second level menu with three options that cascade from the 'Edit boxes' option on the Dialogs menu item.

New flags
New dialog flags is handled by the `cmdSF%:` procedure which is designed to use a dialog to repeatedly alter its appearance and characteristics in response to new flags settings, changed through user input using the dialog itself. The new flags are for:

- Dialog buttons arranged on the vertically right rather than along a horizontal line.
- Dialog title or no title switching.
- Full screen or normal dialog.
- Drag or no drag of the dialog box.
- Dense packing or not of dialog items except buttons.

Text editor
Long text editing using the new `dEDITMULTI` dialog item is handled by the `cmdSE%:` procedure. Text entered through the dialog is held in a long integer array (four bytes per integer) that is sized to allow for the maximum text expected, plus an additional four bytes at the start of the buffer to hold the length of the data entered. Each byte of the text entered is accessed using the `PEEKB` function and displayed on the screen. Note that a button is required to complete the editing process since non printing key presses such as 'Enter' are taken as valid characters.

Date/Time
Editing time fields with the new time flags is handled by the `cmdD%:` procedure. Two new flags are used, a time field with no hours and an absolute time in 24-hour format.

Filename
Filename editing is demonstrated by the `cmdF%:` procedure which illustrates the use of selection and editing control flags, including the following new flags:

- `64 ($40)` don't display file extension
- `256 ($100)` allow ROM files to be selected
- `512 ($200)` allow files in the System folder to be selected

Notes:
Using `LOCK ON` and `LOCK OFF` surrounding the use of the `DIALOG` keyword will tell the system that the application cannot currently process system messages. Attempting to send

shutdown messages etc. while a dialog is open (and marked with LOCK ON) will result in an 'xxxxxx is busy' message; this is a limitation imposed by OPL32.

Wherever possible program data and information should be saved automatically without the user having to do it explicitly. Unless of course you wish to provide options for the user to quit the application without saving or revert to a previously unchanged version.

View menu

Options are: **Show toolbar**

Toolbar visibility on or off is toggled by cmdT%: procedure which simply calls routines in the Toolbar.opo module to hide or display the Toolbar. The procedure uses a global variable TbVis% to store the current state of the Toolbar visibility. Changing the state of the Toolbar will cause the check box next to the 'Show toolbar' menu item (on the View menu) to be ticked or not. Any change to the state of the Toolbar is saved in the program .INI file on exit from the program, and is restored whenever the program is invoked again.

Graphics menu

Options are: **Clockwise, Anti-clockwise, Grey scales**

Clockwise and Anti-clockwise
The clockwise demo is handled by the cmdC%: procedure and the anti-clockwise demo is handled by cmdA%:. The twelve 'EPOC' windows are created during the program initialisation and are retained throughout the duration of the program. When the windows are not visible it is simply because they are obscured by the main window. The clockwise and anti-clockwise procedures work by bringing each of the 'EPOC' windows to the front in an appropriate sequence.

Note the use of a negative value for the Anti-clockwise menu hot-key; it results in the display of grey line underneath the menu item to separate it from the item below.

Grey scales
The grey scales demonstration is handled by the cmdG%: and bands: procedures. After receiving input from the user via a dialog, the cmdG%: procedure creates two windows that occupy the top and bottom halves of the whole screen. The top window is created in four colour mode and the lower window in sixteen colour mode. The bands: procedure is called to draw a sequence of 'coloured' bands in both windows. The width of each band and the starting gCOLOR is as specified in the dialog. Of course there are no actual colours displayed, just shades of grey from white through to solid black. The range of greys actually displayed will depend upon values used by gCOLOR, and also on the colour mode of the window used. All sixteen grey levels used (i.e., 0 to 255 in increments of 16) will not be visible in a four colour mode window, and so an approximate 'dithered' value will be displayed i.e., where not all of the pixels are used and hence an approximation to the grey level is achieved.

Note that on Series 5 the concept of grey and black planes has gone. The 'colour' that is displayed when drawing in a window will depend upon its colour mode and the gCOLOR value. Intermediate greys can also be achieved by using different values for the three arguments in the gCOLOR command, although it is more normal to achieve this in the way demonstrated.

When drawing graphics by copying bitmaps it is the grey levels in the bitmap, the colour mode of the window used, and in some cases the use of a so-called mask, that will determine the final visual effect. For example, with ICON and gBUTTON the bits that are set in the mask specify the bits in the bitmap that are to be used. Bits that are clear in the mask specify the bits that are not to be used. This allows the effect a particular bitmap will create to be varied by supplying different masks. For example, in ICON mbm$, each icon bitmap is paired with a mask in the multi-bitmap file mbm$. Only pixels that are set in the mask are drawn in the final icon. The pixels that are clear in the mask are not drawn, allowing any background pixels to 'show through'.

Events menu

Options are: **Display events**

Display events is handled by the cmdV%:, clrEv: and showEv: procedures. Instead of reacting to events the cmdV%: procedure receives them and uses the showEv: procedure to display the nature and characteristics of each event. The only exception to this behaviour is if the user presses the Esc key which will quit from the procedure (and only Esc with no modifiers such as Shift or Ctrl). Not all events will set every element of the event array, so clrEv: is used to fill the event array with zeros to ensure that information left over from a previous event cannot be confused with the most recent event.

The show event is quite a complex procedure, but it is worth close study since it illustrates how to detect the event type and how to use the additional information that is supplied in the event array. I have extensively commented the code to assist with understanding its operation.

OPX menu

Options are: **Stopwatch demo**

The Stopwatch demo is handled by the cmdS%: procedure which uses calls to the Date OPX to implement a timer with micro-second resolution (i.e., millionth of a second). Two OPX procedures are used, DTNOW&: is used to get a snapshot of the current date and time to the nearest micro-second. Then a loop is entered which repeatedly calls the same procedure to get updated information; the second procedure DTDATETIMEDIFF: is called to calculate the difference between the start time and the current time to the nearest micro-second. Time differences are displayed to the nearest milli-second by dividing the time differences by 1000.

Obtaining timings that are truly resolvable down to a single micro-second using the above method is most unlikely to be possible. However it is very probable that the system timer itself is capable of that degree of resolution.

Tools menu

Options are: **Help and Sound**

Help

Pressing Fn+Help on a Series 5 will bring up information that is related to the Series 5 system and the built-in applications. This behaviour is distinctly different from SIBO systems, where well designed programs will invoke application specific help. Application specific help is handled by cmdSH%: procedure.

It is now recommended that help is implemented using EPOC32 database files that contain two fields - a subject field and an information field. Help is called by running the Data application, via a the RUNAPP&: procedure in the System OPX, passing the name of your help data file as a parameter. Application related help should now be provided as a menu option, via hot-key press (Ctrl+Shift+H is recommended) and preferably also via a help button on the application's Toolbar.

Simply exiting from help (via the menu or with Ctrl+E) will dump you back into the system screen, instead of returning to the application where you called for help. If the help database file in your application is given a .hlp filename extension the behaviour of the Data application will be modified. The options on the Data menu will be restricted, and will include a 'Go back' option. Also the Toolbar options will be different and a 'Go back' button will be included. The help Data file provided with PPCOPL32 contains advice on the stages involved in creating help files for your own applications.

When the help option from the Tools menu is selected or Shift+Ctrl+H is pressed the cmdSH%: procedure is invoked. A test is done to see if help is already running by examining the value of HelpThrdID&, if it is equal to zero the System OPX procedure RUNAPP&: is used to start up the Data application using the fully PARSE$ed help file name as a parameter. The call to RUNAPP&: will return a 'thread ID' that can be used to identify the application's help 'thread'. Another OPX procedure LOGONTOTHREAD: is used with a status word HStatus& which the system can update to indicate whether the help thread is running (pending) or not.

If the value of HelpThrdID& is not zero, a call to IOYIELD will allow the system to update the status word for the help thread. If help is still running (the user may have closed it) the status word will be returned equal to KStatusPending32&, so help is brought to the foreground with the SETFOREGROUNDBYTHREAD&: procedure. However, if the help thread had ended for any reason the status word would be zero. In this case the HelpThrdID& variable is set to zero and the procedure recursively calls itself to restart the help thread.

When the program ends the cmdE%: procedure tests to see if the help thread is active, if so an OPX procedure ENDTASK&: is called to send a shutdown message to the window group identified by the thread ID. Hence application specific help is not left running when the main application has finished.

Note:

For multi-lingual applications you will need to supply language specific versions of the help Data file. Each file should have a name unique to the language - see the `Getlang:` procedure for an example of constructing language specific file names.

Sound

Sound on or off is toggled by `cmdSS%:` procedure which simply uses a global variable `snd%` to store the current state of the application sound. Changing the state of the sound flag will cause the check box next to the 'Sound' menu item (on the Tools menu) to be ticked or not. Any change to the state of the sound flag is saved in the program .INI file on exit from the program and is restored whenever the program is invoked again. All calls within the program to issue a beep sound (i.e. via the `sound:` procedure) will only take effect if the `snd%` sound flag is set to true.

Toolbar options

Options are: **Clock, Anti, Popup demo, Exit**

Program exit, clockwise and anti-clockwise graphics options are available from the Menu and the Toolbar buttons and are described above. However, the Pop-up menu demonstration is only available from the Toolbar button and is handled by the `cmdTbDownP%:` procedure.

Pop-up demo

A simple demonstration of an independent pop-up menu is given by the `cmdTbDownP%:` procedure. Pop-up menus are (and should always be) used independently of normal menus.

Clock and title

Tapping on the Toolbar clock will toggle the format of the clock between analogue and digital formats (using a Date OPX procedure). Touching the Toolbar title will bring up the task list (using a System OPX procedure). Both of these actions are handled from within the `Toolbar.opo` module.

Support procedures

`Getlang:`

Determines and displays the file name for a program resource file. This incomplete procedure is discussed in more detail in the 'Language text' section earlier in this chapter.

`waitkeypen:`

A simple procedure to wait for any key press or pen tap before returning. It uses `GETEVENT32` to test for a system shutdown message and calls the `cmdE%:` procedure to exit the application if one is received.

`sound:`

Makes a beep sound if program sound is enabled.

Read_ini:

Sets up the default settings before trying to open the application's .INI file. If the .INI file is found the stored settings are used in preference to the defaults. Note the use of fully PARSE$ed file names and the 'hard coded' drive C: for the location of the .INI file, as recommended by Psion.

Save_ini:

Deletes the application's current .INI file, if one exists, and creates a new file containing the current application settings. Note the use of fully PARSE$ed file names and the 'hard coded' drive C: for the location of the .INI file, as recommended by Psion.

pferr:

Used to display error messages, either supplied by the application or by using the system generated error codes. The program exit procedure is called if an unrecoverable error has occurred.

15 Programming Techniques

Application files

The format of the files created by the applications 'built-in' to Psion machines are described to varying levels of detail in a number of sources on disk, the key sources are described below. Where possible, information on file format conversion is given. The key examples that illustrate how to access the application data files from within your own programs are described in this chapter.

In addition, a number of DOS-based utility programs are available to convert between various file formats. Virtually all of the conversion utilities are provided on disk and are described below.

File formats, EPOC16

The Psion SIBO C SDK contains the definitive source of information on virtually all of the EPOC16 file formats. However, for those who do not own the SIBO C SDK, the following directories contain information files describing the format of most of the key application files.

PSIONICS
An excellent source of EPOC16 file format information, plus a host of other valuable data, can be found in the so-called 'Psionics' files that have been assembled over a number of years by Clive D Feather. The 'Psionics' files are provided on disk in the PSIONICS directory. However, the information included is being continually improved and expanded so please refer to Clive Feather's web site for the most up-to-date versions, see the 'Contacts and Sources' chapter for the URL.

FORMATS
File formats details for Psion 3a Agenda, Database, Word and Spreadsheet files in RTF, TXT and Word for Window versions. See also the OODOC201 directory for resource file information.

DOC
Documents in Microsoft Word for Windows format.

HEXVIEW1
A file and memory segment viewer and editor, works in text or hexadecimal mode, useful for investigating the detailed construction of a file at a binary level.

Format conversion, EPOC16

PsiWin Versions 1.0, 1.1

The Psion Manager in PsiWin 1.x provides drag and drop management of files and directories, plus seamless conversion of a range of file types to and from Psion formats to your preferred PC equivalents. For example, from Psion Word format to Microsoft Word format and vice-versa. More information on PsiWin is provided in the chapter 'Linking to a PC or Printer'.

Writing PsiWin converters

For those who wish to write additional EPOC16 file converters, Psion produced file conversion documentation and example source code in C++. The additional converters are designed to be used with PsiWin 1.x (Windows 3.1 version). See the FILECONV directory on disk.

File formats, EPOC32

The file formats for Series 5 applications have not been published (not even in the OPL32 or C++ SDKs). It is unlikely that Psion will ever publish the formats, because the mechanism Psion recommend for access to an application's data (documents) is through the application engine itself, as described below and in the 'Series 5' chapter.

Format conversion, EPOC32

Programmers are encouraged to make use of the 'services' provided by an application's engine to read and write the data. C++ programmers can make direct use of the engine, but OPL32 programmers must use the engine via a suitable OPX. Information on how to do this is beginning to emerge from Psion - see Agenda files later. PsiWin 2 also uses this mechanism to convert from Series 3 files to Series 5 formats.

PsiWin 2

A CD-ROM is supplied with every Series 5 system, it contains the Windows 95 'Explorer' software from Psion. PsiWin 2 integrates itself into the Windows 95 Explorer file manager and provides a connection between a Series 5 and a PC. Bi-directional file transfers and format conversions are an integral part of the system. PsiWin 2 actually runs under WINC, a specific 'communication' variant of EPOC32. WINC uses the 'built-in' Series 5 application engines to do file conversion from/to the Psion file formats and those of other applications. For example, between Microsoft Word for Windows format and Psion Series 5 Word format and vice-versa. PsiWin 2 is discussed further in the chapter 'Linking to a PC or Printer'.

Agenda files

Agenda files on the original Series 3 follow a standard DBF format, but from the Series 3a onwards the format changed. Series 3a files have the same basic file and record nature as DBF files, but the internal record structure and file signatures are not the same. Series 3c and Siena Agenda files incorporate additional information to help with the synchronisation between the Agenda records and those held in PC based organisers/schedulers.

The AGNFILE.DOC file in the DOC directory is a document in Microsoft Word format that describes the Series 3a Agenda file format. The same information can also be found in the FORMATS directory as three different file types, i.e. AGNFILE.DOC, AGNFILE.TXT and AGNFILE.RTF.

In the PSIONICS directory, the AGENDA.TXT and AGENDA3A.TXT files discuss all of the Series 3 and Siena formats.

Also, see the OPL source code from Mark Esposito in the PELAGN directory which demonstrates how to read Agenda files from OPL.

For Series 5 Agenda files, see the notes above under 'Format conversion EPOC32'. An OPX that makes use of the Agenda 'engine', to read and write data, is available from the Psion EPOC World web site - see the 'Contacts and Sources' chapter for access details.

Database files

EPOC16 'native' databases are binary files containing typed, variable length records. See DBF.TXT in the PSIONICS directory and DBFFILE.DOC (or .TXT or .RTF) in the FORMATS directory for database format information.

The following directories contain example code illustrating access to database files.

DBFEXAM
Two examples illustrating C access to .DBF files. DBFED2.C uses DbfQuickOpen which, although documented, its use is not demonstrated in the C SDK manuals.

ISAMEG
Contains a demonstration of an Indexed Sequential Access Method (ISAM) database in OPL using the ISAM.DYL library from Psion.

ISAM
Contains a demonstration of an Indexed Sequential Access Method (ISAM) database in C using the ISAM.DYL library from Psion.

DBS Database Server
For more advanced DBF database handling, plus access to dBaseIII and dBaseIV format files see the DBS_105 directory system. The DBS system is 'built in' to OVAL, although version 1.04 had some problems (see the DBSPATCH or PSIONINC\OVAL\DBASE\SERVER directories for patches).

Database conversion

The following directories contain utilities for database file format conversions.

OPLTRAN

A set of DOS-based utility programs for EPOC16 file conversions including:
DBF2TEXT.EXE   Convert a Psion database to a delimited text file.
TEXT2DBF.EXE   Convert a delimited text file to a Psion database.

DBF2TEXT

Converts a Psion database file to a delimited text file – useful as an intermediate step for exporting Psion database data to other formats. This version of the program is more recent than the copy in the OPLTRAN directory.

DBFC103

Converts a delimited text file to a Psion database file - useful as an intermediate step for importing databases in other formats to Psion format.

JBdata

An excellent Freeware database for Series 3a/c that has many more facilities than the built in Data application, in particular it has the ability to load data files with field types other than string. JBdata can also export a Series 3a/c database as a delimited text file, useful for transfer to other systems e.g. Series 5.

Series 5 Data files

Details of the format of Series 5 Data files are not available, see the notes above under 'Format conversion EPOC32'.

PsiWin 2 will convert EPOC16 Data files to Series 5 format. However, files containing field types other than strings cannot yet be converted by PsiWin 2. For example, database files created by OPL applications that have non-string data fields.

An interim solution might be to use **JBdata** to export the EPOC16 database (e.g. on S3a/c) as a delimited text file, transfer the file to a Series 5 and use the delimited file import in the Series 5 Data application.

Word files

For information on the format of EPOC16 Word files see WORD.TXT in the PSIONICS directory and WORDFILE.DOC (or .TXT or .RTF) in the FORMATS directory.

The C source code for a DOS program to convert Psion Word files to text files is located in the W2TSRC directory. The EPOC16 Word application itself provides options to export/import Word files to/from text files. In fact, the OPL editor on EPOC16 machines is just an alias of the Word application that operates on plain text files. Aliasing in EPOC16 is discussed later in this chapter.

Series 5 Word files

Details of the format of Series 5 Word files are not available, see the notes above under 'Format conversion EPOC32'. The Series 5 Word application itself has the option to export/import Word files to/from plain text files.

PsiWin 2 will convert EPOC16 Word files to Series 5 Word format.

Spreadsheet files

For information on the format of EPOC16 Sheet files see SPR.TXT in the PSIONICS directory and SPRFILE.DOC (or .TXT or .RTF) in the FORMATS directory.

Series 5 Word files

Details of the format of Series 5 Sheet files are not available, see the notes above under 'Format conversion EPOC32'.

PsiWin 2 will convert EPOC16 Sheet files to Series 5 Sheet format.

Text files

Plain ASCII text files can be edited in the EPOC16 Word application, or with the OPL program editor. Therefore, transferring text files between a PC and a SIBO system is very simple.

Programs in OPL16 are plain ASCII text files, whereas OPL32 source files are considered to be 'documents' on the Series 5 and so have a UID header, hence they may not be directly readable by a PC text editor. OPL32 source files have to be exported as text files from the Series 5 program editor. Text files can also be imported into the Series 5 program editor.

The Series 5 Word application is able to import/export plain text files.

Sound

In SIBO systems, sounds produced by the buzzer (or buzzer emulation) are generated via the PLIB p_sound function, the GenSound OS call, the OPL BEEP function or the Oval Beep function. Sounds made via a speaker (if fitted), such as DTMF dialling tones, are controlled via I/O functions using the SND: device driver. The SND: driver can produce two distinct notes at the same time allowing the generation of a wide range of notes and note sequences.

All Series 3 and HC models have an internal amplifier driven loudspeaker that can be driven by the SND: device driver. The original Series 3 and the HC also have piezoelectric buzzers for emitting warning beeps and other simple sounds. The piezoelectric buzzer is emulated via the speaker on the later Series 3 models, however it takes more power to drive. On the first Series 3 the sound driver is limited to providing DTMF dialling tones or simple alarm sounds.

On the 3a and 3c the SND: driver can produce two distinct notes at the same time, allowing the generation of a wide range of sounds. Although the sound quality is not as high as with digital sound files, the memory requirements are much less. For example, to play a tune lasting six seconds, at around 8Kbytes per second, would require a digital sound file of size 49,184 bytes. A comparable figure using the SND: device driver would be less than 1 Kbytes for the data required.

The 3a/c systems also include a microphone and can record sounds into compressed digital sound files that can be replayed. The Siena and Workabout have only piezoelectric buzzers and so are restricted to emitting warning beeps and other simple sounds, they do not have speakers or microphones and cannot record or play digital sounds. The HC does not include a microphone or the CODEC hardware necessary for digital sounds.

Series 5 machines have a speaker, microphone and CODEC hardware. Sounds can be generated as tones synthesised from a combination of sine waves according to an algorithm, and are generated directly by the sound driver. Series 5 machines can also record sounds into EPOC32 compressed digital sound files that can be replayed.

Sound files

EPOC16

Playing and recording of digital sound files (.WVE files) on suitably equipped SIBO system is achieved in different ways depending on the language:

In OPL16, by using appropriate EPOC16 operating system calls - see key examples below.

In OVAL, using methods associated with a 'hidden' Sound control i.e. Cancel, Play, PlayAsync, Record, RecordAsync.

In C, using calls to PLIB library functions, for example:
For recording - p_recordsounda(), p_recordsoundw(), p_recordsoundcancel().
For playback - p_playsounda(), p_playsoundw(), p_playsoundcancel().

Key sound examples on disk are:
Files in the PPCOPL16 directory demonstrate playing a sound file asynchronously in OPL16. Examples in the TSMP10 directory demonstrate recording/sampling sounds in OPL and C. The sound examples use a SYS$SAMP.LDD logical device driver to provide access to a SMP: I/O device. See SYS1.TXT in the PSIONICS directory and OSCALLS.DOC in the DOC directory for details of the EPOC16 O/S calls required for recording and playing digital sound files.

Note:
Digital sounds cannot be recorded to Flash SSDs, although once copied to a Flash SSD they can be played back.

EPOC32

EPOC32 digital sound files contain data encoded using the Alaw standard for encoding sound. Sound recording (sampling) facilities are provided by EPOC32. Sampled digital sound files can be generated using EPOC32's sound recording facilities. Like all 'document' files in EPOC32, sound files do not have filename extensions.

In C++ a number of sound classes are available, with associated methods for sound replay/recording and for producing sounds algorythmically.

In OPL32, playing of digital sound files is achieved through calls to the procedures in the System OPX:

`PLAYSOUND:(file$,volume&)`, `PLAYSOUNDA:(file$,volume&,statusWord&)` and `ret&=STOPSOUND&:` to play a sound file synchronously, asynchronously and to cancel the replay of a sound file respectively.

Sound recording OPX functions are not yet available.

Sound file formats

On Series 3a/c machines, digital sound files have a .WVE filename extension (and they may be grouped in a \WVE directory). A set of sample sound files are provided in the WVE directory on disk.

Series 3a/c sound files are compressed and hold one second of sound per 8Kbytes of disk space. For information on the format of EPOC16 (.WVE) sound files see the SOUND.TXT file in the PSIONICS directory on disk.

PC-based wave sound files have .WAV filename extensions. Conversion between EPOC16 and PC type sound files can be achieved using one of the two PC-hosted conversion programs, provided in the OPLTRAN directory on disk.

- WVE2WAV.EXE   Convert a Psion WVE file to a Windows WAV sound file.
- WAV2WVE.EXE   Convert a Windows WAV file to a Psion WVE sound file.
- WAV2WVE.CPP   The C++ source code for a version of the WAV2WVE.EXE conversion program.

Series 5 sound files are treated as documents and do not have filename extensions. The format of Series 5 digital sound files is different to EPOC16 (.WVE) files, they are more compact and can hold a choice of 2 minutes (standard compression) or 4 minutes (ADPCM compression) of sound per MByte. In other words, 8.5Kbytes or 4.3Kbytes per second.

A new sound file conversion utility WVECONV.EXE (Windows 95/NT only) has been provided by Psion to convert Series 3a/c sound files to Series 5 and vice-versa.

You should find the WVECONV.EXE utility on the PsiWin CD-ROM in the \EXTRAS\UTILS directory.

Combined with the other two conversion utilities described above, WVECONV gives full interchange capability between the PC .WAV format and the various Psion formats.

Bitmaps, icons and fonts

For a discussion of EPOC16 bitmaps and bitmap files see the 'User Interface' chapter. For details of EPOC32 bitmaps see the 'Series 5' chapter. Using program icons is described in the chapters on OPL techniques, production of bitmap files and program icons is described later in this section. Standard and custom text fonts are also described later.

Bitmap files, EPOC16

Options for producing bitmap files, for icons in particular, are described in the 'Icon for EPOC16' section below. The format of EPOC16 bitmap files (.PIC) is detailed in BITMAP.TXT in the PSIONICS directory on disk.

Bitmap utilities, EPOC16

A utility program, WSPCX.EXE in the OPLTRAN directory, will convert Windows PCX files to EPOC16 bitmap (.PIC) files; it will also bind multiple EPOC16 bitmaps into one file.

A more recent version of the WSPCX.EXE program, than the version located in the OPLTRAN directory, can be found in the WSPCX314 directory.

Another conversion utility, by Andrew Baldwin, is located in the FIREPIC directory. It is a bitmap loader/viewer/saver for the Psion 3/3a/c and Work*about* that offers a few extra features over other similar programs. It can load and save multiple file formats by the use of plug-in DYLs (currently supplied DYLs for PIC and PCX formats). Full source code is supplied, in C and OPL that demonstrates how to write and use DYLs called by an OPL program.

Note:
PCX files are ZSoft Paintbrush format files, a format understood by many PC-based bitmap edit programs.

Screen capture, EPOC16

Screen captures are useful for including Psion screen shots in manuals or web pages or for extracting parts of the Psion screen for use as icons.

On SIBO systems Shift+Ctrl+Psion+S will capture the whole screen into to an EPOC16 bitmap file called LOC::M:\screen.pic. If the machine has a grey plane the file will contain two bitmaps, the first to store the black plane information and the second to store the grey plane.

Icons for EPOC16

To produce bitmaps and icons on a Series 3a/c, a pixel oriented drawing package is needed. An excellent shareware application, Draw version 2.84 by Rick Andrews, is included in the DRAW284 directory for your evaluation (please register Draw if you intend to keep it).

A Windows (version 3.x) based icon editor, that is very easy to use, is included in the PSICON directory (please read the notes included with the program files).

A SIBO based icon editor is located in the ICONED directory. The program was produced by Psion as part of the C SDK and was been placed in the public domain. The HWIF C source code is included with the executable program.

The OVAL IDE has its own icon editor built in.

A collection of 48x48 icons for use with your own applications or program groups can be found in the ICONS directory (please read the notes included with the files).

Bitmap files, EPOC32

Options for producing Series 5 bitmap files, for icons in particular, are described in the 'Icons for EPOC32' section below. Series 5 multi-bitmap files (.MBMs) may contain from one to many bitmaps. Files produced by the Series 5 Sketch application are not the same as MBM format files. Sketch uses its own 'document' file format for drawings. However, Sketch is able to import and export MBM files that contain a single bitmap. If a multi-bitmap file, containing more than one bitmap, is imported into Sketch only the first bitmap is loaded. Details of the format of Series 5 multi-bitmap files (.MBM) or Sketch files are not yet available.

A new bitmap file conversion utility BMCONV.EXE (Windows 95/NT only) has been provided by Psion to convert Windows BMP files to Series 5 MBM format and vice-versa. In addition to converting BMP files to MBM, BMCONV is able to combine individual MBM files into multi-bitmap MBMs, it will also disassemble a MBM file into a series of individual BMP files – see the 'Icons for EPOC32' section below.

You should find the BMCONV.EXE utility on the PsiWin CD-ROM in the \EXTRAS\UTILS directory. It is also under the PPCOPL32 directory on the disk supplied with this book.

Screen capture, EPOC32

Screen captures are useful for including Psion screen shots in manuals or web pages or for extracting parts of the Psion screen for use as icons.

On the Series 5, pressing Shift+Ctrl+Fn+S will capture a complete screen image as an MBM multi-bitmap file (containing a single bitmap) into a folder and file of your choice.

Icons for EPOC32

Series 5 icons are typically held in a multi-bitmap file (.MBM), that contain up to three bitmap/mask pairs. The three sizes are 24x24, 32x32 and 48x48 pixels to accommodate the different zoom levels in the system screen. When an application is 'built' the icons are placed in an .AIF file, the system then reads the most suitable size for the 'zoom level'. If the exact size required is not provided, or if some sizes are missing the most suitable size is used.

Each icon bitmap is paired with a mask of the same size. Only pixels which are 'set' in the mask are drawn in the final icon. The pixels which are 'clear' in the mask are not drawn, allowing the background to be displayed in these pixels.

In an OPL32 application header you can use MBMs containing just one bitmap as produced and exported from the Sketch application.

For example in OPL32, you could specify them individually:

```
APP ...
    ICON  "icon24.mbm"
    ICON  "mask24.mbm"
    ICON  "icon32.mbm"
    ICON  "mask32.mbm"
    ICON  "icon48.mbm"
    ICON  "mask48.mbm"
ENDA
```

or with an icon/mask pair in each MBM:

```
APP ...
    ICON  "iconMask24.mbm"
    ICON  "iconMask32.mbm"
    ICON  "iconMask48.mbm"
ENDA
```

Or with all of the bitmaps and masks in one MBM, as would normally be the case if the icon and masks were prepared on the PC, and then processed using the BMCONV.EXE utility. For example:

```
APP ...
    ICON  "filename.mbm"
ENDA
```

Once the application is 'built', the icon .MBM file is embedded into the .AIF file and so does have to be supplied separately.

In the OPL32 example application, PPCOPL32, the DOS and Series 5 bitmap files needed to build the 'zoomable' program icon are provided, plus the other graphical items used by the application such the 'EPOC' logo and the bitmaps for the Toolbar buttons. DOS batch files are available to build the .MBM files on a PC. All files are located in the directory structure named PPCOPL32.

The translated application is located in \PPCOPL32\SYSTEM\APPS\PPCOPL32. Other support files for building the icon and the other .MBM files are located in sub directories such as \PPCOPL32\DOSUTILS\ICONMBM etc.

The multi-bitmap file PPCOPL32.MBM contains three bitmap/mask pairs for three icon sizes, to allow for 'zooming' of the system screen display. The component bitmaps and masks in this file were built as PC-type .BMP files using the Windows Paint program. All six files were then converted and assembled into the compressed .MBM file using a batch file and list file with the BMCONV.EXE utility from Psion. All of the files described are located on the disk.

If required, BMVCONV can create a header file that may be used in program source files to identify the component bitmaps within a multi-bitmap set.

Displaying MBM bitmaps

When drawing graphics by copying bitmaps it is the grey levels in the bitmap and the 'colour mode' of the window used that will determine the final effect, and in some cases the use of a so-called mask. Bits that are set in the mask specify bits in the bitmap that are to be used. Bits that are clear in the mask specify bits that are not to be used. This allows the effect a particular bitmap will create to be varied by varying the mask used. For example in icons, each icon bitmap is paired with a mask in the multi-bitmap file. Only pixels that are set in the mask are drawn in the final icon. The pixels that are clear in the mask are not drawn, allowing any background pixels to 'show through'.

Disassembling MBM files

To re-create icon components, or access other Series 5 bitmap components from .MBM files containing multiple bitmaps, you can use the BMCONV.EXE utility 'in reverse'.

For example:

　　　BMCONV /u mbmfile.mbm bitmap01.bmp bitmap02.bmp etc.

will pull the specified .MBM file apart, generating a Windows bitmap file for each of the Series 5 bitmaps in the multi-bitmap (.MBM) file. Since you may not know how many components are in the .MBM file, you may have to experiment with the number of .BMP file names you supply on the BMCONV command line. Using a list file with a long list of potential file names is a good way to disassemble unknown .MBM files. You can then edit the component .BMP files to your needs using a program such as Windows paint. Then convert and reassemble the .BMP files again into a .MBM as required using BMCONV.

Hint, for icon files use the custom zoom option in Windows paint program to set the 'zoom' level to maximum, and set the grid to on.

Series 5 clipart

As stated above, the Sketch application may be used for producing icon components. Sketch has a number of 'standard' clipart images within the application. The S5ART directory contains a set of Series 5 Sketch files that may be used as an additional source of clipart graphics images.

Fonts

A number of font related utilities are supplied on disk for use with EPOC16 machines.

A utility to display all of the characters, their ASCII codes and fonts available on a Series 3a/c is located in the CHARM directory.

A simple program for viewing some text in all of the different built in fonts on the S3a/c can be found in the FONTVW directory. The OPL16 source code is included. Fontview, by Mark Esposito, is very helpful during screen design, to decide which typeface will look best.

A shareware font file editor by Steve Godfrey, for producing new fonts or graphics characters, is located in the FONT172 directory for your evaluation (please register Font172 if you intend to keep it).

A utility for producing/compiling new EPOC16 font files is located in the WSFCOMP directory – see later under 'Custom fonts'.

ROM based fonts

The table below lists the fonts provided in the system ROMs.

In the table below:

* Swiss and Arial refer to fonts without serifs (also known as sans serif - a serif is a slight projection which finishes off a stroke).
* Roman and Times fonts either have serifs (e.g. font 6) or are in a style designed for serifs, but are too small to show them (e.g. font 5 on the Series 3c).
* Courier is a mono-spaced font, i.e. has characters that are all the same width (and have their pixel size as **width x height**).
* With proportional fonts, each character may have a different width.

Fonts on EPOC16 systems are identified by a 16-bit value representing the font position in the ROM as on EPOC16 systems, whereas on the Series 5 they are identified by a 32-bit UID.

Font	Name	Pixels WxH or H only	System	Name Series 5 only	Pixels WxH or H only
1	Series 3 normal	8	S3, S3a/c, Siena, WA	N/A	
2	Series 3 bold	8	S3, S3a/c, Siena, WA	N/A	
3	Series 3 digits	6x6	S3, S3a/c, Siena, WA	N/A	
4	Mono	8x8	S3a/c, Siena, WA	Courier	8
5	Roman	8	S3a/c, Siena, WA	Times	8
6	Roman	11	S3a/c, Siena, WA	Times	11
7	Roman	13	S3a/c, Siena, WA	Times	13
8	Roman	16	S3a/c, Siena, WA	Times	15
9	Swiss	8	S3a/c, Siena, WA	Arial	8
10	Swiss	11	S3a/c, Siena, WA	Arial	11

11	Swiss	13	S3a/c, Siena, WA	Arial	13
12	Swiss	16	S3a/c, Siena, WA	Arial	15
13	Mono	6x6	S3a/c, Siena, WA	Tiny (mono)	3x4

Fonts 1 to 3 are the Series 3 fonts, and are used when running in compatibility mode on the Series 3a/c, Siena and Work*about*. The original Series 3 fonts are 1 = Standard, 2 = Bold, 3 = Small digit for numbers 1 to 9 including the space character.

Initially font 4 is used on the text screen of the Series 3a/c and Siena, Courier 11 is used on the Series 5.

The special font number $9a is set aside to give a machine's default graphics font; this is the font used initially for graphics text. The actual font may vary from machine to machine - e.g. it is font 1 on the Series 3 and font 11 on the Series 3a. The default font is 11 (Swiss 13) for the Series 3c and 12 (Arial 15) for the Series 5.

For EPOC16 OPL programmers the ROM based font IDs are numbered from 1 upwards to the number of fonts available. Whereas, C programmers start with WS_FONT_BASE for the first font, then WS_FONT_BASE+1 etc. for as many fonts as are built into the ROM.

The default font sometimes called the system font, is in most cases the first font in the ROM - with ID WS_FONT_BASE. On the Series 3, the system font is determined by the $WS_SF environment variable which should contain a WORD binary value of 0 for WS_FONT_BASE and 1 for WS_FONT_BASE+1 and so on.

In version 4 of the SIBO window server, which started with the S3a, the system fonts are determined by the $WS_FNTS environment variable. This contains a series of words each containing the fonts used by the window server in various situations.

The full list is:

 System font
 Notifier/Alert font
 Status Window font
 Symbols font used for the status window diamond symbol
 Medium 2 digital clock font
 Medium 2 date font
 Notifier/alert button font
 Small status window clock font

The EPOC16 character set is compatible with the IBM code page 850 character set for character codes in the range 32 to 255. In some proportional fonts the code page 850 block graphics characters (for example, the box drawing characters) are absent. The characters with codes less than 32 are not compatible with any standard and vary from font to font.

In EPOC32, on the Series 5, fonts are identified by a 32-bit UID, OPL32 programmers should refer to ROM based CONST.OPH file. On the Series 5 the character set (in the English version of EPOC32) is intended to be with compatible with code page 1252 as used by Microsoft Windows.

The following style modifiers are available.

style	value	effect	OPL32 constant
G_STY_NORMAL	0	normal style	KgStyleNormal%
G_STY_BOLD	1	bold	KgStyleBold%
G_STY_UNDERLINE	2	underlined	KgStyleUnder%
G_STY_INVERSE	4	inverse	KgStyleInverse%
G_STY_DOUBLE	8	double height	KgStyleDoubleHeight%
G_STY_MONO	16	mono	KgStyleMonoFont%
G_STY_ITALIC	32	italic	KgStyleItalic%

These styles can be combined by ORing their values, for example, to set underlined and double height and Times Roman 8 point, use:

```
2 OR 8
```

Alternatively add the style values together. For example, to set bold underlined and double height use:

```
1+2+8=11
```

Note that the Series 3 fonts (font numbers 1 and 2) are the normal and bold font versions of each other and G_STY_BOLD should not be used with them. Also G_STY_MONO was designed for use with these two proportional fonts to change them to mono-spaced fonts algorithmically.

Font numbering is **different on the HC** from that of the rest of the SIBO family. The HC fonts are listed below.

Font	Name	Pixel WxH or H only	System
1	HC standard font	15	HC
2	HC small font	11	HC
3	HC Mono	6x8	HC
4	HC Mono 2 font	7x10	HC
5	Series 3 normal	8	HC
6	Series 3 bold	8	HC

Custom fonts, EPOC16

SIBO font files are bitmap files that provide the pixel patterns used for drawing characters on the display.

A utility for producing/compiling new EPOC16 font files is located in the WSFCOMP directory, along with a number of example font source files (.FSC) and some helpful notes. Font source files are just plain text files that are compiled by WSFCOMP.EXE into font files that have .FON extensions.

A shareware font file editor by Steve Godfrey, for producing new text fonts or graphics characters, is located in the FONT172 directory for your evaluation (please register Font172 if you intend to keep it).

Custom fonts, EPOC32

Series 5 font files are bitmap files that provide the pixel patterns used for drawing characters on the display. To conserve memory EPOC32 uses files in its own font store file format (.GDR).

Two methods can be used to produce a .GDR file:

The font details can be specified as a text file (a .GD file) that can be compiled into a font store file, using the FNTTRAN.EXE utility (Windows 95/NT only).

Custom EPOC/16 font source files (.FSC) can be converted into a .GD source files using the FONTCOMP.EXE utility, which can be compiled into a .GDR file using the FNTTRAN.EXE font compiler (Windows 95/NT only).

The FNTTRAN and FONTCOMP utilities are supplied with the EPOC32 SDKs from Psion.

Resource/help files

Application resource files are typically used for the following reasons:

- To hold all of the program specific text and data separately from the program code, including menu items, menu accelerators, dialog items, user prompts etc.
- Providing program help text (EPOC16 only) - which may be context sensitive.
- Simplifying the production of multi-lingual applications.
- All application written in SIBO C based on the HWIM OOP library assume the use of a resource file.

Advantages of resource files

Use of application resource files has a number of very significant advantages:

- Removing the data from the program itself reduces the size of the data segment required, thus reducing the RAM requirements at run-time. The required data or textual information can be loaded into the program as required, the process is usually very quick and will not be noticed by the user. Each resource item is tagged with a unique resource identifier that is used in the program source to refer to it as required.
- Resource files can be compressed to further reduce the storage overheads, system functions decompresses the information automatically during the loading process.

- If the text strings are not embedded in the source code they can be used in multiple places throughout the code. A common resource file could even be used for multiple applications.

- Isolating the program data and text from the source code enables minor changes to be made without requiring program re-compilation, and can help to ensure any changes were complete without the need to search multiple source files.

- Program text, without the source code, can be passed to a language specialist to be translated. Thus also avoiding multiple copies of the program source for each language variant in a multi-lingual application.

- Allows applications to be produced as mono-lingual at first and later adapted very easily to be multi-lingual.

Resource/help definition files

An application's resources (strings, dialog data etc.) are defined in a text source file with a .RSS extension.

In EPOC16 applications, help information is typically included in the resource file. EPOC32 applications differ because the help information is usually placed in a help Data file – see 'Help file utilities, EPOC32' later in this chapter.

If other languages are to be supported, the text in the .RSS file will have to be translated into each of the supported languages, being very careful to stay within the text sizes indicated in the file itself.

The .RSS files are converted into a .RSC files by the DOS-based resource compiler RCOMP.EXE. The .RSC file may then be converted into a compressed form (.RZC) using another utility. For EPOC16 system the DOS-based compression utility used is RCHUF.EXE, as supplied with the SIBO C SDK.

Header files are produced by the resource compiler (.RSG) that can be 'included' into program source code to allow the resource identifier names to be used instead of their numeric values.

A program must identify the language code of the machine and load its resources from the corresponding language resource file at run-time. Using and naming of language specific resource files is described in detail in the 'OPL16 Techniques' chapter, and a full list of language codes is available in the Appendix.

On SIBO systems, special resource files (.CFO) are used within the system to hold country/language specific data. System functions are used to access .CFO file data, see the Appendix.

Resource definition files (.RSS), compiled resource files (.RSC) and the resource compiler (RCOMP.EXE) are not interchangeable between EPOC16 and EPOC32 systems.

Resource/help file utilities, EPOC16

The following disk directories contain utilities for using EPOC16 resource files:

HELPKIT
A set of help/resource file production utilities, put together by Jeremy Wakefield (Jezar), is included on disk in the HELPKIT directory. The materials and utilities supplied demonstrate how to build and compile help program resource files, including displaying help from within an OPL16 program. The EPOC16 DOS-based resource compiler RCOMP.EXE is included along with an example resource definition file.

A resource compiler, written in OPL16, suitable for use on a SIBO system is also included.

XFHELP
An OPL 'front end' program for the SIBO-based resource file compiler described in HELPKIT above.

HELPED11
A Windows 3.x based application from Psion (free but unsupported), for the construction and editing of application resource files for program help.

PHCOMP
A DOS-based utility for simplifying the production of application resource / help files.

Resource file utilities, EPOC32

EPOC32 resource files (.RSS) are converted into a .RSC files by the resource compiler RCOMP.EXE (Windows 95/NT only). EPOC32 .RSC files may apparently be converted into a compressed form, although at the time of going to print (September 1997) it was not clear how to do this.

Header files are produced by the resource compiler (.RSG) that can be 'included' into program source code to allow the resource identifier names to be used instead of their numeric values.

Psion's C++ libraries provide classes and methods for using resource files. OPL programmers should refer to the section below on 'Country specific information' and to the 'Series 5' chapter for details of using resource files from OPL32.

Help file utilities, EPOC32

EPOC32 help is typically provided in the form of a 'Data' file of help topics. The 'standard' EPOC32 applications share a single database. New applications may add a database of their own. Groups of applications released simultaneously may share a help database.

A typical help implementation is demonstrated by the PPCOPL32 application, described in the 'OPL32 Techniques' chapter. An example 'Data' file is provided that contains help information about creating program help, it may be viewed on a Series 5 machine independently of the PPCOPL32 application.

The Psion C++ SDK documentation describes a tool called aleppo, designed to support the generation of help databases from source documents. The information states that aleppo will make it convenient and easy to edit the source (in RTF format) documents, and quick to re-generate a help database. Aleppo is said to support localisation and various customisation options, although the aleppo utility was not actually supplied with version 1.01 of the Psion C++ SDK.

Printing

To allow the user flexibility in choice of printer model, printer settings (such as page size, margins headers etc.) and print device configuration (e.g. via serial, parallel, infrared or to a file) an application should provide access to the standard print set-up dialog(s). After invoking the Print Set Up dialog, an application is not normally required to keep a record of the selections or changes made by the user, ROM-based system code will take care of this (on SIBO systems the choices are actually held in environment variables - see the Appendix for details).

Invoking the print set-up dialog from OPL16 is described in OPLPRINT.TXT in the OPLEXAMS directory. In HWIF C a single function call is all that is required i.e. hPrintSetupDialog(). In HWIM, methods in the PRNCTRL class are used.

In OPL32, a printer OPX is provided that provides control over printing and a wide range of advanced printing capabilities to the OPL32 programmer. A sophisticated set of functions are available including access to the four standard print dialogs and facilities for sending text, bitmaps and formatting information to a printer.

It is the responsibility of an application to obtain, and to record, information about the users detailed printing requirement, usually via a dialog. For example, it may only be to confirm that printing is required, or possibly to select what should be printed, or the way in which it should be done etc.

WDR printing, EPOC16

All Series 3 models, the Siena and the Work*about* have a dynamic library called FORM.DYL as part of their ROM. This library provides support for the Psion proprietary WDR based printing services i.e. printing using printer drivers in WDR format, that generate suitable printer command sequences to control printing operations, on behalf of an application for a range of supported printers. Applications need not know which particular driver is in use, because the WDR printer driver will convert printing requests into sequences suitable for the currently selected printer. A utility program is provided in the WDRKIT directory for producing and compiling custom WDR printer driver files.

Miscellaneous topics

This book is fairly ambitious in its scope, but cannot possibly cover all topics. If you are pushing the limits of what is possible it's always advisable to have access to an appropriate Psion SDK and documentation. However, that does not always help if you're trying to solve a specific programming problem. Usually, you can be reasonably sure that someone else has had the same or similar problem and has solved it. This section is a brief description of some of the more esoteric topics and the support materials on disk that describe how some of the more difficult problems have been tackled. However, this section is by no means fully comprehensive. There is a mine of useful information on disk, so always refer to the extensive disk index provided in the 'Disk Contents' chapter. If that fails go 'on-line' where there are many talented and generous people out there who are usually willing to help. The key 'places to go' are detailed in the 'Contacts and Sources' chapter.

Country specific information

Psion machines are produced in a number of language variants and may differ in a number of respects. For example: the language code, the language of the text used by the ROM-based software such as error messages, the month names etc. In SIBO systems, all the above variations are encapsulated in a single configuration file in the ROM called ROM::SYS$CTRY.CFO.

See the Appendix for a complete list of language codes plus methods of retrieving the country specific information from a SIBO machine ROM.

For Series 5 programmer using OPL32, a limited amount of country specific information is available via the Date OPX. The System OPX provides facilities for using program resource files, but does not include a function to return the machine language code. A new OPX due from Psion will address this, plus providing some other requested functions – see the Psion EPOC World web site for the latest information.

The following directories contain some examples of accessing country specific information.

WLD
An OPL16 example of access to the World application database files, via the WLD: device, to get country and dialling code information.

RISET
Using the WLD: device in OPL16 to access the World database for sunrise and sunset information.

CLOCKS
An excellent full HWIM C demonstration application using the World database information to display multiple World time-zone clocks.

Using libraries and other programs

Using DYLs

Mechanisms are provided in OPL16 (through SEND, ENTERSEND etc.) to call dynamic library procedures (methods) written in SIBO OOP C. Three key example are available on disk with full source code on OPL and C.

The simplest example is in the PPCOPL16 directory system and is described in detail in the 'OPL16 Techniques' chapter. A second more complex example is in the FIREPIC directory. A very sophisticated example is provided in the KMAC directory system. The FIREPIC and KMAC examples have explanatory documentation included.

Documents in the OODOC201 directory describe using Object Oriented Programming techniques with the Psion SIBO C SDK (v2.01), including information on writing DYLs.

Calling C from OPL16

Files and example code (in C and OPL) in the OPL_C directory demonstrate a method of calling C routines from within an OPL program.

Calling C++ from OPL32

Calling the operating system or other external code directly through functions such as CALL, OS or USR etc. is not possible in OPL32. Instead the OPX mechanism is provided to allow external library functions, written in C++, to be used by OPL32 programs, thus extending the language. Examples of how to call some of the 'standard' OPX procedures are given in the PPCOPL32 demonstration application described in the 'OPL32 Techniques' chapter.

In the C++ SDK, Psion provide examples of OPX code, in C++ and OPL32 (see the TOPX demonstration in the \EPOC32EX\OPL directory), more examples are becoming available via the Psion EPOC World web site.

Calling EPOC16 functions

The EPOC16 operating system has an extensive system of 'software interrupts' that allow programmers to make use of operating system routines in the ROM. C programmers utilise these facilities through the PLIB and WLIB library functions. OPL16 programmer can also make use of the interrupts using either the CALL or OS OPL functions. The example application described in the 'OPL16 Techniques' chapter demonstrates the use of some of these operating system calls. A number of documents, in Word and text format, are supplied on disk to provide a detailed description of virtually every available system functions.

Refer to the files and documents in the following directories:

PSIONICS	A comprehensive set of text files providing a huge amount of programming related information including operating system calls.
DOC	OSCALLS.DOC, operating system calls explained and detailed.
EPOCALLS	The operating system calls manual from version 2.01 of the C SDK in Word for Windows format.

Running other programs

The OPL16 program in the S3PROC directory illustrates running a named application from within an OPL program, getting a list of all running applications and how to 'kill' a specific application.

Inter-process communications (IPCS)

Since EPOC16 is based on a client/server architecture it provides extensive support for communications between processes and applications. For C programmers the PLIB library provides functions for inter-process message management and for copying data between different process data segments. OPL programmer may use the same function by using operating system calls (software interrupts).

An OPL16 demonstration of inter-process communication is provided in the IPC directory. One program sends messages to another to indicate a change of state or the completion of a task. The example uses one of the 'magic statics' as a message/flag indicator, it also demonstrates asynchronous event handling and extensive use of calls to the EPOC16 operating system.

Link-paste or Bring

An example of a very specific use of inter-process communications is the 'Link-Paste or Bring' capabilities of many of the built-in applications, where data that is highlighted in one application can be brought or pasted into another application, where the user has invoked a 'Bring' command.

An example link-paste server and client, both in OPL and in C, written by Tom Dolbilin is provided in the LPCS directory. It illustrates how to implement 'Bringing' of highlighted data from one application into another.

Since a link paste server (i.e. the supplier of the data) may be requested to provide data at any time - even when it may be currently displaying a menu, dialog or help screen, it is preferable that OPL or HWIF programs should not normally declare themselves as servers. A link paste server would usually be a HWIM process. (On the Series 3 family it is the window server that actually handles the link paste process.)

Supplementary SIBO SDKs

Other specialist Software Development Kits are available from Psion Software and more are appearing with time. A list and brief descriptions of the current supplementary SDKs are given below.

The supplementary kits are not designed as commercial products, and more often than not are made available free to serious developers on request. Psion do like to keep control over the distribution of these SDKs because of the implications they have for consuming support resources within the company. For more information on the supplementary SDKs see the 'Contacts and Sources' chapter for the address of your nearest Psion Software support organisation, or make enquiries via the EPOC World web site.

DBS Database Server

For more advanced DBF database file handling, plus access to dBaseIII and dBaseIV format files see the DBS_105 directory system.

The DBS system is 'built in' to OVAL although version 1.04 had some problems (see the DBSPATCH or PSIONINC\OVAL\DBASE\SERVER directories for patches).

PRC

Psion remote communications supplementary SDK is used to connect a SIBO system (using C, OPL or OVAL) with a remote filing system such as a PC. Facilities for C and Visual BASIC PC programmers are provided in the PRC SDK. An example of the use of PRC is the PsiWin suite from Psion, where the basis of the SIBO to PC link is via PRC.

SMS

The SMS SDK allows application developers (from OPL or C) to use a SIBO system to take advantage of the Short Messaging Services available via many of the cellular telephony service providers.

TCP/IP

Psion provide a TCP/IP SDK to provide Internet and e-mail connectivity to SIBO based applications written in OPL or C.

Uri

The URI Universal Radio Interface SDK is for developers who wish to use a SIBO system to implement a radio based network application.

Aliasing applications, EPOC16

Some file-based applications may end up with large file lists. It may be desirable to separate a file list into two or more separate lists, for example (for the *Word* application) all correspondence going in one file list, all poetry in another, and so on. These file lists could be distinguished, on the System Screen, by having distinct icons, different application buttons could be used to cycle round running instances of these tasks.

Going further, it may be desirable for the behaviour of the application to alter, depending on which type of file is open. For example, the behaviour of the built-in text editor is different for .WRD files (when the application is seen as Word) from .OPL files (when the application is seen as Prog).

The concept of 'aliasing' an application is designed to meet these requirements. For each required new file list, an alias file (.ALS file) should be installed in the System Screen. In practice the user can do this on the Series 3a/c using the 'Create new list' item from the 'Special' menu.

Broadly speaking, the contents of a .ALS file match those of a .SHD file: the Public Name, default extension, and default directory are all defined, as well as the application type number.

However, the .ALS file goes beyond the .SHD file in that it also specifies:

- the name of the application that is being aliased

- (optionally) some alias info that the system screen should pass to the application when it is run, via the command line, to configure its behaviour in some special way.

Active aliasing and passive aliasing

In theory, all applications are capable of being aliased, without them needing to make any conscious provision for this possibility. This is known as passive aliasing. Other applications pay explicit attention to any alias info that may be passed to them on their command lines, and adjust their behaviour according to the contents of this info. This is known as active aliasing. An example of active aliasing is that of the built-in text editor, as described in the following section. This is the only application built into the Series 3 and Series 3a that supports active aliasing. However, in the Series 3c, the Jotter application is just an alias of Data. Any other program that supports active aliasing is free to interpret alias info passed to it in any way that it wishes. There is no obligation to mimic the detailed rules obeyed by the text editor.

Creating .ALS files

An .ALS file is produced from a .MA file and a .PIC file by running the tool MAKEALS. The three files all have the same root name (i.e. disregarding the extensions). For example, the command

```
makeals letter
```

produces the file letter.als from letter.ma and letter.pic.

The .PIC file is the icon to use. The process of creating .PIC files is discussed in the earlier in this chapter.

The .MA file is a source file similar in format to a .MS file. For example, the contents of a file letter.ma could be:

```
Letter.let
\WRD\LET\
3
Word
```

in which there is a fifth line which is blank (MAKEALS will give an error if the fifth line is omitted altogether). See the MAKEALS directory for the Psion utility program for making program alias (ALS) files.

Just as there are multi-lingual forms of .MS files, there are also multi-lingual forms of .MA files. However, in practice these are of limited use, for technical reasons. In most cases, the application type will be the same for the alias file as for the application being aliased. However, the Public Name, the default extension, and the default directory are all commonly varied. Note that the Public Name of an alias must differ from that of the application it is aliasing. Otherwise, seeking to install the alias in the System Screen will have no effect (it is not possible to have two different file lists, each with the same Public Name). Incidentally, no check is made, at the time of installing an alias file, that the application it aliases is itself currently installed. This check is only made when an instance of the alias is to be started.

Active aliasing in the built-in text editor

If the alias info is a null string, the text editor enters Word mode, with multi-level outline facilities, styles and emphases, and so on. Note that it is not unreasonable for an alias to define null alias info. This allows the creation of aliases of the text editor that behave in exactly the same way as the built-in Word application, but differ from each other in terms of their default extensions, default directories, and/or Public Names.

If there is any non-null alias info, the text editor enters one of a number of other modes, with the mode depending on the first character of the alias info. Some of these modes are not available on Series 3 machines. At the time of writing, the allowed first characters and the corresponding modes are:

O   OPL program editor
S   Comms script program editor
$ Plain text editor (not Series 3)
/   Word processor with custom template (not Series 3)

The program editor mode is available on all machines. In this mode there is no access to the style and emphasis subsystems, the corresponding menu commands being replaced by options to 'translate', 'run', 'show error' and set 'indentation'.

In this mode, the first letter of the alias info denotes the nature of the program that is being edited. It actually identifies the program to invoke to effect any 'translate' and (possibly) 'run' commands from the user. The generic name of this program is sys$prg?.img, with the question mark being filled in from the first letter of the alias info. Thus the Prog alias has 'O' for the first letter of its alias info, and so the OPL translate/run program sys$prgo.img is used. In contrast, the Script editor from the communications ROM has 'S' for the first letter of the alias info, so that the program sys$prgs.img is used.

In program editor mode the second letter of the alias info should be 'R' if the program is of a type that understands 'run' instructions in addition to 'translate' ones. Any other second character disables the 'run' command option. The following three letters (e.g. 'OPO' or 'SCO') denote both the expected file extension and the expected top-level directory where any translated output will by default be placed. (This information is used by the editor when offering the user a suitable filename to 'run').

On the Series 3a a final '*' character may be added to the alias info. This has the effect of adding an "S3 Translate" menu option.

The remaining modes are not available on Series 3 machines.

Alias info that consists of a single '$' character selects a plain text editing mode. In this case the program-related menu options are suppressed, with only an 'indentation' option being offered.

A variant on the Word mode is set by alias info that consists of a single '/' character. This behaves in a similar way to the Word application, with the exception that a specific template file is loaded whenever a new file is created. The template must have the same name as the aliased application and must be located on the current drive at the time the new file is created. Thus, an alias created from the following .MA file:

```
Letter.LET
\LET\
1083
Word
/
```

would, on creation of a new file, automatically load the template file \wdr\letter.wrt, provided it exists on the current drive. Note that, in this mode, the value 80 **must** be added into the application type number. If it is not, the automatic loading of the template is disabled.

How aliasing works

Part of the mechanism of aliasing is handled by the System Screen:

- creating a new file list
- listing the appropriate files in the new file list
- allowing the user to assign a new application button to the new file list
- creating a suitable command line to pass to the relevant application, when the user chooses to start an instance of the alias (by pressing ENTER on an entry in the file list).

However, other parts of the mechanism of aliasing rely on the application paying suitable attention to the details of the command line passed to it. Failure to do this will diminish the effect. Thus, even passive aliasing relies on some co-operation from the application being aliased. For example, an application that knows its Public Name (say Word) and blindly writes this to DatProcessNamePtr in all cases, despite a different Public Name being passed to it on the command line, will frustrate the intent of any aliasing application.

Any application button, assigned to the alias by the user, will be ineffective. Instances of the alias, that are running, will appear (in bold) in the wrong file list in the System Screen. This is just one reason why all serious applications should analyse the command line passed to them, as part of their initialisation procedures. There are routines in both the HWIF and HWIM libraries and in OPL16 to assist in analysing the command line.

Object-oriented programming (OOP)

An in-depth discussion of object oriented programming is beyond the scope of this book, but it is worth describing some of the concepts, in particular those that have been applied in various Psion programming environments, using the terminology adopted by Psion.

Grouping of related items into classes is a common way of understanding and organising the world around us e.g. we are all familiar with the concept of classifying the natural world into hierarchies and groupings such as animals, insects, plants etc. Usually because they have things in common e.g. their appearance, habitats, food, behaviour etc. Object oriented programming is an attempt to group the more abstract items that inhabit the world of software; such as display windows, dialogs, database records etc., into classes along with the program code which operates on them. For example, items such an area of a screen, a dialog box or an edit box could all be considered as objects which belong to a specific class called a window. A window will have certain attributes that are common to all objects of the class window e.g. its dimensions, position co-ordinates, and other characteristic such as whether it is currently visible or not. This information (i.e. data), which holds the current dimensions, position, visibility etc., is referred to as the property belonging to the object.

Similarly, there may be certain common operations that are carried out on objects of class window, such as changing the windows size, position and visibility etc. Such operations are called methods (otherwise known as functions or procedures) which belong to that particular class of object. By creating an instance of a window object, a set of 'property' will be created for that instance of class window, and the methods normally associated with objects of class window will become available for use by the programmer.

Using a method, to operate on an object and/or its property, for example in OOP C, is referred to as 'sending a message to the object'. In fact, this simply refers to calling one of the functions associated with that class of object, and should **not** be confused with actually sending a message e.g. using Inter-process Communication or messaging - see earlier in this chapter.

For applications with anything more than a primitive user interface, which aim to emulate the style set by the built-in applications, it is mandatory to use menus, accelerator keys, windows, dialogs etc. The support for such interface objects provided by languages such as OPL and by the built-in system libraries is excellent, and could therefore be said to be object oriented in some senses. However true object oriented programming goes much further than the user interface, and would have a significant influence over the whole architecture of an application.

For programmers working with the SIBO C SDK, Psion have provided the HWIM library, whilst not being fully compliant with all OPP techniques, goes a long way towards providing a complete architecture for an application.

SIBO OOP HWIM C

HWIM, short for Hand-held WIMP (where WIMP represents - Windows, Icons, Menus, Pointing device), is a user interface and application management library built in to the ROM of the Series 3 range, primarily for use by C programs. To develop complete HWIM applications (or re-entrant dynamic link libraries - DYLs) it is necessary to purchase the C SDK from Psion. Building applications based on HWIM, plus the associated supporting libraries, has a lot to recommend it, but it is not simple to master even for experienced programmers. It is a proprietary approach to implementing an object oriented programming system. Thankfully, there are a number of complete HWIM example applications included in the C SDK with source files supplied. In fact, the complete source code is supplied for the Record application that is built-in to the Series 3a. For further details of HWIM programming with the SIBO C SDK, see the documents in the OODOC201 directory. A complete set of Word for Windows documents is included, from version 2.01 of the C SDK, that describe Psion's Object Oriented Programming techniques. A number of other very useful chapters are provided, including information on resource files, DYLs and OOP application design, using the Series 3a Record application as an example.

OVAL OOP

A new object based approach to producing EPOC16 applications became available with the inclusion of the OVAL run-time interpreter into the ROM of the Series 3c and Work*about* in September 96, and the availability of a PC-based OVAL integrated development environment (OVAL IDE).

Applications produced with OVAL are based on objects such as Forms and Controls, which may contain data and can send and receive messages to and from other objects. OVAL is effectively a Visual BASIC programming system for the Series 3c and Work*about*. It is functionally and syntactically equivalent to Microsoft Visual BASIC. Producing an application simply involves the manipulation of interface and control objects. Program code is then attached to the objects (controls etc.) to carry out actions that correspond to the objects manipulated by the user. Although OVAL is not fully object oriented, it draws on many useful concepts from OOP. For example, forms and controls have items of property (data) which determine their appearance and behaviour etc. They also have code (methods) associated with them that provides the functionality and behaviour required by the application designer. OVAL applications can respond to a range of events e.g. from the system screen or events caused the actions of the user. For example, forms may have a hide method that if triggered will cause the form to hide itself or disappear. OVAL is able to hide much of the underlying system and its complexity from the developer.

OVAL is likely appeal mainly to commercial developers, or systems staff with companies, that wish to avoid complex development environments and yet quickly produce sophisticated applications to meet their business needs. It is still early days for OVAL on the 16-bit platforms and OVAL has yet to emerge on the 32-bit Series 5 machines.

C++ OOP

For the Series 5 and EPOC32, Psion Software have changed from using HWIM C to using C++ as their primary application development tool. In fact, they have used C++ to write the majority of EPOC32 itself. C++ is an object-oriented super-set of the C language that has a steep learning curve. However, there are a number of additional compelling reasons for making the effort required to adopt C++ for EPOC32 development. For example:

- It is Psion's primary development tool.
- Object-oriented techniques are now widely used by many serious developers.
- The number of C++ programmers is increasing all the time.
- Other development tools, such as Java, are object-oriented.
- The limits on what is possible in the EPOC32/Series 5 environment are minimised.

16   Errors and Debugging

Introduction

This chapter is written primarily with SIBO and EPOC16 based systems in mind, but many of the concepts and strategies are applicable to Series 5 and EPOC32.

Psion machines and their applications have an enviable reputation for being innovative, but above all users trust them to be stable and reliable. Where memory is used for storing files great care must always be taken to protect the user's data. Psion have designed the operating systems and hardware of their systems with reliability uppermost in mind. Programmers too have a responsibility to produce applications that are reliable, and through good design, handle error conditions without any loss of data.

EPOC16 and EPOC32 are well-protected environments, but errors due to mistakes, design oversights, errors in program code or unexpected user actions are an unfortunate fact of life for software developers. Some types of error, comparatively rare in desktop PCs, are more likely to occur in handheld systems.

An overview of the typical errors is presented with suggested methods of handling them. Strategies for avoiding errors are discussed, plus an overview of debugging and testing of applications.

Avoiding errors

The best way of dealing with errors is to try to avoid them in the first place; which is definitely not the same as ignoring them. With experience many errors are easily anticipated, trapped or designed out. The common types of error, and conditions leading up to errors, are described in the following section. The list is not intended to be exhaustive, but illustrative of the sort of errors that often crop up in programs, or are typical in Psion systems.

Programming errors

Errors due to the use of incorrect parameters in calls to functions or procedures may not appear for some time. Methods for avoiding this type of error will depend on the language used and the facilities provided within the development system. In OPL16 for example, using utilities such as OPLLINT can eliminate most errors of this type. In OPL32 new keywords such as EXTERNAL and DECLARE EXTERNAL have been added to help programmers avoid such errors. In SIBO C, the use of function prototypes is not enforced but is recommended to ensure parameter type checking during compilation.

If the return value from a procedure or function call could indicate an error condition, it is advisable to include extra code to do the appropriate checks. Ignoring return values may save a few lines of code, or allow for simpler code structure, however, it is sure to leap up and bite you eventually.

Accidentally trying to access memory outside of the process data segment will cause the operating system to terminate the process with a corresponding panic number. This type of error is more common in C or C++ programs where pointers are often used. Flawed pointer arithmetic can leave a pointer referring to an illegal address. It is also possible to experience this type of error in OPL programs, particularly if the parameters passed to an operating system call are wrong, or when using OPL keywords such as PEEK and POKE that directly manipulate memory.

Failing to size variables correctly can also attempt to write into areas of memory that are 'not legal'. For example, by concatenation of string variables, where the final string would be too big for the variable used for the result. Keep the number and size of global variables down to save memory. However, don't be too frugal when sizing local variables, because they only exist for the duration of the procedure call.

Choose names for your variables carefully, particularly those for any global variables. Use of too many global variables can lead to problems, particularly if a local and a global have the same name. Your code may not be doing what you think.

OPL programs can be prone to a number of unique errors. Failure to declare a variable before it is used is the most insidious. This often happens due to a simple typing error or because the type specifier character was omitted from a variable name. Undefined variables in OPL programs are only detected at run-time, and therefore may be a long time in showing them-selves. This type of error is missed by the OPL translator and may only 'bite' when an obscure part of the application code or user option is encountered. The OPL translator fails to check that each variable has a corresponding LOCAL or GLOBAL declaration statement. Again OPLLINT used with OPL16 or EXTERNAL and DECLARE EXTERNAL used with OPL32 can avoid these errors - see the OPLLINT directory on disk. OVAL, C and C++ do not suffer from this type of problem.

Attempting to load too many OPL program modules at once (i.e. with LOADM) may also lead to errors, as can trying to load a module that is already loaded, or calling a procedure that is not yet in memory. Juggling lots of small modules is best avoided.

Many of the problems described above will be avoided by adopting or developing a particular programming style or a set of self-imposed 'rules'.

Design errors

Potential errors may arise though failures in application design. All computer systems operate in different ways and impose certain expectations on application designers. Psion systems are no different in this regard, the EPOC operating systems expect applications to conform in a number of key respects. Failure to conform can at best lead to unexpected behaviour and in the worst cases may lead to loss of data.

Directories and files

In contrast to other computers systems, file selectors on Psion systems allow users to specify paths that do not yet exist. This can happen fairly commonly, for example on a SIBO system as follows:-

1. The user inserts a brand new SSD into drive A
2. A 'Save as' or 'New file' menu option is selected
3. The user adjusts the disk selector to drive A: hence the new disk
4. The user types e.g. 'Design' into the filename editor

Assuming the default directory for the application is \DOC\ and the default file name extension is .TXT, the filename returned (after internal parsing) to the application would be: LOC::A:\DOC\DESIGN.TXT even though the directory \DOC\ does not currently exist on the disk in the A: drive.

The user may specify the wrong file name, file type, or a file that is now not available. For example, the storage device may have been removed or swapped, or the file does not exist because the user may have deleted it.

It is the responsibility of application programs to test for such conditions and to create the required directories or files.

Preventing auto-switch off

Under certain conditions it is possible for a program to prevent a machine from being able to switch off. This should be avoided at all costs, since if it goes unnoticed by the user the application will cause the main batteries to go flat. Loss of data can occur under the conditions described. Although Psion machines are well protected against low power situations and have backup batteries, it is undesirable and very risky to prevent switching off. Devices such as SRAMs depend on the main system batteries if their own internal backup batteries have expired.

Conditions that may prevent auto-switch-off are discussed under 'Processes and auto-switch-off' in the 'Processes, Memory and Applications' chapter.

Program resource errors

Data and text used by applications, for example; in user prompts, menus, dialog labels etc. are usually referred to as program resources. Such resources may be embedded in the program code as static data and text strings. A better approach, particularly for multi-lingual applications, is to put this type of data in separate resource files, as discussed in the 'Programming Techniques' chapter. Whichever method you use, it is very important to check the text and data are correct in a number of crucial respects. For example, duplicated menu accelerator keys can cause strange behaviour with application menus and hot-keys. Text strings used for menu titles/items, dialog prompts, information messages, help text, etc. must be sized carefully to avoid strange display effects, or even errors such as 'Too wide'. This is particularly true when translating program resources from the primary language into a number of alternatives. For the benefit of the translator, always clearly specify the maximum size allowed for every item of text. Bear in mind also, that the English variant is not always the best model for determining the maximum size of text resource strings etc.

Ignoring command line and system messages

The command line

Simple applications - especially those that are not file based - have no need to pay any attention to the command line passed to them by the system screen. In this case, the various relevant EPOC16 reserved (magic) statics are left at their default (zero) values.

This fact is picked up by the system screen and by other parts of the operating system, with the following results:

- The name displayed in any status window and in the file list in the system screen is just that of the application .APP or .OPA file
- If the user requests the application to be shut down, from the system screen, the application is shut down by EPOC16, without the application itself being informed of this fact (just as if the user had selected the 'Kill' option in the system screen).

If an application needs to do its own clean up processing in response to a shut down request issued by the user in the system screen, it **must** analyse its command line during its initialisation, this is true even if the application is not file-based.

One final drawback of an application not processing its command line is that users will be unable to assign application buttons with any effect on that application.

New command lines

The first byte of the new command line will be one of `'X'`, `'O'`, or `'C'`:

`'X'`	means the command is a shut down message
`'O'`	means the command is a Switch files message, with a specified file to be opened
`'C'`	means the command is a Switch files message, with a specified file to be created.

In the case of switch-files messages, the remainder of the new command line gives the full path name of the file to open or create.

For OPL programmers one of the c$=CMD$(x%) variants may be used to get the appropriate components of new command line. OVAL programmers use the COMMAND$ functions.

At the time of writing, the command byte is restricted to one of the three values given above. It is possible, however, that some future application might send messages to other applications having different command bytes. In order to be future proof, an application should test explicitly for all expected values of the command byte and should just ignore values other than those expected, i.e. should **not** generate an error on receipt of an unexpected value.

Shutdown messages

Applications can receive shut down messages from the system screen, as an instruction to quit and close down tidily, saving any changes to file as required. These messages can arise when the user presses 'Delete' after highlighting a running task in the system screen. However, as mentioned above, if the application has set its DatLocked to TRUE, the system screen instead presents an 'Application is busy' message.

Incidentally, applications are sent shut down messages only if they have a non-zero value of DatProcessNamePtr. The system screen assumes that any application that has left this EPOC16 reserved static at its default (zero) value is unlikely to be prepared to respond to shut down messages. In that case, the system screen will terminate the application, losing any modified data in the process.

Finally, note that any application which has $4000 included in its application type number will never be sent a shut down message from the system screen; instead, the system screen will display the message 'Cannot quit application'.

Switch files messages

Applications can receive switch files messages from the system screen, as an instruction to close their existing open file, and to open or create another one. These messages can arise when the user presses 'Enter' after highlighting a file within that applications file list in the system screen. However, if the application has set its DatLocked to TRUE, the system screen instead presents an 'Application is busy' message.

Switch file messages will only ever be sent to applications with a basic type number of 2 or 3. Applications whose type numbers include $8000 can receive switch file messages of the Open sort, but not of the Create sort.

System related errors

Out of memory and out of disk space errors can occur through design errors, or through the action of the user. For example, the user may have started other programs, loaded new software or created new large files, etc. Any of these actions may occur while your application is still running. In multi-tasking systems this is just not probable, it is almost certain to happen. An application should check that sufficient resources are available at start up, it should also do checks before any critical actions that may require more resources. In the event that the resources required are not available, the application should be able to warn the user and 'roll back' to a safe configuration.

Also, because other processes are running, files, devices or other resources may not be available because they are in use by another application.

It is impossible on a multi-tasking machine to predict memory availability. It is essential to do extensive testing of 'out of memory' conditions to ensure that the application fails gracefully.

User generated errors

Care should be taken to prevent invalid data entered by a user from generating run-time errors. For example, you may be expecting the user to enter numeric data and by mistake they enter alpha-numeric data instead. Getting input through simple console style functions, such as INPUT in OPL or the PLIB C function p_getch, should be avoided if possible. Dialogs are friendlier for the user and safer, since they handle the validation of data automatically.

File errors can be generated for a host of reasons. The user may specify the wrong file name or file type. A file may not be available because the user has deleted it. The required file or directory may not be available because the user has removed the SSD.

Mass storage devices such as SRAM and Flash RAM can be removed, changed or repositioned at will by the user. In general the filing system itself is robust and reasonably secure. On SIBO systems SSD drive doors have switches that keep the file server informed of possible SSD changes.

If a file is on a remote system, access may fail due to disconnection of the link by the user, or possibly due to a failure on the remote system.

Robust programs can easily be designed to cope with all of the situations described above. Wherever possible allow the user the opportunity to correct a problem and to continue without crashing the application.

Handling errors

You should design the error handling of a program in the same way as the program itself. Applications are usually more reliable when they are incrementally built up from procedures that have been individually tested. Error handling procedures are best constructed on the same basis.

All of the options for programming Psion systems offer facilities for detecting, trapping and processing errors, there is little excuse for not using them.

Each procedure, where things could conceivably go wrong, should normally contain its own local error handling. The error handling statements can then be appropriate to the procedure. For example, a procedure that performs a calculation would have one type of error handling, but another procedure that offers a set of choices would probably handle errors differently.

There are cases when this strategy may not apply. For example, the program may perform some large activity calling several related procedures to open and display all the records in a file. If an error occurs at any stage in this activity, such as failing to open the file or failing to read a record, it may be perfectly reasonable to handle the error centrally in a higher level procedure.

A mixture of these strategies may apply too, for example if the procedure that failed were to establish an error handler to perform any cleaning up (such as closing files) and then let the higher level procedure display the error message.

Another option might be to establish a 'catch-all' error handler in the top-level procedure, in case any unanticipated error occurs. An error of such a general nature is symptomatic of a bug rather than of a legitimate error, and should be investigated by the programmer.

If you use multiple levels of error handling avoid reporting an error more than once.

Certain errors can be treated as fatal. For instance, if program initialisation fails, there is little point in trying to continue. Reporting an appropriate error message indicating the reason for not continuing, allows the user to rectify any obvious problem before trying again.

When modified data has been accumulated in the program, it is not acceptable to terminate the program without at least trying to recover cleanly. A retry or recovery philosophy is much more appropriate: the program should roll back to a previous good state, cleaning up any resources set up in the lower level procedures that led to the error.

Can data get out of synchronisation with itself? If items of data need to be written in more than one place, for example to provide a relational link in a database, it is important to be able to unwind the first write if the second fails.

Errors should be reported to users as clearly and as jargon free as possible. If, for instance, a file is missing it is helpful to say which file is missing, but only if the user is likely to be able to do something about it. So if it is not a data file you might just create the file again, or warn the user and ask if the program should continue by creating a new file.

Alerts are a simple form of dialog that displays a number of lines of text and waits for a response from the user to a limited set of options. For example, an alert can be used to display a simple message such as 'Are you sure?'; offer a choice of two keys such as 'Y' and 'N', then wait for the users input. Alternatively, an alert dialog may display a number of lines of text (e.g. up to 4 on a 3a/c), present three options for the user positioned over the top of three buttons. The button labels are Esc, Space and Enter.

If the error is non-destructive and no user action is required, a brief information message may be sufficient. For example, if the user tries to 'Bring' data when there is no data to bring.

Error codes

Comprehensive listings of all virtually all types of error codes are provided in the Appendix.

In programming environments that can make use of 'include files' (e.g. files with extensions of .OPH or .H), it is common practise to assign 'English like' identifier names to constants such as error codes. Therefore, you may come across terms such as E_FILE_NOTREADY instead of the actual numerical value (i.e. -62) assigned to this identifier. Where possible the both the numerical value and the usual identifier name will be given. In the OPL16 and C SDKs supplied by Psion, the identifiers names used for error codes and other constants are often very similar but not always identical.

Fatal errors

In C programs, errors may be reported back to your application code through the return values from calls to system or library functions. In OPL and OVAL similar mechanisms are available to the programmer through interpreter error functions (e.g. ERR). In all cases the programmer has the opportunity to intercept the error condition and handle it in an appropriate way. In OVAL and OPL a run-time error may occur which the interpreter may consider is not recoverable and the program will be terminated. Similarly the operating system itself may detect unrecoverable error conditions (generated by any type of program) and again it will terminate the process.

System panics

When EPOC16 detects a condition that it determines could only have arisen from a bugged application, it will terminate or panic the process in question. An error code called a panic number, in the range 0 – 255, will be reported to the user. EPOC32 also refers to fatal errors as panics, however the error codes are not equivalent.

See Appendix for a full list of the EPOC16 panic numbers and their meanings.

There is no way for an application to avoid being terminated when a panic has been initiated. Panics are designed to protect the system from errant programs and represent unrecoverable error conditions. Different panic codes will be returned depending on which part of the system code detected the error.

Any particular panic number may be used by more than one piece of code, and therefore may have more than one point of origin. In C programs the SIBO debugger can be used to trap the panic and trace the code back to its origin.

Panic number	Source
0 - 80 and 255	PLIB library – General purpose functions or EPOC16 O/S services
81 - 129	WLIB library – Window Server library
130 - 160	OLIB library – Object Oriented library
161 - 254	Non ROM resident code e.g. ISAM library

Some of the panics, especially those described by 'Invalid function number for ...', are unlikely to indicate a specific bug; it is almost impossible to create code that would produce such a panic by a coding error. However, this type of panic could easily arise from trashing a return address on the stack, with the instruction pointer wandering into arbitrary code. In the lists in the Appendix, those panics that are likely to indicate a specific coding problem are described more fully.

If you get a panic 79, or a panic in the range 81 to 254, it may be due to some other system component. Panics in the range 81-121 are generated by the Window Server. When using object oriented programming, panics in the range 130-158 may be generated.

OPL errors

The OPL run time environment is well protected and panics are rarely generated. Fatal errors are usually (but not always) trapped by the OPL run time interpreter itself. Most of the OPL error codes listed in the Appendix are common between OPL16 and OPL32. The OPL32 constant names in the table may be used in OPL32 programs instead of the numeric values, providing that the CONST.OPH file is 'included' in your source file.

OPL run-time errors

Good facilities for error trapping, recovery and error simulation are provided in the OPL language and should enable a well designed program to cope with most foreseeable error conditions. Examples of error handling in OPL are provided in the 'OPL16 Techniques' and 'OPL32 Techniques' chapters.

OVAL errors

Many structural and syntax errors are detected by the OVAL translator. Fatal errors during run-time are usually trapped by the OVAL interpreter, panics should be rare. See the Appendix for a complete list of OVAL run-time and OVAL translator error codes and their meanings. The error constant names in the table may be used in OVAL programs instead of the numeric values, providing that the CONST.BAS file is 'included' in your source file.

OVAL error codes can have values between 1 and 32767, but not all the values are earmarked for OVAL or application-specific errors. Programmers can adopt any of the unused values for their own user-defined errors. In general undefined error numbers will be those right at the top of the range, so it is best to use numbers from 32767 downwards. The range of error codes between 20000 and 29999 are apparently reserved for controls.

C errors

Many system and library functions return negative values to indicate that an error condition was encountered. Programs can use the return value with the PLIB `p_errs()` function to get a language dependent error description of the problem. The values -1 to -31 are general errors and -32 to -63 indicate I/O device errors: the error code values and their textual identifiers are held in the files p_gen.h and p_file.h respectively, supplied with the SIBO C SDK. The C SDK provides support for the reporting of errors through the PLIB 'notifier services' and via the `p_enter` and `p_leave` function calling mechanisms.

Debugging, an overview

The SIBO C SDK and the OVAL IDE have source level debugging facilities available. Psion have never produced an equivalent debugger for OPL16, although a shareware system (OPP with OPPDBG) is available. No debugging tools currently exist for OPL32, not even an equivalent to OPLLINT.

OPL

Since the OPL16 interpreter has no mechanisms for introducing break points or for tracing the execution of code, it is not possible to debug OPL16 code directly. Debugging in OPL16 and OPL32 often takes the form of including temporary lines of code to pause the program execution at key points and to display the values of key variable. The TRAP, ONERROR and RAISE instructions are also very valuable, see the 'OPL programming' chapter for more details.

The only debugging utility available for OPL16 programmers (apart from the OPLLINT code checker mentioned previously) is in the form of a clever utility program OPPDBG that has to used in conjunction with the OPP OPL pre-processor. Both of these utilities are available as shareware, OPP and OPPDBG are both supplied on disk.

OVAL

Debugging of OVAL applications is hosted on a PC. The debugger has an extensive set of facilities for source level debugging including: break-points, debug messages, step execution, watches and immediate code execution. See the 'OVAL Programming' chapter for more details.

C

Users of the Psion SIBO C SDK have access to the SDBG source level debugger. The debugger runs on a host machine (a PC) and can debug applications running on a connected (remote) SIBO system.

Spy, EPOC16

The Spy application is a utility program (for Series 3, 3a/c) from Psion for presenting a scrolling list of all processes currently running on a system. It can be very useful for debugging and optimising applications. Twelve pieces of data can be displayed (in hex or decimal) for each process including information on the heap, stack statistics, data segment statistics, heap integrity tests, I/O semaphores, process ID's and priorities and more besides. The complete source code for the Spy application is provided with the SIBO C SDK from Psion.

A copy of Spy, with instructions for use, is included on disk - see the SPY directory.

The main display is a scrolling list of processes currently running on the Series 3. The 'Change processes' menu option allows customisation of which processes are shown. 'System' processes are simply ones whose names start with 'sys$', and include:

sys$shll	which the user sees as the system screen
sys$wsrv	the Window Server, which co-ordinates access to the screen and keyboard
sys$fsrv	the File Server, which co-ordinates access to the filing systems
sys$mang	the Manager, which keeps track of all resources used by processes (so that, for example, they can be properly tidied whenever processes exit)
sys$ncp	the 'brains' behind Remote Link (when it is running).

- The Null process, sys$null, which performs the vital task of switching the Series 3 off following sufficient inactivity, is omitted from the list displayed, for various technical reasons.
- First letter matching works in the main window, so that pressing 'C' enough times will position the highlight to the 'Calc' process.
- Arrows are drawn in the top right and bottom right corner, Agenda-wise, whenever there are more processes beyond the visible boundaries of the list.
- The data displayed is updated every time Spy comes into foreground, and also whenever the 'Update' menu option is selected. By default, it is also updated regularly on a timer, though this can be disabled by a menu option. The 'Refresh rate' option governs how frequently updates take place, when the timer is enabled.
- There are in all twelve pieces of data that can be displayed for each process, but only three of these can be seen at any one time. Use the 'Change data' menu option to choose which.
- Many of the data items can be displayed either in Hex or in Decimal.

Spy, EPOC32

An EPOC32 Spy application is a utility program from Psion (supplied with the C++ SDK) for presenting a scrolling list of all processes, threads or heaps currently active in a system. It also has the ability to 'gobble' memory to stress other applications to see how they react to low memory conditions.

Spy can be very useful for investigating and optimising an applications' use of memory and that used by any associated threads. The data items displayed (in decimal) depend upon the mode selected, that is: to spy on processes, threads or heaps. Typical data displayed includes information on the size of heaps, process and thread ID's and their priorities. When in 'heap walk' mode, Spy can dump memory and find text or hex data.

Testing

Many approaches to testing are possible. Its is difficult to say that any individual approach is better than any other, so I can only present my own and recommend it as one that has proved valuable to me.

Start off with a design for your application rather than just writing code and working things out as they develop. I am strongly in favour of testing all the component procedures and functions of an application individually, wherever feasible, before testing them in combination. This may mean writing some extra test code. When particular elements have been tested and 'proved' to be reliable don't change them, even slightly, unless the reasons are absolutely compelling.

Separate an application into well-defined areas and try to avoid any overlap. For example user interface code should be completely separated from engine code. An application engine should not be responsible for displaying information, not even error messages.

Similarly, an engine should not contain any code involved in user input. Try to construct a 'test harness' to exercise the engine code without relying on the existence of a sophisticated user interface.

Emulators are very useful for developing code and initial testing but never rely on them for final testing, after all emulators are just that, they can never fully duplicate hardware. If the application is intended to run on different models of machine make sure it is tested on all machine variants.

If the application is available in multi-lingual formats be sure to have it tested on each foreign machine and to exercise every option in the application. Have the testers carefully note that each screen display, menu cards, dialogs and messages appear as they should.

Use a system of alpha (initial) and beta (pre-release) testing, resist the temptation to change any design elements once at the beta stage. Try to recruit a wide range of individuals to take part in the testing.

Automatic test system (ATS)

Starting with the 3a, the ATS system was introduced to assist with automated testing of HWIM (OOP) applications. Although the process which controls the ATS sequence does not have to be an HWIM application, the process which is being controlled by ATS does have to be a standard HWIM application (or one which mimics the support for ATS). Inter-process messaging is used to implement the ATS mechanism and message types include sending, receiving and recording key presses, running a dialogs etc.

ATS can be used for a number of purposes including the following:

• Testing an application by running a pre-determined sequence of operations, such as displaying all the text strings and dialogs belonging to a program, to check the suitability of the resource files contents.
• Producing a rolling demonstration of one or more applications.
• Macro recording and playback.
• Controlling attached applications.

The ATS system is covered in depth in the 'Object Oriented Programming Guide' manual in SIBO C SDK. An example ATS based Macro recording and playback system is provided with the SIBO C SDK. See the OODOC201 directory on disk. The Macsys Macro system is based on the ATS system and could be used for automated testing of suitable applications. The complete MACSYS system is supplied on disk with several example Macros – see the MACSYS directory. Similarly, the KMAC macro system is based on ATS. The complete KMAC system, including source code, is supplied on disk with example Macros – see the KMAC directory.

17 Distributing Your Software

Introduction

You may decide to release a piece of software, originally written for your own use, to be used by other people. Many people release small personal programs for free and the receivers should expect nothing else from the author. However, if you set out to produce software for other people to use, then designing and writing the application is merely part of the overall process.

A large amount of software for Psion machines has been put into the public domain for free. Some of it offers very high functionality and is also of excellent quality. For those seeking rewards for their efforts the competition is quite tough.

If your application offers something unique, or is of significant complexity, then it is reasonable to expect users to pay for it. However, the standards expected by people who are paying for software will be much higher. Most people have come to expect very high standards from such software, particularly in terms of usability, functionality and above all reliability.

If you expect to receive payment for an application, then there are many things to consider. For example, how is the application to be marketed, supplied, packaged, documented, tested, supported, how much are you going to charge for it and what methods are available for people to pay you.

Application style guides

To increase the quality of your application and your chances of producing a successful product, its advisable to ensure that it conforms to the Psion 'house style'. Close study of the look and feel of the 'standard' applications is very worthwhile. Producing an application that differs markedly from those a Psion owner uses daily will not improve sales of your product.

To assist developers, Psion produce style guides that define the norms for applications, as well as the do's and don'ts. Two style guide documents, produced by Psion, are provided on disk in the DOC directory. APPGUIDE.DOC and CHECK.DOC are slightly different variants of the same guide to writing Series 3/3a applications.

The Series 3 guidelines have changed in a number of ways for Series 5 applications. Interface guidelines are included in the C++ SDK, for example, on Dialogs, Infoprints and messages, Menus, Toolbars, Basic user interface principles and a Glossary of terms. Some guidance is also provided in the OPL32 SDK documentation.

Additional examples, support documents and 'style guides' are becoming available via the EPOC World web site for EPOC32/Series 5 applications.

Distribution options

The simplest option, by far, is to provide the software for free, thus relieving you of almost all obligations - see 'Copyrights and limitations' below. The following discussion therefore is for those who wish profit from their endeavours.

Shareware

A huge amount of Psion shareware exists and is expanding daily. In the main this is due to the inclusion of OPL on all machines.

Shareware is not intended to be freeware, but many people will treat it as such unless they have a good reason to send the registration fee to the author. Many methods have been tried by authors to induce users to register their software. Some approaches are more successful than others, for example:

- By limiting the functionality of the application.
- Having a reminder/nag screen pop up periodically (sometimes of increasing frequency).
- Limiting the number of times the program may run or do certain tasks.
- Or even having an in-built time limit, after which the program ceases to function.

Typically when a user registers a shareware application they will receive a special code to enter into the program that will remove any limits, nag screens or unlock the extra functionality.

Time limited applications are not a particularly good idea, they may be irritating to the user particularly if the time has become out-of-date before the user has ever tried it.

Unlocking functionality may be a reasonable inducement, but be sure not to limit things too much, or the user will never really get to evaluate the application properly. I once tried a shareware card game where the computer was the opponent. The limitation placed on the game was that it didn't score according to the rules, so the user could never win! How was I expected to evaluate the games playing ability?

Offering extras on registration, such as additional modules or a printed manual may add enough value to induce payment.

Determining a suitable price for shareware is always a difficult decision. Asking for too little may be as bad as asking for too much. A decision based on something substantially less than commercial rates and close to the price sought by other shareware authors may be fair. Whatever you decide make the cost clear in the documentation, including how and where the user can send payment.

You obviously want to distribute your application as widely as possible, but keep a note of where so you can provide updates and new editions. For Psion based shareware, sending it to the '3-Lib' shareware library is always good choice. Uploading a zip file into the active Psion forums in 'on-line' systems such as CIX and CompuServe is very likely to lead to a large number of potential registered users. On-line registration is also available through CompuServe and via the Regnet web site – see the 'Contacts and Sources' chapter.

Software licensing

The largest sales volumes of applications software are generated through direct high street sales outlets and via mail order companies. A number of the key software houses and mail order companies, specialising in Psion products, are interested in licensing quality application from software authors. Psion do this themselves, but only rarely and in exceptional cases.

Such companies may be willing to take the risk of packaging and marketing an application that has good potential sales if it is of sufficient quality. Because they may take on a significant financial risk the royalties offered may at first seem less than generous. Balancing the equation involved is tricky. You have to judge the total income likely from lower royalties on larger numbers sold, versus the likely total from a lower volume of shareware registrations at a higher income per unit. As a starting point, see the table of 'Psion distributors and retailers' in the 'Contacts and Sources' chapter.

Self publishing

The most complex and financially risky option is to publish the software yourself, an option only really available to existing organisations or new start-up companies. The various Psion companies, provide a number of services and products to software developers and publishers, most are described below.

Copyrights and limitations

Whatever method of distribution you choose, always make the copyright information prominent in the application and any documentation, clearly setting out any limitation or conditions of use.

Applications written in OPL may be prone to reverse translation, if this is likely to cause concern see the 'Source code protection' section of the 'OPL Programming' chapter for options to prevent reverse engineering of your code.

Distribution methods

For commercial SIBO software, the main distribution media options are SSD or floppy disk.

For Series 5 applications the options are floppy disk and possibly using small compact-flash units. Psion have do not yet have compact flash units available for developers at the time of going to print (September 1997).

Shareware is usually distributed via on-line methods. Other supply options are now being adopted by commercial organisations and shareware authors alike. For example, making software available via down load from web sites, or by distribution in bulk as part of a wide-ranging selection on CD-ROM. Typically, 'unlock codes' are then provided to make the software available when payment has been received.

SSDs

There are three main types of SSD available, from Psion to Developers, as media for software. They are, Solo (one-time programmable) SSDs, masked ROM SSDs, or Developers Flash SSDs. Each has its own benefits, but they differ principally in unit cost and minimum order quantities.

Solo SSDs

One-time-programmable Solo SSDs and masked ROMs are used by software publishers for product distribution. As their names suggest such SSDs or ROMs cannot be reformatted once written to.

The benefits of Solo SSDs are:

* They have a low minimum order quantity.
* They are cheaper than conventional memory SSDs such as Flash.
* They are suitable for low volume specialist market products, where the sales pattern is irregular and application sizes are below 256Kbytes.

The constraints of Solo SSDs are:

* They are more expensive than Masked ROM SSDs and are not suitable for volume markets.
* They are available in only 128K, 256K and 512Kbyte capacities.

Using Solo SSDs

Once the software is thoroughly tested and is bug-free, a master version of the application is made on a Flash SSD of the appropriate capacity. The Flash master is placed in a dual SSD drive unit connected to a PC. This type of drive is available from Psion or their one of their VADs. The DOS-based SOLOPRG.EXE program is used to produce an image master file that is held on the PC. The SOLOPRG software is then used as required to duplicate the software on to two Solo SSDs at a time, using the PC based master file as the source.

Masked ROM SSDs

The benefits of Masked ROM SSDs are:

- They have the lowest unit cost.
- They offer higher capacities (up to 2Mb).
- They are ideal for volume applications, where price points and unit costs are
- important.

The constraints of masked ROM SSDs are:

- They have a larger minimum unit commitment - nominally 3,000 units.
- They have a longer lead-time, typically 10 weeks.
- They have a higher fixed mastering fee (imposed by the silicon foundry, not Psion).

Production of Masked ROM SSDs

Once the software is thoroughly tested and is bug-free, a master version of the application is made on an appropriate capacity Flash SSD. This master is used by Psion to produce a trial master SSD that is sent back for checking. Once the copy is verified as a faithful copy of the software, the mastering process can go ahead. Psion insist on a minimum quantity of units to be ordered (nominally 3,000).

Developers Flash SSDs

Flash memory-based SSDs were not designed as a software release medium for Developers. They are really intended for use during the development and testing of software, as a test and beta release medium for software applications. Flash SSDs are the most suitable format for this purpose as they can be reused application after application and therefore provide a cost-effective solution to testing software. Flash SSDs are available from Psion as blank unlabelled SSDs in quantities of 25 units. Capacities available are 128KBytes, 256KBytes, 512KBytes, 1MBytes and 2Mbytes.

Floppy disk

Many users of Psion the Series 3 family have access to a PC and over 50% of owners have purchased PsiWin. Distributing applications on floppy disk is probably set to take over from SSDs as the most popular supply media.

Psion have produced a Windows based installation utility that is available free of charge to developers. Psisetup, is a Windows 3.x software installation package that controls the communication between a SIBO system and a PC and completes the installation of software from a floppy disk on to an EPOC16 system.

To obtain a copy of the Psisetup contact your nearest Psion Software company or VAD. See the 'Contacts and Sources' chapter for details.

Yellow Computing GmbH have also produced a Windows-hosted installation package. See the 'Contacts and Sources' chapter for details.

Packaging and manuals

Psion can also supply developers with the other elements that make up the final product, for example packaging items. These may include:

- Cartons and trays to holds an SSD/floppy
- SSDs label for the front and back
- A printed license document and a license sticker which is stuck across the SSD in the tray. In order to take the SSD out of the tray the user has to 'break' the sticker and, in doing so, becomes bound by the terms of the licence.
- Generic multi-lingual software licence stickers; to explain what happens if the user removes or breaks the Licence sticker. The production of a formal end-user Licence Agreement is the responsibility of the application developer.

It is the developer's responsibility to write the manual or arrange to have it written.

Psion Software and Accessories catalogue

This Psion catalogue is produced annually and Psion charge relatively modest rates for advertisements. The anticipated 1998 circulation is well over 400,000 copies.

The Software Catalogue aims to:
- Build awareness of the range of software available for Psion personal systems.
- Provide Developers with the opportunity to promote products worldwide, both to existing and new Psion users.
- Open up new markets for Psion systems and software.

The catalogue is distributed worldwide as follows.

- In the UK and other markets to the existing customer base.
- To every new user as part of a 'Welcome pack'
- To potential owners and interested parties in retail stores and in response to direct demand
- To Developers for distribution to their own customer base

18   Linking to a PC or Printer

Introduction

Use of PC based development environments, e.g. those from Psion and some third party utilities, will ultimately require a PC link for file transfer and/or debugging. Transfer of executable and related files to the Psion system for testing can be done in a number of ways. Software such as RCom or MCLink allows transfer of information either 'manually' or in a semi-automated way using batch (script) files. Integrated development environments (IDEs) such as ODE and OVAL have internal communications routines that handle transfer of files automatically. Software suites, such as PsiWin from Psion, provide file manager or explorer type interfaces, file conversion utilities and facilities for printing via a PC. All of the methods and options currently available are described here.

PC link hardware

Whatever PC link or printing method you choose, use of an external power supply for the Psion system is highly recommended. There is a particularly high drain on the internal batteries during communications e.g. to a PC or printer.

Some SIBO systems have micro-switches on the SSD drive doors to inform the system that an SSD may have been removed or changed. Opening a drive door during external communications may interrupt the connection. For example, if an SSD drive door is opened on a Series 3 during communication with a PC, the Series 3 will not be able to communicate with the PC until it is closed again. Although it is unlikely that any information will be lost, it is safest not to open an SSD drive door when a PC link is actually in use, i.e. transferring data.

PC 3Link cable, S3/3a

Also known colloquially as the 'soap on rope' cable, the Psion '3Link' cable connects to the Series 3 or 3a via a 6-pin plug into a port (the Reduced External Expansion Port) on the left-hand edge of the system, near the hinge.

Approximately 50cm along the cable is a lozenge shaped unit containing some electronics and a ROM (Read Only Memory), which appears as Disk[C] when the unit is connected. (Try pressing Psion+* from the System screen, and use the arrow keys to view each of the

Disks). The circuitry converts the very high-speed internal serial interface (used to access RAM and FLASH SSDs) to an industry-standard RS232 serial interface. On the Series 3 this is limited to a maximum baud rate of 9600, this was raised to 19200 baud on the 3a. From the in-line lozenge unit onwards the connection is via a normal RS232 cable terminated in a 9-pin D-type connector (a double ended version with 9 and 25-pin connectors was also available).

The additional ROM in the '3Link' cable electronics also contains communications software and example communications scripts.

Since the 3Link cable electronics are powered from the Series 3 or 3a, use of an external power supply for the Psion system is highly recommended. The additional drain on the internal batteries during communication with a PC can be very significant.

PC link cable, S3c, Siena and S5

An integral RS232 port was introduced on the Siena and the Series 3c. A custom connector was used, the so-called 'Honda' style connector has 15 pins that supply the RS232 signals (and a slightly modified version of the S3a SIBO high-speed serial signals). On the Series 3c the port is on the left-hand-side of the system. Series 3c serial speeds were increased to 57.6K baud.

On the Siena the connector is on the top edge of the system, i.e. when the unit is opened out flat. Initially the Siena could only work at speeds up to 19.2K baud, but Psion plan to increase later Siena models to 57.6K baud as per the Series 3c.

On the Siena, an external power supply cannot be attached directly, however it may be applied indirectly via an optional external SSD drive. It is possible to 'daisy chain' the serial connector cable to the external SSD drive, and then on to a PC to enable the Siena to 'see' the external SSD drive and also the PC connection.

For the Series 5, the same 'Honda' type 15-pin connector is used, but serial communications speeds were increased to a maximum of 115.2K baud. The 'Honda' style connector on the Series 5 is at the back of the machine on the left-hand-side under a roll top dust cover.

The PC link cables are terminated in an RS-232 9-pin D-type connector (PC AT type).

PC to Psion infrared link

At the time of going to print, only Psion to Psion infrared data transfers or infrared printing is possible with suitably IrDA enabled systems.

An infrared Psion to PC link adapter for use with the Series 5 and software such as Psiwin 2 is due to become available (Autumn 97) as an option from Psion.

Note:
The infrared protocols used on the Series 3c and Siena are different to those used on the Series 5. Data transfer between SIBO and Series 5 systems is not possible with the standard system software.

PC to HC connection

Three types of PC connection exist:

- Direct connections to the HC via an RS232 serial port.
- Direct connection to the HC via a LIF (low insertion force) converter.
- Connection via a Docking Station (or Cradle).

Direct connection is via a standard serial cable from the HC serial port (assuming the HC is fitted with a suitable expansion module) and either COM1 or COM2 on the PC.

LIF converters inserted in the HC provide a 3Link-type 6-pin socket suitable for use with the 3Link cable as per the Series 3/3a.

With the HC inserted in a Docking Station, connection to the PC is via a high-speed serial cable connected to a Psion interface card fitted in the PC.

PC to Work*about* connection

Four types of PC connection exist:

- Direct connections to the Work*about* via an RS232 serial port, if fitted.
- Direct connection to the Work*about* via a LIF (low insertion force) converter.
- Connection via a Docking Station.
- Connection via a Docking Holster.

Direct connection is via a null modem serial cable from the Work*about* serial port (assuming it is fitted with a suitable interface module) and either COM1 or COM2 on the PC.

LIF converters inserted in the Work*about* provide a 3Link-type 6-pin socket suitable for use with the 3Link cable as per the Series 3/3a.

With the Work*about* inserted in a Docking Station, connection to the PC is via a high-speed serial cable connected to a Psion interface card fitted in the PC.

Docking Holsters have a 3Link type 6-pin socket suitable for use with the 3Link cable as per the Series 3/3a.

PC link software

During the lifetime and development of the various systems available from Psion they have released a number of machine to PC communications programs and utilities. Some utilities became available as part of the PC Link packages, or with software development tools such as ODE or the SDKs, or as part of application suites such as PsiWin. Each of the communications programs provides different facilities and a summary is given below.

Slink

A very basic PC hosted DOS 'server' program that handles a link between a Psion system and a PC. Slink does not have a command driven interface or support for modems, but is simple and more likely to work with PCs that are less than 100% compatible, and that are not able to run MCLink.

MCLink

A PC based DOS program allowing file transfer and remote file access between the PC and a SIBO system. MCLink has a user command driven interface, and can be driven via batch files on the PC. Once the link is established the PC drives are visible from the SIBO system. MCLink provides modem support.

RCom

An extensive DOS based program that displays its own command prompt. There have been a range of versions of RCom and associated utilities. Later versions of RCom are provided with set up and help facilities, to enable operation under DOS and/or Windows.

When the PC and Psion computer are connected and the RCom command prompt is displayed, the following options are available:

- Enter RCom commands to transfer files to and from the PC and manipulate files or directories on the Psion.
- Use the menu options (or commands) on the Psion to transfer files to and from the PC.
- Format and compress SSDs in the Psion's drives.

The Psion drives are represented by the new drive letters as defined in the RCom set up file.

RCom batch files or scripts

A batch file (or script) contains one or more RCom commands. When the batch file is run, the commands are carried out as if they had been typed in at the command prompt. Batch files for RCom will usually look just like DOS batch files - they may even *be* DOS batch files as RCom's commands are so similar to DOS commands. RCom commands can also be run from within a DOS batch file. For example, the line:

```
RCOM /W /C DIR I:
```

In a DOS batch file will run the RCom command prompt, wait for the link to be established (the /W switch), perform a directory listing of the Psion computer's internal drive and then exit RCom (the /C switch).

ODE link

The OPL Development Environment (ODE) from Psion has its own communications routines included, and provides facilities for most of the stages in the development cycle, including transferring all of the appropriate files to the SIBO system and executing the code. When the code is subsequently modified, ODE will then transfer only those files that have changed during the code translation step.

OVAL link

The Organiser Visual Application Language development environment from Psion has its own communications routines included, and provides facilities for most of the stages in the development cycle, including transferring all of the appropriate files to the SIBO system and executing the code. When the code is subsequently modified OVAL will then transfer only those files which have changed during the code translation step.

SIBO C debugging link

Applications developed with the SIBO C SDK can be generated in debug mode and then run on the SIBO system, but under the control of the PC hosted SDBG debugger (SDBG.EXE). Communication between the SIBO system and the PC DOS based debugger is via a suitable serial link cable – see above.

PsiWin

PsiWin version 1.0 is primarily intended for use with Series 3/3a systems, and version 1.1 was released for use with Series 3c and Siena. PsiWin 1.0 and 1.1 operate in combination with Windows 3.x or Windows 95.

PsiWin version 2 was released for the Series 5 and runs under Windows 95 or Windows NT4 only. Purchase of a Series 5 system includes PsiWin 2 and a PC Link cable as integral components of the Series 5 package.

PsiWin 1.x, SIBO

PsiWin provides 'Psion Manager' a sophisticated Windows based file manager that displays the contents of disks on the PC and on a SIBO system connected via a PC link cable. It forms the main part of the PsiWin version 1 product produced by Psion. In a manner very reminiscent of Microsoft Windows File Manager, Psion Manager provides drag and drop management of files and directories, plus seamless conversion of a range of file types to and from Psion formats to your preferred PC equivalents. For example, from Psion Word format to Microsoft Word 6.0 format and vice-versa. Therefore, files produced during a development cycle on a PC can be moved back and forth very easily. Psion Manager also makes file by file or disk based backups (and restoration) of a SIBO system to a PC extremely easy.

PsiWin also includes Psion Database - a Windows PC version of the Psion Database application that is standard on a Series 3 and Siena. Although Psion Database can work with database files from any Series 3 or Siena, it is based on the 3a/c version of the Database application and has a few menu options not present on the original Series 3. Files produced or modified by Psion Database under Windows can be copied directly to a Series 3 without any need for conversion. It also provides a number of features not present on any of the Series 3 versions like sorting of records, multiple windows for more than one database open at once, extensive printing and much more.

RCom was supplied with PsiWin version 1.0 for DOS based users.

PsiWin 2, S5

Under Windows 95 or NT4, PsiWin 2 integrates itself into Windows Explorer during the installation process. When a Series 5 is connected to a Windows 95 based system, the Psion disks and folder contents become visible in the Explorer window. Drag and drop management of files and folders is possible, plus seamless conversion of a range of file types to and from Psion formats to your preferred PC equivalents. For example, conversion from Psion Word format to Microsoft Word format and vice-versa. Therefore, files produced during a development cycle on a PC can be moved back and forth very easily. File by file or disk based backups (and restoration) from Series 5 to a PC is also extremely easy.

Printing via a PC

See the 'PC link hardware' section above for details of the various Psion to PC link cables.

Whatever PC link or printing method you choose, use of an external power supply for the Psion system is highly recommended. There is a particularly high drain on the internal batteries during communications e.g. to a PC or printer.

MCPrint and RPrint

MCPrint is a PC DOS based 'server' program that allows a SIBO system to print, via its serial printer interface, to a printer that is attached to the PC. The PC hosted printer may be connected via a PC serial or parallel port. MCPrint does not have a user interface.

The RPrint program (supplied with RCom) allows you to print information from a SIBO system to a printer that is attached to a PC. It takes its settings from RCom set up - see above.

To print a file with RPrint:

Use the 'Printer setup' option on the SIBO system and set the 'Printer device' to 'Serial'. Set the same 'Baud rate' for printing as you set in RCom set up. Any Link software on the SIBO system should not be running, i.e. set the 'Remote link' option in the System screen to 'off'. Open the file to be printed on the SIBO system and use the application's 'Printer setup' option to set the model of the printer that is attached to the PC. Use the application's 'Print' option to print the file.

PsiWin 1.x, Psion Print

Version 1 of PsiWin includes Psion Print which allows printing of files created on the SIBO system to almost any printer that is installed under Windows, whether connected directly or via a Network. Psion Print allows the use of TrueType fonts. The Psion Print set up utility is used to configure the printing settings and for installing new printer drivers (e.g. a WDR file).

For example to print from within a Series 3 application:

From the System screen, select the Control menu and set up the printer as serial. Connect the PC Link cable to the Series 3 and the PC (make sure that the Remote Link option on the Special menu is off). Set the Printer model within the Psion application to Psion Print. At the PC end use the Psion Print setup utility to select the type of printer attached to the PC. Run the Psion Print program on the PC and check that a connection is established by the program, printing from within the Psion application should now be possible to the specified printer attached to the PC.

PsiWin 2, printing

Version 2 of PsiWin incorporates extensive facilities to enable printing of files, created on the Series 5, to almost any printer that is connected to a Windows 95 or Windows NT based PC.

Infrared printing, via a PC

At the time of going to print, infrared printing is only possible directly from IrDA enabled Psion systems to suitable IrDA enabled printers.

Printing directly from a Psion system

The number of options that exist for direct printing depends upon the system used. Assuming the presence of suitable interface ports, all systems have the capability to print via at least one serial and one parallel port.

In the case of systems such as the HC and Work*about*, the options available will depend upon the exact expansion/interface adapter(s) installed. Some systems may have more than one interface port available. For example, Work*about* or HC systems may have more than one serial or parallel ports fitted. See the 'PC link hardware' section above for details of the connection options for HC and Work*about*.

Printing on the Series 3 family, Siena and the Series 5 is always via the dual serial/parallel interface port, where necessary using adapter cables to convert the signals into the correct form. Infrared (IrDA) printing only became available with S3c, Siena and S5 systems.

Whatever PC link or printing method you choose, use of an external power supply for the Psion system is highly recommended. There is a particularly high drain on the internal batteries during communications e.g. to a PC or printer.

Serial printing

Printing to serial printers can sometimes be a little difficult, mainly due to the non standard nature of some manufacturers' implementation of the so-called 'Industry Standard' RS232 interface. From the Psion end things tend to be straightforward. For example, setting up for serial printing from a Series 3c would be as follows:

Attach the serial cable into the port on the left-hand-side of the Series 3c. Connect the other end of the cable containing the 9-pin 'D' type connector into the serial port of a suitable printer. A 9-pin to 25-pin adapter will probably be required (Psion supply a range of suitable adapters). From the Series 3c system screen, select the 'Printer' option from the Control menu and set the Printer device to 'Serial'. Ensure the serial parameters such as baud rate and handshaking methods are set in accordance with the requirements of your printer. Make sure that the 'Communications' option on the Special menu is set to 'None'. Ensure the 'Print set up' options within the application match the appropriate (or nearest compatible) printer i.e. the settings for Printer device and Printer model.

Problems with serial interfaces are most often associated with incorrect matching of the serial port settings such as baud rate, parity and handshaking schemes. If the serial port settings are carefully matched at both ends and problems are still encountered, carefully check the pin-out requirements of the connection to the printer, starting with the printer port. It may be that a signal converter such as a 'null modem' adapter is necessary to reconfigure the data transmit and receive lines.

Serial printer cable, S3/3a

On the Series 3/3a, a serial printer cable connects into the port on the left-hand-side of the machines via a small right angled 6-pin plug on one end of the cable. The other end of the cable contains a 25-pin D-type connector (male) suitable for a serial printer port. A 3Link PC cable with a suitable adapter (e.g. 9 to 25-pin) may also be used.

Serial printer cable, S3c, Siena and S5

Connection to the serial port on these more recent systems is via a custom 'Honda' style 15-pin connector. The other end of the PC Link cable contains a 9-pin PC AT style (female) connector, so an adapter may be required to provide a connection suitable for a serial printer port. For example, a 9-pin (female) to 25-pin 'D' type (male) connector.

Parallel printing

Printing via the parallel link is usually very straightforward. Centronics ports, cables and connectors are much more uniform, and there are no awkward parameters and handshaking settings to configure. For example, setting up for parallel printing from a Series 3c would be as follows:

Attach the Psion parallel cable/adapter into the port on the left-hand-side of the Series 3c. Connect the other end of the cable containing the 36-pin 'D' type connector into the parallel port of a suitable printer. The little box on the 'D' type end of the Psion cable contains some electronics that convert the signals available from the Psion port to an industry-standard Centronics parallel interface.

From the Series 3c system screen select the 'Printer' option from the Control menu and set the Printer device to 'Parallel'. Make sure that the 'Communications' option on the Special menu is set to 'None'. Ensure the 'Print set up' options within the application match the appropriate (or nearest compatible) printer i.e. the settings for Printer device and Printer model.

Note:
Problems may be experienced when opening the PAR: device (i.e. the parallel device driver) for printing, for example on the Series 3c or Siena. If you experience an error of the

type 'Device not present' it may be necessary to print using the TTY: device instead, even though a parallel cable is being used - see the text file 'FORUM06.TXT' lines 841-1405 in the \ONLINE directory on disk.

S3/3a parallel printer cable

On the Series 3/3a a parallel link adapter connects into the port on the side of the systems via a small right angle shaped 6-pin plug on one end of the 3Link parallel cable. The other end of the cable contains a 36-pin 'D' type connector suitable for the centronics parallel port of a printer. A small box on the D-type end of the Psion cable contains circuitry that converts the very high speed internal serial interface (used to access RAM and FLASH SSDs) to an industry-standard Centronics parallel printer interface.

Power for the S3/3a parallel link adapter is drawn from the Psion system.

S3c, Siena and S5 parallel printer cable

The parallel link adapter connects via a 15 pin 'Honda' plug on one end of the cable into a suitable port on the Psion system. On the Series 3c the port is on the left-hand-side of the system. On the Siena the connector is on the top edge of the system, i.e. when the unit is opened out flat. The connector on the Series 5 is at the back of the system on the left-hand-side under a roll top dust cover. The other end of the cable contains a 36-pin 'D' type connector suitable for the centronics parallel port of a printer. A small box on the 'D' type end of the Psion cable contains circuitry that converts the signals from the 'Honda' port to an industry-standard Centronics parallel printer interface.

The parallel link adapter is powered from its own battery (9V PP3 type).

File printing

On many systems the printer device may be set to a file name. For example, setting up for printing from a Series 3c into a file is as follows:

From the Series 3c system screen, select the 'Printer' option from the Control menu and set the Printer device to 'File'. A default file name of 'P.lis' will be used, although this may be edited to a name of your choice. Ensure the 'Print set up' options within the application match the appropriate (or nearest compatible) printer i.e. the settings for Printer model. The contents of such a file is likely to include a lot of printer control data as well as the text to be printed. One way of utilising this type of file is to send it (i.e. copy it) directly to the printer device, when you want a paper copy.

Printing plain text to a file from OPL can be done very simply. For example, just use LOPEN("filename.txt") to open the file for printing (remember to include any file directory path as well) and use LPRINT commands as normal.

Infrared printing

Infrared communications on Series 3c, Siena and Series 5 systems (IrDA enabled systems) allow direct 'point and shoot' printing from within suitably enabled applications to similarly equipped IrDA printers.

With a Series 3c or Series 5 this functionality is built in, but the Siena requires additional external infrared device drivers to be loaded first - see the 'I/O System' chapter for more details and the 'Disk Contents' chapter for the Siena drivers.

For example, setting up for infrared printing from a Series 3c would be as follows:

From the Series 3c system screen, select the 'Printer' option from the Control menu and set the Printer device to 'Infrared'. Make sure that the 'Communications' option on the Special menu is set to 'None'. Ensure the 'Print set up' options within the application match the appropriate (or nearest compatible) printer i.e. the settings for Printer model.

Printing to the infrared port can be done from your own applications via the IRP: I/O device. For example in OPL just use LOPEN(IRP:A) to open the infrared device and use LPRINT commands as normal.

19   Disk Contents

Problem solving

A considerable amount of ground has been covered in the previous chapters, but it is almost impossible to anticipate everything a programmer may wish to do. Over the years a large number of programmers have solved a huge range of problems, many have generously put their solutions and example code into the public domain for the benefit of others. Numerous difficult questions have been raised and answered in the key on-line forums related to Psion programming. Answers have come from a range of sources, including Psion's own technical staff, commercial third party developers and from the huge number of talented non-professional developers.

In an attempt to provide solutions for as many potential questions as possible I have scoured all the key sources of programming related information and examples, added in some of my own, and put them all together on disk. This chapter provides a detailed guide to the contents of the CD-ROM containing the collected materials. See the 'Contacts and Sources' chapter for details of the sources used.

Lists and thumbnail sketches of all of the materials and examples are provided below. The lists and descriptions are grouped into topics, in disk directory name order.

For access to a particular programming technique, problem solution or utility program, refer to the disk index at the end of this chapter as well as the main book index. The disk index extensively cross-references the accumulated examples and information by subject matter.

Entries in the disk index will be of the general form:
Keyword plus explanatory text, the category of the information, the directory name for the file or files, followed the name of the file(s) involved, and possibly a line number or a range of lines within the file.

Line number references are given when the information or example code is part of a large ASCII text file. Line number references are general pointers to the location of the information. While every effort has been made to group and order the information be sure to read down the file, below the initial line number / entry, for any related information which may follow on.

All files have been unpacked if they were obtained in the form of a compressed archive. Therefore all files with a .ZIP file name extension are the original compressed archive files provided for convenience. A program such as Pkzip or Winzip is needed to unpack .ZIP archives.

When looking for the solution to a programming problem always check references to the other programming language sections as well. For example: a C programmer may gain considerable insights to a solution from the OPL examples provided and vice versa. Although, it has to be said, that some of the C code can be somewhat obtuse to programmers only familiar with OPL.

Note:
You are referred to Psion's Web-sites for the latest version of all documentation and examples originating from Psion – see the 'Contacts and Sources' chapter for access details.

OPL examples

Aalarms
How to set alarms from within an OPL program (3a onwards); shows how to select and set the built in alarm sounds such as soft bells etc. Illustrates the use of the SND: device.

Aka230
An OPL programmers' utility that compacts variable names, reduces the size of translated OPL programs, speeds them up and makes them less understandable if they are reverse translated.

Appman
Asynchronous handling of menus and dialogs - including nested or multi-level dialogs. Complex code, but very useful if you must have layered dialogs.

Ball
A complete application that demonstrates many OPL techniques, including resource files for multi-lingual programs, icons and bitmaps plus many others - requires the use of the S3atran or S3tran translators, but can be modified to avoid this as all necessary information is provided.

Beepoff
Asynchronous event handling (multiple); detects the switch off key and time to go before the machine will switch off. Demonstrates how to tell whether the processor is busy and if external power is in use.

Bincalc
A hexadecimal, octal and binary calculator written in OPL.

Call870a
A procedure to extract and display information returned by the operating system call FilStatusDevice, $87 Sub $0A. Useful for finding disk space and other details of a storage device.

Dataentr
Use of very long choice lists in OPL dialogs - uses calls to the OOP libraries.

Dbs_105
A supplementary Database Server from Psion for use with OPL or C programs. The DBS SDK is a Database server that runs on Psion machines and access to dBase III and IV format files and Psion DBF files from both C and OPL programs. DBS is the replacement for ISAM. ISAM is a set of routines that provided DBF file manipulation and indexing support.

Dbspatch
On some systems (Work*about* and Series 3c) problems were experienced with the DBS database server, these files were issued by Psion as a fix for the version of DBS v04 in ROM - see the dbspatch.txt file.

Dialog
Enhanced dialog routines in OPL. In particular, performs dialogs asynchronously, i.e. handles key presses and other events outside the dialogs, allows more than eight dialog entries and multi-line entries.

Drawbit
Access to two Window Server routines (gInitBit and gDrawBit) from OPL for the loading and manipulation of bitmaps.

Dun22src
The OPL source code for a dungeon style game.

Editbox
Edit box functions from OPL for text editing with word wrap, cursors, text attributes etc.

Embed
Demonstrates how to embed multiple bitmaps (PIC files) into an OPA and then access them as needed.

Firepic
A picture loader/viewer/saver for the Psion 3/3a/Work*about* that offers a few extra features over other similar programs. It can load and save multiple file formats by the use of plug-in DYLs (currently supplied DYLs for PIC and PCX formats). Source code is supplied (in C and OPL) that demonstrates how to write and use DYLs called by an OPL program.

Fontvw
A simple program for viewing some text in all of the different built in fonts on the S3a; the OPL source code is included. Helpful during screen design, to decide which typeface will look best.

Frame
An application framework/library that supports message-based, event-driven application programming in OPL on the Series 3 or 3a/c computers, includes support for time-based applications.

Freevt05
Emulation of a VT100 terminal in OPL, with source code, useful for studying RS232 serial port communications techniques.

Fsort
Database sorting example in OPL.

Gfxdemo
Graphics effect demonstrations - numerous in OPL.

Helpkit
A set of help / resource file production utilities. Demonstrates how to build / compile help and program resource files; including displaying help from within an OPL program. See Xfhelp below.

Ipc
An OPL demonstration of inter-process communication, where one program sends messages to another to indicate a change of state or the completion of a task. Uses one of the magic statics as a message/flag indicator, uses asynchronous events and extensive use of O/S calls.

Irchat
Two infrared communications examples in OPL. Irchat.opl demonstrates a keyboard based dialog between two infrared enabled Psions. Ircopy.opl demonstrates how to copy a file from one system to another using the infrared serial link.

Isameg
A demonstration of an Indexed Sequential Access Method (ISAM) database in OPL using the isam.dyl library from Psion.

JBsort
A utility to alphabetically sort database files in the background or the foreground. It will sort database files created with Data or by the OPL CREATE command. It can be used by your own programs, and will work on the S3 and S3a/c (and probably the Siena).

Jezar
Examples of directory scanning, asynchronous event handling, access to text files and error handling (all in OPL16).

Kmac
A Macro record / play back system written in OOP C with demonstration use by C or OPL applications, full source code in C and OPL. Example macros are included (kmac\cword) which will count the words in a Word document and will insert the date into a document.

Lib24
An application framework / library that supports event-driven application programming in OPL.

Longlist
Allows building of very long choice lists for use in OPL dialogs. Two OPL examples are given which demonstrate the use of variable arrays and VAFLAT or VASTR array classes. VASTR arrays are smaller but slower to navigate than VAFLAT arrays which are faster to navigate but consume more memory.

Lpcs
An example link / paste server and client - both in OPL and in C. Illustrates how to implement 'bringing' of highlighted data from one application into another.

Makedbf
OPL example code (OPP) to create a .DBF database file including field labels.

Mandel
An example of Mandelbrot set graphics in - OPL and C source code included. Illustrates how to use the floating point maths driver.

Norev14
A reverse translation protection system - see Revtran below.

Nitesrc0
A small Series5 program to automatically switch on the display backlight when the machine is switched on between certain hours of the day.

Online
A large set of text files containing questions and answers from the on-line community of Psion users and technical support. The files include text and code examples that illustrate many techniques, and solve many technical queries - mainly OPL with O/S calls, some OVAL, C and assembler code. All of the files have been indexed by topic related keywords, and numbers quoted refer to the line in the file where the discussion begins.

Opl_c
How to call C routines from within OPL programs; OPL and C source code is included.

Oplcs
OPL code studio – a Windows based editing and template system for writing OPL code.

Oplexams
Numerous OPL source code and text files containing example code and explanatory text to demonstrate a wide range of techniques. All files are referenced by keywords in the disk contents index, and descriptions are given in the READ1ST.TXT file located within the Oplexams directory.

Oplhelp
A programmers' utility to show media types, memory contents and OPL keywords.

Oplhlp
A very comprehensive Windows help file on the OPL language.

Oplinker
The basis of a working linker to link translated OPL modules together into one executable file; OPL source code is provided.

Opllint
An extremely useful OPL source code checking utility – checks OPL syntax and the use of variables and procedure calls.

Oplman
The text of the S3a programming manual, including all the example OPL code in text and Psion Word format, plus a .DBF database of all of the OPL keywords.

Oplman32
The text of the Siena, Series 3c and Series 5 programming manual (from the Psion PLC Website, June 97) in Microsoft WinWord format. The documents include an OPL16 to OPL32 porting guide – see OPLMAN32.DOC.

Note:
You are referred to the Psion Website for the latest version of this document – see the 'Contacts and Sources' chapter for access details.

Oplrad
Notes on speeding up OPL programs, plus an application to store and retrieve program settings.

Opltran
OPL translators and pre-processors for the S3 and S3a/c and Siena.

S3ATRAN.EXE   Translate a Psion S3a OPL source file to a .OPO or .OPA executable.
S3TRAN.EXE   Translate a Psion S3 OPL source file to a .OPO or .OPA executable.

Opp16f
An excellent OPL programmers' pre-processor and utility set for extending the language and using the operating system.

Oppdbg11
An excellent OPL programmers source level debugging utility – requires the use of OPP.

Palmtop
A collection of OPL examples from Palmtop magazine.

Parse$
An example of using the PARSE$ function to get/build all of the components of a file specification.

Pason4e
A utility program with OPL source that demonstrates:

How to enable/disable the switch on password, enable the password after a short period of inactivity, how to switch on the alarm sounds at regular intervals and how to switch off the remote link. The program runs continuously; it does not stop during backups and does not appear when cycling through the list of programs (with Shift-System). Pason4e runs on a 3a/c and the Siena.

Pelagn
Demonstrates how to read Agenda files in OPL.

Plink
A cross-linker for converting C programs to Psion format, which may then be run from inside an OPL program. Useful for speeding up time critical sections of an OPL program.

Ppcopl16

A complete SIBO application that demonstrates a wide range of simple and advanced techniques in OPL16, including calling a DYL from OPL. Full source code provided in OPL and C.

Ppcopl32

A complete Series 5 application that demonstrates a wide range of simple and advanced techniques in OPL32, including handling pointer events, using .INI files, program help and calling OPX procedures. Full source code provided in Series 5 and text formats, plus everything needed to build 'zoomable' Series 5 icons.

Ppcopl32\ppcopl32 and Ppcopl32\dosutils\ppctxt

A small Series 5 utility program (Uidread) for reading the four UIDs from Series 5 files. Source code is provided in OPL32 format in \Ppcopl32\ppcopl32, and in text format in Ppcopl32\dosutils\ppctxt.

Psioninc\opl

OPL examples from the Psion Inc US Web site.

\scan	Sample code to open a channel to the serial port, queue a serial barcode read and a queue a keyboard read.
\serial	Sample code to open a channel to the serial port and queue a read from the serial port.
reorder.opl	Sample code to sort a database file.
linkon.opl	Sample code to turn the remote link on.
xmo.opl	Sample code to terminate the link from within program, the application provides an example of this utility by communicating with an external modem.
longlist.opl	Sample code to use subclasses of the OLIB VAROOT class to implement long choice lists.

Revtran

Reverse translator for OPL programs. Will convert an OPO or OPA file back to an OPL source file. See Norev14 above and the 'OPL Programming' chapter for information on protecting your programs from reverse translation.

Riset

Using the WLD: device to access the World database for sunrise and sunset information.

S3proc

Run named application from within an OPL program, get a list of all running applications and kill a specific application.

Segments

Provides access to memory segments to OPL programs.

Speed

Notes on speeding up OPL programs plus information on some commercial applications.

Spritec

Fast use of sprites for the 3a onwards - uses access to sprites via the operating system to increase the speed of manipulating graphics objects.

Sqr12src
Squares graphics game with source OPL code.

Sunopl
Calculation of sunrise and sunset times based on latitude / longitude information.

Tsmp10
Demonstrations in OPL and C of recording / sampling sounds - uses the SYS$SAMP.LDD logical device driver via the SMP: device.

Watch
Examples of a high-resolution stopwatch (to 1/1024th second) using the free running counter device (FRC:).

Wld
Example of access to the World application database files, via the WLD: device, to get country and dialling code information.

Yam13src
Mine sweeper game application in OPL - full source and support files provided; demonstrates many sophisticated programming techniques, needs S3ATRAN to translate the source.

C examples

Appskel
An example skeleton application for HWIF based C programmers.

Clocks
An excellent full HWIM demonstration application showing multiple world time zone clocks.

Cpocall
An interim C compiler for the Psion, not yet fully functional - see the cpocall\cpocread directory first.

Dbfexam
Two examples illustrating C access to .DBF files, DBFED2.C uses DbfQuickOpen which, although documented, is not demonstrated in the C SDK manuals.

Dbs_105
A supplementary Database Server from Psion, for use with OPL or C programs. The DBS SDK is a Database server that runs on Psion machines and access to dBase III and IV format files and Psion DBF files from both C and OPL programs. DBS is the replacement for ISAM; a library of routines that provides DBF file manipulation and indexing support.

Dbspatch
On some systems (Work*about* and Series 3c) problems were experienced with the DBS database server, these files were issued by Psion as a fix for the version of DBS v04 in ROM - see the dbspatch.txt file.

Fileconv
File conversion documentation and C++ source code examples for producing additional file format converters for use with Psiwin (Windows 3.1 version).

Filetags
File selecting and tagging / marking demonstration in HWIM C.

Firepic
A picture loader/viewer/saver for the Psion 3/3a/Work*about* that offers a few extra features over other similar programs. It can load and save multiple file formats by the use of plug-in DYLs (currently supplied DYLs for PIC and PCX formats). Source code is supplied (in C and OPL) that demonstrates how to write and use DYLs called by an OPL program.

Floatlib
A section of C code for loading the floating-point emulator library.

Funcs
Notes and sections of C code for using library functions for binary searches and sorting.

Getenv
A short and simple C program to show all environment variables on a SIBO system.

Grepfv10
A file string searching program (DOS Shareware) with C source code. Will search a range of files for a text string – excellent for searching the example files for obscure instances of language keywords or functions.

Growbar
A small C application using HWIF with OOP techniques; demonstrating a gauge / growing progress bar.

Hwifeg
A small application in HWIF C with OOP techniques; demonstrating more sophisticated dialog interactions.

Hwimex
A small HWIM C demonstration of customised dialog controls.

Iconed
An icon production / editing program with HWIF C source code.

Isam
A demonstration of an Indexed Sequential Access Method (ISAM) application in C.

Kmac
A Macro record / play back system written in OOP C with demonstration use by C or OPL applications, full source code in C and OPL. Example macros are included (kmac\cword) which will count the words in a Word document and will insert the date into a document.

Lpcs
An example link / paste server and client - C and OPL source code included. Illustrates how to implement 'bringing' highlighted data from one application into another.

Mandel
An example of Mandelbrot set graphics - C and OPL source code are included. Illustrates how to use the floating point maths driver.

Online
A large set of text files containing questions and answers from the on-line community of Psion users and technical support. The files include text and code examples that illustrate many techniques, and solve many technical queries - mainly OPL with O/S calls, some OVAL, C and assembler code. All of the files have been indexed by topic related keywords, and numbers quoted refer to the line in the file where the discussion begins.

Oodoc201
Word for Windows documents describing Object Oriented Programming techniques with the Psion SIBO C SDK. A number of other very useful chapters are included here, including information on resource files, DYLs, OOP application design using the Record application as an example.

Opl_c
How to call C routines from within OPL programs; OPL and C source code is included.

Opltran
The C++ source code for a program (WAV2WVE.EXE) to convert a Windows WAV sound file to a Psion WVE sound file - see WAV2WVE.CPP.

P_crc
C source code to calculate a cyclical redundancy check (CRC) for a data set.

Parent
C code showing a parent process writing information to the window of a child process.

Plink
A cross-linker for converting C programs to Psion format, which may then be run from inside an OPL program. Useful for speeding up time critical sections of an OPL program.

Ppcopl16
A complete SIBO application that demonstrates a wide range of simple and advanced techniques in OPL16, including calling a DYL from OPL. Full source code provided in OPL and C.

Psioninc\csdk

	C examples from the Psion Inc US Web site.
scan.c	Sample code to open a channel to the serial port, queue a serial barcode read and queue a keyboard read.
linkon.c	Sample code to demonstrate use of a 'console' program to start another program using p_exec().
crdtype.c	Sample code to identify whether HC is in old style or new style docking station.

| \modem | Sample code to demonstrate XMODEM and YMODEM communication. |
| \hcdock | Image file to allow HC to communicate with new style docking station. |

Pyrmid .
A card game, full HWIF C source code and support files are included.

RS232_eg
A short demonstration in C of serial port communications - read and write.

S3c111
A SIBO based C compiler and development system – based on the SmallC compiler.

Solipeg
A complete set of HWIM C source code and support files for a Solitaire game: Slp15s is the first HWIM version, Slp21s is an enhanced but more complex release, Slp212 is as per Slp21s but includes Siena compatibility. Excellent examples (from Cade Roux) for studying HWIM programming.

Tsmp10
Demonstrations in C and OPL of recording / sampling sounds - uses the SYS$SAMP.LDD logical device driver via the SMP: device.

W2tsrc
The source code for a DOS program to convert Psion Word files to text files.

OVAL examples

Online
A large set of text files containing questions and answers from the on-line community of Psion users and technical support. The files include text and code examples that illustrate many techniques, and solve many technical queries - mainly OPL with O/S calls, some OVAL, C and assembler code. All of the files have been indexed by topic related keywords, and numbers quoted refer to the line the file where the discussion begins.

Ovaldemo
This directory contains a fully functional OVAL integrated development environment (IDE) from Psion Software; the only restriction is that you can use a maximum of two forms and two modules in each project. To use the OVAL demo package copy the files (except OVALDEMO.EXE) from the OVALDEMO directory on CD into a directory on your PC, run SETUP.EXE and follow the on-screen instructions. (Do not copy the OVALDEMO.EXE file – it is the self-extracting archive file that has already been unzipped, it is only needed if problems are encountered with particular files.) For the most up-to-date copy of the demonstration IDE you should visit the Psion Website - see the 'Contacts and Sources' chapter for details.

Ovaldemo\filename
A small OVAL demonstration of how to get file names from a user.

Ovaldemo\ovalterm
An untested terminal emulator, written in OVAL – useful for studying serial communications techniques and handshaking.

Ovaldemo\psionweb
Some notes and tips on OVAL – from the Psion Software web site, see the readme.txt file for the web address (URL).

Psioninc\oval
OVAL examples from the Psion Inc US Web site.

\barscan	Barcode scanning application to scan a barcode, accept keyboard, search a database and allow user to make additions to database. Intended as a model for an inventory application. Includes error-handling routines to create application databases if they are not present.
\dbase	Sample code to demonstrate handling of dBase III and dBase IV files within OVAL applications.
\dbase\server	Includes database server files necessary to utilise dBase files on the SIBO unit. i.e. patches to DBS04. Read file and database documentation first, i.e. Filehand.doc.
\makedb	Sample code to create a 'Psion native' database file including an index.
\gridapp	Sample application to demonstrate the use of a grid populated with values from a 'Psion native' database.
\dbgrid	Sample application to demonstrate the use of a grid populated with values from a dBase database. Note that the method for populating the grid differs because the dBase file must be opened before being loaded into the grid.
\dbspatch	On some systems (Work*about* and Series 3c) problems were experienced with the DBS database server, these files were issued by Psion as a fix for the version of DBS v04 in ROM - see the dbspatch.txt file.
\modem	Sample application to start the comms process, run the program in background using a script file, and return control to the OVAL application. The script file connects to a modem through the serial port (in a Docking station), dials out and transfers a file using Ymodem. Open the script file using Script Editor, edit to suit your needs, then translate before running the application.

Assembler examples

S3asm2
A full Assembler with support files for producing machine code programs and code segments.

Cpocall\cpocas86
An Assembler is supplied with the CPOC C development system, it is not designed as a stand-alone program and has to be used in conjunction with the CPOC 'front end'.

Online
A large set of text files containing questions and answers from the on-line community of Psion users and technical support. The files include text and code examples that illustrate many techniques, and solve many technical queries - mainly OPL with O/S calls, some OVAL, C and assembler code. All of the files have been indexed by topic related keywords, and numbers quoted refer to the line in the file where the discussion begins.

Macro systems

Kmac
A Macro record / play back system written in OOP C with demonstration use by C or OPL applications, full source code in C and OPL. Example macros are included (kmac\cword) which will count the words in a Word document and will insert the date into a document.

Macsys
Macsys is an application that allows a user to create cross-application macros. Macros are pre-programmed commands that help automate many repetitive tasks. Each Macro, once written and translated, must be installed and assigned a hotkey; thereafter pressing the hotkey from any application will execute the macro. Example Macros are located in macsys\mcr.

Online
A large set of text files containing questions and answers from the on-line community of Psion users and technical support. The files include text and code examples that illustrate many techniques, and solve many technical queries - mainly OPL with O/S calls, some OVAL, C and assembler code. All of the files have been indexed by topic related keywords, and numbers quoted refer to the line in the file where the discussion begins.

Utility software & support files

3lib

Shareware library listings – see the page at the end of the book for details of how to contact the 3Lib Shareware library.

Charm

A utility to display all of the characters, ASCII codes and fonts available on a Series 3a.

CSDK

A database application (DOS based) that provides a very comprehensive index to the whole of the SIBO C SDK manuals, suitable for versions up to 2.20. The C SDK index was produced by EMCC as a commercial product, purchasers of this book are free to use the index for their own individual purposes. However do not distribute the C SDK index to others, doing so by whatever means will be in breach of international copyright laws.

Dbf2text

Converts a Psion database file to a delimited text file – useful as an intermediate step for exporting Psion database data to other formats. This version of the program is more recent than the copy in the \Opltran directory.

Dbfc103

Converts a delimited text file to a Psion database file - useful as an intermediate step for importing databases in other formats to Psion format.

Defines

Defines.dbf is a Psion database file containing a comprehensive set of EPOC16 defines and identifiers with their corresponding numerical values.

Doc

A collection of miscellaneous programming related documents in Microsoft Word for Windows format.

AGNFILE.DOC	Series 3a Agenda file format.
APPGUIDE.DOC	A guide to writing Series 3/3a applications.
CHECK.DOC	A guide to writing Series 3/3a applications.
FLASHFR.DOC	Flash disk friendliness on S3.
OSCALLS.DOC	Operating system calls explained and detailed.
C96.DOC	Interim SIBO C SDK information for Siena and S3c.
OPL96.DOC	Interim SIBO OPL SDK information for Siena and S3c.
UPGRADE.DOC	Interim SIBO C SDK update (September 96) for Siena and S3c.
MANDEF.DOC	Known defects in the SIBO C SDK version 2.10 manuals.
SOFTDEF.DOC	Known defects in the SIBO C SDK version 2.10 software.

Draw284

A graphics / bitmap drawing program - useful for producing icon and other bitmap files for SIBO systems.

Emul3a

A DOS based emulation of the Psion Series 3a.

Epocalls
The operating system calls manual from version 2.01 of the C SDK in Word for Windows format.

Firepic
A picture loader/viewer/saver for the Psion 3/3a/Work*about* that offers a few extra features over other similar programs. It can load and save multiple file formats by the use of plug-in DYLs (currently supplied DYLs for PIC and PCX formats). Source code is supplied (in C and OPL) that demonstrates how to write and use DYLs called by an OPL program.

Font172
A font file editor for producing new fonts or graphics characters.

Fontvw
A simple program for viewing some text in all of the different built in fonts on the S3a; the OPL source code is included. Helpful during screen design, to decide which typeface will look best.

Formats
File formats for Psion 3a Agenda, Database, Word and Spreadsheet files in RTF, TXT and Word for Window versions. See also the oodoc201 directory for resource file information.

Freevt05
Emulation of a VT100 terminal in OPL, with source code, useful for studying RS232 serial port communications techniques.

Getenv
A short and simple C program to show all environment variables on a SIBO system.

Grepfv10
A file string searching program (DOS Shareware) with C source code. Will search a range of files for a text string – excellent for searching the example files for obscure instances of language keywords or functions.

Helped11
A Windows based application from Psion (free but unsupported) for editing application help files.

Helpkit
A set of help / resource file production utilities. Demonstrates how to build and compile help and program resource files. See Xfhelp below.

Hexview1
A file and memory segment viewer and editor – works in text or hexadecimal mode.

Iconed
An icon production / editing program with HWIF C source code.

Icons
A collection of icons for use with your own applications or program groups.

JBdata

An excellent Freeware database for Series 3a/c that has many more facilities than the built in Data application – in particular the ability to load data files with field types other than string. It can also export a database as a delimited text file, useful for transfer to other systems e.g. Series 5.

Makeals

The Psion utility program for making program alias (ALS) files.

Ncp

The NCP documentation and defines covering use of the remote link in Word for Windows format.

Nwtftp

A Excel spreadsheet file with the contents of the Shareware and Freeware on the New World Technology ftp and web site.

Online

A large set of text files containing questions and answers from the on-line community of Psion users and technical support. The files include text and code examples that illustrate many techniques, and solve many technical queries - mainly OPL with O/S calls, some OVAL, C and assembler code. All of the files have been indexed by topic related keywords, and numbers quoted refer to the line in the file where the discussion begins.

Oodoc201

Word for Windows documents describing Object Oriented Programming techniques with the Psion SIBO C SDK. A number of other very useful chapters are included here, including information on resource files, DYLs, OOP application design using the Record application as an example.

Oplman

A Psion database file (SIBO) of the OPL language (see S5data for an OPL32 database).

Opltran

A set of utility programs for file conversions.

DBF2TEXT.EXE   Convert a Psion database to a delimited text file.
TEXT2DBF.EXE   Convert a delimited text file to a Psion database.
WAV2WVE.EXE   Convert a Windows WAV sound file to a Psion WVE sound file.
WVE2WAV.EXE   Convert a Psion WVE sound file to a Windows WAV sound file.
WSPCX.EXE   Convert Windows PCX files to Psion bitmap (.PIC) files; will also bind multiple Psion bitmaps into one file. Also see the \wspcx314 directory.

Phcomp

A DOS based utility for simplifying the production of application resource / help files.

Psicon

A straight forward Windows based icon editor.

Psionfaq
A comprehensive set of text files providing answers to Frequently Asked Questions (FAQ) on all aspects of Psion computers.

Psionics
A comprehensive set of text files providing a huge amount of programming related information such as file formats, operating system calls and the use of a wide range of I/O devices.

S3aspy
A program memory and file inspection utility.

S5art
A set of Series 5 sketch files containing clipart graphics images.

S5data
A Psion Series 5 database of the OPL32 language (see Oplman an OPL16 database). Also included is an Series 5 database of the OPL32 constants.

S5demo
A Windows 95 based graphical demonstration of the new Series 5 system.

Sieirpr
Siena additional device drivers to enable infrared printing (to the IRP: device) plus other infrared I/O capabilities to the Siena.

Siena
A DOS based emulation of the Psion Siena.

Spy
A utility from Psion to monitor all active processes in the system and the resources they are using.

Ssds
Notes on upgrading the storage capacity of SSDs.

Undelete
A small utility which attempts to undelete files from Flash SSDs.

Uri
Microsoft Word for Windows document describing the Universal Radio Interface SDK for implementing a radio based network application.

Wdrkit
A set of utilities for producing / compiling WDR printer driver files.

Wrkabout
A DOS based emulation of the Psion Work*about*.

Wsfcomp
A utility for producing / compiling new SIBO font files.

Wspcx314

Convert Windows PCX files to Psion bitmap (.PIC) files; will also bind multiple Psion bitmaps into one file. This is a more recent version of the WPCX.EXE program than the version located in the \Opltran directory.

Xfhelp

A 'front end' program for the resource and help file compiler in Helpkit.

Zmdmptch

A patch version of the Zmodem protocol library for the S3c. If you have an early (V5.20F) S3c and wish to use the Zmodem protocol from comms scripts then you should install the SCP$ZMDM.DYL file into an \IMG directory.

WVE

A collection of miscellaneous Series 3 family digital sound files (.WVE files).

General Utilities

Grepfv10

A file string searching program (DOS Shareware) with C source code. Will search a range of files for a text string – excellent for searching the example files for obscure instances of language keywords or functions.

Lha213

A set of DOS based utilities for compressing and uncompressing files and archive file sets.

Pkzip

A set of DOS based utilities for compressing and uncompressing files and archive file sets.

Winzip31

A Windows 3.1 based application for compressing and uncompressing files and archive file sets.

Winzip95

A Windows 95 based application for compressing and uncompressing files and archive file sets.

Disk index

Disk index topic	Type	Directory	File	File or line
C SDK v2.1 interim 3c/Siena update	WWord	doc	C96.doc	
C SDK v2.1 known document defects	WWord	doc	mandef.doc	
C SDK v2.1 known software defects	WWord	doc	softdef.doc	
C structs and OPL	OPL	online	usenet01.txt	ln1903
C vs OPL programs	text	online	forum02.txt	ln756-972
C++ with Psion	text	online	usenet07.txt	ln815-844
Cacheing procedures	text	online	usenet01.txt	ln301
Calculator add conversions	OPL	Oplexams	conv.opl	
Calculator memories access	OPL	online	usenet01.txt	ln1429
Calculator; hex; octal; binary	OPL	bincalc	bincalc.opl	
Calendar displaying in OPL	text	online	conf05.txt	ln33-118
Cancelling alarms	OPL	online	forum04.txt	ln181
Cancelling alarms	OPL	online	forum06.txt	ln718-839
Card game in HWIF C	C	pyrmid	various	
Character codes display	OPL	online	forum01.txt	ln1561
Character codes display utility S3a/c	Util	charm	various	
Characters special	OPL	online	conf01.txt	ln283
Checksum / CRC calculation	OPL	online	usenet01.txt	ln2013 / 2101
Child / parent process demonstration	C	parent	various	
Choice items to text box	OPL	online	forum03.txt	ln358
Choice list in dialogs long	OPL	psioninc\opl\	flatlist.opl	
Choice list in dialogs long	OPL	online	conf01.txt	ln1692
Choice lists in dialogs	OPL	online	conf01.txt	ln563
Choice lists in dialogs long	OPL	online	usenet01.txt	ln455
Choice lists in dialogs long	OPL	longlist	various	
Choice lists long with VAFLAT reading	OPL	online	conf05.txt	ln1871-1950
Choice lists long with VARRAYs	text	online	conf02.txt	ln135 / 535
Choice lists very long in dialogs	OPL	online	forum06.txt	ln369-607
Circle drawing	OPL	Oplexams	circlex.opl	
Circle drawing	OPL	Oplexams	circle.opl	
Circle drawing	OPL	Oplexams	circles.opl	
Circle filled	OPL	Oplexams	ex_circ2.opl	readme.txt
Circle filled	OPL	Oplexams	circlef.opl	
Circle hollow	OPL	Oplexams	ex_circl.opl	readme.txt
Clipart collection for Series 5	Util	S5art	various	
Clock to 1/32 second	OPL	Oplexams	getaevnt.txt	getaevnt.opl
Clock type getting	OPL	Oplexams	getclock.opl	
Clock types displaying	OPL	online	usenet04.txt	ln525-602
Clock types displaying	OPL	online	usenet05.txt	ln251-346
Clock types displaying	OPL	online	usenet09.txt	ln222-271
Clocks HWIM C application	C	clocks	various	
Clocks reading the current type	OPL	online	conf05.txt	ln2315-2409
Close down another application	OPL	online	forum01.txt	ln736
Close down another application	OPL	Oplexams	closeapp.opl	
CMD$(5) OPL command return values	OPL	online	usenet09.txt	ln396-426
Comm ports selection of	text	online	conf04.txt	ln1
Comms programs from fax	OPL	Oplexams	seriafax.txt	
Comms routines	OPL	Oplexams	commtime.txt	
Comms script run	OPL	Oplexams	runsco.opl	
Communication between processes	OPL	ipc	various	
Communications examples of code	text	online	usenet02.txt	ln410
Compiler C provisional for Psions	Util	cpocall	various	
Compiler C Small C for Psions	Util	s3c111	various	
Compiling font files	Util	wsfcomp	various	
Compress data files	OPL	Oplexams	cpress.opl	
Compressing files	OPL	online	usenet01.txt	ln277
Compressing heaps	C	online	forum02.txt	ln137
Contrast changing screen	OPL	Oplexams	contrast.txt	
Contrast changing screen	OPL	online	usenet01.txt	ln1

19-24 Disk Contents

Disk index topic	Type	Directory	File	File or line
DYLs and OPL example app PPCOPL16	OPL/C	ppcopl16	various	
DYLs calling from OPL programs	OPL/C	ppcopl16	various	
DYLs calling from OPL programs	OPL/C	firepic	various	
DYLs example C code	OPL/C	ppcopl16	various	
DYLs for Workabout and HC	C	online	forum02.txt	ln1-111
DYLs how to produce & code example	WWord	oodoc201	dylbld.doc; catfile.doc etc	
DYLs using from C	C	online	forum04.txt	ln1-158
Dynamic dialogs OVAL	text	online	conf02.txt	ln442
Dynamic memory use	OPL	online	forum01.txt	ln662
Easter calculation	OPL	online	usenet01.txt	ln923
Easter calculation of date	OPL	online	conf02.txt	ln683 / 759
Edit boxes	OPL	editbox	various	
Edit boxes advanced	text	online	conf01.txt	ln1847
Editing text	OPL	online	conf01.txt	ln3295
Editor for font files	Util	font172	various	
Editor preferences keeping OPL settings	OPL	online	forum05.txt	ln196-238
Editor; OPL; windows based	Util	oplcs	various	
Elapsed timer calculating	OPL	online	conf01.txt	ln2150
Electrical impedances	OPL	Oplexams	atten.opl	
Ellipses drawing	OPL	Oplexams	elipse3.opl	
Emulator detecting PC EPOC operation	OPL	online	usenet05.txt	ln783
Emulator DOS based for S3a	Util	emul3a	various	
Emulator DOS based for Siena	Util	Siena	various	
Emulator DOS based for Workabout	Util	Wrkabout	various	
Emulators Psion in Win95	text	online	conf03.txt	ln75
Encryption / passwords	OPL	Oplexams	encrypt.opl	
Encryption of data	text	online	usenet03.txt	ln121
Entersend0 on S3	text	online	conf01.txt	ln3128
Environment variable for Owner info	OPL	online	usenet11.txt	ln315-377
Environment variable for user info	OPL	online	conf05.txt	ln531-619
Environment variable owner/user info	OPL	Oplexams	user.opl	
Environment variable serial port status	OPL	Oplexams	penv.opl	
Environment variables displaying	C	getenv	various	
Environment variables identified	text	Oplexams	envvars.txt	
Environment variables print settings	OPL	online	forum06.txt	ln940-980
Environment variables reading	OPL	online	forum06.txt	ln940-980
EPOC calls	WWord	doc	oscalls.doc	
EPOC calls	OPLs	Oplexams	oscalls.txt	
EPOC calls interpreting	text	online	conf01.txt	ln695
EPOC operating system calls full manual	text	epocalls	various	
ERR resetting to zero	OPL	online	usenet01.txt	ln1081
ERR value resetting to zero	OPL	online	conf05.txt	ln270-319
Error handling	OPL	online	conf01.txt	ln512
Error handling and I/O commands	OPL	online	forum02.txt	ln1961-2046
Error handling handles and I/O commands	OPL	online	forum02.txt	ln974-1105
Error handling with ONERR	OPL	jezar	upfile.opl	
Error value resetting ERR to zero	OPL	online	conf05.txt	ln270-319
Evaluation command	OPL	Oplexams	ex_eval.opl	
Event handling	text	online	conf01.txt	ln374
Event handling asynchronous	OPL	beepoff	various	
Event handling asynchronous	OPL	jezar	various	
Example OPL file descriptions	OPLs	Oplexams	read.txt	
Examples from OPL prog manual	OPL	oplman	oplexam.wrd	oplexam.txt
Fanfare sound playing	OPL	online	conf01.txt	ln2150
FAQ Psion	text	psionfaq	various	
Fax accessing device from a program	OPL	online	forum02.txt	ln606
Field labels in database files	OPL	online	usenet07.txt	ln363-681
File / memory viewer / editor	Util	hexview1	s3aspy	
File access using I/O statements	OPL	online	forum01.txt	ln1010

Disk index topic	Type	Directory	File	File or line
Game squares graphics	OPL	sqr12src	various	
Gauge progress bar HWIF with OOP	C	growbar	various	
Getevent date change	OPL	online	forum05.txt	ln240-299
Getevent use of	OPL	online	forum05.txt	ln240-299
GIF to PIC file conversion	OPL	online	forum06.txt	ln124-164
Graphics 3D cube	OPL	Oplexams	cube.txt	cube.opl
Graphics animation	OPL	Oplexams	sinus.opl	
Graphics animation driver reference to	text	online	usenet11.txt	ln1-25
Graphics bitmap editor	Util	draw284	various	
Graphics bitmap file converter / combining	Util	wspcs314	wspcx.exe	
Graphics bitmaps embedded in an OPA file	OPL	embed	various	
Graphics card game in HWIF	C	pyrmid	various	
Graphics clipart collection for Series 5	Util	S5art	various	
Graphics demo mandelbrot	OPL/C	mandel	various	
Graphics demonstrations many	OPL	gfxdemo	gfxdemo.opl	
Graphics ellipses	OPL	Oplexams	elipse3.opl	
Graphics file viewer and converter	OPL/C	firepic	various	
Graphics game mine sweeper OPA source	OPL	yam13src	various	
Graphics Mandelbrot plots	OPL/C	mandel	various	
Graphics speed up	OPL	Oplexams	doubleb.txt	
Graphics spiral demo small	OPL	online	usenet01.txt	ln365
Graphics squares game	OPL	sqr12src	various	
Graphics with bitmaps	OPL	ball	various	
Grep program for text in files searching	C	grepfv10	various	
Grep text file search utility	Util	grepfv10	various	
Grey plane in Image file conversion	text	online	forum02.txt	ln388
Grey planes and bitmaps	text	online	conf01.txt	ln2431
GRID class list view of records	text	online	conf05.txt	ln375
Grid control and databases in OVAL	text	online	usenet10.txt	ln722-817
Group names and program names	text	online	conf03.txt	ln280
gUPDATE in OPL	text	online	usenet07.txt	ln100-138
Handshake lines serial port	OPL	online	usenet07.txt	ln193
Handshake lines serial port	text	online	usenet08.txt	ln317
HC serial port access	text	online	usenet03.txt	ln598
HC serial port types	OPL	online	forum02.txt	ln1830
Heaps compressing	C	online	forum02.txt	ln137
Help / resource file compiler front end	Util	xfhelp	various	
Help / resource file editor	Util	helped11	various	
Help / resource file format description	text	psionics	various	
Help / resource file format description	text	psionics	various	
Help / resource file format description	WWord	oodoc201	various	
Help / resource file processor	Util	phcomp	various	
Help / resource file utilities / compiler	Util	helpkit	various	
Help file for Windows covering OPL	Util	oplhlp	opl.hlp	
Help files	OPL	Oplexams	ctrlhelp.opl	
Help files	OPL	online	conf01.txt	ln310
Help files and helpkit	text	online	conf01.txt	ln1478
Help files calling	OPL	online	conf01.txt	ln4969
Help files compiling	text	online	conf01.txt	ln1142
Help files using	OPL	online	forum01.txt	ln1689
Help key and dialogs	OPL	online	usenet07.txt	ln215-306
Help key detecting in menu & dialog	OPL	Oplexams	various	
Help key in dialogs	OPL	online	forum02.txt	ln1549-1612
Help key in dialogs	OPL	online	forum03.txt	ln564-627
Help/resource file releasing	OPL	online	conf05.txt	ln404-469
Help/resource files embedding in OPA's	text	online	conf05.txt	ln2412-2504
Hex to decimal conversion	OPL	Oplexams	oplvars.txt	
Hex; octal; binary calculator	OPL	bincalc	bincalc.opl	
Hexadecimal file dump	OPL	Oplexams	hexdump.opl	

Disk index topic	Type	Directory	File	File or line
Infrared to PC information	text	online	usenet08.txt	ln847-875
Installation program Windows based	text	online	usenet08.txt	ln82
Integer numbers testing	text	online	usenet06.txt	ln1068-1142
Integer rounding techniques	OPL	online	forum05.txt	ln57-161
Integers long splitting	OPL	online	forum01.txt	ln2013
Inter-process communication	OPL	ipc	various	
IOA use of for key presses	OPL	online	forum01.txt	ln1124
IOOPEN advice	OPL	online	usenet01.txt	ln3200
IR port chat OPL program example	OPL	irchat	irchat.opl	
IR port chat program infrared example	OPL	irchat	irchat.opl	
IR port device drivers for Siena	Util	sieirpr	various	
IR port receive file infrared example	OPL	irchat	ircopy.opl	
IrDA information	text	online	usenet03.txt	ln342
IrDA information	text	online	usenet06.txt	ln290-662
IrDA infrared information	text	online	usenet08.txt	ln455-544
IrDA infrared to PC information	text	online	usenet08.txt	ln847-875
IrDA infrared Web page	text	online	usenet08.txt	ln755
IrDA infrared web site	text	online	conf02.txt	ln367
ISAM Database	OPL	isameg	various	
ISAM database example in C	C	isam	various	
Java for EPOC32	text	online	usenet08.txt	ln149-272
Java project references	text	online	usenet06.txt	ln815-843
Jbdata database program	Util	jbdata		
Key click disable	OPL	Oplexams	keycloff.txt	
Key clicks turning off	OPL	online	conf01.txt	ln1
Key detection in dialogs	OPL	online	forum03.txt	ln946-1051
Key press getting the last	OPL	online	usenet01.txt	ln1169
Key press getting the last key pressed	OPL	online	usenet09.txt	ln42-104
Key presses hot keys detecting	OPL	online	conf01.txt	ln2865
Key presses in background	OPL	Oplexams	capture.txt	
Key presses scanning for with I/O funts	OPL	online	usenet04.txt	ln796-883
Key presses simulating	OPL	online	conf01.txt	ln1706
Key presses using IOA	OPL	online	forum01.txt	ln1124
KEY$ OPL function discussion	OPL	online	conf05.txt	ln1 / 19
Keyboard buffer clearing	OPL	online	conf01.txt	ln4805
Keyboard scan codes	OPL	Oplexams	kbscan.opl	
Keypress capture and test advanced	OPL	Oplexams	docap.opl	
Keypress capture and test advanced	OPL	Oplexams	jump.opl	
Keypress capture and test async	OPL	Oplexams	ktest.opl	
Keypresses asynchronous	OPL	Oplexams	getaevnt.txt	getaevnt.opl
Kill run find programs	OPL	s3proc	s3kill.opl	
Language / country code list of	text	online	usenet01.txt	ln2554
Language code	OPL	Oplexams	res&lang.txt	
Latitude / long calcs advice	text	online	usenet01.txt	ln2380
Latitude / long from World	OPL	Oplexams	latlong.opl	
LCD contrast changing	OPL	online	usenet03.txt	ln261
LCD contrast get & set	OPL	Oplexams	contrast.txt	
LCD screen contrast controlling	OPL	Oplexams	lcd.opl	
Leap year test	OPL	online	usenet01.txt	ln1051
Leap years & Y2000	text	online	usenet08.txt	ln1082-1134
LHA213 - DOS zip / unzip utility	Util	lha213	various	
Link / paste or bring advice	text	online	usenet01.txt	ln2431
Link activating	C	online\usenet02.txt	ln141-283 / 355	
Link activating	OPL	online	usenet04.txt	ln483
Link connection detecting	OPL	online	conf05.txt	ln206-268
Link from OPL	OPL	online	usenet08.txt	ln343-452
Link on/off testing	OPL	Oplexams	link.opl	linkon.opl
Link paste	OPL/C	lpcs	various	
Link paste or bring demonstration	OPL/C	lpcs	various	

Disk index topic	Type	Directory	File	File or line
Screen contrast get & set	OPL	Oplexams	contrast.txt	
Screen pixels testing status on or off	OPL	online	usenet09.txt	ln106
Screen printing / capture	C	online	usenet02.txt	ln286
Screen re-drawing faster	OPL	online	conf01.txt	ln1232
Screen re-sizing for status window	OPL	online	conf05.txt	ln2507
Screen using full on 3a	C	online	usenet01.txt	ln2230 / 2469
Script file run from OPL	OPL	Oplexams	script.opl	
Scrolling lists	OPL	Oplexams	listch1.txt	
Scrolling windows	OPL	Oplexams	various	
SDDs upgrading the capacity	text	ssds	various	
SDK Psion remote comms PRC	text	online	conf03.txt	ln59
SDK SIBO C index to manuals up to 2.20	Util	csdk	various	
SDK SMS from Psion	text	online	conf03.txt	ln209
SDK SMS version 2.01 functions	text	online	conf04.txt	ln71
Search for pattern in file	OPL	Oplexams	oposrch.opl	
Search for text string in a file	OPL	Oplexams	ts.opl	
Serial comms technical details	text	online	conf04.txt	ln90
Serial I/O on Workabout for bar codes	OVAL	online	usenet09.txt	ln1155-1215
Serial link enable disable	OPL	pason4e	various	
Serial link / remote comms docs	text	ncp	various	
Serial link activating	C	online	usenet02.txt	ln141-283 / 355
Serial link activating	OPL	online	usenet04.txt	ln483
Serial link checking for installation	OPL	online	conf04.txt	ln42
Serial link detecting	OPL	online	conf05.txt	ln206-268
Serial link from OPL	OPL	online	usenet08.txt	ln343-452
Serial link off	OPL	psioninc\opl\	xmo.opl	
Serial link on	OPL	psioninc\opl\	linkon.opl	
Serial link on	C	psioninc\csdk\	linkon.c	
Serial link on/off testing	OPL	Oplexams	link.opl	linkon.opl
Serial link read / write S3	OPL	Oplexams	s3serial.txt	
Serial link starting	OPL	Oplexams	linkopl.txt	
Serial link starting from OPL	OPL	online	conf01.txt	ln1679
Serial port / modem comms example	OVAL	psioninc\oval\modem\ various		
Serial port access on HC	text	online	usenet03.txt	ln598
Serial port buffers reading data in	OPL	online	usenet05.txt	ln494
Serial port cables S3c	text	online	usenet08.txt	ln661-752
Serial port comms	OPL	Oplexams	commtime.txt	
Serial port comms via VT100 emulation	OPL	freevt05	various	
Serial port communications demo	C	rs232_eg	rs232.c	
Serial port data reading	text	online	usenet10.txt	ln380-407
Serial port file transfer using Xmodem	OPL	Oplexams	txmodem.opl	
Serial port file transfer using Ymodem	OPL	Oplexams	tymodem.opl	
Serial port handshake lines	OPL	online	usenet07.txt	ln193
Serial port handshake lines	text	online	usenet08.txt	ln317
Serial port handshaking	OPL	online	usenet01.txt	ln2329
Serial port handshaking DTR	OPL	Oplexams	dtr.opl	
Serial port I/O on Workabout	C	online	usenet06.txt	ln58-286
Serial port pin outs S3c	text	online	usenet08.txt	ln661-752
Serial port pins information S3/3a	text	online	usenet01.txt	ln3219
Serial port programming example	OVAL	online	usenet09.txt	ln602-622
Serial port reading	OPL	Oplexams	ttyread.txt	
Serial port reading from	OPL	online	usenet01.txt	ln2605
Serial port reading from	OPL	online	usenet04.txt	ln649-793
Serial port reading from	OPL	psioninc\opl\serial\serial.opl		
Serial port reading from	OPL	online	conf02.txt	ln276
Serial port reading/writing	OPL	online	conf05.txt	ln715-1085
Serial port sending Esc etc.	OPL	online	usenet01.txt	ln2451
Serial port settings reading	OPL	online	conf01.txt	ln2911
Serial port status	OPL	online	conf01.txt	ln3671

Disk index topic	Type	Directory	File	File or line
Serial port status from environment var	OPL	Oplexams	penv.opl	
Serial port time outs	text	online	conf02.txt	ln186
Serial port types on HC	OPL	online	forum02.txt	ln1830
Serial transfers Xmodem example	OPL	online	usenet09.txt	ln804-1034
Series 3 family application stds guide	WWord	doc	check.doc	
Series 3 finding which model	OPL	online	forum01.txt	ln2103
Series 3 menu memory loss fix	OPL/Ass	Oplexams	menpat.txt	mnupatch.opl
Series 3 model recognising which	OPL	online	conf01.txt	ln5013
Series 3a DOS based emulator	Util	emul3a	various	
Series 3a or 3c detecting	OPL	online	conf05.txt	ln206-249
Series 3c parallel port printing problems	OPL	online	forum06.txt	ln841-1405
Series 3c programming manual	WWord	oplman32	various	
Series 3c Zmodem patch	Util	zmdmptch	various	
Series 5 backlight control example	OPL	nitesrc0	various	
Series 5 clipart collection	Util	S5art	various	
Series 5 demo program	Util	s5demo	various	
Series 5 programming manual for OPL32	WWord	oplman32	various	
Shareware / freeware Web / Ftp site	Excel file	nwtftp	nwtftp.xls	
Shareware and freeware info Web site	text	online	usenet09.txt	ln1217-1269
Shareware library 3Lib lists	text	3lib	various	
Shareware registration code using CRC	OPL	online	usenet07.txt	ln140-191
Shareware registration method / function	text	online	usenet04.txt	ln605
Shareware registration methods	OPL	online	forum01.txt	ln1448
Shift key and menus	OPL	online	forum01.txt	ln479
Shutdown another program	OPL	online	forum01.txt	ln736
Shutdown message handling	OPL	online	conf05.txt	ln341-372
Siena DOS based emulator	Util	siena	various	
Siena IR port device drivers	Util	sieirpr	various	
Siena numeric keypad	OPL	online	usenet04.txt	ln635
Siena OPL differences	text	online	conf02.txt	ln374
Siena parallel port printing problems	OPL	online	forum06.txt	ln841-1405
Siena printing Infrared drivers for etc.	Util	sieirpr	various	
Siena programming manual	WWord	oplman32	various	
SMP: device for sound recording	OPL/C	tsmp10	various	
SMS SDK from Psion	text	online	conf03.txt	ln209
SMS SDK version 2.01 functions	text	online	conf04.txt	ln71
SND: device example	OPL	aalarms	various	
SND: device playing standard alarms	OPL	aalarms	alarmsnd.opl	
Software copy protection	text	online	conf02.txt	ln480
Solitaire game v1.5 in HWIM C	C	\solipeg\slp15s	various	
Solitaire game v2.1 in HWIM C	C	\solipeg\slp21s	various	
Solitaire game v2.2 in HWIM C	C	\solipeg\slp22s	various	
Sort comb type	OPL	Oplexams	combsort.opl	
Sort database program	OPL	fsort	fsort.opl	
Sort database program	OPL	Oplexams	dbsort.opl	
Sort heap sort	OPL	Oplexams	sort.opl	
Sort re-order data file	OPL	Oplexams	ex_reord.opl	
Sorting advice	text	online	usenet01.txt	ln1461
Sorting an array	OPL	online	conf01.txt	ln2274
Sorting database files	OPL	Oplexams	reorder.opl	
Sorting utility for databases	OPL	Jbsort	various	
Sorts and binary searches	C	funcs	various	
Sound file conversion WAV to WVE	text	online	usenet08.txt	ln641-658
Sound file converter WAV to WVE	Util	opltran	wav2wve.exe	
Sound file converter WVE to WAV	Util	opltran	wve2wav.exe	
Sound Files - miscellaneous .WVE	Util	WVE	various	
Sound files playing	OPL	online	forum01.txt	ln1664
Sound files playing asynchronously	OPL	online	forum05.txt	ln867-1103
Sound key clicks turning off	OPL	online	conf01.txt	ln1

Disk index topic	Type	Directory	File	File or line
Sound playing async problems	text	online	conf01.txt	ln3956
Sound playing standard alarm sounds	OPL	aalarms	alarmsnd.opl	
Sound playing two tone	OPL	online	forum01.txt	ln2054
Sound playing wve files	OPL	ball	various	
Sound recording via SMP: device driver	OPL/C	tsmp10	various	
Sound sampling	OPL/C	tsmp10	various	
Sound setting off or on	text	online	conf01.txt	ln962
Sound testing if off or on	text	online	conf01.txt	ln933
Sound volume control	OPL	online	forum01.txt	ln2054
Special characters control codes	text	online	conf02.txt	ln906
Speeding up OPL	text	online	conf01.txt	ln1015
Spiral graphics demo small	OPL	online	usenet01.txt	ln365
Spreadsheet creating	OPL	online	forum01.txt	ln955
Spreadsheet file format descriptions	text	formats	sprfile.*	
Spreadsheets Word and I/O commands	OPL	online	forum02.txt	ln1107-1546
Sprites advice on multiple	OPL	online	usenet01.txt	ln1347
Sprites and bitmaps	OPL	online	usenet04.txt	ln885
Sprites in OPL fast access	OPL	spritec	various	
Sprites using	OPL	online	forum01.txt	ln327
SSD Disk device type testing	OPL	Oplexams	fildev.opl	
SSD drive name getting current	text	online	conf05.txt	ln2625-2662
Stack implementing one	OPL	online	usenet01.txt	ln2771
Starting up an application	OPL	online	usenet01.txt	ln1097
Status window re-sizing screen	OPL	online	conf05.txt	ln2507
Status windows strange effects	text	online	conf02.txt	ln1
Stopwatch	OPL	Oplexams	ex_watch.opl	
Stopwatch high resolution	OPL	Oplexams	frc.opl	
Stopwatch high resolution	OPL	watch	various	
Sub-process	OPL	Oplexams	various	
Sub-processes	OPL	Oplexams	ctrlhelp.opl	
Summer times settings World data	OPL	Oplexams	zones.opl	
Sunrise / set calculation of	OPL	sunopl	various	
Sunrise / set info via World database	OPL	riset	riset.opl	
Switch off detecting	OPL	beepoff	various	
Switch off detecting	OPL	online	usenet01.txt	ln245
Switch off setting auto	OPL	Oplexams	expow.opl	
Switch off time to go before	OPL	beepoff	various	
System & country info	OPL	Oplexams	getctd.opl	
System date display of	C	online	usenet10.txt	ln977-1023
System screen file lists update	OPL	Oplexams	updflist.opl	
System screen replacing	text	online	usenet10.txt	ln670-719
System screen shutdown messages	OPL	online	conf05.txt	ln341-372
System time and alarms setting	OPL	aalarms	aalarma.opl	aalarma.txt
System time information	OPL	Oplexams	timetick.txt	
System time information and alarms	OPL	Oplexams	aalarm.opl	
Tagged file list	OPL	Oplexams	taggin.opl	
Tagging files from a list	OPL	online	usenet05.txt	ln582-780
Tagging files in HWIM C	C	filetags	various	
TCP/IP stack project	text	online	conf05.txt	ln2172-2211
Terminal emulator VT100 incl OPL source	OPL	freevt05	various	
Terminal program examples of code	text	online	usenet02.txt	ln410
Terminating a process	OPL	online	forum01.txt	ln736
Text and font viewer for 3a	OPL	fontvw	various	
Text entry via edit boxes	OPL	editbox	various	
Text file convert from a database	Util	dbf2txt	various	
Text file from data file	OPL	Oplexams	export.opl	
Text file printing	OPL	online	conf03.txt	ln92
Text file reading from	OPL	online	conf05.txt	ln1560-1697
Text file search utility Grep	Util	grepfv10	various	

Disk index topic	Type	Directory	File	File or line
Text file to database converter	Util	dbfc103	various	
Text file writing records into	OPL	online	conf05.txt	ln1989-2066
Text files from Word files	C	w2tsrc	wrd2txt.c	
Text files reading and word wrap	text	online	conf01.txt	ln2014
Text files using IOOPEN etc.	OPL	jezar	upfile.opl	
Text files using IOOPEN etc.	OPL	online	usenet01.txt	ln127
Text formatting fonts multiple on screen	OPL	online	conf05.txt	ln1089-1105
Text formatting when printing	OPL	online	conf05.txt	ln1540-1556
Text in files searches Grep program	C	grepfv10	various	
Text string search in a file	OPL	Oplexams	ts.opl	
Text strings testing for display width	text	online	conf05.txt	ln2665-2711
Text to database converter	Util	opltran	text2dbf.exe	
Time / clock calculation	OPL	Oplexams	clockcrd.opl	
Time and date getting and formatting	OPL	online\conf05.txt ln1108-1537 / 2215-2311		
Time change from OPL	OPL	online	forum05.txt	ln389
Time conversion	OPL	online	forum02.txt	ln156 / 352
Time getting system settings	OPL	online	conf05.txt	ln1108-1537
Time information from system	OPL	Oplexams	timetick.txt	
Time outs serial port	text	online	conf02.txt	ln186
Time setting from OPL	OPL	online	usenet06.txt	ln986-1028
Time setting system	OPL	Oplexams	various	
Time system get current	OPL	Oplexams	attime.txt	
Time zones dates of Summer/Winter	text	online	usenet10.txt	ln474
Timer and run program	OPL	Oplexams	abstim.opl	
Timer count down	OPL	Oplexams	ex_timer.opl	
Timer example	OPL	online	usenet03.txt	ln70
Timer high res stop watch	OPL	watch	various	
Timer high resolution	OPL	Oplexams	frc.opl	
Timer information and alarm setting	OPL	Oplexams	aalarm.opl	
Timer set absolute	OPL	Oplexams	attime.txt	
Timer setting	OPL	Oplexams	abstim.opl	
Timer setting	OPL	Oplexams	alarms.opl	alm.opl
Timers two	OPL	Oplexams	timers2.opl	
Translating large OPL source files	OPL	online	usenet01.txt	ln60
Translation of large OPL source files	text	online	usenet01.txt	ln1616
Translators DOS based OPL	Util	opltran	various	
Undelete data records	OPL	Oplexams	undel.opl	
Undeleting files on Flash RAM	Util	undelete	various	
Universal radio interface document	WWord	uri	uri_faq.doc	
Upgrading SDDs capacity	text	ssds	various	
User information location	OPL	online	usenet10.txt	ln315-377
User information location of	OPL	online	conf05.txt	ln531-619
User/owner info from environment variable	OPL	Oplexams	user.opl	
VAFLAT OOP function using from OPL	OPL	online	forum02.txt	ln185
VAL OPL function language dependent	OPL	online	forum04.txt	ln162
VAL use of OPL function	OPL	online	forum02.txt	ln1855
Variable arrays use for file tagging	OPL	online	usenet05.txt	ln582-780
Variable arrays VARRAYs	text	online	conf02.txt	ln135 / 535
Variable sizes calculating	OPL	online	conf01.txt	ln4687
Variables compactor for OPL	Util	aka230	various	
Variables contiguous storage	OPL	online	conf01.txt	ln4721-4798
Variables converting	OPL	Oplexams	oplvars.txt	
Variables storage and memory	OPL	Oplexams	oplvars.txt	
Variables tutorial	OPL	Oplexams	oplvars.txt	
VARRAYs variable arrays	text	online	conf02.txt	ln135 / 535
VAT codes checking	OPL	online	conf02.txt	ln560
Videoplus codes algorithm	text	online	usenet03.txt	ln514
VT100 terminal emulator incl OPL source	OPL	freevt05	various	
WAV to WVE file converter	Util	opltran	wav2wve.exe	

Disk index topic	Type	Directory	File	File or line
Ymodem serial read	OPL	psioninc\opl\	xmo.opl	
Ymodem serial read	C	psioninc\csdk\modem\	various	
Zip / unzip DOS utility LHA213	Util	lha213	various	
Zip / unzip DOS utility PKZIP	Util	pkzip	various	
Zip / unzip Win 3.x utility WINZIP31	Util	winzip31	various	
Zip / unzip Win 95 utility WINZIP95	Util	winzip95	various	
Zmodem patch for S3c	Util	zmdmptch	various	

20   Contacts and Sources

Psion

Psion's main source of support, SDK information and updates for developers is through their EPOC World Website.

The SIBO software development kits and related goods are no longer supplied directly to developers. Although for licensees and Value Added Resellers (VARs), who pay annual fees to Psion, alternative arrangements are available.

In the UK the SIBO SDKs and certain other supplies are now only available through approved 'Value Added Distributors' (VADs). Contact details for the three main VADs are listed below.

Psion Software and UIDs

To obtain a reserved UID for Series 5 applications you should contact Psion Software in one of the following ways:

E-mail:	uid_sw@software.psion.com
EPOC World web site:	http://software.psion.com/EPOCWorld/
Fax to:	+44-171-724-4048, attn UID Allocations
Write to:	UID Allocations, Psion Software PLC, 19 Harcourt St, London W1N 1DT, England

EPOC World subscriptions

EPOC World Website	http://software.psion.com/EPOCWorld/
Write to:	Customer Services Department, Psion PLC, 1 Red Place, London W1Y 3RE
Telephone:	+44 (0) 990 143 050
E-mail to:	ew_subs@psion.com.

Psion's key web sites

These locations are the key starting points for the web sites of the Psion group.

Psion PLC main web site	http://www.psion.com
Psion Software's support related site.	http://www.software.psion.com/EPOCWorld/
Psion Inc in the USA	http://www.psioninc.com
Psion Inc free downloads for developers.	http://www.psioninc.com/downloads/samples.htm

Psion UK VADs

In the UK the SIBO SDKs and certain other Psion related supplies are now only available through approved 'Value Added Distributors' (VADs). All UK Psion 'Value Added Resellers' (VARs) must be associated with one of the VADs listed below.

VAD	Telephone & Fax	E-mail & Web site address
Paradigm Technology Ltd 7 Thames Park Lester Way Wallingford Oxford OX10 9TA	Tel: +44 1491 822600 Fax: +44 1491 822601	Sales@paratech.co.uk
Frontline Distribution Ltd Hampshire House Wade Road, Basingstoke Hampshire RG24 8PL	Tel: +44 1256 463344 Fax: +44 1256 479461	info@frontline.co.uk http://www.frontline.co.uk
Hugh Symmons Mobile Data Alder Hills Park 16 Alder Hills Poole Dorset BH12 4AR	Tel: +44 1202 718388 Fax: +44 1202 714410	

Psion International Contacts

European Psion Contacts

Austria

Hayward Computer-Peripherie	tel: +43 662 85870 fax: +43 662 858780	support@hayward.telecom.at

Belgium

Micro Connection	tel: +32 3 232 3468 fax: +32 3 226 1749 BBS: +32 3 226 2079	MCD@innet.be

European Psion Contacts

Cyprus		
Series 5/3/3a/3c/Siena	tel: +357 2 448618	
Synchrotech Limited	fax: +357 2 458345	
Workabout and HC	tel +30 31 327 961	3a-psion-sideris@the.forthnet.gr
3A Company	fax: +30 31 327 962	
Czech Republic		
Point X spol sro	tel: +42 2 2319395, 2310672, 2318636, fax: +42 2 24810821	pointx@login.cz http://www.netx.cz/psion/
Denmark		
Mobi Data A/S	tel: + 48 16 96 00 fax: + 48 16 96 01	info@mobidata.dk http://www.winet.dk/com/mobidata/defaul t.htm
Eire		
SIS Survey	tel: +353 1 4568 650 fax: +353 1 4568 653	
Finland		
Anglo Nordic Series 5/3/3a/3c/Siena	tel: +358 9 819 211 fax: +358 9 811 338	
Hand Held Systems Finland Workabout and HC	tel: +358 5 811 700 fax: +358 5 371 0062	Sales: satu.penttinen@hhs.inet.fi Tech Sup: Pekka.Aikas@HHS.Inet.F
France		
Psion France	tel: +33 1 53 41 12 00 fax: +33 1 5341 12 01	
Germany		
Psion GmbH	tel: +49 6172 6630 fax: +49 6172 663100	Sales:gmbh-vertrieb@psion.com Tech Supt: gmbh-support@psion.com http://www.psion-gmbh.com/
Greece		
INT Electronic Series 5/3/3a/3c/Siena	tel: +30 1 9233013 fax: +30 1 9234273	intelect@cybex.gr http://www.cybex.gr/int_psion.html/
3A Company Workabout and HC	tel +30 31 327 961 fax +30 31 327 962	3a-psion-sideris@the.forthnet.gr
Hungary		
Psion Magyarorszag KFT	tel and fax: +36 1 1851722 +36 1 2093804 +36 1 2093805	psion@hungary.net http://www.hungary.net/weblapok/psion/
Italy		
Video Computer Series 5/3/3a/3c/Siena	tel: +39 11 403 4828 fax: +39 11 403 3325	http://www.videocomputer.it/
Nordelettronica (Division Micra)- Workabout and HC	tel: +39 2 660921 fax: +39 2 6601 3335	Tech queries: psion.tech@nordele.it Comm: nordele@nordele.it
Macedonia		
Duna Workabout and HC	tel +389 91 11 97 55 fax +389 91 41 50 41	pajkovski@duna.com.mk http://www.duna.com.mk/
Malta		
BDS Limited	tel: +356 239200 fax: +356 248603	

European Psion Contacts

Netherlands		
Psion BV	Tel: +31 20 4469444	psionnl-support@psion.com
	Fax: +31 20 4469446	http://www.psion.nl
Tech Support:	Tel: +31 20 4469499,	
	fax: +31 20 4469425	
Norway		
Ucom AS	tel: +47 32 20 33 00	
	fax: +47 32 20 34 59	
Poland		
Centrum Informatyki	tel: +48 22 821 3262	ciesm@elmo.nask.waw.pl
Energetyki	fax: +48 22 821 3263	
Portugal		
Comp 3 Lda	tel: +351 1 797 2259,	
	fax: +351 1 795 1928.	
Russia		
Roditi	tel: +44 171 439 4390	
Series 5/3/3a/3c/Siena	fax: +44 171 434 0896	
Pilot Corporation	tel: +7 095 976 7280	alex@pilot.msk.ru
Workabout and HC	fax: +7 095 976 7235	
Slovenia		
Davos	tel: +386 64 324 223	joze.prosenik@spika.unistar.si
	fax: +386 64 324 223	
Spain		
Paresa SA	tel: +34 3 487 2702	paresa@paresa.es
Barcelona	fax: +34 3 487 2516	http://www.paresa.es/
Paresa SA	tel: +34 1 308 5947	paresa@paresa.es
Madrid	fax: +34 1 308 6719	http://www.paresa.es/
Sweden		
Svenska Industrielektronic	tel: +46 31 709 1600	psion.support@industrielektronik.se
AB	fax: +46 31 478520	http://www.industrielektronik.se
Switzerland		
Excom AG	tel: +41 1 782 2111	infos@excom.ch
	fax: +41 1 781 1361	http://www.excom.ch/
Turkey		
Porcan AS	tel: +90 216 388 84	argune@porcan.com.tr
Workabout and HC	50 fax: +90 216 366 98 29	http://www.porcan-b.com.tr/porcan-b/
United Kingdom		
Psion UK	tel: +44 171 3174100	www.psion.co.uk
Technical Support:	tel: 0990 143061	uk-support@psion.com
Sales:	tel: 0990 143050	
	Fax: 0990 561046.	
	Doc faxback service:	
	fax: 0891 515432	

North American Psion Contacts

Canada		
Syscan International Inc	tel: +1 514-521-0482, fax: +1 514-521-0949	Web site: http://www.syscan.com/
Mexico		
TDT	tel: +52 5 361 3755 fax: +52 5 361 3755	
United States of America		
Psion Inc - Sales hotline Concord (Head/Office), MA	1-800 997 7466 tel: +1 508 371 0310 fax: +1 508 371 9611	Tech Sup: usa-support@psion.com http://www.psioninc.com/
Burlingame (West Coast Office), CA	tel: +1 415 373 1234 fax: +1 415 373 1233	

Psion distributors and retailers

The following list is not exhaustive, it simply represents some of the key third party dealers or producers who supply products useful to programmers.

Clove Technology 43 Springbank Rd Bournemouth BH7 7EL Suppliers of Psion systems, software and accessories.	+44 1202 302796 +44 1202 300419 (fax) 100255.3642@compuserve.com http://www.clove-tech.co.uk
Exportech PO Box4499 London SW17 8XQ Suppliers of Psion systems, etc. Specialist in large SSDs and SSD upgrades. Also Compact Flash RAMs.	+44 181 682 3313 +44 181 682 4414 (fax) 100121.1165@compuserve.com
New World Technologies Inc 110 Greene St. (#5100) New York NY, 10012, USA Suppliers of Psion systems, software and accessories.	+1 800 886-4967 (US toll-free) +1 212 941-4633 (Int'l) +1 212 274-8527 (Fax) info@nwt.com http://www.nwt.com/ FTP server: ftp://ftp.nwt.com/pub/
POS 143 Streatham High Road, London SW16 6EG Psion approved repair company	+ 181 677 9246 + 181 769 9293 (fax) 0831 194985 (mobile) 106051.2651@compuserve.com
Purple software Ltd PO Box 7535, London NW1 6AT Software development house offering a wide range of applications. Manufacturer and supplier of the Cyclone floppy disk drive for Psion systems.	+44 171 387 7777 + 44 171 387 1188 (fax) purple_software@compuserve.com http://www.purplesoft.com

Widget Software Ltd 121 London Road Knebworth, Herts SG3 6EX Suppliers of Psion systems, software and accessories.	+44 1438 815444 +44 1438 815222 (fax) info@widget.co.uk http://www.widget.co.uk
Yellow Computing Computersysteme GmbH Hanns-Martin-Schleyer-Str. 1 D-74177 Bad Friedrichshall, Germany Software house and supplier of the Yellow application installer.	+49 0 7136 9511 0 +49 0 7136 9511 11 (fax) info@yellow.de http://www.yellow.de

Getting 'On-line'

The best way of keeping up to date with all that is happening in the world of Psion programming is to join the main 'on-line' discussion groups, particularly if you are 'new' to the Psion environment. Many questions and answers are to be found in this arena which may save you hours of head scratching. It is advisable to aim straight for the FAQ's (frequently asked questions) section, if there is one, before posting questions yourself, to avoid irritating the regulars with questions that have been asked many times before. A copy (September 1997) of the excellent FAQ maintained by Daniel Pfund is in the PSIONFAQ directory on disk. For the most up-to-date version of this FAQ see Daniel Pfund's web site, the URL is listed in the key web site section.

On-line sources

Psion EPOC World news groups	Accessible to EPOC World subscribers only. The news server is 'ew-news.software.psion.com' and access is via your EPOC World user name and password. There are a number of groups including C++, OPL, OPXs.
Usenet groups See your internet service provider for access	The current groups on Usenet are:- comp.sys.psion.announce comp.sys.psion.misc comp.sys.psion.comm comp.sys.psion.apps comp.sys.psion.programmer comp.sys.psion.marketplace comp.sys.psion.reviews
CIX: 0845 355 5050 (UK) admin@cix.co.uk http://www.cix.co.uk/	The conference is called 'Psion', it contains numerous topics and extensive file lists available for download.

CompuServe Tel: 0800 289378 (UK) http://www.compuserve.co.uk/homepages/	The forum is called 'Psion' and contains numerous message boards and file libraries with huge lists of files for download. On-line shareware registration services to users and authors - GO SWREG.

Key programmers' web sites

The following list of web sites represent some of the key Psion related pages that are oriented towards programming (apologies to those not listed). Starting at any of the addresses in the table below should take you to virtually all of the key web sites. All of the sites below have extensive links to other Psion related pages.

Steve Litchfield   http://3lib.ukonline.co.uk
Probably the best page on the web for Psion programmers. A great starting point. Home of the 3-lib shareware library, including Steve's renowned Mapper application.

John Boyce   http://www.compulink.co.uk/~jbsoft/
One of the most productive Psion programmers offering a wide range of excellent freeware.

Rick Andrews   http://web.ukonline.co.uk/Members/rick/
Author of Draw284, probably the best drawing program for Series 3a/c. Series 5 version due any day.

Palmtop Magazine   http://www.palmtop.co.uk & palmtop@aol.com
A finely crafted dedicated magazine, literally packed with Psion related material, including some programming related stuff.

Mark Esposito (Pelican Software)   http://www.pelicansoft.com
A long established and highly respected Psion programmer, producer of the renowned Notepad deluxe application.

Andy Clarkson   http://ourworld.compuserve.com/homepages/andyc
Author of OPP and OPPDBG, the widely used and highly renowned OPL program development utilities.

Daniel Pfund   http://www.geocities.com/SiliconValley/8130/
Maintainer of the excellent and comprehensive Psion FAQ.

Clive Feather   http://www.cityscape.co.uk/users/cdwf/psion/psionics/
Compiler of the Psionics files, the most detailed and comprehensive set of programming related information files outside of the Psion SDKs.

Cade Roux   http://ourworld.compuserve.com/homepages/cade
Probably the most knowledgeable individual on object-oriented programming outside of Psion. See the excellent Solipeg on disk.

Steve Godfrey   http://www.users.dircon.co.uk/~steveg/
An expert Psion C programmer. See the excellent HWIM clocks application on disk.

Konstantin Saliy   http://sunny.aha.ru/~kis/
Author of the renowned keyboard re-mapping program and Hexview1, supplied on disk.

Softbase   http://www.softbase.co.uk/psion/ A very slick Series 5 specific site. Wide range of information including SDK document searches.

Total S5   http://homepages.enterprise.net/livewire
An excellent Series 5 specific site. Wide range of information including links to Series 5 software and S5 FAQs

REGNET   http://www.swregnet.com/
A shareware registration web page – on-line registration of shareware using your credit card.
A service to authors and users. E-mail info@swregnet.com for more information.

EMCC http://www.compulink.co.uk/~emcc/

The publisher of this book. Visit this site for the latest information on this book and CD-ROM, including news of any updates or corrections.

E-mail addresses

Some miscellaneous e-mail addresses you may find useful.

Marco Aicardi, author of OPLprot the anti-Revtran program can be contacted via maicardi@mbox.vol.it

Leigh Edwards, can be contacted via ple@cix.compulink.co.uk or 100533.1726@compuserve.com or during CompuServe access using 100533,1726.

Acknowledgements and credits

As I outlined in the introduction, I am very grateful to many people. I owe considerable thanks to the many individuals who have provided help, example code, answers to questions, numerous utilities, proof reading, artistic design, time and effort expended on my behalf. Without the help of others this book would never have been produced. I have attempted here to acknowledge as many of the key individuals as I could and can only apologise to anyone I may have missed.

I intend to keep this book current and relevant to future developments from Psion and third party developers. If you have any constructive comments, contributions or corrections to this work I would be very grateful to receive them, preferably by E-mail. All significant contributions will be credited, any major contributions will warrant a free copy of a revised edition.

In alphabetical order by Surname:

John Arundel, Rick Andrews, John Boyce, Andrew Baldwin, Jeremy Burton, Steve Clack, Andy Clarkson, Clive Craske, Tom Dolbilin, Simon East, Mark Esposito, Clive D Feather Psionics, Steve Godfrey, Richard Harrision, Les Huett, Steve Litchfield, Ali Manson, Colly Myers, Joe Odukoya, David Palmer, Daniel Pfund, Dave Ponsford, Howard Price, Rosemary Rolfe, Dan Ramage, Cade Roux, Mike Rudin, Konstantin Saliy, Martin Stamp, Martin Tasker, Jeremy Wakefield (Jezar), David Wood.

Appendix

Panic numbers, EPOC16

When EPOC16 detects an error condition that it determines could have only arisen from a bugged application, it will terminate or panic the process in question. An error code called a panic number in the range 0 - 255 will be reported to the user.

Panics, operating system

Panic Code	Description
00	Used by test code when a test fails
01	Invalid function number (semaphore manager)
02	Invalid semaphore handle
03	Semaphore not allocated
04	Initial semaphore count is negative
05	Signal count is negative
06	Invalid function number for process manager
07	Invalid process ID
08	Task tried to create a task
09	Invalid function number for time manager
10	Invalid function number for segment manager
11	Segment size was negative
12	Type was not one of E_SEGMENT_LOW E_SEGMENT_HIGH E_SEGMENT_DEVICE or E_SEGMENT_LOCKED
13	Invalid segment handle
14	Segment copy is out of range
15	Invalid function number for heap manager
16	Heap not initialised
17	A heap cell is being reduced by more than its size
18	Attempt to set heap granularity greater than E_MAX_GROWBY
19	A heap cell address is outside the boundaries of the heap (the heap has probably been corrupted – try calling p_allchk to catch the corruption sooner)
20	Invalid function number for inter-process message manager
21	Inter-process messaging has already been initialised (i.e. p_minit has

Panic Code	Description
	been called twice)
22	Inter-process messaging has not been initialised (i.e. `p_minit` has not been called)
23	Cannot initialise with zero messages in the queue
24	Invalid function number for I/O manager
25	Invalid I/O channel (possibly because you did not test that the previous `p_open` succeeded or you have closed the channel or you overwrote the variable containing the channel)
26	Device requested panic
27	Invalid wait handler handle (possibly nothing to do with wait handlers and just indicative of a low address overwrite of the 4 bytes at address 2 - as a result of an un-initialised pointer)
28	Key and pointing device already hooked
29	Key and pointing device requesting process is not a task
30	Invalid function number for device manager
31	Invalid device handle
32	Invalid function number for file manager
33	Process already connected to file server
34	Reserved for future use
35	Invalid function number for library manager
36	Invalid library handle
37	Invalid function number for library
38	Invalid LIB file channel
39	Invalid DYL index number
40	Invalid message to file server
41	Process has not connected to file server
42	Invalid function number for conversion manager
43	Invalid function number for general manager
44	Attempt to unhook from notify when not already hooked
45	Invalid revector address
46	Invalid function number for conversion manager
47	Leave called before a call to enter (possibly because you were unaware that the function you were calling could call `p_leave`)
48	No method available to handle message (OOP)
49	Invalid reclass attempted (OOP)
50	Unknown category in `LibHandle` (OOP)
51	Unknown class in `LibCreate` (OOP)
52	Supersend called from outside a method (OOP)
53	Attempt to get a handle before being linked (OOP)
54	Missing external categories in `LibLink` (OOP)
55	Object does not point to a valid class (OOP)
56	Invalid link layer completion code
57	Invalid function number for window server

Panic Code	Description
58	Invalid function number for hardware manager
59	Unexpected interrupt
60	Attempted to write outside of process data segment (possibly because of an un-initialised pointer or a corrupted data structure)
61	Interrupts have been disabled for too long
62	Reserved for future use
63	Divide by zero interrupt
64	Overflow interrupt
65	Invalid function number for Dbf manager
66	Invalid DBF I/O channel
67	Invalid parameter for DBF function
68	Address zero overwrite (possibly because of an uninitialised pointer)
69	The operating system detected less than 0x100 bytes of remaining stack (this amount is reserved for hardware interrupts to run). You probably have declared large data structures as automatics. Consider making them static variables or allocate them from the heap.
70	Environment name size > `EnvMaxNameSize`
71	Single step interrupt (INT 1)
72	Break point interrupt (INT 3)
73	A request was made while an asynchronous request of the same type and on the same channel was already pending
74	Invalid function number for serial I/O manager
75	Call to an ASIC1 function on an ASIC9 machine
76	Attempt to find a DYL not in a visible bank
77	Floating point emulator exception
78	Semaphore count exceeds 0x7fff
80	Library fatal error – preceded by a notification of the specific error
255	The function `p_allchk` detected a corrupted heap

Panics, window server

Panic Code	Description
81	Font does not exist
82	Illegal window or bitmap ID
83	Illegal window ID
84	Null handle given to server
85	Illegal graphics context ID
86	Illegal `GMODE` value (V2 only)
87	Illegal `TEXTMODE` value (V2 only)
88	Illegal font ID (V2 only)
89	`wBeginRedraw` called while already in a redraw

Panic Code	Description
90	Mouse icon does not exist
91	Illegal bitmap ID
92	Window tree is already initialised
93	WendRedraw called when there isn't a redraw to end
94	Attempted to change the background of a backed-up window
95	wInitialiseWindowTree called when the *parent* window is not initialised
96	Illegal parameters passed to wsAlertW wsAlertA or wsAlertUpdate
97	Illegal length in gPeekBit (V2 only)
98	Illegal x+length value in gPeekBit (V2 only)
99	Illegal ypos in gPeekBit (V2 only)
100	Tried to connect a second time
101	Tried to access a permanent graphics context while a temporary graphics context exists
102	Illegal opcode in message
103	Command buffer received by wserv is too long
104	Generally bad message received
105	wFree was called with an ID that doesn't refer to a freeable object
106	Illegal DYL ID
107	Out of range count sent to wSetWinBitmap
108	A bitmap was freed while still in use by a wSetWinBitmap command
109	Illegal window-bitmap ID
110	Bad data or version in connect message
111	Called wGetEvent while the previous call was still pending
112	Function not available
113	Illegal clock ID in wsSetClock
114	Illegal sprite ID (V4 only)
115	Client already has a sprite (V4 only)
120	Corrupt control block (possibly not connected)
121	Function number out of range

Panics, object oriented programming (SIBO)

Panic Code	Description
130	Record in flat variable array is out of range
131	Number of record to insert new record before in flat VA is out of range
132	Attempt to set capacity of flat VA less than current number of records
133	Number of record to delete in flat VA is out of range
134	Record in segmented VA is out of range
135	Outside range of segmented buffer
136	Tried to delete outside segmented buffer

Panic Code	Description
137	Record in string VA whose address is sought is out of range
138	Attempt to set capacity of string VA less than current number of records
139	Number of record to insert new record before in string VA is out of range
140	Number of record to delete in string VA is out of range
141	Did not read correct number of bytes from resource file
142	Image fails to contain built-in resource file
143	Stray signal death in Application Manager
144	Request to clear area outside character map
145	Bad type/length binary file record header
146	Read on serial port already outstanding or read buffer not allocated
147	Serial port read buffer too small for requested read
148	Write to serial port already outstanding or write buffer not allocated
149	Serial port write buffer too small for requested write
150	Read on serial port outstanding when tried to see no. of characters available to read
151	Read on serial port outstanding when tried to flush serial read buffer
152	Read or write outstanding when tried to set serial port characteristics
153	Control to set/get not supported
154	OPL translator invoked with empty command line
155	Unrecognised code for setting the console
156	String passed to console is too long
157	IPCS Message read failed
158	Stray signal death in IPCS server list

OPL errors

Good facilities for error trapping, recovery and error simulation are provided in the OPL language and should enable a well designed program to cope with most foreseeable error conditions. See the 'Errors and Debugging' chapter for further details.

OPL errors, general (-1 to -25)

Error Code	Description	OPL32 Constant
-1	General failure	KErrGenFail%
-2	Invalid arguments	KErrInvalidArgs%
-3	Operating system error	KErrOs%
-4	Service not supported	KErrNotSupported%
-5	Underflow (number too small)	KErrUnderflow%
-6	Overflow (number too large)	KErrOverflow%
-7	Out of range	KErrOutOfRange%
-8	Divide by zero	KErrDivideByZero%
-9	In use (e.g. serial port being used by another program)	KErrInUse%
-10	No system memory	KErrNoMemory%
-11	Segment table full	KErrNoSegments%
-12	Semaphore table full	KErrNoSemaphore%
-13	Process table full/too many processes	KErrNoProcess%
-14	Resource already open	KErrAlreadyOpen%
-15	Resource not open	KErrNotOpen%
-16	Invalid image/device file	KErrImage%
-17	No receiver	KErrNoReceiver%
-18	Device table full	KErrNoDevices%
-19	File system not found (e.g. if you unplug cable to PC)	KErrNoFileSystem%
-20	Failed to start	KErrFailedToStart%
-21	Font not loaded	KErrFontNotLoaded%
-22	Too wide (dialogs)	KErrTooWide%
-23	Too many items (dialogs)	KErrTooManyItems%
-24	Batteries too low for digital audio	KErrBatLowSound%
-25	Batteries too low to write to flash/disk	KErrBatLowFlash%
-26 to -31	Unknown error	

OPL errors, file and device (-32 to -69)

Error Code	Description	OPL32 Constant
-32	File already exists	KErrExists%
-33	File does not exist	KErrNotExists%
-34	Write failed	KErrWrite%
-35	Read failed	KErrRead%
-36	End of file (when you try to read past end of file)	KErrEof%
-37	Disk full	KErrFull%
-38	Invalid name	KErrName%
-39	Access denied (e.g. to a protected file on PC)	KErrAccess%
-40	File or device in use	KErrLocked%
-41	Device does not exist	KErrDevNotExist%
-42	Directory/folder does not exist	KErrDir%
-43	Record too large	KErrRecord%
-44	Read only file	KErrReadOnly%
-45	Invalid I/O request	KErrInvalidIO%
-46	I/O operation pending	KErrFilePending%
-47	Invalid volume (corrupt disk)	KErrVolume%
-48	I/O cancelled	KErrIOCancelled%
-50	Disconnected	
-51	Connected	
-52	Too many retries	
-53	Line failure	
-54	Inactivity timeout	
-55	Incorrect parity	
-56	Serial frame (usually because Baud setting is wrong)	
-57	Serial overrun (usually because Handshaking is wrong)	
-58	Cannot connect to remote modem	
-59	Remote modem busy	
-60	No answer from remote modem	
-61	Number is black listed (you may try a number only a certain number of times; wait a while and try again)	
-62	Not ready	
-63	Unknown media (corrupt SSD)	
-64	Root directory/folder is full (on any device the root directory has a maximum amount of memory allocated to it)	
-65	Write protected	

Error Code	Description	OPL32 Constant
-66	File/media is corrupt	
-67	User abandoned	
-68	Erase pack failure	
-69	Wrong file type	

OPL errors, translator (-70 to -95)

Error Code	Description	OPL32 Constant
-70	Missing "	
-71	String too long	
-72	Unexpected name	
-73	Name too long	
-74	Logical device must be A-D (A-Z in OPL32)	
-75	Bad field name	
-76	Bad number	
-77	Syntax error	KErrSyntax%=
-78	Illegal character	
-79	Function argument error	
-80	Type mismatch	
-81	Missing label	
-82	Duplicate name	
-83	Declaration error	
-84	Bad array size	
-85	Structure fault	KOplStructure%
-86	Missing endp	
-87	Syntax Error	
-88	Mismatched (or)	
-89	Bad field list	
-90	Too complex	
-91	Missing ,	
-92	Variables too large	
-93	Bad assignment	
-94	Bad array index	
-95	Inconsistent procedure arguments	

OPL errors, specific (-96 to -120)

Error Code	Description	OPL32 Constant
-96	Illegal Opcode (corrupt module - translate again)	KErrIllegal%
-97	Wrong number of arguments (to a function or parameters to a procedure)	KErrNumArg%
-98	Undefined externals (a variable has been encountered which hasn't been declared	KErrUndef%
-99	Procedure not found	KErrNoProc%
-100	Field not found	KErrNoFld%
-101	File already open	KErrOpen%
-102	File not open	KErrClosed%
-103	Record too big (data file contains record too big for OPL)	KErrRecSize%
-104	Module already loaded (when trying to LOADM)	KErrModLoad%
-105	Maximum modules loaded (when trying to LOADM)	KErrMaxLoad%
-106	Module does not exist (when trying to LOADM)	KErrNoMod%
-107	Incompatible translator version (OPL file needs retranslation)	KErrNewVer%
-108	Module not loaded (when trying to UNLOADM)	KErrModNotLoaded%
-109	Bad file type (data file header wrong or corrupt)	KErrBadFileType%
-110	Type violation (passing wrong type to parameter)	KErrTypeViol%
-111	Subscript or dimension error (out of range in array)	KErrSubs%
-112	String too long	KErrStrTooLong%
-113	Device already open (when trying to LOPEN)	KErrDevOpen%
-114	Escape key pressed	KErrEsc%
-115	Incompatible runtime version	
-116	ODB file(s) not closed	
-117	Maximum drawables open (maximum 8 windows and/or bitmaps allowed)	KErrMaxDraw%
-118	Drawable not open	KErrDrawNotOpen%
-119	Invalid window (window operation attempted on a bitmap)	KErrInvalidWindow%
-120	Screen access denied (when run from Calculator)	KErrScreenDenied%

OPL32 errors (-121 to -126)

Error Code	Description	
-121	OPX does not exist	KErrOpxNotFound%
-122	Incompatible OPX version	KErrOpxVersion%
-123	OPX procedure not found	KErrOpxProcNotFound%
-124	STOP used in call back	KErrStopInCallback%
-125	Incompatible update mode	KErrIncompUpdateMode%
-126	In transaction	KErrInTransaction%
-127	Include file cannot contain procedures	
-128	Too many OPX's	
-129	Too many OPX functions	
-130	Undefined variable	
-131	Undefined procedure	
-132	Icon mask missing	
-133	Incompatible declaration	
-134 -	Unknown error	

OVAL errors

Many structural and syntax errors are detected by the OVAL translator, fatal errors during run-time are usually trapped by the OVAL interpreter. The OVAL run-time environment is well protected and panics should be rare. See the 'Errors and Debugging' chapter for details of how to avoid and detect errors.

Error Code	Description	OVAL Global Constant
0		ERR_NO_ERR
3	Return requires GoSub	ERR_RET_NO_GOSUB
5	Illegal function argument	ERR_ILLEGAL_FUNCTION_CALL
6	Overflow	ERR_OVERFLOW
7	No system memory	ERR_OUT_OF_MEMORY
9	Subscript out of bounds	ERR_INDX_OUT_OF_BOUNDS
11	Divide by zero	ERR_DIVIDE_0
13	Type mismatch	ERR_TYPE_MISMATCH
14	No string memory	ERR_OUT_OF_STRING_SPACE
19	Resume missing	ERR_NO_RESUME
20	Resume outside error handler	ERR_RESUME_NO_ERR
28	No stack memory	ERR_OUT_OF_STACK_SPACE
51	Internal error	ERR_INTERNAL
52	Invalid file name/number	ERR_BAD_FILE_NUMBER
53	File not found	ERR_FILE_NOT_FOUND

Error Code	Description	OVAL Global Constant
54	Invalid file mode	ERR_BAD_FILE_MODE
55	File already open	ERR_FILE_ALREADY_OPEN
57	I/O error	ERR_IO
58	File already exists	ERR_FILE_ALREADY_EXISTS
59	Invalid record length	ERR_BAD_RECORD_LENGTH
61	Disk full	ERR_DISK_FULL
62	Input beyond end of file	ERR_INPUT_PAST_EOF
63	Invalid record number	ERR_BAD_RECORD_NUMBER
67	Max files reached	ERR_TOO_MANY_FILES
68	Device not available	ERR_INVALID_DRIVE
70	Access denied	ERR_ACCESS_DENIED
71	Disk not present	ERR_DISK_NOT_READY
75	Invalid path or filename	ERR_FILE_ACCESS
76	Invalid path	ERR_PATH_NOT_FOUND
91	Object not Set before use	ERR_OBJECT_VARIABLE_NOT_SET
93	Invalid match pattern	ERR_PATTERN_INVALID
94	Invalid Null argument	ERR_INVALID_USE_OF_NULL
321	Unknown file format	ERR_INVALID_FILE_FORMAT
340	Control array element does not exist	ERR_CA_ELEMENT_NOT_EXIST
341	Invalid control array index	ERR_INVALID_CA_INDEX
343	Object is not an array	ERR_OBJ_NOT_ARRAY
344	Object array requires index	ERR_NO_INDEX_FOR_ARRAY
360	Control array element already loaded	ERR_OBJ_ALREADY_LOADED
362	Design time controls cannot be unloaded	ERR_CANT_UNLOAD_CONTROL
365	Form unload disabled	ERR_CANT_UNLOAD
380	Property value is invalid	ERR_INVALID_PROPERTY_VALUE
381	Property array index is invalid	ERR_INVALID_ARRAY_INDEX
383	Cannot write to property	ERR_PROPERTY_READ_ONLY
385	Property array requires index	ERR_NEED_INDEX
386	Property only available at design time	ERR_NOT_RT_PROP
394	Cannot read property	ERR_PROPERTY_WRITE_ONLY
400	Cannot show form modally	ERR_CANTSHOWMODALLY
401	Cannot show form non-modally	ERR_CANTSHOWNONMODALLY
402	Close or hide topmost modal form first	ERR_MUSTCLOSEMODAL
422	Property does not exist	ERR_PROPERTY_NOT_FOUND
423	Property or control does not exist	ERR_PROP_CONTROL_NOT_FOUND
3001	Invalid argument	ERR_DA_INV_ARG
3002	Could not start DBS server	ERR_DA_SESSION

Error Code	Description	OVAL Global Constant
3006	Database ' ' is locked	ERR_DA_DB_EXLOCKED
3008	Table ' ' is locked	ERR_DA_TB_EXLOCKED
3009	Table ' ' could not be locked	ERR_DA_TB_IN_USE
3010	Table ' ' already exists	ERR_DA_TB_EXISTS
3011	Could not find item ' '	ERR_DA_OBJ_NOT_FOUND
3015	Table does not contain index ' '	ERR_DA_TB_NOT_INDEX
3017	Field too long	ERR_DA_FLD_TOO_LONG
3018	Field ' ' not found	ERR_DA_FLD_NOT_FOUND
3019	No current index	ERR_DA_INV_NO_INDEX
3020	Update requires Edit or AddNew	ERR_DA_BAD_UPDATE
3021	Operation requires current record	ERR_DA_NO_RECORD
3022	Duplicate key	ERR_DA_DUPLICATE
3023	Edit or AddNew already called	ERR_DA_ADD_EDIT
3024	File ' ' not found	ERR_DA_FILE_NOT_FOUND
3026	Disk full	ERR_DA_NO_DISK_SPACE
3027	Database is read-only	ERR_DA_DB_READ_ONLY
3040	I/O read error	ERR_DA_DISK_IO
3044	Invalid path ' '	ERR_DA_INV_PATH
3046	Table locked	ERR_DA_LOCKED
3051	File ' ' could not be opened	ERR_DA_FILE_OPEN_FAIL
3070	Failed to bind name ' '	ERR_DA_BIND_NAME
3113	Field ' ' not updatable	ERR_DA_NO_UPDATE
3125	Invalid name	ERR_DA_NAME
3146	Table open when deleting index	ERR_DA_ODBC_FAIL
3159	Invalid bookmark	ERR_DA_BMARK
3162	Field cannot be Null	ERR_DA_INV_NULL
3163	Field data too long	ERR_DA_DATA_TOO_LONG
3170	Installable ISAM not found	ERR_DA_ISAM
3191	Duplicate field name	ERR_DA_FLD_TWICE
3204	Database already exists	ERR_DA_DB_EXISTS
3218	Record locked	ERR_DA_UPDATE_LOCKED
3219	Illegal operation	ERR_DA_ILLEGAL
3250	Index could not be built	ERR_DA_BAD_KEY
3259	Invalid field type	ERR_DA_TYPE
3264	Cannot append table with no fields	ERR_DA_NO_FIELDS
3265	Collection item not found	ERR_DA_NOT_FOUND
3266	Cannot append Field	ERR_DA_FLD_APPEND
3267	Invalid use of property 'Value'	ERR_DA_FLD_PROPERTY
3268	Property cannot be set	ERR_DA_DB_PROPERTY
3269	Cannot append Index	ERR_DA_IDX_APPEND
3273	Method not available	ERR_DA_METHOD

Error Code	Description	OVAL Global Constant
3283	Primary index already defined	ERR_DA_PRIMARY
3284	Index already exists	ERR_DA_IDX_EXISTS
3290	Syntax error	ERR_DA_SYNTAX
30009	Row value invalid	ERR_GRID_INVALID_ROW
30010	Column value invalid	ERR_GRID_INVALID_COLUMN
30011	Grid/database synchronisation error	ERR_GRID_DB_ERROR
31000	Unknown error[0]	
31001	General failure	
31002	Invalid arguments	
31003	O/S error	
31004	Service not supported	
31005	Underflow	
31006	Overflow	
31007	Out of range	
31008	Divide by zero	
31009	In use	
31010	No system memory	
31011	Segment table full	
31012	Semaphore table full	
31013	Too many processes	
31014	Resource already open	
31015	Resource not open	
31016	Invalid image/device file	
31017	No receiver	
31018	Device table full	
31019	File system not found	
31020	Failed to start	
31021	Font not loaded	
31022	Too wide	
31023	Too many items	
31024	Batteries too low for digital audio	
31025	Batteries too low to write to Flash	
31026 – 31031	Unknown error[-26 to -31]	
31032	File already exists	
31033	File does not exist	
31034	Write failed	
31035	Read failed	
31036	End of file	
31037	Disk full	
31038	Invalid name	
31039	Access denied	

Error Code	Description	OVAL Global Constant
31040	File or device in use	
31041	Device does not exist	
31042	Directory does not exist	
31043	Record too large	
31044	Read only file	
31045	Invalid I/O request	
31046	I/O operation pending	
31047	Invalid volume	
31048	I/O cancelled	
31050	Disconnected	
31051	Connected	
31052	Too many retries	
31053	Line failure	
31054	Inactivity timeout	
31055	Incorrect parity	
31056	Serial frame	
31057	Serial overrun	
31058	Cannot connect to remote modem	
31059	Remote modem busy	
31060	No answer from remote modem	
31061	Number is black listed	
31062	Not ready	
31063	Unknown media	
31064	Root directory full	
31065	Write protected	
31066	Media is corrupt	
31067	User abandoned	
31068	Erase disk failure	
31069	Wrong file type	
31070	Missing "	
31071	String too long	
31072	Unexpected name	
31073	Name too long	
31074	Logical device must be A-D	
31075	Bad field name	
31076	Bad number	
31077	Syntax error	
31078	Illegal character	
31079	Function argument error	
31080	Type mismatch	
31081	Missing label	
31082	Duplicate name	

Error Code	Description	OVAL Global Constant
31083	Declaration error	
31084	Bad array size	
31085	Structure fault	
31086	Missing endp	
31087	Syntax Error	
31088	Mismatched (or)	
31089	Bad field list	
31090	Too complex	
31091	Missing ,	
31092	Variables too large	
31093	Bad assignment	
31094	Bad array index	
31095	Inconsistent procedure arguments	
31096	Illegal Opcode	
31097	Wrong number of arguments	
31098	Undefined externals	
31099	Procedure not found	
31100	Field not found	
31101	File already open	
31102	File not open	
31103	Record too big	
31104	Module already loaded	
31105	Maximum modules loaded	
31106	Module does not exist	
31107	Incompatible translator version	
31108	Module not loaded	
31109	Bad file type	
31110	Type violation	
31111	Subscript or dimension error	
31112	String too long	
31113	Device already open	
31114	Escape key pressed	
31115	Incompatible runtime version	
31116	ODB file(s) not closed	
31117	Maximum drawables open	
31118	Drawable not open	
31119	Invalid window	
31120	Screen access denied	
31121 – 31127	Unknown error[-121 to -127]	
31500	' ' is not an OVAL application	
31501	OVAL application ' ' is corrupt	
31502	Unable to locate OVAL extension	

Error Code	Description	OVAL Global Constant
	' '	
31503	Cannot find OVAL component ' '	
31504	Incompatible version of OVAL component ' '	
31505	' ' cannot be run. It is only for design	
31506	' ' cannot be run. Incompatible translator version	
31507	Unable to locate OVAL extension ' ' in RAM	

Magic (reserved) static variables

The EPOC16 reserved statics (commonly refered to as magic statics) are variables with fixed, known, addresses, existing in the process data space (i.e. a unique set for each process) between addresses 0x00 and 0x40. They are 'magic' in the sense that they are accessible from all parts of the process code, even from dynamic library code (which does not have any data space and therefore may not normally access statics).

Some of these variables are used by the operating system as part of the process context. Others are used by system code such as the window server, and the graphics user interface libraries. The specific usage differs depending on the model of SIBO machine.

The remaining reserved statics are freely available for use by the process code. A common use is to provide access from dynamic library code to application-specific data, without the need for it to be passed in function parameters.

Magic static	Purpose
0x00 DatWordDead	The word at this address contains the value 0xDEAD. This value must not be changed by application code. Many operating system calls check for this value and will panic the process with panic reason code PanicDead0 if it has changed. A change in this value is symptomatic of a common software bug; the unintentional use of a NULL pointer.
0x02 DatHandNext 0x04 DatHandPrev	The data at these two addresses are used as pointers to a queue of wait handler function descriptors. This data should not be modified by application code.
0x06 DatCountrySeg	This holds the segment handle of the data segment containing the country and language specific fold tables for the process. This data should not be modified by application code.
0x08 DatClassHandle 0x0a DatClassPtr	In applications which use any of the object oriented

Magic static	Purpose
	programming calls (this includes use of HWIF programs) these locations hold data required by the operating system to work out how to send a message to an object's superclass. It is recommended that application code does not modify the contents of these locations.
0x0c DatEClassHandle 0x0e DatEClassPtr	In applications which use any of the object oriented programming calls (this includes use of HWIF) these locations hold data required by the operating system to work out how to perform a p_exactsend. It is recommended that application code does not modify the contents of these locations.
0x10 DatEnterFramePtr	The enter and leave mechanism provided by the operating system uses this address to store the pointer to the last enter frame generated on the stack. When a leave occurs this pointer is used to unwind the stack and restore the register set. This location should not be modified by application code.
0x12 w_ws	In applications that use system user interface libraries this location is assumed to hold the object handle of an instance of the 'wserv' object. The application is responsible for ensuring that this location is set up correctly, normally by calling system code on application start-up.
0x14 w_am	In applications that use the application manager object (all object oriented programs and HWIF programs) this location is assumed to hold the object handle of an instance of the application manager object. The application is responsible for ensuring that this location is set up correctly, normally by calling system code on application start-up.
0x16 wClientData 0x18 wserv_channel	These locations are used by the window server process to store information about your application. If you use any graphics functions you should not modify the contents of these locations.
0x1a T	This location is used by the OPL language translator. If your application does not use OPL then this location is free for use by application code.
0x1c r	This location is used by the OPL language runtime code. If your application does not use OPL then this location is free for use by application code.
0x1e DatOsFramePtr	This location contains a pointer to the last member of a linked list of operating system calling frames. Following this linked list will show which functions called which operating system services. This location should not be modified by application code.

Magic static	Purpose
0x20 DatATFlag	This byte location contains the current address trap status for the process. Certain operating system calls cause address trapping to be turned on or off and the operating system sets or clears this flag to record the current address trap hardware status. Just setting the flag to zero will *not* disable address trapping. This location should not be modified by application code.
0x21 DatHeapLocked	This byte location contains the current state of the heap locked flag. While the heap is being modified (for example, being resized, due to a memory allocation request) the heap is locked. This prevents the operating system from compressing the segment while the data structures used by the operating system to run the heap are in an inconsistent state. This location should not be modified by application code.
0x22 DatProcessNamePtr	System user interface library code assumes that this location contains either NULL or a pointer to a zero terminated string that the application wishes to be displayed as its name. Otherwise it is free for use by application code.
0x24 DatCommandPtr	This location contains a pointer, set up by the operating system. It points to an alloc cell that contains the full path name, as a zero terminated string, of the *.img* or *.app* file from which the process was loaded. Immediately following the zero terminator, the alloc cell contains leading byte counted initial command line data.
0x26 DatTest	Psion's test system library code assumes that this location contains the object handle of the test code. Otherwise it is free for use by application code.
0x28 DatApp1 0x2a DatApp2 0x2c DatApp3 0x2e DatApp4 0x30 DatApp5 0x32 DatApp6 0x34 DatApp7	These locations are free for application code to use.
0x36 DatDialogPtr	System user interface library code may assume that this location contains a pointer to the current dialog structure. Otherwise it is free for use by application code.
0x38 DatGate	System user interface library code may assume that this location contains an object handle. Otherwise it is free for use by application code.
0x3a DatLocked	System user interface library code may assume that this location contains a flag indicating whether the application is capable of receiving termination or switch files messages. Otherwise it is free for use by application code.

Magic static	Purpose
0x3c DatStatusNamePtr	System user interface library code may assume that this location contains a pointer to a zero terminated string that will appear in a status window. Otherwise it is free for use by application code.
0x3e DatUsedPathNamePtr	System user interface library code may assume that this location contains a pointer to a fully parsed file name. Otherwise it is free for use by application code.

Language and country data

Psion machines are produced in a number of language variants, and may differ in the following respects:

- the language code
- the language of the text used by the ROM-based software (for example, the error messages returned by p_errs and the month names returned by p_nmmon)
- character type and conversion tables
- the keyboard layout
- the default country and country-dependent data

A particular language variant will always have a different language code and text, but may not differ in all of the above.

Systems are designed to be produced in a variety of languages and, as far as SIBO system services are concerned, all the above variations are encapsulated in a single configuration file in the ROM called ROM::SYS$CTRY.CFO. Depending on the machine, there may be further files (for example, 'resource files') containing language-dependent data for higher-level system components.

Unlike the language-dependent data, the country-dependent data may be altered from the language-dependent defaults.

Get machine language code

```
INT p_getlanguage(VOID);
lang% = CALL($1b8b) REM as called in OPL16
```

Return the language code from the ROM configuration file. The language code can be used by applications that contain the text for more than one language to determine which language to present. The language codes, defined in p_config.h, are as follows:

Notes:
With Series 5 systems, there are slight differences from the SIBO language codes. Constants for the language codes are supplied in CONST.OPH for OPL32 .

Code	Country, SIBO	Country, EPOC32	OPL32 Constant
1	English	English	KLangEnglish%
2	French	French	KLangFrench%
3	German	German	KLangGerman%
4	Spanish	Spanish	KLangSpanish%
5	Italian	Italian	KLangItalian%
6	Swedish	Swedish	KLangSwedish%
7	Danish	Danish	KLangDanish%
8	Norwegian	Norwegian	KLangNorwegian%
9	Finnish	Finnish	KLangFinnish%
10	USA	American	KLangAmerican%
11	Swiss French	Swiss French	KLangSwissFrench%
12	Swiss German	Swiss German	KLangSwissGerman%
13	Portuguese	Portuguese	KLangPortuguese%
14	Turkish	Turkish	KLangTurkish%
15	Icelandic	Icelandic	KLangIcelandic%
16	Russian	Russian	KLangRussian%
17	Hungarian	Hungarian	KLangHungarian%
18	Dutch	Dutch	KLangDutch%
19	Belgian Flemish	Belgian Flemish	KLangBelgianFlemish%
20	Australian	Australian	KLangAustralian%
21	New Zealand	Belgian-French	KLangBelgianFrench%
22	Austrian	Austrian	KLangAustrian%
23	Belgian French	New Zealand	KLangNewZealand%
24		International French	KLangInternationalFrench%

Often, language codes are included as part of file names to load language specific information e.g. with resource files. When the language code is less than 10 it is usual to pad the number with a leading zero in making up the file name. For example, to load a French resource file, with a country code of 2, the file name would typically become MYTEXT02.RSC instead of MYTEXT2.RSC.

Get O/S error text

```
INT p_errs(TEXT *pBuffer, INT n);

REM in OPL16
AX%=              REM set to negative error number n
bx%=              REM points to a 64 byte data buffer
r%=CALL($068b,bx%)
```

Get the error string n from the ROM configuration file and write it to pBuffer. Returns zero if successful or the 'Unknown error' if n is outside the range of error text strings in the configuration file.

Get O/S message text

```
INT p_gettext(INT n, TEXT *pBuffer);

REM in OPL16
AX%=              REM set to message number n
bx%=              REM points to a 64 byte data buffer
r%=CALL($148b,bx%)
```

Get the nth string from the ROM configuration file and write it to pBuffer. Returns zero if successful or the negative E_GEN_ARG if n is outside the range of the text strings in the configuration file. This function is called by specific text retrieval functions such as p_errs and p_nmmon.

Applications only need to use p_gettext when retrieving text associated with a higher level of system software (in which case the documentation of the higher level software will list appropriate values of n).

Get country-dependent data

```
VOID p_getctd(E_CONFIG *pcfg);

bx%=                REM points to a 40 byte data buffer
r%=CALL($058b,bx%)  REM as called in OPL16
```

Write a copy of the system E_CONFIG struct to pcfg where the E_CONFIG struct is defined in p_config.h as:

```
typedef struct
    {
    UWORD countryCode;
    WORD gmtOffset;
    UBYTE dateType;
    UBYTE timeType;
    UBYTE currencySymbolPosition;
    UBYTE currencySpaceRequired;
    UBYTE currencyDecimalPlaces;
    UBYTE currencyNegativeInBrackets;
    UBYTE currencyTriadsAllowed;
    UBYTE thousandsSeparator;
    UBYTE decimalSeparator;
    UBYTE dateSeparator;
    UBYTE timeSeparator;
    UBYTE currencySymbol[9];
    UBYTE startOfWeek;
    UBYTE summerTime;
    UBYTE clockType;
    UBYTE dayAbbreviation;
    UBYTE monthAbbreviation;
    UBYTE workDays;
    UBYTE units;
    UBYTE spare[9];
    } E_CONFIG;.
```

The countryCode specifies a country by its international dialling code.

EPOC16 identifiers

Details of many identifiers or defines, environment variables and reserved (magic) statics are given here to assist the reader, however the current value of any of the identifiers referred to here should always be confirmed by reference to other relevant documentation e.g. header files (i.e. .h or .g files) provided with the appropriate SDK.

For defines/identifiers see the **defines.dbf** (in the DEFINES directory) Psion database file on the supplementary disks for a comprehensive set of defines with their corresponding numerical values.

Identifiers	code	Description
E_MAX_NAME	12	maximum length of an EPOC16 process name
E_MAX_ENV_SIZE	16	maximum length of the name of an environment variable
E_MAX_PROCESSES	24	maximum number of active processes running under EPOC16
P_FNAMESIZE	128	maximum length of an EPOC16 file specification see EPOCDEFS.H
E_PRIORITY_FORE	128	the default priority of a foreground process
P_ENVMAX	256	maximum size of an environment variable in bytes

EPOC16 Environment variables

A list of all the SIBO system and application environment variables and their functions.

The following table lists all environment variables on SIBO systems that are created or read by Psion's software. All Psion environment variable names contain the $ character, any your own applications may create should never contain the $ character.

Name	Environment Variable Function
EM$	Used by the CLIB and PLIB startup modules. Contains a string that specifies a search path for the 8087 floating point emulator.
$WS_FL	On HC with V3.5 of the window server, and all machines using version 4 or later. The initial value of the internal parameter that is set by wSystem is loaded from the $WS_FL environment variable when the window server starts. Ensures the window server will:- provide the notifier service, report low battery voltages, present a hung-up status window if an application hangs, report a process that terminates with a panic or with a negative reason number.

Name	Environment Variable Function
$WS_FNTS	Contains a series of words, each of which includes the index of a font used by the window server, as follows:- system font, notifier/alert font, status window font, symbols font used for the status window diamond symbol, medium 2 digital clock font, medium 2 date font, notifier/alert button font, small status window clock font.
$WS_IF	HC: the font used for output that is not graphics context directed is determined by the $WS_IF ("Internal Font") environment variable. Should contain a WORD binary value of 0 for WS_FONT_BASE, 1 for WS_FONT_BASE+1, etc. If you change the value of $WS_IF, you must reset the machine. The "factory" setting of $WS_IF is 4 (which selects the S3 font).
$WS_SD	Pressing shift-ctrl-psion-s on MC, S3, S3a/3c, Siena or Work*about* saves the current screen to a file called screen.pic in the current path of the window server. An existing file of the same name is replaced. The current path of the window server on a SIBO machine is always LOC::M:\. If an environment variable with the name $WS_SD exists, the window server uses its value to open the file to be created. E.g. running the following program: ```\n#include <p_std.h>\n\nGLDEF_C INT main(VOID)\n {\n p_setenv("$WS_SD","B:\\SCREEN.PIC");\n return(0);\n }\n``` subsequently causes the screen dump to be written to the root directory of the local *B:* drive. If the save fails for any reason, the file is not produced and no notification of the failure is given. You can use this behaviour to disable the shift-ctrl-psion-s screen dump key by setting up $WS_SD to contain an illegal file specification. E.g. inserting the following line of code:- p_setenv("$WS_SD","");disables the screen dump key.
$WS_SF	Determines the system font, which should contain a WORD binary value of 0 for WS_FONT_BASE, a WORD binary value of 1 for WS_FONT_BASE+1, etc. If you change the value of $WS_SF, you must reset the machine
M$V	Evaluator format preferences, stored as an HWIM EXTENDED_MEM_VALUES structure. Read and written by the ws_eval_env method of the WSERV class.
D$X	Values may vary in non-English machines. Telephone dialling preferences, stored as a DIAL_ENVAR structure. Read and written by ws_dial_env method of the WSERV class. Normal default values are: toneLengthTicks = 8, delayLengthTicks = 8, pauseLengthTicks = 48, dialOutCode[] = "9".

Name	Environment Variable Function
L$X	Read by the S3c only, to provide an extra option for the 'Use' choice list of the System Screen's 'Communications' dialog. Should contain three leading byte counted items which are:- text for the extra option, which will be appended to the choice list; full file specification of the file to `p_execc` if the new option is selected; additional command line data. E.g. to add an 'IRcom' option that executes the file `loc::m:\sys$irc.img`, passing it the command line "-P1", the environment variable could be set (using an HC-style Command Processor).by: set `L$X=\05IRCom\13LOC::M:\SYS$IRC.IMG\03-P1` Additional command line options can be appended to any specified using the 'Extra parameters' line in the System screen's 'Communications' dialog.
P$D	Type of the port used for printing, held as a zero terminated character containing a single ASCII digit. The possible port types are:- `PRINTER_PORT_PARALLEL` = `'0'`; `PRINTER_PORT_SERIAL` = `'1'`; `PRINTER_PORT_FILE` = `'2'`; `PRINTER_PORT_FAX` = `'3'`. The default value represents `PRINTER_PORT_PARALLEL`. Set/created by the `PRINTER pr_set_port_type` method, got by the `PRINTER pr_port_data` method.
P$F	File to which printing is to be directed, held as a zero terminated character string. The default print file name is `p.lis`. Set/created by the `PRINTER pr_store_srchar` method, got by the `PRINTER pr_port_data` method.
P$S	Characteristics of the serial port when used for printing, held as a `P_SRCHAR` structure. Default values are: tbaud = `P_BAUD_9600`, rbaud = `P_BAUD_9600`, frame = `P_DATA_8`, parity = `0`, hand = `P_OBEY_XOFF|P_OBEY_DSR|P_IGN_CTS`, xoff = `oX11`, xon = `oZ11`, flags = `0`, tmask = `0`. Set/created by the `PRINTER pr_store_srchar` method, got by the `PRINTER pr_port_data` method.
P$M	Specification of the current printer model, held as a zero terminated character string, which contains an ASCII digit, followed by the name of a printer driver (`.wdr`) file. The digit specifies the index number, starting from zero, of the model within the printer driver file. The default value is `"OBJ.WDR"` (the file `bj.wdr` is in the ROM of relevant machines and contains only one model - for the BJ-10e printer). Set/created by the `PRINTER pr_set_model` method, got by the `PRINTER pr_sense_model` method.
P$P	Contains two bytes of data that specify the display preferences for print preview. The first byte is an ASCII digit specifying the number of pages to display, which must be in the range '1' to '4'. The second byte is also an ASCII digit, which may be '1', indicating that margins are to be visible during print preview, or '0'. Set/created by the `PRVVIEW wn_init` method

Name	Environment Variable Function
P$PP	Port used for parallel printing, specified as a single ASCII character, for example, 'B'. Should only be set on machines that have more than one port, such as the Work*about*. It is read, but not created, by the `pr_sense_port` method of the `PRINTER` class.
P$SP	Port used for serial printing, specified as a single ASCII character, for example, 'A'. Should only be set on machines that have more than one port, such as the Work*about*. It is read but not created, by the `pr_sense_port` method of the `PRINTER` class.
P$Z	Paper size, stored as a single ASCII digit. It is normally '0' (A4) or '4' (Letter). Only used on the Siena & 3c. It is not supported on Siena, version 4.20 or below.
P$IP	Single ASCII character, specifying the port letter for the IR printing device. Used on the Siena & S3c only.
P$PX	Contains device type & serial characteristics for 'Parallel' printing. Used only on the Siena and the Series 3c, which communicate with the Parallel cable via a serial interface. Contains a one byte device type (0 is parallel) followed by a `P_SRCHAR` struct, as defined in `p_serial.h`. Used on the Siena & S3c only
C$CALC	Used on Siena & S3c machines only, stores Calculator display preferences.
M$0M0 to M$9M9	Contain the current values of the ten (Advanced view) calculator memories. The names are dependent on the names of the memories, as seen from within the Calculator application, e.g if memory M2 is renamed to "Memory2", the environment variable `M$2M2` will be replaced by an environment variable with the name `M$2MEMORY2`. The names will never exceed eleven characters.
TW$S	Contains permanent data for the Tips application. The data consists of a single byte containing two flags: `0x02` = if set, the display of tips is enabled `0x04` = if set, tips are displayed once per day, otherwise they are displayed whenever the machine is turned on
W$C	Contains display preferences for World application, as three `WORD`s:- clock type: `WS_CLOCK_FORCE_ANALOG` or `WS_CLOCK_FORCE_DIGITAL` map colour: `TRUE` for grey map `FALSE` for black map distance units: `WR_UNITS_MILES` (0), `WR_UNITS_KILOMETERS` (1) or `WR_UNITS_NAUTICAL` (2)
W$R	Stores permanent data for the World database. Content has 3 elements:- a signature for the world database file, including file version; data specifying home city; data specifying default country, that is, the country to which telephone numbers are assumed to belong if a country is not specified.

Name	Environment Variable Function
SP$DRV	Identifies the drive that contains the Spellchecker's global dictionary, as set from the Spell application's Install menu option. It contains a single ASCII character that may be 'A', 'B' or 'M'.
SP$OPT	Stores the preferences settings from the Spell application as a series of flags, stored in a single UWORD. Contents affect spellchecker & thesaurus (not necessarily used by both). The content is an ORed combination of the following set of values, selected by the user from the Spell application's Preferences menu option: 0x0100: if set, ignore words all in upper case 0x0200: if set, ignore words containing punctuation 0x0400: if set, ignore repeated words 0x0800: if set, ignore the case of repeated words 0x1000: if set, show the definitions window
WP$SPEL	Used by all applications that may wish to access Spellchecker. The content is a single byte with a value of zero, but has no significance. Its existence indicates that Spellchecker is installed.
WP$THES	Used by all applications that may wish to access the Thesaurus. The content is a single byte with a value of zero, but has no significance. Its existence indicates that the Thesaurus is installed.
F$X	Contains two bytes of preferences. The first byte contains one of the ASCII characters 'M', 'A' or 'B', representing the drive that is currently used to store the application's intermediate files. The second byte contains a combination of the following flags: 0x01: if set, a new fax job is created on selection of 'Print to fax'. Otherwise, the document is simply processed to produce an intermediate file, for later sending 0x02: if set, intermediate files are automatically deleted after they have been sent
F$XM	Contains the current 3Fax modem parameters.
F$XP	Stores power usage data for the 3Fax device. Contains time on batteries and time on mains.

Name	Environment Variable Function
MAIL$ST	Used, with some differences in content, by both the Corporate and the Internet PsiMail applications. It is created by an email application whenever a mail session completes, to contain data passed from the message transfer agent (MTA) to the mail client. It is not a permanent store of data, as it is deleted and recreated every time the MTA starts. A MAIL$ST environment variable created by the Corporate mail application will not disrupt the Internet mail application, should it be run on the same machine, and vice versa. The content for the Corporate application consists of a sequence of five UWORDs, in the following order:- a count of the messages that were sent; a count of the messages that were received; a count of the messages that were not sent; a count of the messages that are marked as read; a flag which, if set to TRUE, indicates that some messages were not received The content for the Internet application consists of a sequence of eight UWORDs, in the following order: a count of the messages that were sent; a count of the messages that were received; a count of the messages that were not sent; a count of the messages that are marked as read; a count of messages that were deleted from the mail server; the return code from the MTA; the return code from the sending process (normally 0); the return code from the receiving process (normally 0). The first 4 items are common to both variants of MAIL$ST.
S$SVER	Contains a text string representing the Workabout System Screen version number, for example, "1.00F". Only used on Workabout
C$P@	Set when exiting from the Workabout command processor. It contains a single ASCII character representing the current drive, default value of 'M'. Only used on Workabout.
C$PA to C$PZ	C$PA may be set when exiting from the Workabout command processor, to contain a text string representing the current path on drive A. It is not set if the drive A path is to the root directory. Similar environment variables may be set for all other possible drives - C$PB to C$PZ inclusive. Only used on Workabout.
C$P£	Contains parameters used by Link when accessed from the Workabout System Screen and/or Command Processor. Only used on Workabout.
CP	Set following selection of the keyboard from the Command Processor or the System Screen. It contains a single byte whose binary value is either 0 (Standard keyboard selected) or 1 (Special keyboard selected). Only used on Workabout.

Utility programs, SIBO C SDK V2.20

All of the following programs and utilities are located in the \SIBOSDK\SYS directory.

Utility	Program Function
CTRAN.EXE	Generates a .C source code file from a .CAT file in an application project using Object Oriented Programming (OOP) techniques e.g. when using HWIM applications or producing DYL's.
DEBUG.APP	Debugging tool e.g. used in the DOS based Psion 3a Emulator
ECOBJ.EXE	Converts .OBJ files for Object Oriented Programming based (OOP) applications to place the class descriptor data into the code segment. It is run automatically, should not be directly executed.
ECONFIG.EXE	Converts .FIG files, source files containing country specific data, such as default international dialling code, currency symbol, into .CFO files, used in building a new country specific version of a ROM.
ECPPFX.EXE	A C++ compiler support utility. Used to patch object files for EPOC16 after compilation by the Topspeed compiler. Called automatically from the project system (see TSPRJ.TXT) Should never be executed directly.
EDUMP.EXE	Dump/display the details of an .IMG or .APP file. See EMAKE.
EMAKE.EXE	Makes the .IMG file and used to add additional files into an executable image file (.IMG) e.g .PIC, .RSC or .RZC, .SHD files. For example to add icons, resources and shell data files into an executable file. Up to four named files can be added into a .IMG file, which is then normally renamed to a .APP file. The files to be added into the .IMG file are specified in a .AFL file. If building the application by using a project file (.PR) the EMAKE utility is called automatically if a .AFL file is found. See EDUMP. Also used by the build process to convert the .EXE file produced by the linker to a .IMG file. Can be used to convert the .EXE file to other Psion file types e.g. Logical device driver (.LDD), Physical device driver (.PDD) and Dynamic library (.DYL). Can also be used to set the version number and/or the initial priority of the executable.
EMAST.EXE	Detailed in the HC programming guide, Vol 1 of the C SDK. It is a mastering tool, for transferring an image of the HC ROM, onto an SSD, for use as a master repro disk.
EREMAKE.EXE	Used to change the files added into an existing executable file. See EMAKE.EXE.
EROM.EXE	Creates a master file image of the HC rom. Used when producing customised versions of the HC rom.
FATD.EXE	A FAT file system integrity checker
FE.EXE	A TLV file editor
FLASHD.EXE	A Flash SSD integrity checker
FLMAN.APP	File manager used during debugging.
LPREP.EXE	Used with RGCOMP and RGPREP in the production of .RG files from .RE

Utility	Program Function
	resource externals files. LPREP is a general pre-processor (see TSPRJ.EMP). Should never be executed directly.
MAKEALS.EXE	Produces .ALS files from .MA files. See the Series 3a programming guide 'Aliasing applications' in Vol 1 of the C SDK
MAKESHD.EXE	Make a shell data (.SHD) from a source (.MS) file. Specifies the application type e.g. 'File type' or 'No file type', the default application name and icon size expected.
MASTCPY.EXE	See EMAST for details
MCLINK.EXE	Link PC to Psion via a com port.
MCPRINT.EXE	Link PC to Psion to use PC as a print server.
RCHUF.EXE	Compiled resource files (.RSC) can be compressed by RCHUF.EXE to save space on the SSD supplied. The Psion will automatically uncompress the data when it is loaded by the appropriate operating system call or C function call
RCOMP.EXE	Compiles a .RSS file into a .RSC files.
RGCOMP.EXE	Used with RGPREP and LPREP in the production of .RG files from .RE resource externals files. RGCOMP (see TSPRJ.EMP) Processes .I files to ????. Should never be executed directly.
RGPREP.EXE	Used with RGCOMP and LPREP in the production of .RG files from .RE resource externals files. RGPREP (see TSPRJ.EMP). (Processes .RE files to .REX files ????) Should never be executed directly.
SDBG.EXE	Symbolic debugger.
SLINK.EXE	Simplified version of MCLINK to connect a PC to a Psion.
WAV2WVE.EXE	Converts PC type sound files (.WAV) to Psion (.WVE) sound files
WDTRAN.EXE	Compiles .WDR printer driver files from a .WD source file as described in Chapter 3 of the Additional System Information, vol 1 of the C SDK.
WSDUMP.EXE	A window server debugging aid that converts window server dump output to human readable form.
WSFCOMP.EXE	Font compiler for producing specific fonts from .FSC files.
WSPCX.EXE	Bitmap and PCX file conversion utility. Can be used to link multiple .PIC files into one file.
WVEDMP.EXE	Provides header info from a .WVE file. Usage WVEDMP <filename.ext>.

File types, by extension

Ext	File Description
.AFL	Add file list files (.AFL) are used to add resource files (RSC or RZC), graphics or icons (.PIC) files and shell data (.SHD) to an .IMG file which by convention (not automatic) are renamed to an application (.APP) files.
.AGN	Format of agenda files, S3
.AIF	Application information files (Series 5)
.ALS	Program alias file for allowing an application to generate a separate list in the system screen and possibly to have modified behaviour. The OPL editor is just an alias of Word which operates on text files with a default extension of .OPL
.APP	Executable application file which has added files included e.g. an icon file (.PIC) and possibly others such as .RSC or .RZC files and a shell data file (.SHD). Executable application files for Series 5 (EIKON or OPL)
.ASM	Assembly language source file
.BMP	PC type bitmap files.
.BTF	HC command shell (batch) file.
.C	C language source code files.
.CAT	Category files for HWIM applications or DYL libraries.
.CFO	Language configuration files – country specific
.CL	Sub category files HWIM
.DBD	Debugging file information for the symbolic debugger produced during the compile and link step. The debugging information is only produced when the VID debug pragma is enabled.
.DBF	Psion 'native' Data application database files.
.DFL	Add file lists for DYL
.DYL	Dynamic library file.
.EXT	Category file include file for HWIM or DYL projects
.G	Include file HWIM or DYL projects – resource Ids
.HLP	Help files, applications specific help for Series 5 (Series 5 data files)
.IMG	Applications - image files
.ING	ASM include file HWIM
.INI	Application information files (Series 5 and MS Windows based systems)
.LDD	Logical device driver files
.LIS	Category listing file HWIM
.MA	Alias files source files S3
.MAP	Generated during the linking process, contains symbolic information.
.MAS	HC ROM build
.MBM	Multi bitmap files (Series 5)
.MS	Text source file used to generate a Shell Data file (.SHD) using MAKESHD.EXE.
.OPA	OPL translated application programs
.OPH	OPL header files SIBO and Series 5 (formats differ)

Ext	File Description
.OPL	OPL source code files SIBO
.OPO	OPL translated program files
.OPX	OPL language extension library files OPXs (Series 5)
.OXH	OPX header files
.PCX	PC type graphics bitmap/picture files.
.PDD	Physical device driver file
.PH	Multi bitmap header files SIBO (used with WSPCX)
.PIC	Psion bitmap files which can be used to store icons and other graphics objects.
.PLK	Multi bitmap files list specifier files (used with WSPCX)
.PR	Project file used to control the compile / link / build process SIBO C.
.RE	Resource externals file used with application resource (.RSS) files.
.RED	The re-direction file used by the Topspeed compiler etc to locate the various files such as #include files (e.g .H and .G files) etc.
.RG	Produced from .RE files during the build process.
.RH	Resource header files in SIBO OOP
.RSC	The compiled form of a .RSS file. In multi-lingual applications there may be several of these files supplied, one for each country supported. e.g. myapp01.rsc for English, myapp02.rsc for French, myapp03.rsc for German. SIBO and EPOC32 formats vary.
.RSG	Resource generated files – resource ID inforamation
.RSS	A resource script specifier file. Used to specify program constants, string data, menu data, dialogue data and help resources etc. used within a programe. e.g. typically used to store all the static or language specific data and strings used by a program, particularly useful when producing multi-lingual applications.
.RTF	Word processor file format (rich text format)
.RZC	The compressed form of an .RSC file. Compiled resource files can be compressed by RCHUF.EXE to save space on the SSD supplied. The Psion will automatically uncompress the data when it is loaded by the appropriate operating system call or C function call.
.SHD	Shell data files specify the application type e.g. 'File type' or 'No file type', the default application name and icon size expected.
.SPR	Format of spreadsheet files
.SYM	Created by the EMAKE utility when it makes the .IMG file. The debugging information is produced during the compile and link step if the VID debug pragma is enabled.
.TRM	Serial port parameters
.TXT	Format of text files
.WAV	PC Windows type sound files.
.WD	WDR printer driver source files SIBO
.WDR	Printer driver file for SIBO
.WRD	Format Psion word processor
.WRT	Word template files (SIBO)
.WVE	Psion digital sound files. (EPOC32 sound files do not have a .WVE extension)

Special Keys

SIBO system special keys

On SIBO systems the Psion key is identified by the ⌶ symbol.

On SIBO, Psion+Esc will quit from any console based process e.g. OPL or HWIF program, unless it has been disabled by the application e.g. by using ESCAPE OFF in OPL or HWIF uEscape(FALSE).

Control+S pauses the foreground application and any other key resumes.

Shift+Ctrl+Psion+S - captures the screen on a SIBO system to a file called LOC::M:\screen.pic

The so-called 'Key of death' which kills the foreground process on SIBO systems is Ctrl+Shift+Psion+K. Be careful with this key combination it will kill any process rather than shutting it down.

Series 5 / WINS special keys

OPL32 has different keypresses for WINS and the Series 5, to avoid clashes with the Windows task list keys.

For OPL32 or other 'console' based process, the 'Kill' key is:

WINS: Shift+Esc

Series 5:   Control+Esc

The 'Pause' and 'Resume' keys are:

WINS: Control+Alt+S and Control+Alt+Q

Series 5:   Control+Fn+S and Control+Fn+Q

Shift+Ctrl+Fn+S - Capture the screen on a Series 5 system to a file and folder of your choice.

The so-called 'Key of death' which kills the foreground process on Series 5 is Ctrl+Shift+Fn+K. Be careful with this key combination it will kill any process rather than shutting it down.

Glossary of terms

Term	Description
3Link	Psion's Serial link package (the Psion Parallel link package is sometimes referred to as a "Parallel 3Link").
API	Application Programmers Interface – a library provided for programmers, typically to provide access to operating system functions and facilities.
ARM	Advanced RISC Machines
ARM 710a	Advanced RISC Machines Processor, Series 5
ASCII text or characters	The American Standard Code for Information Interchange system for assigning a numeric code for displayable and non-displayable characters.
BCS	Binary Counted Strings. String variables that are preceded by a value that gives the current length of the string (usually a byte value, which limits the string length to 255 characters).
C	A compiled programming language
C++	An object-oriented super-set of the C language
CF	Compact flash - non volatile storage media, used on Series 5
CISC	Complex Instruction Set Computers
CLIB	'C' Library. This library is very similar to standard 'C' libraries from other development systems such as Borland or Microsoft. Developers can consider using CLIB if they are unfamiliar with Psion's proprietary languages, such as PLIB, or if they have to port some existing code from another project in another development environment.
CODEC	Coding and Decoding of Analog data streams to and from digital data.
Compact Flash	CF - non volatile storage media, for Series 5
DMA	Direct Memory Access controller
DRAM	Dynamic Random Access Memory
DSP	Digital Signal Processor
DTMF	Digital Tone Multiple Frequency
DYL	see Dynamic library
Dynamic library (DYL)	OOP based library code modules used on SIBO systems
EIKON	The default Graphical User Interface on Series 5
Environment variable	Unit of storage used on SIBO system. Globally available through system functions.
EPOC	Psion's operating system – usually referring to SIBO systems.
EPOC16	Psion's operating system – specifically referring to SIBO systems.
EPOC32	Psion's operating system – specifically referring to 32-bit systems.
FIFO	First in, first out
Flash RAM	Flash SSD storage not needing power to maintain the data
Flash SSD	Solid State Disk designed to store information that is unlikely to be altered frequently.
FMFS	Flash Memory Filing System used in Flash SSDs.
FORM	A DYL providing screen layout, formatted text and printing.
GDI	Graphics device interface
Heap	An area of memory used for dynamic storage of program data

Term	Description
HWIF	Handheld Wimp InterFace library. This contains library routines for creating menus, dialogs and edit boxes, and for carrying out printing. It has the style of traditional 'C' programming, in contrast to the HWIM library. It allows some measure of access to the user interface software in the ROMs of the SIBO computer range, but not as much as the HWIM library does.
HWIM	Handheld Windows Icons and Menus library. This is a DYL that exists in the ROMs of most SIBO systems, and also refers to a particular style of programming, in which the full power of the user interface software in the ROM is accessed. This programming style is fully object-oriented, in contrast to HWIF, which basically provides a wrapping layer around the object-oriented programming features.
I/O	Short for Input / Output
I/O Semaphore	Flag used to indicate the status of a processes I/O requests
Interrupt	Hardware - physical signal to a processor of an external event. Software- system of calling system related functions
IrDA	Infrared Data Association
ISAM	Indexed Sequential Access Method.
ISAM.DYL	Indexed Sequential Access Method, object library
Magic (reserved) static variable	A static variable private, but available to a particular process and any sub-processes (tasks) on SIBO systems only.
MMU	Memory management Unit
OLIB	Psion's Object Library that provides the basis of application architecture and the foundation for other DYLs.
OOP	Object-Oriented Programming.
OPL	Organiser Programming Language
OTP	One-time programmable SSD.
OVAL	Object-based Visual Application Language
PCMCIA	Interface to miniature PC cards and peripheral
Pixels	Short for picture elements.
PLIB	PLIB is Psion's proprietary version of a standard 'C' Library. It differs from CLIB by being more suited to the particular demands of programming SIBO systems. It provides a closer binding to the ROM software than CLIB.
PLL	Phase Locked Loop, Series 5
Process control block	Segment of memory used by the operating system to manage a process
Process data segment	The area of memory used for a programs data and variable storage.
RAM	Random Access Memory (as opposed to sequential access)
RAM SSD	Solid State Disk used for storing information that is likely to be altered often. These SSDs require a power source.
RCOM	The communications program in Psion's 3Link package.
Reserved (magic) static variable	See magic static
RISC	Reduced Instruction Set Computer processor. CPUs with less complex instructions, but where each is highly optimised for speed, e.g. execute in the smallest number of CPU cycles.
RLIB	A library used automatically by the SIBO C SDK
ROM	Read Only Memory

Term	Description
RTF files	Rich Text Format files - a word processor interchange format
SDK	Software Development Kit.
Semaphore	A software flag, typically used by an operating system.
SIBO	Psion's hardware architecture SIxteen-Bit Organiser e.g. the Series 3, 3a/c Siena, Workabout and HC.
SIR	Serial Infrared - transmission of data
SRAM	Static RAM
SSD	Solid State Disk - see Flash RAM and RAM SSD
Stack	Area of memory used for temporary storage e.g. by a processor
Static variable	A variable that retains its contents between function calls
Text files	see ASCII text
UART	Universal Asynchronous Receiver Transmitter – serial comms
UIDs	Unique Identifiers, Series 5 applications
URL	Universal Resource Locator – used for World Wide Web addressing on the Internet
Usenet	A system of discussion or 'news groups' on thousands of topics taking place via the Internet.
VAD	Value Added Distributor, Psion nominated main distributors.
VAR	Value Added Re-seller, typically suppliers of Psion computers with specialised software or hardware added.
Variable static	see Static variable
WDR printing	A system for using printer drivers on SIBO system
Web site / page	Personal or business oriented pages on the Internet located with URL addresses.
WIMP	In the widest sense, WIMP means Windows Icons Menus and Pointing device, in other words, modern styles of user interfaces.
WLIB	Window Server Library – SIBO
WYSIWYG	What You See Is What You Get - usually applied to applications that display information exactly as it will appear in the final form e.g. when printed.
XADD	A SIBO DYL for Print preview classes, grid classes etc.
ZTS	Zero terminated string, a zero or null character (ASCII 0) is added to the end of a string to mark its end.

Index

G

M

N

O

Index

P

Y

Z

Index

Notes

Notes

Notes

Notes

CD-ROM request form

Programming Psion Computers

FREE if not supplied with the book.

Requests __must__ be on this form

Please complete this order form,

carefully cut it from the book and

send it to the address over the page.

For destinations outside of Europe

Please include £2.00 postage.

Please send files on CD to:	
Name	
Address 1	
Address 2	
Address 3	
City	
Post code	
Country	

CD-ROM Supplied
by Bookseller
Please use this form to register
your book with EMCC for news
of updates and revisions

Files on CD-ROM

EMCC

PO Box 109

Sale

Cheshire

M33 4TA

England

Files on other media

Programming Psion Computers

Orders <u>must</u> be on this form

Please complete this order form,

carefully cut it from the book and

send it to the address over the page.

For destinations outside of Europe

Please include £2.00 postage.

Please indicate your preferred format:	
Floppy disk	**£10.00**
Iomega Zip disk	**£12.00**
Name	
Address 1	
Address 2	
Address 3	
City	
Post code	
Country	

Files on other media

EMCC

PO Box 109

Sale

Cheshire

M33 4TA

England

Palmtop Magazine

The journal for today's Psion user

Please complete the order form over the page

visit http://www.palmtop.co.uk

e-mail palmtop@aol.com

A finely crafted magazine, dedicated to Psion and packed with Psion related material, including some programming related stuff.

Subscription options for Palmtop magazine

£5 off the listed prices if you subscribe using the form over the page.

1 year (6 issues)		1 year + 6 back issues		1 year + 12 back issues	
UK	£24	UK	£44	UK	£60
Europe	£27	Europe	£50	Europe	£70
Worldwide	£33	Worldwide £60		Worldwide £85	

Order forms

Palmtop Magazine

The journal for today's Psion user

Please complete this order form, carefully cut it from the book

and send it to:

Palmtop Publications

25 Avocet Way

Bicester

Oxon OX6 0YN

England

Please start my subscription to Palmtop magazine

£5 off the listed prices if you subscribe using this form.

I would like to subscribe for: years

and I enclose my payment of £   UKP

Name	
Address 1	
Address 2	
Address 3	
City	
Post code	
Country	

Order forms

The 3-Lib Shareware Library

The biggest collection of Psion shareware in existence, maintained by Steve Litchfield.

visit http://3lib.ukonline.co.uk

Probably the best page on the web for Psion programmers.

A great starting-point.

Home of the 3-lib shareware library, including Steve's renowned Mapper application.

Please complete the order form over the page

Order forms

The 3-Lib Shareware Library

Please complete this order form, carefully cut it from the book
and send it with a self addressed envelope to:

3-Lib Shareware Library

22 Greys Crescent

Woodley

RG5 3EN

England

Please send me a 3-Lib library listing	
Name	
Address 1	
Address 2	
Address 3	
City	
Post code	
Country	